The New Essential Guide to Lesbian Conception, Pregnancy, & Birth

STEPHANIE BRILL

Director, Maia Midwifery & Preconception Services

Foreword by Preston Sacks, M.D.

alyson books
NEW YORK

I Dedicate This Book to Love.

This book is intended as a reference volume only. It is not a medical manual. The information contained in this book was written to help readers make informed decisions about conception, pregnancy, and birth, and health issues associated with conception, pregnancy, and birth. It is not designed as a substitute for any treatment that may have been prescribed by your personal health care provider. If you suspect you have a medical problem, see a competent heath care provider to discuss your concerns.

Please note that the image of the pacifier on the front cover should not be taken as an endorsement of pacifier use either by the author or publisher. Please consult your pediatrician, midwife, or other health professional to understand the risks and benefits associated with pacifiers.

A previous version of this book entitled *The Essential Guide to Lesbian Conception, Pregnancy, and Birth* was published by Alyson Books ©2002 by Kim Toevs and Stephanie Brill.

Manufactured in the United States of America.
This trade paperback original is published by Alyson Publications, P.O. Box 1253,
Old Chelsea Station, New York, New York 10113-1251.
Distribution in the United Kingdom by Turnaround Publisher Services Ltd., Unit 3, Olympia Trading Estate, Coburg Road, Wood Green, London N226TZ England.

First Edition: July 2006

06 07 08 09 [a] 10 9 8 7 6 5 4 3 2 1

ISBN 1-55583-940-1
ISBN-13 978-1-55583-940-6

An application for Library of Congress Cataloguing-in Publication Data has been filed.

Book design by Victor Mingovits.

CREDITS
Illustrations by Suzann Gage (pages 258–59) from *A New View of a Woman's Body* (1991), Courtesy of the Federation of Feminist Women's Health Centers.
page vi photo courtesy of Maia Midwifery & Preconception Ser vices
page 1 photo by Jennifer Loomis
page 67 photo courtesy of Maia Midwifery & Preconception Services
page 143 photo by Cathy Cade
page 213 photo courtesy of Maia Midwifery & Preconception Services
page 317 photo courtesy of Maia Midwifery & Preconception Services
page 387 photo courtesy of Maia Midwifery & Preconception

Contents

Acknowledgments

I AM ETERNALLY grateful to have been given the opportunity to do the work that I do. To be fully immersed in helping people to bring children into their lives and to parent from as openhearted a place as possible is my greatest joy. To have had the honor of helping thousands of queer families into being is a privilege I hold with the utmost care. I would like to thank all of the families with whom I have worked—I offer this work back to you. I also deeply appreciate those of you who have been willing to share photos of your family. A book is always made better with images of love.

I have had some amazing help in the researching and reworking of this book. I was completely humbled by the time and assistance given by Doreen Zorenick, A'maya Pettibone, Eve Alpern, Caroline Lowry, KC Bly, Ali McCallum, Emalee Danforth, Tomi J. Knutson, Hasmig Minassian, Lisa Rae Vickey, and Sharon Katz. But most especially, I would like to thank Deirdre Wood for her tireless dedication to this project. I cannot thank all of them enough.

I am also grateful to the people in my own Bay Area community who are also doing groundbreaking work in support of our families who have helped me with specific questions—Shannon Minter of the National Center for Lesbian Rights, Alice Ruby of the Sperm Bank of California, and Leland Tremain of Rainbow Flag Health Services.

Then there are the people closer to home without whom I could not have accomplished this undertaking—Kristina Wingeier, Robin Winn, Allen Brill, Wendy Brill, and my parents. Of course, my greatest inspiration comes from my children—Gi, Anna, Daniel, and Prana. This book and all of my creative endeavors are for them. And I absolutely could not have completed this revision without the unwavering love of my partner, lover, best friend, and editor, Kristin Kali, to sustain me. I thank her, my sweet love; she is my heaven.

And, of course, this book would not have been possible without the help of my editor at Alyson, Shannon Berning. Thank you.

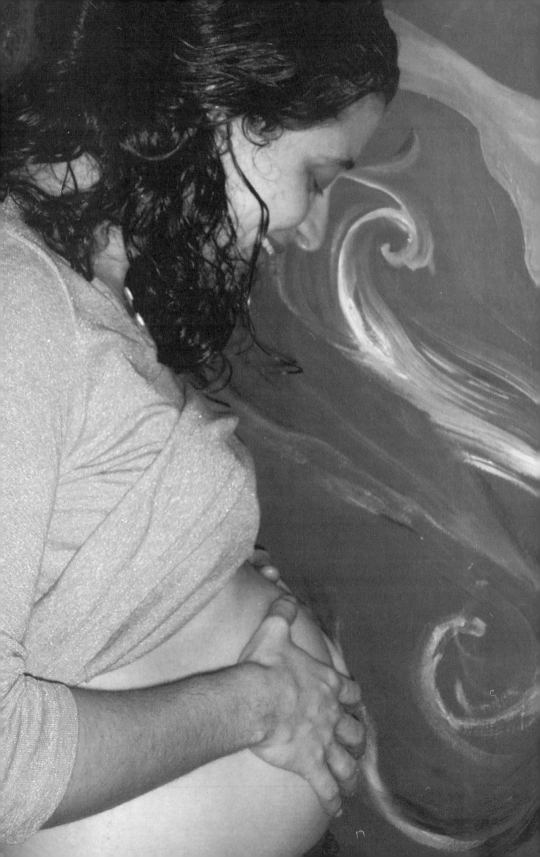

Foreword

A FEW YEARS ago, I was in the gay and lesbian section of my local bookstore, looking for a book on conception and pregnancy that I could recommend to my patients. As an infertility specialist practicing in downtown Washington, D.C., I have a large number of single and lesbian patients seeking my help in building their families via donor insemination. As I browsed through the selections, I came upon *The Essential Guide to Lesbian Conception, Pregnancy, and Birth.* It was apparent that this book was the best one on the shelf and that the depth of information in this book was far superior to any of the others on lesbian health.

Now, it is my pleasure to introduce *The New Essential Guide to Lesbian Conception, Pregnancy, and Birth,* which has been fully revised to bring readers up to date on everything they need to know about family planning. As co-founder of Maia Midwifery and Preconception Services, Stephanie Brill draws upon her expertise in the field of women's health and translates this knowledge into a highly readable book.

The New Essential Guide is a roadmap to the process of conception for any woman, and in particular assists single or lesbian women, as well as transgender people, through the steps involved in donor insemination. Brill focuses on the socioeconomic and legal aspects of building a family via donor insemination, and covers in detail the often-difficult concerns of how to discuss these unique family-building issues with extended family, friends, partners, and potential donors.

Brill gives equal weight and respect to all possible alternatives, not directing the reader but allowing the reader to construct a plan that meets her own specific goals. This not only broadens the applicability of the book, but also increases the reader's awareness of alternative lifestyles and the particular issues that they may raise. This is especially true for transgender parents-to-be—where there is a general lack of information.

I continue to be impressed at the accuracy and timeliness of the medical information. The section on how to prepare your body for pregnancy should be studied by all women (regardless of sexual orientation) prior to attempting conception. All too often, women come to me for fertility consultations who have no idea about their own menstrual cycles. The guidance in this book allows the reader to understand and identify their fertile window, which is the first step to successful conception. The section on reproductive function is well presented and provides ongoing reference throughout the fertility process.

The New Essential Guide to Lesbian Conception, Pregnancy, and Birth also gives advice on when to seek the counsel of a fertility specialist. Brill prepares the reader for this visit, listing what is involved in a fertility evaluation and the potential treatments that may be recommended. The treatment approaches, risks, side effects, and expected success rates are outlined.

Lastly, the chapters on how to have a successful pregnancy draw on the experience at Maia Midwifery and gives detailed recommendations for the pregnant woman and her partner, friends, and family.

The information is presented in a clear and concise manner, and is often interjected with humor and humility. Brill makes the process of lesbian conception less daunting, and, as a result, places the reader in a relaxed and comfortable state. I feel confident that this new edition of *The New Essential Guide to Lesbian Conception, Pregnancy and Birth* will be as well received as the original.

I will continue to recommend this book to my patients as they journey through the process of conception, pregnancy, and ultimately begin their journey as parents. I congratulate Brill on a fabulous job helping the countless readers expand their families and pave the way for our next generation.

— PRESTON SACKS, M.D.

Introduction

QUEER FAMILIES ARE popping up everywhere! Since the publication of the first version of the *Essential Guide,* in 1999, we have seen so many more families walking through our doors every week and provided phone consultations for families across the country and the world. It is a very exciting time to be a part of this growing acceptance that queer people are having with their innate right to choose to parent.

One of the goals in writing this book was to make the wealth of information we have accumulated over the years accumulated at Maia Midwifery and Preconception Services, in Orinda, California, available and easily accessible to queer folks everywhere. Whether you've always wanted to be pregnant or just recently started to explore the possibility, this book is a useful resource guide, both emotionally and practically, for the entire process of becoming a queer parent—from trying to conceive through the first stages of parenthood.

This book is intended for any person—lesbian, bisexual, transgender, genderqueer—and their family members. This book is also for single heterosexual women. The information in this book is quite helpful for anyone trying to conceive. Because our scope is so broad, and because it takes up a lot of space to keep saying "lesbian and bisexual women and single and transpeople of any sexual orientation," we have decided to use the word "queer." We are fully aware that some people do not resonate with that word, but using an acronym such as LBTS just didn't feel right either. So bear with us as language evolves; we are in an in-between phase right now.

In addition, we sometimes use both female and male pronouns to refer to people who are pregnant in order to be inclusive of the many female-to-male transgender people, or transmen, who choose to become pregnant.

At Maia, we want everyone to have the information and tools they need to follow their own unique path to creating a family. So much of the information covered in this book is available nowhere else. It comes from the real-life learning experience of having worked with thousands of queer families. It also comes from being natural fertility specialists. And, because queer people often wait until their forties to try to get pregnant, it comes from our expertise in helping people over forty to get pregnant with their own eggs. As midwives, we value not only the outcome of pregnancy but also the transformational process of becoming pregnant and growing a baby. We want you to keep in touch with your capacity to share big, openhearted love, which is the original inspiration to parent.

Homophobia and transphobia are still very much a force in our society. Homophobia and transphobia can be defined as an irrational fear of or contempt for or prejudice against queer and transgender people or our lifestyle or our cultures. Self-love is the most fundamental tool queer folks have to combat external and internalized homophobia/transphobia—and the subsequent self-doubt, shame, and low self-esteem that homophobia/transphobia can cause. A healthy love of self helps all individuals celebrate their power to conceive, birth, and raise children, without falling victim to the message that they are unfit to parent.

We emphasize communication skills and exercises throughout the book, to help you clarify your desires and foster closer relationships with your partners, coparents, and other family members. Communicating clearly increases joy and happiness, and improves the stability and longevity of the family unit. Skills that support your family's emotional health and integrity are important in light of the additional strains a homophobic world can place on queer families.

To get the most out of this book, read it from front to back, and then use it as a reference guide. Use the exercises and questions we pose as tools for discussions with partners, donors, or coparents. Read it for inspiration to remember that others have walked down this path before you. Even if you feel you're past making your initial decisions, the exercises and ideas in the book's first section provide a good opportunity for you to take a step back and survey the decisions you've made thus far.

———

IN 1992, KIM TOEVS and I founded Maia Midwifery and Preconception Services. We were inspired midwives with a vision for our community. Together we wrote the first edition of this book in 1999. Kim left Maia in 2000 to focus on different aspects of queer health care.

Since then Maia has grown with the times. We continue to offer classes, groups, and individual preconception, fertility, and infertility care. We also facilitate known donor and coparenting negotiations and offer counseling to families in the childbearing cycle. The client base has increased in the past seven years. One of the greatest parts of this evolution is the obvious increased comfort that queer people feel in their ability to be themselves. We see this especially in the ever-growing expression of gender. The queer community has always pushed the socially accepted boundaries of gender expression—indeed, this is the root of homophobia. However, one remarkable change I have seen in our parenting communities is the increased comfort in just being who we really are, not only within our families and microculture but also in the world at large. Gender identity is a large and important part of self-expression. Stemming directly from the feeling of increased personal comfort is the dramatic increase of so many more out dyke daddies, femme mommies, gender- fluid parents, and transgender parents of every sexual orientation changing the world by being themselves.

A strong part of Maia's mission is to improve health care for queer families. To these ends we provide training for medical and mental health care professionals and regularly make presentations at conferences.

In addition to my experience as a midwife, I bring sixteen years of queer parenting to my work. I have four children ranging in age from 5 to 16. I have a big, beautiful, blended family. All of our children are amazing and continue to be my inspiration. I am personally dedicated to changing the world for our children. So in addition to being a midwife, a mom, and a writer, I work intimately in the schools. I have helped to develop inclusive curriculums. I co-founded a charter school based on anti-bias principles. I regularly provide staff in-services on issues of sensitivity regarding queer issues. I am dedicated to eradicating the limitations of gender. I lead groups for parents of gender-variant children and provide training to educators on ways of making schools a safer place for gender-variant and transgender children.

Congratulations! You are on your journey to expand your family—whether with your first child or your fifth. I have two wishes for you: stay connected to love and be yourself—all else will follow.

Part One
Many Choices, Many Decisions

CHAPTER 1

Creating New Types of Family Structures

BECAUSE LESBIAN AND bisexual women and single and transgender people of any orientation must reach beyond mainstream models and definitions of family, we have the opportunity to create profoundly new models of family. Traditionally, adults who parent together have been sexually and romantically linked to each other, and biologically related to their children. The very nature of how we make family debunks the myth that these relationship components are inextricably linked, thereby liberating each of us to create family structures best suited to our needs and ideals.

Children and parents alike are well served by the ability to choose the number of parents in a family as well as how the roles of parenting, home keeping, and income earning will be divided. All may benefit as well from creative decision making about the nature of extended family and the structure of community support networks. The multitude of ways in which queer people are building families speaks to how unique each of us is. Along with our diversity, we are fundamentally united in knowing that, ultimately, love is indeed what makes a family.

Creating Our Family Relationships

If you're just beginning to explore the possibility of parenthood, now is the perfect time to look more closely at your ideas about various family structures. In this chapter we give you some new ideas and ask some essential questions to help you clarify your vision, even if you've already made some decisions about how you would like to create a family. Most of us retain some assumptions and unexamined ideas about the concept of family that may subconsciously restrict the choices we make. Take this opportunity to explore the different components of parenting relationships and look at some of the following examples of how others have created their families.

Although most lesbian and bisexual women and transmen who are considering parenthood either plan to be single parents or partnered parents, there are numerous options for including other parents and coparents in families that step outside these two models. No matter what your initial parenting vision may be, traditional or more complex, it's helpful to carefully examine the nature of the bonds that are traditionally associated with family. In so doing, you can give more thoughtful attention to your choices about your own family in the making.

Biological Relationships

An adult can be biologically related to a child, whether by providing the sperm or egg for conception or by carrying the child in utero and giving birth. This adult may or may not be an active parent, if we define "parent" as someone who takes on daily primary responsibilities for the child. Conversely, a biological relationship isn't necessary for one to be considered a parent.

Hopefully you can see, through the following examples, the multitude of possibilities that exist for creating family. When we break apart the connections between the building blocks of biology, love, sex, and parenting that society often suggests are inseparable, we can form an almost infinite number of new family models by recombining them. To our great benefit, the many choices we have allow us to create families that suit our individual needs and lifestyles.

EXAMPLE: Tanya and Leslie choose to parent together. Tanya conceives with sperm obtained through a sperm bank that will release information about the donor when the child turns 18. Although the child may have a relationship with the donor after he or she reaches that age, the donor will have no contact with the child previous to that time and therefore no parenting role. Both Leslie and Tanya equally and fully identify as mothers, even though only one of them is biologically related to the child.

ANOTHER EXAMPLE: Jill and Tamika have always wanted their close friend Andre to donate sperm to them and be actively involved in their child's life in a coparenting capacity. When his initial preconception tests reveal that he is HIV-positive, they initially lament the loss of his involvement in their family. Over time, though, they realize that his special role as their best friend and the baby's key male role model isn't contingent upon his biological relationship with the child. They choose an anonymous donor and invite Andre to become a coparent.

Romantic Relationships

Often a romantic relationship between two adults is a key element in their decision to parent together. Two people, from their love for each other, can choose to raise a child together, regardless of their respective biology or gender. Although this frequently is accompanied by an equal desire to raise children, sometimes one partner has a much stronger interest in being a parent than the other. It is quite common for two people with unequal interests to enter into parenting together because they want to stay together as a couple, and one of them decides to have a child regardless of the partner's lack of desire to parent.

Some queer people have difficulty believing that two people who are romantically involved can raise a child together while having different levels of commitment to parenting. Perhaps this unequal level of responsibility too closely resembles stereotypical heterosexual models of parenting, where, regardless of how much both partners profess to want children, the woman finds herself in the obligatory role of primary caretaker, with little option to prioritize her career or other personal needs. Standing in contrast to the stereotypical heterosexual model are the thoroughly explored and clearly communicated arrangements that queer families have the opportunity to consent to before conception. This kind of negotiation can become a meeting ground for couples who want to stay together. Sometimes the more reluctant partner finds that she wants more parental involvement over time, and sometimes she does not.

EXAMPLE: Peggy and Yolanda live together as romantic partners, but only Yolanda is fully committed to parenting a child. Peggy decides that although her life will be affected by having a baby in the house, she doesn't want to take on the primary responsibility of raising the child. She is past her own childbearing years and feels her life has a different focus now. Although partnered with Yolanda, Peggy plans to act more as a supportive secondary parent than a primary parent. Yolanda conceives with sperm from a gay male friend. He and his male partner, who live nearby, also actively parent the child. As the child grows older, she spends a substantial amount of time at both homes.

Occasionally, none of the people involved in parenting a child are romantically connected.

EXAMPLE: Ellen, who is straight, and Jim, who is gay, are parenting together. She self-inseminated at home with his sperm to conceive, and they share a home.

EXAMPLE: Barb and Anne are good friends who share parenting responsibilities. Barb is the primary parent, while Anne is an active coparent who spends slightly less time with the kids and defers to Barb for primary decisions, such as those concerning the child's health and education. Barb and Anne don't live together, but when Barb and the children relocate to a new town, Anne moves with them to continue her involvement in the family.

Sexual Relationships

A sexual relationship initiated for the purpose of conceiving doesn't necessarily imply a desire to share parenting responsibilities.

EXAMPLE: Dana, a lesbian, has sex with her male friend Mateo to get pregnant. She becomes a single parent, and he doesn't have an ongoing partner relationship with her or a parenting relationship with the child.

Many bisexual women coparent with men they're sexually involved with, whether or not other parents are also present in the family. Sometimes conception occurs between queer-identified people who share both a sexual relationship and a parenting relationship.

EXAMPLE: Inez is a male-to-female transsexual. She and her bisexual partner, Akiko, conceive a baby together before Inez completes her sexual reassignment surgery and loses her ability to make sperm, and they both parent their child together.

The Challenges of New Family Structures

There are many inherent challenges to creating new and different models of family. One of the primary struggles is finding in others the recognition and validation of the legitimacy of our families. When we step outside of the culturally familiar to such extremes, we also need to create new language to define our family relationships. This requires ongoing awareness. Because our family structures are often new and different, we may find very little social support for them. This can be quite stressful on the family unit as a whole. Breakups in "alternative" families caused by pressures from an unsympathetic culture are truly tragic.

If you plan to have a family that is considered "alternative"—and I assume that includes most readers of this book—it's valuable to plan ahead as to how each of you, individually and as a family unit, will get the support you need to be a family outside of, and sometimes against, the mainstream. Regular counseling for all relevant family members often helps to keep lines of communication open and strong. Using the time before conception to advance your communication skills creates a strong foundation for parenting. Personal self-reflection will also help you to deepen your own commitment to parenting. Additionally, finding queer families to connect with helps to break feelings of isolation. And perhaps most important, a carefully thought-out vision that is honestly shared by all involved will go far in helping you to feel confident in your choices. Crafting such a vision and gaining clarity about mutual desires and goals can take many, many months or even years to develop.

If you don't wish to take that much time to clarify your desires and goals in the planning stages, it's all the more important for you to establish mechanisms for keeping decisions and emotions clear among all adults involved throughout the process of parenting.

||||||||||||||||||||||||||||||||||||||||||||||||||||||||||||||||||||||||||||||||||||||||||

"I'm a bisexual woman who wants to be a mom. I've never been in a long-term romantic relationship and would be fooling myself to think that I'm ready for one now. I don't even want one. However, I live close to my parents and siblings, and we all want to raise my children collectively. So, although I'll be a single mom, I feel like I actually have more support than most partnered parents I know."—TERRI, 37, LAS VEGAS, NEVADA

||||||||||||||||||||||||||||||||||||||||||||||||||||||||||||||||||||||||||||||||||||||||||

Naming Our Family Relationships

Crucial to our parenting identity is the language we use to identify our relationships to our children and the rest of our family. We also are greatly affected by how we are named by our children, our community, and the broader culture.

Because as queer parents we are at the edge of a cultural frontier, many terms haven't yet been created or standardized for our family-structure concepts and definitions of family members. It's vital and empowering to claim our own language and find ways to make our names accurately reflect our relationships. Because language is so fluid, careful clarification of exactly what you mean by a term will help prevent miscommunications and misperceptions.

Language and the Needs of Children

The language you establish for naming your family relationships before your child is born provides the initial framework within which your child will understand his or her family and relationships. The language you choose should help to clarify donor negotiations, discussions with your partner, and how you identify yourself to coworkers, your families of origin, and neighbors. What follows is an accounting of the more common titles we at Maia have heard used. There is great diversity in how queer people identify themselves and their kinship relationships. Pay attention to your reactions as you read; they will give you a lot of insight into your own philosophies and assumptions.

Choosing parenting titles you feel accurately reflect your family relationships, and using those names with pride, are the first steps in communicating to others that their use of your chosen titles is important, not only to you but also to your children.

MOM

All lesbian couples raising children are confronted by one question from strangers as well as new friends: "But who's the real mom?"—meaning, "Who gave birth?" Once you've heard this question one or twenty times, you'll start to understand what a vested stake people have in fitting our personal relationships into the familiar heterosexual paradigm. For lesbians, who gave birth doesn't define this reality. Both moms are real. The use of the word "real" in place of "biological" demonstrates how difficult it is for many people, even those with the best intentions, to step outside the heterosexual model of procreation. Many people meeting a lesbian couple with children feel the need to identify for themselves who is "more the mom." This identification, if not made on the basis of biology, is often made on the basis of which partner stays home more with the kids, which partner is more femme, or some other concept rooted in heterosexual stereotypes. Depending on who asks this question and why, you may give a number of different responses. But what's most important is how you answer the question to yourself, your partner, and your children.

Most women who are parenting the child they birthed self-identify as Mother or Mom. If their female partner is also the child's parent, they're in a unique parenting category, which the dominant culture may struggle to recognize. Some nonbirth moms refer to themselves as "second mom," "other mom," or "coparent." Some go by a chosen "mother" name such as Ima or Mere, or simply by their own first name. Many nonbirth mothers we've worked with identify themselves as Mom, just like the mom who gave birth, but often with a subtle distinction (for example, Mama versus Mommy). When both women choose the same title, they confront our culture's inability to conceptualize a "nuclear family" with two moms and children instead of one with both a mom and dad. If you would like to be called Mom or Mommy or Mama, don't let your fear of homophobia color your choice of how you refer to yourself. Claim the title or name that feels right for you. Your child might give it a special twist in order to provide distinction when calling for you or referring to you. Most children naturally come up with distinctions in the terms they use by age four, such as calling one parent Mommy and the other Mama.

DAD

Some women who are fully parents haven't been able to find any title that rings true for them. Some butch or gender-fluid women who are nonbirth parents identify more with the name Dad, feeling that the image invoked more accurately reflects the image of themselves as parents. Additionally, some butch women who give birth also identify more with the term "Dad." Likewise, transmen are dads whether or not they gave birth. Numerous gender-fluid parents we work with identify more closely with "Dad" or come up with their own titles.

More than one family we have worked with has chosen the term "Dadmom" to refer to this parent. These families have felt it makes it easier on their children to refer to their mom and their dadmom. Of course others in the community have felt this only increases the old stereotype that one of us is always the man and one is always the woman. Our families are our own, we will not be able to please everyone in our choice of language to describe ourselves and our family members, nor is it our responsibility to do so—choose what feels right for you.

DONOR, COPARENT, DAD

At Maia we've seen tremendous variation in the terms people use to refer to the role that the biological father has in their life. If an anonymous donor through a sperm bank is used, the title "donor" or "sperm donor" is often used when referring to him. "Biological father" works for some families who want to specify a man's connection to the child, implying that he isn't taking on additional aspects of fatherhood. When working with a donor they know, some women refer to him as the father of the baby, whether or not he'll have a parenting role. Some are called "donors", "known donors," some "uncles," "special uncles," or "super uncles." Some are called "coparents."

Although all these titles in some way reflect the nature of the relationship the man has with the child, what exactly these titles reflect isn't always obvious to someone outside the family. For example, some children's donors become key family members. These donors hold a unique position in the children's lives different from that of other men. Their only title may be "donor," which in other families may refer to the man who donated sperm but has no relationship with the child. Whereas in other families, the men may be called coparents, though they may see the child just once a month and may or may not feel like family to the child. Some children refer to their coparents as Dad and others don't.

|||||||||||||||||||||||||||||||||||||||||||||||||||||||||||||||||||||||||||||||||||||||||||||||||

"I know some lesbians feel compelled to have a man involved in their family so that the child can have a male role model. Whatever. We really want nothing to do with men in our immediate family. We have enough love between us to nourish a small country. We're not lacking anything. Our family is complete with the two of us and any kids we have."—ANGELA, 36, CULVER CITY, CALIFORNIA

|||||||||||||||||||||||||||||||||||||||||||||||||||||||||||||||||||||||||||||||||||||||||||||||||

Occasionally we'll hear a story about a known donor without parenting responsibilities who self-identifies as Dad to family and friends, to the great consternation of the moms, who would never dream of calling him that. Having a more thorough initial discussion with the donor about names and their power helps to avoid this type of unexpected, and sometimes messy, situation.

In reality the names and titles chosen initially often evolve as relationships evolve. This is often directed by the child or by changes in life circumstances.

EXAMPLE: Samara and Ntonia have a son and used a known donor who lived in another state. Their agreement had been that the donor would be available to answer questions for the child. They were open to some sort of relationship developing organically over time, but as they weren't in each other's lives, they were doubtful that this would happen for many years, if at all. Initially their donor would visit when he was in town—once or twice a year for a few hours. Then, through unexpected surges of love, he moved in with them when the child was 4. For months they continued to refer to him as the donor. Then they referred to him as an uncle. Initially, the child was very clear the donor was not his dad whenever someone would ask, but now he is unable to answer those questions as clearly. As the donor is establishing a deepening emotional bond with the child, the family realizes that their son may end up with a dad after all.

The titles designated for the men involved in your family often speak to some deep desires you may have about family ties—regardless of how day-to-day parenting logistics work out. Whether consciously or not, many of us are greatly influenced by our feelings about the presence or absence of our own fathers and/or stepfathers in our rearing. Bringing these feelings into the light can help you to communicate more clearly exactly what you mean when you use these different words. Communicating about this is vital initially within yourself and your partnership, then in your negotiations with a known donor, and finally directly with your child and the world at large.

FAMILY

"Family" has many meanings in the queer community. At pride events we often hear the recording of Sister Sledge singing "We Are Family" as our unofficial anthem. In this context, the lyrics ask us to celebrate the adult kinship systems that queer people form, especially those of us who are distanced from our own biological families by homophobia and our sexual orientation and/or gender presentation. Gay people often use a question such as "Is your coworker family?" to mean "Is he or she queer-identified?"

When we include children in our families, we again recognize the malleability of language. "Family" may have a nuclear-family connotation, meaning two adult partners and their children. It may refer to the people who sleep under the same roof and have an interconnected living arrangement, regardless of their kinship to each other and their children. Family may refer to the extended biological family. To some, family includes all of the people who have unique relationships with the children, perform regular and committed child care, and actively participate in either daily or weekly life with other family members.

Although laws in many countries limit the notion of family to relationships of blood or marriage, unless specifically contested, many cultures (both inside and outside the United States) are more flexible. For example, some cultures identify special child-to-child relationships with the term "cousin," and special adult-to-child relationships of nonmaternal females with the term "aunt." These inclusions are also common among lesbian families, especially in single-parent households.

Besides needing names to refer to their primary parents, children often need special names or titles to give to other important people in their lives, especially for relationships they don't see reflected or valued in popular culture. Examples we've heard of are "stepmom," referring either to a mom who comes into the family when the child is older; or "my lovee" and "my special," referring to a mom's partner, former partner, or housemate who doesn't identify as the primary parent. Friends and family members need to understand that supporting your child's sense of family means recognizing and participating in using the names you and your child use for important family members.

The use of these names may be crucial to a 2- or 3-year-old who is just learning how to describe his or her world in concrete terms, but may be different for a 13-year-old who is making her or his own decisions about how to come out to friends. Our children may answer the question "Who's in your family?" differently according to their developmental stage, how many words they feel like using, and how they perceive they will be responded to. As children age, they often use shorthand and commonly used terms to refer to their complex family structures in situations where knowing all of the details of interconnectedness is not vital. The solid foundation of your family is created from the work you do before your baby's birth. When you're as clear as possible in your own vision and choices, you'll be able to maintain inner confidence that will naturally allow for more flexibility and acceptance of your child's creative expressions of family.

THE BIG EXERCISE: YOUR VISION

To create the family of your dreams, it's important to identify your unexamined, ingrained beliefs about family. This exercise will help you distinguish between your underlying, often unconscious, belief system and how you would choose to create your ideal family. You probably can't tackle the following questions all at once; they aren't merely an item on a to-do list, but are instead tools for ongoing discussion and reflection. As you write or discuss your answers, ask yourself what has influenced your beliefs over the course of your life. Your own family experiences? Images from TV? Opinions of other queer and/or single parent families who are already in your community? Notice the opinions you cling to most rigidly, since they may point to your unspoken fears. Notice also the opinions you feel most passionate about, since they may point to your heart's truest yearnings.

- What, from your childhood memories, was beneficial about your family structure?
- What was challenging about it?
- What seemed to work or not work in terms of roles for each parent?
- As a child did you have friends who had alternative family structures? What were the benefits and drawbacks to their models, both for the children and the parents?
- How many people, ideally, should parent a child? How many people should parent two or more children?
- Does a child need both a male and a female parent?
- Should a child have male and female role models who aren't primary parents?
- Does a child need access to information about who he or she is biologically related to?
- Does a child need the opportunity to have a relationship with the people he or she is biologically related to?
- Can people actively involved in parenting live in more than one household? Does this necessarily mean the child should live in more than one household?
- Can you imagine sharing an intimate and lifelong parenting relationship with someone with whom you aren't romantically partnered?
- Can you imagine sharing an intimate and lifelong parenting relationship with someone with whom you are romantically partnered?
- Can you imagine people who are committed, connected participants in a child's life who aren't primary parents? Would you consider these people family members?
- What would an adequate support system for a single parent encompass?

When you've answered the above questions, summarize by describing your vision of the ideal family, whether in writing, drawing, or some other method of recording, such as tape recording. You'll probably want to be able to refer back to your ideas at a later date.

After you're finished with this exercise, come together with relevant family members and compare your answers. Can you take your visions one step further by combining them? If you decide to do this, save it: It's your family's mission statement and probably contains some of your most heartfelt beliefs.

Keep this document available as your own personalized family template. Hold clear the essence of your vision and why it's important to you. As you move along your pathway to parenthood, you may lose sight of not only what you're trying to achieve, but also why. When you're at an impasse while making decisions about all the various details, or feel overwhelmed, pressured, or uninspired, return to this original vision. Let it rekindle your passion to parent.

Change the vision as you grow, if it seems appropriate. Expand it and clarify it as your understanding of your goals deepens. Use it to ensure that the decisions you make are aligned with your truest intentions. Inherent in families is the concept of change. Our families are similar to heterosexual families in that after five or ten years they don't necessarily look like they did at the beginning. Households may evolve as people redefine their relationships. New lovers connect and blend their families, including stepparents, new children, and ex-lovers. While keeping this in mind, remember that you have the power to thoughtfully choose your initial family structure. Your family mission statement is a living document that reflects your hearts' desires. Keep it updated and it will continue to inspire you for years to come. Share it with your children as they grow.

||||||||||||||||||||||||||||||||||||||||||||||||||||||||||||||||||||||||||||||||||||

Sample Family Mission Statement: We are committed to raising our children in a loving and nurturing home. Alice, Cathy, Manuel, and Jeff are planning to parent our incoming child equally. To us that means we will support Alice throughout the pregnancy and early-newborn period. When the baby is old enough we all eagerly look forward to being with our child for as much time each week as our respective schedules permit. We know that time isn't the only requirement of being a parent. Some of us earn more money and will put this toward supporting our child. Some of us will have more time to be with our child in his or her formative years. We are committed to parenting together even if Alice or Manuel turns out to be infertile. We will try together all of the various options that we can come up with in order to make a baby. This may include using another man's sperm or even considering adoption. If our couples should break up in the future, each of us remains committed to parenting this child throughout his or her life. As four loving parents we welcome our baby.

||||||||||||||||||||||||||||||||||||||||||||||||||||||||||||||||||||||||||||||||||||

CHAPTER 2

Coparenting

COPARENTING PROVIDES MANY wonderful, creative parenting opportunities as well as options for innovative family structures. Still, coparenting almost always takes more work, communication, and lifelong commitment than most people initially expect. A growing number of queer people are choosing to have and raise biological children outside the model of the traditional spousal two-parent family. This is a particularly appealing option for single parents and for parents who aren't interested in bearing full-time parenting responsibilities. We look at various types of coparenting arrangements and their challenges and benefits. Finally, we offer tips for negotiating coparenting contracts and clarifying expectations, and present a number of anecdotes that exemplify the best and the worst scenarios. If you are planning to use a donor/coparent who will also be biologically connected to the child through his sperm it is vital that you also read the relevant chapters in part 2 that address the additional intricacies of this form of coparenting relationship.

What Is a Coparent?

A coparent is what you and your family members define it to be. It may be difficult to find family role models with coparenting relationships similar to your ideal ones unless you live in a large, diverse queer community with many parents and children. You may find some useful coparenting role models in families with parents in which divorces have occurred and stepparents are present, extended-family relatives are key relatives, or best-friend "aunties" or uncles play important roles. These parents, however, rarely start out intending to have the family structure they end up with. So, depending on where you live, you may find yourself in uncharted waters if you're interested in a coparenting or group-family situation.

The term "coparent" often refers to someone who takes responsibility for a child's care and well-being but isn't a primary parent. Occasionally the term refers to someone who does equally share responsibility with other parents but isn't romantically involved with the birth parent. A coparent may be a stepparent, an ex-spouse, a housemate, or a friend. A coparent may or may not be biologically related to the child. If the birth and non-birth parents are lovers, living together, and sharing equal responsibility for the child, they often refer to themselves simply as parents instead of designating the nonbirth mom as the coparent. Occasionally both will call themselves coparents. Some nonbirth moms do refer to themselves solely as coparents when they want to identify themselves specifically as the nonbirth parent and feel hampered by not having any other positive title to choose from in our culture. However, this is becoming less common and we at Maia discourage its use in this way as it minimizes the nonbirth mom's role.

Often when queer and single women coparent with a man or multiple men they talk about him as "my coparent, Dan" rather than "my son's dad." This clarification of language establishes that the child's father is not romantically involved with the child's mother. If a gay male couple and a gay female couple are all sharing parenting responsibilities they may refer to one another as coparents. Some people use the word as a verb, as in "The children have four parents; we all coparent the children." Others use the terms parent and coparent as nouns: A parent is an adult with primary responsibility for the child, while a coparent has a secondary responsibility.

When we consider that housing arrangements, time, finances, and labor divisions vary from family to family, we begin to understand how the imprecision of the term "coparent" can lead to confusion and lack of clarity about who plays what role. At the same time, this lack of a rigid definition can provide wonderful opportunities to create a unique family structure suited precisely to the needs of your family members—in other words, a coparent can be whatever you define it to be.

Types of Coparenting Arrangements

Two-Couple Families

If two people have more resources than one to put toward raising a child, three or four have even more. For example, Elena and Martha coparent with Raul. Elena stays home full-time while the other two work. When their jobs and career goals change, Elena and Raul work half-time and perform child care half-time, while Martha continues to work full-time. Elena and Martha live together; Raul lives in the same apartment building. Their child lives with Elena and Martha. They all share a portion of living expenses informally to allow their work and child-care arrangements to be flexible.

Coparenting does not always mean sharing expenses. Gema and Karen are raising older children from Karen's previous marriage. Gema decides she'd like to get pregnant and give birth. Her partner is encouraging but doesn't feel she can fully commit herself to sharing the responsibility of a baby when she has two kids already. She suggests that they find some other people for extra support in raising the child. They know they want to get sperm from someone they know personally, and they want the baby to have a relationship with his or her father. So they ask Bruce and Toby, a couple they met in a queer coparenting discussion group, if they would be interested in coparenting with them. Bruce, who's very excited about parenting, offers his sperm, and Toby (who feels a little less committed) is supportive of the arrangement but will wait to see how his relationship with the child evolves. The two men live nearby and help out tremendously in the early infancy of baby Isaac so that the older children can keep receiving quality attention from Karen and Gema. Over time the men develop a special relationship with the older children, though their primary relationship in the family is with Isaac. They see him once or twice a week on an informal basis, but do not contribute financially.

Single Parents

Maryam, a single woman, has committed parenting participation from someone other than a lover. She and her friend Davide coparent together. As a female-to-male (FTM) transgender person, Davide is not able to produce sperm. They used a sperm bank to conceive. Davide primarily spends time with their child at night and on weekends. He has more job flexibility than Maryam if one of them needs to take time off work when their child is sick. Davide shares a close emotional bond with their child, and Maryam enjoys the parenting relationship and mutual support she and Davide share.

Kaya, a single woman, lives with two men in a duplex. One is Manuel, her best friend from college; the other is his lover, James. Manuel and James intend to be the primary parents for their soon-to-be-born baby. Kaya wants to return to work soon after giving birth, and the two dads plan to take care of their child during the day. Manuel is a student; James telecommutes two days a week. The fathers have arranged their schedules so that one of them will be home between 8 A.M. and 6 P.M. daily. All three parents have decided to share equally the costs directly associated with the child. The truth about sharing financial responsibility for a child is that the average earning potential of a man still far exceeds that of a woman, and adding the income of one or two men to a one- or two-woman family can be of substantial benefit.

Group Households

In group families, a number of people may live together, each bearing a different amount of responsibility for the child. For example, Noelle and Jackie live in a house with their child, Jonah, and three other housemates. They all identify themselves as a family. One of the housemates has a regular weekly committed "special time" with the child, while the others have more casual connections. The housemates all help out with the child as needed, although the two primary parents are fully financially responsible for the child and make all important decisions in the child's life, such as those re-garding discipline style, bedtime, education, and health care.

In a different situation, two couples, each primarily parenting their own kids, move into a house together and form a social and support unit for each other, each couple acting as coparents to the other couple's kids. For example, they share the responsibility of driving their kids to extracurricular activities, and they share meal preparation and shopping duties. Sometimes they take vacations together, but they split up to visit grandparents. These relationships may be similar to those of close godparents or comadres and compadres.

Coparenting with Men

Queer women choose to coparent specifically with men for many reasons. Lesbian or bisexual women who feel strongly about their children having fathers, not just uncles or donors or male friends, can arrange father-rela-tionship opportunities for their children without being heterosexually part-nered. Some single women, both gay and straight, have had a solid stable relationship with a male best friend for longer than any lover they've had. They realize their best choice right now for a parenting partner isn't a lover. Male coparents need not necessarily be biologically related to the child, but they often are.

The differences between a coparent and a known donor vary from family to family, and this is where the flexibility of coparenting can be a weakness. Often the expected level of participation in making parenting decisions of the parties involved differs. People may be willing to have their known donor develop a close relationship with their child over time, but if they choose the biological father to be a coparent, they're specifically asking him to make a parental commitment from the start. In so doing, they state their willingness not only to share the child's daily life with him but also possibly to share in making decisions about how to raise the child. The challenge lies in the fact that what is entailed in the commitment to shared parenting needs to be spelled out clearly—often before everyone involved knows much about parenting. In fact, some families find it quite helpful to attend parenting classes together and to read parenting books together before deciding to coparent together. In this way they are able to determine if their parenting philosophies are compatible. A coparenting relationship requires the structure of clearly defined roles and expectations as well as the fluidity necessary to accommodate change. The more people are involved, the more difficult it can be to negotiate change successfully.

Who Makes the Parenting Decisions?

Some women and transmen who are the birth parents and primary parents are willing to share decision making equally with their coparents, while others want to retain the right to be the "bottom-line" decision maker in decisions about schooling, health care, discipline, diet, bedtime, weaning, and social activities. Some moms and trans-dads with coparents decide that the birth mom and birth dad (and their partner, if they have one) will be the primary decision makers until the child turns 7, at which point the primary parents and coparents will share ultimate decision-making authority and the child will be old enough to provide some input. In some coparenting situations, everyone is comfortable with the idea that house rules and parenting styles may vary between parents, knowing that, within reason, children have a capacity to understand that different adults interact with them differently and each household may employ a somewhat unique set of rules. Too much variation in parenting styles, or in fundamental parenting philosophy, however, can be very challenging for a child, and therefore should be avoided, so these beliefs and convictions warrant thorough discussion.

Claire is seven and lives primarily with her moms, Kelly and Annette, her older sister, and two other housemates in a large house. She spends Thursday night, Sunday afternoon, and Tuesday evening at the apartment of her dad, Robert. Robert and Claire spend most of their time together one-on-one and have a set of routine activities they enjoy, including eating out, watching videos, listening to music, and playing computer games. At her main house Claire is around more people and noise, and participates in multiple activities, including crafts and hiking. She has somewhat different diets at the two houses, including how much sugar and junk food she is allowed to eat, although she sticks to a vegetarian diet all the time. At each house Claire has similar household responsibilities and is disciplined in a similar manner, and all parents have similar expectations regarding her manners and behavior. Some of the topics all parents have recently discussed as a team—although Kelly and Annette have the final say—are their approaches to spirituality, discussions about sexuality, ideas for helping Claire resolve conflicts with school classmates, and when Claire might be old enough to stay home alone. Kelly and Annette have made primary decisions recently about Claire's health care and extracurricular activities.

EXERCISE: CLARIFYING ATTITUDES ON COPARENTING
Examine the following topics and consider the opinions you have about them in regard to child raising. Which values do you feel so strongly about that anyone you would coparent with would need to share them?

⊙ Health care
⊙ Religion and spirituality
⊙ Diet
⊙ Expenses
⊙ Household responsibilities
⊙ Discipline style
⊙ Day care; preschool; education
⊙ Urban, suburban, rural living
⊙ Housing arrangement
⊙ Playtime activities: videos, music, TV, movies, etc.

Now think of families you know who have coparenting arrangements and glance back at the examples of family structures you have just read. In relationship to household structure, division of income and child expenses, time spent with the child, and naming of relationships, which examples do you like or find insightful? Which sound completely distasteful to you? For each topic in the list above, finish this sentence: "My ideal would be _____." Then complete the sentence "I would be willing to consider _____ if _____ ." Finally, write a working definition for yourself that fits your values: "A coparent is _____."

||||||||||||||||||||||||||||||||||||||||||||||||||||||||||||||||||||||||||||||||||

"As a forty-year-old single woman I realized it was now or never. I asked a close older friend of mine if she'd like to coparent with me. She is straight, retired, and has grown children. After many months of talking we've decided to buy a house together and go for it! I will be the child's mom and she will be the grandma." —ALICIA, 40, RURAL MONTANA

||||||||||||||||||||||||||||||||||||||||||||||||||||||||||||||||||||||||||||||||||

||||||||||||||||||||||||||||||||||||||||||||||||||||||||||||||||||||||||||||||||||||||

"We had worked out all of the coparenting agreements with Maurice before we started to inseminate. Pregnancy was great. But when it came time to sign off for the adoption—he refused. It was a living nightmare for a few months while we got to the bottom of his fears with a therapist. Finally, he signed the papers. He has parented our son every Thursday for the past five years and we are all trying for baby number two."
—RUBY, 34, AND VANESSA, 37, NEW YORK CITY

||||||||||||||||||||||||||||||||||||||||||||||||||||||||||||||||||||||||||||||||||||||

Prior to parenting it's often difficult to realize that a shared parenting relationship is an intimate relationship. This is one of the most important points to consider when evaluating whether coparenting is right for you. This intimate relationship is unique in that it often occurs between people who haven't chosen to be intimate in other ways. Thus, coparents need to communicate frequently. Coparenting seems to work best in families where the parents are both skilled at open, direct, respectful communication. Whether or not they live together, coparents are affected by events in each other's personal lives and are affected by each other's idiosyncrasies—communication style, decision-making style, punctuality, etc.—just as if they were life partners. Some people feel strongly that coparenting is easier than romantic partnership because the unspoken expectations of one another to meet each other's emotional needs are much fewer.

Living Arrangements

Many coparents don't live in the same house but share a duplex or live in the same neighborhood. Some people live far away from each other, but this is rare and is usually the result of a job-based move. Where the child will live should be a detailed point of initial negotiations. Not all coparenting relationships include the desire for the child to spend any nights away from her or his primary house, especially in the child's early years. If you desire this option, read on carefully.

Many prospective parents don't realize that a baby's needs are different than those of an older child. People who have created a clear image in their minds of parenting an elementary-school-age child need to trust that that image may manifest itself eventually but will not look anything like the day-to-day life of raising an infant or toddler. This misconception often causes tension and insecurity during the first years of shared parenting. With a realistic view of how a baby's needs evolve, you can incorporate flexible arrangements into your parenting agreements.

If the parent who gave birth is breastfeeding, she'll find it difficult for the child to spend the night away from home until the child is eating quite a bit of solid food, which begins usually at eight to fourteen months of age. (Although a baby may start eating solid food at five to six months, breastfeeding frequency won't immediately decrease. Many children and primary parents are not emotionally ready to have the infant sleep away from home until he or she is two or three years old. Likewise many children nurse for up to four—or even more—years.) Nursing is a very intimate and important bond. In our practice we've seen birth parents, before or during pregnancy, commit to wean the baby at six months, so that the child could start spending the night regularly at the dad's house. Once these women actually started parenting and felt the strength of mothering instincts, they were miserable being under the pressure of a rigid timetable. In fact, any promises about nursing versus bottle feeding that come with dates attached are a setup for hard feelings, whether or not they relate to sleepover arrangements. Therefore, we strongly recommend that you make no specific commitments about breastfeeding timelines.

If your ultimate goal is to have actively involved coparents who live in different houses, it's crucial to include the above information about breastfeeding needs when you discuss how the first year will work. Using "half-time," "equal-time," or "50/50" language to conceptualize the living and time-sharing arrangements of the first few years is unrealistic. If the baby nurses every hour to three hours in the beginning, your coparents may be spending all their time with the baby at your house. Although some nursing parents feel comfortable pumping milk so that others can feed the baby with a bottle, most first-time birth parents feel the need for time at the breast to be crucial for establishing a strong and healthy immune system and for proper emotional and physical development. The bond of the birth parent to the baby should not be undermined. For more information about the value of the bond of biology see *The Queer Parents' Primer*.

On the other hand, some birth parents feel quite committed to de-emphasizing the biological bond and feel that by pumping there is increased potential for the other parent(s) to bond with the baby. It is important to make sure that the baby has formed secure attachments with each parent, regardless whether or not feeding the baby is a formative element in the establishment of that bond.

Is it feasible for them to see the baby four times a week or more, for several hours each time, in your living room? Have you ever spent that much intimate time with your potential coparent(s)? If not, you'd better go camping together for a week and see what happens.

Finally, some parents are fine leaving their infant with a grandparent, aunt, coparent, or best friend for an occasional night. Others won't consider having their child sleep away from them until he or she is three or four years old. Even if your potential coparents don't expect the infant to spend the night regularly at their house, they may have many fantasies of special sleepover parties occurring later that may or may not come to pass on the timeline they expect. It's not too soon to discuss this in your pre-pregnancy negotiations. On the contrary, this kind of discussion of expectations is essential.

As they grow older, some children adapt well to living in two households, while others find it disruptive. If you'd like your child to live in more than one household, it will be difficult to plan in advance at what age your child will be ready for this arrangement, if at all. Some parents don't want their child to spend equal amounts of time at each household, or they feel it would be unfeasible, so they plan instead on their child spending one weekend a month at the second house or having impromptu sleep-overs and participating in regular daytime visits and outings. Other families find that an equally divided schedule will work fine at some point. How much participation the child will have in choosing for him or herself as he or she grows older is an important question to consider in your living-arrangement discussions.

Often people are quite far into the negotiation process before they realize the assumption is that they're committing to live in the same town as the coparent(s) for the next eighteen years, no matter what happens with their careers or personal lives. Once again, this is an opportunity to clarify whether all of the coparents will be primary parents or if the coparent(s) will be auxiliary parents. This can impact who ultimately gets to make decisions. Auxiliary parents usually do not share equal decision-making power with primary parents when it comes to bigger decisions, such as what schools the child will attend or the style of discipline to use.

MAIA'S RECOMMENDATIONS FOR BUILDING LASTING CO-PARENT RELATIONSHIPS: The time you put into your negotiations with potential coparents prior to pregnancy is invaluable. Don't let your "baby lust" alone govern your choices of coparents; take the time to explore together whether you're truly a good match. We've found that coparent relationships that last more than just a few years are the ones that have followed these guidelines:

- Agree that each individual will seek counseling about the kind of family he or she wants to create prior to inseminating.
- All couples involved need to have clear lines of communication and solid, healthy relationships with each other.
- Agree that all involved coparents will attend family counseling sessions every six weeks for the duration of your child's life — starting before conception.
- Agree to stay out of court if conflicts arise. Commit to counseling first, then mediation if needed, or agree on a new model such as a family council.
- Take the time to draw up thorough, personalized contracts, estate planning, wills, and other pertinent legal documents.
- Agree to uphold the intentions that are laid out in your contracts.
- Discuss in depth your opinions on religion and spirituality, medical and health approaches, education, values, and other important issues.
- Make provisions for possible career changes and/or relocation.
- Be clear in your contracts about mutual expectations about finances, decision making, and time commitments with the child.
- Clarify not only to yourselves but also to lawyers, therapists, extended family members, and friends what your agreements and intentions are for your family. This framework will help to hold you all accountable in times of tension.

Issues with Families of Origin

Coparenting almost always includes negotiating holiday plans. When your child is in school, the one- or two-week winter holiday may not afford him or her enough time to see all the grandparents. You'll have to decide how to handle this. Perhaps you'll all visit the relatives together. If you don't, you'll need to decide if your relatives will see your daughter only with you, or with you and your partner, or with her other coparents as well. If, for example, your extended family never sees your child with her dads, they may have a difficult time acknowledging your child's relationship with them. By the time all the relatives get visited, you may not have time to take your own family vacation. Through working out specific examples like this, you and your potential coparents can begin to understand the level of communication necessary to make your relationships work and use these topics as practice exercises to get the feel of one another's expectations, and communication and conflict-resolution styles.

Finances

We've witnessed many creative financial arrangements between coparents. Some families decide that all parents will contribute a percentage of their income to the child's expenses, based on how much each makes individually. Others pay a monthly amount each, which may or may not vary with the income of the parent. Some split the costs of parenting among the adults who are working, exempting the person or persons doing the primary child care. Some families make financial arrangements that reflect the amount of time each parent has with the child or how parental decision-making power is distributed. It's a good idea to discuss how arrangements might change if someone gets a large pay raise, gets laid off, or goes on disability. Financial discussions are often charged and can lead to conflict, which often arises from a difference in opinion about the child's needs. A common conflict occurs in regard to specific expenditures: One person thinks private school is worth $12,000 a year, while the other parent can't or won't pay, feeling it's an unnecessary expense.

Negotiation Dynamics

In your discussions with a potential donor, be honest about exactly why you want a coparent; then you may ask for the same level of honesty in return. Good negotiating builds trust and betters communication skills, which will help you resolve problems together more smoothly later on. You'll probably want to discuss what everyone's family life was like growing up, whom each of you hold as your parental role models, and why. Discuss how you imagine the details of a regular day in your child's life and what might happen in the event of everyday surprises. For instance, what will happen when your child needed to stay home sick from school and you all have busy schedules?

If you're having deep and detailed conversations before deciding to parent together, you'll almost certainly experience initial misunderstandings, feel threatened, or doubt each other's intentions. You can realistically expect these feelings to arise during such important conversations, but you can also use these tense moments to deepen your communication if you openly acknowledge the tension and work through it. Often you both may subconsciously skirt around possible points of contention for months, because ultimately no one wants to find a point that is nonnegotiable. When people are wedded to the idea of parenting together, possibly believing it's their only option for creating a family, the stakes can feel very high.

Thoroughly discussing all the variables will help each of you to develop an accurate vocabulary for understanding what you each feel is your ideal vision of family and parenting. Often it's helpful to negotiate in the presence of another person, so that you'll have a third party involved. Many alternative family specialists can help you with this project. Be aware, however, of the bias this third party may bring to the conversation (no one is completely objective), in terms of how well this person knows each of you or whether they've had personal experience with the topic at hand. Also, remember, this is your life: if you find you've offered too much right away, you're not stuck. Simply have another conversation and clarify what you feel. This will allow you to create the family you want and will also set the stage for honesty and for dealing with the emotional and circumstantial changes inherent in raising a child.

Contracts and Legal Issues

A contract benefits a coparenting family in a number of ways. Some think of it as a bureaucratic task; others approach it with dread, fearing it will cause conflict, and others feel that drawing up contracts will take away from the natural flow of the relationship. We encourage you to regard a parenting contract as a powerful tool. Approaching it in this spirit, most parents find the process of creating the contract deeply rewarding. The security of having a parenting contract is invaluable.

Many people believe a parenting contract isn't necessary because they share a high level of trust and communication. In reality, what we've seen is that people who go through the process of writing a contract—clarifying on paper their intentions about roles, responsibilities, values, and conflict resolution—feel even greater trust and a higher level of communication when they finish. Developing a contract can provide you with guidance through important initial conversations so that crucial pieces aren't overlooked. Furthermore, if and when a time arises that a coparenting group or couple don't communicate as well as hoped, a contract will clearly state beyond the ambiguities of memory what the original intention of the family was. It can serve to protect the nonlegal parents of the child, when used in mediation or other conflict resolution strategies that do not involve custody litigation.

Legal parents are defined as the biological parents of a child, unless a second-parent or stepparent adoption has been completed and the birth certificate has been amended. The legal parents are the parents on the birth certificate. In most states there can only be two legal parents. The contract serves as an essential tool for reminding everyone to act with the utmost integrity, especially if it's not written in "legalese" but in a language that conveys your heartfelt intentions when you agreed to parent together.

Planning for Disagreement

At some point you'll likely reach an impasse in making a parenting decision. This may happen prior to pregnancy or when your child is much older. Perhaps you differ in your opinion on vegetarianism, your comfort with Western medicine versus alternative health care, or whether the child will spend a month of the summer with a specific grandparent. What will you do when conflict arises? Having a well-articulated plan of action will help put all of your minds at ease. An agreement to see a family counselor is a good example. In your parenting contract it's wise to work out all the details, such as who will choose the counselor, who will pay, and whether all need to agree that counseling is necessary or if one party can demand it. A number of families we've worked with see a therapist as a team every six weeks to keep channels of communication open, to maintain healthy relationships, and to prevent the need for crisis intervention.

Legal Status of the Contract

A coparenting agreement is not likely to hold up in a court of law. If there is any way to become a legal parent to your child, through marriage or adoption, we encourage it strongly. If there is no such avenue available, a coparenting document will clearly outline your intentions. This document has strength when used in formal mediation. Please remember to have statements that acknowledge everyone's prior knowledge and acceptance of each parent's gender identity and sexual orientation. This increases your security against such personal attributes becoming weapons used against you in a time of conflict.

Contract Content

Besides containing a detailed plan for conflict resolution, your contract may include a communication plan, specifying how and why you'll keep these channels open. The contract should specify the details you've worked out in the areas we mentioned earlier: finances, decision-making, household and living arrangements, and special areas of importance. It may also include some history about how you all came together to parent and why you specifically chose one another. It could also list the reasons why each of you want to parent, what the concept of "family" means to you, and what commitment each of you is making to your child now and in the future. Write the contract in the language you could imagine reading to an older child as a beautiful tribute to the love you brought to creating family; this will keep you writing your own truth, not what you imagine a legal document should sound like.

Dealing with Change

After you set up a coparenting relationship, it will inevitably change, no matter how you expect it to turn out, because the rest of life continues in its dynamic way while you parent. People who aren't yet parents have a difficult time understanding both the permanency of the relationship and the inevitable flux the relationship will undergo. You must, however, prepare yourselves for the unexpected. If you aren't someone who can adapt well to unexpected change, you'll want to either develop these skills or seriously consider not entering into a coparenting situation, since when you parent with other people, changes are bound to arise.

Issues for Single Parents-to-Be

Single parents-to-be often choose coparenting as a way of starting off their parenting with a strong base of support. We commonly see single moms–to-be choosing to coparent with their donors. We also commonly see single parents-to-be choosing to coparent with close friends or family members. The arrangements that we have most commonly seen involve the birth parent as the primary parent with other supporting parents, in other words: only one legal parent, only one ultimate decision maker, but others who have committed to her or him and to the child. Some of these arrangements are more formal than others. Unfortunately, we have also seen a fair number of empty promises in situations where the parties did not take the time to formalize agreements and expectations. Take the time, prior to pregnancy, to clarify each possible coparent's commitment and expectations. Make sure that you clearly state if you are simply asking for support in the early years of parenting or if you are asking for a lifelong, day-to-day commitment to the child.

New Relationships

If a coparent becomes partnered, the existing parents may feel uncomfortable with the new partner taking on a close role with the child when the primary parent(s) barely know this person. This is, in effect, a stepparent situation with all the opportunities and difficulties of a blended family. If a couple who share parenting with a coparent break up, the child now potentially has three households. This can result in the child having many stepparents if both people in the prior couple partner with new people. Not all possible scenarios can be worked out in advance, but in general the point is that coparenting situations have the potential for many complicated relationships.

In conclusion, no matter how clear you think your vision is, ask honest questions of yourselves and your potential coparents. More discussion is far better than less. Use your contract as a means to achieve even deeper discussion. Examine how solidly you trust your own communication skills as well as your ability to be flexible and to compromise. You'll need to rely on all of these skills if you choose to coparent. We also remind you that coparenting with anyone means a lifelong commitment to each other as well as the child. Two truths exist about coparenting: The struggles are real, and with enough creativity the opportunities are broad. For sample coparenting contracts, please see the Maia website www.maiamidwifery.com.

CHAPTER 3

Making Decisions and Creating a Plan and a Timeline

QUEER FAMILIES STARTED from scratch are intentional families. That means that our children are wanted children, children brought into this world from the great love we have to share with them. Anytime you are confronted with internal doubt or external questioning about whether or not you have the right to parent, remember that your child is a much planned, deeply loved, and wanted child. That is the greatest gift that anyone can give to their child.

As you start out on your path to parenthood, you'll face many decisions unique to queer families. The sheer number of these decisions, as well as their importance, may simultaneously empower and intimidate you. Whether you struggle through these decisions or make them with ease, you're creating your own unique approach to parenting that will carry you through the years ahead. Most of us experience at least a few instances when we can't seem to make a decision, doubt a decision we thought we had firmly made, or can't reach a mutual decision with a partner or prospective coparent. This chapter will help you develop specific decision-making tools and skills. It will advise you on how to create your own plan and timeline for your journey to pregnancy. This timeline and the information included on what to do when you're stuck making a decision are the essential tools you'll need to keep yourself moving forward toward your goal of creating a family.

The first part of this chapter discusses why some decisions seem so difficult to make. The second section focuses on how to make decisions well. The third part guides you through creating a personal plan and timeline, describing when to make each decision. The final section outlines ideas about what to do if you're procrastinating or can't seem to move forward with your decisions.

Self-Love

By the time your child is growing up, you'll be used to making many daily decisions, both big and small, about his or her life. Some you will undoubtedly agonize over; most you'll make easily. Right now you may feel overwhelmed about the fact that parenting involves making decisions that will permanently affect another person's life. Sometimes, especially in the beginning, the staggering weight of this responsibility immobilizes people. "What if I don't make the best decision about something very important?" is a fundamental question parents and parents-to-be ask themselves again and again.

You'll parent most successfully and joyfully when you approach decisions from a place of self-love instead of fear or guilt. Learning to trust and believe that you'll make the best possible decisions you can at the time, with the best intentions for your family and self, is a crucial element of self-love. Self-love includes acknowledging that some of your decisions may seem like mistakes later. If you can commit to being as honest as possible in your self-reflection and communication, you'll do well. Women who approach the many parenting decisions ahead of them from this perspective more easily avoid becoming burdened by regrets or immobilized with indecisiveness.

If you've made many other important decisions in your life, you may feel awkward now if you find yourself challenged by the decisions before you. Don't worry: this awkwardness is a sign that you're on the right track; feeling awkward is a natural part of learning and growing. We honor growing babies with love instead of judgment as they learn to walk, hesitatingly, taking clumsy tentative steps, falling, and trying again. We need to honor ourselves in this way as we learn to make parenting decisions, because we not only grow our babies, we also grow our parent-selves.

Obstacles to Clear Decisions: Internalized Homophobia and Transphobia

Homophobia and transphobia are still very much a present force in society. Homophobia and transphobia can be defined as an irrational fear or contempt for or prejudice against queer and transgender people or our lifestyle or our cultures. Due to cultural homophobia, internalized homophobia, and the lack of easy access to sperm, women and transmen without biologically male partners have to claim their right and renew their commitment to have children at each step toward getting pregnant. They constantly must call upon their courage to go forward, in the presence of many messages that say they shouldn't. When a person has internalized society's homophobia, self-doubts can take on a life of their own, carrying an emotional charge that's sometimes difficult to recognize and understand.

Often queer and single parents-to-be feel they must be perfect before they parent, not only to provide the best for their children but also to prove to everyone who may wonder whether we can be excellent parents. This self-expectation of being 200 percent perfect can reveal itself in various forms.

In the early stages of deciding to parent, women appear to be especially vulnerable to the effects of both homophobia and single-parent prejudices. Queer people who spend many years wanting to parent but not taking the necessary steps to start inseminating are often immobilized by unprocessed internalized homophobia. Homophobia is insidious because it's often invisible. It's important to examine whether internalized or external homophobia is a factor when you're unable to take the necessary steps toward becoming a parent. Sometimes therapy or counseling is needed to help you explore these issues, as their impact on your life can feel paralyzing.

Internalized homophobia and external homophobia can arise once you begin to inseminate and again when you're pregnant and parenting. Therefore, it's important to actively address these influences now and begin to dismantle their power over you. You do a service to yourself and your children when you eradicate shame and move into pride.

Difficulty Making Donor Decisions

Donor decisions are the most common area in which many people reach an impasse in their decision-making process. The foundational and often subconscious reasons for this phenomenon usually involve homophobia and single-parent shame. Only some of the influences of homophobia stem from its internalized forms; the external structures of society's homophobia impact how we make decisions. For example, societal homophobia has created a legal system that greatly affects how we make decisions about donors and sperm, in that the system doesn't automatically protect queer parenting relationships. If you want to use sperm from a known donor, you may choose to inseminate in a doctor's office or freeze your donor's sperm at a sperm bank solely to secure legal protection.

If making decisions about sperm isn't easy for you economically or philosophically, you may get stuck at this decision-making point, unable to reconcile your fear of unsecured custody with your desire to conceive with sperm that doesn't come from an anonymous donor.

Internalized heterosexism may also affect you at this juncture. You may feel secure in your decision to conceive with sperm from a sperm bank. Yet as you look at the lists of potential donors at a sperm bank, you may feel suddenly sad. Some women feel sad or disappointed at the thought that their child won't have a father in his or her life. Others feel sad at the realization that they've been considering their own single or partnered female household to be less valid because there is no father. It's important to reframe these forms of thinking from a perspective of lack to an appreciation of all you have to give your child. Exploring your own issues surrounding men, fathers, and society's expectations may be necessary in order for you to find the donor you wish to use.

Challenges for Single Parents-to-Be

Single parents-to-be—whether they be trans, straight, lesbian, or bisexual—who are at an impasse in their journey to parenthood often need to sort out a variety of internalized messages. If you're single and waiting for a partner to arrive before you parent, try to disentangle your parenting needs from your ideas about the stigmatization of single parents so that you can truly consider different arrangements of feasible parenting that suit your situation. If you have a clearly articulated understanding of which resources you specifically bring to parenting, not just in comparison with a two-parent family, you'll be less likely to make decisions about donors and other issues on the basis of internalized feelings of inadequacy or shame.

Is It Desirable to Remain Closeted?

Queer people choose many different strategies of being out or closeted about their sexual identity. Often someone will choose to express her identity in different ways depending on the situation. The same is true for transgender parents. In some situations you may choose to disclose your sexual orientation or true gender identity. In others you may choose to "pass" as heterosexual/or the gender of your birth. Many lesbians are afraid to parent while they are closeted but are also afraid to come out. But being closeted isn't necessarily something you want to continue to do as a parent. Still, finding the courage and strength to come out may seem overwhelming. The desire to remain closeted often stems from a combination of internalized homophobia/transphobia and perceived risk of external homophobic/transphobic actions.

Before pregnancy, fears of homophobia or transphobia may make it difficult for you to interact with sperm-bank employees or health-care providers who offer services you need, especially if you don't have an active plan for how you'll present relevant information about yourself, your partner, or other family members. Of course, as unjust as it continues to be, in many areas these concerns are very real. Coming out may result in a lack of access to much-needed services. Deciding whether to come out is always a personal decision. Give this issue attention from the beginning, and if you're partnered, make sure that you both share an approach that feels inclusive yet safe for both of you. Deciding in advance how you'll present yourself to others will reduce homophobia's or transphobia's power over you, which would otherwise cause you to delay entering potentially uncomfortable situations.

When deciding whether or not to come out about your sexual orientation, be aware that many people will assume you're straight when you mention planning a family, even if they don't assume so already. If you're partnered, how you respond to questions about the father is always an opportunity for you to come out. If you're a woman partnered with a woman and you don't come out—whether or not your partner is with you at the time—you negate her importance in your life and family.

When deciding whether to cross-live as a pregnant man—sometimes living as a man, and sometimes as a woman depending on the situation—or to live full-time within your gender identity, there are numerous considerations at hand.

It is greatly valuable to make the necessary changes in your life to be able to live in a community where you and your child will be accepted prior to conception.

Examining Your Internalized Homophobia/Transphobia

It's helpful to become more consciously aware of the impact internalized homophobia or internalized transphobia has on you. As you read the following section, examine what you think you need in your life before you're ready to parent. You may realize you hold yourself to a standard you wouldn't expect others to maintain. Or perhaps you'd expect other queer parents, but not straight parents, to match your standards. These expectations are unfair both to you and to others. But holding yourself to impossibly high standards is understandable, since many of us are asked by others to justify our decision to parent in ways that straight people are not. You may not even be consciously aware that heterosexual parents are not often asked to validate their parenting choices in the way lesbian, bisexual, trans, and single parents often are.

EXERCISE: HOMOPHOBIA AND PARENTING
Explore these questions in your journal or through discussion with a friend or partner:

⊚ Is it fair to give birth to a child who may be stigmatized because of his or her family members?
⊚ How much homophobia will my child suffer because of my choices?

- If my child were gay or trans, how would I feel about that?
- When I'm a parent will I lose control of who I'm out to?
- Do I have to lose my current gender identity to gain an identity as a parent?
- Do I have the right to have children?
- Can children be healthy if raised by lesbians?
- Can children be healthy if raised by a trans-parent?
- Can children be healthy if raised by one gay woman?
- Can I be a good parent?

These are reasonable questions, and how we answer them is influenced by how each of us grapples with homophobia. If you find that your answers reflect a strong level of internalized homophobia, you may find the resources listed at the end of the book very helpful. At Maia we've found that as a necessary part of the journey to parenthood, women need to explore the impact of external and internal homophobia on their decision to parent. Women who don't address these issues often get delayed in their decision-making process. We also see that if these issues are not addressed prior to conception it leads to a greater tendency towards depression and isolation both during pregnancy and postpartum.

Decision-Making Styles

Time spent actively reflecting on how you make decisions will not be wasted. You have so many decisions ahead of you: some small, some large, some reversible, some permanent. Stress over making decisions often stems from a fear of the consequences of your decisions. Stress may also stem from the fact that your style of decision making isn't the healthiest for you.

If you're partnered, making big decisions can place a strain on your relationship. It's valuable to explore together how each of you makes important decisions and how you've made decisions together in the past. Such reflection will give your relationship a much more solid footing for parenting discussions to come. After reading through the following descriptions of some common approaches to decision making, try the accompanying exercise to help you determine your decision-making style.

Analytical: You create budgets, timelines, and lists of pros and cons. Your approach strictly adheres to cost-benefit analysis, meaning you balance the potential cost of decisions against their potential benefit. You may focus on the probabilities of risk.

Intuitive: You take a spiritual approach to decision making, perhaps through prayer, art, tarot, or your own intuition. You may write in a journal in a stream-of-consciousness style to clarify your feelings and ideas. You may sit by a stream or in a temple or church or wherever you go to ponder and listen to your soul.

Body-based: Your approach is visceral, on the "gut-level." You're aware when decisions make you feel peaceful and calm or agitated and unsettled. You get information from whether a choice you make leads you to relaxed deep breathing versus shallow breathing. You notice if your decisions cause an upset stomach or headache.

Default: Your fear of making a decision leads you to make no decision. You think often about worst-case scenarios. Perhaps you procrastinate until your lover decides for you, or you're forced to make a last-minute decision, or you miss the opportunity entirely. Most commonly your decisions are made by default.

Experimental: You try things on for size and don't hesitate to change your mind and try again. You gather information about what works and doesn't work for you through the experiential process.

External-input: You ask for opinions from your community, your friends, therapist, your parents, and spiritual guides. You organize an "advisory committee" or "board of directors" of friends, coworkers, and family members. Perhaps you generalize from anecdotal stories you read or hear about, or people you interview.

If you aren't sure how you make decisions, think back in time. What big decisions have you made in the past? Have you been happy about how you made them? Have the decisions you've made given you a feeling of achievement or confidence? Have you rushed through the process of making a decision because it was uncomfortable for you? Do you feel you took an unreasonably long time to make your decision? What feedback have you gotten from others about how you make decisions? Has their feedback been useful or rung true?

A sophisticated decision-maker can consciously employ a mix of the above styles in the process of reaching a decision, with the balance dependent upon the type of decision. How would you like to make decisions?

Decisions in a Partnership

So often lovers fall into the habit of speaking in emotional shorthand. You may assume you know your partner so well that she isn't obliged to fully articulate her thoughts, needs, and desires. For her part she may feel that the familiarity she has with you allows her to take for granted many aspects of communication. Moving into parenthood, though, means moving into a completely new territory of life. You may discover things about yourself and each other that you hadn't yet realized. Who your parents were to you, what family means to you, and how you want to create new life are some of the biggest, deepest, and most personal topics you can explore. What you learn through this exploration—and how you integrate the influence of your upbringings into your joint parenting choices—may require levels of communication and skill that your relationship hasn't yet needed.

Clear decisions within a partnership support greater intimacy. A relationship is strengthened when both partners feel included and invested in making decisions. Creating a unified vision of your intentions and plans to parent will help you not only negotiate each of your roles and expectations throughout the process, but also help you negotiate clearly with potential coparents or donors.

Roles in Decision-Making

You'll probably notice, if you haven't already in your relationship, that each of you occasionally falls into predetermined roles, whether consciously or unconsciously. Perhaps one of you is the worrier, so the other becomes the reassurer. The worrier doesn't get to feel her own confidence and trust, and the reassurer has no room to name her own fears. Perhaps one is the initiator, more aggressively pursuing information and pushing for making decisions, while the other holds back. The initiator feels unsupported and alone in manifesting the parenting vision, and the one holding back feels rushed or even guilty for not doing her share of the work. Perhaps one of you expresses passion and intuitiveness about your decisions, so the other plays the role of the rational thinker to maintain a sense of balance.

When you have set roles, it's common for neither of you to feel completely whole in your approach to the decision at hand. Be aware of who takes on which role, name it, and bring it into the conscious realm. When making decisions, choosing roles that balance each other is often helpful. If you don't want the role you find yourself in, remember that you can change that. Look for other ways to find balance within the partnership, or even try out some new roles as an exercise for expanding your perspectives. Evaluating each of your decision-making styles and how they mesh will give you valuable insight into the dynamics of your relationship roles.

Honoring Different Discussion Styles

Often one partner will want to discuss the baby-making process more frequently than the other. Perhaps one of you prefers to set aside a block of uninterrupted time during the weekend to update each other and share feelings, while the other calls at work a number of times a day to share late-breaking news and thoughts on the subject. If this is the case, you may need to set aside times for baby-free discussion as a way to keep space for the other aspects of your life together. You may also need to create some structure for the baby discussions you do have, to make sure each of you gets a chance to express your feelings fully.

Many people find the following listening practice helpful. For five minutes at a time, take turns actively listening to each other without interrupting. At the end repeat to your partner what you heard her say, without her interrupting to correct you. This practice will reveal the subtle differences between what you say and what your partner hears. This fine attention to clear communication will lead to more harmonious conversations and a deepening of your relationship.

EXERCISE: PARTNERS AND DECISIONS

Think about a few important decisions you've made together in the past, one at a time. For each decision, reflect on how you think the decision-making process went. Thinking about it now, do you notice any unresolved feelings? If so, why? How did your partner communicate (or not) what she wanted? Did the process of making this important decision elicit a feeling of greater intimacy? What style of decision making did you use in each situation? What style of decision-making did your partner approach the decision with? How would you describe the style of decision-making that you ultimately used together to come to your final decision? What would you do differently if you could?

Next, make some active and explicit commitments with your partner about how you'd both like to approach making decisions about having a baby. If you feel your current communication style is effective, discuss with your partner what in particular works for you. If you feel you'd like to improve or try a new approach, articulate specifically how you intend to change your communication style and in what way you'd like to see hers change. Ask her to tell you in her own words what she heard you say; to make sure you're both clear. Ask her to let you know if she shares these intentions, and then ask her to tell you her own intentions so that you can repeat them back to her.

Positive feedback about the specific successes of your communication together will not only make each of you feel appreciated for your efforts, but also will help reinforce what works in your communication together. Making difficult decisions together can be some of the most challenging yet rewarding work in your relationship.

Embodied Decisions

Conception, pregnancy, and birth are body experiences. Our bodies hold ancient wisdom in the form of instinct about how to conceive, grow, and birth a baby. Learning to notice your body responses will help you access a lot of important information. When you have trouble implementing a decision you've made, notice how your body feels when you think about that decision. If you hold ambivalence about your decision, you should reexamine it: you may notice your body feeling tense, closed up, or uncomfortable instead of soft, relaxed, or open. Your body speaks for your heart, not your mind. Your heart is where you hold your truth about what is most important to you. Your mind can get caught in details and limited options that may hinder your ability to solve problems creatively.

The specific type of information that your body can best give you is regarding whether you feel safe. Checking in with your body will help you discover how safe you feel about a certain decision, both consciously and subconsciously. If you commit yourself to doing something that feels unsafe, whether it's working with a specific sperm donor or trying an infertility treatment, you'll eventually have to disconnect or numb yourself from your body's discomfort and danger signals in order to continue with your choice.

Disconnection is a powerful coping mechanism for dealing with difficult situations. It is often an old coping strategy left over from childhood. Unfortunately, many of us use disconnection in challenging situations that we actually could change. Making decisions that are validated by your body—embodied decisions—allows you to make strong choices. Such choices support you in being present rather than employing patterns of disconnecting or "checking out." When you prioritize choices that make you feel embodied, your process of becoming a parent will feel much more rewarding, and you'll be able to model this embodiment for your own children.

Past Influences on Decision-Making

Sometimes when we make decisions solely from external information or pressure, we make choices that aren't appropriate to us as individuals. To make a decision that's right for you, you may find it helpful to take into account your past experiences. Recognizing and acknowledging what has been particularly joyful or painful about your experiences with men, your reproductive cycle, and the medical system will help you understand what makes you feel safe or unsafe about the process of getting pregnant and giving birth. We encourage you to notice how you feel in your body while thinking about any of these past experiences. Using your body to gather information about your past experiences is time well spent, as they will affect your decisions both consciously and subconsciously. Our life experiences greatly affect our sense of safety and comfort—both positively and negatively.

Making Your Preconception Plan

The following section outlines specific areas in which decisions often need to be made in order to help you devise a personal pre-pregnancy plan that includes a timeline. As you read through these topics, take notes on which issues are pertinent to you, which decisions you've already made, and any additional things that arise that you need to make decisions about. The next step is to create a working plan and timeline for making these decisions and moving toward your goal of getting pregnant.

For many prospective parents, breaking down a pregnancy plan in this way makes the process much more manageable. Working with a checklist can help to greatly shorten the time it takes to move from wanting to parent to actually getting pregnant.

Preparing-for-Pregnancy Checklist

- Have I thought about homophobia/transphobia and its role in my decisions?
- Do I need to come out to people in my life?
- Do I need more support structures in place before I begin inseminating?
- Am I clear about my family vision?
- Have we thought about how we would coparent if we split up?
- Do I have a workable financial plan or budget?
- Do I need to research insurance plans and parental leave benefits?
- Do I need to change jobs?
- Is my housing situation adequate?
- Do I have personal issues I'd like to resolve before pregnancy?
- Do we need to do anything to strengthen our partner relationship?
- Are we clear about which one of us will get pregnant first?
- Do I have a plan for improving my health and fertility?
- Have I started to monitor my fertility?
- Do I need to make any health-care appointments or have tests performed?
- Do I need to research how legal issues in my state affect my donor and parenting choices?

- If I'm using a sperm bank, have I completed all preliminary registration steps, including having health tests performed and sent to the bank?
- Have I selected my three donors?
- If I'm working with a known donor, have we negotiated expectations, reviewed his/her health history, received sperm-count results and the results of other necessary tests, and written a contract?

Family Structure

Having read through the information in chapter 1, you've been exploring your visions of ideal family and the support structures you'll need to be a good parent. How you envision your family will not only affect your sperm options, but also may affect some of the issues covered in the following sections, such as work and housing options. It's crucial to clarify your desired family structure before you make any permanent decisions. Take your time thoroughly exploring your own family history, personal motivations, and ideals. If you're partnered, communicate with each other clearly so that you'll understand each other's needs and desires.

Finances

People often feel great pressure to guarantee financial security for their children before they conceive. As you may guess, a lot of variation exists as to how much money is adequate. You may choose to plan a budget for conception costs, prenatal care costs, and even the first months of parenting. As you read on, though, you may expand your pregnancy and conception budget to include nutritional supplements, acupuncture visits, and ovulation test kits. An awareness of your financial limitations will be helpful in making decisions further down the road, but also remember that creative financing has included everything from taking out loans, throwing insemination fundraising parties, and sharing child-care responsibilities with others.

Work

Some parents-to-be have concerns relating to their job that they would like to resolve before getting pregnant. These concerns can usually be addressed by creating a task list. Work-related tasks may include exploring your insurance and parental-leave options. Your list may include wanting to find a job that pays more or gives you adequate health coverage, or negotiating better maternity or family-leave benefits. You might discuss working part-time from home or job sharing for a few months after the baby is born. Consider how difficult it may be to stay at your current job while you're pregnant if your workplace isn't gay- or trans-friendly or you aren't out to your coworkers or boss. If loyalty to your company means remaining in the closet to employees or clients, know that being closeted and pregnant in the workplace is a daunting challenge for many people.

You may initially choose not to let your boss know that you're trying to conceive. You may choose not to share your baby plans with your boss because you're aware of the discrimination women face in some work environments when they're perceived as being on the "mommy track" instead of the "career track." Unfortunately, pregnancy discrimination, combined with homophobia, can make job stability shaky at a time when you want and need stability.

Some feel that becoming perfect at their job is the only action that will provide adequate security in the face of such discrimination, and thus they delay pregnancy indefinitely in their quest for perfection. If this is your case, it will be most helpful to give yourself a definite timeline to follow in order to make your work environment feel stable enough for you to move forward with having a baby. In chapter 21 we'll give you information about being an out pregnant lesbian in the workplace. If this is a significant concern for you, you may want to read ahead before you make a work task list as part of your overall baby plans.

Many people take this time prior to pregnancy to create a worklife that is more supportive of parenting. This might involve a job change to reduce commuting, finding a job with flexible hours, or finding a less demanding job. Learning to decrease the stress associated with your work is also a beneficial goal. Learning to leave work at work and to set appropriate boundaries at work are also skills to develop at this time that you will need when you are a parent. If you make every effort to shift your priorities now, both pregnancy and parenthood will proceed more smoothly.

Housing

Creating an action plan for housing issues is important for many people. Will your current housing situation be adequate or appropriate after you give birth? If you feel you need a lower mortgage payment or rent, enough room to grow into with a child, good schools, child-friendly roommates, or a smoke-free environment, what is your action plan? Consider carefully if it's essential that you move before starting to inseminate. Financial reality and financial dreams are often separated by many long years. Include only the necessary steps in your overall plan and timeline.

Personal Emotional Growth

Some prospective parents feel they need to break a pattern of addiction or stabilize their depression or other mental health issues before they can conceive. Others feel they haven't had all the experiences they need and want for personal growth as child-free adults, such as traveling or dating. Having children doesn't preclude you from pursuing your personal endeavors, but it certainly changes the focus of your life.

It's unrealistic to think you'll have completed your personal emotional growth before parenting. Sometimes this desire to be "issue free" is related to the internalized-homophobia "perfect parent" pressure discussed previously. Sometimes it stems from wanting to be fully healed from issues of abuse or dysfunction that you're afraid to repeat in the next generation. Parenting is a process of personal growth; you grow while your children grow. If these issues are pertinent to you, do the necessary reading, therapy, or self-reflection you need to be able to move forward. Creating emotional milestones that you must pass before you get pregnant may be important to you; realize, however, that emotional work rarely agrees to follow a given timeline. In fact, feeling a sense of pressure, deadline, or urgency often hampers emotional growth and change. Therefore, consider your goals carefully and decide whether it seems reasonable to consider your life a work in progress rather than to force yourself to wait indefinitely to move forward toward parenthood. The dedication to becoming a parent may be just the incentive you need to leave an unhealthy relationship or to find more healthy solutions for current behavior patterns.

Partner Issues

If you're in a committed relationship with someone who isn't sure they want to parent, you're in a tricky—and common—situation. There are a number of approaches to this challenge. You may choose to keep discussing it with your partner, hoping for a clear solution to arise. You may choose to leave the relationship in order to start a family. You may start inseminating anyway, with a "wait and see" approach but no guarantee from your partner that he or she will necessarily stay and participate in the process. If you're in this situation, it may be helpful for you to review some of the ideas for creating family structures discussed in chapter 1. Explore in depth your partner's concerns about parenting as well as your desires. A couple's counselor may be able to assist you in sorting through these issues and establishing a realistic timeline for doing so.

At Maia we have seen greatest success in situations of unequal interest when the partners do not live together. When partners who are not equally committed to parenting live in the same home, resentment can build quickly on both parts, and it can be confusing to a child to try to understand why one of their parents doesn't care for them as much. This lack of involvement can easily translate into that parent not loving them as much, and these children can internalize this as a reflection that there is something wrong with them. On the other hand, when unequally committed partners live separately, it eases the stress levels and expectations on all sides. The child can more clearly understand the roles and relationships as reflected in a parent's presence or nonpresence in the home. In such a situation, the less involved parent may choose to become more involved over time and even move in at some point in the future, or she may decide to remain a secondary coparent or just "mom's partner."

Perhaps you need to decide whether you or your partner will get pregnant first. If only one of you is able to conceive or doesn't want to get pregnant, no discussion is needed. If you both want to conceive at some point, however, there are a variety of factors to consider. In many couples where both partners would like to give birth, they decide that the older partner should try to conceive first. If your age difference is great, this can be a key factor in your decision. Some couples decide that if one person has chronic health issues, only her partner should conceive. If a couple thinks they'd like to have more than one child and they'd both like to conceive, the person with greater health issues might be well served by trying first so that the "healthy" partner's support and resources can be solely focused on her needs in pregnancy. Sometimes people in an interracial relationship make their decision based on the ethnicity of their available donor and the preferred ethnicity of their child.

Often one person desires the experience of pregnancy and birth much more strongly than her partner, but other rationales exist to suggest that her partner should conceive instead. For example, the woman desiring pregnancy may have greater health concerns, take medicine that may cause birth defects, suspect she is infertile, or have inadequate health insurance coverage. She may earn more money than her partner or have fewer maternity-leave benefits. Sometimes the woman who is less passionate in her desire to parent wants to give birth as a way of making sure she creates a strong bond with the children. Occasionally, someone who has never desired pregnancy becomes fascinated with it as an option for herself as of result of watching her partner try to conceive.

Communication is key to staying connected through these sometimes volatile discussions. Explore with your partner what exactly is influencing your decision. If you feel you're acquiescing or are ambivalent about your joint decision, be creative in exploring alternatives. We worked with one couple, Janet and Martha, through their decision-making about which of them should conceive. They strongly believed that a child needs one stay-at-home parent. The problem was, however, that Janet earned significantly more money than Martha but wanted to be pregnant anyway. After some creative thinking they decided that Janet would become pregnant and take eight weeks of maternity leave after the baby was born. When Janet returned to work, Martha quit her own job and became the stay-at-home mom. Janet used a breast pump at work to provide bottles of breast milk for the baby. They now have two children, both birthed by Janet and both cared for during the week by Martha. Their plan has worked beautifully, but initially it took them a few months to conceptualize such an arrangement.

Prospective Single Parenthood

If you're single and waiting for the right romantic relationship to come along, you may choose to go ahead and parent instead of waiting for the perfect relationship to arrive. Because there's no guarantee that any relationship is "stable enough" to last the many years of parenting, anyone wanting to parent should acknowledge that she may at some point become a single parent. Approaching dating with a burning desire to quickly determine whether the relationship will develop into a long-term, healthy, life-partner and coparent situation can place an unrealistic amount of pressure on both of you. In our practice we've seen many ways in which single women can create viable support options, and we've seen many single parents become coupled during pregnancy or the first few years of parenting. There are numerous books and support and information groups for single mothers by choice. They may help you reframe your concerns about being a single parent. They also dispel many myths about single parenthood and offer creative ideas about forming various kinds of support networks.

At Maia we celebrate single moms by choice. People who choose to become single parents are incredibly strong individuals and amazing people as a result. However, we also strongly counsel prospective parents about the realistic challenges of single parenthood. Many of the prospective single parents (and partnered prospective parents) we encounter prior to conception do not realize how essential it is to develop a network of community, be it friends or family, to help support the raising of a child. Some prospective single parents have a well-established circle of support in their lives. But others are much more private people. Learning to reach out and ask for help at this point will provide much-needed skills for the future. Finding support groups and other community building activities in your areas of interest are good ways to start establishing deeper relationships. Likewise, we always recommend that prospective single parents ask their friends directly what kind of support they can expect from them in their parenting. This helps to create the extended family of your choice and to recognize the weaker links before relying on them.

Sperm Choices

When people ask how you'll get pregnant (and believe me, you'll get a lot of questions), they usually mean "Where will you get sperm?" This decision depends on your original vision of family that chapter 1 helped you begin to explore. Once you have a sense of the type of family structure that feels right to you, you'll know whether you'd rather have the biological father be an active coparent or just a donor. Part 2 of this book will help you thoroughly explore the issues surrounding sperm-donor decisions; it covers the steps of each of these processes in detail and includes exercises to help you articulate exactly what you're seeking. Once you've decided whether you want a coparent or a donor, we recommend that you plan to take no more than three months to figure out where and how you'll get sperm. Three months will afford you a great deal of time to brainstorm a list of possible known donors-coparents, if you think you might want one, and have initial conversations with them. Either you'll find some promising leads, or you'll use the rest of the time to research information from various sperm banks.

If three months seems too short a time, understand that people often find themselves stuck *for years* making decisions about how they'll obtain sperm. Our goal is to help you keep moving forward. Even though sperm-donor decisions are important, they don't need to hold you up interminably. Set your own time frame—one that makes sense to you—and reevaluate as necessary. Keep in mind that making a decision over many months or years doesn't necessarily mean it is better than a decision made more quickly.

Chronic Health Issues

All sorts of health issues can impact a person's decision to parent. Whether it's chronic back injury, asthma, or a partner's health condition, we recommend getting a reliable professional appraisal from a health-care provider concerning possible health risks to and of pregnancy and parenting. Have realistic discussions with your health-care provider about any special support or disability services you may require and any financial issues that may arise during pregnancy. Discuss with your health-care provider, as well as a midwife or obstetrician, which health goals you want to reach before conceiving and create a reasonable timeline for reaching those goals.

Preparing Your Body

Preparing your body for pregnancy has the potential to both optimize your fertility and strengthen your body. Most helpful changes made in regard to nutrition, exercise, or herbal medicine take a good three to six months—some even longer—to fully benefit your body, so now is the perfect time to read part 3 and implement any changes you'd like to make. Many of these changes, such as giving up coffee, can significantly increase your chances of conceiving. Even if you've been inseminating for a number of months already, your body can benefit from any positive changes you make now. If you're still in the planning stages, however, be aware that it's best to make these changes a full six months prior to conception.

WEIGHT LOSS

Many people tell us they wish to achieve a certain body weight before becoming pregnant. We'll speak to this issue directly in chapter 10; for now, be aware that rapid weight loss immediately prior to pregnancy may negatively impact your fertility. If you decide to try to lose weight before becoming pregnant, give yourself ample time so that you can both lose weight in a healthy way and let your body readjust its metabolism and hormone levels before you inseminate.

FERTILITY MONITORING

Many people need to complete a minimum of three months of charting their fertility cycles before they feel familiar with the nuances of their cycles. Over these months, they review their charts carefully and plan their optimal time of insemination. If you have irregular cycles, it may take you up to six months to determine the signs that indicate when you should inseminate. If you haven't already sought ways to help balance your menstrual cycle, it is helpful to know that it can take a few months to give any changes or treatments a chance to work fully. The importance of fertility monitoring is discussed in depth in chapter 11. However, the more months you have charted before you start inseminating, the more familiar you will be with your body, thereby increasing the likelihood of perfect timing right from the start.

HEALTH AND FERTILITY TESTS

Most sperm banks require that you complete lab tests for sexually and maternally transmitted infections before you can purchase sperm. But whether or not you're required to, you may wish to have a number of these tests performed. See chapter 5 for information about these tests and general reproductive and sexual health. Have any tests performed a couple of months before you start to inseminate so that you can seek any treatment you need if your results are abnormal. You can see any physician, nurse practitioner, physician's assistant, or midwife for health screening tests, so unless you want or need specific infertility tests, you do not need to see an obstetrician or gynecologist, which is fortunate, as some obstetricians and gynecologists are booked for months in advance. If you have to schedule a visit with your primary-care provider or gynecologist, make an appointment as soon as possible.

The Value of Creating a Timeline

A timeline for planning when you'll start to inseminate is useful for a number of reasons. First of all, it will help you notice if you're not moving forward toward your goal. If you set a deadline for a certain step you need to complete, you'll pay attention if you pass the deadline without moving forward and can evaluate both why you're stuck and what to do to move forward. If you don't have the structure that a timeline provides, weeks, months, and years may slip by without your making progress toward your goal.

A timeline gives you a manageable perspective on the entire process. You can plan a reasonable length of time for each step on your personal checklist and come up with a realistic date to start inseminating. As you mark the steps off your checklist, you can reassure yourself that you're making progress in the midst of what sometimes feels like a discouragingly long journey.

A timeline also gives your mind some peace by predetermining points when you'll step back and reevaluate the process and decide whether you need to change directions. For example, if you know you'll gather information for three months by charting your fertility cycle, you can rest the worried part of your mind, the part that wants to scrutinize the chart daily, sure that you will find some sign of infertility. You can let that part of your mind know that at the end of three months you'll have a comprehensive picture and will then give the interpretation of your chart your full attention. Reevaluation points also help partners make timely and effective decisions when each of them has different approaches to making decisions, especially in terms of pacing. Whether you've been contemplating pregnancy as long as you can remember, or only since age 35, or just since your partner mentioned she wants to have children, your plan and timeline will move you forward systematically.

Remember, your timeline shouldn't be a source of stress: You can always extend it or rework it when you reach a reevaluation point or even before. The timeline's job is to keep you making conscious choices.

Using Your To-Do List to Create a Timeline

Reviewing the notes you made when reading the previous section, about creating a plan, will help you devise your timeline. For each section, evaluate carefully what your personal vision or goal is. This step isn't necessarily completed quickly. The exercises throughout the book will help you clarify your desires and help you accomplish this step. If you need to, write your thoughts in a journal, talk with friends, or see a therapist or couples counselor as you clarify your vision for each area that requires a decision or action prior to your conceiving. Set aside a specific time at least every two weeks to focus on this part of the process, individually and with a partner, if you have one.

As you clarify each goal, you'll be able to make a list of smaller steps that you need to take to reach that goal. For each smaller step allocate a time length that seems reasonable for the step's completion. In this way you'll create a realistic sense of the overall time frame needed to complete your pre-insemination goals. Be sure to build in some time for actually creating your timeline!

Once you've finished creating the complete task list of everything you want and need to do prior to inseminating, examine your goals and see which you can work on concurrently. For example, you may be able research parental leave benefits and medical benefits at work while also taking active steps to make your housing situation feel stable enough to raise a child. You may chart your fertility cycle while you work on improving your eating habits or exercise program. Combine and overlap the goals as necessary until you've reached the end of the timeline—when you will start inseminating.

When Your Timeline Isn't Working

Choosing to parent isn't a rational decision. It's a choice to enter the unknown, jump off a cliff, commit to a lifelong relationship with someone you've never met (your child!). Choosing to parent is deciding to open your heart wider than you may have ever opened it, with an ecstatic amount of love to experience, and therefore there's a terrifying risk of loss. It's about trust and willingness to grow and change in unforeseen ways. It's a lot of hard work. It's about giving up old identities and activities to make room for new ones. Children challenge us to live our lives with integrity. As you make each decision necessary to begin inseminating, you inch closer to that cliff edge of parenthood, which may feel so daunting that you hesitate. You may need to deal with many personal and emotional issues before being able to move steadily toward your goal.

If you feel you're not moving forward because you're just plain stuck, articulate to yourself why you want to have children. (Many women have toddlers before they ever consider putting their desire for children into words.) This isn't your response or justification to society's challenge, but your words of inspiration to yourself. Your reasons for wanting children are deeply personal, and grounding yourself in this desire can help you move forward.

Although the emotional reality of becoming a parent may be all that is stopping you, practical concerns may also arise. Sometimes you may feel backed into a corner without any options. This may be because you're single but want a partner with whom to parent. It may be because you live in a state that has many legal restrictions about unmarried women parenting, and this scares you. Perhaps you feel you don't have enough financial resources to parent or even to conceive.

Often you actually may have an option but may be reticent to choose it because you feel you'd have to compromise more than you're willing to. Are there creative ways to modify the situation, taking more options into account? Brainstorming all possible options, no matter how crazy they seem, will open you up to new possibilities. Get some outside perspectives by spending time in a lesbian- or single-parent or trans-parent on-line chat room or even just talking with a friend. More than likely, you'll come up with some creative solutions.

For example, if you really want to use a known donor but your friends have declined, how about asking a relative of your partner, such as a cousin or brother? Are you willing to use the sperm of someone you don't know very well? How about your best friend's circle of good friends? Are any of your original reasons for wanting a known donor modifiable, or are there other ways to satisfy these reasons without using a known donor? Each chapter in this book offers creative solutions to conundrums that may arise in your journey toward pregnancy.

Sometimes women can't move forward, even though multiple options are available. This is often because these decisions can seem so permanent, and have such important consequences, that it's too scary to take the responsibility to make them. Welcome to the world of parenting. Yes, being a parent is an awesome responsibility, but if you allow your already-existing love for your child to guide you, you'll feel strong in your decisions. Trust that you'll always be able to share with your child that the decisions you've made have been made from love.

Differing Opinions in a Partnership

It can be nearly impossible to move forward if you reach an impasse with your partner about a specific decision, which commonly occurs when discussing donor options. If you and your partner are unable to move forward due to a difference in opinion, it's important to figure out whether you actually differ in your preferences or if you simply employ clashing decision-making styles. Sometimes one partner makes decisions much faster than the other. The slower partner may dig in her heels because she feels pressured or wants to research the options more thoroughly, or wants to make it "her own" in some way as an active participant. Other times it's truly a discrepancy in heartfelt desire.

Communication is essential to partnered decision-making, as are generosity and an honest awareness of which things you really could compromise on versus which you feel strongly about. Try to have compassion for how each other's past history may be impacting the current decision. What are your emotional stakes in this decision? What are your partner's? Can the needs of both partners be met in ways you haven't considered? Having your concerns acknowledged and validated can go a long way toward reaching a compromise. Relationship dynamics may color your perceptions of your choices and how absolute those choices seem. But by becoming aware of the context within which you're trying to make a decision, and addressing the tensions inherent in the decision at hand, you'll find greater room for compromise.

Ambivalence

If you've made a decision but catch yourself procrastinating about implementing it, perhaps you're ambivalent about the decision. Revisit it. Change your mind if necessary. Renegotiate with your partner. Better now than later.

Pulling It All Together

Use the resources you have available to help you make decisions effectively, whether they are the exercises we suggest, a relationship counselor, a support group, an on-line chat room, or other parenting books. Determine your decision-making style and tailor it to suit your needs. Communicate as honestly and fully as possible with your partner, if you have one, so that you can make healthy decisions together. Create a personal timeline of all your pre-insemination tasks and objectives, and really use the timeline as a working tool. Recognize if you haven't moved forward on any decision related to conceiving or parenting and get help you need to move forward. Finally, trust in your own ability to build a wonderful family and fill it with love.

CHAPTER 4

What You'll Want to Know about Your Health Before You Conceive

IT'S A GOOD IDEA to get a general physical exam before trying to conceive. Many of the standard tests you receive in early pregnancy as part of prenatal care are actually more informative before pregnancy, when you have more options to treat any abnormal results. Planned pregnancies are great for so many reasons, not the least of which being that we can know our health status and make any necessary adjustments prior to conception. Bring this list of tests to your health care provider, and you can decide together which ones you may want to have done before pregnancy. A general exam will reveal other health problems these tests don't cover that might affect your health or your baby's health during pregnancy. Some sperm banks require you to take some or all of these tests before you purchase sperm.

Pap smear: Contrary to popular belief, a Pap smear does not test for "everything vaginal." It's a specific test (developed by Dr. George N. Papanicolaou in 1953) that examines a sample of the cells on and in your cervix to make sure they're growing in a healthy way. It's a screening test, therefore, for cervical cancer.

It is a myth that lesbians, transmen, or asexual straight women don't need to get Pap smears. Although most cancerous cervical changes are related to infection by a sexually transmitted virus called HPV (the same virus that causes genital warts), not all are; some cervical cancers have an unknown cause. We know that HPV can be transmitted years before it causes symptoms, lying dormant. Therefore, a person may have been infected through sex that wasn't recent. Also, no one has proved that HPV cannot be transmitted between women. Or that lesbians are immune to cervical cancer. In fact, lesbians are considered to be at increased risk for cervical cancer based on population risk factors such as clinical obesity, smoking, and alcohol abuse. Furthermore, it is more likely for occurrences of cervical cancer in transgender people to go undiagnosed, owing to lack of access to trans-positive health care.

If you get a Pap smear and learn that your cervical cells are very abnormal or cancerous, it's best to seek treatment before pregnancy, as the hormones of pregnancy can cause the abnormalities to worsen rapidly if untreated.

Once pregnant, you won't want anyone performing any procedure or treatment on your cervix that could disrupt pregnancy.

For more information on safer sex, see chapter 7.

CBC — complete blood count: A CBC test looks at qualities of the cells in your blood. It tells whether you're anemic or have an abnormal type of hemoglobin such as sickle cell and provides other information about your general health.

RPR; Hep B surface antigen; HIV: These test for syphilis, hepatitis B, and HIV, respectively. All can be tested for from one tube of blood, and all are sexually transmitted infections (spread by shared needles as well) that are transmittable to a fetus during pregnancy.

Rubella: A rubella test tells whether you are immune to German measles. If you find out you aren't immune, you may choose to get vaccinated before pregnancy, as German measles is very dangerous to a fetus. You shouldn't conceive for one month after getting the shot.

Blood type and factor: If your blood type is Rh-negative, you may want to choose a donor who's also Rh-negative, although you don't have to. Your health-care provider will explain the consequences of this blood type for conception in more detail.

Chlamydia and gonorrhea screen: This test can be performed using either a urine sample or with a swab sample from the cervix.

Tests for genetic diseases: Hemoglobin electrophoresis checks for abnormal hemoglobins such as sickle-cell anemia or thalassemia. A variety of abnormal hemoglobins appear in people of many different ancestries, least frequently in people of Northern European descent. Cystic fibrosis occurs most often in those of Northern European descent, and Tay-Sachs disease is associated primarily with people of Jewish or French Canadian ancestry. A physician or genetic counselor can describe these tests in detail. This may inform your choices of donors as well.

Ureaplasma/mycoplasma: This is a test that checks for the presence of specific kinds of bacteria that occasionally live in men and women, can be sexually transmitted, and are not accompanied by symptoms. Some studies suggest a connection between infection with any of these and a higher chance of early miscarriage and missed implantation. Treatment is a one-week course of oral antibiotics. Unless you always have protected sex with your partner, she'll also have to undergo treatment. Unfortunately, the value of testing for and treating this type of infection is not commonly understood by many health-care practitioners, therefore obtaining this care may require advocacy on your own behalf.

Cytomegalovirus (CMV): Cytomegalovirus is a member of the herpes virus family. In healthy adults and children, this virus, which is spread through contact with infected secretions, can cause mild flu-like symptoms that resolve without complications. However, infection of a fetus during pregnancy can cause serious problems. Nearly all adults will be exposed to CMV in their lifetimes. Antibodies are found in 60 percent of the adult population, indicating previous infection. It is helpful to know your antibody status when selecting a donor. The risk of contracting CMV from a donor who is antibody-positive due to a past infection is extremely low. However, some people find that having the information about themselves is helpful when selecting donors from a bank that tests for CMV. You may want to discuss CMV with your medical provider, as there may be indications in your particular case that would influence your choice of donor.

Cholesterol: Some people choose to find out their cholesterol levels as a part of their preconception health assessment, as this can be a good marker of overall health. High cholesterol levels can be aided with fish oil supplementation. On the other hand, if your total cholesterol is low—under 140—it could contribute to problems with your progesterone. Raising cholesterol is fairly easy to do with dietary changes such as an increase in dairy fat (always use organic), meat consumption (once again organic as the hormones used in factory-farmed meats can cause additional problems), or one tablespoon of coconut oil a day.

Heavy-metal toxicity: Some people choose to have themselves tested for lead, mercury, and other heavy metals, and if necessary they can undergo heavy-metal detoxification prior to becoming pregnant. Blood tests or hair analysis seem to be the most common ways of diagnosing toxicity.

Glucose: Some people also like to have their fasting blood sugar tested as a screening for type 2 diabetes or insulin resistance.

Celiac: Celiac disease is gluten intolerance. When people with celiac disease eat gluten, their immune systems attack the villi lining the small intestine at the site of absorption. If the villi are destroyed or damaged, nutrients from food are unable to be properly absorbed and reach the bloodstream. There's no cure for the condition except following a gluten-free diet. If the condition is undiagnosed and gluten is ingested, it can lead to a decrease in fertility and complications during pregnancy. Blood tests can help you to diagnose celiac disease. People who have chronic digestive difficulties or lots of grain sensitivities should consider having this test.

Choosing to learn more about your health prior to pregnancy empowers you to make conscious choices about your health and the health of your baby. This is one of the advantages of a planned pregnancy. Take the time that you need to get to the bottom of any lingering health issues that you may have prior to pregnancy so that you can support a pregnancy that is as healthy as possible. A healthy pregnancy is worth the wait!

CHAPTER 5

Age Considerations

OFTEN, WOMEN START their conception process in their late thirties to early forties, and many of these prospective parents are concerned that they may not be fertile simply because they're 35 or older. No matter how fertile or healthy these people might feel, there's a common perception that women who are 35 and older are at high risk for infertility. The medical terminology applied to a woman giving birth after her thirty-fifth birthday is that she is of "advanced maternal age." How do you make sense out of the perception that your body's fertility rapidly declines after age 35, and even more so after age 40, if you feel healthy and menstruate regularly?

As you grow older, the challenges to conception and risks that go along with pregnancy increase. Societal prejudices and assumptions about women over 35 also influence medical opinion, despite its putative objectivity. Your state of health and fitness can greatly influence your fertility at any age, including your late thirties and early forties. As lesbians become ready to parent in their late thirties and early forties, they often have questions about the actual risks to conception, pregnancy, and birth that their age may influence. For example, the miscarriage rate increases as a woman ages. Trying to differentiate between the causes of miscarriage that can be prevented and the pregnancies that miscarry for genetic reasons is one example of the exploration needed for many lesbians choosing to parent as they get older.

This chapter will help you explore how aging may create fertility challenges that can affect both your timeline and the need for initial fertility tests. For ideas on how to optimize and increase your fertility, be sure to read part 3.

Egg Changes

Eggs and chromosomes change as a woman ages. Over time this can result in decreased ovulation, ovulation problems, and increased chances of miscarriage and fetal anomalies such as Down syndrome. Female infants are born with all the eggs their body will ever produce. At birth this is around 1 million to 2 million eggs. Throughout her life eggs are lost through a process called atresia. At the start of puberty, ovaries usually contain about 300,000 to 400,000 eggs. About 1,000 eggs are used during each menstrual cycle, but only a few are prepared for ovulation and usually only one of those is released. The unreleased eggs are reabsorbed by the body and thus can't be fertilized. Therefore, women may actually ovulate about 400 to 500 eggs over the course of a lifetime. By menopause, which occurs at different ages for different people, only a few hundred eggs remain in the body. About ten to fifteen years before the onset of menopause, the rate at which eggs are used up increases. This rate change is related to a subtle change in the menstrual cycle: Between ages 37 and 38, many women notice that the first half of their menstrual cycle (from menstruation to ovulation) grows shorter by a few days.

Increased difficulty in getting pregnant as women age seems to be related to a decrease in their total number of eggs. In addition, increased difficulty in conceiving—as well as a higher rate of miscarriage—is related to changes in egg health. Among other factors, "egg health" refers to whether or not the egg is able to respond to the hormone message from the brain that tells it to mature and ovulate. Sometimes eggs don't have enough hormone receptors on the outside to recognize hormone messages. Women usually ovulate the eggs that have the most receptors earliest in life, leaving the eggs with fewer receptors for later ovulation. Thus, egg health decreases with age, along with the total number of remaining eggs.

Egg health also refers to the genes inside the egg. The ovaries and eggs of women 35 and older have received more exposure to toxins and radiation than those of younger women. As a result, more of their eggs may contain damaged chromosomes. Also, older eggs more frequently have trouble dividing properly once fertilized.

Causes of Fertility Decline

Because of these factors, fertility rates start to decline after women turn 35, and decline more rapidly by their late thirties and even more so in their early forties. One scientific study showed age-related rates of conception per cycle for women attempting to conceive with frozen donor sperm by intrauterine inseminations (an insemination method that is often used with frozen sperm to increase the chance of pregnancy). For women younger than 35, the rate of pregnancy was 20 percent per cycle. For women ages 35 to 40, the rate was 12 percent. For women over 40, the rate was 6 percent.

Because of these factors, as women grow older they're also more likely to give birth to babies with chromosomal abnormalities and variations, as well as have still births. For example, the risk of having a baby with Down syndrome for a woman age 20 is one in 1,177; for a woman age 35 it's one in 296; and to a woman age 41 it's 1 in 65. Many of these chromosomal abnormalities cause the embryo to stop developing in the first few weeks of life; thus, the early-miscarriage rate for women in their late thirties and early forties is significantly higher than for women in their twenties and early thirties. By age 35 the early-miscarriage rate is 1 in 4 to 5 pregnancies; by age 40 it's approximately 1 in 2.

Amniocentesis, chorionic villi sampling (CVS), and newer ultrasound technologies are procedures a pregnant woman can undergo to check for certain chromosomal anomalies. Most of these tests have inherent risks, and many people have difficulty deciding whether to have them performed. If you choose genetic testing and learn that your fetus has chromosomal abnormalities, you have the option to terminate your pregnancy anywhere between twelve and twenty weeks.

The Maia Approach to Age

At Maia we work with many, many women over 40 each year who conceive with their own eggs—some of them with fresh sperm and some with frozen sperm, some of them with medical infertility treatments and many of them never having seen a doctor. We have also worked with people who are under 35 who are unable to conceive, no matter what we do. Our experience shows us that individuals are not statistics. Your egg health and overall fertility may be better or worse than the average person. Age alone by no means determines fertility.

At Maia we tend not to take statistics at face value, but rather to discerningly interpret statistics within the context of the studies used to formulate them. It is heartbreaking to hear women come to our office and tell us that they have been informed they have just a 3 percent chance of conceiving using their own eggs, just because of their age. These statistics are thrown around without any consideration of diet, lifestyle, menstrual health and history, genetic tendencies around fertility, or hormonal test results. It is true, when a woman is over 42 we are more concerned that it may be more of a challenge for her to conceive, but unless we have reason to believe otherwise, we assume she is fertile.

At Maia we also focus on decreasing the miscarriage rate of women in their forties. We have had less luck with this. Although our miscarriage rate is not one in two for women over 40 (another commonly cited statistic), it is certainly close to one in three. We assume that this is mostly due to chromosomal abnormalities. However, hormonally originated miscarriages and some unexplained miscarriages can be prevented through fertility enhancement. All of the fertility enhancement suggestions that we make in part 3 support regulation of the hormones and balancing of the reproductive cycle.

Studies have shown that at least 50 percent of healthy women who do not conceive in the first year will conceive in the second year. Fewer than one in ten women between 35 and 39 failed to conceive after two years. These studies were done on married heterosexual women who were not using medical fertility treatments. And, they conceived without the help of fertility medication. Most of the readers of this book will not have endless access to fresh sperm each month and thus our chances might be slightly lower because of decreased access. However, with all of the fertility enhancement advice that we provide and the finely attuned fertility awareness that we teach, we firmly believe that your chances are not only as good as those of the studies' subjects, but better!

After all, studies show that women can produce better eggs by simply taking a multivitamin daily. In fact, an in vitro fertilization (IVF) study showed that taking a multivitamin increased likelihood of conception by up to 40 percent. If you follow the Maia approach to fertility enhancement—which is much more comprehensive than just taking a multivitamin—just imagine what the results may be. Our success rates are hard to quantify as many families don't report their pregnancies to us. However, we know that our success rate for women over forty using their own eggs is at least 60 percent. The keys to our high success rates seem to be the following:

- Belief that you can do it
- Fertility enhancement
- Fertility awareness
- Fantastic timing

Hormone Tests Before Inseminating

If you're over 37, you may benefit from undergoing initial hormone tests before you begin inseminating. Many women who have participated in complicated infertility tests and treatments regret not having had initial hormonal tests performed when they first became serious about wanting to get pregnant. Had they had information early on indicating that their fertility was declining, they may have made different decisions or sped up their timelines. But bear in mind that no test can predict your success at conception. If you're over 40, fertility specialists agree, hormone test results that show normal values don't necessarily guarantee good ovarian function. By the same token, the fact that these tests aren't definitive also means that some women with suboptimal lab numbers, even occasionally with very infertile numbers—do conceive.

Benefits of Hormone Tests

Initial testing has numerous benefits. If your lab values show that you're less fertile than you'd hoped, you can choose to be assertive about creating a comprehensive plan to optimize your fertility, instead of taking your time and trying something new every few months. This may include adopting diet changes, a new exercise plan, a spiritual practice, in-depth emotional work, and healing modalities such as acupuncture all at the same time. Although Western medicine suggests that egg age and egg health cannot be made "younger" by healthy lifestyle changes, people who make these types of changes often see significant improvements in their hormone test results. More important, their overall fertility often increases, which is much more significant in the long run than a set of lab values that may be inaccurate.

If you have information that suggests your hormone levels aren't optimal, you may be spurred to start inseminating as soon as possible. Fertility can decrease rapidly, often over a period of three to six months. To speed up your timeline, you may reprioritize which decisions require lengthy consideration and which can be made more quickly. You may choose to move directly toward receiving medical assistance, whether from intrauterine insemination (IUI), fertility drugs, or assisted reproductive techniques such as in vitro fertilization (IVF). Some women choose to do IVF with an egg donated by a younger woman.

Some people choose to undergo initial hormone tests before they start to inseminate, because if their results suggest decreased fertility, they might choose to adopt or have their partner conceive. If your test results might be significant to you in this way, make sure the person who explains them to you has specific training in fertility and can accurately advise you on your realistic chances of conception. Not every obstetrician-gynecologist or primary caregiver can adequately provide this service. It may pay off to do some research on you own or to get a second opinion; you can schedule a consult at Maia.

Choosing to Forgo Hormone Tests

Some people may feel comfortable choosing to forgo initial hormone tests if they have alternative ways of assessing their fertility. You may prioritize your intuition or "body feeling" or other methods of understanding your body, such as Chinese medicine and applied kinesiology, more than the significance of medical lab values. Furthermore, you may feel that lab values would label you as subfertile or infertile before your body even gets a chance to try to conceive. You may want to avoid information that casts doubt on your body's ability to conceive or erodes your self-confidence.

If you know you have no interest in using medical technology to help you conceive, and you're working to achieve optimal fertile health, lab values may be irrelevant to you—which is to say, test results may give you new information but won't affect your decision to inseminate.

Basic Types of Tests

Here we provide descriptions of various hormone tests related to fertility. You may gain a deeper understanding of these tests if you read about hormones and the menstrual cycle in chapter 1. Additional diagnostic fertility tests and procedures are described in chapter 1. For general health-screening tests you may want to consider before pregnancy, see the previous chapter.

If you aren't experiencing regular menstrual cycles or any noticeable signs of fertility, you may want to undergo these tests regardless of your age. You may also consider them if you've been inseminating for a number of months without achieving pregnancy. In chapter 17 we'll review what it means to have "premature ovarian failure" or other fertility challenges.

ESTRADIOL; FOLLICLE-STIMULATING HORMONE (FSH); PROGESTERONE

Two hormone levels that can be checked at the beginning of the cycle, the third day after your menstrual period starts, are estradiol and follicle-stimulating hormone (FSH). Estradiol is a form of estrogen made by the ovaries. FSH is produced in the pituitary gland in the brain. It sends the message to the ovaries to prepare the eggs and their sets of helper cells, called follicles, to ovulate. If either of these hormone levels is too high, the eggs and ovaries may not respond well to your hormones or you may not have many viable eggs left (ovarian reserve). FSH results are a measure of ovarian reserve; a result of under 6 is excellent, 6 to 9 is good, 9 to 10 is fair, 10 to 13 indicates that things are moving more quickly in your body toward perimenopause, and at over 13 it can be hard to conceive. Levels of FSH can fluctuate if you have irregular menstrual cycles. As follicles mature they produce estradiol, which helps the uterine lining to thicken. Expected estradiol ranges are usually under 50 (for most labs). Ideally you want both your FSH and estradiol to be low. A high estradiol can indicate either a cyst or diminished ovarian reserve. A normal FSH and a high estradiol result may indicate that the estradiol is suppressing an FSH level that would otherwise be higher, thus masking poor ovarian reserve.

Progesterone, a hormone that helps regulate the second half of your cycle, is tested at seven to ten days past when you think you may have ovulated, which for many people is about six days before they expect their next period. Your progesterone values can suggest whether or not you've actually ovulated. A high progesterone level indicates that an egg was released and the rest of the follicle has turned into a little progesterone-making gland. A low progesterone level may indicate that an egg was not released. It also may suggest that the follicle didn't get mature enough to turn into a sufficiently effective gland or that your body has an insufficient level of progesterone building blocks. Even if the egg ovulates, a borderline low progesterone level prevents the uterus from keeping its lining well nourished and well attached. This can cause early first-trimester bleeding or miscarriage.

Multiple tests increase accuracy. One progesterone blood test drawn during one cycle may not be enough to give you accurate information about whether your progesterone level is high enough to sustain an early pregnancy or whether you'd benefit from supplements. Because progesterone, like other hormones, is released by the body in pulses instead of at a steady rate, your level will swing up and down throughout the day. Whether your level happens to be at a high or low point at the moment your blood is drawn can significantly affect your results. Some people feel a blood draw first thing in the morning before you eat is the most accurate. Tests taken from saliva are considered more accurate as hormone levels in saliva don't vary as much as those in the blood and multiple samples from multiple days are usually checked at once.

LUTEINIZING HORMONE (LH); THYROID; PROLACTIN LUTEINIZING HORMONE (PLH)

Luteinizing hormone, produced by the pituitary gland, triggers ovulation. Some women choose to have their LH checked, though levels of this hormone don't usually change drastically until a woman is fully into menopause. High levels may also indicate polycystic ovarian syndrome (PCOS), which is thoroughly explained in chapter 17. Some women also have their thyroid levels tested. The thyroid regulates rate of metabolism and other hormones in the body. More often than you may think, a woman's thyroid level may be somewhat out of balance, which can affect many functions of the body, especially fertility. Western medicine and many other healing practices offer treatments to help balance thyroid hormone levels. Check with your health-care provider to learn about available options. Another hormone, prolactin, is a secreted by the brain and is most commonly known for its role in breast-milk production. Prolactin also stimulates the production of progesterone. Prolactin levels are naturally higher in the second half of your cycle. Elevated prolactin levels can interfere with ovulation and progesterone synthesis, which may make it challenging to maintain a pregnancy. An abnormally high prolactin level in a woman who isn't breastfeeding may indicate that her fertility is inhibited.

Pressures on Women

Many older women are given blanket advice—from family members, friends, coworkers, and doctors—because of their age but without any consideration for their unique circumstances. You'll hear frequently that "time is of the essence." Please balance these alarmist statements with the knowledge that each of us ages, reproductively speaking, at different rates. We tend to inherit our rate of aging from our mother's lineage.

Although women's fertility can decrease quickly, you alone know your body and can make the decisions best for you. One of our clients received normal results after having her FSH levels tested by a health-care provider, but the following appeared at the bottom of her lab form: "Reassuring results, but advise aggressive management due to age." Don't be rushed past your point of comfort by external pressure to try things that you're not ready to try, simply because of your age.

For example, many sperm banks recommend that any woman over 35 skip vaginal insemination altogether and move directly to intrauterine insemination (IUI). This method involves washing the sperm to separate it from the semen, then placing it directly into the uterus with a sterile plastic tube that is passed through the cervix. You may prefer IUI, since it might reduce the number of inseminations needed for you to get pregnant. On the other hand, it may actually decrease your chances of conception if your timing isn't extremely accurate. If you feel it's important to give at-home, nonmedicalized insemination a try first, go for it! Your intuition is just as valuable a fertility signal as any other. Because of your age, you may modify your decision by planning to try inseminating vaginally for two to three cycles before moving on to IUIs, instead of the six to nine cycles you might give vaginal insemination if you were younger.

Do Everything You Can to Increase Your Fertility

Carefully read part 3, "Optimizing Your Health and Fertility," and start taking any supplements and incorporating the necessary exercise and lifestyle changes now, so that you'll have time to get the most benefit from them. Fertility enhancement is your ticket to increasing your odds of conception. Visualize yourself as fertile. Visualize your uterus and ovaries bathed with beautiful, radiant, fertile light. Trust that you know the most about your body, because you live in it!

In preparation for this edition of the book we contacted as many of our over-40 clients as we could reach to see what they thought was the essential piece that helped them to conceive. Some people came to us before they had started inseminating, others after unsuccessful IVF attempts. We work regularly with people who use many infertility services and conceive. We also work with many people who either don't want to seek such services or have tried them unsuccessfully. Following is some of the most common feedback from people who conceived using their own eggs and no fertility medications.

- "Eighty percent of what worked was having someone out there who believed I could do it [after] two years of trying, 7 cycles after Maia consult" (44 years old).
- "Fresh sperm, one IUI and one ICI a month. Cut out sugar and caffeine. Added fresh, organic fruits and vegetables. Supplemented with fish oil, prenatal vitamins, and Chinese herbs. Did acupuncture. Conceived in fifth cycle" (41 years old).
- "I cleaned up my life emotionally. Conceived in fourth cycle" (41 years old).
- "I moved through the grief of my mother dying. Increased exercise. Acupuncture and chi-nei tsang. Eliminated caffeine. More conscious eating. Fertility tea, Vitex, flax seeds, prenatal vitamins. I switched to fresh sperm. A long process over a three-year period" (44 years old).
- "Maia was the only place that told me I didn't have to stop breastfeeding to conceive. I'd had two miscarriages in the two years trying to conceive prior to Maia consult. I started to eat every four hours. Vitex, sensual feelings and dreams, checked my cervix daily, trusted myself and inseminated earlier. Conceived and held pregnancy on third cycle after my initial consult"(42 years old).
- "Changed jobs and worked part-time. Disregarded my ovulation predictor kit and trusted my sex drive and mucus. [Conceived on] third cycle" (42 years old).
- "Had a spiritual shift and used two different OPKs [ovulation-predictor kits] each month, four tries" (43 years old).

Begin Inseminating as Soon as Possible

Based on our experiences working with many women age 38 to 46, we encourage you to move more quickly, if possible, through the many months to years women often take making decisions about becoming pregnant. If you are already seeing changes in your menstrual cycle or your period itself, this is especially important. Signs to watch out for include a shortening of your cycle and a shortening of the amount of blood with each period. Look at which obstacles loom like mountains in front of you and devise an action plan to get around them. Necessity is the mother of invention. Be creative in your problem solving so that you can start inseminating as soon as possible. Your fertility can change quite quickly, so time often truly is of the essence. Unfortunately, we've seen a number of women who have trouble conceiving even earlier than age 38. Fertility challenges are on the rise, so use your time wisely.

Make Your Donor Choices Carefully

When you're making your donor choices, be aware that fresh sperm (if your donor has a healthy sperm count) has a much higher success rate than frozen sperm. Because frozen sperm is less fertile than fresh sperm, if you're using it consider doing at least one IUI each month. Once you know your cycle well, you may increase the number of IUIs per cycle. If you unsuccessfully inseminate with frozen sperm for a number of months, consider using fresh sperm if at all possible. Reevaluate your approach to insemination frequently, in response to the results you are getting and changes in your body.

Work the System

If you want initial hormone tests performed, be pushy, if necessary, with the medical and insurance systems in order to expedite the process. Often, long delays in the insemination process are caused by a woman having to wait weeks to months to see specialists and having endless debates with insurance companies. Be assertive and clear about your timeline with care providers and insurance representatives. While you wait for your appointments, use the time wisely. Do what you can to optimize your fertility. There is no reason why you can't start inseminating on your own while you wait, even if you think you will be using fertility medications in the future.

EXERCISE: BODY CHECK-IN
Now that we've reviewed some information on age considerations, take a moment to check in with your body. Take a deep breath, relax your shoulders, and really feel your body. How is all of this information affecting you? Does it simply reiterate what you already know? Does it feel discouraging? Thought-provoking? Find a way to let the information filter in to its own place in your mind. Don't put it in the

place where you may keep the negative stereotypes you've received about middle-aged and older women.

Often we don't realize how much of our perceptions of ourselves are shaped by our culture. How women's bodies are understood and valued as they age varies greatly from culture to culture. Keep in perspective that this society, which values youthful physique over wisdom from experience and acts as if women's sexuality (closely tied to reproduction) stops by the time they're in their forties, isn't the norm worldwide. Your interpretation of how your body changes as you age is probably a complicated mixture of personal truth and internalized societal prejudice. The information you receive from others about your fertility contains the same mixture. Keep this in mind as you decide how you will approach conception. What matters is how you feel about your fertility. Does it feel like your fertility is waning? Do you still feel fertile? Only you can answer those questions.

Although each person's body is unique, and each person's approach to the challenge of infertility is unique, some common truths exist: fertility can decrease rapidly with age, and diagnostic tests are limited in their ability to produce accurate results. These truths are tempered by another truth: overall health and fitness, as well as specific fertility-boosting practices, can play a significant role in increasing fertility. If you're choosing to parent later in life, it's helpful to establish an assertive action plan best suited to your own needs that enables you to approach the entire insemination process efficiently and reevaluate your methods in a timely manner.

Part Two
Sperm Options

Introduction

IT IS OF utmost importance for you to read the following chapters, on sperm choices, before you begin the insemination process. If you already have a known donor or a coparent who has agreed to help you get pregnant, be sure to read chapter 9, "Increasing Male Fertility"; it takes three months for sperm to be produced, so any changes to improve the quality should be started immediately!

Decisions about how and where you'll acquire sperm carry lifelong consequences. Reading chapters 6, 7, 8, and 9 will help you make sure you're thoroughly informed of your options, and completing the exercises in each chapter will help you clarify your values, assumptions, and expectations. You may find making decisions about where and how you'll obtain sperm to be challenging. We recommend that you set a goal of making your final choices within one to three months so that you aren't indefinitely stuck at this decision point. If you find that it's taking you longer, consult chapter 3, "Making Decisions."

Remember, you can gather information about multiple options while you explore emotionally which one seems most right for you. In fact, if you are having trouble making decisions, gather more information. As you obtain information from sperm banks, you can also interview potential donors. Saving as much time as possible in the decision-making process becomes increasingly important as you grow older, since you'll want to start inseminating before your fertility begins to decline.

In our experience, people often start with a particular plan for their sperm source, then find for a variety of reasons that it changes over time. Your plan may change before you start inseminating or even a number of months after you've begun trying to conceive. Reading the first three chapters in this section will familiarize you with the diversity of possibilities if you decide you need to change your path.

CHAPTER 6

Donor Coparents

COPARENTING WITH A donor dad can serve your family in many beautiful and long-lasting ways. Your child or children will have the benefit of knowing their biological parents intimately alongside any non-biological-ly related parents. For some children this can serve to significantly increase their sense of self-esteem and belonging.

Coparenting with a Donor-cum-Dad

In this chapter we discuss families that include the biological sperm donor as coparent. Compared with that of other coparents, the biological father's role is unique because he is automatically granted certain custody rights other coparents rarely have. We also explain the differences between a coparent dad and a known sperm donor. We recommend that all coparenting families-to-be involving the biological sperm donor read not only this chapter but also chapter 2, "Coparenting." If you will be using a donor-coparent, please also read chapter 7, "Known Donors," and chapter 9, "Increasing Male Fertility."

Choosing a Coparent You Do Not Know Well

Many people wanting to get pregnant choose to get sperm from and to co-parent with a good friend whom they know well and wouldn't consider par-enting with people they don't know well. Still, more and more parents-to-be who are specifically looking for men to be biological fathers or coparents do not already know them but instead meet these men in support groups or on-line groups devoted to arranging such relationships. The problems we've seen arise in coparenting relationships are exponentially more likely to occur in a situation in which the adults involved don't have a lot of shared history on which to draw. We would like to caution you from entering too quickly into a coparenting situation with someone you have just met.

We must emphasize, once again, this relationship will be lifelong. Di-vorce is not an option in legal coparenting arrangements—for better or for worse, you are stuck with each other for the rest of you life. Take great care in making a decision of this magnitude. We recommend tossing around a year as a good period of time to be getting to know someone new before starting to inseminate. Invite him or her to meet your circle of intimates—be that friends or family. Ask your circle for feedback and reflection. Consider seeing a therapist together.

All too often we hear from prospective parents that they are relieved that they did not conceive with a donor coparent they had been inseminating with because the more they got to know each other, the more his guard came down and they realized that they actually did not like the person they were choosing to parent long-term with.

When Your Known Donor Becomes Your Coparent

Often coparent dads start out as known donors who discover they'd like more involvement in the child's life. The switch from known donor to coparent usually happens after the child is born, and often occurs when the donor grows to love the child and the lesbian parents feel closer to the donor. Or the donor may later be unable to conceive children due to HIV infection or a health problem that limits his fertility. Having your donor suddenly want to be a coparent once you're pregnant or once the child is born can be stressful for all involved, in part because you don't have the sense of a relaxed timeline that you would while negotiating before conception. At Maia we have seen these situations go both ways. Some donors are seamlessly worked into the growing family. It is a natural and organic process that all consent to—an expansion of family that enhances life for each family member.

We have also seen situations that are heartbreaking. Parents who felt they had negotiated very clearly with their donors—drawn up contracts, had lengthy meetings, etc.—then after the baby is born, the donor decides to sue for partial custody. Many years of financial and emotional draining occurs as the primary parents are dragged through court to try to retain full custody of their child. Every situation where this has gone awry that we have encountered has occurred in families where the prospective parents did not know the donor for very long ahead of time prior to inseminating.

Choosing a Coparent

One of the main challenges of entering into coparenting is that the birth parent-to-be usually doesn't know a coparent as well as she would know a life partner, nor does she have as much experience with him (or perhaps with men in general) in making important decisions about intimate topics. It's essential to realize that no matter how smooth or rocky the relationship is, *coparenting is a lifelong connection and commitment.* Coparenting is a complex relationship that requires trust, mutual respect, some level of shared values, and the ability to creatively work through the unexpected as a team.

Coparent Negotiations

Think carefully about the initial points of negotiation and discuss these points clearly with your partner, if you have one, before moving on to negotiations with a potential coparent. Without this preparatory work, many people find themselves quickly acquiescing to an agenda they may not feel comfortable with. Sometimes this is due to feeling pressured in the moment, not wanting to say no to a friend, or feeling a tremendous urge to get pregnant and to get your donor/coparent to commit so that you can move forward. If a couple is seeking a coparent, it's crucial that they're in agreement about their desires and their limits so that they don't feel undermined or betrayed by each other when talking to potential coparents. Read over the next sections carefully and then take time to clarify your visions individually and as a team if you're partnered.

Initial Topics of Discussion

Health Issues and Logistics

GENERAL HEALTH ISSUES

If you're seeking a coparent who will be the biological father, the same health issues and conception logistics that apply to known donors apply to coparents. In the next chapter, "Known Donors," you'll find detailed information on safer sex, sexually transmitted infections, and lab tests for infections as well as information on sperm counts and semen analysis. Often it's easier for people who are just asking a man to donate sperm to request lab tests and a sperm count from him than it is for them to ask the same of a coparent. When you're interested in having a particular man both donate sperm and help you raise a child, discussing your desire for health screening can sometimes go by the wayside, which in part stems from the fact that there's so much other information to discuss. Many people are so thrilled that they have found a suitable coparent that they wish to avoid the bad news of his having a low sperm count or other health problems. Often people don't want to offend a man by asking for a sperm count before they discuss other key coparenting topics, as they fear he may feel objectified.

GETTING A SPERM COUNT AND OTHER TESTS EARLY ON

Because his health may affect your health and the health of your baby and partner, we recommend that you overcome any hesitations you may have and ask your potential coparent to get the health tests for sexually transmitted infections recommended in chapter 4 before you proceed in your negotiations. A borderline low sperm count may be improved through changes in diet, vitamins, or Chinese medicine (see chapter 10). Having a semen analysis performed early on will give the man a few months to seek treatment if necessary and see if it works, while you continue negotiations. It takes three months to make sperm so it usually takes at least this long to see the result of fertility- enhancement measures and treatments. A low sperm count may also lead you to consider different methods of insemination that concentrate the sperm—such as IUI—right from the start. Likewise, finding out that someone is completely infertile early on will allow him the time to find a diagnosis and possible treatment, or will save all of you the emotional heartache of building a very close relationship on a potential that doesn't exist. If you discover the donor is infertile, but you're still wedded to the idea of coparenting with him, you'll need to make other choices about where to obtain sperm. This will take time if you've been considering him your only suitable option for a biological father for your baby.

If you are using a transwoman on hormones as your sperm donor and coparent, see chapter 15 for more information about the feasibility of this option.

Financial Power

This is an area worth spending time examining. We have worked with quite a few single moms-to-be who are quite heartened by finding potential coparents who are financially much more secure than they are. However, we caution you to remember that in our culture at this time, money is power. This does not mean that the situation will be unworkable. On the contrary, it may be fantastic. The access to wealth that you do not have may enable you to provide an upbringing for your child that otherwise would have been out of reach. Or it may mean that you won't have to feel so much stress over finances knowing there is a safety net or a college fund available. In situations of financial inequity, we recommend that you spell out financial commitments in writing prior to pregnancy. For example, if your coparent is offering to purchase you a home to live in, get it in writing that he will not evict you during a set period of time and that a set amount of notice will always be given before needing to relocate. Putting your financial relationship in writing reduces the likelihood of money being offered with strings attached. This may be an area where it would be best to seek legal advice.

Stick to Your Vision

When negotiating with coparents, people often don't bring up all the issues they initially had planned to. Too often they find themselves telling a potential coparent they can have as little or as much participation in parenting as they want. Most people have preferences, as well as limits, about how much participation they desire from a coparent, especially if they've done some preliminary thinking before starting negotiations. Presenting potential coparents with an option to create a family and giving him or her carte blanche to decide its structure can often confuse and put pressure on them. They probably haven't been thinking about parenting as long as you have. If they have, they are probably already prepared to compromise a great deal and will feel reassured when you articulate your desires and limits.

Stay Connected to Your Truth

Women often think men have the essential ingredient: sperm. Men who want to parent but aren't partnered with a female would argue that a uterus is harder to come by. It's much easier to get sperm from a sperm bank than to find a surrogate mother. We mention this because we see women negotiate from disempowered positions unnecessarily. In our practice, we've seen that women have a tendency to want to be very fair and to not take advantage of someone. This tendency causes them to avoid starting a conversation with a discussion of their own desires. When you're creating your family, however, your desires are central. It's crucial for you to lay out for your potential coparent(s) what your ideal vision is, as well as parts on which you can compromise or negotiate and which are firm. If you can directly and clearly communicate your desired family structure and the framework of your relationships, your conversations will be much more efficient and fruitful. Your potential donor-coparent will then have a specific image to work with when asking themselves, Can I imagine this being my future? If he says no, you can reevaluate your limits and see whether you might be willing to compromise, or you can thank this person for considering the arrangement, and move on.

Partner Dynamics and Biological Fathers

When a lesbian couple negotiates parenting with a man, the nonbirth mom-to-be commonly feels more threatened by the role of the biological dad than the birth mom does. This difference can certainly affect negotiation dynamics. The nonbirth mother's insecurity can be heightened if the woman conceiving is better acquainted with the man. If the nonbirth mother is more interested in the man having a known-donor role instead of a "father" role, her insecurity can also increase. The mom who won't conceive often places less importance on the child's needing a biological father. She may feel that two parents are enough, regardless of gender, and that she can adequately fulfill the role of second parent. If a man is involved, she may feel she has no place in the family.

If you have a partner, clearly discuss any feelings of threat, discomfort, or concern either of you may harbor about the role of the biological father or male coparents. Sometimes it will take extensive conversations for both of you to get to the root of these emotions. When you can name the cause specifically, you'll be able to actively address it. If one woman doesn't know the man as well, arrange ways for her to spend time with him, perhaps even without her partner present, so that they can develop their own relationship and communication style. Keep in mind that it will be harder for many people to recognize the nonbirth mom as a primary parent if a man is involved in any way, especially if he is called Dad.

To assure a sense of safety for the nonbirth mom, it may be helpful to choose a donor whom she already knows well. This may be especially important if you live in an area where you won't be able to secure parental rights for both moms. If the donor-father retains his legal parenting status, you and your partner need to be sure that he will honor your intentions as a family. If the man in question is closer to the biological mom-to-be, this may be too large of a leap of faith for the nonbirth mom to make.

Sometimes partners, even though they may be in firm agreement about what they want, when it comes to negotiating will fall into the roles of "good cop" and "bad cop" when they present their needs to a potential coparent. One is firm about clearly stating and enforcing boundaries with the potential coparent, whereas the other compromises and smoothes over emotions. Unfortunately, the nonbirth mom often falls into the "bad cop" role, which, if she has already been feeling marginalized, can further alienate her and the others. Within the partnership, agree on boundaries and limits as well as which specifics you feel you might be willing to compromise on. Choose who will present during each part of the conversation each time. To keep the power dynamic more equal, consciously take turns expressing the topics that are the most difficult to bring up.

Courting a Donor or Coparent

The process of negotiation can feel a lot like courtship. Occasionally, it may actually bring up the romantic feelings common with exciting and new relationships. In a couple, both partners may not equally feel this "romantic" aspect. One may feel "swept away" while the other remains pragmatic. Sometimes sexual attraction springs up between a mom and a male coparent, even if the mom is exclusively lesbian. Boy, does this surprise people! We've even seen women end up in counseling, concerned that they're really heterosexual. The conception and coparenting relationship is intimate, and creating new life is profoundly cosmic. This intimacy can move naturally into sexual energy and doesn't necessarily signify a change in sexual orientation or the need to act on these feelings. Sometimes one person in a couple feels she must hide the depth of these feelings from her partner; the partner, however, is usually consciously or subconsciously aware of the situation. If these issues arise, discuss your feelings honestly in order to reduce the emotional charge that secret feelings often generate.

Issues for Single Parents-to-be

Many people make an apparently solid agreement about parenting roles that is then challenged by unforeseen change. We've seen single women choose to coparent with a man or two men in order to share child-rearing responsibilities. In some cases the woman was very close to the men; in others they were not. If the woman later becomes partnered, everyone has to do a lot of work to sort out the new relationships. The new lover can feel like he or she's a fifth wheel in an intimate preexisting family dynamic, which can spur a lot of jealousy and insecurity if she develops a close relationship with the child. The father may feel resentful or "used." He may feel that he and the birth mother went through all sorts of negotiations to determine whether they could parent together well, while a new lover is allowed access to a parenting role solely based on the mother's recent attraction to him or her. The birth mother may feel under great pressure if she becomes the mediator between the new partner and the male coparent.

> EXAMPLE: Beth wanted to parent and felt under pressure to get pregnant right away, since she was in her early forties. Although single, she wanted to share financial and parenting responsibilities with someone. She met Alan at a meeting of gay men and lesbians interested in parenting together, and they started to talk. It took a year for them to feel they were a good match. From the onset of the process, Beth met

with us often to clarify her desires and concerns, and to receive suggestions about how to approach meetings with him. Once Beth and Alan started talking in earnest, she brought him in to see us for a joint consultation so that they could benefit from facilitated discussions. In our private sessions, we reviewed with Beth what her heart desired versus what her mind told her was appropriate, fair, or polite to ask for. She did a lot of personal work to realize that she was creating her family and coparenting relationship from the bottom up; therefore, she could negotiate from her highest vision without apology. She needed to remember that she didn't have to protect Alan in her negotiations, that he, as an adult, could take care of communicating his own needs to her, and that he was responsible for not agreeing to arrangements that didn't feel fair to him.

One of their main points of discussion concerned finances, especially since his income was higher than hers. He wanted them to buy a duplex together so they could live next door to each other, but she couldn't afford to buy a house; at the time, she was renting a small studio. In divorce situations, the person who has less child-care responsibility usually contributes more financial support. But in coparenting relationships, people often feel that whoever spends more time with the child should hold more financial responsibility. In Beth and Alan's situation, Alan had the money and wanted to contribute substantially to the child's expenses, but Beth didn't want to feel dependent upon him. She wondered whether financial dependence would result in her feeling a debt toward Alan, and she feared it might lead to an unequal power dynamic in their parenting. She wanted to be the primary parent but was concerned that he would feel he could buy decision-making power. She didn't want to feel disenfranchised in her parenting.

In her early meetings with us, Beth said she felt it would only be fair to give Alan 50 percent of the decision-making capacity. In her heart, however, she felt strongly that she needed to retain authority as the primary parent, especially when the child was young. We encouraged her to state honestly in her communication with Alan what she wanted. He could agree or disagree. If he disagreed, she could decide to negotiate further, or not. It was difficult for her to conceptualize that wanting more than "half" wasn't "wrong." When she expressed her desires, she found that Alan agreed that, for the child's early years especially, she would be the primary parent.

They had explicit conversations about Alan's sexual practices with his new lover, who was younger and not ready to be a primary parent.

Alan's lover was HIV-positive, and for Beth to feel safe inseminating with Alan's sperm, she needed him to agree to practice safer sex within her definitions. When Alan's lover felt left out of this new evolving primary relationship, he would pressure Alan to have sex that was less safe, in effect to demonstrate that he was more important than Beth. Alan discussed this situation frankly with Beth and committed to a plan of how he would handle it, including being honest with Beth if, in the moment, he did have sex that was less safe than the standard to which he had agreed.

One of the most beautiful things that come out of their negotiations was a written agreement that set down not only the nature of the relationship they would share, but also the nature of love and why they were choosing to bring a child into the world.

Beth became pregnant after two months of inseminations, and at four months of pregnancy became involved with a new lover, Dora, who wanted to participate in raising the child. Dora resented Beth's previous commitment to a man, who would be an ongoing, intimate part of Beth and Dora's family life. Alan felt some resentment that he had had to go through such extensive negotiating with Beth but that Dora was allowed to move right in and become actively involved in the baby's life solely because of her romantic connection to Beth. Beth felt exhausted at times trying to keep peace and harmony between all the members of their parenting team. She appreciated Alan's taking care of the child and giving financial support, and she acknowledged that the situation is more complicated and time-consuming than she'd ever imagined.

Contracts

When you use a donor or coparent, the contract portion of the coparenting agreement is critical.

Legally speaking, if you find yourself in court in a custody dispute, your contract won't be binding. In a court of law, a notarized contract serves only as a document stating your original intentions. In the state of California, for example, a biological father has a claim to paternity even if he isn't listed on the birth certificate, even if he signed a "sperm donor only" contract, and even if the mother was inseminated by a physician. All the biological father needs to do is prove that he has a unique relationship with the child that is recognized by the child or the community, based on his paternity status. He has even more of a claim if you had intercourse with him to conceive.

Many states do not legally recognize lesbian mothers as parents if they didn't give birth to the child. Therefore, these families can't complete a second-parent adoption in order to legally secure their parenting status. Nonethe-less, they can still request that the biological father sever his paternity rights. Some women choose a male coparent with whom they feel comfortable listing on the birth certificate and acknowledging legally his paternity. The nonbirth mom may still feel that her relationship with her child is very vulnerable. Legally speaking, it is. If the biological father has a partner who's an active coparent (in our experiences, usually a man), his relationship with the child is also not legally recognized.

The current legal system holds all of your written and verbal family arrangements secondary to the will of the court, if you end up there. The court doesn't make decisions on the basis of its interpretation of your original intentions but on what it deems to be in the best interest of the child. Few legal precedents have been set by coparenting families arguing in court.

If a dispute occurs and you all agree to resolve it through binding arbitration or mediation, a notarized contract will be a powerful tool for you. One of the most useful aspects a coparenting contract can contain is specific language that spells out a process for conflict resolution, including an agreement by all parties to partake in family counseling first, followed by mediation or binding arbitration if necessary, to avoid staying out of a usually homophobic court system.

The best source of current legal information on this topic is the National Center for Lesbian Rights. Additionally, sometimes lawyers and social workers, or other alternative family specialists, will partner with you and agree to work on the development of such contracts—giving you an opportunity to draft something that speaks to more than just the legal concerns. The family specialist can help facilitate and negotiate a contract between all parties before it gets to the expensive lawyers who have a much narrower field of interest.

CHAPTER 7

Known Donors

A KNOWN DONOR is someone you know who donates sperm to you to help you become a parent but will not serve as a parent to your child. There are numerous reasons for choosing a known donor. In this chapter we will cover the advantages, the drawbacks, and also the logistics of working with a known donor.

Do Sperm Banks Offer Known Donors?

It is important to clarify the definition of a known donor. You may have heard that some sperm banks offer so-called "known-donor" options. Indeed, there are a few sperm banks that allow the child to contact the donor when he or she becomes 18, but not before, and one unique bank, Rainbow Flag Health Services, releases the donor's information to you when the baby is three months old. This is not the way we are using the term "known donor."

In this book, a known donor is someone in your life who has agreed to provide sperm to you in order to help you become a parent. This person may or may not have any ongoing contact with you and your child after the time of conception. A non-operative or pre-operative male-to-female (MTF) transgender person can sometimes be a donor, but in this chapter we will use male pronouns to refer to sperm donors.

Why People Choose Known Donors

There are many reasons why people choose to use a known donor to conceive their child. The most common reasons that we see for people using known donors are discussed in the following sections.

The Donor-Child Relationship and Guaranteed Access to Donor Information for Your Child

The most common reason that people choose to use a known donor is to secure a possible relationship for their child. Many people feel daunted by the decisions parenting requires them to make before they even give birth to their child. One of the first decisions you may struggle with is how much information about and contact with the genetic sperm donor of your child you think should be available to your child while he or she grows up and later as an adult. Some people feel strongly that it wouldn't be ethical to make a choice about sperm donation that limits in any way a child's ability to have potentially meaningful information about him or herself. Some people aren't sure whether or not they might regret their child's having limited or no access to knowledge of his or her biological father. If you have strong feelings about your child's right to know his or her donor, it's important for you to acknowledge and explore these feelings.

Some people want their child to have personal contact with the donor, although they don't want the donor to fulfill the role of father. Perhaps they plan for the donor to have a special relationship with the child: "uncle" or "super-uncle" are common terms women use to describe this role. They don't define their donor as a coparent, though, since he will not have parental responsibilities. They would, however, like the donor to be involved in the child's life—not as a parent but as an extended-family member.

Other people do not assume that there will be any familial connection between the donor and child, but they like the idea that if the children at some point in his or her upbringing have questions about the donor, they will be able to have them answered.

Avoiding Parallels with the Adoption Experience

People often choose a known donor when adopted people in their lives (perhaps even they themselves) have had painful experiences with adoption and not knowing their biological parent or parents. Wanting to prevent a child from feeling "half adopted" and needing to seek the other half of her or his biological heritage can lead these parents to choose a known donor. Most lesbians who choose to use sperm banks do so with a spirit of openness rather than secrecy. They explain to their children from an early age about the nature of their family and conception. They explain that their children's conception was carefully planned and incredibly desired, and that the man who donated sperm gave a gift so that their family could come into existence just as it has. In this way they work to prevent their child from developing feelings of shame, emptiness, and inadequacy that are common in some people who have been adopted.

Some children who are conceived with anonymous-donor sperm never wish to seek out their biological origins, while others feel a great lack if they can't contact the donor or learn his identity. Many children have both kinds of feelings, depending on what developmental stage they're in and how much understanding they receive from friends and community about their family. There's no way to predict your child's feelings on these issues, although you can decide how you'd like to address their emotions and concerns. Therefore, make sure you feel comfortable with your decision so that you can share it with your child from a place of clarity and love.

Ability to Assess the Donor's Character

Many people feel it's imperative to meet a person to determine whether they are a "good person." The anonymity of a sperm bank does not work for such people. Many of our clients have told us that, at the very least, they want to ensure that their baby will receive half of his or her genetic material from someone they feel has "good energy" or "the right vibe," is "a person with integrity" and "someone who feels like a good connection," or is "not an ax murderer." This desire brings up fundamental questions of nature versus nurture. Which traits are genetic? What are the results of childhood family dynamics and environment? Can your loving support as a parent counterbalance inherited tendencies in personality and character from the sperm donor? Obviously, there are no universally known answers to these questions; we must each find our own answers. For some people for whom this assessment is important, the detailed sperm bank questionnaire an anonymous donor fills out seems sufficient data to decipher the man's character. Others, however, feel that meeting the man directly is imperative, and thus, they decide to go with a known donor instead of an anonymous one from a sperm bank.

Ability to Feel a Spiritual Connection with the Donor

A number of people we work with feel that there is something inherently spiritual in conception. These same people often feel that the intention and focus of the man donating is important to them. Part of what goes into selecting a known donor for them is more of a match of spirit, beliefs, or energy. This may be a subtle and unspoken quality they are looking for, or they may choose to meditate or pray with their donor as a preparation for conception. Likewise, some people feel that the freezing and defrosting aspect in using a sperm bank somehow interferes with vital essence or life force. If this is the case for you, working with a donor whom you know and resonate with can be an essential component of your conception.

Inexpensive and Available

Using a known donor's sperm is usually the most cost-effective way to get pregnant, since it's usually much less expensive than buying sperm from a sperm bank. Most people don't pay their known donor more than a token amount, if anything at all. Any major costs incurred will probably arise from obtaining a health screening and sperm analysis, travel, and the freezing of sperm, if warranted. Since using a known donor is usually inexpensive, people who choose this option can perform many more inseminations each month and are able to cover a wide window of fertility, if their donor's schedule allows it.

Sperm from a known donor is also more readily available if you live in a state or country where you can't access insemination services through the medical system unless you're heterosexually married. Unless you're willing to travel to a lesbian-friendly sperm bank and see a lesbian-friendly practitioner, your access to sperm is limited to personal arrangements and home inseminations: known donors or coparents.

Gay and Bisexual Donors

Some people feel strongly that they would like to have a gay or bisexual donor for their child. They're proud of their sexual orientation and feel more comfortable with the idea of obtaining sperm from a gay man than that of a straight man. Many queer people believe that we are "wired" differently—and prefer our own kind of wiring! Few sperm banks allow gay or bisexual men to donate sperm. Rainbow Flag Health Services in Alameda, California, is the only sperm bank that currently labels the sperm from gay and bisexual donors as such. People who want to use the sperm of a gay or bisexual donor usually must work with a known donor.

Better Chance of Conception with Fresh Sperm

There are many key benefits to using fresh sperm instead of frozen. For one, fresh semen from a known donor's ejaculate almost always contains significantly more and longer-living sperm than a vial of frozen sperm. With fresh sperm you'll often have much more semen to inseminate than with a vial of frozen sperm. Frozen sperm is stored in quantities of 0.5 or 1.0 cc, a portion of which is buffer solution. The volume of semen in one ejaculation received from a known donor is usually 2.0 to 5.0 cc. Furthermore, freezing lowers the sperm count per cc of semen. On average about 70 percent of sperm don't survive the freeze and thaw process. Fresh sperm live longer (two to three days) than frozen sperm (eighteen to twenty-four hours), allowing you to cover a longer stretch of fertile days with fewer inseminations. Thus, pregnancy is achieved more quickly with insemination of fresh sperm.

Risks and Challenges of Using a Known Donor

A number of serious factors must be considered when deciding to work with a known donor. The most significant of these are the health and legal risks associated with using fresh sperm from someone you know. The rest of the concerns we've encountered are less frightening but can none-the-less significantly affect the life of you and your child.

Health Risks

When inseminating with fresh sperm, you can never know for sure whether you're exposing yourself to the risk of contracting a sexually transmitted, potentially life-threatening disease. No matter how much pre-insemination risk assessment you've done with your donor, you may have forgotten to ask something, or he may not have told you the entire truth, or he may think he is monogamous when his partner actually has sex with others. There's always the chance when using fresh sperm that the donor has acquired an infection too recently to show up on lab tests or that he will contract a disease in the future (but before you conceive) and thereby put you—and your baby—at risk. This potential health risk is one of the primary reasons people choose not to use known donors. Later in this chapter you can read about recommended tests and questions to help decrease your chances of contracting an infection if you choose to work with a known donor.

Frozen sperm that has gone through the quarantine process has statistically the lowest chance of transmitting an infectious disease to you or your fetus. The quarantine process involves retesting a donor for infectious diseases six months after his sperm is first frozen. If his test results come back negative at the six-month mark, his sperm is released for use. It is worth noting, however, that despite these risks, no one has reported to us having contracted hepatitis, HIV, or other sexually transmitted infections from their known donor.

Legal Risk

The other primary reason lesbians choose not to use known donors is the potential legal risk that the donor will claim parental rights. Until he has formally terminated his parental rights, he is a legal parent to your child, whether or not he is on the birth certificate. This means your donor could gain custody rights. Although the legal procedures of both severing paternity rights and formalizing second-parent adoption are supposed to ensure that a donor will not be able to gain custody, laws and the attitudes of judges vary from state to state and county to county. Not all states grant second-parent adoptions or other legal means for same-sex couples to secure legal parenting rights to their child. Likewise, some states leave single mothers more vulnerable as well. In some states, it is impossible to use a known donor without the donor being a legal father. For current information on your legal options contact the National Center for Lesbian Rights, www.nclrights.org.

Additionally, the parents of a donor may sue for custody as the child's grandparents. Unfortunately, in some parts of the country, homophobic and transphobic attitudes are so strong that a queer or transgender parent can lose custody simply over sexual orientation or gender identity. Although the donor contract and other legal documents you draw up prior to insemination will assist you, there's no guarantee when you conceive with sperm from a known donor that you'll retain sole custody of your child.

The longer you know someone prior to choosing him as a donor, the more thorough and explicit the conversations you have with him regarding each of your roles and intentions, and the more documentation you have clearly stating your mutual intentions, the less room there will be for confusion in the future. There's often no way to predict the life changes that may influence your donor to want to be a participatory or legally recognized parent.

Although we have seen innumerable positive known donor relationships, they tend to have an unexpected element to them at some point in time. Unfortunately, we have seen a number of known donor relationships go horribly awry. So once again, we caution you to always be on the lookout for any red flags that arise during the preconception period and take them seriously.

Other Issues to Consider: Unexpected Developments

By asking a friend, coworker, or associate to donate sperm, you're inviting change in your relationship with that person, which may be for the better or for the worse.

Disturbing Knowledge

Unfortunately, we've heard a number of stories from women who wished they'd never asked the intimate questions necessary when screening a potential known donor. These women discovered information about their potential donors' characters that drastically affected their friendships with them. Often the discovery was accidental, and sometimes the donor did the great service of disclosing the information directly. Many of these men disclosed disturbing information about their sexual proclivities, pedophiliac behavior, and participation in sexual assault. These are but a few of the stories we've heard directly.

Change Happens

No matter how clear you feel you've been prior to insemination, the nature of your relationship with the donor may change because the child changes it, you change it, or the donor changes it. After the child is born, there's no guarantee that a donor won't change his mind about the role he will play. For example, suppose you have a mutual understanding that the donor will participate in the child's life during holidays, barbecues, or even more often, but he gets a job in France. Or perhaps he has said he has no interest in children, until later: he is diagnosed with a terminal disease, faces his mortality, and wants to become an active parent to your child. It's essential to realize that change happens and to plan for it whenever possible.

It's precisely this human element of the unknown that makes using the sperm of a known donor very different from using frozen sperm. With a sperm bank, your relationship to the sperm donor isn't going to change. If you use one of the identity-release donors available at some sperm banks it may change after your child turns 18 (or when the baby is three months old if you use Rainbow Flag Health Services).

With known donors there's always the chance of change. Perhaps it will be for the better; perhaps it will be a struggle. Part of the nature of parenting is that you often won't know for sure what you really want until you actually are a parent. Before the birth of your child, try not to lock yourself into commitments with the donor that can be tricky to get out of later.

Last-Minute Change of Heart

It is not uncommon for a donor to back out at the last minute. If a donor backs out before you have inseminated, you'll probably feel rejected, abandoned, or overwhelmed at having to start the process all over. Sometimes these feelings arise because the donor isn't very direct in communicating; he stops returning phone calls or showing up for meetings. Sometimes he gets cold feet at the last minute. This can often cause a tremendous amount of wasted time, energy, and money.

If this happens, don't let it devastate you. It's much better for him to back out now than change his mind in the future over key issues such as custody. Try to take this in stride and use it as an opportunity to reevaluate your options and move forth with either new known-donor possibilities or with a sperm bank. In the long run his changing his mind now, rather than later, is a gift to you! This type of loss is often hard to find support for and can feel like being left at the altar. Unfortunately, this is fairly common.

The Logistics of Donation

Another challenge to using a known donor is that of coordinating logistics. Often people choose donors who live far away. The geographic distance provides the benefit of parenting security but also introduces travel costs and timing challenges or the costs and limitations of freezing the donor's sperm. Sometimes, too, even a local donor may be just too busy to adapt to your schedule or may have to travel frequently. These are significant issues to focus on before moving ahead too quickly.

It's helpful to sit down with your calendars and plot out what this form of commitment to each other might look like. When planning, remember that your time of ovulation can at best be narrowed down to a few days of the month and even that may not be a sufficient window. Many people are devastated if they're unable to inseminate one month because of scheduling conflicts. It may be necessary to rule out an otherwise viable donor simply because of his schedule.

What Do You Want from a Known Donor?

Once you've decided to try to find a known donor, it's essential to clarify exactly why you're choosing this option. If you're partnered, you need to make sure both of you are communicating clearly with each other about this decision. Being able to articulate your feelings will help you remain clear when you negotiate with a potential donor. We recommend you do this internal exploration and external verbalization before you even make a list of potential donors.

Some people first need to discuss what they want from a donor with someone they trust in order to clarify their needs and desires. If this is the case for you, use a good friend, a therapist, or an "advisory committee" of family or friends—anyone who can actively listen and provide feedback but won't try to impose their agenda upon you. (Don't use your potential donor in this capacity.) Again, clarifying what you want prior to negotiating will dramatically increase your chances of establishing the relationship you desire from the start.

How to Find a Donor

Prospective parents use a variety of approaches to ascertain who would make a good donor. Some feel they can intuit a man's character and feel comfortable proceeding even though they don't know each other well. Others feel they need to have known the man for a long time prior to considering him a potential donor, since he will be in their lives from that point on. Some feel comfortable simply trusting character recommendations from close friends or coworkers. Some women even intuit that a donor may be a "good connection" if they can imagine being sexual with him.

You may find a potential donor anywhere in your life: coworkers, current friends, old friends from school or work, relatives of your partner (such as a brother or cousin), nonblood relatives, etc. A trusted friend may introduce you to his or her circle of relatives, friends, or colleagues. We've known more than one woman who pulled out her Rolodex and called everyone in it, asking whether they'd consider being a donor or if they knew anyone who might be interested. Sometimes people place personal ads in queer publications or on-line. Sometimes men who would like to be known donors or coparents also place ads.

Make a list of any men you know whom you could imagine being your donor. Try to make this list as freely as possible to start with. Get creative or even silly, and try to add people you might have forgotten from earlier in your life. As soon as you start weeding out some of them, you'll be surprised by how many you cross off, so think big. Flip through a few of the men on your list, putting them into the donor role like slides in a slide show. Do you have a visceral body response that gives you more information than you've had so far? Sometimes at this point people realize they actually want an unknown donor. Sometimes they come to such a realization even later, after they've approached or interviewed a few men.

If you're partnered, you should each make your own list. You might each agree to have veto power upon review of the other's list, no questions asked. If you read through each other's lists and reject everyone, you may need to reexamine your criteria. Are they impossible to meet? On the other hand, you may trust all the reasons you said no, so try to get even more creative and make a new list of possible donors. Check in with yourself at this point to make sure that you aren't saying no out of fear of having a child. You may find that discussing your reasons for eliminating potential donors will help you or a partner further clarify your desires.

Please remember, all parents must feel comfortable with the choice of known donor. This is not a place to abdicate your decision-making power, as the potential risks are great and all of you need to be on board with this important decision.

Unequal Power Dynamics

Unequal power dynamics may exist between you, a partner, and the potential donor. We recommend that you take the time to explore whether these dynamics are actually repeating an unhealthy pattern for you. Make sure you approach this life-changing decision from the most centered and honest place within you.

EXERCISE: DONOR POWER DYNAMICS
Write down the names of your potential donors. Then write in a free-association style about the power dynamics that may exist between you and each donor. Next, write about past relationships that mirror these dynamics. What was the quality of these relationships? Do you feel centered when you're in this role? Is it a place of safety? A place of insecurity? A place that makes you feel better than or worse than your donor? Is it a typical relationship you've had with other men in your life? Now include your partner, if you have one, in this picture. Does this produce any additional power dynamics? Although not all relationships with unequal power dynamics are bad, it's important to enter these types of relationships with care. Some examples follow.

RELATIVES

Sometimes people ask their partner's brothers, stepbrothers, in-laws, or cousins to be donors. You may trust relatives more than you do other people in your life. Blood relatives of your partner specifically may be appealing because your child would share genes with both of you. This can be especially important for interracial couples or for people looking for their partner's exact ethnic mix. At Maia, we have seen these situations go both ways. It usually is much more complex than initially imagined.

There are a few things to seriously consider as a couple: Think through the following questions: How will your extended families view this situation? Will this seem like incest to you, or your families, or the outside world? Will you tell your friends and coworkers or will it remain a family secret? Will your child feel comfortable with the dual role of his or her uncle/donor/father?

People often think that using their partner's family member will make the partner's extended family more likely to see this child as hers. In fact, some of the drive to choose a genetically related donor is often connected to seeking out a feeling of family recognition and acceptance. The odd twist is that this type of arrangement may unintentionally undermine the ability of your partner and you to view the baby as belonging to both of you.

As the partner of the pregnant parent-to-be, you may see the traits of your brother or cousin unfolding in your child and have a complex range of emotional response to the genetic tie that is so close to you and yet not you. Likewise, at family gatherings your extended family may choose to emphasize the similarities between your partner and your *cousin's* baby— effectively leaving you out of the picture altogether. Likewise, the continual emphasis on the genetic connection at all family gatherings can get old fast. And, not the smallest point to consider is that well-meaning family often are the ones to tell your child "where they came from" and "now, you know who your daddy is, right?" even if you have decided to use other language.

We have also seen family donors take inappropriate extensive liberties in telling their sister/cousin/stepchild how to raise "his" child. Please also consider the current or future children of your donor and his partner, if he has one. If they experience jealousy or homophobia, it will all be a part of your child's self-image.

Usually, women don't choose a donor from their family's previous generation, as many cultures have an incest taboo about intergenerational conceptions. Even if the potential donor isn't genetically related to the birth mother—for instance, he may be her or her partner's stepfather—the situation may create feelings of shame for the child or parents. We caution you about choosing a situation where you feel the conception of your child needs be held as a family secret.

CLOSE FRIENDS

Close friends are often the ideal coparents or involved donors because they are already intimates in your life and thus will naturally be extended family for your child. For people who ask a close friend to be a completely uninvolved donor, we have found this works best if they live far away. Otherwise, any connection they form with your child can be construed as overstepping their bounds. Sometimes when using a close friend it is challenging to know what exactly you want from them.

Discussions and Negotiations with a Potential Donor

The First Conversation

Every initial conversation with a potential donor is unique, with no universal formal structure. You may first ask a man by calling him, writing him a letter or email, or asking in person. If you and the donor live near each other, it's probably best to meet in person. It's normal to feel nervous, vulnerable, and awkward. There's no established model for this kind of request. Keep in mind, however, that there's nothing wrong or embarrassing about asking someone to be a donor. If you act self-confident, you'll set a good tone for the conversation. Many people start by telling the donor they're planning to have children, and then ask him if he'd consider donating his sperm to help them. This is the best place to start. If he immediately responds favorably, you could then have an initial conversation discussing why in particular you're asking him, what you envision as his involvement after the baby is born, and what might be the logistics of the process (he may have misperceptions and be shy to ask). Most men, however, need time to consider the prospect before discussing any details. You may wish to provide him with information to read on the subject.

You aren't obliged to discuss with him whom else you've asked, whether he is first or fifth on the list, or why you aren't asking other, perhaps more obvious, people. Do set a tone of candor and direct communication for him to follow. If he needs time to think about it, arrange a time to check in, perhaps in two weeks, so he'll know you want him to seriously consider the proposition. Let him know you can meet again to discuss the details you'll both need to know to decide mutually whether this will work.

Don't expect this first meeting to necessarily be long. Keep in mind that occasionally a man may think your request is some type of sexual proposition and feel very uncomfortable. Plan a way to provide a comfortable end to the meeting for both of you. If you're partnered, remember to include her in this process. If she can't be present at the initial conversation, at least include her in your donor planning. We find that it's common for one partner in a couple to ask a man to be a donor without first consulting with her partner. Sometimes the person who's planning to conceive will start interviewing people informally without even thinking about involving her partner. This is usually innocently done but can easily hurt the partner's feelings and increase feelings of being marginalized. The arena of donor negotiations can be very tender for nonbirth parents.

Remember, in general, that the nonbirth partner may be concerned about not feeling involved enough. She may also feel that her parental role won't be securely recognized by the birth parent, the child, or society in general. This is especially true when a known donor is used, since it can resemble a heterosexual connection. Be communicative with each other from the very start; you'll both appreciate it later. When you speak with a potential donor, plan ahead that neither you nor your partner will agree to anything in the moment but will confer privately after the meeting. Either of you can put the other on the spot if you speak enthusiastically on behalf of both of you when your partner might actually disagree. Once your potential donor agrees, you're ready to initiate more in-depth negotiations.

Asking for a Sperm Count

As forward as it may appear to be, we advise you to ask your donor to undergo a semen analysis before you enter into in-depth negotiations. This is a practical first step. If his sperm count is low, he can get an exam to try to discover the cause and begin a program of herbal or vitamin supplements, nutritional changes, or Chinese medicine to improve his fertility. This type of program needs to be undertaken for three to four months before you will begin to see results. Depending on the situation, it may take more than six months to be the most beneficial. If you discover his sperm count is completely not viable, then you'll have saved everyone a tremendous amount of emotional energy and time. Many prospective parents cringe at the thought of asking their potential donor to get a semen analysis. They are afraid it will make their request seem conditional. It actually is conditional, and it's best to get to the bottom of whether or not he will be a viable donor before either of you gets too invested! If your donor procrastinates getting a semen analysis, after numerous direct requests from you, see it as a red flag.

Clarity of Vision

You're trying to negotiate what's possibly going to be one of the most important decisions you'll make in your lifetime. Don't let this overwhelm you; many people successfully choose known donors. Once more, however, we'll remind you that if you haven't fully articulated your desires for yourself, you may find yourself acquiescing to things you normally wouldn't. Clarify your vision before you ask, "What role would you like to have?" You may hear him answer, "Well, I'd like to see the child one night a week, or one weekend a month from the time he or she is six months old." You may hear yourself responding on the spot; "Okay, I think I could work with that" before you honestly know whether you can or even want to. Often a woman will feel very strongly about choosing a known donor, but after realizing she has few potential donors in her life, she feels desperate to make the situation she puts together work. Sometimes women start negotiations from an unexamined place of internalized sexism: "Whatever you want is more important than what I want. As long as I can get the sperm, I'm willing to do whatever it takes. I need to be fair. I need to be grateful." People often fall into two traps: agreeing to things they don't want and refraining from stating what they do want. We even go so far as to offer things they'd rather not give, before he has even requested anything. It's common to feel indebted to your donor and to want to please him, but don't second-guess your donor at your own expense. It is also worth mentioning that some people choose donors because they cannot afford a sperm bank. If this is the case, remember to continue to engage your discernment and choose the right donor for you. The extra time taken now will pay off later.

Clear Communication

Entering into this level of dialogue with someone can bring up many emotions. In fact, many women report experiencing the same exhilarating and nervous feelings that arise when they begin to date someone. This is a very powerful thing you're considering doing with each other. In our practice, we've noticed that many lesbians don't have much experience talking with men about intimate issues. It isn't uncommon to have these types of discussions at a very adolescent level. If you feel this may be the case for you, consider bringing a friend or having a third party facilitate these conversations.

When negotiating with a potential donor, stop and reflect back to each other frequently to make sure you understand one another: "What I hear you saying is" Some people find themselves involved in negotiations for years, but this isn't necessary. If you're dragging out the process, get some help from a therapist or friend. Either find a new donor or understand why you're holding up the process. If your potential donor is the one taking months to decide whether or not to donate, this should be a red flag. (Months of discussion about a coparenting relationship, on the other hand, can be reasonable.) Re-examine how direct you're being with him. Does he have a specific understanding of your needs and wants, and when you'd like to start trying? Early on in your discussions, ask your potential donor to bring his partner if he has one, so that you can discuss together how the commitment he makes to you will affect his intimate relationship(s). If your donor's partner isn't equally committed to the process, his or her resentments about impositions on their schedules and sex life may create substantial tension in their relationship. It's helpful to meet the partner and get a direct sense of how she or he feels about this joint project, so that your donor doesn't surprise you by bowing out later in deference to his primary relationship.

Partner Issues

Many couples fall into certain roles when working through initial conversations with a potential donor. Perhaps one partner knows the donor better. Perhaps the other feels a little more wary. Perhaps because she doesn't know the donor as well, she'll have an easier time asking the tough questions. Perhaps one partner is a softer negotiator, more prone to acquiesce or compromise in the moment. The other may find herself needing to draw all the boundaries, having to say what they both really mean.

If two partners haven't known a potential donor for an equal length of time, this inequality might benefit or hinder them in terms of how comfortable they each feel. A nonbirth mother may feel especially left out if the birth mother is very close to the donor. It's important to try to resolve this rather than ignore it. The nonbirth mother can share her feelings with her partner and arrange to spend more time with the potential donor on her own to feel more comfortable with the arrangement. If the choice of donor continues to make her feel left out even prior to the start of insemination, it may be best to seek out a more suitable donor or to re-examine the possibility of using a sperm bank.

It is not uncommon in a couple for only one prospective parent to want to use a known donor and for the other to prefer a sperm bank. This issue warrants thorough exploration, as the source of the sperm is one of the only decisions you cannot change. As mentioned previously, we encourage prospective parents to participate fully in this decision and not acquiesce to a partner's desire. Stay in your truth and come to resolution together. Many couples end up realizing that their sovereignty as a couple is paramount and end up using a sperm bank in these situations.

Issues for Single Women

It's important to present a clear message to potential donors, but this should be within clear boundaries. Tempting as it may be, a single-mom-to-be should not use her donor as her primary confidante. If you aren't sure what you want from a donor, use a friend or therapist to help you clarify your desires before going further.

Establishing Boundaries

Since the donor is the only other person involved in making the baby when you're single, this relationship can often seem like a heterosexual relationship, which may be confusing to you and others. This can be even more complex if you have sex with him to conceive. Single women are more likely to put the donor's name on the birth certificate under "father" than partnered women are. It's common to slip into more of a coparenting relationship with a donor than you might have otherwise. This often becomes painfully apparent when a woman later meets a lover with whom she wants to coparent, and wants the donor/coparent to become less involved. At that point it's often difficult to change things.

> EXAMPLE: Yasmine is a single 41-year-old bisexual woman. She tries to get pregnant for six months using frozen sperm. Her best friend, Josh, has been her primary support person throughout her preconception period. In a moment of despair after getting her period, again, Yasmine asks Josh if he'd give her sperm. He agrees. They don't feel like they need to draw up contracts, as their relationship is so good. Nothing will change; he'll remain her friend and support her as such in her motherhood. The only difference is the source of sperm. After two months Jasmine conceives.
>
> The complete emotional turnaround that Yasmine experiences in pregnancy comes as a total shock for Josh. Suddenly, Yasmine expects him to be there for her all the time. She tells him she plans to give the baby his last name. She cries when he says it's not his child—it's her child. She wants more and more from him. He feels overwhelmed and resentful. To him, he has lost his friend and is being treated like he is a man unwilling to step up to the plate of fatherhood. Yasmine does not feel like she has changed her expectations of him. They seek counseling together but it is only marginally helpful. The child is now four years old. They have worked things out, but Yasmine is still disappointed in Josh and Josh still harbors resentment at feeling like he was set up.

Romantic Feelings for the Donor

Just as with coparents, discussed in chapter 2, we've seen some women develop romantic feelings for their donors. In fact, it isn't unusual for negotiations with known donors to feel like a courtship. Sometimes a single woman, or either person in a partnership, will feel like they are falling in love with the donor, which can be a rather awkward surprise. The emotions may not contain any sexual component—more of a cosmic, romantic "Ah, I want to make a baby with you" theme. Or they may be distinctly sexual in nature. These feelings can bring up jealousy or cause some women to question their sexual orientation. They can also bring about a thrilling sense of expansion—you may feel like you've already begun to grow your family just by expanding your life to include your donor (or coparent), and you don't even have the baby yet. This same attachment may leave you feeling vulnerable, insecure, deeply grateful, or humbled by his commitment to you and your family. Sometimes your partner recognizes the energy before you do. If you've never been romantically involved with men, or if the connection you're feeling isn't explicitly sexual, it may be awhile before you can name the dynamic. If you used to date men unsuccessfully, you may find yourself revisiting your old but familiar gender dynamics and patterns of interactions, which may be both insightful and uncomfortable. Usually, these feelings subside when the baby is born.

Contracts

We encourage people to draw up contracts as a process of clarification. Documenting all agreements is a good exercise and provides greater legal safety. We find that the document is more meaningful if it's written in language that is legally clear yet heartfelt. This way it will be accessible if you ever want to share the contract with your child. Take note that most of your personal papers will be discovered by your children at some point, so make sure your contract reflects your truest intentions in conceiving your child so that it doesn't serve to undermine your child's self-esteem.

This contract can include a statement of intention on the donor's part to sever paternity rights. The contract needs to state in no uncertain terms what each person's role will be and who will be considered the child's parents. Create the contract in such a way that, as the child grows and can verbalize her or his desires, you'll have room for renegotiating any of the decisions to meet your actual circumstances.

Establish guidelines in the contract for handling conflict between the parties. These guidelines, and the explicit instructions as to the process whereby changes in the contract will be negotiated, are the most important part of the contract. Everything else can change over time, but if you have problems, it's essential to have established mechanisms to keep you out of court. Change is fundamental to parenting, therefore, the points in the contract are only your intentions. When change occurs, established agreements about how to work through them will be monumentally helpful.

Some people resist drawing up contracts as they feel like their spiritual connection is what is most vital. To put it into legal terms would diminish the connection that they feel or would disrupt the flow they have established with the one another. We encourage you to sign contracts anyway. We recommend that the parent(s) and the donor each write a brief letter to the child about what his or her intentions are. These are declarations of love you can attach as cover letters to your contracts. They serve two purposes: to make it clear to your child when he or she discover these papers that love is guiding your decisions, and to state your intentions from the start. This way, if you and your partner split up, or your donor tries to sue for custody, you all have declarations of your intentions in your own words to refer back to.

Specific Topics to Discuss with Your Donor

Will Your Donor Be Known?

As you'll recall, many people choose a known donor so that their child will have options about meeting and knowing him. Don't assume that the donor has the same understanding. He may want to remain anonymous, except to you, of course. Bring up this topic with him before you tell close friends about your negotiations with him, especially if you and your donor share some of the same professional and social circles.

Does your donor have strict guidelines about who may know his role in your baby's conception, either during the time of trying to conceive or afterward? Do you have strict guidelines about whom your donor may disclose the information to? Does your donor understand the importance of your guidelines and will he respect them? Do you plan to disclose the donor's identity to your child? If so, bear in mind that as soon as your child is old enough to talk, you'll lose control over who knows and who doesn't.

You will want to consider that keeping his identity from your child, or asking your child to keep his identity a secret from others will create a sense of shame for your child. We recommend that both parents and the donor be open to everyone knowing at some point. If this feels uncomfortable, it may be a sign that he is not the right choice for your family.

EXAMPLE: My partner and I chose a donor for our son (now four) who was an old boyfriend of a close friend. Our friend lives a few hours away. The donor was a world traveler. In ten years of knowing each other through our mutual friend our paths had not crossed. He was loving, smart, beautiful, kind, and not in our lives—the perfect choice. Well, our son was a few months old when people in our circle started to report having met our donor. We even met someone on a trip to Thailand who could identify our donor's connection to us upon meeting our family. It turns out he was dating a woman in our area who had ties to every one of our communities. The identity of our donor became known to all.

What does your donor plan to tell his biological family? Will your child be viewing these people as grandparents? Do his family members pose any legal threat to the security of your family? It isn't uncommon to rule out a donor because his family is homophobic. In fact, it's a very important consideration when selecting a donor.

Language

Take the time to decide what you'd like to call the donor, what you'd like the child to call him, and how you'd like the donor to refer to himself. What will the title be for the nature of this relationship? For example, will it be "our donor Greg"? "Uncle Greg"? "Greg"? "Dad"? This is important to discuss. You and your donor may have a discrepancy in terminology. Even if your understanding of the role is similar, the language you each naturally choose to use may be unintentionally different.

You need to know that the donor will support your choice of terminology and will use the same language both in public and directly with the child. Many donors innocently refer to themselves as fathers when the child's parents would never consider "father" to be the appropriate term. The donors often mean no harm in such situations; rather they are using commonly understood shorthand. Be very clear if you feel strongly about him not using these forms of appellations and be sure to give contextual examples.

Even if you have a donor agreement stating that he won't share custody, it won't always hold up in court. According to the National Center for Lesbian rights, it's vital to know that if your donor took you to court and could demonstrate that he has a unique role in your child's life based on donor status, or that the words "dad" or "father" have been used by people to name his relationship to the child, this testimony may take precedence over any agreements you have made.

Amount of Time in Your Child's Daily Life

How much time would you like this man to have in your life? You need to answer this before you ask yourself how much you would like him in your child's life because for many years this is one and the same. Will the child occasionally sleep over at his house? Will the donor see the child once a month? Once a week? On birthdays or holidays? What's important to you? Will your child get to decide when he or she will see him? If you or the donor moves away, how often will the child see the donor? Who decides? Who will pay the travel costs?

The Nitty-Gritty of Sperm Donation

Time Commitment

Prior to inseminating, you should clarify with the donor how many months he will commit to helping you. If your donor is providing fresh sperm, ask if he'll commit to one year. Six months often feels very rushed; it could very well take less than that, but don't limit your options prematurely. You'll want to be clear about whether the specified time period includes months in which you won't inseminate. The more clarity at this point in discussions the lesser chance for resentment on either part in the future.

If you're freezing sperm for safety reasons or because your donor lives far away, decide on the minimum number of vials you'd like to freeze. Depending on his volume of ejaculate, he may be able to produce one to five vials per ejaculate. Most sperm banks recommend that a donor on average make three to five visits to deposit sperm there. Would you like to have a second child from this donor's sperm? If so, consider freezing enough now for both children. Many men can make a deposit every forty-eight hours, provided they don't ejaculate at any other time outside of their sperm bank visit—some need a few more days to rebuild their count before another donation. But please read the section on the pros and cons of freezing donor sperm.

Availability

It's essential that your donor have a clear picture of what will be expected of him on a monthly basis. Make sure he is aware that you can give him a best guess at the start of the cycle but that you often won't know exactly when your most fertile time is until one to two days before or even the day of insemination. Also, be sure that he knows you will be asking for two to three donations a cycle. How flexible is his daily schedule? Is he willing to rearrange his day with little or no notice? Does he travel often on business? Will he try to arrange to be in town every month during your fertile days? If he will be flying to your location, a flexible schedule is key. Who will pay for his travel costs? Is he available if you need him to inseminate at 10 P.M. or 6 A.M.? How easy is he to reach? Will he return calls promptly? How much advance notice might you receive if he won't be available? Once you start inseminating, you might find it emotionally difficult to skip a cycle. Discuss this with him from the get-go.

It is also worthwhile to discuss how he likes to be contacted. We have had numerous prospective parents lament how difficult it is to get in touch with their donors, but their expectations were extreme: they wanted immediate contact. The donors in these situations report being overwhelmed by six increasingly frantic phone messages and emails over the period of an hour while they were in a meeting or at the gym. Please discuss this and establish what each of you needs to feel comfortable.

Abstinence and Your Donor's Sex Life

You'll need to ask your donor not to ejaculate for forty-eight to seventy-two hours before he donates for you. If he has ejaculated more recently, his sperm count may be significantly lower. Asking a donor to make this commitment may greatly affect his sex life, and thus it's important to discuss it in your initial conversations. It is common for the donor's sexual partner or partners to feel jealousy or resentment when you request this. The partner may pressure the donor to have sex when he's supposed to be abstaining, in order to prove his loyalty to the romantic relationship. Eventually, the pressure may become too great, and your donor may feel he can no longer donate for you. Likewise, some men ejaculate very frequently—a few times a day. For such men the abstinence you request can have a significant impact on his sexuality—especially if it takes a while for you to conceive.

||||||||||||||||||||||||||||||||||||||||||||||||||||||||||||||||||||||||||||||||||||||||||||

Creative Semen Analysis and Abstinence: At Maia we

have learned to handle abstinence in a creative way. We request that every potential sperm donor get a sperm count from an initial semen analysis. For men for whom abstinence will be an issue we suggest that they get two or even three analyses. The first one is done after he has abstained for forty-eight to seventy-two hours; if the sperm count is good, then we suggest he resume his normal ejaculatory habits for the next few days and then go back for a repeat test. Some men—especially gay men, we have noticed—have no decrease in their sperm count or volume with their normal ejaculatory behaviors. This is a great relief as it means he does not have to alter his personal behaviors. The other way we use serial semen analysis is to see how much a donor's ejaculate decreases if he donates a few times in a row. This is incredibly helpful when trying to ascertain the best timing approach. For example, if you know there is no significant decrease in his semen, then he is a donor who could donate a few days in a row. However, if his sperm count drops dramatically each time he donates unless he waits a day in between to rebuild, you would plan your insemination timing differently. This is vital information and can often be the difference between an extended conception period and a short conception period.

||||||||||||||||||||||||||||||||||||||||||||||||||||||||||||||||||||||||||||||||||||||

Financial Arrangements

It is customary for the prospective parents to cover any donor expenses. Getting to the donor or bringing him to you may involve transportation, lodging, and food costs. Medical costs may often be incurred if you ask the donor to undergo health screenings. If your donor is depositing sperm in a sperm bank, you'll have a sizable up-front cost to have the donor receive the necessary medical screenings and to freeze and store the sperm. If you store the sperm longer than one year, you'll be charged an annual storage fee as well. You can be creative, however, with some of these costs. If you want the donor to undergo initial medical tests, his health insurance may cover a portion of the costs if his primary-care doctor orders the tests. If he doesn't have insurance, he may be able to get basic health screening and sexually transmitted infection (STI) testing for low or no cost at a community health clinic or at a Planned Parenthood office. Payment of such costs reinforces the validity of a legal contract. Some people pay their known donors a token amount, or pay them with something other than money, such as food or gifts. Often this exchange helps both prospective parents and the donor to feel that they're not indebted to their donor. Another creative option we have seen is for prospective parents buy their donor a special gift if they feel that donor resentment could be developing. One family gave their donor frequent-flyer miles for a trip to Hawaii after he donated to them for a year. Another family purchased an iPod for their donor. These gifts are certainly not necessary, but it made the parents-to-be feel less awkward about continuing to ask him for sperm over an extended period of time.

Health and Safety Screening

When considering a known donor, it is very important to do a thorough exploration of his health. This involves asking numerous questions about his health history and his past and present behaviors. Please read on. If you find these questions too daunting to ask on your own, ask a doctor to provide this screening for you. However, you will also want to make sure that the doctor asks thorough enough questions about sexual practices and lifestyle behaviors. We mention this as the health-care provider in question may only have worked with married couples, where it is assumed that the couple already knows of and accepts a certain level of risk.

Since you and he will be doing something intimate together—handling his semen—it may also be worth your while to get more comfortable talking to him *now* about potentially awkward or embarrassing topics, as it could help to break the ice for future exchanges.

HEALTH HISTORY

Find out very specific information about your donor's personal and family health history. Women who are involved romantically with men rarely would reject a relationship with a partner because of concern over an inheritable disease. Yet you may choose to make such decisions about a potential donor, for it could affect your health or that of your child.

For example, you may feel it's important that the donor not have a family history of asthma because you yourself have a family history of asthma, allergies, or eczema. Or the mental health of his family members may be important to you if chronic depression runs in your family. You may have an understanding of disease that emphasizes environment and lifestyle over genetic predisposition. It's up to you to choose how specific to be when you ask questions, and how relevant the answers are to your decision.

An alternative to doing this detective work for yourself is to ask him to get a physical exam from his health-care provider and to give you a copy of his medical-history (his health-care provider will have this document).

DRUGS AND ALCOHOL

It's important to inquire about your potential donor's drug, alcohol, and cigarette intake. Marijuana use can significantly decrease men's sperm count and motility. Stimulants and alcohol can also decrease fertility. Alcohol, cocaine, and other recreational drugs such as crystal meth and ecstasy have been shown to affect not only sperm count but also the health of each individual sperm. Cigarette smoking is detrimental to sperm health, especially if a man has a borderline semen analysis. A man's drug and alcohol use can be particularly relevant in relationship to safer sex. Many people practice safer sex until they have a few drinks. When unsafe sex occurs under the influence of drugs or alcohol, a man may have no memory of it. This is an important issue to discuss with all potential donors. Make sure that your donor agrees to inform you if he has had unsafe or risky sex.

Sexual Health History

For the sake of your own health as well as that of your sexual partner(s) and your unborn baby, it's important when inseminating to minimize your risk of contracting an infection. This risk, in fact, is what deters most people from using fresh sperm. Your health risks can be significantly decreased if you know what questions to ask your potential donor. Therefore, we want to give you detailed information to prepare you so that you can approach this sometimes touchy subject with your donor. Please do not overlook this crucial piece of the screening process—failure to do so could leave you and your baby at serious risk. Broaching the subject will also lay the necessary groundwork for ongoing open communication regarding STI risks during the insemination process.

Many women have inadequate safer-sex discussions with their donors not because of a lack of information on the subject but because of their own discomfort with the intimacy of the topic. If you don't feel comfortable discussing sex practices and sexually transmitted infections, you can ask a health professional to do this type of screening for you. Perhaps you could see a health professional with your donor. If you have any concerns, for extra safety you may want to consider freezing and quarantining his sperm.

If you think you'd like to ask the donor about his safer-sex practices yourself, or just be better informed, please read on. The amount of information we provide is not to overwhelm you, but to make sure you don't have any gaps in your knowledge that may jeopardize the health of you or your unborn child. Again, the key to a positive experience with a known donor is taking the time to communicate carefully.

Monogamy

If your donor is monogamous (he and his partner only have sex with each other), and he and his partner have both clearly tested negative for HIV and other infections, they have no risk of contracting these diseases, except from the nonsexual ways that infection is transmitted. You should be aware that people have varying definitions of monogamy. Some define monogamy as having sex only within their primary relationship. Others define it as limited and specified kinds of sex outside of a primary relationship. And still others define monogamy as having sex within a primary relationship, but also having group sex with their partner present.

Some people may be sexually exclusive within their relationship but haven't been tested for STIs prior to the beginning of that relationship. Some may have been tested initially but not long enough after exposure to previous partners for the test to be fully accurate. If your donor has been in any of these situations, he should be tested again. Remember, your donor may be monogamous, but his partner may not be, and your donor may not know this.

If your donor's partner isn't monogamous, your risk of infection—and your child's risk—substantially increases, unless he or she always practices safer sex with other partners. As you can never know 100 percent that someone is monogamous or otherwise risk-free, using a known donor is always a leap of faith. Thus, the more testing and the more talking you do, the better.

Safer-Sex Practices

HIV and all other STIs are transmitted by infected blood (including menstrual blood), semen, vaginal secretions, female ejaculate, or other body fluids that enter the bloodstream through tiny invisible openings in the mucus membranes of the mouth, rectum, or vagina during sexual contact. These openings may be sores or irritations from other types of infections, abrasions in the vagina or rectum incurred through inadequate lubrication, or openings in the mouth from recent flossing, brushing, or gum disease. It may also enter the bloodstream via blood transfusion, needles shared for drug injection or tattooing, or some S&M (sado-masochism) practices.

Penetrative penile intercourse, whether vaginal or anal, is unsafe if a latex condom isn't used, whether or not ejaculation occurs. The risk of infection is higher for the receptive partner. Oral sex without a latex barrier has been found to be a source of transmission of HIV, although it occurs much less frequently than with intercourse. Before a man ejaculates, he secretes a little bit of pre-ejaculatory fluid, also called pre-come, which may also be a source of infection. If a man puts another man's penis in his mouth, there are a variety of ways in which it could be more or less safe. The least safe is if someone ejaculates in his mouth. He may reduce his risk, but not eliminate it, if he doesn't let his partner ejaculate but still puts the head of the penis in his mouth, because he will still be exposed to pre-ejaculatory fluid. Not putting his mouth on the head of his partner's penis reduces his risk even further.

Donors wanting to be "safe" when having oral sex with women and non-operative transmen need to use a dental dam or plastic food wrap so their mouths don't come in contact with vaginal secretions, female ejaculate, or menstrual blood. Oral-anal contact is also considered a less-than-safe sexual practice, most notably for the partner using his mouth. Those wishing to partake in this activity may also use dental dams or plastic wrap. In addition, body fluids can be exchanged if shared sex toys are not washed between use.

Condoms

There are a few things your donor needs to know about condoms: Lamb-skin condoms aren't effective barriers against viruses; latex condoms are. Latex condoms can only be used with water-based lubricants, as oils will dissolve the latex. Some people are allergic to the latex in condoms. If so, more recently invented polyurethane condoms can be used. They're more expensive, but they have another benefit in that they can be used with oil. Condoms lubricated with spermicide are slightly more effective in preventing HIV infection and can also be used, except by those who experience reactions to the spermicide.

Talking About Sex Practices

It's often challenging for lesbians to question men in detail about their sex lives. Usually, our donors are fairly well known to us, and we may have difficulty being as explicit as possible. You may feel you're invading their privacy. You may also feel that this type of discussion adds yet another level of intimacy to a relationship that would feel more comfortable remaining less intimate. Having a conversation about sex may also seem inherently sexual. Or you may be invested deeply in working with this donor and not want to discover information that may jeopardize your decision. Finally, you may fear appearing ignorant about gay or straight men's sexual practices.

Many women are able to have the following conversation:

"So, do you practice safer sex?"

"Yes, I do."

"OK, all the time?"

"Yeah."

Often that is the extent of their discussion. To be thorough, though, read through the above section on safer sex again, thinking about how you might phrase specific questions to find out what you need to know. You might ask the following:

- "What does safer sex mean to you?"
- "What is your definition of 'monogamous'"?
- "Do you have oral sex with other men or women who have penises, and if you do, do you use a condom?"
- "Do you put your mouth on the head of the penis? Do you do that

before ejaculation? During ejaculation?"
- "Do you ever drink or do drugs when you have sex? Do you ever have sex when you're intoxicated? Can you be certain you adhere to the same safety standards at those times?"
- "Do you have anal sex? Do you use a condom?"
- "Do you use gloves or bare hands with anal penetration?"
- "Do you have oral-anal contact? Do you give, receive, or both? Do you use a barrier?"
- "Do you have oral sex with women or transmen? Do you use a barrier or condom?"
- "Do you use bare hands or gloves with penetration?"
- "Do you use gloves to clean up after sex?"
- "Do you share sex toys?"
- "Do you practice BDSM (bondage & discipline/domination & submission/sado-masochism)? What are your safety parameters in your practices?"
- "Are there other situations where you come in contact with body fluids?"

It may help to bring a copy of this book when you interview your donor and his partner and read it together. Create your own list, adapted from this one, and he can read it at home before discussing it with you. This conversation is difficult or awkward for many women (and men too!).

The definition of safer sex differs from person to person. For example, in the gay male community, for years a debate has raged about the risk of unprotected oral sex. Some people feel it's a negligible risk. You can find information from your local health department, the San Francisco AIDS Foundation, and national AIDS hotlines. Your focus in these discussions, however, should be what makes you (and your partner) feel safe and whether your donor can agree to these restrictions, whatever they may be.

Once you both have established exactly what kind of sexual practices your donor can engage in, you need to discuss with him his commitment to tell you if something changes. If you've been through all the testing and negotiating and have started inseminating, he may feel an immense pressure not to admit that he's done something that doesn't adhere to your guidelines. You need to let him know that you trust him to tell you immediately.

If you aren't comfortable with his answers to these vitally important questions about sexual practices, you may want to consider looking for another donor. If you're set on working with a specific donor, but decide after your sex discussion that you feel unsure of his risk of contracting a sexually transmitted infection, consider freezing and quarantining his sperm.

Freezing and Quarantining Donor Sperm: Advantages and Disadvantages

If you bring your donor into a sperm bank to have his sperm frozen, it's very much like getting other sperm from the sperm bank except that it is your donor's sperm and it is only released to you. In sperm-bank lingo he is called a "directed donor."

CONVENIENCE

People ask their donors to have their sperm frozen for many reasons. They may have concerns about his health or lifestyle practices; he may not live in their area; he may be planning to have a vasectomy; or they may want to have a second child with his sperm. People using sperm from a male-to-female (MTF) transgender person may choose to freeze her sperm prior to hormone therapy or surgery.

REDUCED CHANCE OF INFECTION

You may choose to freeze and quarantine your donor's sperm if you're unsure of his health status. If his sperm freezes well, he can donate a number of vials over a few weeks and have them stored. For his sperm to be released, he'll need to test negative for all the tests for sexually transmitted infections the particular sperm bank requires at the time of donation, and another sample must be taken again in six months and tested. If all tests come back negative after six months, his sperm has an almost 100 percent likelihood of being infection-free at the time it was frozen. From that six-month point on, you may use any of that frozen sperm. If you run out before you become pregnant, you'll need to repeat the process.

With most banks the six-month quarantine can be waived with a directed donor.

LOWER SPERM COUNT AND EFFECTIVENESS

Unfortunately, freezing may lower sperm count or motility so substantially that it's not a useful option for your particular donor. It is advisable to do a semen analysis and freeze-thaw test as soon as you choose a donor whose sperm you plan to freeze so that you may find out how well his sperm survive freezing.

Whenever possible, we recommend using fresh sperm because of its increased effectiveness. You may, however, have a found the perfect donor and feel he warrants this kind of creative problem solving.

Freezing sperm is expensive, so plan to put aside at least $2,000 to $3,000 for this service, plus any courier delivery costs. If you have a long-distance donor, freezing sperm may in the long run be less expensive or stressful than paying travel expenses for multiple months of insemination.

Pros and Cons of Long-Distance Donors

Many prospective parents consider using a donor who lives far away. This desire can stem from wanting to ensure as little contact between the donor and their family to decrease the chance for confusion over roles. Having the donor live in another state or another part of the country can be emotionally reassuring for some people who are considering the known-donor option. Others have not choice but to take a long-distance donor because the person whose sperm they want lives far away.

Some people choose to freeze sperm because they don't live near their donor. He could donate at a sperm bank near him and have the sperm transferred to a bank near you, or you could order his frozen sperm monthly by mail if you don't live near a sperm bank. He may also travel to a sperm bank in your area and freeze a number of vials. Frozen sperm can be brought home in a liquid nitrogen tank, where it will remain frozen for up to one week. You can use the sperm whenever you're ready to thaw it.

There's a method for preparing fresh sperm that allows it to be mailed overnight unfrozen without its losing its much of its viability. The technique requires that you inseminate by intrauterine insemination. You may consider this method if your donor's sperm doesn't survive freezing well or to avoid the other disadvantages of freezing. This is an exciting new option.

When the costs of travel versus couriers and freezing are added up, many people discover that the cheapest way to achieve conception with a long-distance donor is if they travel to the donor or have him travel to them.

Gay or Bisexual Directed Donors

Most sperm banks interpret the FDA regulations to mean that they cannot accept any gay or bisexual directed (known) donors, but a few are willing to do so. Some of the banks we spoke with were very clear that if donors "indicate" that they are gay on the application form, they will not accept them, but if they do not "indicate" they are gay on the form the same lab work and testing is done as for any other donor. Thus, the health concerns that would disqualify a donor are the same for everyone and would not be based on sexual orientation. However, the state of New York will not allow any frozen sperm known to be from a gay or bisexual man to enter the state.

Medical Testing for the Donor

Semen Analysis

We recommend that you get a semen analysis (sperm count) and health screening for any potential donor as soon as he agrees that he is open to being a donor and that you'll be having further talks. If he doesn't have a high or functional sperm count, you'll want to know immediately, so that you both can come up with a plan. There are a number of possible reasons for a poor result of a semen analysis (see page 111 for further information). You may know instantly from the results that you want to choose another donor, or you may be committed to this donor and want to wait and see if his sperm count can be raised. Your donor would probably want a physical exam for his own information and peace of mind. We know of donors who learned they had testicular cancer when they underwent an exam after a semen analysis gave abnormal results. Some men find their infertility is caused by a dilated blood vessel in the testes called a varicocele, which often can be surgically repaired. If Western medicine gives no answers, studies have confirmed the efficacy of acupuncture and other non-Western approaches to improve fertility in many subfertile men.

A semen analysis usually costs $100 to $200 and can be performed by a sperm bank or in a private physician's lab. At a sperm bank, your donor will probably be given a small container and shown to a private room. If he's working with a private lab or physician, he'll be given a small container and lid, he'll ejaculate at home, and then he'll drop the sample off at the lab within twenty to thirty minutes of ejaculation. Prior to a semen analysis, he should abstain from ejaculating for at least forty-eight hours but not more than a week.

Accuracy of the Semen Analysis

Sperm quality can fluctuate greatly from day to day and is also influenced by stress, sleep, drugs, and eating habits. Therefore, if your donor receives abnormal test results, he should have the test repeated so that his fertility can be more accurately assessed. Although a semen analysis is a good starting place to assess a donor's fertility, it isn't the be-all and end-all of fertility tests. If your donor's sperm count is normal and you don't conceive after a number of inseminations, don't assume that you've ruled out all the problems with his sperm with one analysis. Some studies suggest that a sperm count isn't a very accurate predictor of the sperm's fertilizing capacity, beyond identifying obviously abnormal sperm samples, because numerous men with "normal" sperm counts have other infertility challenges. Other tests, such as those that assess how the sperm swim through fertile mucus or whether the sperm can fertilize a hamster egg in a Petri dish, often can more accurately tell you whether the donor is infertile or subfertile.

WHAT EXACTLY DOES SEMEN ANALYSIS TELL ME?

Normal semen contains sperm, hormones, sugars, salts, and secretions. During the semen analysis, a semen sample is examined under a microscope shortly after ejaculation, and then hourly for up to three hours. Sometimes the semen is incubated at human body temperature for twenty-four hours and then the sperm are counted again.

A number of factors are evaluated in the semen analysis, not just the number of sperm. The most important quality is motility (movement), followed by count and morphology (size and shape). We'll describe these factors, but don't expect to read the following descriptions and then be able to easily interpret your donor's semen analysis. If the results are questionable to you, or clearly low, seek further expertise. If your donor has the analysis performed at a sperm bank, they should explain the results to both of you. Some will even invite him into the lab to look through the microscope and see what they're measuring. If his private doctor orders the test, she or he may be able to do some basic interpretation, although male infertility will probably not be the doctor's specialty.

- *Volume.* Two to five cc is average volume. Volume can vary quite a bit depending on the man's mood, whether he has ejaculated within the past twenty-four to forty-eight hours, and his state of arousal. Volume is often dependent on arousal. If your donor has a low volume, to increase volume he should take longer to build up to climax. He should spend at least thirty minutes masturbating prior to ejaculation. Studies have shown that if a man witnesses another man ejaculating, his volume increases. So, porn or mutual masturbation with another man may help as well.
- *pH level.* pH level, or the amount of acidity, should be similar to that of fertile cervical mucus, slightly alkaline. A score of 7 to 8 is

normal. If the acidity level is too high he may want to evaluate his diet and strive to eat more alkaline foods.

⊙ *Viscosity*. Semen first gels and then liquefies after ejaculation, which makes it easier for the sperm to swim. Fifteen to thirty minutes after ejaculation, the desired viscosity is plus 1 on a scale of 1 to 4.

⊙ *Agglutination/clumpy sample*. If you are working with a donor whose sample remains clumpy, agglutination is a factor. Agglutination can decrease fertility if more than 25 percent of the sperm are clumped together. Clumpiness prevents movement. Usually increased hydration (drinking more water on a daily basis) and supplementing with vitamin C help dramatically. If not, IUI might be necessary.

⊙ *Motility*. Normal motility (movement) is 60 percent or greater with good forward movement within two hours of ejaculation. If your donor has low motility, consult chapter 9 "Increasing Male Fertility."

⊙ *Sperm count*. This is the actual number of sperm, motile and nonmotile, per cc of semen. Currently, 20 million to 160 million sperm per cc is normal. Sperm banks usually guarantee a minimum of 20 million motile sperm in each vial for both vaginal and intrauterine insemination. A donor's fresh (not frozen) complete ejaculate will ideally have considerably more than this because you get an entire ejaculate (not just 0.5- to 1.0 cc), and none of the sperm are lost during freezing.

⊙ *Morphology*. This describes the shape of the sperm; for example: two tails, no tail, two heads, wrong-size head, or tail not as long as normal. You may be surprised at how many sperm, on average, are abnormally shaped. It's helpful to understand that the body's approach to sperm production focuses on quantity more than quality. Millions upon millions of sperm are produced constantly by the body. Most of these sperm that are misshaped do not move as effectively through the fertile mucus into the uterus, and therefore are naturally filtered out during intercourse or vaginal insemination. If too many of the sperm are abnormally shaped, the number of normal, functional sperm may be significantly low, even if the overall sperm count is high. The World Health Organization classifies a "normal" semen sample as one with more than 30 percent of its sperm normally shaped. Some men have few sperm that are very abnormally shaped but many that are just slightly abnormal.

A different type of classification that counts even slight differences in shape and size as abnormal is called a strict Kruger assessment. Kruger analysis classifies borderline sperm as abnormal. Thus with a Kruger analysis a count greater than 14 percent is considered excellent. Kruger analysis is very helpful for IVF and may or may not be helpful in your situation. Some studies indicate that morphology is not as important when using IUI. This is probably due to the number of sperm placed directly into the uterus. It is also possibly because a lot of the less motile sperm are also the poorly shaped sperm and they are more likely to be washed out of the sample. Slight abnormalities may actually be significant factors in the ability of sperm to fertilize an egg. Therefore, a semen analysis that includes a strict Kruger assessment can give you more detailed information.

There are three main causes of poor morphology: a genetic trait, exposure to toxins, and increased scrotal temperatures. If your donor has a high number of abnormally shaped sperm, find more information about how to increase normal morphology; see chapter 9, "Increasing Male Fertility."

⊙ *White blood cells (WBCs).* These are part of the body's immune system. More than five showing up per high-powered microscope field could indicate an infection of the reproductive tract. This should be treated prior to insemination.

Putting It All Together

The number of cc's in the ejaculate multiplied by the number of motile (moving) sperm per cc will give the total number of motile sperm for that fresh donation. For example, if an average volume of ejaculate for one man is 3 cc's and his average count is 70 million motile sperm per cc, then an average ejaculate will contain 210 million motile sperm total. Factor the percentage of motile sperm into the equation and you have a pretty good sense of the quality of the sample.

You want to have at least 20 million motile sperm per cc. That is the recommendation of the World Health Organization and most sperm banks stick to that recommendation. The WHO also says that anything less than 20 million per cc is subfertile. It stands to reason, then, that we have seen very clearly that the people who get pregnant fastest often are the ones using sperm where the motility is much greater. If you are using a known donor with fresh sperm he should have a minimum of 40 million motile sperm per ejaculate or you should consider at least one IUI per cycle. This recommendation is following the assumption that he has already taken three months to boost his fertility.

Freezing viability (when applicable): A semen analysis is repeated after sperm have been frozen for forty-eight hours and then thawed. Remember, even men whose sperm freezes well can expect to lose 50 percent of their live sperm through freezing and thawing, which means that starting with a high sperm count is essential. In fact, one sperm bank tells men that, on average, only one man out of six has sperm that will freeze well, and another sperm bank turns away 80 to 90 percent of donor applicants, primarily because their sperm won't freeze well enough. In other words, most men won't be giving you an optimally fertile sample if their sperm will be frozen. Any sample that is less than 20 million motile sperm per cc is considered subfertile. Less than 5 million per cc is infertile. If you are planning to use a subfertile count for IUI the count must be absolutely no lower than 10 million per cc.

Herpes

If your donor has herpes, medical opinion is that it is safe for him to donate as long as he isn't having any symptoms. Herpes cannot infect the sperm. The only way the baby could get herpes would be from the pregnant mom. There seems to be a 3 percent risk of herpes shedding, in the absence of symptoms. The risk of herpes being transmitted to the semen recipient would be much lower than 3 percent as long as the donor is not having any symptoms.

Other Tests

The following is a comprehensive list of the medical tests required of men who donate sperm at sperm banks. You may choose to ask your donor to have some or all of these, depending on your budget, his insurance, and his sexual or health history. Most tests come back from the lab with the normal healthy results printed next to your donor's results for reference. We provide brief descriptions here for your information; however, the health practitioner who orders the tests should explain the results to you or your donor. Speak up if you don't completely understand.

HIV-1, HIV-2, HTLV 1 and 2. HIV-1 is more prevalent in the United States than HIV-2. HIV-2 is a different strain of the virus and is much more common in Africa. If a donor is tested at an "anonymous" testing center, he will probably only be tested for HIV-1. The "regular" blood test isn't a test for the actual virus, but a test for the antibody that one's immune system makes after it has been infected. One never has the HIV antibody without being infected. The time between infection and seroconversion (when the antibody being tested for will actually show up in the blood) is usually two weeks to three months, although it can take up to six months. The test very rarely shows negative when someone is actually infected. If the test comes back positive, it's retested twice, once with a more specific and expensive test, before results are released. Thus, a positive HIV result is confirmed by three tests.

⊙ *Rapid HIV Tests.* Many people using known donors have found rapid HIV testing to be of great use for them. All rapid HIV tests are screening tests (they test for indications of infection, not the actual virus). They are comparable to the standard enzyme immunoassay (EIA) screening test in terms of accuracy (99 percent) with regard to both sensitivity (99 percent) and specificity (99.8 percent). Generally, rapid HIV tests are approved only for HIV-1; however, the FDA has approved some specific brands for testing for both HIV-1 and HIV-2

Rapid HIV tests use urine, oral fluid (from a mouth swab, not saliva), or blood (from a finger stick) as the testing sample. Rapid HIV tests are widely available over the Internet, at pharmacies without a prescription (but behind the pharmacy counter), and anonymously at clinics. Depending on the type of rapid test, results are available quickly, typically in from twenty minutes to a few days, as compared to one to two weeks for EIA (also called ELISA) tests. All positive rapid tests require additional testing for confirmation of the result.

Even though rapid tests are easily available, they still require that anyone taking the test be in contact with a clinic, physician, or counselor to get the results. After taking the sample the person taking the test has to wait at or return to the testing site or send the test to a lab for processing. The oral- fluid-type tests take just twenty minutes. For the other types of rapid testing the person taking the test has to return in a day or two for the result. Home tests require that the person taking the test call in with their customer number to access the results. If the test is positive they are connected with a counselor.

You do not need a prescription for an HIV test, and most clinics that offer HIV testing now offer a rapid-test option (sometimes at a cost, but generally not). The availability of rapid HIV testing varies from area to area, so you may have to travel a bit to get a quick test. The quick tests may have a high percentage of false positives, so all positive results need to be confirmed. There is no evidence of a false negative results.

USING AN HIV-POSITIVE DONOR

Since 1987 there have been thousands of documented cases of women getting pregnant via either IUI or IVF, using processed sperm from HIV-seropositive men and no seroconversion of the mother or baby. HIV is not in the sperm but in the seminal fluid, and so very specific sperm washing techniques are used to remove the semen from the sperm. Not many clinics perform these washes, but they are available. It is important to note that in the comparative sperm research, men with HIV tend to have poorer sperm quality. But if you are completely wedded to using a donor who is HIV-positive, it may be possible to conceive.

- *RPR.* This blood test, also known as VDRL, STS, or serologic test for syphilis, is for syphilis, a sexually transmitted bacterium that can be treated with penicillin.
- *Hepatitis B surface antigen and antibody, core antibodies.* This is a blood test for the sexually and blood-transmitted virus that causes hepatitis B, an infection of the liver that can cause serious liver damage. Someone who has been vaccinated against hepatitis B will show positive surface antibodies.
- *Hepatitis C antibody:* If a person tests positive for hepatitis C antibodies, they're considered to be infected with hepatitis C. An entirely different virus than hepatitis B, hepatitis C is transmittable sexually and especially through blood exposure (sharing any kind of needles, for example). After many years, hepatitis C can cause severe damage to the liver. Statistics show that 5 percent of pregnant women infected with hepatitis C transmit it to their infants in the uterus.
- *Cytomegalovirus (CMV), IgG, and IgM.* CMV is a virus that many of us have been exposed to at some point in our lives. It usually will only make you sick if your immune system isn't working well. Once exposed, you'll test positive for IgG antibodies for the rest of your life, meaning that your immune system has a memory of the infection. Active infection will give you a positive test result for IgM antibodies in the bloodstream. Getting an active CMV infection while pregnant can cause birth defects such as central nervous system damage, brain damage, and hearing loss.
- *Chlamydia, trichomonas, gonorrhea.* Tests for these STIs are usually conducted by means of both urine and genital culture for bacterial infections that can be treated with a short course of antibiotics.
- *Myco/ureaplasma.* The test for the presence of myco/ureaplasma can reveal the need for antibiotics as well. Undetected in women the bacterium can interfere with fertilization and implantation and

can be a cause of miscarriage.

⊙ *Urinalysis, complete blood count (CBC), and chem panel (blood chemistry)*. These are tests with many components that assess someone's overall health. Most laboratories print out a range of normal values next to the results of the tests, so that you can fairly easily see when a result is abnormal. Interpretation of what that information means requires help from a health-care practitioner.

Some of the inheritable diseases that can be tested are Tay-Sachs, cystic fibrosis, and abnormal hemoglobins such as those that cause sickle-cell anemia and thalassemia.

When Will You Know You're Ready to Start Inseminating?

You may start to inseminate as soon as any important health test results come back, or you may all know months in advance that you're ready, just waiting for the month to arrive that you plan to start inseminating. You'll know that you're either stuck at an impasse or don't actually want to use this donor if the month that you were going to begin inseminating comes and goes without insemination. Likewise, when you've worked out all of the logistics but cannot bring yourself to call or e-mail the donor, you'll know some hidden feelings may need to be examined.

You have the right to decide at any time that you don't want this man to be your donor. This is your family you're creating, and if at any time you don't feel fully at ease, you need to speak up. If you're partnered and both of you have different senses of comfort with the donor, you need to have some careful, honest, specific—and possibly uncomfortable—conversations. Not feeling safe about the sperm you put in your body, or your lover's body, for whatever reason, isn't conducive to conception. Be sensitive to the fact that your donor has feelings, too, and through this process he has undoubtedly grown emotionally invested. Be kind, considerate, and prompt in letting him know that you no longer wish to use him as your donor.

You also have the right to declare that you're ready whenever you feel so, regardless of the cautious advice you may get from others. Listen to their advice, decide if it merits some attention, and then move forward. You're the one(s) who are making a baby. The initiative to jump off that cliff into parenthood can only be taken by you. Trust your intuition. Go forward. You may have spent six months or four years planning with your donor, or you may have spent two weeks or two days.

THINGS TO WATCH OUT FOR IN DONOR NEGOTIATIONS

It pays off to take the time you need to find the right donor for you. Please do not rush into any known donor relationship. You are looking at a lifelong decision that cannot be changed. Choose with great care.

⊙ What does your heart say? Is he the right donor?
⊙ What does your body say? How does your body feel in his presence?
⊙ Does he want secrecy around his donor status?
⊙ Is he getting his health tests or is there always a delay?
⊙ Is it taking him months to decide?
⊙ Is his partner on board?
⊙ Do his responses to your questions keep changing?
⊙ Do you trust him?

A comprehensive Known-Donor Health Screening Questionnaire is available on our website (www.maiamidwifery.com).

Having decided to use a known donor and finally having all of the negotiations completed is a wonderful achievement. Take stock of everything you have gone through to come to this place. The clarity that most families feel about their choices has deepened quite a bit by this stage in the journey. Despite this clarity of vision we encourage you to read through the chapters on coparenting and sperm banks as well—you never know where life will take you. Parenting is an exquisite blend of the planned and the unexpected.

CHAPTER 8

Sperm Banks and Unknown Donors

THE PROLIFERATION OF sperm banks friendly to queer and single women in the last two decades has introduced new possibilities and decisions into the realm of conception options. Lesbians started their own sperm banks for several important reasons. Unmarried women, both now and in the past in many states and nations, have often had limited access to sperm-bank services and infertility treatments. When the first overtly lesbian-friendly sperm bank opened in 1982, the AIDS epidemic was just beginning. Lesbians were seeing their male friends getting sick and dying from a disease whose modes of transmission were not yet well understood. Lesbians wanted to be able to choose sperm that had been quarantined and retested. They also wanted easier access to sperm from anonymous donors, which would eliminate the risk of being sued for custody by the biological father. Up until that point, many lesbians relied on go-betweens to choose and screen a donor, arrange the sperm exchange, and maintain each party's anonymity. Some people still choose to use a go-between.

Purchasing sperm from a sperm bank has become a common choice for many families. Despite the benefits sperm banks offer, finding one's way through a medicalized, profit-driven business often feels confounding. Working with a sperm bank requires that prospective parents entertain the philosophical and spiritual questions raised by choosing to conceive in a fashion that precludes a child's access to information regarding the identity of their biological father. In this chapter, we focus mainly on sperm banks as the primary option for people seeking anonymous donors, although we also address working with a go-between and anonymous sex. In this section we cover in detail the benefits and drawbacks of sperm banks, how sperm banks work, and offer tips and tricks for optimizing your relationship with them.

Sperm-Bank Benefits

Sperm banks may offer you the best chance of finding healthy sperm that is free of transmittable infection. Although there is no system that can completely guarantee your safety, the exhaustive method of testing, quarantining, retesting, and releasing is the standard used today by sperm banks. Any donor option that doesn't involve freezing and retesting the sperm must rely upon the donor's word that he practices safe sex.

Using sperm from a bank ensures that you won't have to worry about the threat of a custody dispute from the donor or any of his family members. Of all available options, many people feel most secure obtaining sperm from a sperm bank. Some don't want to have to interact directly with any men when choosing how they would like to conceive their child. This option certainly removes the need for interacting with donors. But interactions must occur with all sorts of other people, including health-care practitioners, the sperm-bank receptionist, and the sperm-bank health educator.

A number of prospective parents wish to select sperm from a sperm bank because they may select a donor on the basis of many details of his identity: ethnic background, height, weight, education, religion, aspects of his medical history, and so forth. In addition, sperm banks won't change their minds as known donors can, and you can count on their regular business hours for scheduling. Still, if you need to pick up sperm from the bank, you may be inconvenienced by their hours. Having sperm shipped to your home or doctor's office may be easier, although you'll incur cost and have to send the liquid nitrogen tank back as well as make plans for where and when the tank will be delivered.

Ethical Considerations of Using Sperm Banks

People who choose to work with a sperm bank often need to make some kind of peace with the idea that neither they nor their child will have access to the donor, even if they're very happy about the other advantages the sperm bank offers. In fact, many people who are pleased about not having to interact and negotiate with a man about the sperm still feel a sense of fear or loss about making a permanent decision to give up access to their donor's identity. Making peace with your decision will allow you to convey pride in your choices regarding your child's creation.

Many people find that their attitudes toward anonymous sperm donors are influenced by their conversations with friends who have been adopted. Some adults who were adopted as children feel adamant about reserving a child's right to access information about their biological parents, while others feel their adoption has led to their belief that love, not biology, is what makes a family. Many feel it's important to distinguish between the experience of someone whose biological parents gave them up for adoption and the experience of someone raised by people who actively chose to create him or her assisted by a donor who also consciously chose to contribute to the child's creation. All these ethical questions are very personal and intimate, with no clear right or wrong answers. Making a final decision about using a known or unknown donor is, in fact, where the majority of prospective parents reach an impasse in moving toward their goal of getting pregnant; they feel incapable of making such a big and permanent decision about someone else's life. Feeling secure in your decision requires trusting your own beliefs and values as well as your thoroughness of researching what you need to know to make an informed decision and your good intentions to make the best choice for your future child and family. Making this decision takes self-love and confidence. If you're partnered, it also requires clear communication and respect for each other's points of view. If you feel paralyzed about making a decision about where to obtain sperm, review chapter 3, "Making Decisions and Creating a Plan and a Timeline."

As we've mentioned, several sperm banks offer open identity programs that provide your child access to donor contact information when he or she turns 18. These programs allow women to choose to use sperm banks while alleviating some of their concerns about not having a known donor.

Sperm-Bank Drawbacks

Frozen sperm is less fertile than fresh sperm for a number of reasons. First, the freezing process somewhat reduces the sperm's capacity to fertilize an egg, in part because of the solution added to the semen to help it freeze better. Also, instead of thriving in the cervix for two to three days post-insemination, sperm that has been frozen usually only lives eighteen to twenty-four hours, due to changes caused by the freezing process. A number of the sperm die during the freeze-thaw process. Furthermore, the amount of sperm purchased in a vial is only one portion of the ejaculate. Thus, both the total number of sperm and their longevity are reduced.

Because of these limitations, people using frozen sperm must chart their cycle carefully to take advantage of optimum timing for their inseminations each month. Many people choose intrauterine insemination (IUI) instead of vaginal insemination, in hopes that it will increase the efficacy of each insemination. Depending on your particular situation and your knowledge of your body, IUI may or may not be the best choice for you. For more information see chapter 14.

For all of these reasons, it often takes more cycles to conceive with frozen sperm. On average, the probability of conception by having intercourse is 20 percent per cycle. By vaginal insemination with frozen sperm, the probability is 4 to 10 percent per cycle. By intrauterine insemination with frozen sperm, the probability is 8 to 18 percent per cycle. These statistics vary with age. These statistics also vary with the number of inseminations per month and the accuracy of your timing. Very little data exist for the probability of vaginal insemination with fresh sperm, but it's probably equal to or slightly lower than that for intercourse.

If a person lives in an area where doctors refuse to provide fertility services to unmarried women or are limited in their ability to do so, she may not be able to find a provider who can help her perform an intrauterine insemination. We have heard such reports from Georgia, Oklahoma, Florida, Mississippi, Texas, and Tennessee. However, some of the people we have spoken with have gotten creative and crossed state lines or gone to major cities for their inseminations.

The high cost of buying sperm at a sperm bank can be prohibitive. It is usually a minimum of $1,000 a month. It's also difficult to budget for an expense that could be incurred for one month or 12. Many people charge all of the expenses on their credit cards, wondering how they'll start to pay off the bill when they're in mid-pregnancy, while simultaneously saving for maternity leave and the expenses of their newborn child. And women who wish to inseminate with more than two vials per cycle may need to buy three to four vials of sperm per cycle.

Almost all sperm banks choose to deny men who have had any sexual contact with other men in the last seven years the opportunity to donate, regardless of their sexual-practice history or their disease-screening results. Many queer women would prefer to use sperm from gay men. The only sperm bank that releases the sexual orientation of its donors is Rainbow Flag Health Services. Their contact information is listed in "Resources."

Sometimes people have trouble trusting a business, and the strangers who work there, to do such important screening and maintain the high level of integrity necessary in regard to sperm quality. Some people choose to be inseminated at their doctor's office instead of at home, just so they can see the sperm under the microscope to verify that it's actually moving. Others buy an inexpensive microscope at a toy store or use a fertility lens for this same purpose at home.

Often sperm donors are in their early twenties. As they get older, donors may discover things about their health history that would be significant for you to know. In extreme situations, sperm banks try to contact women who have received the donor's sperm and update them; this can only happen, however, if the donor contacts the bank about a change is his health. This is a valid concern for anyone working with a young donor, whether known or unknown. If the donor is known to you, however, you may feel assured that you'd be contacted by him in such an event.

Choosing a Donor from a Sperm-Bank Catalog

Choosing a sperm-bank donor is different from choosing a known donor. A sperm bank can offer a more in-depth interrogation about personal and family medical health history than social convention easily allows between two people who know each other. Sperm banks offer a wider range of options in terms of ethnic background and inheritable characteristics of the donor than many people have available in their circle of potential known donors.

Most people find the concept of choosing a donor based on height, weight, ethnicity, skin tone, age, eye color, hobbies, or level of education to be somewhat surreal or even uncomfortable. People wonder how to make a decision based on these characteristics and what that says about themselves and their values. External value is placed on certain qualities by the sperm banks themselves through their pricing system. Some banks charge more for open-identity donors (see below), subtly placing more value on these donors. Other banks charge more money for donors who have higher education and more prestigious occupations. Sweden and the United Kingdom both require that all people using sperm banks use open-identity sperm donors. Only through a sperm-bank catalog has a whole new method of selecting the genetic profile of one's child become possible.

Open-Identity Donors

Open-identity donors have given permission to a sperm bank to release identifying information about themselves to the child when the child turns 18. Only a few sperm banks offer open-identity donors. Remember, these donors will only be known to you if your child pursues this option at 18. At that time there's no guarantee that the donor will still be living.

Some sperm banks, under consumer pressure to offer comparable policies, have policies that when the child turns 18 he or she can request that the sperm bank attempt to contact the donor and ask permission at that time for his identity to be released. There's no guarantee of how hard the sperm bank will work to find the donor or how the donor will respond. Many pregnancies may result from one donor's sperm, depending on the sperm bank's policy. A donor might need to plan in advance how he wants to respond to numerous young adults calling him up within a year or two of each other.

Matching Your Partner's Characteristics

Sometimes people choose a donor on the basis of their desire to match his characteristics—skin tone, hair color and texture, height—to their partner's. This often comes from a desire to create a likeness that will publicly symbolize family, since many will then perceive the child as being of the same or similar ethnic background as the nonbirth mother. Many lesbian couples share a common desire with heterosexual couples that their child look similar enough to either mother that a biological connection might be assumed. In this way lesbians often hope to lessen how often they need to answer questions about family structure and biology as mothers of adopted children or interracial children often must: "Are you her real mother?" Creating a basic family resemblance reduces the amount of basic education queer women and their children have to do with strangers in casual situations. For these same reasons, heterosexual transmen using sperm banks may choose to match the sperm donor to look like their female partner. In fact, if this is important to you, an ever-growing number of sperm banks actually offer photo matching. You can provide a photo of your partner to the bank, which will then find the best visual match.

Single Women's Freedom to Choose

In many ways single women aren't as bound by these concerns. Many single women choose a donor who looks similar to them, on paper at least, although the baby will share half of his or her genetic makeup, and therefore some physical characteristics, with his or her mother, no matter what the donor looks like.

Multiracial Couples' Choice of Ethnicity

In this day and age, race and ethnicity are still areas of discrimination. Thus children of color will usually have noticeably different social experiences than Caucasian children. Children of color will have different experiences from one another based on their ethnicity. This is important to keep in mind when selecting donors, not from the standpoint of trying to avoid racism but rather from the perspective of creating a family unit. If you are in a relationship where the biological parent is Caucasian and the partner is a person of color, we recommend that you strongly consider using a donor to match the partner's ethnic makeup. This will strengthen the parent-child bond in innumerable ways throughout life. In multi-ethnic families of color it is important to do the same. One thing to consider is the possibility that the other parent may choose to give birth in the future. If this is the case you may balance it all out by ending up with donors of different ethnic backgrounds for each of your children.

Donor's Interests and Passions

Some people choose a donor not because of physical characteristics but because of other qualities, such as physical or intellectual capabilities or temperament. The information available on the donor form may include years and type of formal education, self-reported hobbies and crafts, and interest in sports. People may extrapolate from this to form a picture of the donor in regard to his innate capacities. Or they may perceive instead that education and abilities are as much mitigated by circumstance, opportunity, and culture as by inheritable capacity. You may have numerous realizations about the assumptions you make along these lines, especially if you see your assumptions reflected back to you or contrasted by your partner's choices or your friends' opinions about your donor list.

Identifying Positive Attributes

Some people feel that a substantial shortcoming in the anonymous-donor choice is not being able to get a sense of the donor's personality—inner qualities such as generosity, compassion, kindness, patience, or any other trait that feels important. Many people feel that at least some aspect of these traits is a matter of inherited potential, not environmental upbringing. They pore over their donor forms trying to infer a sense of these qualities from his volunteer or political activities or even his handwriting style. Some people put a lot of trust in their own intuitive sense or that of the workers at the sperm bank.

To address this stumbling block, an increasing number of banks are providing more and more information about donors to prospective parents and their future children about the donors. Some banks offer handwriting samples, audio CDs, baby photos, adult photos, phone interviews, and videos. This is making the prospect of choosing a donor more comfortable for many people.

Examine Your Donor Selection Process

Take a careful look at your ideas about what exactly influences people to be who they are fundamentally so that you can be clear about how you're making your choices. If you and your partner are at odds about how you're going about the process, understanding your own and each other's preferences and beliefs will help you both to communicate more effectively and less defensively. Choosing a donor usually will not be a casual decision where compromise is easy.

It's natural for your criteria for choosing a donor to change over time. Personal characteristics often become less important than sperm count and motility if you've inseminated a number of times without conceiving. That doesn't mean that your earlier choices were awry or that you care less now about who the donor is. Your priorities are merely shifting to focus more directly on your primary goal: getting pregnant!

How Are Donors Screened?

Accepting a Sample

A prospective donor must provide a semen sample. If the sample meets the sperm bank's criteria, it's frozen for forty-eight hours to one week. It's then thawed and reexamined under a microscope to see how the post-thaw sample compares to the unfrozen sample. If the sperm survive in high enough numbers, a donor undergoes a physical as well as extensive blood and urine tests.

How Many "Siblings" Are Permitted?

Each bank has it own policy regarding the number of pregnancies each donor can supply. Some have as few as five and others as many as a hundred. Some banks make provisions that after a donor has reached his pregnancy limit, a family that used his sperm can still use it conceive siblings. These banks save the extra samples as "sibling sperm." If you are potentially interested in using the same donor for any future children, it is a good idea to buy up as much of it as you can once your baby is born.

Everyone relates differently to this concept of other children conceived with the same sperm. Some banks have special sibling registries where you can contact other families who have used the same donor. Some families like this sense of extended family. Other families do not think of those children as family—for them family is not about biology in that way. However, a recent study revealed that the majority of the children interviewed who had been conceived from donor sperm from sperm banks would like to meet these siblings. For many of them, knowing that there are possibly as many as fifty or more siblings makes them feel simultaneously overwhelmed and does a number on their self-esteem. They feel more like a commodity and it is disconcerting. This is the first study of its kind.

How Are My Parenting Rights Legally Protected?

Your donor will never have access to your identity. If you choose an open-identity donor, your child may request his name she or he reaches the age of 18. Even if you were to discover who your donor is, state laws require that a man severs his paternity rights when he donates sperm anonymously to a medical facility and must sign a written contract of formal consent to do so. He would not be able to sue for custody; you would not be able to sue for child support.

The Trend to Great Access to Information

The Sperm Bank of California (TSBC) was the bank that took the risk to spearhead the new open-donor trend, in recognition of the growing movement two decades ago to give adopted people more access to information about their biological parents. Children from the very first open-identity sperm donors turned 18 in 2001. Since that time, TSBC has been conducting and publishing studies reflecting the first generation of children to be raised with openness about their origins. They have found that lesbians and single moms of any orientation tell their children about their conception at an early age. These children then grow up securely knowing that their parents really wanted them. Almost all of the teenagers interviewed express comfort with how they were conceived, probably due in part to knowing about it from such a young age. Most of the teenagers interviewed expressed interest in meeting their donors. Some expected to initiate contact at 18; others just knew they would at some point. The driving force for most of them was to learn more about their donors in order to learn more about themselves. All of the research reflected children who are well adjusted and possess a strong sense of self.

How Sperm Banks Work

When you first contact a sperm bank, they'll usually set up an orientation meeting for you if you're local. You'll need to fill out some paperwork, usually pay a fee for the orientation or to set up your account, and talk to a health educator, who will not only explain the process but will also give you some basic information about charting your cycle.

You'll be given brief biographical sketches of the available donors. Most sperm banks offer you copies of additional lengthy questionnaires filled in by the donors for a $15 to $50 fee. After reviewing the donor profiles, you let them know your top donor choices and when you want to start inseminating.

Some sperm banks encourage or permit you to purchase a number of vials of sperm in advance from a preferred donor. In this way, you can be assured that his sperm will be available for you when you need it. Otherwise, his sperm may run out temporarily before more is released from quarantine, or permanently if he stops donating or if he has reached the maximum number of pregnancies allowed from one donor. In this case you either wait or choose a different donor for those months.

Doctor Sign-off

Before the sperm is released to you, there is a form you need to get signed by your health-care provider stating that you're in "good health," or possibly indicating that specific health tests have been done. Some sperm banks insist that the form be signed by a physician rather than a nurse practitioner or midwife. There is no state that requires that sperm be sent only to a doctor's office, it can always be shipped to your home. However, if you have a problem securing a doctor who will sign your forms or a doctor who will allow for the sperm to be sent directly to you, please know that it need not be a doctor from your own state.

New York only permits sperm banks licensed by New York to ship sperm within or to New York State. However, under certain circumstances, if someone is unable to find a suitable donor through banks that are licensed in New York, a New York doctor can submit paperwork for exemptions, which would permit them to use donor specimens from a bank not licensed through the state. If such a written exemption is obtained then most banks will ship there.

Pickup and Timing

At the beginning of the cycle during which you wish to inseminate, you'll phone the sperm bank to let them know when you may be inseminating, which donor you want, how many vials you would like, washed for intrauterine insemination or unwashed for vaginal insemination. If they're sold out of your preferred donor, you may be put on a waiting list for the next month. You may have to use the sperm of your second or third or even fourth-choice donor. Then, as soon as you know exactly when you'll need the sperm, at least one to two days in advance, you call the sperm bank to arrange either to pick it up or to have it shipped to you or your doctor.

If you're going to pick up your vials and use the sperm within the next twenty-four to forty-eight hours, you can get them in a small cooler with pieces of dry ice inside. If you need the vials shipped to you, they will arrive in a liquid nitrogen tank where they will stay cold for four to seven days. If you're unsure when exactly you're going to ovulate or need to pick up your sperm early because you'll be bringing it with you out of town, or simply want to have it early for peace of mind, ask if your sperm bank has a liquid nitrogen tank that you can borrow or rent.

Tips and Tricks

Here are some suggestions that may help you obtain the highest-quality sperm samples with the fewest number of unpleasant surprises. Each sperm bank has its own personnel, policies, and attitudes. You may choose a sperm bank because of proximity, cost, donor selection, or how safe or helpful they feel. As a client you should also be treated with utmost respect, regardless of your sexual orientation, gender identity, partner status, race, age, class, ability, choosiness about your donor, irregularity of menstrual cycle, or emotions about the entire process. By all means, change sperm banks if you're frustrated with the quality of service you're receiving and have already tried other methods of addressing your concerns.

MAIA'S RECOMMENDATIONS
- Get the sample with the highest number of motile sperm per cc.
- Get vials from the same ejaculate.
- Get newer samples.
- Use a donor who has proven pregnancies.
- Use IUI-ready sperm only for intrauterine inseminations and ICI-ready sperm for self-inseminations.
- Factor morphology into the equation.
- Buy the best sample available.

What Counts as "Quality Sperm"?

See if you can obtain the samples from your selected donor that have the highest motility or concentration. This information is kept available, and can be looked up by a worker, if he or she is willing, when your monthly samples are released. Some banks will release this information if you ask and others will only provide the specific information when they send the sample to you. If the latter is the case, save those sheets of paper. This can serve to help you select donors in the future.

Sperm banks vary in their parameters for accepting donor sperm. Usually sperm banks guarantee 20 million to 30 million motile (moving) sperm per sample. The higher the motility, the better the sample. Remember, sperm banks ship all over the country, so it's worthwhile to comparison-shop; you don't have to use your local sperm bank. Many sperm banks offer samples from donors in the 40 million to 70 million range, so get the best samples available.

If you're going to inseminate more than once each cycle, ask for all the vials you'll use in one cycle to come from the same ejaculate if possible or from dates close together. These may be the most biochemically compatible with one another as they will have been in the donor's body at the same time.

When you order the sperm, request sperm that has been donated the most recently.

Avoid the Two-for-One Deal

Certain banks will offer you two subfertile samples for the price of one. This certainly increases the volume of sperm, which can assist greatly. However, usually a high number of nonmotile sperm is what makes it subfertile, there are millions of dead or not effectively moving sperm in the way for the healthy ones to swim through. Go for one really optimal sample instead.

Post-thaw Numbers

In attempt to make the sperm look better than it actually is, some banks only release to you the fresh or "raw" numbers on your donor. These numbers are completely irrelevant to frozen sperm. The only numbers that matter are the numbers that reflect how well the sperm is functioning after it has been frozen and then thawed.

Choose a Donor with a Strong Track Record

You'll undoubtedly have many of your own personal criteria for choosing a donor. It's best to work with a donor whose sperm has resulted in successful pregnancies, so one question that may be useful is to ask how many pregnancies have resulted to date from your top donor choices' sperm. Many variables can affect this number, including one donor being more often selected than another for a variety of reasons. But if, say, one favorite of yours has been on their catalog just nine months and resulted in four pregnancies, and the other has been available for two years with no pregnancies, you'll probably want to go with the first one.

If you set your heart on a donor whose sperm has resulted in nine pregnancies to date at a sperm bank with a ten-pregnancy limit, you may be setting yourself up for disappointment if he reaches his limit before you achieve pregnancy. The reality of sperm banks is that demand often exceeds supply. Donors of certain ethnicities are often hard to find. Open-identity donors are in high demand at sperm banks that offer these programs. You may be amazed at how long you spend choosing your initial donor, and how often your top choice isn't available.

If you don't get pregnant after three to six cycles of inseminating with your donor, move on to a new one. Your "chemistry" may just be incompatible.

Use IUI-Ready Sperm for IUI and ICI-Ready Sperm for ICI

At Maia the trends we see are somewhat different than those reported by some of the sperm banks. We have yet to see a pregnancy achieved by someone using IUI-ready sperm (sperm washed for intrauterine inseminations) when they are self-inseminating. Now we are sure that it happens, but after so many people trying it with no success we strongly discourage the practice. When sperm was not quite so expensive we used to recommend that if the desired donor only had IUI-ready sperm, to use two vials each time you self-inseminated, or four vials for two inseminations. This did not result in any pregnancies. However, many of these same people then changed to ICI-ready sperm (unwashed semen samples) and immediately conceived.

Why? We think there are two reasons. First, the quantity of IUI-ready sperm is so low. It is purchased in 0.5 cc amounts. Thus, even if you were to use two vials it would still only amount to 1.0 cc—which is a small portion of an average ejaculate. Second, we feel that for vaginal insemination there are other substances in the semen that help to buffer the sperm in its journey to the cervix. These are washed out in the IUI-ready preparation.

Anonymous Donors

Using a Go-Between

Before sperm banks were accessible to lesbians, many women chose to make private arrangements with a go-between in order to obtain anonymous sperm. The go-between was usually a friend, a friend of a friend, a community yenta, or a midwife who would screen the donor to some extent and maintain confidentiality by picking up and dropping off the donated semen. A smaller number of people still prefer this arrangement to any other sperm-donor choice, although along with its benefits, it does have some drawbacks.

BENEFITS

Your go-between may be able to find a man who will donate sperm to you for free. This in and of itself is appealing or essential to many prospective families. If you really want an unknown donor but can't afford to use a sperm bank, you might consider using a go-between. You may also consider this option if you want anonymous sperm and need it to be fresh in order to increase your chances of conception.

You may be intrigued by the go-between option if you're philosophically opposed to working with the legal and medical systems or getting their permission to conceive your baby. Likewise, you may prefer anonymity but not like the idea of using frozen sperm. You may know your go-between well enough so that her character assessment is more credible to you than that of a sperm bank.

When your go-between negotiates terms of donation with your donor, she may have some flexibility in negotiating that you won't have with a sperm bank. For example, you might arrange that if you or your child ever wanted to meet the donor, your go-between could find the donor and ask him if he is willing to be contacted. Your go-between could let him know from the start that when your child reaches puberty or becomes a teenager, she or he would probably want to meet him. You could make any arrangement, potentially, that you all agree to before your donor gives you sperm.

DRAWBACKS

One drawback concerns confidentiality. You need to be able to trust your go-between to maintain the anonymity of the donor from everyone she knows for the child's whole life, or until the year on which you all agree. Many people feel itchy holding a secret like that. If you crossed social paths with your donor—which could happen if you live in the same area—could either of you figure out the other's identity, either intentionally or unintentionally? If he decided he wanted to figure out who your family is, could he? Probably, depending on how determined he is. If he discovers your identity, he becomes a known donor. He would become a known donor without your having had the legal opportunities to draw up a contract that you would have had if you use a planned known donor. In this way, you may be signing on for the eventual potential risks of a known donor without the benefit of planning and negotiating.

The second area of concern for many people considering using an anonymous donor with a go-between involves potential health risks. You could have your go-between ask the donor about his medical history. You'd need to trust your go-between's ability to interpret the donor's medical history and repeat it to you accurately. You could then find a medical person to ask about it if you had questions. You couldn't directly see the donor's test results or a note from his health-care provider attesting to his good health or family medical history, unless he gave a copy to your go-between that had his identifying information removed. You'd have to rely on your go-between to ask the detailed questions and give the detailed information sometimes necessary to reach an agreement on safer sex that feels secure to you. You'd have to trust the donor to uphold these agreements without having met him in person.

You may find scheduling fresh sperm donations between yourself, your partner if you have one, your donor, and your go-between to be very difficult, depending on your work and vacation schedules.

Recently we met a teenage boy who told us that he and his donor met for the first time at a party. The boy was talking about his family to a person at the party. He said he had lesbian moms. The donor said "Oh, I once donated to some lesbians a long, long time ago." The man asked if he had a known donor. The boy said "No, my moms had a friend who would get the sperm and bring it to them. It was all very secret. All I have from my donor is the jar they used to inseminate in. It's this cute little jar with rainbow stickers plastered all over the lid." The man he was speaking to almost fell over. They realized that by pure chance they happened to meet one another *and* realize their connection. They went on to have DNA tests to confirm; now they are forming a friendship.

Anonymous Sex

Some people become frustrated with their known-donor prospects or with the financial realities of using a sperm bank. The thought often crosses someone's mind to pick up a man at a bar and have casual or anonymous sex as the easiest way to conceive. Casual or anonymous sex does, however, pose substantial health risks. Still, despite these risks, people do have casual unsafe sex all the time in our culture. Often women who imagine this scenario are sure they'll conceive the first time they have unprotected intercourse with a man. More often than not, however, they don't conceive on the first try. The more times a woman has sex in this situation, the more she exposes herself to the risk of contracting a sexually transmitted infection.

Picking someone up may not be as anonymous as you'd like it to be. How many times have you been surprised by how small the world is? Unless you travel to a distant city to find a sex partner for conception, you may live in fear that he'll show up on your doorstep one day. Legally, you wouldn't have any redress against a custody suit from him because (1) he wouldn't have formally consented to be a donor instead of a parent; and (2) conception by intercourse undermines even those arrangements where this agreement is made.

If you're considering this option, first examine if you feel any ethical obligation to the man involved. It's also important to make sure that you feel comfortable with the idea of having sex with a man. You don't want to feel ambivalent later about the circumstances of your baby's conception.

Finally, imagine this situation down the road and ask yourself just as you would with other possible sperm options: What story will you tell your offspring and others?

Anonymous-Donor Considerations

Using sperm from an anonymous donor requires thoughtful consideration of your feelings about the permanence of the anonymity and how it may impact your child. Any deep reservations you have in this department usually arise as ambivalence or procrastination about choosing a donor or actually beginning to inseminate. If you feel comfortable with the anonymity, there are many strong benefits to using sperm banks as your donor source.

Using a go-between or having anonymous sex has benefits as well as substantial health risks that should be considered carefully. No matter what you choose as your most perfect donor option, you'll be interfacing and negotiating with someone, be it the known donor, the sperm bank staff, a doctor performing the inseminations, or a go-between.

Keep in mind that the emotional work of clarifying why you feel right with your choices is work toward the creation of your child. This will allow you to be assertive and clear in creating the arrangements that make you feel safe and comfortable with the above people. It will also provide you with the clarity and confidence you need to tell your child the beautiful story of how you chose to create her or him, and how he or she came to be in the world.

CHAPTER 9

Increasing Male Fertility

IN THE LAST fifty years, male fertility rates have dropped significantly worldwide. Statistics show that the average sperm count is decreasing by 1.5 percent every year in the United States, and 3 percent per year in Australia and Europe, more than likely as a result of environmental toxins. Many men have suboptimal fertility without experiencing any symptoms or having a medical history that suggests there is anything wrong with their health. We recommend having your donor undergo a semen analysis early on, precisely because low fertility is so common. If your donor's semen analysis results are not optimal, the test can be repeated for greater accuracy. Also, a more highly detailed analysis called a Kruger strict morphology, as well as a sperm-penetration assay, may help more fully explore the quality of his sperm.

If you're considering working with a donor with fertility problems, think over this choice carefully before starting to inseminate. Unfortunately, Western medicine has very little to offer in terms of fertility treatments for sperm enhancement, except to manipulate sperm and egg either through intra-uterine insemination (IUI) or by combining the sperm with an egg in the laboratory and transferring the resulting embryo directly into the uterus (in vitro fertilization, or IVF).

Non-Western healing practices, however—especially acupuncture and traditional Chinese medicine—have a lot to offer men who want to increase their fertility. In addition to seeking alternatives in health care, some commonsense lifestyle changes and a specific focus on good nutrition can significantly increase sperm fertility.

The information provided in chapter 11, "Choosing a Fertile Lifestyle," about environmental toxins found in home and in the workplace is crucial to men's healthy fertility. Toxins can not only lessen a sperm count to the point of infertility but may also alter sperm so that the egg is fertilized but grows in an unhealthy way, leading either to miscarriage or birth defects.

Just as for women's, for men's hormone levels to stay constant it is important to get regular and sufficient sleep and keep levels of stress to a minimum.

If Your Donor Has a Poor Semen Analysis

When the first semen analysis that your donor receives is not very good, the first thing to do is to repeat the test. Sometimes something as simple as a lab problem can cause a faulty analysis. Make sure that the analysis is being done by either a sperm bank or at least a lab that has the capacity to examine the sperm on-site. All too frequently a sample sits in the office and then is transported to another lab at the end of the day. This sitting around will not affect the total count or the morphology of the sample, but it can easily impact the motility—how many of the sperm are moving. Also keep in mind that if your donor has been sick in the past six weeks, it can have a strong negative impact on his semen sample. As time is usually of the essence, it may be worthwhile for him to see a urologist, as well, to rule out any medical complications that could be reflected in the poor quality.

If the second analysis also shows that his sample is quite low or is borderline, reading on in this chapter about the many things that are known to both inhibit and enhance sperm quality. Don't lose hope! Sperm is being made all the time. The sample you see today has been made over the past three months. *A poor semen analysis can be turned around in three months with careful attention to diet, supplements, and lifestyle.* See Part Three: Optimizing Health and Fertility for more information. Acupuncture in tandem with these lifestyle changes can boost male fertility even more. If you have seen a good turnaround in three months, by six months the results are amazing. If your donor changes his eating habits and lifestyle and there is still little or no change after three months, then it is more likely a genetic cause, and you should think about finding a different donor.

Fertility Inhibitors

Sperm Temperature

The testicles hang in the scrotal sac outside the body to keep the developing sperm cooler than normal body temperature, which is 98.6 degrees Fahrenheit. Regularly overheating the sperm at any time during the sixty-seven or so days they take to develop can negatively affect sperm count and function. To avoid overheating their testicles, potential donors should not wear tight underwear, pants, or exercise shorts and should avoid spending long periods of time in hot tubs, hot baths, showers, or saunas. Frequent long bike rides also heat the testicles and can have a negative impact on fertility. Making the simple change to boxer shorts, for daytime and sleepwear—is often all that is needed. Studies are showing that men who sit at a desk all day have lowered sperm counts as well. Those same studies show that if a man gets up periodically throughout the day, at least every two hours, and walks for a few minutes so that his testicles can return to normal temperature, the counts improve.

Caffeine, Alcohol, and Drugs

Studies show a direct link between marijuana use and lowered sperm count and a significant increase in malformed sperm. Caffeine and other stimulants such as sugar or amphetamines can also detrimentally affect sperm quality and count. Caffeine concentration is highest in coffee but is also abundant in cola drinks, black teas, and even chocolate, depending on how much is consumed.

Alcohol use can decrease both the health and count of sperm. Ideally, your donor should not consume more than one alcoholic drink per day. The use of cocaine and other recreational drugs can directly damage sperm.

Cigarettes

Cigarette smoke, as well as secondhand or environmental smoke, seems to have a devastating effect on sperm count and quality if the semen is already borderline infertile. If there is a good sperm count to start with, the sperm will not be affected quite as significantly by exposure to cigarette smoke. Studies have shown, however, that if both the biological mother and father smoke, or if just the biological father smokes, the chance of miscarriage may increase by as much as 64 percent.

Prescription Medicine

Some medicines can temporarily decrease sperm count and motility and should not be taken within two and a half months of sperm donation. These include some antifungal and antidiarrheal medications as well as the antibiotics erythromycin and nitrofurantoin.

Air Pollution

A large study on 18-year-old men was conducted in the Czech Republic on the adverse effects of air pollution on male fertility. One group of subjects lived in the country where the air was considered to be of good quality, and one lived in an industrialized city with poorer air quality all year round and predictable periods of the year when there was an increase in the air pollution. The findings were fascinating. There was a noticeable decrease in sperm quality following periods of elevated air pollution without a change in the number of sperm in each ejaculate. In other words, the count remained the same but the number of motile sperm and the number of appropriately shaped sperm (morphology) was significantly decreased and there was noticeable chromosomal damage following periods of increased pollution. The specific toxins in the air were not evaluated in this study, but the implications are obvious and far-reaching.

Exposure to Industrial Chemicals

Exposure to the common industrial chemical trichloroethylene (TCE) has been shown to decrease hormonal development of sperm and cause infertility. It is found in paints, adhesives, rug cleaners, paint strippers, and other chemicals used in the home, office, and workshop.

Heavy-Metal Toxicity

High levels of lead, mercury, and other heavy metals can interfere with the ability of sperm to fertilize the egg. Blood tests or hair analysis can help to determine if there is an overload of heavy metals in your body.

Steroids

High levels of anabolic steroids have been shown to decrease motility and increase abnormally shaped sperm.

Phthalates

Phthalates are compounds derived from naphthalene, used in manufacturing dyes, explosives, moth repellents, and as a solvent. Men with higher phthalate levels have reduced sperm counts, lower sperm motility, and more deformed sperm.

Cell Phones

Preliminary studies are revealing that cell-phone use may indeed be decreasing male fertility. The issue is most likely the heat coming from the radio frequency energy. The radio frequency energy can heat tissue and the testes appear to be especially vulnerable. There has been evidence of decreased sperm counts and motility in men who are heavy cell-phone users and keep their phones in their pants pockets. Where the cell phone is worn seems to be the crucial factor at this point.

Laptops

Laptops increase scrotal temperatures when placed on laps for one hour or longer. It is unknown whether years of frequent laptop use cause irreversible damage. It is therefore best to use laptops on a desktop rather than your lap.

Dental Composites

In ice studies it is clear that both dental composites and dental sealants decrease sperm count and production. Dental work most likely has a negative effect on male fertility.

Oxidative Stress

Oxidative stress refers to damage in the body at a cellular level, and is the basis for including anti-oxidant fruits and vegetables in the diet. There is strong clinical evidence indicating that men diagnosed with infertility have high levels of oxidative stress that may impair the quality of their sperm. In fact, some fertility specialists propose that as high as 40 percent of men with unexplained infertility have high levels of free-radical activity in their bodies. Thus strategies for lowering oxidative stress help to increase sperm quality. Anti-oxidants help to remove free radicals from the body.

Fertility Enhancement for Men and Pre- or Nonoperative Transwomen

Frequent Ejaculation

Frequent ejaculation stimulates the testicles to keep up a higher level of sperm production than that of men who don't ejaculate often, so this method can be used to increase fertility. Leland Traiman of Rainbow Flag Health Services provided us with this tip that we have come to find invaluable for improving sperm quality. At this point we suggest it to all people using known donors and especially emphasize it to people who are dealing with a suboptimal semen analysis. It is especially helpful to transwomen coming off of hormones and wanting to increase their sperm quantity and quality. We ask men and transwomen to ejaculate at least once a day—preferably two to three times a day. This is done every day of the month except the two to three days proceeding and the days of his donation of sperm to you. In other words, he ejaculates frequently every day except when he is donating to you. On the two to three days leading up to his donations for you he continues to get sexually aroused—just not to the point of ejaculation.

Vitamins and Nutrients

In order to function properly, the reproductive system requires the proper vitamins and minerals. In fact, many micronutrients and minerals are essential for the glands in the testicles to be able to constantly produce so many millions of sperm cells. Further, the incredibly active motion of sperm constantly swimming requires a high amount of the micronutrients that allow liberation of cellular energy. Finally, the entire sperm-growth process is mitigated by a variety of male hormones, including testosterone, luteinizing hormone (LH), and follicle-stimulating hormone (FSH). These hormones require building blocks from the diet, just as they do in women. Nutritional deficiencies can impair hormone function, decrease sperm production and increase abnormal sperm. Fresh, nutritious foods, adequate calories and a well-balanced diet positively influence sperm quality and number. Supplements to a healthy diet can also increase quantity and quality of sperm.

- *Vitamin C.* Vitamin C has been demonstrated to radically improve sperm count, motility, and morphology. Vitamin C also decreases agglutination (clumping). Vitamin C protects sperm from oxidative stress. The recommended dose is 1,500 mg twice daily.
- *Zinc.* Zinc is essential for testosterone synthesis in the testes. Even mild zinc deficiency has been linked to lower sperm counts. Sufficient zinc can increase sperm count and motility. Thirty to 50 mg zinc picolinate is the recommended supplemental dosage. It is recommended that it be taken for no more than six months at a time.
- *Folic acid and B-12.* A lack of B vitamins can affect the pituitary gland in the brain, where LH and FSH are made, and which stimulate sperm production in the testes. Folic acid plays a critical role in normal DNA synthesis. Two thousand mcg of vitamin B-12 and 800 mcg of folic acid in a multi–B vitamin containing B-1, B-2, and B-6 can decrease sperm malformation and increase sperm production.

- *Vitamin E.* Vitamin E is a proven anti-oxidant that aids in the absorption of selenium. Vitamin E has been shown to increase sperm motility and increase the ability of the sperm to penetrate the egg. You may want to consult with your health-care professional if you take aspirin or other blood thinners, because these medications can be dangerous when interacting with supplemental vitamin E. The recommended vitamin E dose is 400 IU daily.
- *Selenium.* A deficiency in selenium can lead to defective motility. Almost half the male body's supply of selenium is located in the testicles and seminal ducts. The sperm cells contain significant amounts of selenium and zinc, which are lost upon ejaculation. The recommended daily dose is 200 mcg; not more than 300 mcg of selenium should be consumed in one day.
- *Arginine.* Arginine is an amino acid needed to make sperm. The recommended dose is 1,500 mg twice daily to raise sperm counts.
- *Coenzyme Q10.* This is a vitamin-like nutrient with a key role in producing adenosine triphosphate (ATP), which is needed for energy production in every cell of the body. It is also a powerful antioxidant.
- *L-carnitine.* This helps in the breakdown and removal of transfatty acids, which allows for greater sperm motility. The recommended daily dose is three to four grams.
- *Glutathione.* Glutathione is a powerful anti-oxidant that can increase sperm quantity, motility, and morphology.
- *Pycnogenal.* Pycnogenal has been shown to help with proper formation of sperm in people who have abnormally high rates of poor morphology.
- *Essential Fatty Acids.* Essential fatty acids, known as EFAs or good fats, are need for all healthy functioning of the body, including proper sperm production.

High-Quality, Clean Drinking Water

Seminal fluid is more than 80 percent water. It is vital to drink at least two quarts of water daily—more if you exercise or exert yourself. Chronic dehydration can lead to problems with agglutination (clumpy semen) and decreased volume.

Water contaminated by pesticide runoff contains organochlorine compounds mistaken by the body for estrogen compounds, and therefore decreases sperm counts. Drinking water also may contain hormones from a variety of sources in our environment, including hormones used to grow large cattle or keep cows lactating for dairy production, or the hormones that women excrete in their urine after taking birth control pills or menopausal hormone-replacement therapies. We strongly encourage men to use high-quality water filters on both drinking taps and shower heads. Filtered water is preferable to bottled water, as bottled water varies greatly in terms of how well it's been filtered and the minerals it contains from its source; furthermore, water sitting in plastic containers may become contaminated by chemicals leaching from the plastic.

Organic Foods

To further reduce pesticide and hormone exposure, men should increase their intake of organically grown foods. High levels of pesticides, hormones, and antibiotics can be found in nonorganic meat and dairy products and should be avoided whenever possible. In addition, exposure to unnecessary chemicals can be avoided by limiting intake of processed foods, including those with artificial dyes, sweeteners, and preservatives.

||||||||||||||||||||||||||||||||||||||||||||||||||||||||||||||||||||||||||||||||||||||

Maia Recommendations for Fertility Enhancement

- ⊙ Eat plenty of fresh fruits, vegetables, whole grains, nuts, seeds, legumes, and lean meats.
- ⊙ Eliminate processed foods.
- ⊙ Drink half your body weight in ounces of water a day; a 150-pound person would drink 75 ounces, or about 9 cups of water.
- ⊙ Avoid saturated fats and hydrogenated oils.
- ⊙ Take a fish oil or flax oil supplement daily.
- ⊙ Consider doing a liver cleanse in order to increase the overall function of the body.
- ⊙ Take a good multivitamin and liquid mineral supplement daily
- ⊙ Consider acting on the specific supplemental recommendations discussed in this chapter.

||||||||||||||||||||||||||||||||||||||||||||||||||||||||||||||||||||||||||||||||||||||

Part Three
Optimizing
Your Health
and Fertility

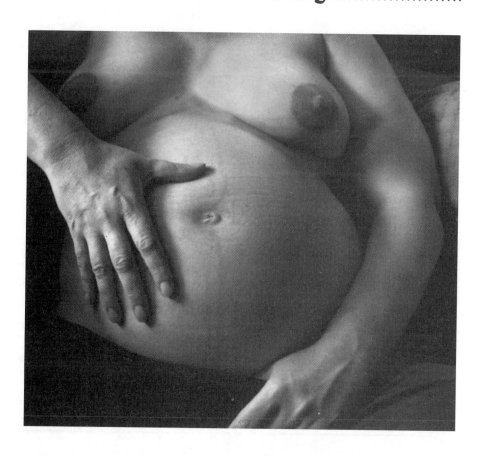

CHAPTER 10

Nourishing Yourself with Food

AT MAIA WE don't subscribe to one particular fertility diet. We recognize that eating is a very individual experience aimed at creating health and pleasure in your body. What is right for one person may not be right for another.

What we do subscribe to is the general conviction that healthy eating will significantly increase your fertility, ease your early pregnancy discomforts, and decrease your risk of miscarriage and birth defects. As you read though this chapter you will gain a much better understanding about the relationship of food and digestion to hormonal functioning. Please do not skip this chapter, as healthy eating is all too often the missing link in the fertility equation.

It is best to eat as if you are pregnant—in terms of quality and frequency-for at least three months before you conceive. This will give your body the best chances for a healthy conception and pregnancy. Having all the necessary nutrients available in your body will increase the functioning of your hormones and provide the basis for early cell division. If there is a time in your life to optimize your diet it is pre-pregnancy through the end of your breastfeeding time. Your baby is grown on the food you ingest. Your investment in diet at this time is investment in your child's future.

Establishing Healthy Eating Habits

The desire to have a baby is an excellent incentive to make any diet changes you've previously been interested in and to educate yourself about your body's specific nutritional needs during preconception and pregnancy. A well-balanced diet comprising healthy foods creates well-balanced hormones. Balanced hormones increase your chances of conception and decrease your chance of miscarriage. Remember, when you're actively trying to conceive, the second half of every menstrual cycle is potentially the beginning of the first trimester of pregnancy. Pregnancy brings a feeling of urgency to making changes for the health of your baby. Prior to conception, you can make changes at a pace that works for you. Improving eating habits is much easier before the mood swings, hormone changes, and morning sickness of pregnancy set in. In fact, healthy eating habits help decrease those first- trimester discomforts.

Even before pregnancy, healthy eating will help stabilize the emotional roller coaster that the insemination process inevitably brings. If you're still some months away from starting to inseminate, even better to start making positive dietary changes now. Diet suggestions for increasing fertility take three to six months to produce the maximum benefit. Diet is frequently the missing link in fertility challenges. In order to give yourself and the baby the best shot, improve the quality of your eating habits as much as possible. It is an excellent time to work with a nutritionist if food is a challenge for you.

Slow Changes Are Lasting Changes

Creating healthy eating habits is a slow, evolving process. The amount of time it takes varies from person to person. There's no right way to eat that is appropriate for everyone; we each conduct our own personal experiments. Some people make dramatic changes overnight and then adjust emotionally to those changes over time. Others integrate small changes one step at a time.

We strongly recommend approaching change gradually and gently, in a way that makes sense to you. If you make too many changes at once, you may not be able to sustain them. Dramatic diet overhauls can manifest a fanaticism similar to that characterizing eating disorders. Our goal is to help you create long-term healthy habits, not to offer a magic "fertility diet." Rapid changes aren't necessarily healthy. Slow change avoids unwanted metabolic shifts and the potential toxic release into the bloodstream that can occur when you make too-dramatic changes in your diet.

Hunger as a Motivator

At Maia we have observed a very interesting phenomenon. A number of women whom we have worked with seem to be driven by hunger. Their motivation, their drive to accomplish what needs to be done in their lives, is partly fueled by their hunger. For these people, when they start eating more calories throughout the day they feel heavy and sluggish. They feel full and unmotivated. Sometimes it is an issue of food allergies, but often it seems to be the loss of borderline hypoglycemia (low blood sugar). Hypoglycemia—before it causes emotional crashes—can bring a sense of mental clarity. When you have lived in a state of chronic hunger, nourishment can initially feel bad. However, over time it creates a much greater sense of well-being and balance.

Many of the people we have worked with who have lived off the high of hunger are not aware of a feeling of being hungry. It is obvious from their caloric intake and their caloric output that they are not getting enough calories. These women often have a very hard time conceiving and implanting. The work we do is to get them to eat more food and to increase their healthy fats. Usually within three months they are pregnant.

Weight Gain and Loss

Often people want to diet immediately prior to pregnancy. Some people are told by their health-care providers that losing weight will increase their fertility. However, dieting can suppress estrogen production, progesterone, and luteinizing hormone. Likewise, rapid fat loss pumps stored estrogen into the system, potentially blocking ovulation. The reduction in hormones may mean that the corpus luteum (the ovarian follicle after ovulation) is too small, increasing the risk of miscarriage. Preconception is not the time to diet. On the other hand, slow weight loss may be effective for increasing your fertility if you are a larger person. However, please see page 174 for a more thorough discussion.

Times of great metabolic shifts do not create optimal circumstances for your body to get pregnant and your risk of miscarriage is higher in these instances. Being as stable and consistent as you can is important. If you're going to diet, maintain your final weight goal for at least three months before you start to inseminate. This will stabilize your metabolism. Also, understand that the building blocks for hormones are stored in our body's fat. Without sufficient fat or with too much excess fat, hormone levels for both conception and pregnancy are difficult to maintain. You need to weigh enough to feed your baby from your body during both pregnancy and breastfeeding. Therefore, if you're underweight, gaining even ten pounds may increase your fertility.

Exercise

When people start to eat more they often increase the amount they exercise in order to balance calorie input and output. Beginning a rigorous exercise program or drastically increasing your exercise routine can change your metabolism significantly. As with dieting, metabolic shifts may be beneficial in the long run, but they don't facilitate fertility in the short term. Please see the section on exercise in chapter 11.

Eating Disorders

Many women have had or still have eating issues, whether they identify them as such or not. While you are inseminating and while you are pregnant, old habits may arise quite silently and surprise you. For example, your self-image might go askew and cause self-deprecating patterns to arise. Unable to see an accurate reflection of yourself and your body, you may stop eating, overly control your eating, or start bingeing. Use this time to identify and practice strategies for avoiding falling into compulsive eating behaviors. This type of preparation will be immensely helpful for both pregnancy and parenting. The emotional charge of food's role in your life may be lessened if you make sure you have sufficient nonfood-oriented ways of being nurtured and receiving love.

A number of the people we have worked with who have a history of severe eating disorders spend quite a bit of time and attention planning for pregnancy. Knowing that stress and hormonal states are often the triggers for eating disorders, they can exercise forethought, which can go a long way toward managing these impulses. Once the cycle of negative habits such as bingeing, withholding food, or overeating and the accompanying negative consuming mind-sets have been activated it is hard to stop. It is much easier to prevent this from happening. Here are some of the ideas that clients have utilized in the past:

- Create more time in your life to prepare food. It is easier to slip into old habits if you are eating on the run.
- Schedule regular times to eat in each day, knowing that pregnancy will require three larger meals and three smaller meals each day.
- Study pregnancy and breastfeeding nutrition prior to pregnancy so that you are familiar and comfortable with the increased needs of this special time.
- Create a plan with your partner, friends, or family for helping you to feed yourself. Provide these people with your particulars about your diet and food preparation requirements. Many people make up a schedule that they can rely on. For example, my sister will cook on Tuesdays. I eat at Donna's house every other Wednesday. My partner cooks Monday, Wednesday, and Friday.
- Devise a plan for what will happen if you get morning sickness and all food looks unappetizing or causes you to throw up. Make meal plans for the week and stick to them or ask a friend or partner to review your food intake with you.

Signs of Hunger and Low Blood Sugar

Many people in our culture, especially women, aren't aware of their body's hunger signals. One study shows that women frequently don't recognize hunger signals, misinterpreting them at first as a need to urinate. They recognize hunger as a body-function signal but aren't initially aware of which one. Hypoglycemia (low blood sugar) is the step beyond hunger and gives its own signals. It occurs when you haven't eaten enough food for your body's needs. Signs of hypoglycemia include: irritability, light-headedness, panic, exhaustion, insomnia, nausea, mood swings, headache, and extreme emotions such as rage, dizziness, and the inability to think clearly.

Too many people go for extended periods of time, sometimes all day, without eating. In these situations the emotional instability is even more extreme. It is common to feel overwhelmed and unloved when you have allowed your body to get overly hungry. Insomnia can be a symptom of not having eaten enough during the day. If you find that you are suffering form insomnia try feeding yourself in the middle of the night. Also pay more attention to the quality, frequency, and caloric intake during your day. Likewise, if you find you crave sugar or caffeine in the afternoon it is usually indicates an unfulfilled need for protein earlier in the day.

When trying to conceive and while pregnant, it's best to maintain a steady blood-sugar level so that your body doesn't experience blood-sugar extremes. Maintaining a balanced metabolism is also important. Consistency helps maintain balanced hormone levels. If the body is stressed from going without food or is experiencing extreme blood-sugar swings, it becomes reluctant to embrace pregnancy as being healthy for the body—that is, if a body is focused on self-preservation, it's more likely to reject a pregnancy. Also, babies in the uterus can be severely stressed by blood-sugar swings in the mother's body. In fact, frequent extremes in blood-sugar levels can affect their organ development.

Learning to avoid low blood sugar during preconception will benefit you significantly in early pregnancy. Look at the of signs of hypoglycemia again. How many of these are what our culture views as symptoms of a "normal" pregnancy? Hormone changes play a role in these discomforts and are unavoidable, but low blood sugar, the main culprit, is avoidable. You don't have to feel sick for twelve weeks!

How Often Should I Eat?

Every three hours you should eat food with nutritional value. You don't have to eat a lot, but you should eat something. How many meals do you eat each day? Do you go for long stretches of time without eating or with eating foods of limited nutritional value? Are you not sure what counts as nutritious? Many people who theoretically understand the necessity of eating regularly still find increasing their food intake to be challenging. Unfortunately, for many women, eating has become optional.

Bring Food with You

Frequently, we go out in the world without bringing along food or planning to stop to eat. Many people leave the house without having eaten breakfast and come back eight or more hours later not having eaten at all. During the day, some people subsist only on coffee and "munchies."

To avoid going longer than three hours without food, you'll need to bring food and drink with you wherever go. Some people have access to food nearby, whether at a vending machine, a fast-food drive-thru, or a restaurant. The first two of these options are not, generally speaking, nutritious food. When you are at work or outside the house, however, you may not have access to nutritious food. If you don't eat often, start with steps that seem manageable—steps that will enable you to eat something of value, even if you only take two bites every four hours, for instance, some prepared apples, oranges, nuts, or a piece of cheese. To integrate changes that are truly viable, you'll have to get really practical.

‖‖

Maia Recommendations for Nutritious Snacking

- Eat something nutritious that contains protein every three hours
- Shop mindfully
- Plan ahead
- Bring food with you
- Always have an extra stash of food in your car and your bag for those times when you are out longer than expected

‖‖

What to Bring When You Leave the House

Planning is the key to eating well. Consider what time your last meal or snack will be before you leave your house and how many three-hour periods will pass until you eat next at home. How many meals or snacks is that? Now, how will you carry your food with you? Are you only willing to bring a purse? Are you willing to bring a lunch bag? A cooler? Will you bring food only if it fits in your backpack or doesn't take up room in your briefcase? Do you have a water bottle? A thermos? Answer honestly so that you can realistically plan what types of and how much food you'll bring. Do you have a refrigerator at work? A microwave? Hot water?

Now that you've considered your limitations, let's think about what kind of foods are nutritious, starting with snacks. Many people have a piece of fruit for a snack. Fruit will give you vitamins and perhaps some fiber, as well as some fruit sugar. However, fruit is digested fairly quickly, isn't particularly substantial, and gives you very little, if any, protein. If you enjoy fruit, try supplementing it with a cup of yogurt (plain, not sugary; read the label). How about a handful of peanuts, almonds, or sunflower seeds? Supplementing what you already enjoy and are accustomed to is always better than trying to change what you eat completely.

If your in-between-meal food is fruit juice, consider exchanging it for whole fruit and other foods. The natural sugar in fruit juice is very rapidly absorbed by the body. Furthermore, many fruit juices have added sugars; do not drink these. Think about investing in a good juicer and making your own fresh fruit-vegetable juice. Drinking fruit juice when you need a quick pick-me-up after lunch or breakfast will give you immediate energy. Unfortunately, as we mentioned, the body's response to easily absorbed sugar is a yucky-feeling sugar low and an emotional plummet soon after. The same process occurs with refined sugars in soda and candy bars, although these contain none of the beneficial vitamins in fruit juice. Substituting a smoothie made with yogurt or protein powder for fruit juice keeps the same liquid fruit element in your body while adding protein and staying power.

Look at the list of suggested snacks and see which ones you could add to your diet, taking into account your cooking and carrying restrictions. Do you need to purchase containers to bring food in? Then think about the preparation time a snack may require. Would it be more convenient to prepare your food the night before rather than in the morning? Consider bringing a small serving of the previous night's leftovers for a snack if it isn't already going to be your lunch.

HEALTHY SNACK SUGGESTIONS
- ½ cup precooked canned kidney beans or garbanzo beans (chick peas), seasoned at home
- ⅓ cup hummus with raw carrots or broccoli, pita bread, or crackers
- ⅓ cup tuna salad with whole-wheat crackers
- ¼ cup almonds with a piece of fruit
- Tortilla chips and bean dip
- Peanut butter and jelly sandwich made with whole-grain bread
- ½ cup trail mix, including any of the following: raisins, banana chips, walnuts, almonds, dried coconut, cashews, dried apricots, sunflower seeds (make your own trail mix or purchase from bulk bins at the grocery store)

- 1 cup plain yogurt
- 1 cup cottage cheese with fruit
- Small container of leftovers: stir-fry, lasagna, soup, etc.
- Chopped raw vegetables with salad dressing for dipping: celery, bell pepper, zucchini, broccoli, and carrots
- Cheese and crackers

Practical Steps to Improving Your Nutrition

Preparing Your Own Food

Many people rarely cook, especially those who live in large cities, have hectic schedules, or live and work near restaurants. These people eat out, order in, or defrost and microwave prepared meals for lunch and dinner. At breakfast they may only grab a piece of fruit or a bagel. While eating something is better than eating nothing, the benefits of cooking for yourself are numerous. In fact, many people find they feel more connected to their bodies and their food when they take the time to cook the food they eat. The experience of cooking can be quite meditative and people usually get greater nourishment from home-cooked foods. Home-cooked food is usually fresher and healthier than you'd find elsewhere, with fewer preservatives and saturated fats. The food you use to cook with will be less processed and better quality than most of what is available elsewhere. And we cannot overlook the love that can be poured into home-cooked food.

Do you enjoy cooking? Are you willing to cook? If so, how often and when? Could you plan meals for the week and cook them on the weekend? Could you freeze meals in one- to two-serving portions so they can be thawed easily? A pot of soup, beans, or a casserole not only serves as a lunch option, but also a fast nutritious dinner, ready when you get home. When you cook dinner, make enough so that you'll have leftovers for the next day. When you clear the table, pack the leftovers directly into lunch containers so that your food will be ready to go in the morning. You may want to keep some prepared healthy food stocked in your kitchen that you can fix quickly if you get in late or if your blood sugar drops. Many cookbooks provide quick, easy-to-follow, healthy recipes.

Shop with a Plan

Of course, if you plan to cook, prepare, or bring food with you, you'll need to shop. Keeping a list helps to avoid impulse buying, thereby saving you money. It takes some practice and effort to plan ahead what to buy at the store so that your kitchen is full of nutritious foods you enjoy. For some people the hardest part of making diet changes is the planning required. This is sometimes challenging, because it means acknowledging that you consider feeding yourself to be a priority. Many people find that creating a computer-generated list of all the foods they need on hand in their kitchen helps them organize and simplify their kitchen and shopping needs. As you run out of something you can just check a box next to the item and have a ready-made list at the end of the week.

Divide Labor Between Partners

If you live with a partner, examine and evaluate how your household food tasks are divided. Who does the shopping? Who does the cooking? Is the division of labor fair? Or does one person end up doing it by default, and is this arrangement full of tension? Is there no cooking or shopping at all? Can your partner help with or take over food preparation and planning? Please examine your roles in relation to food. One of the best ways to support the person who will be conceiving and growing the baby is to participate in the cooking and shopping. If you do not know how to cook, or if the birth parent is the primary chef in the house, it is vital for you both to understand that this may need to change as soon as pregnancy arrives. Morning sickness and exhaustion of early pregnancy can make it impossible to prepare food and still be able to eat that very same food. In anticipation of this role reversal, take the time to learn to cook now when there is not quite so much pressure attached.

Offering to share the extra focus and time required to make healthier eating choices, especially at the beginning, can feel very supportive. Making food and diet changes is a sensitive area in which respect for each other is key. Discussing how you both can support the new choices you'll be making about food can make all the difference. In your partnership are you both committed to making these changes? Will both of you give up your morning coffee ritual or nightly glasses of wine? Will you both change your eating schedules? Or will just one of you make these changes? Look at the potential impact these changes may have on your social and personal lives and your life together. This can be a joint growth process. We've seen many couples use healthy diet changes to strengthen their relationship. It's one way of making a joint commitment toward the baby that the whole family will benefit from.

Eating Alone When You Are Single

People who are becoming single parents can feel isolated when given a list of nutritional recommendations. They may miss the practical help as well as the enthusiasm for creative food preparation that a partner can provide. Some people find eating by themselves or cooking for themselves a lonely activity. Therefore, many solo eaters don't eat meals at home. Does cooking for one person seem like too much work for you? It's helpful to get a few good cookbooks designed for single people, since the recipes in most cookbooks are for multiple servings. It can be disheartening to follow a recipe, especially when you're just learning how to cook, and find that you're going to be eating the same soup for seven days! If you're single, do you have a friend to cook with one night a week for company? Can you swap half of what you made for half of what she or he made to add variety to your menu? A good way to form and strengthen your Single Moms by Choice group is to have a weekly group cooking date. You can rotate homes or go to the home with the best kitchen. Finding the inspiration to cook is well worth the results.

Seek Community Support

It's wonderful to bring your community into the experience of your growing family. One particular way to ask for help is to let friends know if it's difficult for you to get up the energy to cook when you're in certain phases of your menstrual cycle, such as going through the depression of starting your period or the chaos of timing your insemination. It's really nice to be fed; it feels nurturing and supportive.

Getting Specific About Food

What Do I Need to Budget for Food?

When you focus on the food you eat, your eating habits will change. This doesn't need to inflate your food bill, although it easily can. The cost of food usually increases just before and during pregnancy because people begin eating higher-quality food, and they inevitably eat more. Food costs continue to increase because of the increased nutritional needs of nursing and then because there is another mouth to feed.

It's worthwhile to put extra discretionary money toward food. In fact, most families find that this is the area of life with the biggest cost increase. Luckily, some of your new eating habits will actually lower your food costs. You can make healthy meals inexpensively at home, more cheaply certainly than eating out or buying fast food. Cooking can be less expensive when you buy in bulk or from farmers markets. Decreasing coffee and fast-food consumption will also save you money. If the only way you can get food into yourself is to purchase it already prepared, then a significant increase in food costs is fairly unavoidable— but worth it, if the food is healthy.

Some people with extra money who don't cook get homemade meals delivered or hire someone to cook for them. Others buy healthy prepared food that only requires heating up. Work within your means and needs. Quick eating often costs more, since it isn't planned ahead of time. Forethought truly saves. Remember, healthier eating makes your body feel better.

Specific Healthy-Eating Suggestions

It's important to strive for realistic improvements in your eating habits. Read the following sections and look for suggestions that sound good to you.

VEGANS AND VEGETARIANS

Vegans are vegetarians who eat no animal products whatsoever. They need to make sure they have a regular source of vitamin B-12, which is found in animal products or synthesized by microorganisms. Brewer's yeast is an excellent source of B-12, and you can add it to your diet by sprinkling it on casseroles, toast, popcorn, cooked vegetables, and soups. Another source of vitamin B-12 is fermented food, such as tempeh, miso paste, and high-quality tamari soy sauce. Other sources of vitamin B-12 include fortified cereals, fortified soymilk, fortified soy products, and vitamin B-12 supplements. Vitamin supplements are available that do not contain animal products. If you eat organic vegetables, you'll receive some B-12 from the microorganisms living on the plants. Pesticide-sprayed vegetables are not a source of B-12.

Women who eat no meat need to be more aware of eating iron- and protein-rich foods. Unfortunately, a number of people who are vegan or vegetarian eat diets high in starch and sugar but consume relatively few fresh vegetables. Vegetarians who eat many vegetables and whole foods should have little trouble meeting the caloric, protein, vitamin, and mineral requirements of conception and pregnancy. Many prenatal care providers are insufficiently trained in nutritional counseling to be able to accurately advise vegetarian women about meatless pregnancy diets. Contrary to popular belief, with adequate knowledge and planning, vegetarian and vegan diets can be very healthy for pregnancy. For helpful tips you can share with health-care providers and family members consult *Macrobiotic Pregnancy and Care of the Newborn,* by Michio and Aveline Kushi, and *The Vegetarian Mother and Baby Book,* by Rose Elliot.

WHOLE FOODS AND COMPLETE DIGESTION

Good digestion is key to fully absorbing the nutrients you've worked so hard to get into your body. Our hormone levels are negatively affected by poor digestion. Much of the basis of our hormones comes from plant hormones and hormone-building blocks. If our food isn't well digested, we won't get what we need from it. Eating whole foods aids in digestion and reduces the danger of colon cancer. Whole foods are whole grains that haven't been processed and thus have not had much of the fiber and protein removed, such as whole wheat and brown rice. Whole foods are also whole fruits and vegetables with their skins and peels and pulps, instead of fruit juices.

There are many fertility diets available designed to improve digestion. Most schools of health around the world believe that digestion is the seat of health and that poor digestion is actually the cause of infertility. There is a lot of common sense behind this line of thinking. If your body cannot absorb or utilize the nutrients you ingest then it is unable to convert your food into the necessary building blocks for reproductive hormonal balance.

MAIA RECOMMENDATIONS FOR HEALTHY EATING

- Eliminate caffeine, soda, aspartame and other sugar substitutes, and preservatives from your diet.
- Eliminate sugar.
- Eliminate "bad fats," meaning saturated and trans fats
- Reduce mercury-laden fish.
- Stop drinking alcohol.
- Eat locally grown meat and vegetables whenever possible.
- Eat organically grown meat and produce whenever possible.

IMPORTANCE OF WATER

Most Americans are perpetually dehydrated. How many glasses of fluid do you drink during one day? How many glasses of water specifically? We are talking about water, not juice, tea or soda. We encourage women—both preconception and pregnant—to drink at least eight eight-ounce glasses a day. Carry water with you. If you use a container that you can refill, you can keep track of how much you drink during the day. There are even some bottles with straps that can make carrying water with you wherever you go less cumbersome. Try to use glass bottles or metal bottles such as Klean Canteen as plastic leeches into the water and into your body.

Water helps both kidney and liver function. When you're pregnant your body is the filtration system for your developing baby; thus, it becomes even more essential to drink enough to support this filtration process for both you and the fetus. There's a difference between plain water and other beverages such as soda, fruit juice, coffee, tea, or milk. It is all ready to start working without itself being filtered by the kidneys. Water serves a unique purpose in our bodies that other beverages do not.

High-quality water is vital for health. The wide array of chemical contaminants in public water contributes to miscarriages, developmental abnormalities, and degenerative diseases, among other health problems. Regulations for bottled water are notoriously weak. Hot water used for baths and showers releases contaminants into the air, where we breathe them directly into our bloodstream, so people absorb 5 to 100 times more chemicals from the water they bathe in than from the water they drink. A good filter for drinking and cooking water, and a shower filter for bathing water, will help protect you and your baby from contaminants.

REGIONALLY GROWN FOODS

Amazingly enough, if you shop at a supermarket, the food on your table has traveled an average of 3,000 miles to get there. This dramatically redefines the concept of "fresh" food. When food travels such distances from field to table it loses many of its vital nutrients along the way. Needless to say, in order to survive such travel it must be picked unripe. For maximized nutritional value, focus on eating what is in season and what is grown in your own region. This theory comes from macrobiotic eating, which is founded on the belief that the foods that grow in our environment at different times of the year are the foods that are appropriate to our bodies, as the foods and the people move through the same yearly cycles and seasons.

Consider shopping at your local farmers market or seeing if any of your local farms has a delivery service. The fresher your foods, the healthier your foods. They also taste remarkably better.

ORGANIC FOODS

Organic foods are grown without the use of synthetic pesticides, hormones, antibiotics, or other additives. Organic foods are obviously much better for your body, but often only people with chronic or terminal illnesses or "health nuts" strive to eat organic foods. Strongly consider growing your baby on organic foods and continuing to feed your baby organic foods through your breast milk and as your child grows. The vast majority of pesticides in use today haven't been approved for human consumption; in fact, they haven't been tested on humans at all prior to use. Environmental toxins are also on the rise. Eating as organically as possible is one way to support your body to be as strong and healthy as possible.

Many fruits and vegetables are now genetically engineered. The long-term effects of eating these foods are unknown. Organic foods are usually not genetically engineered. Be aware that one of the most heavily genetically engineered foods is made from soybeans. Most of these preparations are also heavily processed.

Pesticides cross the placenta. There have been numerous studies on the affect of pesticides on young children. For example, a study conducted by the Centers for Disease Control, in 2003, found that there was twice the level of pesticides in the urine of children than that of adults. The immune systems and livers of developing babies and children have greater difficulty ridding their bodies of contaminants. Likewise, a study conducted at the University of Washington, Seattle found that preschoolers who were fed a conventional diet had six times the levels of certain pesticides than those preschoolers who were fed organic diets.

Organically grown foods are getting easier to find. If your mainstream market does not carry a broad selection of organics they are always available in health food stores and farmers markets. As people continue to ask supermarkets to carry them, however, accessibility to organic foods will increase. Organic foods can be expensive. If you are on a limited budget and need to prioritize which types of organic foods you can afford, the order we recommend is: meat, dairy, eggs, fruits, vegetables, grains. Toxins are more concentrated in foods that are higher up on the food chain. Meats that come from animals that have been given antibiotics and growth hormones are less healthy choices for our bodies. Ingesting such medications and hormones on a regular basis can have long-term effects, such as suppressing our own hormonal and immune systems. In addition, recent studies have suggested that the ingestion of growth hormones found in meat and dairy products may contribute to the onset of early puberty in children.

Organic milk, cheese, and butter may cost twice what conventional dairy products cost, but they don't contain the pesticides that cattle have eaten and then concentrated in their bodies. In fact, various carcinogens (cancer-causing agents) such as dioxin are concentrated in fat cells. Thus, they're concentrated in a cow's milk and when ingested by us they become concentrated in the fatty tissues of our breasts, and subsequently in our breast milk. These toxins may become quite concentrated in the small bodies of breast-fed babies. Besides being pesticide free, organic dairy products are free from growth hormones such as Bovine Growth Hormone and antibiotics, which are pumped into nonorganically raised cattle. Ingesting synthetic hormones can throw your own hormones out of balance, which may affect your ability to conceive. In addition, organic meat and dairy products usually come from farms or facilities in which animals are treated humanely. When possible, buy milk from reputable local dairies and avoid ultra-pasteurized milk, which is created using a process that reduces the milk's nutrients in favor of a longer shelf life.

Eggs from chickens that are organically fed are significantly higher in quality than their counterparts. We still know very little about the long-term effects of pesticides, hormones, and antibiotics on the human body. Meat and dairy production is big corporate business, with large lobbies and media campaigns that often make information difficult to access. Many fruits have been sprayed with pesticides up to twelve times before you eat them. If you choose not to buy organic foods, or they aren't available to you, washing your fruits and vegetables to remove as much external pesticide residue as possible is important. However, in thin-skinned fruits and vegetables most pesticide residue cannot be washed or peeled away. A study conducted at the Columbia Center for Children's Environmental Health found a link between pesticide use around New York apartment buildings and impaired fetal development.

VEGETABLES

We are going to sound like your mother here, because we are mothers: Eat lots and lots of vegetables. Essential vitamins and minerals for the functioning and integrity of your reproductive system are only found in fresh fruits and vegetables. In order to ingest the recommended daily allowance you must eat at least nine servings of fruits and vegetables a day. A serving is half a cup. This takes effort. We suggest the rainbow approach: Eat as many colors of vegetables and fruit as you can each day. This is a simple way to ensure that you'll get the entire variety of trace minerals and vitamins you need. Eat three to four servings of green and leafy vegetables daily—dark leafy lettuces, spinach, kale, collard greens, mustard or dandelion greens, tatsoi, broccoli, or chard—and one to two servings of red, orange, or yellow vegetables—squash, red pepper, and sweet potato.

Fresh vegetables contain many more vitamins and minerals than frozen, and frozen vegetables and fruits have more retained vitamins and minerals than canned. This is particularly true for vegetables you buy that have been grown locally, since vegetables that are shipped from far away are picked unripe and lose vitamins as they sit in boxes and on shelves. Fresh-frozen vegetables may have more vitamins and minerals than "fresh" vegetables that were picked unripe and traveled thousands of miles to get to your store. Overcooking can quickly reduce the content of some vitamins and minerals, such as folic acid, in vegetables. The brighter the green of the vegetable, the healthier. Vegetables do not need to be cooked until they are olive drab. In addition, steamed vegetables retain more vitamins than those that have been boiled or fried. And the vegetable water can be used for making soups.

We know that some of you do not like vegetables and do not eat them daily. The key will be learning to use them. Learning to like them will follow this. Start by buying already washed and prepped vegetables and salad mixes. Always order a side of veggies when you eat out. Even if vegetables are not on the menu the waiter can fix you a side order. Consider buying a juicer.

||||||||||||||||||||||||||||||||||||||||||||||||||||||||||||||||||||||||||||||||||||||

Maia Recommendation for Vegetables: Some people cannot bring themselves to prepare, cook, or eat vegetables. If this is the case for you we suggest you juice your vegetables. It will not be as high in fiber, but it is much, much better than no vegetables and much better than canned or frozen vegetables, as well. Get a good book on juicing and get to work. We have had a number of clients who get eight servings of vegetables a day through their juicer. You will come to love the juice, which is delicious. You can add ingredients that are packed with goodness that you can't find in any prepared juice, such as beets, fresh ginger, or horseradish or daikon radish. Make the investment of getting a good juicer with a powerful motor, such as Acme or Omega. Trust us: Like millions of others, you will love the difference in your body after a month of juicing

||||||||||||||||||||||||||||||||||||||||||||||||||||||||||||||||||||||||||||||||||||||

HEALTHY FATS

We recommend that you focus on using monosaturated fats and cold-pressed oils in your diet. Olive oil, nuts, seeds, and fish are all healthy ways of ingesting fat. Saturated fats such as butter and coconut oils can certainly be ingested in moderation. Processed foods such as fast foods and potato chips are the main culprits containing bad fats. We encourage you to do your reading on healthy and unhealthy fats.

Polyunsaturated fats are extremely important for the body. Two of the individual polyunsaturated fats known as omega-3 and omega-6 are called "essential fatty acids." These cannot be manufactured by the body and must be eaten in foods. Essential fatty acids are necessary for the healthy function and development of most of the body's tissues, including the brain, heart, blood vessels, kidneys, and liver. Deficiencies can lead to infertility in women and men, reduced growth, and decreased cell integrity. Hormonal regulation is disrupted if the correct balance of essential fatty acids is not present in your body.

Making sure you get enough essential fatty acids is one of the most important things that you can do to increase your fertility and regulate your hormones and to provide a good start for your growing baby once you are pregnant.

The ratio of omega-3 to omega-6 fats in your diet should be 1:5. This is approximately the ratio of fatty acids in breast milk. The current dietary ratio of most people's diets is about 1:14. It is important to adjust this ratio. Reducing cooking oils that contain large amounts of omega-6 such as sunflower, safflower, and corn oil and replacing them with oils that are high in omega-3 such as canola oil or low-level omega-6 such as olive oil will improve this ratio.

Food sources of omega-3 oils include flaxseeds, oily fish, walnuts, green leafy vegetables, pumpkin seeds, canola oil, and mustard seed oil. Because the modern diet often has the wrong balances of these essential fatty acids the necessary synthesis of other fatty acids from the essential ones is often disrupted.

Eight out of ten people are deficient in docosahexaenoic acid (DHA), a derivative of omega-3 that is essential for maintaining the integrity of the cell membranes in the ovaries and for optimal fetal development. DHA can be obtained from fish oil supplements, which are often necessary to rectify the imbalance. Unless you are a vegetarian, we highly recommend one teaspoon a day of fish oil as the preferred supplemental form. Our favorite company is Nordic Naturals; they seem to be the most regulated and ethical of the companies we know of. If you are a vegetarian you can supplement with flax oil; however, for some people it cannot be converted in the body and there remains a deficiency even after months of adding flax to the diet.

It takes up to three months for the balance to be redressed. Evening primrose oil, borage oil, and black currant seed oil are often needed with the flax or fish oil supplements for complete benefits.

FLAX SEED

Flax seed is a phenomenal plant seed with many important properties: it fights cancers, increases progesterone, and reduces allergies. Another primary benefit of flax seed is how it aids digestion of food, especially protein, in the stomach itself, before it reaches the intestine. Flax seed is inexpensive and organically grown seed can be found in the bulk section of health-food stores. Two tablespoons of ground flax seed equal one tablespoon of flax seed oil and contain the fiber that the oil doesn't. Taken daily, it not only provides hormone building blocks but also helps our bodies better absorb the hormone-building blocks of other plants we've eaten. It also has the pleasant side effects of improving bowel regularity and vitality of skin, hair, and nails. We recommend that all women add ground flax seed to their diet. You must grind your own, as it needs to be ground daily in order to retain its potency and nutritional properties. Flax seed is tasty sprinkled on oatmeal, with yogurt, and in smoothies. It has a pleasant, nutty flavor.

Vitamins and Minerals

Although we recommend that you start taking a food-based prenatal vitamin and a liquid mineral supplement three months prior to conception, we do not recommend that you try to count on getting the bulk of your nutrients through vitamin and other supplements. Vitamins and especially minerals in pill form are often hard to absorb effectively. Ideally, your primary source of vitamins should be fruits and vegetables, with supplements as a backup to fill in the gaps.

Some megadose vitamins don't contain the correct balance of vitamins and minerals, and therefore can inhibit the absorption of other vitamins. For example, large doses of calcium need to be balanced with magnesium and vitamin D. Vitamin A should be balanced with vitamin E. Some vitamins taken in high doses can be toxic and tax the liver and kidneys. When you're inseminating or pregnant, it's best not to ingest more than 8,000 IU of vitamin A, 4,000 IU of vitamin D, or 1,000 mg of vitamin C on a daily basis.

Prenatal vitamins contain much more than you need if you aren't pregnant. Therefore, hold off on taking prenatal vitamins until two to three months before you start inseminating. If you don't conceive after a number of months, take a break from prenatal vitamins and switch to a regular multivitamin and a folic acid supplement so that your total folic acid dose equals 800 to 1,000 mcg. Some people experience negative reactions to the iron contained in prenatal vitamins, including diarrhea, constipation, or stomach pains. If this is the case for you, see the following section on iron for alternative sources and try a regular multivitamin plus a folic acid supplement instead of prenatal vitamins.

IRON

Low iron is the main cause of anemia. Anemia can impact the timing and strength of your ovulation. In addition, your blood volume increases by 50 percent during pregnancy, so it's important to begin pregnancy with a high iron level. Because iron supplements are often difficult to absorb and may cause negative side effects, eating iron-rich foods is a good way to start boosting your iron profile, instead of taking supplements, if you aren't significantly iron-deficient.

Often anemic people find it helpful to take a food-based liquid iron supplement such as Floradix or to make herbal teas rich in iron as well as increase their intake of iron-rich foods. If you're low in iron (which you can tell from a simple, inexpensive blood test) you'll need to eat a higher level of iron daily for two months to replenish your body's reserves. Foods rich in iron include eggs, beef, pumpkin seeds, prunes, beets, lentils, tofu, blackstrap molasses, dried apricots, and seaweed. The U.S. recommended daily allowance (RDA) of iron for nonpregnant women is 18 mg per day.

FOLIC ACID (FOLATE)

Many women who do not eat a lot of fresh leafy greens do not get enough folic acid. Low folic acid during the first few weeks of pregnancy correlates with increased rates of neural tube defects—spinal and nervous system problems in the developing fetus. Eight hundred to 1,000 mcg a day is the standard recommended dose during pregnancy, and that's what you'll usually find in prenatal vitamins. If you are taking a regular multivitamin you may need to supplement to reach the recommended amount. It is recommended that you take folic acid for at least three months prior to conception and throughout the first trimester.

There are many natural ways to get folic acid: dark leafy greens, dried peas and beans, whole grains, whole-grain breads and cereals, citrus fruits, bananas, and tomatoes. If you have a diet rich in fresh whole foods, you may well be getting enough folic acid.

VITAMIN C

Vitamin C helps the body absorb iron and also in tissue repair. It also assists in the formation of healthy gums, teeth, and bones for the baby. Foods high in vitamin C include broccoli, blueberries, asparagus, citrus fruits, green and red peppers and chilies, strawberries, and cauliflower. Eating nine servings of fruits and vegetables daily will adequately meet your needs for vitamin C. Do not take more than 1,000 mg a day as supplements, as it can reduce fertile mucus and induce miscarriage.

PROTEIN

Proteins are the building blocks for our cells, so they are crucial to the mother's and fetus's health. Sufficient protein also helps to balance blood sugar.

Proteins are made up of amino acids. A full supply of amino acids is essential for proper egg production and LH and FSH regulation. Sources of protein include animal products, dairy products, nuts and seeds, legumes, and beans. If you eat a diet of fresh foods and vegetables, you're likely to get sufficient protein. We've noticed, however, that many people's diets overemphasize carbohydrates. This is especially true with vegetarians. In fact, many vegetarians are chronically deficient in protein. Try increasing your proteins and decreasing your carbohydrates and notice if your body feels more alive. Protein-rich smoothies are easy to make at home in a blender. Try yogurt or milk, fresh fruit or juice, and "silky" tofu. Add protein powder, chlorella, or spirulina for a big boost. But remember, moderation is the key to a healthy diet. If you aren't pregnant yet, be careful not to overindulge in protein (no more than 100 grams of protein on a regular daily basis), since some studies indicate that excess protein consumption can hinder the body's ability to absorb calcium.

CALCIUM

Calcium is essential to creating a strong skeletal system and good muscle function. It is also vital for hormonal balance. Low calcium can affect egg production and ovulation. High-calcium foods include sesame seeds and tahini; sunflower seeds; almonds; dairy products; greens of turnip, radish, mustard, and beets; kidney beans; tofu; miso paste; and sea weeds ("sea vegetables"). Many seafoods are high in calcium, especially sardines or anchovies that one eats with the bone included. If you cook soup, putting an egg (still in its shell) in your soup stock with a tablespoon of vinegar will dissolve the calcium out of the shell and into the water. You can then fish out the egg after twenty minutes and eat it hard-boiled.

Many sea vegetables (seaweeds) are high in calcium, iron, and protein. Look for them in any store that carries Asian food. Nori is the sea vegetable dried in sheets that is used for sushi. Other sea vegetables are kombu, wakame, arame, dulse, and hijiki. Some have a mild flavor, like nori or kombu, and others such as hijiki have a stronger flavor. Kombu can be added to grains, beans, or soup stocks. If added to beans in a strip (which can be removed after cooking, as you would do with a bay leaf), it will reduce the flatulence and indigestion often caused by beans. Most seaweeds can be found in powder form or you can grind them at home into powders and sprinkle on foods as a condiment; this is especially tasty if mixed half and half with ground toasted sesame seeds. This Japanese mixture, called gomasio, is incredibly rich in minerals, has a salty flavor imparted by the seaweed, and can be used in place of table salt. It is especially good on boiled potatoes or rice.

VITAMIN A

Beta carotene is converted to vitamin A by the liver, and it promotes healthy skin, eyesight, and bone growth. Vitamin A is essential for producing reproductive hormones. Beta carotene is found in most orange vegetables and fruits, including carrots, squash, sweet potatoes, apricots, melons, and chili peppers. As mentioned earlier, vitamin A should not be taken in supplement form in doses exceeding 8,000 IU per day. The beta carotene content in food alone, however, is not high enough to cause physical problems, even if you drink carrot juice daily.

VITAMINS

The B vitamins are crucial for fertility. Many people find that they need to take a vitamin B supplement at this time in life. Stress inhibits the appropriate absorption of B vitamins. All the B vitamins play a role in fertility.

Vitamin B-1 (thiamin) deficiency has been associated with reduced implantation and ovulation. Foods richest in thiamin are Brewer's yeast, lean meats, egg yolks, leafy green vegetables, whole grains, wheat germ, berries, nuts, seeds, and legumes.

Vitamin B-2 (riboflavin) deficiency has been associated with increased rates of miscarriage and low-birth-weight babies. The best sources of riboflavin are liver, milk, meat, dark green vegetables, whole-grain cereals, pasta, bread, and mushrooms.

Vitamin B-3 (niacin) helps to regulate the production of all the reproductive hormones, thus impacting fertility if in short supply. The best sources of niacin are poultry, meat, salmon, whole grains, dried beans and peas, and nuts. The body also makes niacin from the amino acid tryptophan (found in such foods as milk, turkey, and tuna).

Vitamin B-5 (pantothenic acid) is essential for fetal development. It is found in sweet potatoes, broccoli, oranges, strawberries, and pecans.

Vitamin B-6 (pyridoxine) is essential for proper hormonal functioning and balance. Adequate B-6 can prevent luteal phase defects by balancing the estrogen-to-progesterone ratio. It also helps to regulate FSH and LH by increasing serotonin and dopamine. This helps to regulate the strength and quality of ovulation. The best sources of pyridoxine are whole grains, cereals, bread, liver, avocados, spinach, green beans, and bananas. Pyridoxine is needed in proportion to the amount of protein consumed.

Vitamin B-12 may help regulate irregular menstrual cycles. It is also needed to work in conjunction with folic acid. The best food sources include salmon, tempeh, miso, and lamb.

||||||||||||||||||||||||||||||||||||||||||||||||||||||||||||||||||||||||||||||||||||||||||||

Maia Tips for Healthy Eating

- ⊚ Drink half your weight in ounces of water a day.
- ⊚ Take probiotic supplements every night before bed.
- ⊚ Take 1 teaspoon of fish oil every day.
- ⊚ Eat something with protein every three hours.
- ⊚ Eat three to four servings of green vegetables every day.
- ⊚ Eat one to two servings of red, yellow, or orange vegetables a day.
- ⊚ Eat two to three servings of fruit a day.
- ⊚ Eat whole grains daily.
- ⊚ Eat from as many colors of the rainbow a day as possible.

||||||||||||||||||||||||||||||||||||||||||||||||||||||||||||||||||||||||||||||||||||||||||||

Food and Extended Conception Periods

If it takes more than a few cycles for you to get pregnant, you may start to resent the diet changes you've made. Often people only intend to temporarily eliminate their consumption of caffeine, alcohol, or sugar. As this period lengthens, any changes you've made can trigger resentment, the need to be in complete control of your food intake, and monthly bingeing.

Every month many people try to "perfect" their diets (and for that matter their whole beings) under the assumption that if they merely eat better they'll become pregnant. Then they work to control their eating even more. Rather than making healthy choices, many people become fanatics. The emotional undercurrent of stress and self-blame is incredibly defeating. All the pleasure is taken out of eating. It becomes a pass/fail exercise instead of a source of nourishment and nurturance.

Attempting to control anything tends to greatly increase stress. Many people have a natural tendency to try to control anything they can during a time of feeling out of control. Don't be hard on yourself and fall into the trap of trying to control how much you're trying to control. If you find yourself in this place, slow down and honor yourself. You're doing the best you can. Let love, nurturing, and self-compassion flow in. It may be helpful to review your diet on a regular basis with a trusted friend, nutritionist, or partner if you find yourself falling into a place of overcontrol. That person can serve to help you keep a balanced perspective.

The resentment people often feel toward their bodies when they don't get pregnant overflows into the changes they've made in their diets or toward their partners or others who encouraged, pushed, or suggested these "ineffective" changes in the first place.

There is a potential at some point to want to stop all fertility-related changes in your life if they haven't "worked." With this usually comes a desire to binge on all of the "forbidden" foods and substances. It's fine to do whatever you need to do. Just be kind to yourself afterward. This is part of why you should incorporate slow changes that establish long-term, lifelong patterns. If you've made slow changes, it won't feel like you're sliding down a mountain when you do slip. This is also one reason why, if you're partnered, it's beneficial to make these changes together.

Nutritional Needs for Conceiving While Breastfeeding

If you are still breastfeeding while you are inseminating, or if you will have been breastfeeding until a few months before you try to get pregnant again, it is even more important for you to focus on your nutrition. Please know that you will need to increase your caloric intake to equal that of a person pregnant with twins. In order for you to conceive with ease and to make it through the first trimester without miscarriage you must have the nutrients available in your body. The years of pregnancy and nursing can serve to deplete your body of its stores of nutrients. Please do not proceed without paying special attention to increasing the calories, quality, and fats in your diet. It will result in greater fertility, and a healthier pregnancy and postpartum period for you. The primary reason we see for "secondary infertility"—troubles getting pregnant the second time around—is depletion. We will cover this more in the next chapter.

Conclusion

We want food to be nurturing and loving for you, and we want to remind you to approach the topic slowly and thoughtfully. Gradual changes are the strongest. Try not to chastise yourself if you're not yet ready to give up your cherished coffee (try switching to decaf); we're merely offering suggestions. For now, implement the ones that feel right. Don't try to do a complete overhaul. Baby steps are the right-size steps. Eventually, your healthy eating habits will be lifelong. You've got plenty of time.

Most people we work with feel fantastic from making healthy changes in their diet! Even those who have been eating in a healthy way for a long time find areas that they can improve for greater health. When you make changes in your diet you feel it and it is noticeable to others. It's validating to respect the impact that making food and diet changes has on our bodies and psyches. Take the time to write in a journal and share with your friends and lovers what comes up, both initially and along the way. If necessary, consider joining or starting a support group of women who examine the role food plays in their lives. Any choices you make toward greater health will improve the quality of your life and your pregnancy. Good luck!

MAIA TIPS FOR ADDING FRUITS AND VEGETABLES TO YOUR DIET

- Add fruit or applesauce to pancake batter or to oatmeal.
- Add a fruit smoothie with whey powder, flax oil, and spirulina to your morning routine.
- Juice fresh fruits or vegetables every day.
- Add vegetables such as spinach and mushrooms to your eggs.
- Add fruit or dried fruit to your salad: pears, pomegranates, persimmons, oranges, and apples are all good
- Add a dark leafy green mix and grated carrots to your salad.
- Eat salad or raw vegetables as a snack or with your lunch
- Drink a vegetable juice pick-me-up in the afternoon or when you return home from work.
- Add lettuce, shredded cabbage, spinach, or sprouts to your sandwiches.
- Stuff leftover vegetables or salad into a pita pocket with cheese — or add to a bagel with cream cheese.
- Buy ready-made carrots or celery for snacks.
- Buy precut vegetables for stir fries.

CHAPTER 11

Choosing a Fertile Lifestyle

A FERTILE LIFESTYLE promotes balanced hormones, regular menstrual cycles, monthly ovulation, and a healthy uterus. It also optimizes health before conception occurs, which increases healthy development of the baby during pregnancy and decreases chances of miscarriage, birth defects, and pregnancy complications. The first part of this chapter discusses how to check on aspects of your overall health, including sexual and reproductive health, before you conceive. The middle part focuses on exercise, sleep, sex, and reducing stress. Although many people realize there's a connection between nutrition and fertility, many don't realize that these three other lifestyle factors are also essential to optimal fertility. As we explore each of them in this chapter, you'll notice that the common thread is consistency. Maintaining equilibrium in your body will keep your reproductive hormones in equilibrium—probably the most important aspect of optimizing fertility. We'll then move on to discuss choices about taking antidepressants and anti-anxiety medicines during preconception and pregnancy. And we'll end the chapter with a thorough review of things you can do to enhance your fertility and things to avoid that inhibit fertility.

All too many people approach fertility as if it is something they need to conquer, a task to check off their to-do list. This is especially common for both Type A personalities and for people who have been in the workforce for their adult lives and are now facing a pregnancy in their late thirties or forties. At Maia, one of our greatest challenges when speaking to our clients is to find the way to connect someone to a new approach to life. You see, pregnancy cannot be scheduled. Fertility is not a thing—it is a state of being. Perhaps the best way to show this is by example.

Ava's Story

Ava called Maia because after eight months of trying she finally got pregnant, only to miscarry a few months later. Since then she had been unable to conceive and it had been six more months. Ava is 39 years old. She and her partner live in Chicago. They have been together for ten years and are quite in love. They both quit their jobs a year and a half ago to start a chocolate café. They work together now.

The first round of questioning uncovered nothing unusual—Ava reported herself to be quite healthy, her hormonal tests were all within range, her timing looked great. We did notice that since her miscarriage her cycles had been getting more irregular. She wanted to know whether she should see a fertility doctor. We decided to dig deeper and explored each area more fully to see what would be revealed. Looking for why someone is not getting pregnant is often detective work.

Upon further questioning we learned that these past two years since the café was opened had been incredibly hard but rewarding work. It had been a very stressful few years. Both women worked upwards of twelve hours a day. They ate a lot more chocolate than they used to. Ava was not going to the gym anymore but she was running around on her feet all day. They were too exhausted to have sex. They ate regularly, but they only ate at home one or two meals a week. They were in a gourmet ghetto so they ate well, but it was all take-out. They were very high on life, but they did not get much sleep. Since the miscarriage Ava had had two root canals.

This information gave us a lot of insights. We spent the next hour coming up with a fertility plan. We actually started with the dental work. Extensive dental work throws off fertility and can cause miscarriage. So we recommended that Ava complete all dental work before trying to inseminate again. Then we discussed her relationship to food. Ava missed cooking terribly. One way she and her partner used to spend time together was through long, beautiful, candle-lit delicious dinners that they would cook together. It was their love of food and their love of each other that inspired them to start their chocolate café. The irony was now they became too busy to spend time just the two of them together. Then we moved on to exercise—Ava missed not only her workout at the gym but her yoga practice she had on the days in between. She used to feel very connected to her body. This feeling of contentment in her body enhanced her sex life. They used to have sex at least three times a week with long lovemaking sessions on the weekend. Now she couldn't remember the last time they had made love. We also discussed the value of sleep in regulating fertility. Through our conversation Ava could recognize what was going on—she was living at a much higher level of stress and her satisfaction with herself and her life were greatly reduced. In fact, she felt quite depleted.

This was the plan we came up with:

⊙ Ava will complete her dental work.
⊙ The two women will eat breakfast at home every day together.

- They will hire assistants to help them at the café — possibly even a part-time manager.
- Ava will cut her hours back significantly.
- Ava will come home early from work two nights a week to cook dinner.
- They will both take Sundays off and spend the day together at home.
- Ava will return to her workout and yoga routine.
- They will remember to make love on Sundays and hopefully throughout the week.
- In any event, Ava will masturbate regularly for uterine tone and pleasure.
- They will get at least six hours of sleep a night and one good nap on Sundays.
- If this plan hasn't worked and Ava is not pregnant after four months of insemination, she will see a fertility doctor.

It took eight weeks for the dental work to be complete. This was a blessing in disguise because it allowed for these changes to take hold over those two cycles. The first month they inseminated again she conceived! They now have a beautiful nine-month-old baby.

Specific Ways to Increase Fertility

Four issues are key to optimizing your fertility: exercise, sleep, sex, and stress reduction. These factors alone, combined with a healthy, nutritious diet, vitamins, minerals, and fish oil, will greatly improve your fertility.

Physical Exercise

People in today's industrialized world lead more sedentary lives than those of their ancestors. What to their ancestors was movement necessary for the work and play of daily life is compartmentalized in the modern world into activities called exercise. Some people do a substantial amount of exercise in daily work: in fields, on construction sites, at restaurants, or in factories. Many people, however, have sedentary jobs and don't have much time or energy for exercise at the end of the workday. Those that do exercise may do so in a binge form: heavy frequent exercise for a short period, followed by little or no exercise — much like the pattern of American dieting. We want to reframe the idea of the "chore" of exercise into the enjoyment of an active lifestyle.

FERTILITY AND PREGNANCY BENEFITS

Regular, moderate exercise optimizes fertility and benefits the body in many ways. At Maia we used not to focus on exercise very much. In the past few years, however, we have seen a marked difference in the conception rates of those who exercise and those who do not. We highly encourage everyone hoping to conceive to start a regular exercise regime. Regular exercise helps keep the blood pressure in a safe range, which supports the kidneys. It also balances the metabolism, which in turn balances hormone levels. Some studies show that in chromosomally healthy pregnancies, *regular exercise decreases the miscarriage rate by as much as 40 percent!* The deep breathing performed during exercise increases lung capacity, keeping body tissues well oxygenated. Regular aerobic exercise strengthens the heart, allowing it to beat more slowly, which increases its longevity. Regular exercise keeps your body flexible and strengthens the back and the abdomen, which significantly increases comfort in pregnancy. Aerobic exercise increases stamina, crucial during labor and new parenting.

MODERATION

There can be too much of a good thing when it comes to exercise and fertility. When women and transmen exercise very heavily, especially while restricting their calorie intake, their body-fat percentage can drop so low that the body has nowhere to synthesize and store its hormones, so it stops menstruating. This issue may appear to be more about body fat and weight, but to reduce body fat to the level of amenorrhea (when menstruation ceases) usually requires substantial exercise as well, unless starvation is the issue.

Studies have shown that a low percentage of body fat can detrimentally influence fertility, even if regular ovulation occurs. In these cases, gaining just five to ten pounds can significantly increase fertility.

Starting a heavy exercise program as you begin to inseminate can change your body's metabolism and thyroid levels, which in turn will affect your fertility hormones. If increasing your daily exercise is important to you and you decide not to postpone starting to inseminate for a few months until your exercise regimen is stable, then make sure you start lightly and increase your exercise level in small steps. Be aware that you may need to increase your caloric intake as you increase your exercise so that your body doesn't go into diet or starvation mode.

Once you begin inseminating, for half of each month you may possibly be in early pregnancy. After inseminating, take your pulse occasionally to monitor how fast your heart is beating during exercise. During pregnancy, your heart should beat no more than 140 beats per minute. You can get a good workout while achieving this pulse rate by exercising at a medium level for a longer time compared to exercising at a more difficult level for a shorter time. Monitoring your heart rate will also keep your core body temperature from getting too hot, which is especially important in early pregnancy. Moderately priced heart-rate monitors are now available at most sporting-goods stores.

FOR THOSE WHO ABHOR EXERCISE

You are not alone if you do not enjoy exercise. At Maia we have two standard approaches to exercise. Either exercise for twenty minutes beyond the time you break a sweat three times a week, or exercise for five minutes every day. As you get more and more in shape it will take a little longer to get you to the point of breaking a sweat. But the harder you exercise, the shorter that time will be. The five-minutes-a-day approach is usually used by people who like to madly clean their house, or run like a maniac from work to their transportation. With support you will find one of these approaches doable. Find an exercise buddy to motivate you to get out the door. Hire a personal trainer. Join a gym. Walk at your lunch hour. Create a reward system for yourself. Do whatever it takes to get your body moving.

FEAR OF EXERCISE

You may have heard some inseminating women express concern about exercising in the second half of each cycle, from ovulation to period or pregnancy. They often fear they'll "shake the embryo loose" and cause an early miscarriage. They end up exercising regularly for two weeks, then stop completely for two weeks; this confuses the body. For the first six to ten days after conception, the embryo hasn't yet implanted in the lining of the uterus; it's still migrating down from the top of the fallopian tube. Once it implants, it embeds into the thick endometrium, which eventually grows into the placenta. We advise people to avoid particularly bouncy or strenuous exercise at this time but to continue exercising in other ways to provide the body with consistency, such as talking a brisk walk or riding a bike or exercise bike. Also, do not swim in a pool for twenty-four hours after inseminating, as the chlorine in pools may hinder the sperm's viability.

We know that some of you will still decide not to exercise when you could be pregnant. Remember that an active lifestyle supports hormonal regulation. Make a point of walking briskly every day, walk to work, park farther away from work than you need to, and always take the stairs. These are some of the small ways you can stay active even if you are avoiding formal exercise.

Fertility and the Myths of Size and Weight

Obstetric approaches to weight gain and pregnancy are constantly changing. Our mothers, if they went to obstetricians in the United States for prenatal care, were advised to gain little weight during pregnancy in order to retain their feminine figures. Often they were given prescriptions of amphetamines to suppress their appetite or told to smoke during pregnancy for the same effect. Obviously, people at that time weren't given the healthiest advice about weight gain and pregnancy. You may still hear this advice from older relatives. Obstetrics now still takes the approach that there is an "ideal" weight gain for pregnancy, although the "ideal" is somewhat higher than it used to be. Obstetricians also commonly have had a limited amount of training in nutritional counseling (one study found the average to be three hours), so you may hear a lot of nonsense and little valuable information from both doctors and friends as you plan for pregnancy.

If you feel you're overweight you wouldn't be alone if you wanted to lose some weight before you gain it back during pregnancy. But trying to lose weight by dieting just before conception can be challenging to your fertility, as the body can move into a starvation mode. In fact, for some dieting can actually impair fertility. Instead of dieting to lose weight, concentrate on eating healthy foods without limiting your intake and exercising regularly; this will keep your body balanced as you try to conceive.

If you haven't lost any weight before conceiving, don't panic. Larger women who eat healthy foods when hungry during pregnancy often gain less weight than skinnier pregnant women following the same pregnancy diet. In our practice we've noticed that the most slender women often gain the most weight, as the body needs to have a minimum amount of fat to store hormones to support pregnancy and the milk production of breastfeeding. Postpartum exercise will slowly use up the fat you've acquired throughout pregnancy in a way that doesn't throw your body out of balance.

Some women are told that being skinny increases their fertility. This is more about American fatphobia rather than sound medical knowledge. A woman needs a certain amount of fat to sustain the hormone levels necessary for ovulation. Usually, if a woman is slender, gaining a few pounds will improve her fertility.

For larger women, weight loss can help the body recognize hormones and fine-tune the hormonal balance. Thus, if you weigh 200 or more pounds and are having trouble conceiving, an increase in exercise and a diet rich in protein and low in carbohydrates may facilitate conception. We have worked with plenty of larger people who eat in a healthy way and exercise regularly who have absolutely no problems conceiving.

It cannot be denied, however, that for some larger women there is a link between fertility and being overweight. It is not necessarily the extra weight itself that is the cause of fertility problems; rather, often there are other issues that are associated with the extra weight and that also cause the fertility problems. The primary problem seems to be a production of excess estrogen. This can throw the whole balance of the reproductive system off. It can show up in fertility tests as low progesterone. Fat cells store and secrete estrogen throughout the menstrual cycle. This can interfere with ovulation and implantation. For some it can even cause a person not to ovulate.

If you are overweight and experiencing irregular cycle lengths, or have luteal phases of less than eleven days (the luteal phase is the time between when you ovulate and you get your period), you think you may not be ovulating, or you keep experiencing missed implantations or early miscarriages, then weight loss may help. A moderate weight loss of 5 to 10 percent of body weight can restore hormonal balance without additional medical intervention. However, the weight loss needs to be based on a balanced program of healthy eating and exercise. It needs to be slow weight loss, no more than a half pound to a pound a week.

You may find that when you implement a plan for natural hormonal regulation, you may start to rapidly lose weight from this alone. If your diet is healthy and your exercise regime is stable, this is not a problem. It will likely stabilize on its own after a few weeks. However, if you experience this form of rapid weight loss, wait until it has stabilized back to a rate that you can manage (1/2 pound to 1 pound a week) before inseminating. Rapid weight loss can cause hormonal mayhem. If you are experiencing rapid weight loss, try to slow it down. One solution may be to receive acupuncture treatments to help balance your hormones during this time, resulting in less rapid weight loss.

Another issue with larger people can be polycystic ovarian syndrome (PCOS), a condition resulting from a hormonal imbalance. But beware that this diagnosis is often too broadly given to anyone who is larger and experiencing hormonal fluctuations. Be wary of such diagnosis. For a more thorough discussion, please see chapter 17.

Sleep

Sleep serves the body in many ways. The time your body spends sleeping is an essential restorative period when damaged cells are repaired. Your immune system needs plenty of sleep to do its work cellularly to prevent infection. Lying down at night relaxes the muscles that are used all day to hold the body and head upright. It takes a lot of work to hold our bodies erect for so many hours, whether we're sitting or standing. Adequate sleep is key in the body's recuperation process. Finally, sleep is when the psyche gets some unfettered time to come out and play. Dreamtime plays a crucial, if not well understood, role in emotional and cognitive functioning.

The body's circadian rhythms—its daily clock—can be thrown off by irregular or insufficient sleep. Many hormone levels in the body have a twenty-four-hour pattern that differ between night and day. Getting regular nightly sleep helps keep hormone levels balanced.

There are different types of sleep, each with a different type of brain-wave pattern. Each type is essential for the successful carrying out of a specific bodily function. You need a good balance of all types of sleep for your body to complete its nighttime healing and re-energizing functions. Different types of sleep occur in a cycle of set sleep patterns. If the body is interrupted before it gets through a whole sleep cycle, which is three to four hours, it can't complete all aspects of its functioning.

When people chart their basal body temperature, they often immediately see how interruptions and changes in their sleep pattern affect their temperature, making it higher or less predictable. Sleep plays many roles in balancing and maintaining the body, many of which are yet to be discovered. You might be someone who feels rotten if your sleep is interrupted, or you may have adapted to getting very little sleep. In either case, sleep deprivation causes your body to draw on other resources to maintain itself. The goal of a fertile lifestyle is to optimize the state of your body's health, not just give it the minimum it needs to keep functioning. Regular, plentiful sleep is an essential element of a fertile lifestyle.

Ovulation and Sleep

Studies show that the amount of light you sleep in can affect your ovulation. It can also affect your production of fertile mucus. Before electric lights came along, the amount of light emanating from fires and candles at night was minimal. The light of the full moon is significantly brighter than when the moon is new, and women often menstruated when the moon was full—

it was apparently triggered by the changing cycle of nighttime light. (Women also didn't use all the deodorant products we use now, and most didn't bathe as frequently as we do; thus, women's cycles were also more in sync with each other through more exposure to each other's pheromones.) Current studies demonstrate that sleeping in light one night out of many dark nights can trigger ovulation. This practice is called lunaception. Women who sleep in darker rooms have more regular cycles.

LUNACEPTION: HOW ELIMINATING LIGHT CAN AFFECT HORMONES AND OVULATION

- Eliminating light while sleeping fosters hormonal regularity in many ways.
- People who do not reliably ovulate start to ovulate when they sleep in darkness.
- Fertile signs line up more completely.
- Irregular cycle lengths become more predictable.
- Hormonal imbalances such as high FSH and low progesterone rebalance.
- Fertile mucus becomes more copious.

Some studies have shown that you can delay or prompt ovulation by sleeping in total darkness and then sleeping in low-level light for a night. Do you use a nightlight or does light come into your bedroom from the hallway? Does light stream in through your bedroom window from streetlights or lighted signs? Do you have a digital clock? Does light shine under your door? If so, try to minimize the light you're exposed to at night. Some women choose to sleep in complete darkness, using heavy curtains to block out any extraneous light.

If you are someone who experiences multiple days of fertile mucus then you should sleep in total darkness until you have experienced one to two days of fertile mucus or wet vaginal sensations. Then, for the next three nights, you should sleep with passive light shining into your room. This will bring on ovulation. If you do not reliably have multiple days of fertile mucus, then add the passive lighting twenty-four hours before you expect your peak fertility signs to encourage your ovulation.

Sex

Recently at Maia we have been recommending that people have orgasms at least three to four times a week, and since our clients have started doing so the fertility rates have been dramatically on the rise. The reasons for this are many. First, orgasm brings release. It is an amazing stress reducer; it physiologically reduces stress by releasing endorphins into the system. It also releases oxytocin, creating the love feeling throughout the body. Oxytocin is the hormone responsible for lactation and labor contractions. Oxytocin is also released with vaginal and cervical stimulation. The sexual stimulation brings about a chemical and hormonal shift in the body.

The second reason why we think increased orgasms increase fertility rates is directly related to the workout the uterus is getting. The uterus is a muscle. Proper exercise of any muscle provides adequate blood flow and tone to that muscle. So part of the theory is that you are simply strengthening the uterine muscle, making it more toned for pregnancy. This uterine tone also helps with alignment of the uterus. Many practitioners around the world believe that it is actually poor uterine alignment that causes infertility. Uterine contractions also help to expel the contents of the uterus, perhaps making it less prone to endometriosis.

The third reason is sexual intimacy. Fertility and sexuality are inherently linked. Historically it has been through sex that babies are conceived. There is a sexual intimacy linked with conception. Couples who take on this exercise of sex at least three times a week find their sexual intimacy deepens. This also deepens the emotional intimacy as they often go hand in hand. Many a couple has said that the sex made all the difference. It made them feel like they were actually making a baby. It brought baby making back to the bed. If you are single, the sexual intimacy with yourself is just as rewarding. So please, have many, many orgasms. Now that's good homework, don't you think?

Stress

Stress has a tremendous affect on fertility and is so common in everyday life that many people barely notice it. Please note that virtually all studies on stress have been on men, which means we do not know exactly how stress affects a woman's body. The following conclusions are based on the limited information we have on chemical reactions that occur in the male body.

The "stress response," called fight-or-flight, evolved as a reaction to imminent danger. Fight-or-flight refers to the way the body physically changes almost instantaneously when experiencing what it perceives as a threat. Many biochemical and hormone shifts occur, the greatest being the immediate release of adrenaline directly into the bloodstream. Stress activates the adrenals to release adrenaline, cortisol, and dehydroepiandrosterone (DHEA)—all three of which can interfere with proper hormone production. Adrenaline, cortisol, DHEA, and other biochemicals cause the blood pressure, pulse, sense of smell, vision, and pattern of blood flow in the body to switch to "survival mode." This survival mode causes the brain to focus sharply on the threat and not notice much else in the surrounding environment. Fight-or-flight allows the body to release the most energy and strength in the moment possible, to either fight back or flee from the threat. The fight-or-flight response is not under our conscious control; it is, however, powerful and very useful in specific situations. It takes a lot of the body's resources to respond in this way, and it is not meant to be a sustainable state of being but a temporary response to a dangerous situation.

Stress is the "emotional state" you feel when you're having some level of fight-or-flight response to something in your environment. These stressors—situations or people causing stress—can be momentary, such as a near miss on the freeway or a boss raising her voice at you. Stressors can be long-term, such as poverty, racism, or an abusive relationship. Often, stressors are things you feel you have little control over; you feel you can only respond and react but not necessarily change your stressors.

Positive events in your life can be stressful, too, since they involve a great deal of change or expectations, or you don't feel in control. In fact, three of the most stressful events, on average, in adult lives are getting married, buying a house, and having a baby—all of which are usually considered joyful occasions.

Long-term, chronic stress can contribute to a variety of health problems and culminates in adrenal overload.

Stress as a Tool

Most people perceive stress as a negative influence, and yet many adapt to it and even use it subconsciously as a life tool. Because of the stimulation of the adrenaline involved in stress, if you pay attention you may find that you use stress as a motivational tool to complete a task you know you need to get done. If you don't feel stressed about it, you might not have the energy required to do it. The stress response, like many other body responses, can be learned and patterned so that certain things trigger it. Since it is recognized and accepted as a common physical state, people can actually fine-tune their control of the level of stress they permit themselves to feel about certain things. In other words, the type of stress response in non-life-threatening situations becomes a conscious choice.

Examine How Stress Serves You

When you make a plan to reduce the amount of stress in your life, you need to recognize how you use stress as a tool and what you'll replace it with. This might include examining the framework of your life in general. You may feel that the number of commitments you have requires you to use a low level of stress throughout the day just to get you out of bed and through your schedule. If this is the case, you may realize that your normal mode is stress and that brief moments of relaxation are the exception. This, unfortunately, is the case for many people.

Quick stress-reduction techniques can substantially calm and relax you, but if stress is the cornerstone of your emotional and physical state, you ultimately need to reframe how you organize your life in terms of scheduling, work, productivity, and play. Reducing your stress will help you to prepare for parenthood.

Using Stress to Numb Feelings

Although stress is a mind-set and feels like a specific emotion, stress in and of itself is not a true emotion. It's not one of our innate feelings. It's a learned response to a biochemical state. Stress numbs people from feelings of fear, anger, sadness, and even happiness. If you use stress this way, even subconsciously, you may have many self-protective reasons for doing so. Feeling great sadness, fear, or anger isn't something most people are raised to do in a healthy way and having these emotions isn't usually comfortable. Any emotion felt very strongly can seem "out of control," which often doesn't feel safe. Avoiding the depths of these emotions is often about avoiding feeling vulnerable.

Acknowledging the depths of your feelings about a situation can sometimes give you the impetus you need to change the situation. You may be in uncomfortable or untenable situations in terms of love relationships or work commitments but not be ready or even know how to change these situations. If you aren't going to change a negative situation, it's easier and safer not to feel the emotions brought on by the situation. Even feeling great happiness is difficult for many people, as irrational as this seems. Sometimes feeling really happy brings up fears from the subconscious: "I don't deserve to be this happy" or "If I let myself be this happy, I'll feel even worse when the happiness goes away." Stress is a non-emotion that masquerades as a feeling, dampening the effect of the real feelings you may be experiencing. A commitment to reducing stress often means a commitment to feeling more.

How Stress Affects Fertility

The chemicals released in the body while under stress affect reproductive hormones in a variety of ways, many of which are yet undiscovered. The immediate hormonal response to stress is the production of adrenaline. If the body is in an ongoing or long-term stress state, it uses up a great deal of cortisol, which is a hormone that helps to stimulate the production and storage of glucose, reduces inflammation after trauma, and is vital to immune function. When the body starts to run out of cortisol, it takes progesterone and turns it into cortisol. Hormones are very interchangeable in this way. For example, testosterone and other androgens are turned into estrogen in the ovaries in the first half of the menstrual cycle. A deficiency of one set of hormones often causes depletion of others through the body's ability to re-form hormone molecules. The body regards stress as a greater priority than fertility, in terms of allocating hormone resources. This makes sense if we think of it in terms of evolution: you wouldn't want to compromise your safety by putting your energy into pregnancy when you are in the midst of a dangerous situation. Long-term stress can cause subtle long-term imbalances in fertility hormones. If a woman is stressed enough during one menstrual cycle, her stress can be powerful enough to stop her body from ovulating altogether for that month or to lengthen or shorten her menstrual cycle that month.

Stress can cause an overproduction of prolactin, which can cause problems with ovulation. Stress hormones directly affect the hypothalamus and the pituitary glands. Through a complex set of interactions, this can also lead to complications with LH and FSH production. These hormones directly affect fertility and ovulation. There can be an excess of estrogen and a decrease of progesterone with chronic stress as well. And stress can lead to menstrual cycle irregularities.

Stress is also hard on fetuses, since the changes that adrenaline causes in heart rate and other physiological functions are significantly more difficult for a growing baby to withstand than for an adult body. Also, the biochemicals that affect brain function set up many of the basic patterns of how the brain works while a baby is still in the uterus. As it develops, a baby will adapt to excessive chemicals to which it is exposed. When born, however, its body will feel imbalanced if it isn't exposed to this same level of chemicals. The same is true for sugar and drugs the mother may ingest while pregnant. The placenta isn't an effective barrier for any of these. Children exposed to excessive levels of certain chemicals or drugs may seek out similar brain-chemical states from their environments as they grow older, which puts them at higher risk for attention-deficit problems, substance use, or thrill-seeking behaviors.

Adrenal overload can impair fertility dramatically, even when your hormonal lab work looks to be within normal range. If you suspect that you may have adrenal stress, the most accurate form of testing is saliva testing. Blood testing does not reflect the status of adrenal function throughout the day, but rather for just one moment.

BENEFITS OF YOGA

Yoga is one of the oldest systems of mental and physical enhancement practiced in the world today. Yoga is based on the principle of mind-body unity. If the mind is chronically agitated, the health of the body will be compromised. Thus, the practices of yoga can help restore mental and physical health and radiance. Research shows that if practiced regularly, yoga can prevent and manage chronic stress-related health problems. It's also helpful in optimizing fertility and counterbalancing infertility.

One aspect of yoga that distinguishes it from other exercises and sports is the attention it gives the endocrine and nervous systems of the body. These systems are toned and regulated through the physical postures of yoga, thus aiding the regulation of all hormones, including the reproductive hormones. Yoga also tones and firms the body's muscles and aids in proper digestion and regular elimination.

Yoga is highly recommended for all women preparing to conceive. Once pregnancy is well established, yoga postures can be adapted for pregnancy. Although books and videos on yoga postures are widely available, it's best to begin and augment any personal practice under the guidance of a trained yoga instructor, then supplement your program at home with videos or books.

NOTICING WHEN YOU ARE STRESSED

Learning to deconstruct your stress responses is important when you are striving to increase fertility. One of the most common causes of "unexplained" infertility is the affects of cumulative stress on the body. Learning to incorporate stress-reduction techniques into your daily life is vital for health.

Do a body check-in as described in chapter 5: Do you feel tension in your jaw, neck, or shoulders? How does your stomach feel? Is your digestion disturbed? Does your breath fill your lungs deeply or stop at the top of your chest? Are your shoulders hunched? Are your arms crossed tightly in front of you? Is your heart beating quickly? Often people don't fully realize their stress level until they sit quietly for a moment and focus on their bodies, away from distractions. If you do a check-in like this throughout the day for a few days in a row, you'll start to get a realistic feel for how much stress you experience in your everyday life.

STRESS-MANAGEMENT TECHNIQUES

The process of insemination is inherently stressful. The longer it takes you to get pregnant, the more stressful the experience. In order to take care of yourself, you'll need to incorporate stress-management techniques into your daily life. Relieving stress can be as simple as taking five deep breaths and as complicated as finding a new job or housing situation. We'll discuss the quick, simple ways here. Keep in mind that utilizing a variety of approaches will be the most effective.

Breathing. Put your hand on your chest and take a breath so that your chest rises and pushes your hand out. Now put your hand on your abdomen and bring your breath down lower so that your belly pushes your hand out. This second type of breathing is called abdominal breathing. It triggers your nervous system to relax your body and create a physical state that is the opposite of the stress state. Try breathing abdominally, keeping your hand on your belly if you need to, five times in a row. Do you feel different? You can do deep breathing anywhere whenever you feel stress.

Muscle relaxation. Lie on your back and take a couple of deep breaths. Starting at the top of your head, contract all the muscles in your face, shoulders, neck, chest, arms, pelvis, legs, and feet. Scrunch up everything as tightly as possible and hold it as you slowly count to five. Then let everything fully relax, and see how soft and loose you can make all the different parts of your body. If you need to modify this exercise, do it on just your hands, shoulders, and face.

Aromatherapy. Aromatherapy means treatment using scents. When inhaled, botanicals work on the brain and nervous system through the stimulation of the olfactory nerves. Through the olfactory nerves, essential oil molecules have direct access to the limbic area of the brain. Stress-relief studies have demonstrated very clear results in people who are exposed to the aromas for only five minutes. The essential oils lavender, chamomile, and clary sage are good stress-relieving essential oils. You can buy a diffuser, place a few drops on some toilet paper and inhale deeply for a few minutes, or place a few drops on a light bulb.

Unstructured time for yourself. Find a little time every day when you won't be interrupted by people, the phone, or anything else. This may be as little as five minutes, although ideal would be a half-hour or more. If you only have a few minutes, you might just choose to sit quietly and take some deep breaths. If you have more time, choose something that is just for enjoyment with no expectation of the outcome. For example, don't choose to do a project that involves finishing and cleaning up; choose a bath instead. Pamper yourself and give yourself permission to experience whatever thoughts come into your head. Don't judge or analyze them; let them slip on by like a movie you can watch without interacting. You may notice some feelings arising. This time for yourself has no "shoulds" attached, and you don't need to have structure or goals for it. This free time is essential for letting your mind unwind. Sometimes you'll find that your mind really needs more than five minutes to relax, so when you can, schedule an hour or more just for being, not doing.

Exercise. As we mentioned earlier in this chapter, physical exercise is a wonderful way to mentally and physically reduce stress. Movement is the means by which the body works adrenaline out of its system and gets out of the fight-or-flight response. It also helps to put the mind into a different state; many people report that regular exercise helps to "clear their head" and allows them to feel calmer.

Therapy. Seeing a therapist or counselor can help you recognize patterns in your life that are stressful. Therapy will help you to unlearn your automatic stress responses and help you to develop tools to cope with stress more effectively.

Acupuncture. Acupuncture also helps to rebalance and counteract the effects of stress on the body, mind, and emotions.

Other effective stress relievers include meditation, yoga, martial arts, and sex. Please remember that stress uses up B vitamins, so be sure to increase your intake of these foods rich in these vitamins in order to compensate for this loss.

Prescription Medicine During Preconception and Pregnancy

Antidepressants and Anti-anxiety Medication

Many people who struggle with anxiety or depression regularly take Paxil, Prozac, Zoloft, Celexa, Effexor, Wellbutrin, or other medications to help them feel chemically balanced. Some people continue to take their medication throughout pregnancy and breastfeeding, while others feel strongly that it is imperative to get off these medicines before conception occurs. There is not enough information available to truly know what the long- and short-term effects of these medications are on fetuses and babies.

Whether or not to continue taking your medication is a personal decision that should be made carefully, on the basis of an assessment of the strength of your support system and coping mechanisms, your past history with depression or anxiety, whatever information you obtain about the impact of the medication on the fetus, your personal philosophies, and input from your therapist as well as your partner.

Safety of Prescription Medicines

For obvious ethical reasons, prescription medicines cannot be tested on pregnant women. Information about the safety of medicines on fetal development is obtained through animal testing and data on pregnancy outcomes once the drug has been approved for use. Drugs are classified into five categories in terms of the risk they pose for pregnancy. Most drugs are like Paxil and Prozac: classified as category B, which means that animal studies on mice and rats have shown no fetal development problems but that no studies have been performed on humans. But because human bodies don't always behave like those of mice, these drugs should only be used if their potential benefit clearly outweighs their potential risk. Category C drugs are those for which there is insufficient data to make conclusions about safety in pregnancy. Many doctors and midwives question the value of this drug classification system for Selective Serotonin Reuptake Inhibitors (SSRIs). SSRIs are antidepressants.

Making a decision about taking these drugs can be difficult because we don't know the actual risks involved. Most of them are very new in the United States, so data go back only a few years. A few of these medicines have been used in England and Europe for a longer period of time and thus have longer track records there. If you decide to continue taking your medicine, be aware that the least risky drug to take while pregnant may not be the same as the least risky drug to take while breastfeeding. Some people in their late second trimester taper off one type of medication and begin another for this reason.

There are growing concerns about people taking SSRIs in late pregnancy and potential adverse effects on newborns. The Federal Drug Administration (FDA) issued a warning as did Canada reflecting these concerns and the lack of conclusive information about the safety of these drugs. Working with a psychiatrist who is familiar with the concerns surrounding both pregnancy and breastfeeding is essential. If your psychiatrist is not up-to- date on the latest findings of the effects of these drugs on the childbearing cycle and the current research, find another psychiatrist to consult with.

Coping Skills

If you suffer from anxiety or depression, you had coping skills before you took this medicine and you may have learned new skills or refined others since then. In fact, some people find their medicine so effective that they no longer need to focus on their other coping skills. If this is your case, it might take some careful thinking as well as asking your therapist, partner, family, or close friends to reflect back to you practices that they've noticed seemed to support a healthy mental state for you. They may also be able to remind you which practices seem specifically detrimental to your well-being.

For many people, regular exercise, regular sleep, and stress management are essential to avoid anxiety, depression, or obsessive-compulsive behavior without their having to take medicine. For many, a sense of balance is more easily maintained when they avoid caffeine, alcohol, excess sugar, and other drugs. Eating regularly to avoid low blood sugar will help maintain mental constancy. Supplementing a healthy diet with a B-vitamin complex can also help avoid depressive feelings brought on by vitamin-depleting stress. Many studies point to the profound results of an increased intake of essential fatty acids (fish oil or flax oil supplements).

Some people have refined techniques such as affirmations, visualization, meditation, yoga, or nondepressive thinking that they can put into daily practice with great success. All of your coping skills will be useful in dealing with the stresses of conception, pregnancy, and birth, whether or not you also take medication. An assessment of your coping skills will help you decide whether you have adequate alternatives to taking medicine to maintain your mental health. Many people who choose to go off of their medication during the childbearing time find that acupuncture is an invaluable aid. Be aware that St. John's wort and some Chinese herbs administered to fight depression are not safe to take during pregnancy.

Support Team

Assess the strength of your support team if you're considering getting off your medication. Include your key support-team members in your decisions on the topic, and enlist their help throughout your baby-making process, whether or not you stop taking your medicine. If you haven't gone through a rough time recently, the people in your life may not realize that your mental health will need to be a primary focus for you if you stop taking antidepressants or anti-anxiety drugs.

Your support team may include your partner; good friends; family members; a body worker, acupuncturist, or other health- care provider; your therapist or psychiatrist (or other M.D. who prescribes your medicine); and a fertility specialist, ob-gyn, or midwife. Your team may also include your boss, church or spiritual group, Twelve-Step community, or other support-group members. Ask the important people in your life for their commitment to help you through this process. Unfortunately, because of the misinformation and prejudice that surrounds mental illness, you may have chosen self-protectively to be quite private about any medicine you take or special needs you have. Revisit your choices now to see who might be an ally if you discussed your situation with them. Ultimately, trust your judgment if you don't feel safe sharing this information with someone.

Fertility Drugs and Psychotropic Drugs

If you're taking fertility drugs, make sure that both your psychiatrist, therapist, or prescribing M.D. and your ob-gyn or infertility specialist know you're taking or have recently taken antidepressants or anti-anxiety drugs. Let them know you need to discuss specifically and accurately the emotional side effects that your fertility drugs may have in store for you. You need a fully informed team. If at all possible, don't taper off your antidepressant or anti-anxiety medicine right when you start taking fertility drugs such as Clomid or injectables, since the physical and emotional changes may be too difficult to handle all at once.

Getting Off Antidepressant or Anti-Anxiety Medicine

Many people want to wait until the last minute to stop taking their medicines. We advise a slow process of tapering off, after informing your partner and support team, being completely off for at least two to three months before the beginning of your first insemination cycle. This timeline will let you more fully adjust to getting off your medicine before you experience the emotional ups and downs of the insemination process. Many psychotropic medicines have a long half-life, and take three to six weeks to fully leave your body. We recommend you prioritize your alternative coping skills before you stop taking your medicine so that as few changes as possible will be happening concurrently. Take a few months to make this transition thoughtfully and gently; your mental stability is worth your patience, and your body needs time to restabilize before trying to achieve pregnancy. Acupuncture can be vital at this time to help you restabilize without your medication. You will need these months to truly be able to take stock of whether or not you will be able to effectively cope without your medication. It is best to have your dose stable in your body when you conceive rather than to have to start again in mid-pregnancy.

Monitoring Your Mental Health

The insemination process has its own innate cycle of excitement and depression, and you may confuse these feelings with signs of depression or anxiety. Hormonal changes that you notice from early pregnancy, fertility drugs, or regular premenstrual syndrome (PMS) may also confuse you in this way. Talking to a health-care provider who has experience with both fertility issues and mental health issues can help you (and your partner) gain perspective on the possible causes of the changes in your mental state. If you start to feel depressed or feel your mental state is "out of control," evaluate whether you're using your other coping skills and your support system to the best of your ability.

You may need to make significant decisions, such as cutting back on your work week or increasing your therapy sessions, to reduce your stress sufficiently to protect your mental health throughout conception and pregnancy. Often these choices incur financial costs. Your mental health is worth it, however, and is crucial to your ability to bond with the baby you're creating. Allow yourself to shamelessly make your mental health needs a priority for both you and your baby-to-be.

How each person taking antidepressants or anti-anxiety medicine approaches pregnancy is uniquely defined by her own circumstances; nevertheless, prioritizing exercise, sleep, nutrition, and stress management, as well a having a reliable support team will offer immeasurable benefits for weathering the highs and lows of insemination and pregnancy. This is the case whether you choose to stop, continue, or restart taking your medications.

Indeed, anyone focusing on the areas of healthy living discussed in this chapter can experience a powerful enhancement of their fertility. Any incremental change you make has potential effects not only on your fertility but also on your pregnancy health, fetal development, and general physical and emotional well-being. Include your family members and friends as much as possible in any new, positive habits you choose to start or reinforce for a lifetime of health.

CHAPTER 12

Fertility Inhibitors and Enhancers

THIS CHAPTER WILL cover numerous things that can help to increase fertility. However, the things recommended here are unlikely to be effective if you have not made the lifestyle changes covered in the previous two chapters needed to deeply support your fertility. We cannot overemphasize how essential nutrition; sleep, regular orgasms, exercise, and stress reduction are for fertility enhancement. Establishing a healthy, fertile lifestyle and mental and emotional approach to life are the foundations of health and thus greater fertility.

The true goal of fertility enhancement is health enhancement. The two are inextricably linked. This is what is missing completely from the medical approach to infertility. The success we have at Maia with older women conceiving naturally with their own eggs is due in great part to the willingness to commit to living a fertile lifestyle. For many that includes a complete overhaul in their approach to life. Take Peggy, for example, a 38-year-old single woman when she came to see us at Maia.

Peggy had been at the top of her career for years. She owned her own home. She knew a fair amount about nutrition and health but work and getting through the week had been of greater priority for her since she took this job five years ago. On the weekends she took long walks and cooked lots of healthy foods. The rest of the week she ate well, but infrequently, and often from foods she picks up when she was at work. She had frequent insomnia. She saw a therapist. Since she turned 36 her menstrual cycles had gotten a little shorter and she did not menstruate for as many days each month.

One day Peggy woke up and realized that if she didn't become a mother soon she might not ever do it. She realized that she didn't just want a child to fit into her busy life; she wanted to be a mother and work her life around that. She felt it was time for a complete overhaul. As part of this plan of hers she came to Maia. When she came in she had just given notice at her job. She had decided to downsize her expenses and not work for six months in order to prepare for parenthood. She was tapering off of her antidepressant with the help of her therapist. She decided to learn to meditate. She was taking a meditation class at her community center every week. Peggy planned to spend her days exercising, taking naps, doing creative projects, cooking healthy foods, and reading. She was planning to take in a roommate to offset her bills. She was changing her approach to life.

At her first appointment we primarily covered fertility awareness and congratulated her on her major life changes. We also helped her clarify what her sperm options were.

For the first two months after stopping work she had an identity crisis. She was afraid this was from going off her medication. However, she also realized that she had been working all of her life. She had never realized how wrapped up in work her identity was. She felt like she was grasping at straws—who was she? She decided to give it a few more months before deciding if she needed to go back on her medication.

By the third month she was loving life. She came back in to see us. We looked at her charting and were able to point out the menstrual irregularities. She felt like she was eating amazingly well. Her stress was markedly decreased. She was sleeping more than she had ever imagined was possible. She was exercising regularly. We recommended the following things: regular orgasms, taking a yoga class, drinking a quart of fertility tea a day, and acupuncture. We also suggested vitex, an herb also known as chaste tree berry, but suggested that if she was going to get acupuncture she first see if her acupuncturist would include it in her herbal blend.

By the fifth month she felt that she had never been so happy, healthy, or relaxed. Her menstrual cycles were evening out and her fertility signs were strong. She decided it was time to start inseminating. She realized that if she could take in another roommate, do very part-time consulting, continue to live simply, and use a known donor, she wouldn't need to return to work until the baby was two years old. A good friend of hers was willing to be a donor.

She self-inseminated at home with two inseminations a cycle. She got pregnant on the fourth month. She gave birth to her baby two days before she turned 40. Peggy is convinced that she may never have gotten pregnant if she'd stayed in her past life—or at the very least would have ended up in a fertility clinic.

The following information builds upon that in the previous two chapters. These three chapters together present a comprehensive picture for making the most of your body's innate resources to conceive and grow a healthy baby. First we will cover which chemicals, medicines, and products to avoid, both during preconception and in pregnancy, and then provide specific suggestions for enhancing your fertility.

Our bodies interact with our physical environment in thousands of invisible yet profound ways. How the environment influences our hormonal balance specifically is, to a great extent, still shrouded in mystery. Advances in technology and industrialization have introduced new chemicals into the environment at a rate that exceeds our ability to track the long-term negative consequences to our bodies. Nevertheless, you have at your fingertips many simple ways to lower your exposure to toxins and chemicals that may inhibit your fertility. Many ancient and recent healing philosophies offer insight into optimizing fertility health, and easy-to-obtain supplements and herbs can have a far-reaching impact on regulating an irregular menstrual cycle.

Fertility Inhibitors

Foods to Reduce or Avoid

Quite a few of the foods people regularly ingest are known to decrease fertility. The following sections will review these fertility inhibitors.

STIMULANTS

One of the most direct ways to increase your fertility is to remove all stimulant intake: caffeine, cigarettes, sugar, and any other stimulants. We will discuss addiction to adrenaline and stress later on. Giving up stimulants is often the hardest change for people to make in their lifestyle.

Stimulants serve many purposes, including acting as appetite suppressants. Stimulants allow us to function at a level we wouldn't usually be able to maintain without the assistance of artificial energy. Many people have ingested stimulants on a daily basis since their teenage years or even earlier, and thus stimulants have become an integral part of their lives. In addition, stimulants such as coffee are central to many social interactions.

Stimulant cessation may prove to be a major lifestyle change for you. Please transition gently, with compassion for yourself during the inevitable withdrawal period. Know that stimulant withdrawal is often accompanied by headaches or severe mood swings that can last for a number of days. Many people find that homeopathic remedies and acupuncture ease this transition. Also, don't forget to increase your water intake during this time.

Sugar. One of our most important recommendations—and something that may be a daunting prospect—is to eliminate refined sugar from your diet. Sugar is an appetite suppressant and immediately raises blood-sugar levels after ingestion. In response to higher blood-sugar levels your body secretes a lot of insulin. As soon as the insulin starts to work your blood swings toward a sugar low. A sugar low makes you feel tired, sluggish, and emotional. Often this causes you to eat more sugar and thus continue the yo-yo cycle of high and low blood sugar. If you reread the section on low blood sugar earlier in the chapter, you'll see that ignoring your body's signals of hunger for nutritious food will cause a sugar craving.

One way to eliminate sugar is to approach the problem indirectly. We recommend that you focus on regular eating of nutritious food instead. For example, we recommend that you eat some protein every three hours. If you regularly eat protein-rich foods, you'll probably reduce the frequency of your sugar cravings. Our next suggestion is to restrict eating sugar to times following a protein-rich meal or snack. This decreases its impact and the quantity that you are likely to ingest. Sugar needs to play a supporting role in your diet, not a leading role.

It's essential to monitor and reduce your intake not only of refined sugars but also of "natural" sugars. Dried fruit and fruit juices contain high amounts of quickly absorbed sugar. Eating whole grains, fresh fruits, fresh vegetables, and healthy meats while eliminating sugars helps to stabilize your blood sugar and insulin levels. For more information on regulating your blood sugar, read *The Zone*, by Barry Sears. It's much easier to weather the mood swings of conception by keeping as many aspects of your life and physical being as consistent and stable as possible.

Aspartame. Aspartame is an ingredient in most "diet" and "sugar free" foods and drinks. Aspartame should very carefully be avoided by those trying to conceive and pregnant. Read labels vigilantly. Aspartame has been found to be detrimental to every stage of reproduction. It is suspected of causing birth defects and possible DNA damage. It affects fertility and sexual functioning in both women and men. It can also lead to miscarriage by triggering an immune response that attacks the fetus. In the digestive process aspartame is naturally heated to a level where it becomes poisonous to the body.

Caffeine. Giving up caffeine may dramatically increase your fertility. Studies have shown that caffeine can cut both female and male fertility by up to 50 percent. Caffeine intake can also significantly increase your chance of miscarriage. Caffeine consumption depletes the vitamins and minerals in your body by interfering with absorption; it reduces iron absorption by up to 50 percent. So if you're using a known sperm donor, be sure to ask him to give up caffeine or reduce his intake as well. Just removing caffeine from both of your diets may significantly decrease the amount of time it will take for you to conceive. Giving up caffeine now means you won't have to go through withdrawal headaches during pregnancy. This means giving up caffeine throughout the whole cycle, not just the first half. It has the greatest benefit if you stop caffeine at least three months prior to conception.

Caffeine comes in many forms; chocolate, soda, and coffee are the most popular. Black tea has less caffeine than coffee, green tea even less. Unless you're buying water-filtered decaffeinated coffee, decaf coffee beans have been soaked in acetone, the primary chemical in nail-polish remover, as part of the decaffeination process. Green tea has beneficial herbal properties, including powerful antioxidants, especially if steeped less than three minutes; thus, switching from coffee to tea may be better for you than switching from coffee to decaf. Green tea has been shown to increase fertility. However, as it has caffeine it is still best not to drink it once you have a confirmed pregnancy. We recommend that you use the Maia fertility blend of teas (see page 207).

Take some time to examine the purpose caffeine has served in your life. For some it's a social ritual. For others it feels like it feeds the soul. For still others it's a reward they look forward to in the day. Others simply love the taste of coffee. Unless you determine what role it plays in your life and substitute something for it, you'll more than likely feel emptiness and a sense of deprivation when it's gone. If you like the treat of coffee, try some of the more exotic herbal teas, and add half-and-half, rice milk, honey, or lemon.

Many people don't realize that when they first stop drinking coffee they're going to feel exhausted by midafternoon. Some form of revitalization is necessary. To boost your energy, substitute healthy, nutritious protein-rich food. If you take a five-minute break to go for a walk, you'll raise your energy level by increasing your blood circulation. Some women take lunch walks with a coworker or get regular massages; others take tai chi classes. These suggestions also substitute an activity for the ritual break and socialization that coffee drinking usually involves.

It's often hard on a partnership if one partner gives up caffeine and the other doesn't. It's always a good idea for family members to engage in healthy patterns together; it makes change seem possible and lasting change more likely. For some, giving up caffeine is too large a step, and that's their personal decision. If you aren't able or willing to give it up completely, at least reduce your intake. Your goal is to reduce caffeine consistently, not just during the second half of each month you inseminate.

Alcohol. In moderation, alcohol ingested before pregnancy shouldn't have harmful effects on the pregnancy. However, regular nightly or binge drinking before pregnancy can impair absorption of many vitamins necessary for reproductive health, thus decreasing fertility and increasing the chances of miscarriage. If regular drinking is a part of your lifestyle, decide to eliminate it at least a few months before conceiving.

It's best to figure out how you can modify your lifestyle in a thoughtful way, one in which you can substitute other pleasurable activities or healthy coping skills—than to feel rushed to adapt because you find yourself pregnant sooner than expected. During pregnancy it's important to avoid all alcohol consumption.

OTHER FOODS ISSUES

Unhealthy fats. There is so much to learn about fats and our bodies. We highly recommend reading about healthy and unhealthy fats. It is best to eliminate all trans-fatty acids from your diet, as the FDA had decided that there is *no* safe amount of trans-fatty acids (TFAs). TFAs are formed when liquid vegetable oil goes through a chemical process called hydrogenation. This process converts some of the unsaturated fats into saturated ones. The process also rearranges some of the remaining unsaturated fats so their natural shape is turned into an abnormal shape. TFAs are only found naturally in minute amounts. Any amount is detrimental to health. Fortunately, trans-fatty acids are easy to avoid. They are found in commercially fried foods, high-fat baked goods, margarine, potato chips, corn chips, and processed crackers. To avoid use of the words "trans-fatty acids," as that has become a negative buzzword, companies also call them partially hydrogenated oils, and vegetable shortening.

It is also best to reduce the saturated fats in your diet. Saturated fats are found in meat and dairy products. Saturated fats are fats that turn solid at room temperature. When eaten in large quantities they can lead to obesity, heart disease, high cholesterol, and an increased risk of certain cancers. Eating a diet of fresh fruits and vegetables that is high in whole grains and low in processed foods and mass-produced baked goods such as cookies and chips will eliminate many of the trans-fatty acids and place the saturated fats in a healthy balance in your diet.

Wheat. Some diet experts are firmly convinced that the over ingestion of wheat can decrease fertility. We would concur that the ingestion of processed wheat in the form of flour does create a tendency toward decreased absorption of nutrients and thus decreased fertility. Likewise, there is some evidence that the over ingestion of wheat throws off the natural estrogen balance in the body. In fact, many of the women we have worked with who take wheat out of their diets do, indeed, conceive a few months thereafter.

We do not believe that everyone needs to eliminate wheat in order to get pregnant. However, in order to reset your digestive system and to observe whether or not you have a wheat sensitivity we recommend the following: for at least three weeks completely eliminate wheat from your diet. You will find that you will need to familiarize yourself with other grains such as brown rice, quinoa, amaranth, and millet. Notice how you feel. Notice your mental functioning. Notice your emotional balance. After this resetting of your system you may find that you choose not to return to wheat at all or to reduce the amount of wheat in your diet. Using a wide variety of foods creates a wider palate from which to draw vital nutrients.

Dairy. There are some people who claim that there is evidence that eliminating dairy dramatically increases fertility. We have seen that this can be effective for some people. If you want to try eliminating dairy, take the same approach as for wheat. Avoid eating dairy in any form for at least three weeks. If your diet is heavily based on both wheat and dairy, we suggest that you stagger the experiments. The intention is not to trigger feelings of deprivation but to allow you a chance to observe the effect on your body. Dairy has been known to increase inflammatory response in the body. Inflammation of any form decreases fertility.

Lactose intolerance. Many experts feel that most adults experience some form of lactose intolerance, meaning that they don't digest dairy proteins well. This can lead to stomach pains, flatulence, and bloating, and sometimes food allergy symptoms such as asthma or eczema. Ethnic groups with higher rates of lactose intolerance have generally developed dairy-free or dairy-light cuisines. Unfortunately, mainstream American cuisine is dairy-rich. Calcium is found in many sources other than milk, cheese, and ice cream.

Sufficient intake of calcium is crucial prior to pregnancy for hormonal regulation and during pregnancy for fetal development. Lactose-intolerant women who haven't yet focused on calcium in their diets should look at our calcium-rich food list (see page 164) and make sure they include non-dairy sources in their diets. Indeed, no one should rely solely on dairy for their calcium intake, as dairy products are one of the leading food allergens and contain high levels of pesticides, hormones, and cholesterol. There is evidence that the number of people suffering from some level of food allergy or lactose intolerance, both of which effectively limit the absorption of calcium, is actually quite high, suggesting further that all should work to include a variety of nondairy calcium sources during preconception and especially during pregnancy and lactation.

Environmental Toxins

Because of the difficulties inherent in assessing one's true risk to toxin exposure, we encourage you to take seriously what information is available and to err on the side of caution when exposing yourself (and possibly your baby) to toxins during preconception, pregnancy, and breastfeeding. Ultimately you must make your own choices about what level of risk you're comfortable exposing yourself to. Often, avoiding certain environmental toxins is out of anyone's individual control. You may react to this by not making any changes, as the changes you can make may seem insignificant compared to what you can't change. Our belief, however, is that any reduction of your toxin exposure is significant, and there are all sorts of creative yet simple ways to reduce your exposure to all sorts of fertility-inhibiting toxins.

Toxins abound in work and home environments, outdoors and indoors. People may be exposed to toxins through specific hobbies and activities they enjoy. Toxins are found in food, water, air, and soil. Our environment is full of numerous pollutants and toxins that can inhibit both male and female fertility. Unfortunately, the information available to the public on toxins and reproductive health is inadequate. Some chemicals cause little damage if exposure is minimal, yet many have a cumulative effect whereby years of low exposure can concentrate them in the body to a significant and potentially harmful level. The effects of many chemicals are not immediately apparent, and obtaining unbiased information about the possible toxic reproductive effects of chemicals is often difficult, since researchers and scientists are often heavily pressured from various industries to underreport problems. In addition, it's difficult to sort out exactly which chemical out of thousands may be linked to a birth defect over the course of a pregnancy. In their first few weeks of development, fetuses are much more susceptible to low doses of chemicals than grown adults. Little is known about the toxicity of chemicals to developing fetuses, and even less is known about how chemical exposure affects fertility.

REDUCING TOXINS AT HOME

Housecleaning. Using nontoxic cleaning products is a significant and simple change you can make to reduce your daily interactions with toxic chemicals. Many common cleaning products are quite toxic, not only to you but also to children and pets. Studies are now showing that hazardous chemicals used in everyday household products end up in the bodies of unborn children (as verified through umbilical-cord blood).

Chlorine combines with organic compounds to cause a variety of negative effects on fertility. Chlorine is found in chlorine bleach, bleached menstrual products, chlorinated water, and water contaminated by pesticide runoff. We recommend that you do not use chlorine bleach. Use gloves when cleaning, and open windows for good ventilation. If you're starting to inseminate, have a housemate or partner trade household responsibilities so that you won't be exposed directly to toxic cleaning products. Environmentally safe cleaning products are available in health- food stores and on-line.

Laundry detergents. It is essential that we all start using natural detergents and avoid continued use of the cleaning agents called nonylphenol ethoxylates (NPEs), use extensively in the manufacture of laundry detergents. Canada and the European Union have both banned their use. But in 2004 alone the U.S. used 260 million pounds, and the use is growing. NPEs have been found in more than 60 percent of the streams tested. Detergents are the biggest source. According to the Sierra Club, "Extensive research indicates that even tiny concentrations of NPE metabolites interfere with the ability of fish and shellfish to grow, reproduce and survive. By mimicking the natural hormone estradiol and disrupting the endocrine system, these chemical compounds cause organisms to develop both male and female sex organs; increase mortality and damage to the liver and kidney; decrease testicular growth, the formation of sperm, and testosterone levels in male fish; and disrupt normal male-to-female sex-ratios, metabolism, development, growth and reproduction." If this is the hormonal affect on fish, imagine the effect on humans and fetuses. Effective substitutes can be found in your local health-food store.

House repairs. When making repairs and improvements around the house, keep in mind that many toxic chemicals are found in paint, caulk, solvents, glues, and finishes, and should therefore be avoided. If someone is using these products in a space you plan to be in, at the very least open a window so that the area is well ventilated before you enter it. Ideally, depending on the toxicity of the product being used, you should thoroughly ventilate the area for a minimum of two days before reentry. Whenever you use paint products, be sure to follow the safety guidelines of your public health department or paint store to avoid exposure to old lead-based paint. Nontoxic paints are available at many hardware and home improvement stores. Be aware of the off gassing of carpets, foam, particleboard, flame retardant mattresses and other products made with formaldehyde.

Dry cleaning. Dry-cleaning chemicals are particularly toxic. Environmentally friendly dry-cleaning businesses, however, are beginning to appear. If you can't find one, at least throw out the dry-cleaning bag after you pick up your clothes from the cleaner and air your clothes outside, if possible, before putting them in the closet. Don't leave your dry cleaning sitting in a hot car. The off-gassing of the chemicals in an enclosed space increases the intensity of your exposure to them.

Gardening. While gardening, you'll want to minimize or eliminate your use of chemical fertilizers and pesticides. Use organic fertilizers and employ natural methods to control garden pests. Wash store-bought fruit and vegetables—whether they're organically or conventionally grown—with soap and water. Many resources exist to help you find alternatives. For helpful tips, visit www.backyardorganicgardening.com or www.greengardener.co.uk.

REDUCING TOXINS IN YOUR PERSONAL CARE

Tampons. Many women are unaware that toxins are present in brand-name pads and tampons. Most tampons contain absorbency enhancers that may include polyester, rayon, or asbestos, as well as metals linked to infertility, such as boron. Synthetic fibers in conventional tampons can cause vaginal inflammation and irritation. The rayon in many tampons depletes natural magnesium from the vaginal tissue, leaving it more susceptible to infection from bacteria such as *Staphylococcus aureus*, which is linked to toxic shock syndrome. To make their products white, tampon manufacturers bleach the materials with chlorine, which gives off a by-product called dioxin. Dioxin is most highly absorbed through mucus membranes—the vagina. Dioxin builds up in the body over time and has been linked to reproductive cancer and birth defects.

Perfumes and fragrances in deodorizing tampons can upset the naturally healthy microbial balance of the vagina and cause irritation and an allergic reaction. Super-absorbent tampons absorb not only blood but also vaginal fluids that help cleanse and balance the vagina's natural bacteria. If the natural bacteria aren't in proper balance, vaginal infection can occur. Infection increases the amount of white blood cells in the vagina, but large numbers of white blood cells will attack sperm, recognizing them as "foreign." Thus, infection makes the vagina less "sperm-friendly" and can reduce your chances of conception. Many natural fertility specialists consider tampons to decrease fertility by decreasing the production of fertile mucus.

Nowadays women have a large selection of improved products to choose from. If you choose to use tampons we suggest that you use eco-friendly tampon brands that have no fragrances and are unbleached. Use the lowest absorbency possible, and change tampons frequently. Don't sleep all night without changing your tampon. Instead, consider using pads at night. If you're using disposable pads, use fragrance-free unbleached pads, available at health-food stores or on-line.

Consider using washable cloth pads, a menstrual sponge (a natural sea sponge you can rinse out and reuse), or menstrual cups such as the Keeper (which is reusable) or Instead (which is disposable).

Douching. The vagina has a unique immune system composed of healthy bacteria that keep its pH balance very acidic, so that other bacteria (such as those in the rectum) have trouble growing there. The vagina naturally self-cleanses with an outward flow of vaginal secretions and cervical fluid. Douching is unhealthy for the natural balance of bacteria in the vagina, since it washes out healthy bacteria. If a douche is store-bought and contains perfumes, deodorants, or dyes, it can chemically irritate the vaginal tissue, causing an inflammation that is not conducive to conception. Finally, douching can be dangerous during pregnancy, as it may push fluid up through the cervix and into the bloodstream, interrupting pregnancy and potentially causing harm to the mother and baby.

Other personal products. During preconception, pregnancy, and postpartum, avoid using nonorganic hair dyes and hair bleach as well as chemicals used for permanents. Be aware that the fumes from most nail polish and nail polish removers are toxic and very readily absorbed when you breathe them. Nontoxic nail polishes are available at health-food stores and some fashion boutiques. If possible, paint your nails outdoors. If you get pedicures and manicures, make sure the room is well ventilated. Avoid using pHisoHex or any other antiseptic skin cleanser containing hexachlorophene, which is considered toxic for pregnancy.

Phthalates. Phthalates are industrial chemicals used in cosmetics, as solvents, and to soften plastic. Phthalates can be absorbed through the skin, ingested as fumes, ingested when leached into foods, or when children bite or suck on toys or pacifiers. Phthalates are found in many leading beauty products, from perfume to deodorant to hairspray. Hundreds of animal studies have shown that phthalates can cause liver damage, kidney damage, lung damage, and reproductive harm. Also, studies are indicating harm to the developing fetus. The people with the highest level of exposure are women age 20 to 40. There are things that you can do to reduce your exposure. Store your food in glass containers, only purchase body products that are known to be phthalate-free (see www.nottoopretty. org/resources.htm), avoid purchasing new vinyl products or vinyl flooring, purchase cloth shower curtains, microwave with glass and not plastic, and avoid the fumes out-gassed by new products by letting them air out for a few days to a few weeks before use.

REDUCING TOXINS IN ARTS AND CRAFTS

Think carefully about any crafts or other projects in which you partake regularly and whether you need to modify them. Many reproductively toxic chemicals are found in solvents, glues, paints and varnishes, dyes, and detergents. Also, many crafts require chemicals that contain toxic metals such as lead, mercury, and boron. Consider using alternative products during preconception and pregnancy, reduce the frequency of your projects, or reduce your exposure by wearing protective clothing and ventilating your workspace.

CIGARETTE SMOKE

During pregnancy, smoking increases the likelihood of low-birth-weight babies, preterm labor, stillbirth, and miscarriage. The toxic chemicals in cigarettes target the lung cells so that babies born to smoking moms may have precancerous changes in their lung tissue at birth, even though no cigarette smoke has directly entered their lungs. The nicotine to which a baby is exposed in the uterus permanently changes the biochemistry and nerve patterns of his or her brain. This appears to be related to the higher rates of criminal activity, drug addiction, and attention-deficit disorders of children born to smokers. Also, on average, children whose mothers smoked while pregnant demonstrate lower IQ scores.

Smoking while trying to conceive can negatively affect how the cilia (tiny fibers) in the fallopian tubes work to move the egg and then the embryo toward the uterus. The chemicals inhaled in cigarette smoke also cause many vitamins and nutrients—especially vitamin C—that are important for optimal fertility to be leached from the body. Nicotine penetrates the body's tissues so deeply that it has been found in Pap smears. Smoking also destroys estrogen.

If you smoke, start decreasing how much you smoke several months before you start trying to conceive. This is important if you use smoking as a response to stress, since trying to conceive can be quite stressful, and you'll want to have enough time to implement healthier ways of dealing with stress before you feel challenged by the emotional roller coaster of inseminating. Also, as you cut back and eventually quit, take a daily multivitamin that contains vitamin C, the B vitamins, and E to help replace the vitamins you've lost from cigarette use. Eliminate any exposure you may have to secondhand smoke from family and friends as well as at social events or in the workplace.

Smoking requires deep, slow breathing, so be sure to focus on continuing to breathe deeply and slowly a few times a day after you quit. Although you may not realize it, in this way smoking is similar to a relaxation exercise. Smokers also have an excuse to go outside during the workday. When you quit smoking, coworkers might not understand that you should be entitled to that time and fresh air also. Smoking is also often a social connecting point, so when you quit you need to find alternative connecting points. Know that quitting smoking can feel like a big loss—just from the point of socializing. Whatever perk smoking brings, you need a substitution.

Having a cigarette or smoking a joint often relates to communication patterns. If a conversation gets too intense, you may be used to leaving to go smoke as a way of ending the conversation. It's important to recognize if you use smoking in this way. Because you no longer have an easy excuse to leave the room when you need a break, you might find yourself feeling trapped or angry and not knowing why.

Ask for the support you need during the preconception period, just as you would if you were pregnant. We understand that quitting smoking often takes a number of tries and a lot of support, whether through smoking-cessation programs, friends, or family. Consult your local public health department or the American Lung Association for resources. Herbal and homeopathic smoking-cessation remedies are also available in most health-food stores.

Over-the-Counter Medicines and Herbal Remedies to Avoid

Many medicines are best avoided in pregnancy, especially in early pregnancy. A few days after conception, blood flow has not yet been exchanged between embryo and mother. By six to ten days after conception, however, the embryo has implanted itself in the wall of the uterus, and the exchange of blood has started. At this point the embryo is most susceptible to exposure to drugs or toxins, up through about eight weeks from the last menstrual period. Once you begin inseminating, you're spending each second half of your cycles in the possible pregnancy zone, so it's a good idea to take a careful look at the medications you take.

The United States Food and Drug Administration has created a drug classification system that assigns each drug to one of five categories—A, B, C, D or X—relating to is effect on pregnancy. To determine what classification a drug is, look it up in the *Physicians' Desk Reference*.

ANTIHISTAMINES AND DECONGESTANTS

Avoid antihistamines and decongestants, including Sudafed, Ma-huang, Ephedra, and Osha root, as they can dry up mucus, including fertile mucus, which you need to conceive. Avoid cold and flu formulas, most of which contain antihistamines and decongestants. The herb echinacea is safe to take during pregnancy, but goldenseal root (which often is compounded with echinacea in herbal preparations) should be avoided.

LAXATIVES AND DIURETICS

Avoid most laxatives, including senna, aloe, castor oil, turkey rhubarb, buckthorn, and cascara sagrada.

It's also best not to take over-the-counter diuretics (products that make you urinate more) nor herbal diuretics such as buchu, horsetail, and juniper berries. Avoid motion sickness or antinausea drugs (Bendectin) as well. Do not ingest large amounts of herbs containing steroid-like ingredients, including agave, ginseng, licorice, hops, and sage, which can suppress your fertility hormones. For these same reasons, in the first trimester avoid eating copious amounts of basil or parsley.

When you see a physician or other health practitioner, let him or her know if you're going to start inseminating soon, or are already, as some medicines have a long half-life, meaning they stay in the body for a number of hours or days before being fully metabolized. Some vaccinations should be avoided for up to three months before conception in order to prevent infection-related birth defects in the first trimester. If in doubt, ask your health-care provider.

PAIN RELIEVERS

There is strong evidence that use of aspirin, ibuprofen (Advil, Motrin), naproxen (Aleve), and other pain relievers and nonsteroidal anti-flammatory drugs (NSAIDs) hinder implantation and significantly increase the chances of miscarriage. In fact, risk of miscarriage may increase by up to 80 percent if these drugs are taken around conception or used for longer than one week. Thus, when trying to conceive, it's best to avoid aspirin and ibuprofen. These medicines inhibit prostaglandin production, which in turn can inhibit both ovulation and implantation. Prostaglandins are natural chemicals essential to the working of the muscle in the ovary to release the egg and are necessary for successful implantation. Acetaminophen (Tylenol) is preferred by obstetricians, although it taxes the liver. Some clinics routinely use baby aspirin to increase implantation. Please only take baby aspirin under the care of your physician.

Dental Work and Mercury

At Maia we consistently see a decrease in fertility, a probable decrease in implantation, and a likely increase in miscarriage rates in women who are having extensive dental work. This is most likely related not only to the dental composites and the jarring to the body of the drilling, but also to the use of pain relievers that decrease fertility. There have been studies on mice that suggest that leached components from dental composites adversely affect female fertility and reproduction. On the other hand, getting your teeth cleaned regularly, preferably in a mercury-free dental office, is important for preventing tooth decay that can cause miscarriage or preterm birth.

Mercury is a highly toxic element that is found both naturally and as an introduced contaminant in the environment. Most Americans are exposed to mercury through consumption of contaminated fish. Mercury is released into the atmosphere through the coal burned at power plants, which falls into our water sources through rain. Mercury is particularly dangerous to developing embryos, which are up to ten times more sensitive to the effects than adults. It can alter the nervous system, which can result in delayed onset of walking, talking, cerebral palsy, and mental retardation. The Environmental Protection Agency estimates that one in six women of childbearing age in the United States has mercury levels in her blood high enough to put her baby at risk. Currently, the EPA recommends avoiding shark, swordfish, king mackerel, or tilefish altogether, especially for those planning to become pregnant, during pregnancy or breastfeeding, and for young children. Environmental groups contend that these recommendations aren't nearly stringent enough, and to this list they add tuna steak, sea bass, Gulf of Mexico oysters, marlin, halibut, pike, walleye, white croaker, and largemouth bass. Because fish offers important nutrients and protein to the diet, environmental groups suggest that pregnant women eat fish low on the mercury scale such as wild salmon. It is probably best to stay away from farmed fish as well, many of which have been fed with hormones and dyes.

Electromagnetic Fields and Radiation

Electromagnetic fields (EMFs) are present wherever electricity flows. Much controversy has surrounded the potential risks of living under power lines and near transistors, but strong evidence shows a link between increased EMF exposure and cancer. Studies also show increased miscarriage rates in pregnant women who use electric blankets. To enhance fertility and avoid miscarriage in early pregnancy, we recommend avoiding electric heating pads and electric blankets. If you have an electric blanket that you love, turn it on to heat up your bed before you get in, and then turn it off. If you regularly use a heating pad, try using a hot water bottle instead or fill up a tube sock with rice and heat it in the oven until warm.

Microwaves

Many microwave ovens leak as they get older. If you have one, have it checked for radiation leaks. And, of course, don't stand in front of a microwave oven when it's on.

Computers and the Workspace

A link between laptop use and decreased male fertility has been established, but it is harder to study the impact on female fertility. Nonetheless, for many reasons related both to repetitive stress injury and to the difficulties of accurately assessing factors that contribute to miscarriage risk, be mindful of the number of hours you spend in front of a computer and do not place the laptop on your lap if you use one.

Chemicals in the Workplace

The Occupational Safety and Health Administration (OSHA) requires all workplaces to provide information on any unsafe chemical to which a worker may be exposed. This includes chemicals that are unsafe during pregnancy. Employers are also legally required to follow standard safety procedures to minimize risk to workers. In spite of this, many workers—and this may include you and your coworkers—feel pressure not to take the time to comply with safety standards or do not have adequate protection available on the job. Unfortunately, employers' profit motive doesn't always prioritize worker health.

If you work in an area in which you're regularly exposed to chemicals and you choose not to tell your management that you're trying to conceive, it may be difficult for you to get the extra protection you need. Minimizing your chemical exposure is crucial not only during pregnancy but also for the months preceding pregnancy. We understand that being out about both being lesbian or bisexual and trying to conceive can feel like a threat to your job security at a time when you need it the most. Think carefully about what your best solutions may be, whether it's transferring temporarily to different tasks or being more careful about toxic exposure in your work routine.

Fertility Enhancement

Many diverse healing practices offer a variety of approaches to optimizing fertility. At Maia we have our favorite areas of complementary health and healing practices that we find especially effective for increasing fertility. For persistent menstrual irregularities, missed implantation, secondary infertility, polycystic ovarian syndrome (PCOS), endometriosis, short luteal phases, and fertile signs that don't line up we have seen many instances in which alternative medicine has helped to dramatically increase fertility. Used in tandem with healthy eating and fertile living these modalities can work wonders!

Practitioners of alternative healing practices are often found in the Yellow Pages, especially in large urban areas. Information about non-Western healing practices is also available on-line and in books. The descriptions that follow give a simple introduction to the philosophy of each healing approach, which may sound odd or difficult to understand if your conceptualization of how the body works has been limited to a Western medical perspective. Exploring alternative healing modalities for their potential benefits to your fertility is worthwhile for a number of reasons: (1) Non-Western alternatives to Western medical treatments often have fewer risks or side effects; (2) non-Western practices can work in conjunction with Western medicine to increase its effectiveness and ameliorate its side effects; (3) non-Western practices can increase overall fertility, health, and comfort, even if you don't suspect that you have a fertility "problem" requiring treatment. After our descriptions, we'll focus more specifically on the properties of various herbs and on ways to cleanse your body.

Acupuncture

Acupuncture and Traditional Chinese Medicine (TCM) is a system of healing and health enhancement that has been used widely throughout China for thousands of years. Acupuncture is often combined with Chinese herbs for greatest effectiveness. Chinese medicine strengthens a person's constitution through addressing areas of depletion or excess in the vital essence. Acupuncture also increases circulation. Chinese medicine views the entire body as interconnected with the mind and spirit. If you are having difficulty conceiving or want to begin your conception period in the strongest health we recommend undergoing a few months of regular acupuncture treatments to enhance your fertility.

Chiropractic

Chiropractic is much more than help for backaches. Chiropractic views the nervous system as the primary regulator of the body's other functions. Nerve patterns, and therefore other body processes, can become imbalanced by lack of alignment in the skull, spine, and pelvis, causing pain, illness, and less-than-optimal body functioning. By releasing the pressure on the spinal nerves that connect to the uterus, fertility is enhanced. Likewise, hormonal imbalances can be created by restriction of movement that can affect the pituitary. Adjustments made manually can realign the bones, nerves, and support tissues, thereby rebalancing the body, which may greatly enhance fertility.

Chi-Nei Tsang

Chi-nei tsang is a form of abdominal massage that utilizes breath, touch, and imagery to improve body functioning. It enhances the functioning of many systems of the body including the metabolic, digestive, respiratory, lymphatic, endocrine, nervous, urinary, musculo-skeletal, and reproductive systems. It is a very gentle form of massage that is also quite effective at releasing old emotional issues that are often stored in our abdominal areas. Chi-nei tsang sees these emotions as "undigested." It is very subtle, yet powerful work. It is especially useful for unblocking old scar tissue from ruptured cysts, em-dometriosis, and past surgeries. It is also particularly helpful for anyone who regularly experiences digestive difficulties. Fertility and proper functioning of the abdominal organs and intestines are intricately related. Chi-nei tsang helps to regulate and improve blood flow and releases stagnation from the area while simultaneously subtly adjusting the placement of the reproductive organs. We highly recommend it as a fertility enhancement treatment.

Maya Abdominal Massage

Maya abdominal massage was brought to the United States by Rosita Arvigo, who studied for twelve years under a Mayan shaman. Maya abdominal massage is a slow, deep, penetrating technique that releases deep muscle tissue spasms in the entire abdominal area, corrects uterine displacement, and facilitates increased blood and lymph flow to the reproductive organs and the whole body. These techniques help to adjust the regulation of the hormones as well. It is an external, noninvasive form of bodywork. Maya abdominal massage, like chi-nei tsang, can bring about amazing results. We highly recommend it for anyone who is over 35, anyone who has had abdominal surgery, anyone with painful periods, endometriosis, fibroids, anyone who has been told they have a retroverted uterus, and anyone having difficulty conceiving. Likewise, like chi-nei tsang, we recommend it for anyone who has given birth before, whether or not they plan to give birth again.

Osteopathy

Osteopathy is based on the premise that mechanical imbalances in the neuro-musculo-skeletal system predispose the body to ill health by reducing circulation of vital fluids, i.e., blood and lymph. On a practical level, osteopaths work with their hands, using highly developed palpatory and manipulative skills to get the best possible alignment of the spine and musculo-skeletal system. Osteopaths check the movements of the central nervous system to locate any areas that aren't moving freely. The treatment is used to assist what already exists in the body; helping to release the changed stresses and tension buildup. Osteopathy increases fertility by realigning the structural elements that if in misalignment can lead to fertility problems. As the treatments have a cumulative effect, a series of sessions is usually of more benefit than just one. Many people feel much more deeply aligned and receptive to pregnancy after receiving a series of osteopathic treatments.

Herbal Support

Herbs can encourage conception and healthy pregnancy by nourishing and toning the uterus, nourishing the entire body, relaxing the nervous system, and balancing the hormonal system, in part by providing a wonderful source of easily absorbed trace minerals and vitamins. One characteristic of tonic herbs is that they are safe for long-term use and they are gentle in effect.

When considering using any herbal supplement, it's important to understand how they work, for whom they work, and when to use them. Fertility herbs need three months or more to reach their full effect. Taken on a daily basis, the herbs we suggest will increase your overall health. The herbs we suggest are safe to use in tandem with fertility medications.

HERBAL TEAS

Red clover, nettle leaf, red raspberry leaf, and oat straw can be safely taken at any time in life. Because they are nourishing and toning herbs, they can be safely ingested as a tea on a daily basis. Since they have an overall ability to enhance the functioning of the female reproductive system, these herbs—taken together or alone—can be used during preconception and through pregnancy. We recommend that everyone planning to conceive drink a tea made of these herbs on a daily basis and keep drinking it throughout pregnancy and breastfeeding. Daily use over time significantly increases their effectiveness. Drinking daily herbal infusions is an inexpensive, relatively effort-free means of fine-tuning your hormones and inner balance.

There are a few animal studies that indicate that in high doses red raspberry leaf, red clover, and nettles may lead to anovulation and undue uterine activity. However, one to four cups a day prepared as we suggest is far below the level of concern.

IIIIIIIIIIIIIIIIIIIIIIIIIIIIIIIIIIIIIIIIIIIIIIIIIIIIIIIIIIIIIIIIIIIIIIIIIIIIIIIIIIIIIIIIIIIII

Maia Fertility and Pregnancy Tea: Always try to purchase or harvest organic herbs. Put a small handful of each herb in a one-quart glass jar, then fill it with boiling water and cover with a lid or saucer. Let it steep for a minimum of four hours; overnight is preferable. Strain the leaves out and store the tea in the refrigerator, where it will stay fresh for three to four days. Drink one to four cups a day.

Red clover is known for its ability to balance hormones. It's a rich source of calcium, magnesium, and trace minerals and supports various hormone-producing glands. Red clover also relaxes the nervous system.

Nettle leaf strengthens and nourishes the uterus and body. It also tones the blood, especially by providing large amounts of readily absorbed iron and vitamin C. It also helps increase the transportation of waste products from the blood and improves the functioning of the kidneys.

Red raspberry leaf nourishes the uterine muscle and endometrial lining of the uterus, as well as the other reproductive organs. Because of its effect on the uterus, one cup a day of raspberry leaf infusion throughout pregnancy has been shown to decrease the likelihood of a long labor or necessity of cesarean delivery.

Oat straw is very nourishing and calming to the nervous system. It is very high in calcium and can be combined with the above herbs to make a tasty and effective blend.

||||||||||||||||||||||||||||||||||||||||||||||||||||||||||||||||||||||||||||||||||||||

VITEX

Vitex is an amazing herb that is most readily utilized when taken in tincture form. It is derived from two plants of the genus *Vitex*. Vitex has a direct effect on the female reproductive system. It is a gentle, but incredibly effective herb. Vitex must be used for at least three months to start seeing results. Many herbalists feel that the results seen with vitex increase over time. Vitex is especially effective if you are experiencing luteal-phase defects—in other words, if the second half of your cycle is shorter than the first half of your cycle. It is also helpful if you have a progesterone imbalance, as seen in your short luteal phase; if your basal body temperature dips below your cover line in the second half of your cycle; as demonstrated through lab work or saliva tests; or if you have had miscarriages due to insufficient progesterone. Vitex normalizes the length of the luteal phase of the cycle and encourages greater progesterone synthesis. In this way it is also effective for people who do not ovulate.

Vitex works predominantly in two ways: it works with the balance of luteinizing hormone and follicle-stimulating hormone. This results in a shift of estrogen and progesterone ratios. Thus it indirectly increases progesterone during the luteal phase of the cycle. The second way that it functions is by modulating the secretion of prolactin, which can also produce the desired effect of a lengthened luteal phase.

Vitex is considered to be a very safe herb. Many herbalists recommend staying on it throughout the first trimester if you have known progesterone insufficiencies or if you have had miscarriages related to progesterone insufficiency in the past. Although most people experience no side effects, we have seen a number of people experience a month or two of menstrual mayhem while the body reorganizes the hormonal balance to a more effective one. Some people experience transient nausea or headaches while first using vitex. These side effects seem to be ameliorated by taking vitex after food rather than on an empty stomach. We have found the best results when people divide their dose up equally four times a day.

Detoxifying

Detoxifying is the process of releasing toxins stored in the body, especially those in the intestines, colon, and liver. A well-functioning liver processes the chemicals that enter your body and also helps to process the waste produced by the body itself. The liver is responsible for removing toxic substances from the bloodstream. If the liver is not functioning up to par these toxic substances circulate for longer in the body, causing all kinds of imbalances, including painful and irregular menstruation, heavy bleeding, low energy, acne, and general poor health. The hormonal balance needed for fertility relies upon good liver function.

At Maia we recommend that anyone hoping to conceive do a liver cleanse as part of preconception preparation. You need to do a liver detoxification program at least three months before you'd like to start inseminating. This is because the detoxifying process moves toxins from the deeper recesses of the body into the bloodstream and intestines on their way out of the body. As these toxins move into the bloodstream, they can cross the placenta and come in contact with your baby if you're pregnant. Therefore, once you are or may be pregnant, it's best to use remedies that support and nourish your liver, intestines, and kidneys instead of trying to detoxify them.

Acupuncturists and homeopaths offer sound treatments for helping to stimulate the body to clear itself of a number of chemicals, including heavy metals. Detoxification methods include the use of herbal and homeopathic remedies, acupuncture, enemas, juicing, fasting, and diet changes. Detoxifying your body is best attempted under the guidance of a trained professional.

Grain Elimination Cleanse

As part of your liver cleanse, we recommend that you also try a grain elimination cleanse. Once again, this should not be done when you are or could be pregnant. Many people have grain sensitivities that they are not aware of. Likewise, most people have chronically overloaded their bodies with excess carbohydrates, especially in processed forms. This is very hard on the body. Excess grain intake also creates insulin imbalance. Our clients have had life-changing results when they eliminate grain from their diets for three weeks—this is the grain cleanse. The repair of the intestinal track is complete within three weeks. However, if you eat any grain during that time the cleanse should be started again.

Many people find that after their cleanse they feel as though their digestion works much better, headaches are gone, eyesight is clearer, fatigue is gone, their thoughts are clearer. After you complete your liver and grain-elimination cleanse, it is important to reintroduce high-allergen foods and each of the grains one by one. The high-allergen foods are wheat, corn, soy, dairy, eggs, and nuts. Take three days to a week to notice the impact of each allergen and grain before introducing another. This way you can isolate and reduce the foods that your body is sensitive to. If you have a reaction to one of the foods, try eliminating it from your diet for three months and then try introducing it again. It is best to avoid foods that your body is sensitive to because allergic reactions create inflammatory responses, which in turn decrease fertility.

Priobiotics and Leaky Gut Syndrome (Intestinal Permeability)

The intestinal lining is a barrier that, when functioning well, only lets properly digested fats, proteins, and starches through to enter the bloodstream. The spaces in between the cells that line the intestines are usually sealed. However, if the intestinal lining becomes irritated, unwanted, larger molecules can pass through these normally sealed areas into the blood. The immune system registers these unwanted substances as foreign and triggers an antibody reaction. The more permeable the intestines, the more toxins enter the bloodstream. The more permeable the intestinal lining, the less the body is able to utilize the minerals it ingests. So no matter how many vitamins and the minerals you ingest, your body will not able to utilize them.

Causes of intestinal permeability include chronic stress, food allergens, intestinal infections, small intestine bacterial overgrowth, environmental toxins, excess alcohol, poor diet, and NSAIDs and other medications. This problem can be healed by removing the cause of the phenomenon and building bowel health with probiotic therapy.

"Probiotics" refers to healthy bacteria that contribute to the health of the intestinal tract. These hard-working bacteria keep us healthy by increasing absorption of minerals and vitamins and by improving digestion, especially of milk products. Probiotics improve our immune systems by producing antimicrobial substances that deter various bad bacteria. Probiotics produce B vitamins. Probiotics support healthy liver functioning. And probiotics help with reproductive hormonal regulation. It is important to supplement with probiotics at least a few times every year. Choose a high-quality supplement such as PB-8 brand, from your local health-food store, and take the supplement before bed for greatest effectiveness.

MAIA'S FERTILITY TIPS
- Drink one quart of fertility tea a day.
- Take essential fatty acids daily (Nordic Naturals is a well-regulated brand free of mercury and PCBs).
- Take a tincture of vitex.
- Do a three-week grain cleanse.
- Do a three-week liver cleanse.
- Take probiotics daily.

Take Charge of Your Fertility

We wish to leave you with the awareness that you have great influence over the state of your fertility. While a number of environmental toxins are decidedly detrimental to fertility, many creative options exist for avoiding and reducing your overall exposure to toxins. Beyond this, you have a world of diverse resources open to you to explore how to increase your fertility beyond its current state. Whether your focus is physical, emotional, spiritual, or a combination of all three, you'll find many ways to optimize your hormone balance and the functioning of your uterus, ovaries, cervix, fallopian tubes, brain, and other aspects of your body that are essential to conception and pregnancy. Optimizing your fertility is up to you and is within your power. We encourage all people planning to get pregnant to employ as many of the suggestions in these three chapters as possible for an easier conception and a healthier baby.

Part Four
Conception

CHAPTER 13

Welcoming the Baby

THE PROCESS OF making, growing, and parenting a baby is transformative. Just as your child will change your life when she or he arrives, the mere intention of expanding your family changes your life as well. You may be well on the pathway already and aware of how you've grown and changed so far. Perhaps you're at the beginning of the process and are just starting to imagine what your life as a parent may be like.

Acknowledging change is crucial to surviving and flourishing from it. A good metaphor to use is the idea of making space in your life for the baby, which includes making space for the changes that come with a baby. Most people imagine making room for a baby physically in their home, but we also mean making room in your heart, your relationships, and your day-to-day schedule, even during the preconception phase. How might you do this?

Intentionally set and affirm your priorities regularly, with both yourself and your partner, if you have one. Discuss not only what kind of parent you would like to be and why you'll make a good parent, but also specifically how you'd like your conception to be. Make sure your conception vision aligns with your values and worldview.

Regularly setting and reevaluating your intentions helps you affirm the place inside yourself that so dearly knows you want to be a parent. It keeps your desire for a child vital and vibrant, as a positive part of your life. Encouraging and strengthening your vision of family helps ease all parts of the decision-making process and keeps your relationship healthy. This is especially valuable in the face of naysayers and cultural pressure against queer families, single parents, and women trying to conceive who are older. The practice of naming and embracing your desires allows you to build a strong base upon which to center yourself, and will allow you to weather any difficult and unexpected challenges that arise.

Many parents-to-be make room in their home for their baby-to-be by setting up a special area or altar where they place items that remind them of the desired baby. This can be a physical place to center yourself and remind yourself of your love-for it's always love that draws us to make children. Some people find that making collages of the qualities they hope to carry forth in their child, or collages that represent the journey of egg and sperm, or any other part of their journey they would like to visually conceptualize. Some people find it helpful to consult other cultural or religious fertility preparations in order to discover something meaningful for themselves. Whatever form it takes, this place can be an area where you connect with the strength of your love and desire by visualization or communication with the baby-to-be, or it may simply serve as a visual reminder of your desire to parent. We know one couple who kept a menorah at their baby altar, and every night before going to bed they lit a candle and said a prayer about the baby. They continued this ritual from the preconception period through pregnancy. They felt it not only allowed them to feel connected with their intentions and the baby, but it gave them a time and place to connect with each other. It's helpful to set up some sort of visual prompt or ritual from the beginning. This practice will be especially meaningful if it takes longer than expected for you to conceive. Established rituals can help carry you through as time marches on.

Things to Work on Internally Prior to Insemination

There are a number of topics that are helpful to examine in your life prior to insemination. Not all of these pertain to everyone. Although we feel that finding peace in these areas is significant to increasing fertility, you may be unfamiliar with or wary of the idea that your mind and body have a reciprocal relationship. Regardless of your views on this topic, an awareness of your feelings about the following topics is at the very least interesting and may well help you gain insightful information about yourself.

If you've already been inseminating for a while with no success, examine the following issues and see if you feel any tension about them. The premise is that this tension is constricted energy, held in your body, that could otherwise be freed to encourage pregnancy. This is not a blaming approach. It comes from us to you in alignment with the theme of the book: Approach everything with self-love. Use only what you find useful.

Whether you've started inseminating or have yet to begin, you'll find it's beneficial to engage in self-reflective activities such as keeping a journal, receiving bodywork, getting in touch with your body through yoga or chi gung, or going to therapy or couples counseling. Only you know which of the following issues may concern you. In the following sections we describe a number that arise time and again for many women.

Your Relationship to Sperm

In the history of humanity to date, a woman or transman must put sperm into her or his body in order to conceive. Sperm is available in various forms—straight from a penis through sexual intercourse or deposited into a receptacle such as a jar; frozen in a solution; or centrifuged, washed, or otherwise separated from semen. Regardless of its form, it is sperm. A drop of semen contains millions of sperm. It's amazing. It's alive. It potentially contains the perfect component to help you start making your baby. Sperm, so microscopic, has a cosmic component: it will ultimately bring your baby to you.

Despite its amazing qualities, lesbian and bisexual women and straight transmen have a variety of responses to the idea of interacting with it. Some of these responses are similar to the responses some women have toward men in general. Many women and transmen are uncomfortable just thinking about sperm, let alone touching it. Often sperm reminds us of anger we may have that we, as women and transmen, are dependent on something outside ourselves and our love relationships to make babies from. Also, sperm has a particular smell that some people say revolts them. Many people are surprised by their reactions to sperm, since either they've never come in contact with sperm before, or it's been so long since they have that they've forgotten its unique odor. Most experience a visceral response to sperm, either positive or negative.

Some people can feel its aliveness. This can feel wonderful and powerful or "creepy-crawly." Some resent feeling as though there's another presence in the room with them; others feel that presence as the baby. Some women adamantly experience sperm as bad. Others experience it as sacred. Many women try to disconnect the concept of sperm from the concept of men.

For some it is difficult to connect with the potential of the sperm. It looks so unimpressive, how can it be the key to creating a baby? When the sperm seems so unimpressive, it is easy to feel disconnected from having faith in the process of conception. In such instances you may find it helpful to look at the sperm under a microscope to see its aliveness. This can be done at a clinic, or even by using a fertility lens or a child's microscope. Also looking at your or your partner's cervix being open and gushing fertile fluid can make the journey of the sperm seem more possible and real.

We encourage you to examine your feelings about sperm. Try to come to peace with the concept of sperm prior to insemination so that any charged feelings about it won't negatively affect your insemination experience. Make peace with it so that you can welcome it into your body rather than reject the very substance that will allow you to realize your dreams.

Both the woman or transman who will be putting the sperm into her or his body, and their partners, if they have one, should work to discharge any negative feelings they may have about sperm. We've worked with a number of families who've chosen clinic inseminations based solely on the fact that their partner wouldn't have to come in contact with sperm. We've also worked with people whose partners find sperm so offensive that they will only touch their partner with gloves on and can't imagine being sexual with her for days after she's been inseminated. This kind of response from your partner can feel humiliating and invalidating. Conception is usually a time when you not only need great support but also want to feel connected as a couple. It's a time to feel that you're in this process together.

We've heard multiple stories of women who discharged any negative hold sperm had on them by renaming it. Names such as "little spermies," "swimmers," "little guys," and "animalitos" are common. We've noticed a tendency in the English language to refer to individual sperm in the masculine, which is interesting since just 50 percent of sperm have male chromosomes and the other 50 percent have female chromosomes. Our culture portrays the egg as patient, immobile, receptive, and "feminine," while sperm are individual, competitive, powerful, dynamic, and "masculine," even in scientific writings. Recently, scientists have found that a large number of sperm must act cooperatively in order for one sperm to reach the egg, penetrate it, and achieve conception. Perhaps some of us would find it easier to embrace the sperm's role in conception if it weren't portrayed through a sexist perspective. Reenvision it for yourself if you need to.

The Child's Sex: Preference and Selection

Although both science and folk wisdom have devised many methods of influencing the conception process, none of these methods can guarantee that you'll conceive a child of a specific sex. (Likewise, just because you birth a child of a specific sex does not mean you have birthed a child of that gender.) Therefore, if you think you must have a boy, or a girl, it's extremely important that you closely examine the reasons for this before you get pregnant.

People who want to influence the sex of their child often have fears or concerns about raising a child of the "undesired" sex. Some are afraid of passing on sex-specific diseases to their child. Some are afraid of raising daughters; some are afraid of raising sons. Some hope to "balance" their family.

It no longer seems to be true that lesbians are giving birth to a disproportionate number of boys. According to current sperm-bank statistics, and those of our own practice, it seems to be balancing out, with female births and male births being about fifty-fifty. It is, however, slightly more common to give birth to a girl when using fresh sperm and slightly more common to give birth to a boy when using frozen sperm.

EXERCISE: SEX PREFERENCE
Whether or not you have a preference about having a boy or a girl, take some quiet time to explore the following questions and the feelings they bring up. Allow yourself to write freely and completely. No one has to see these pages, so try not to censor yourself.

⊚ What is a girl to me?
⊚ What is a boy to me?
⊚ Do I have a preference? Why?
⊚ What exactly am I looking for in my child?

Part of this discussion concerns our own histories and how our personal experiences have informed our desire to have a child of a specific sex and gender. It's important to explore our enculturation as female and our experiences as lesbian and bisexual women. Exploring the sexism involved in our histories is often particularly poignant for women who consider themselves butch, and people who consider themselves cross-gender, transgender, gender-fluid, or gender-queer. Continue writing for a few minutes or more on your history as a female and as a lesbian or bisexual woman. We have great power to change the labels and differences in treatment based on gender if we start exploring these issues in ourselves before we conceive. Gender enculturation begins in the womb. We can choose if and to what extent we would like to buy into this concept.

Conversations about gender often reveal past wounds and unexamined internalized sexism and homophobia. We feel it's equally important and equally challenging to raise feminist boys as it is to raise feminist girls. It's important to note that sex is the physiology we're born with. Gender is each culture's meanings and perceptions related to physical sex. With the growing recognition of transgender identities in our culture comes a greater understanding of how complex gender is and how someone's gender identity doesn't always match the sex they're born with physically.

At Maia, when we enter into these conversations with clients, we frequently hear things such as "I want someone I can play football with" or "I want someone I can dress in pretty clothes." Other beliefs have been shared with us:

- They're separatists and believe they'll be kicked out of their community if they have a boy.
- They have an unexplainable, tremendous dislike of one gender or the other.
- One partner has threatened to leave if the other partner births a baby of the "wrong" sex. In this case it's your relationship that needs examination. Are you ready to have children together if such a threat is involved?

Please talk to as many parents as you can about their experiences in parenting children of any sex and gender. If you want to nonmedically increase the chances of giving birth to a baby of a particular sex, read the following section for ideas. Do think carefully, however, about the above questions and how you'll feel if any techniques you try don't result in your having a baby of the sex you prefer. If, after exploring your feelings and the sources of your feelings, your preferences remain unwavering and a child of the undesired sex is unappealing, perhaps adoption is more appropriate for you. However, before becoming a parent, some introspection is needed about the core of these preferences. Because the "correct" genitalia does not guarantee anything but that. At Maia we sponsor a support group for the parents of transgender and gender-variant kids, so we can state unequivocally that some children are cross-gendered. This is a fact of life and will remain a fact of life while we live with a binary gender code.

Past Pregnancies

If you've been pregnant before, you'll have a different history in your body than people who haven't been. It's important to explore your feelings about that part of your past. It's also important to explore your body memories about these past times.

Those of you who have been pregnant and given birth before may have given birth during a time in your life when you were straight. If you've raised your child or children, you may wonder if it's fair to want children again. If you haven't raised the children you gave birth to, you may question your capacity and deservingness of parenting again. If you've given birth and given a child up for adoption, thinking about getting pregnant again may bring up suppressed guilt and other feelings about that time of your life. From a body-memory point of view, your body may still be weeping from that loss. We've seen women effectively prevent future pregnancies by experiencing "unexplained infertility," which ceases to be a problem after they're able to finish the emotional processing of that loss, or choice, or set of experiences.

If you've had past abortions, the experience can be similar to having given up a child. Often there are overlapping issues: If I chose no before, do I deserve to choose yes now? What if that was the one opportunity I was given? Will I now be punished for not wanting that baby?

Many women have developed ovarian and uterine symptoms after abortions, unwanted pregnancies, and miscarriages. Examples of this include endometriosis, ovulation pain on one side of the body, and ovarian cysts. Painful reproductive cycles are often related to suppressed anger, sadness, and feelings of betrayal. This is not to downplay in any way the seriousness of these situations, but rather to emphasize that we live in our bodies our entire lives, and the experiences we have are recorded like a map. Roadblocks come from areas of stagnant energy. Releasing those energies through movement, either emotional or physical, can free the pathways again.

EXERCISE: PAST PREGNANCIES
If you've been pregnant before, take some quiet time alone and allow yourself to write freely about this time in your life. Write about how you feel now, emotionally and physically. Is there anything you'd like to say to those babies or potential babies, born or not? Is there any healing you'd like to give yourself? Hold yourself in your heart and visualize yourself getting all the healing and support that you needed then and may still need now.

Past Surgeries

Our bodies need to recover from the traumas of surgical procedures that have helped us heal. Anesthesia masks the pain, but it still is logical that the body may retain memories of trauma that the mind might not remember. Because we don't remember the pain of the incision and internal manipulations, we often don't realize the long-term impact surgery may have on us.

Doing bodywork, meditating, spending time rubbing the part of your body that was cut, and writing in a journal are all helpful methods of clearing stress. Once again, the theory is that when your energy is not tied up elsewhere, you'll have more energy available for pregnancy. Cut down on the many messages your body is receiving and make pregnancy your focus.

We have actually seen amazing results when people seek help from particular healing modalities when they have had surgeries. If the surgery was not on your back or abdomen we have found that a series of osteopathic treatments can help to release the trauma and realign the whole body. If the surgery was on your abdomen, back, or uterus, we have found that some very specific massage techniques will greatly assist whatever work you do on your own. We have seen the best results from people receiving visceral manipulation, chi-nei tsang treatments, and Maya abdominal massage. All three of these modalities specifically help to realign the organs and to break up any scar tissue. Scar tissue can adhere to ligaments, the uterus, or fallopian tubes, any of which can impede fertility. Practitioners of each of these modalities can provide you with self-help techniques you can use at home between treatments for greater results.

Getting Comfortable in Your Body

Pregnancy is, of course, an extremely physical experience. Getting comfortable in your body helps to prepare you for a healthier, easier pregnancy. It's a great time to receive massage, start exercising, take a dance class, do yoga, make love, or masturbate. It's a great time to touch your own body lovingly, give self-massage, use lotions, and appreciate your body for the wonder it is. Do what makes your body feel good!

By focusing on nurturing your body, you can come to appreciate how amazing this body of yours is. Can you believe you actually have the capacity to make and grow a complete human being inside your body?! Celebrate this amazing truth prior to conception by fostering activities that connect you with the strength and beauty of your body. Doing so helps temper the emotional elements of self-doubt that can creep into an extended conception period.

Lesbian Conception

Some lesbians feel a strong initial aversion to the idea of lesbian conception. People report it feeling "unnatural," "unhealthy," and "wrong." The idea of "autonomous" conception threatens the ideas at the core of male-dominated society. If women can buy or borrow sperm, we can essentially conceive on our own. This threatens the fabric of our society and may feel disquieting. We have, however, the power to define conception in whatever way we choose. This realization can feel just as life-changing and difficult as coming out. For some people, coming out is painful and earth-shattering. For others, the transition is more gentle.

Allowing the mind to entertain the idea that you can conceive in any way that feels right to you—and that sexual intercourse with a man is not the only or "right" way—can take time. Often heterosexist ideas are so deeply ingrained in us that we don't recognize them. Letting go of this idea seems to be especially challenging for bisexual women and for women who were previously heterosexual.

Take the time you need to explore these ideas until you—and your partner, if you have one—feel comfortable with the idea that there are many valid ways to conceive. Once you've achieved this, you'll be ready to imagine how you'd like to conceive.

What Exactly Is Conception?

Once you've established where you'll obtain sperm, you're ready to conceive. Many people share with us that it wasn't until they felt connected with the spiritual aspects of conception that they were finally able to conceive. So what exactly is conception? The actual act of conception isn't discussed much in our culture. This silence appears to be linked not only to sexual taboo but also to cultural taboos surrounding life, death, and spiritual mysteries that prohibit us from talking about the unknown. Women who have intercourse with men often get pregnant "by accident." This may happen with lesbians who sometimes have sex with men, but more frequently lesbians fall to the other extreme: delaying pregnancy by painstakingly planning it. All people who get pregnant outside of using IVF (in vitro fertilization) have conceived, yet serious consideration is rarely given to how we'd like to conceive, to the act and meaning of conception itself.

Before you consider where you'd like to conceive or which method you'd like to use, spend some time examining your beliefs about conception. From a spiritual place, a religious place, a scientific place, what is conception to you? How does it happen? When does it happen? What are the answers you find inside yourself? Each culture and religion passes down a set of beliefs about when and how life becomes, and science adds a whole new dimension to it. But what holds meaning for you?

In Tibetan tantra, a baby is called into your body by your desire; it comes into your body through an energy vortex down through your head. Scientists say sperm from a penis reaches an egg in a fallopian tube, union occurs, and cell division begins. Some Native American traditions believe that babies were once little stars in Spiritland. Australian aboriginal culture explains that babies come from the earth itself. Some cultures believe a baby can only be conceived when two people have simultaneous orgasms. Others believe the entire future of a baby is determined at conception.

Some people think conception can't occur until a number of hours after insemination, because it takes time for the sperm and egg to meet. Yet others swear they feel it happen the moment sperm enters their body, or even just before. What do you believe? Have you thought about it?

Although you might not approach making a baby from a spiritual place, bringing life into your body often brings up these questions. Why is it that sometimes you succeed in conceiving, and other months you don't? Are you the one who controls your conception through timing, health, and a good sperm source? Or does something outside you determine this? Is it predetermined? Or is it just chance?

How you approach conception initially is often quite different than how you approach conception after you've been trying to get pregnant for many cycles. Your experience, your ideas, and your ideals may all change. There's no predictable quality to this change, but your approach to conception will more than likely deeply transform over time.

It's helpful to review your beliefs about conception if it's taking you many months to conceive. Doing so can give you new insights, deepen your faith, and help you remember things you may have forgotten.

CHAPTER 14

Timing Is Everything

AS LESBIAN OR single women, we almost invariably have limited access to sperm. This is sometimes the case for bisexual women and transmen as well. As a result, many of us choose to spend large amounts of money to procure this vital elixir. How much sperm you have available, however, is meaningless unless you inseminate at the right time of the month for your body. Therefore, *timing is everything*. This chapter covers in detail the steps you can take to make sure you're inseminating at the optimal time each month. By studying and claiming your own fertility, you take control of your most valuable resource: yourself. By familiarizing yourself with the information your bodies gives you, you can come to trust yourself and your decisions more fully. Your fertility cycle is so individual that the only way you can reach a comprehensive understanding of it is to explore your own body and its changes. You, and only you, have the ability to be the expert on your fertility. Don't abdicate this right—claim it!

Anatomy, Conception, and the Menstrual Cycle

To track your fertility effectively, it's important to have a working understanding of your anatomy and menstrual cycle. This will allow you to have the same basic understanding and working vocabulary as that of the fertility health care providers you may encounter. Many of us are carrying around limited, misguided, old, or incomplete information about our menstrual and fertility cycles. For example, plenty of people don't realize that all women don't ovulate on day fourteen of their cycle.

We'll provide an overview of anatomy and the menstrual cycle, and then discuss the tools you'll need to more deeply explore your own fertility cycle. You may wish to examine the diagram on page 240 before you read any further, in order to maintain a visual image of the inside of your body. It may also be helpful for you to rent *The Miracle of Life*, a beautiful and informative video on conception filmed with the use of special cameras.

The Anatomy of Conception

Let's start by describing your reproductive organs. Inside your vagina, if you reach deeply with your finger, you'll feel a protrusion that is slightly firmer than the walls of your vagina. This firm, round protrusion is your cervix, the opening of your uterus. The opening of your cervix is called your os. When you put millions of sperm into your vagina, about 10 percent of them will swim up through your cervix, into your uterus, and then about two hundred will make it into each fallopian tube. The journey from vagina to fallopian tube is about four inches and takes between a half hour to an hour to complete. Your uterus is an upside-down pear-shaped organ, usually the size of an apricot, which will become the home for your baby when you're pregnant. Your uterus grows as the baby grows.

At the top of your uterus on the right and left sides is a narrow area from which the fallopian tubes branch forth. These tubes are four to five inches long but are extremely narrow; the inner diameter is about the width of a needle, and they are open at the ends. Floating close to the ends of each tube are your ovaries. Each ovary is about the size and shape of an almond. Your ovaries contain all the eggs your body will ever release. In fact, as a fetus inside your mother's body, you already had in your ovaries all the eggs you would be born with. Eggs mature over our lifetime, but we never create more eggs. Each month many eggs begin to mature in each ovary, each within its own follicle. As the follicles grow, one follicle ripens most rapidly and becomes the dominant follicle. When the most dominant follicle is ready and an egg within it matures, the egg is released from the ovary. Ovulation is the moment the egg bursts forth from the follicle. Following ovulation, the egg is outside the ovary in the pelvic cavity, where it's immediately swept into the fallopian tubes by small feathery protrusions from the tubes called fimbria. The egg is then guided along the fallopian tubes into the uterus by tiny hair-like fibers called cilia, which line each tube.

Conception occurs after ovulation, usually inside the fallopian tubes. The egg is gently pushed through the fallopian tube, and the sperm swims into the tube via the uterus. Here they meet no more than twenty-four hours after ovulation. Conception is not an easy task. The egg is designed to allow only the strongest and healthiest sperm to penetrate it. It takes up to four hours for the sperm to attach itself to the egg and burrow its way in through the surface area, called the zona pellucida. If conception occurs, cell division begins and the embryo travels all the way down the tube and into the uterus, dividing cells and growing rapidly as it goes. This takes four to five days. Shortly after the embryo enters the uterus, it implants into the uterine wall.

Every person has a slightly different menstrual cycle. For some women, the first part of their cycle is longer or shorter than average. For others, the second part of their cycle is longer or shorter than average. For still others, the menstrual cycle is a varying combination of lengths depending on multiple factors. A normal menstrual cycle varies from about twenty-four to thirty-five days. For the sake of keeping this information simple, we've chosen to describe a twenty-eight-day menstrual cycle with one ovulation. The following is an overly simplified yet working overview of the menstrual cycle.

Many hormones in the brain and ovaries affect our fertility cycle. Four basic hormones, however, are at play in the menstrual cycle: follicle stimulating hormone (FSH) and luteinizing hormone (LH) from the brain, and estrogen and progesterone from the ovaries.

Follicle-stimulating hormone causes the egg to ripen and mature. Estrogen is at play predominantly in the first half of the cycle and helps regulate the release of FSH and *luteinizing hormone*. Progesterone is at play primarily in the second half of the cycle. It's secreted from the corpus luteum, in the ovary, and, coupled with estrogen, prepares the uterine lining to receive the fertilized egg. Progesterone maintains the lining of the uterus after conception and implantation, until the placenta is formed at around eight to ten weeks of pregnancy. At that time the placenta produces the majority of the necessary progesterone to support the pregnancy.

FSH gives the signal that encourages the follicles in the ovary to begin to mature. These follicles in turn secrete estrogen. Over the next seven or so days, the follicles ripen and secrete more estrogen into the bloodstream.

Estrogen signals the uterus to prepare its lining to receive and nourish a fetus. It simultaneously signals the cervix and cervical mucus to change and become receptive to sperm. Estrogen also sends the message back to the brain that the ovary heard the message from the FSH to begin follicle maturation and is responding.

Mid-cycle, around day fourteen for many women, a sharp increase in estrogen causes a surge in LH. This hormonal dance then stimulates ovulation of the body's ripest egg. This first part of your cycle, which is high in estrogen, is known as the follicular phase; it can vary in duration quite a bit, depending on how long it takes your body to reach its estrogen threshold.

After ovulation, the luteal phase begins, marked by high levels of progesterone. This phase usually lasts twelve to sixteen days. Following ovulation, LH signals the body to initiate the formation of the corpus luteum, which is the gland formed by the ruptured follicle following ovulation. The corpus luteum continues to produce progesterone to support an early pregnancy until the placenta is formed. If egg fertilization does not occur, the corpus luteum degenerates within twelve to sixteen days and a new menstrual cycle starts.

The luteal phase is more finite in length if your body produces adequate progesterone. Just as estrogen begins the preparation of the womb to receive a potential fetus, progesterone completes it. Over the next two weeks the uterine walls thicken. If pregnancy and implantation do not occur, progesterone levels fall, the uterus sheds its lining, and your period begins.

Fertility Awareness

Once you have a working understanding of the female body and the menstrual cycle, you can move on to learn the Maia approach to monitoring and recording your personal fertility information. Fertility awareness allows you a profound understanding of the workings of your own body and your unique fertility and menstrual cycles. The methods we outline are highly accurate and effective in identifying your fertile days. When you effectively chart your body's fertility signals, interpreting your chart and deciding when to inseminate can be approached in a straightforward manner.

The Rule of Three

There are many ways to establish your peak fertility time. None of them is entirely foolproof as an indicator on its own, but when used together as a "team" of fertility indicators, they will guide your timing for effective insemination. Through a combination of record keeping and various tests and self-exams, you will be looking for three indicators that are in alignment showing fertility, and that will be the time to inseminate.

For people who aren't partnered with a man with whom they wish to conceive a baby, good charting and proper interpretation are crucial to achieving pregnancy. This is because you'll only be inseminating one to three times per month, compared to the multiple times that partnered heterosexual women, and bisexual and trans-people dating men with penises might have sex. We strongly encourage you to start charting as early as possible — ideally *at least* three months prior to insemination — in order to maximize its value.

Fertility Awareness Can Be Empowering

Fertility monitoring and charting is something you do in the privacy of your own home. You're the only one needed to gather this information. You aren't dependent on anyone else to recognize your signals of fertility and how to interpret them. Despite this, many people find themselves relying on doctors to tell them when they're fertile. A doctor, however, can only know the fertility information of the generic woman. You are not generic, and with a brief amount of self-study, you can become the true expert on your fertility and thus an active participant in your health care.

Adequate Charting Is Crucial

The majority of the clients that we see don't chart anywhere near enough, if at all. You'll probably need at least three months to gather vital and appropriately useful information about your body. You should allow up to six months if you have irregular cycles. This means that like fertility enhancement, it's most valuable to begin thorough fertility tracking up to half a year or more prior to the time you plan to start inseminating. You can make any other decision about insemination overnight, if you have to. Fertility awareness, however, is not a decision. It's a simple system of gathering information about your body that, to be most effective, requires months of research.

Charting well from the beginning is the single most important tool you have to shorten the time it will take for you to get pregnant. Thus, even if you're certain you're incredibly fertile and that you'll get pregnant on the first try, chart anyway. If you don't get pregnant the first time, by the time you're ready to start charting, you'll have already lost valuable months of gathering information about your fertility cycle.

Charting is invaluable and must be done every cycle in which you plan to inseminate. It allows you to determine your fertile window, peak fertility, ovulation symptoms, and signs that ovulation has passed. Ovulation rarely occurs on the same cycle day from one cycle to the next—even in the most regular of menstrual cycles. So the most valuable information is always your most current information.

DO I NEED TO CHART EVEN IF I'M SEEING A FERTILITY SPECIALIST?

Yes! Everyone needs to chart. Fertility doctors have ultrasound and lab work to help you assess how your follicles are developing. However, no one has a crystal ball to see what exactly your rate of development will be. Therefore, any additional charting that you do will only serve to assist you in determining the best timing for you. Think of doctors as helping you to ascertain the best timing. Doctors may be experts on fertility, but you are the expert on your body. Please chart even if your doctor may not understand the significance of what you are paying attention to—you simply have complementary areas of expertise.

WHAT SHOULD I TRACK?

The purpose of charting is to ascertain not only when you ovulate, but the signs from your body that indicate approaching ovulation. Insemination occurs just before ovulation, thus it is essential to learn to predict your fertile window. You'll want to know when your egg comes out and what happens in your body to forewarn you that the egg is about to be released. Many people have an innate sense of their own fertility. Others don't have any sense of this at all. Even if you are clear about your fertile window, you may not know your body well enough to accurately plan for IUI timing. In the next section we'll examine the various signs of fertility—outlining for each how to observe and chart it—and examine the practical challenges and advantages of tracking each signal. When three of these signs line up, you're in a peak window for insemination.

IS FERTILITY CHARTING OBJECTIVE?

A fertility chart is a reflection of your personal fertility cycle. Therefore, your chart is inherently subjective. It's an illusion that certain signals are more objective and therefore somehow more valid than others. The signals that the medical profession tends to validate as being the most important are basal body temperature and the results of ovulation-predictor kits (for a description of an ovulation-predictor kit, sometimes called an OPK, see pages 252–57. Because these signs are externally obvious, they're somehow deemed more valuable. As you'll see, these signs are just as subjective as other signs you'll monitor. Yes, the average woman does experience a dip and a rise in her basal body temperature. And the average woman does experience an LH surge that can be detected by ovulation-predictor kits. But what these signs indicate in terms of each person's fertility cycle is different. There is no standardized body. Thus, we recommend charting many fertility signs to see which ones prove the most helpful and revealing for you. Ovulation-predictor kit results and basal body temperature changes may be useful indicators for you in combination with other fertility signals, but they may not be so useful on their own.

HOW MUCH OF THE MONTH DO I NEED TO CHART?

It's essential that you chart for the full month. For a chart to be most helpful, you need to be able to see your low, high, and peak fertility signals, as well as learn the signs that indicate that you've ovulated and that your fertile window has closed. As some people ovulate more than once a month and some women's cycles vary significantly in length, it's important to continue charting until you once again see your menstrual blood. Once you've charted in this complete fashion for three full cycles, you'll most likely be able to narrow your charting window to a ten-to-fourteen-day period.

DOCUMENTING VS. INTERPRETING

When you log everything you feel, notice, and observe, resist the urge to interpret the data as you go and to discard certain sensations as invalid. Record your complete experience without censoring it. Interpret it later as a second, separate step. When it's time to interpret your chart, you can reengage the discretionary part of your mind and determine what all the information means.

WRITE DOWN EVERYTHING

It's important to write down everything—both significant and what seems insignificant—when tracking your fertility. In our midwifery practice, we've worked with so many people who've conceived at unexpected times that we've come to appreciate the true breadth of fertility and understand that each person's body is unique. Many of the straight women we've worked with have gotten pregnant when they were menstruating, because they'd assumed that menstruation afforded them a window of infertile sex. How could they be ovulating when they're bleeding? It's remarkable how many women get pregnant when they're bleeding or at other unlikely times of the month. This phenomenon is caused by double ovulation.

DOUBLE OVULATION

According to the Western medical interpretation of female fertility, ovulation only happens once, mid-cycle. Although it's recognized that some women ovulate twice in one month, it is only considered to be possible only within twenty-four hours of a woman's first ovulation. Our experience has proved otherwise. We, and many other practitioners around the world have come to realize that for some women, and for some cycles, ovulation occurs more than once a cycle, often seven to ten days apart.

We've heard many women say, "Sometimes I have signs of fertility such as fertile mucus when I don't expect it, so I figure I'm checking it wrong." While showing our client Denise her cervix with a speculum one day, we observed a very open os with copious fertile mucus. When we asked her if she thought she was ovulating, she replied, "No, it's day eight." Then with raised eyebrows she looked at her partner and told us, "I always get fertile mucus on day eight and just ignore it, figuring I'm doing something wrong. On day fifteen it returns, and I inseminate." Denise went home and ran her ovulation-predictor kit out of curiosity: it was positive! It turned negative again and then turned positive once more with the return of her fertile mucus on day fiftenn. She'd been charting for a year and a half and had managed to convince herself each month that on day 8 she had forgotten what she was doing. We recommended that she expand her thinking, begin to document everything, contemplate the fact that she probably had a double ovulation cycle, and inseminate at each fertile window. The next cycle she inseminated on day eight and conceived.

Using the Maia Fertility Chart

At the end of this chapter is a copy of the Maia Fertility Chart. We feel that this chart is the most comprehensive and effective method of documenting your fertility cycle. Many people note their fertility signs in their date books or on scraps of paper. Visually reviewing a comprehensive, condensed, and consistent record of your fertility signals will allow you to interpret the information more effectively. It allows for an easy comparison of patterns that arise month to month. It also makes it easier for an outside professional to review. We recommend that you make photocopies of this chart and use it to monitor your cycles for at least three to four months before deciding whether it's useful for you. People with computer skills have found they can tailor our chart to their specific needs. We also recommend that you save all of your charts in a folder or binder. Be sure to also include the year. Please resist the urge to throw them away at any point. If your partner is also charting menstrual cycles, be sure to note whose is whose on each chart. Also, write legibly so that others can help you interpret them and you won't have to redo them in order to get reflection. At Maia we offer long distance chart review services for anyone who is not able to find knowledgeable providers of such services in their area.

Specific Fertility Signs and How to Chart Them

Begin a new chart on the first day of your menstrual bleeding. This day you'll call day 1, regardless of the date.

Basal Body Temperature (BBT) and Charting Fertility

Basal body temperature (BBT) is your body's resting temperature after at least three hours of uninterrupted rest. In the follicular phase of your cycle, the time leading up to ovulation, your BBT temperature is on average lower than your temperature during the luteal phase of your cycle—the time following ovulation until your next menses. Progesterone warms the body as it nurtures the growing embryo. It's essential for you to take your temperature at the exact same time every morning before you fully wake up, talk, or move around. Use a digital BBT thermometer available in any pharmacy. Many set an alarm, take their temperature, and go back to sleep. Although it's important to take your temperature daily, it isn't necessary to take your temperature on the days of your menstrual cycle. When your reading is at least two tenths of a degree higher than the highest reading of the previous six days, draw a long horizontal line over this number. This is called the "cover line" and is a demarcation in the chart between follicular temperatures and luteal temperatures. Many on-line fertility websites will help you to chart and interpret your BBT and assist you in determining your cover line and its relevance.

Some people notice a dip in their temperature with or preceding ovulation. Not everyone experiences this dip. The vast majority of ovulating women, however, experience a rise in temperature following ovulation. Tracking your BBT can be useful for a number of purposes.

You can use a BBT chart to determine when ovulation has occurred. Ninety percent of all people have ovulated when their temperature has risen above the coverline. BBT is most helpful retrospectively as a means of confirming and validating your other preovulatory signals. People who are able to use this tracking method find it an easy means of monitoring their fertility. BBT readings alone, however, are not a useful means of planning insemination because body temperature usually rises post-ovulation, which is often too late. But if you've done additional corroborative monitoring of your fertility and have found that your dip in temperature correlates consistently with the day that your ovulation-predictor kit (OPK) or fertility monitor reads positive and the day when your mucus is most fertile, then perhaps you can use this information for timing purposes.

You can also use your BBT readings to confirm that you do indeed ovulate. If you consistently record a biphasic chart—a chart that has lower temperatures in the first half of the cycle followed by higher temperatures in the second half of the cycle, you can feel quite confident that you're ovulating. A rise in temperature that stays elevated for twelve to sixteen days indicates a strong ovulation. However, if your elevation persists for less than twelve days, it may be revealing other hormonal imbalances.

BBT FOR IDENTIFYING A SHORT LUTEAL PHASE

BBT can be used to determine whether you're experiencing a short luteal phase of your cycle. People whose BBT stays high for fewer than twelve days more than likely have a short luteal phase (the time from ovulation to menstruation) and may have trouble sustaining a pregnancy to the point of implantation. This most frequently indicates a progesterone imbalance. Progesterone imbalance is the most easily recognizable and most common hormonal imbalance in women. Identifying a short luteal phase can be critical information, as you may not have any problem conceiving but may have difficulty maintaining a pregnancy.

If you suspect your progesterone is low you could choose to get a blood test or a saliva test to confirm. As progesterone is secreted in different amounts throughout the day, however, a blood test is less accurate than a saliva test and may show a normal reading when your progesterone is actually low. Other people use their BBT as all the reflection they need to start addressing the imbalance.

There are a number of ways to address progesterone imbalance. It may be quite helpful to check your cholesterol level. If both your cholesterol and progesterone levels are low, then low cholesterol could be a culprit—cholesterol needs to be at least 140 in order to help regulate progesterone (see chapter 4). Likewise, it may be a good idea to test your adrenal-stress index. When adrenals are overtaxed, the body must utilize progesterone to produce the cortisol necessary to respond to chronic stress. Finally, a very low-fat diet can also depress progesterone levels.

Reducing stress and supporting the adrenals can help to support progesterone levels, naturally. One herbal tincture that encourages progesterone production, if taken daily, is vitex. This is our favorite course of action at Maia because it has the fewest side effects. Another means of naturally increasing your progesterone is to use a liquid supplement, produced by Biomatrix, which is placed under the tongue daily following ovulation until menstruation or throughout the first trimester with pregnancy. As your progesterone comes into balance, you may find your menstrual-cycle length increasing, your overall sense of warmth in your body increasing, and your sex drive increasing as your body begins to produce more progesterone.

Progesterone vaginal suppositories may be prescribed by your doctor to treat progesterone insufficiencies. If you take suppositories, your menstrual cycle may be unusually extended. In fact, some people have to stop taking the progesterone in order to bleed. The side effects of progesterone supplementation can mimic pregnancy. Before discontinuing progesterone each cycle, some women like to have a blood test to confirm that they aren't pregnant.

If you conceive during a cycle in which you've been using a vaginal or liquid progesterone supplement, continue to use the supplement throughout the first trimester of pregnancy until the placenta is ready to take over progesterone production.

BBTS DIPPING BELOW THE COVERLINE AFTER OVULATION

Another indicator of progesterone imbalance is BBTs that dip to or below the coverline in the second half of the cycle. If these dips do not follow an explainable pattern—such as a night of drinking, a night of insomnia, being in a different bed, traveling, or some other variation from your normal routine—then it is safe to say that you are observing inherent hormonal fluctuation. This form of lowered progesterone can prevent implantation. If this is a consistent pattern for you, please either treat as a hormonal imbalance, or confirm with a saliva test and then treat—this phenomenon is too fleeting to be spotted on a blood test done on only one day of the cycle.

BBT FOR IDENTIFYING A WEAKER OVULATION

From our experience, when a person's temperature rises in a slow stair-step fashion and reaches its peak after two or more days, this is an indication of weaker ovulation—in other words, an ovulation that is less likely to result in conception. Strong ovulations are accompanied by strong, fast temperature rises. If you have a slow rise, consult the fertility- enhancement section of this book to boost this function, as this indicates less than optimal hormonal functioning. This is not likely to show up on blood tests, but would most likely show up on a saliva progesterone or adrenal panel. Vitex is quite effective in such cases.

BBT FOR IDENTIFYING PREGNANCY AND EARLY MISCARRIAGE

Some people track their BBT to try to determine whether they're pregnant or about to get their period. If your temperature remains high and does not dip when you'd ordinarily expect your menstrual blood, you're probably pregnant. If you experience a dip when you're expecting your menstrual blood, you'll most likely begin bleeding within twenty-four to forty-eight hours.

If your temperature has been consistently elevated for eighteen consecutive days, you can safely assume that you're pregnant. Although it's always terribly disheartening to miscarry, if you find that your temperatures drop significantly and you start to bleed following more than eighteen days of elevation, you'll be able to know that this is a miscarriage and not simply a late period.

BBT FOR IDENTIFYING A THYROID IMBALANCE

A consistently lower or higher BBT than average may indicate a thyroid imbalance. Many women's BBT is in the low 97 range, not 98.6 degrees. If your temperature is usually in the 96's, your thyroid level may be low, which can affect fertility. We rarely see conception occur in people who have a BBT lower than 97.3. We usually recommend doing tests to either establish or rule out thyroid issues and then boosting with enhanced nutrition and acupuncture. Likewise, if you have a consistently elevated BBT, you may have a thyroid imbalance. This can be easily determined with a blood test.

DRAWBACKS OF BBT

Although tracking BBT provides clear, readable charts for some people, for others it doesn't provide anything other than a confusing and seemingly random set of points. This variability is usually due to the numerous influences that can significantly affect temperature readings. For example, to have accurate readings you may need to (1) go to sleep at the same time every night and wake up at the same time every morning; (2) sleep soundly through the night; (3) avoid sleeping with pets that are in and out of your bed during the night; (4) sleep in the same bed throughout the week; (5) sleep in a room with consistent air temperature; (6) not get up to urinate; or (7) not drink alcohol before going to sleep. Unless these factors are consistent, there's a good chance that when you look at your chart you might not see a meaningful pattern.

Because BBT tracking is such a widely recognized method of monitoring fertility, many people feel like failures if it doesn't work for them.

Don't lose heart. A random-looking chart doesn't necessarily indicate that you aren't ovulating or that you have other fertility problems. More than likely it simply means that temperature charting doesn't work for you, which isn't uncommon.

At Maia we don't consider BBT tracking to be one of the most useful fertility signs for determining when to inseminate, especially as resting temperatures aren't reliable in predicting ovulation or preovulatory fertile days. Many people who do experience a dip in their temperature aren't able to know if they're at the bottom of their dip until a rise occurs a day or two later, by which time they're no longer fertile. Others experience more than one dip and are unable to know which one is the most significant until after the fact. Thus, the best use of basal-body-temperature tracking is to confirm that ovulation did take place and to help determine when that may have happened in alignment with your other signs. You can usually assume that you ovulated just before the rise. On the other hand, 10 percent of people ovulate after the rise. If your cycle is extremely regular—which isn't true for most women—you can make an educated guess as to when ovulation may occur during your next cycle.

The majority of people seem to be most fertile during the day preceding and the day of their deepest temperature dip. These are the best days to inseminate. If you have a known donor and you have only inseminated one time that cycle and you wake up with a clear spike in your temperature, you still have a chance of conceiving if you inseminate right away that morning. The egg will most likely still be viable. The same is true for IUI. If your temperature has already risen, you can still do an IUI as early as possible that day, but no later. For most people, though, resting body temperature readings aren't a primary fertility signal and are best used in conjunction with other fertility signals when deciding when to inseminate.

Phases of the Moon

Although most people are unaccustomed to tracking the phases of the moon, the moon phases play an important role in cultures with strong ties to lunar phases. Moon cycles are useful in determining many things, including insemination timing and the preselection of a baby's sex. At the very least, we suggest that you note in your chart the full moon and the new moon. If this is within a few days of when you usually ovulate, you may notice something meaningful—the mystery of why your signs are a little late or a little early some months may be solved. Many people's fertility is affected by the pull of the moon. Bear in mind that the moon exerts a pull on all the water on earth, including the water in your body. For example, if the full moon is two days after your usual ovulation time, you may ovulate a little later that cycle. Incorporating this phenomenon can help to reduce stress and increase awareness around variability in your cycle.

The Czech Psychic Institute has used the scientific elements of astrology to time ovulation and lunar fertility cycles. This methodology is built upon the belief that a woman ovulates not only mid-cycle, but also when the moon is in the exact phase it was in when she was born. For example, if you were born two days after the full moon, then every month, two days after the full moon, you are particularly fertile. They've also discovered that if you're menstruating at this same time, you're highly, highly fertile and even more likely to conceive. (Perhaps this is why so many heterosexual women conceive when they're menstruating.) If you choose this method, you must ask an astrologer which day of the moon cycle you were born on.

This same research strongly indicates that if you inseminate during "feminine" moon signs, you'll carry a girl, and if you conceive during "masculine" moon signs you'll carry a boy. These moon signs relate to the astrological sign that the moon is in during the actual time of conception, not the moon sign when you were born.

We share this information with you because often in Western culture it isn't easy to access information about radically different means of fertility monitoring and insemination timing. Perhaps this information will open up new possibilities for you. Charting this is optional but can be remarkably useful.

Mid-cycle Bleeding

Take special note of any bleeding you experience during the month. If you bleed at any time of the month other than menstruation (such as after sex or during the middle of your cycle) write down when it occurs, its color and quantity, and the days when you spot. This information may later be useful if you're unable to get pregnant right away.

Ten percent of all women experience mid-cycle bleeding, for which there are a number of causes. Mid-cycle bleeding can be as simple as a little spotting following or preceding ovulation, or it may indicate something more significant such as endometriosis, a sexually transmitted infection, hormonal imbalance, or cervical cancer. If endometriosis is the cause and it's severe, you may need minor surgery to clear out the buildup causing the bleeding. It's also common to bleed following an office procedure such as a Pap smear or sometimes following an intrauterine insemination. If you regularly bleed at times other than your menses, you may wish to get an initial hormonal panel before you begin inseminating to ensure that your hormones aren't significantly imbalanced. For safety's sake, you should bring any unexplained bleeding to the attention of a medical professional.

When you've inseminated and are newly pregnant—even if you don't necessarily know it yet—you may experience mid-cycle spotting following embryo implantation into the uterus. This is perfectly normal. Always share information about your bleeding with your fertility specialist. For some people, mid-cycle bleeding is a predictable fertility signal.

Ovulation Sensation

People experience ovulation sensation in a number of ways. It is common to be more sensitive to the feelings of ovulation on one side of the body than the other. Many people feel no obvious physical signs of ovulation. When you begin to focus more deeply on body awareness through the fertility monitoring and charting process, you may be surprised to note that you actually do experience ovulation sensation.

WHAT DOES OVULATION FEEL LIKE?

Ovulation sensation is a primary fertility signal. Some people are aware of approaching ovulation because of certain sensations in their body. Some feel only the actual ovulation, whereas others are aware of the impending ovulation several days prior. Some people feel a twinge or a small sensation of release—some feel this on both sides, some on just one side. This appears to be a distinct awareness of the sensation of ovulation. For some, ovulation is simply an open feeling or awareness of the area of their body near their ovary. Some may experience a buildup of sensation that lasts moments or increases over hours or even days. This may be a physical heaviness or ache, which is actually a response to the rapid growth that the dominant follicle is doing over the twenty-four hours preceding ovulation. Still others perceive ovulation sensation on a more spiritual level. More than one woman we've worked with has reported a momentary but intense depression accompanying ovulation, while others feel an intense high.

Some women experience cramping with ovulation. Ovulation occurs when the egg breaks through the wall of the ovary, which can cause cramping from the little bit of blood that gets into that peritoneal space surrounding the ovary. For some this cramping is momentary, but for others it can last a few hours. The pain can range from slight to intense. If over time you consistently only feel ovulation on one particular side or if it is a very painful, sharp feeling for you, then it is quite possible that you have either scar tissue or ligament tension in your pelvic area. Paying attention to this level of sensation in your body can help you to address potential fertility problems before ending up with "unexplained infertility." The best treatment we have found for addressing this situation is abdominal and uterine massage, specifically Maya abdominal massage or chi-nei tsang (see page 206).

NOTICE AND VALIDATE WHAT YOU FEEL

When you start to notice and write down the feelings you experience, without censoring yourself, you may become aware of many sensations you'd never noticed before. Many people note in their chart comments such as "Day 16: sharp twinge on right side; might be gas"; or "Day 18: slight achiness on left side. Day 19: lots of achiness on left side increasing

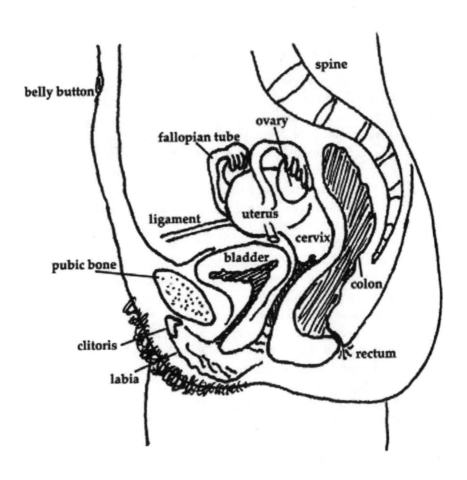

SIDE VIEW OF A NON-PREGNANT FEMALE

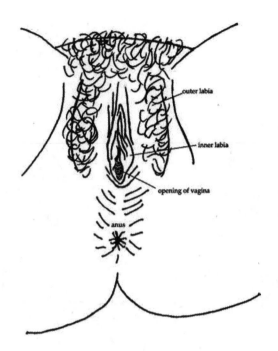

A FEMALE WHO HASN'T GIVEN BIRTH

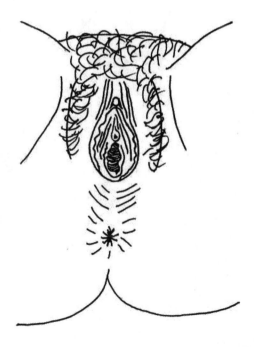

A FEMALE WHO HAS GIVEN BIRTH VAGINALLY

INSIDE THE OVARY, THE
CELLS IN A FOLLICLE
NURTURE A MATURING
EGG CELL AND PRODUCE
HORMONES.

CONCEPTION OCCURS
INSIDE THE FALLOPIAN
TUBE. CARPET-LIKE FIBERS
PUSH THE EGG DOWN THE
TUBE TO THE UTERUS.

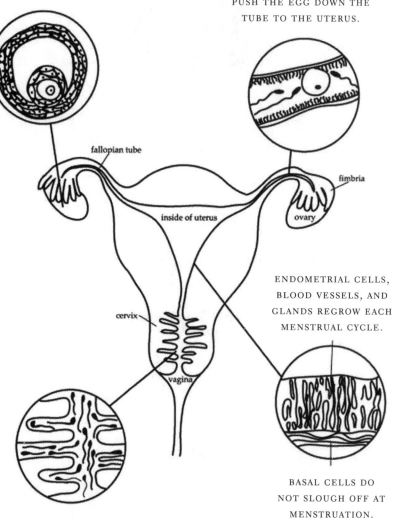

fallopian tube

inside of uterus

fimbria

ovary

ENDOMETRIAL CELLS,
BLOOD VESSELS, AND
GLANDS REGROW EACH
MENSTRUAL CYCLE.

cervix

vagina

BASAL CELLS DO
NOT SLOUGH OFF AT
MENSTRUATION.

THE CELLS THAT LINE THE
CHANNELS BRANCHING OFF
OF THE CERVICAL CANAL
PRODUCE FERTILE MUCUS.
AFTER INSEMINATION, MANY
SPERM LIVE HERE UNTIL
THEY FIND THEIR WAY TO
THE FALLOPIAN TUBES.

as the day progresses." When you pay attention in this way you'll most likely discover a wealth of information that can help you determine which signals may indicate ovulation. Don't be confused if you don't feel that the side you ovulate from alternates monthly. Some people ovulate in an alternating fashion, but many don't have any distinguishable pattern. Likewise, if you don't experience any conclusive ovulation sensations, don't worry—if you have other strong fertility signs, you probably ovulate when you are sleeping.

INSEMINATION RECOMMENDATIONS

People who feel physical sensations leading up to or with ovulation can easily time inseminations for that period. We caution you not to use these sensations as your sole indicator of when to inseminate, as you may not have enough warning to coordinate the logistics, or it may come when you're sleeping and you may miss it altogether. Likewise, you may need to take a few months lining up all of your signs to be able to determine if the sensation you feel is pre-ovulatory buildup or post-ovulation sensation or the feeling of ovulation itself. One helpful clue is that the pre signs will increase in intensity over time whereas the post signs start off stronger and get weaker. If you discover that you are able to feel ovulation, plan your final insemination around your ovulation symptoms—this is your peak fertile window.

Cervical Changes

The cervix, located inside the vagina, is the neck of the uterus. In the center of the cervix is an opening, called the os, which leads to the uterus. If you've never given birth and never had an abortion, your os will look like a round opening. If you have given birth, your os will be more of a slit or an L shape. The os undergoes monthly changes that are obvious when viewed with the assistance of a speculum, or are palpable to the touch if you're monitoring your cervix by feel.

The influence of increasing estrogen, which peaks at the time of ovulation, causes the cervix to both soften and slightly dilate or open. Simultaneously, the cervix produces fertile mucus that can be seen pouring out of the os during your most fertile days.

The changes in your cervix are concrete and are an accurate, inexpensive way to monitor your fertility. *Because this information is so amazingly helpful, monitoring cervical changes, particularly via speculum, is a primary fertility signal.*

HOW TO MONITOR CERVICAL CHANGES

There are two ways of monitoring your cervical changes: by feel with a finger or by viewing with a speculum. Because we aren't used to monitoring our cervices, it may take you a while to get the hang of it. Don't worry, with time it will be quite natural. The first month that you start to monitor your cervix, it's best to start immediately following the arrival of your menstrual blood and to continue daily until you bleed again. Once you've isolated your usual fertile window, you'll be able to limit your cervical monitoring to an approximate seven-to-ten-day period. Many people, however, find this sign so incredibly valuable that nearing ovulation and insemination they may monitor their cervix several times a day. Please note that your cervix may be higher upon waking and more open following a bowel movement.

Your cervix will be softer and more open when you're fertile. Most people find that it pulls up high and out of the way when they're fertile and is easier to reach and closer to the vaginal opening when not fertile. Because these changes are what you're hoping to track, it's important to begin your monitoring each month before your cervix begins to open and soften so that you can fully note its changes. Some people's cervices are naturally lower in the vagina and some are higher. Sometimes the cervix will alter its placement in the body from month to month. This is normal and nothing to worry about.

MONITORING BY TOUCH

Monitoring your cervix with your fingers is easy, once you've learned to identify where your cervix is and to feel the opening of the cervix. This is most readily done while in the squatting position or with one leg raised on the side of a bathtub or bed. You may find, however, that your cervix is too far back for you to monitor with your own fingers. In this case either you'll either need someone else to feel it for you or you'll need to use a speculum. Always wash your hands with soap before checking your cervix. Likewise, for consistency of feel, always check your cervix in the same position each day.

What you should record each day is how easy your cervix is to reach, how far back or high up it is, what direction it's facing, how soft it is, and how open it is. Your cervix will open as your fertility increases and you're about to ovulate. Immediately following ovulation, it closes. This monitoring is incredibly useful, since you can familiarize yourself with these internal changes. For the first month or two these changes may be quite subtle as you are familiarizing yourself with a whole new level of monitoring your body; but over time it becomes both recognizable and obvious. You may also notice the quality of mucus remaining on your finger after touching your cervical os.

Monitoring your cervix with a speculum is an easy, inexpensive, and amazing fertility tool. However, for some it can be quite an emotional leap to imagine choosing this option willingly. Because of the amount of information monitoring by speculum provides, many people overcome their ambivalence and learn to use a speculum. *Speculum monitoring is a primary tool for logging fertility signals.*

A speculum is the instrument used to open your labia wide in order to see deeply inside your vagina. It has two bills that you can open and a latch to keep it open and in place. The same instrument is used when you get a pap smear. Speculums can be ordered on our website. See the drawing for a greater understanding. Looking deep inside your body is an incredibly intimate experience. Thinking of doing so can make you feel very vulnerable. It can feel scary for people who are uncomfortable with vaginal penetration, or for those who have a history of sexual abuse or assault. You're not a failure if you choose not to use a speculum to monitor your cervix. There may be another time in your life when it's much easier and exciting. If you do have a lot of anxiety about vaginal issues, however, this may be the perfect opportunity, in the safety of your own home, to become more comfortable with your vagina. It's always helpful to work on your vaginal anxieties when you're planning to give birth, and it is much easier to do before you're pregnant.

Many people or their partners find that looking inside their bodies with a speculum is the most concrete form of feedback they can obtain about their fertility cycle. Being able to see your cervix opening and watching the fertile mucus pour out can seem so much more simple and believable than charting the phase of the moon, observing little changes in this or that, urinating on a stick, or taking your temperature. People who observe their cervices wonder why they would do those other things when they can just look inside themselves and see when they're about to ovulate. The most common feedback we get from clients is frustration that they didn't start using a speculum earlier, as doing so clarified so much about their fertile window.

To use a speculum, you'll need pillows, a flashlight, a mirror, lubrication, and a speculum. It can take a little while to get the hang of using a speculum. One of the most important elements to success is being able to relax your body. Lie down on a bed or on the floor—many people find that the firmness of the floor makes observing the cervix much easier. Place supportive cushions underneath your knees. This allows your leg and pelvic-floor muscles to relax.

With your finger, locate the placement and position of your cervix before inserting the speculum, so you know in which direction to angle the speculum, as your cervix is not always centrally positioned. Hold your labia apart so that the speculum doesn't pinch your skin. We suggest that you use a fair amount of lubrication, such as KY jelly, when you're using a speculum for the first time. Hold the speculum fully closed with the handle facing the ceiling. To slide it into your body most comfortably, it's best to angle downward toward your backbone.

Near the opening of your vagina is a really strong muscle band. Easing the speculum in over this band is usually the most uncomfortable part of inserting the speculum. Be sure to slide the speculum over that band and all the way in or it will remain uncomfortable. If you don't insert the speculum fully, it will feel similar to partially inserting a tampon. If you're having difficulty with the insertion, use your breath to help you relax more deeply. If you spend a few moments directing your breath to your vaginal muscles with the intention of relaxation, they will soften and stretch. Push the speculum in as you exhale.

Once you've inserted the speculum, take a deep breath or two before you open the bills of the speculum. When you're ready, gently push the bills open. If you're doing this by yourself, you'll need to click the speculum open and shine the flashlight directly into the mirror. This will make it easier to see than to angle the light into your body. Adjust the angle of the mirror until you can see clearly into your body. Whether you're looking for your cervix on your own or with the help of another person, it can take a few minutes or even a few tries with the speculum before you're able to see your cervix. You'll usually need to pull the speculum out a bit, always in the closed position, angle it in a slightly different position, reinsert, and reopen. Eventually your cervix will come into view.

When you're ready to remove the speculum, be sure to close the bills of the speculum before you attempt to take it out of your body. So as not to pinch your cervix, you may want to slide it partially out first and then close it. The cervix is sensitive, so if it gets touched, it will move right out of the way. Likewise, sometimes you'll be up against the edge of it and won't see the opening, so you won't necessarily know that you're there. Have patience; locating your cervix is a skill that often takes time to develop. Once you get used to doing it, though, it will take less time and you'll become familiar with the color variations inside your body. Locating your cervix will also become easier. It's helpful to know that the rugae—the folds of the vaginal walls—look different than the cervix does. The rugae are textured, whereas the cervix is smooth and shiny and often a slightly lighter shade of pink than your vaginal walls.

If you're having difficulty locating your cervix, remove the speculum, stand up, and jump for thirty seconds. This will bring your cervix down and relax your pelvic floor. Remember that feeling first for your cervical placement with a gentle finger can help you find the needed angle. When you insert the speculum, try opening the bills fairly widely, then wait patiently for a few seconds, and quite possibly the cervix will naturally slide its way into view. Likewise, some women find it's helpful to bear down a little or to cough in order to bring the cervix into view. If you still can't find your cervix, you may want to call a midwife or nurse practitioner and ask them to guide you to finding your cervix on your own. An excellent book to help you become more fully informed about female anatomy, with fantastic diagrams and photographs, is A New View of a Woman's Body (Federation of Feminist Women's Health Centers, 1991).

BUMPS OR REDNESS ON YOUR CERVIX

In general it's normal to have some bumps on the end of your cervix. These are small cysts and are generally considered harmless. If you see or feel such cysts and haven't had a recent Pap smear, it's always best to have a Pap smear so that you can feel more relaxed when doing cervical monitoring.

INSEMINATION RECOMMENDATIONS

After monitoring your cervix through several cycles, you'll be able to recognize when it's the softest and most open. The peak fertile window is when your cervix is wide open and fertile mucus is coming forth. For most, this is a one-to-three-day period, allowing time for multiple inseminations.

Sperm Options

With frozen sperm, it's best to time your inseminations as close to your time of ovulation as possible. Thus, becoming familiar with the changes in your cervix will allow you to inseminate on the day when your cervix is most open and has the most fertile mucus. This is especially helpful if you are someone who has a few days of fertile mucus. Speculum monitoring is also very helpful if your signs are scattered over a few days. If you are self-inseminating with frozen sperm you absolutely need to inseminate when there is fertile mucus. However, for some people their bodies no longer produce much fertile mucus by the time their os is fully open and they are ready to ovulate. If this is the case for you there is nothing wrong with your body—it is simply designed to use fresh sperm, which would last in your cervix during that time. When you are using frozen sperm, however, this can become a problem, as without the fertile mucus the sperm cannot make it into the cervix. If there is more than twenty-four hours between the time when you can visualize the peak of your mucus until the time of ovulation then you have three choices: use IUI, increase your fertility to enhance your mucus, or switch to fresh sperm.

If you're inseminating twice, the inseminations should be twelve to eighteen hours apart.

When you're using fresh sperm, you have a much more flexible window for inseminating, since fresh sperm lives longer. There's less of a need to analyze if your cervix is as open as it can be. Once your cervix begins to open and your mucus is fertile, you're in a peak fertility window to inseminate.

If you plan to use IUI as your method, or one method, of insemination, it's not as crucial to plan around your fertile mucus but it is essential to inseminate when your cervix is open. This can be a fine line, because you want to inseminate within six hours of ovulation. So it is best to really monitor your cervix during your peak fertile window so that you can observe the more subtle changes right around ovulation. If you are in your late thirties or forties your cervix will close up and cloud over within no more than twelve hours after ovulation, often sooner. If you are in your twenties or early thirties then it may stay open for twenty-four hours following ovulation and close and cloud over more slowly. Monitor very carefully with your other signs to be able to recognize the most fertile time and the time immediately following, as that will be the best window for insemination. But you do want to make sure you don't miss your peak fertile window by waiting too long to inseminate.

Tracking Fertile Mucus

Fertile mucus is a primary fertility signal. Fertile mucus is produced by your cervix and serves as a natural filtration system that allows healthy, well-formed sperm into the cervix. The fertile mucus comes out of the cervical opening and pools in the bottom of the vagina. The mucus then guides the sperm into the cervix. It provides a comfortable pH for the sperm and gives them the energy they need to keep swimming.

Understanding the role of fertile mucus often helps people relax during vaginal inseminations. Our bodies are perfectly designed to guide sperm into our cervices during our fertile periods and keep sperm out of our cervix during rest of the month. Once the sperm has been guided into the cervix, it's stored and nurtured there, where there are special crypts in which the sperm are nourished and then time-released into the uterus. Thus, fertile mucus serves an invaluable role in conception. In fact, without fertile mucus the body environment is detrimental to sperm. During the rest of the month the vagina is kept at a pH of 3.8 to 4.5. This acidic environment kills sperm. The pH of semen is 7.1 to 8.1, which is alkaline. The pH of fertile mucus is 7 to 8, matching that of semen. In other words, if you are hoping to get pregnant there is very little point in putting semen into your vagina unless you have fertile mucus. Sexual arousal and orgasm also increase the alkalinity of the vagina, making it more hospitable for sperm.

Because fertile mucus is so vital to conception, tracking the progress of your fertile mucus is of great value when you are having intercourse or performing vaginal inseminations. By monitoring your fertile mucus, you'll be able to effectively time your inseminations based on the organic processes that facilitate the transportation of sperm in your body. Within twelve hours after ovulation, your fertile mucus has decreased by 50 percent and is replaced with cloudy, sticky secretions. These secretions form a thick, impenetrable net that prevents sperm from moving into the cervix. Therefore, you must perform your vaginal inseminations when you're producing fertile mucus.

HOW TO TRACK FERTILE MUCUS

There are two ways to check your fertile mucus, by touch and by speculum exam. What you monitor is the progress of your mucus throughout the month. You don't need to check your mucus when you're menstruating. Likewise, you can't accurately check your mucus when you're sexually aroused. When you are not aroused, note the color, consistency, and amount of your mucus. Usually there are a number of pre-ovulatory days when the mucus becomes cloudy white or yellowish and is sticky but not stretchy. Then, immediately before ovulation, are the "wet days"—when your mucus increases in volume, is extremely slippery and stretchy or stringy, and has an egg-white consistency. These are your most fertile days. To determine the most fertile of these days, it's valuable to actually stretch the mucus between your fingers and measure the distance it stretches. The other secretions during the month are predominantly vaginal secretions whereas fertile mucus comes forth from the cervix.

Some women produce less mucus as they grow older. Many women of all ages—especially those who don't eat dairy products or are using antihistamines—don't find any mucus in their underwear or feel any mucus when they reach inside. Others find that their fertile mucus gets mixed in with their day-to-day vaginal secretions and is difficult to isolate. If this is the case for you, looking at your cervix with a speculum will help you clearly see the mucus that's secreted from your cervix. You can then use a Q-tip to see how far the mucus will stretch, or when you take the speculum out there may be fertile mucus on the bills that you can touch and stretch. It's best to check your mucus in the same manner each day, whether by checking your vaginal opening, touching your cervix with your finger, or using a speculum.

Some people never have stretchy mucus. This does not mean that they do not have fertile mucus. Other signs to look for include a wet spot on your underwear or days when it is particularly slick or slippery when you wipe your vagina after using the toilet. Likewise, it is helpful to clarify that some people mistake their early secretions for their most fertile secretions. With careful monitoring it is easier to notice that the secretions move from sticky (which will trap and stop sperm), to stretchy which is good for sperm, to more wet and also stretchy (which is great for sperm). Some people describe their most fertile day as looking like a waterfall is pouring out of their cervix. These same people may or may not ever have stretchy mucus. Now other people have this amazing seven-inch-stretch mucus that is impossible to miss. They are both fertile.

NOT ENOUGH FERTILE MUCUS?

If you find you're not producing much mucus that is clear, wet, or stretchy, then this may actually be inhibiting your fertility. If you feel that the quantity of your mucus is inhibiting conception, there are a few approaches you may take. Antihistamines dry up fertile mucus, as does chlorine, so avoid these. Likewise, if you haven't eliminated sugar and refined flour from your diet, now is the time to do so. Many nutritionists have found that vitamin A and potassium supplements can help dramatically. We've seen acupuncture and Chinese herbs have a marked affect on increasing fertile mucus production, as well as an amazing increase in people who drink our fertility blend and take Vitex. Please reread Part 3 on optimizing your fertility.

Some of our clients swear by the assistance of room-temperature organic egg whites inserted into the vagina prior to insemination or intercourse. This is one of the only mediums that's friendly to sperm, has the same pH as semen, and enhances sperm motility. This method is worth practicing prior to insemination as it takes a few tries to ascertain how much egg white to use. The goal is to have a slightly lubricated vagina. We recommend that you insert the egg whites about twenty minutes prior to insemination.

If you see a medical doctor about this problem, he or she may prescribe estrogen supplements. If you choose, you can simply bypass the need for fertile mucus and proceed directly to intrauterine insemination. However, keep in mind that even though a natural reduction of fertile mucus is expected with age, it is also a sign of (perhaps subtle) hormonal imbalance.

Having scant or not noticeable fertile mucus is not necessarily an indication of decreased fertility. Many people don't readily find fertile mucus yet get pregnant after their first insemination. However, these people may not be monitoring with a speculum. If they were to do so they might be surprised to see how much mucus is actually there. Many people can only observe their fertile mucus with a speculum.

INSEMINATION RECOMMENDATIONS

The days when your mucus is the wettest, clearest, and stretchiest are your high-fertility days, the last day of clearly fertile mucus being the peak day for vaginal insemination or intercourse. Your peak fertile days are usually one to two days before your temperature rise. *We could easily argue that fertile mucus is the single most significant fertility signal.*

Fertility Lens

A fertility lens is a pocket microscope that can be used to monitor your fertility. On the days of your cycle when estrogen is prominent—during your most fertile days preceding ovulation—your body produces a fernlike pattern in both your fertile mucus and saliva. This pattern can be observed on a lens or with a 50X microscope. If you observe the pattern of your mucus or saliva throughout the month, you'll see that it changes. Around the time of ovulation, the entire screen is actually filled with a crystal pattern that looks exactly like fern leaves. Then, immediately following ovulation, usually within twelve hours, it's replaced with a beadlike pattern with only a few ferns remaining. As people age the amount of time that ferning is present decreases. A person in their twenties may have full ferning for four to five days, whereas we have worked with some women in their forties who only fern for a few hours

MONITORING YOUR FERNING

Each person has a slightly different ferning pattern. Many have slight ferns creeping into the screen of the lens for a few days before the entire screen is covered. This usually correlates with the time of increased mucus that's just beginning to become clear and stretchy. Then, depending on your body, you may find that you have one day of full ferning or several. These day(s) usually correlate with your peak day(s) of fertile mucus. It helps to replicate with a sketch what you see on your chart so that you can easily track your ferning from month to month.

A clear and obvious ferning pattern is a primary fertility signal. Some people, however, are either unable to detect ferning or have full ferning for seven or more days. In these instances, the usefulness of the lens as a fertility tool decreases since it isn't specific enough.

It is common to experience frustration when first learning to use the lens as it takes time to be able to read it. Once you see the ferning it is hard to imagine you ever couldn't see something so beautiful and obvious, but it happens to almost everyone. Have patience and be sure to look on the fertile days. Sometimes looking a few times a day while you are getting the hang of it helps

INSEMINATION RECOMMENDATIONS

When your lens is completely covered with ferns, you're highly fertile. If you fern fully for half a week, however, you'll need to match up this sign with others for it to be most useful. For the people who fern for only a few hours, we have reliably performed an IUI in that window with great success! This is especially helpful for those who do not get a positive result from an ovulation-predictor kit. However, for some the ferning is a pre-sign that can signal them to alert their donor or order their sperm from the bank. It is only through careful monitoring that you will be able to see what it signifies for you.

Ovulation-Predictor Kits

Ovulation-predictor kits (OPKs) are used to monitor the level of luteinizing hormone (LH) in your urine. Depending on age and frequency of use, a surge of LH in the urine may occur prior to ovulation. Thus, if you use a sensitive OPK, you'll have a sign that indicates a hormonal shift in your body that precedes ovulation. Many people love this method since it appears to be so easy and objective. As with a pregnancy test, you simply pee on a stick and it tells you whether or not your LH level is above the control level. But that's the full extent of what it tells you. It doesn't tell you when you're going to ovulate or if you've already ovulated. OPKs show a positive reading when the amount of LH in your urine exceeds that of the control line, but this is a generic level of LH to which your urine is being compared. You are not a generic person.

EFFECTIVE USE OF OPKS

To get the full benefit from your OPK, it's important to follow a few instructions that aren't included in the kit manuals. First, begin testing early enough in your cycle to ensure that you are able to determine the onset of the luteinizing hormone surge. If your kit shows a positive or almost positive reading the first time you test, you've begun testing too late in the cycle to gain complete information. Begin your testing earlier in your cycle next month and keep testing until you get your period. If this is your first month testing, start on day eight just to be sure.

Second, if you plan to use these kits, we recommend that you only use them if you're willing to test your urine twice a day. If you test your urine only once daily, as is generally recommended, and you have a negative result the first day and a positive the next, you have no way of knowing how long your LH has been surging. If you started to surge a few hours after your first test, it's possible that by the time you get a positive the next day, you've already ovulated, as most women ovulate eighteen to thirty-six hours following an LH surge.

Third, use the same brand of kit, and ideally sticks from the same kit, for a complete cycle. If you mix and match, you can't accurately interpret the information you're getting because there are slight differences in the products. Likewise, stop testing once you get a positive reading. The first positive is the only valid positive. The LH may remain in your urine for longer, but that information isn't useful in any of your decision making. Always try to test your urine at the same time every day. For some, the first morning urine is not as accurate. There appears to be a natural surge around 2 P.M. that makes testing then a good idea.

When used with these guidelines, we consider this method to be a significant fertility signal, if tracked in conjunction with other fertility signs to help you to narrow down your peak fertility window. By no means, however, do we consider this method to be more valid than the other aforementioned signals.

The brands of kits that we currently recommend are Ovuquick, Clear Blue Easy, and First Response. First Response has the lowest LH trigger of these tests, thus it often reveals a positive result up to forty-eight hours before the Clear Blue test would do so. For younger clients, this First Response can give them the early warning of pending ovulation—although ovulation may easily be forty-eight hours away. In older clients, when all of the fertility signs don't match up or aren't consistent from cycle to cycle, we have had them test twice a day using both First Response and one of the other kits. We have used this information effectively in the following ways: if First Response is positive before the Clear Blue, we have people inseminate within

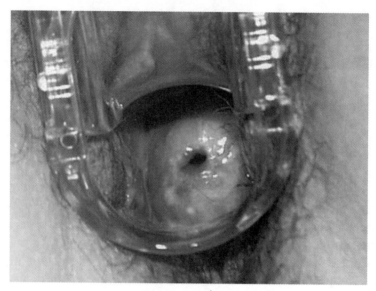

THIS CERVIX, VIEWED THROUGH AN OPEN SPECULUM, SHOWS SIGNS
OF FERTILITY: ABUNDANT CLEAR MUCUS AND AN OPEN OS.

twelve hours of the first positive. The next insemination is then timed within eighteen hours of the first insemination or when the Clear Blue reads positive. If both kits go positive at the same time, we recommend inseminating immediately and again ten to eighteen hours later.

DRAWBACKS TO OPKS

In our experience, many people inseminate too late. One of the primary reasons this happens is that they wait for their OPK to turn positive before beginning to inseminate. All their other signs may have lined up beautifully, but they're reluctant to inseminate until after their kit turns positive. By that time many women are no longer in their peak fertility window, and many of them have already ovulated by the time they inseminate.

Another significant drawback is that these kits are expensive, ranging in price from $20 to $80 for a five- to seven-day kit. Both of these drawbacks lead many people to choose to use the kits for only a few months in order to see how the information they're gathering from their other tracking methods line up with their LH surge.

Other important things to consider include that some people experience mini LH surges preceding their actual surge, which can make the readings inaccurate. Likewise, some people approaching menopause have increased LH but aren't necessarily ovulating. Also, some fertility medications skew

OPK results. If you're taking fertility drugs, check with your health care provider and the manufacturer about any possible interference. And lastly, although the control level of the kits reflects the "average" amount of LH for most women under 40, your body may release slightly higher or slightly lower levels of LH into your urine. This would skew the value of the ovulation predictor kits, as they wouldn't provide an accurate positive reading for you. Due to these inconsistencies, we predict that within the next five years there will be different kits for women in their twenties, women in their thirties, and women in their forties.

INSEMINATION RECOMMENDATIONS FOR OPKS

The most important thing to remember about OPK results is that they're not more significant than your other signs. You are looking for any three signs to line up at the same time. When they do, it's best to inseminate right at that moment.

VAGINAL INSEMINATIONS WITH FRESH SPERM

If you have learned to monitor your fertile mucus, you will want to inseminate with your best day of mucus for your first insemination. This is often twelve to thirty-six hours before your OPK results turn positive. The next insemination would be with the OPK positive result. If you are doing three inseminations, the last one could be up to twenty-four hours later—depending on all other signals of fertility.

VAGINAL INSEMINATIONS WITH FROZEN SPERM

We recommend inseminating when you have a faint positive. That is, when your line is equal to the test line, or almost equal to it. Your next insemination would be within eighteen hours following the first insemination.

IUI WITH FRESH OR FROZEN SPERM

The decision as to whether to use fresh or frozen sperm is really dependent upon age. For people who are nearing 40 or are in their forties, we recommend the first IUI with the positive OPK, or earlier if three signs line up before getting a positive OPK, and the second insemination no later than twelve hours following the positive reading. For people in their twenties and early thirties we recommend one IUI twelve hours after the positive and another one twelve to eighteen hours later—assuming all signs line up with this timing. And for women in their mid- to late thirties it is somewhere in between the other suggestions, dependent on the results of the other signs being monitored. For example, if your temperature has not risen in the morning following the positive OPK the night before, it is safe to still do an insemination that night. Pushing it to the next morning would be too late. On the other hand, if the kit is positive in the morning and the mucus is starting to get cloudy that evening, the next insemination would be no later than early the next morning.

In summary, OPK results alone won't provide you with enough information to time your inseminations accurately.

Fertility Monitors

If you'd like to make a larger financial investment ($200 to $600) toward tracking your fertility, a fertility monitor may be right for you. The monitors are personal computers that track levels of LH and estradiol in your urine or oral and vaginal temperature. According to the information that is gathered from your body's signals and your unique rhythms, the monitor displays a daily reading of fertility. This is a nice benefit, because it's attuned to your personal levels of hormonal surge and can detect that surge for you. Often you can rent these monitors from companies if you can't afford to purchase one. For more information on price and how to order a fertility monitor, visit www.clearplan.com or www.zetek.net. The Clear Plan Monitor is widely available in pharmacies, whereas the Ova Cue is only available on-line.

BENEFITS OF FERTILITY MONITORS

This method of tracking fertility can be more accurate than using monthly OPKs. Many people find the "peak" readings to be affirming. With the Clear Plan Monitor, your daily urine results are interpreted for you, so you don't have to squint at color variations on a stick and interpret sometimes subtle shifts. The monitor calibrates itself against your test month. Thus, your highest LH surge will show a "peak" reading even if it's lower or higher that what the OPK might call positive. In this way it truly is personalized to your body and not that of an "average" woman. Many people inseminating with fresh sperm find this method effective, as not only the peak but also the high-fertility windows are more clearly defined than they are with OPKs. It also makes it easier to plan IUIs.

The benefit of the Ova Cue is that it predicts your optimal fertile window in advance. This is especially effective for people using fresh sperm. Also, it seems to be much more accurate than the Clear Plan monitor. There is only one purchase, as it doesn't require strips, and their customer service is excellent.

DRAWBACKS OF FERTILITY MONITORS

As mentioned, these monitors are quite expensive, although if you end up using one for more than a few months or if you plan to get pregnant more than once, they can end up being more cost- effective than OPKs. For the Clear Plan, the sticks that are needed each month are often difficult to find in stores, so it might be necessary to order them. Likewise, you can only test once a day. This leaves you with the same possible scenario as with OPKs: not knowing when your surge actually happened within a twenty-four-hour period. A real drawback is that these monitors read "peak" for two days, regardless. For some people these two days are the peak days. But for older women ovulation coincides only with the first peak day.

With the Ova Cue it can be difficult to interpret when to do an IUI. Therefore it is essential to monitor other signs to see how they all add up. However, it does seem to be the best predictor on the market as it indicates fertility three to five days in advance. This is perfect for vaginal inseminations. Most people find it harder to plan an IUI from using the Ova Cue, but still find it very useful.

Overall, these monitors seem to be more helpful than OPKs and could be considered a primary fertility tool.

INSEMINATION RECOMMENDATIONS

If you use the Clear Plan monitor, it's best to time your frozen sperm inseminations twelve to eighteen hours before it reads "peak" and within six hours of the "peak" monitor reading. Knowing when your monitor will read "peak" is impossible to predict for sure; therefore, you should also use your other fertility signs. If you're using fresh sperm, your final insemination should be timed for within six hours of the monitor's "peak" reading. You can start to inseminate as soon as the monitor says "high." For IUI it is best to aim for as soon as the monitor says "peak" and again twelve to eighteen hours later. If you are young, it may be best to time your first IUI eight to ten hours after the first peak and the second one twelve to eighteen hours later, depending on other signs.

Fertility Drugs

If you're taking fertility drugs, it's important to note this in your chart. Fertility drugs can significantly alter your fertility signals. Depending on the medication, your fertile mucus may be significantly reduced or may be greatly increased. Likewise, your peak fertility window may be shifted by multiple days in either direction. At Maia, we've seen numerous clients who were taking the drug

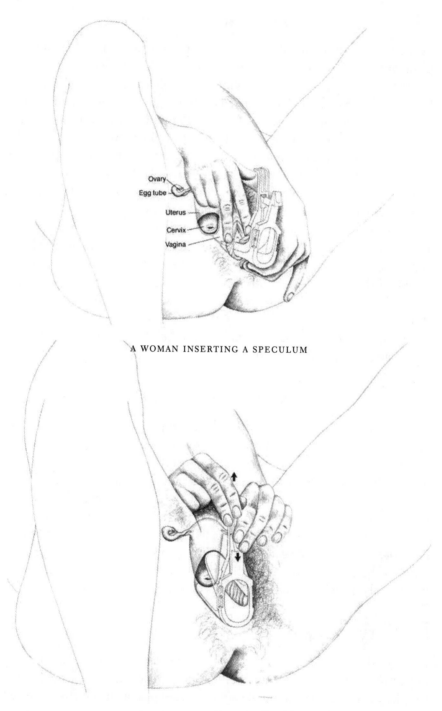

A WOMAN INSERTING A SPECULUM

A WOMAN OPENING A SPECULUM

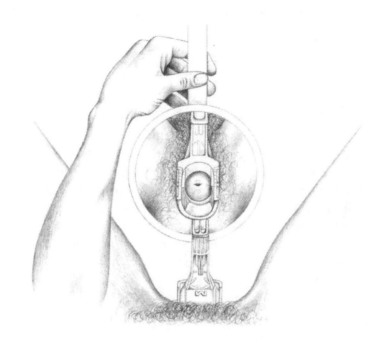

A VIEW OF THE CERVIX IN A MIRROR

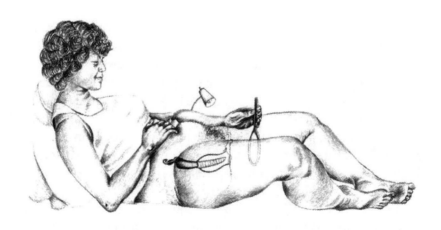

A WOMAN USING A DESK LAMP, HAND MIRROR, AND SPECULUM
TO LOOK AT HER CERVIX

Clomid and were informed by their doctors to expect their ovulation around day seventeen to day twenty-one, whereas in fact some people actually ovulate much earlier while taking this drug—around day ten or eleven. Be sure to monitor your fertility signals from the time that you stop bleeding, as you don't know how your body will respond to the medication during each new cycle.

Mood Changes

Some people find it helpful and insightful to chart their mood cycles throughout the month. Many people are familiar with the premenstrual mood changes they experience but have never noticed whether they experience predictable mood changes prior to ovulation. When paying attention to this, many find they're assertive, energetic, creative, and confident around their time of peak fertility, while others feel internal and introspective. Still others experience brief but intense depression at this time, lasting a few minutes to a day or two. We also notice an intense need to do housecleaning during the optimal fertile window.

Sex Drive

Tracking your sexual desire is also a useful guide to fertility. We consider libido to be a primary fertility signal. Many people experience significantly increased sexual desire on the days immediately preceding and during ovulation. People who have a high libido all the time often report a distinct shift in the quality of their desire or in the kind of sex they're interested in around the time of ovulation.

Although you may not act on your sexual desire, you may notice that you feel sexier at this time of month. Many report having sexual dreams as they near ovulation. Some lesbians report having sexual fantasies involving men around this time of the month. Tracking your sexual desire will give you essential information, so be sure to write down your feelings, even if they're subtle. Numerous studies document that a woman's increased exposure to pheromones increases her chances of conception. Pheromones are smells that we emit that are probable instigators of sexual attraction; they've been called the "flames of desire." In fact, some experts say that a woman's sense of smell is a hundred times sharper than normal during her time of peak fertility. Likewise, frequent sexual activity increases a woman's fertility. We, of course, feel this applies to all people who have the ability to be pregnant—men or women. And perhaps the most compelling of all the studies are those that have documented spontaneous ovulation in response to sexual arousal. Be sure to monitor not only your level of sexual desire, but also your partner's level of attraction to you and your general level of attraction to others. Partners have reported being unable to stay away when their partner is ovulating. Some have described their smell as intoxicating.

INSEMINATION RECOMMENDATIONS

Using your sex drive to help confirm your timing is indispensable. When your sex drive or feelings of sexiness increase, your fertility increases. If you're using fresh sperm, we recommend inseminating when your libido increases, especially if your other signs corroborate this timing. This is biology working at its best.

If you're using increased sexual desire as a fertility signal, you'll discover that it often precedes your other signs. Therefore, if you're using frozen sperm you should probably wait to inseminate until you show strong signs of fertile mucus, whether or not your sex drive is high.

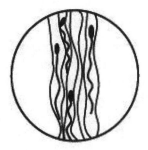

NONFERTILE CERVICAL MUCUS   FERTILE CERVICAL MUCUS

Appetite Changes or Food Cravings

Some people have predictable food cravings during their menstrual and fertility cycle. Many people are already aware of their food cravings around the time of the month that they menstruate but have never paid attention to their cravings at other times of the month. In fact, many have just as distinct cravings for a few days nearing their time of ovulation. Some people crave comfort foods; others crave salads and fresh vegetables. Some crave chocolate; others notice a general appetite increase. Some people are not hungry at all while they are fertile. Since you're noticing and keeping track of so many other things throughout the month, pay attention to these cravings as well to see whether there's a pattern.

Breast Changes

Some women notice that their breasts become more physically or sexually sensitive preceding ovulation, and many notice that their nipples actually darken when they're fertile. Many report erect nipples as a fertility sign. It is common to have a change in the way their nipples feel or look immediately following ovulation. Some experience this as a change in color, while others know it to be a heaviness or sensitivity that does not go away until they menstruate. For some, these breast changes are so significant that they're able to use this information as a primary fertility signal. Others notice no or only subtle shifts that wouldn't constitute primary information.

Stress

In your charts, it's important to document times of increased stress. Stress can greatly affect your fertility. See chapter 16 for more information.

Dreams and Sleep

Many people report having dreams that are highly sexual, In "Technicolor," or filled with fertility symbols. People have told us that their dreams are particularly vivid or memorable when they're fertile. Pay attention to your dreams; for some this is one of the clearest signals that ovulation is approaching or even occurring and can be used as a primary fertility signal. People also often report nighttime restlessness or insomnia when they are most fertile.

Don't Ignore Your Own Signs

Since you're focusing on your monthly cycles and rhythms, feel free to add additional entries to track. Some people like to track their headache cycles, others track constipation, and still others track their arguments with their partners. You can learn so much about yourself through careful charting that it's helpful to track anything that might give you additional insight into in your body and your life.

Charting for Partners and Singles

Women and transmen who are partnered don't always want to share every detail of their bodies with their partners. It's certainly not every person's dream to have their partner ask them about the consistency of their vaginal discharge on a daily basis. On the other hand, the partner who isn't inseminating can feel frustrated if her partner is not charting thoroughly or if they disagree on how to interpret body signals. This can lead to uncomfortable or unhealthy relationship dynamics if left unchecked.

Some people are reticent to do speculum exams to observe their cervix, since they're afraid that if their partner sees their cervix with a speculum and has to interact with them in a more clinical or scientific manner, it will take the magic out of conception and birth or from their sexual and romantic relationship. Others are thrilled to look at their cervix but feel offended if their partner is reticent to share the experience with them. Oftentimes a partner is quite nervous to wield a speculum for the first few times as she is concerned about hurting her partner with the speculum exam.

We often find that the way a partner can be meaningfully involved in the fertility process is to be the keeper and organizer of the charts.

Both Women Charting in a Lesbian Partnership

We encourage partnered women who menstruate to each keep a chart, even if one is not planning to conceive. You can both see how your overlapping cycles influence your relationship fluctuations. This can become a shared project of self-exploration. It also takes the burden off the woman who's inseminating and turns it into a shared adventure. It can become a journey for both of you to learn about yourselves and each other. Of course, some partners have no interest in engaging with their bodies in this way. This often stems from a gender identity and should be completely respected. Sometimes charting is stressful enough and the partner or couple decides to focus on the intended birth mom. However, if partners do chart, this information will come in handy should you decide to switch who is trying to get pregnant or for the future if she plans to get pregnant as well.

Charting for Single Parents-To-Be

It can be emotionally challenging for a single parent-to-be to find the motivation to continue charting month after month. This is by no means due to lack of initiative, but rather because the shared aspect of learning is absent. As a result, we recommend that single women find another person in their life with whom to chart. This doesn't have to be someone who's planning to get pregnant. Many people are excited to learn more about themselves and their bodies and would love to do this kind of project with you, sharing both discoveries and frustrations. Charting buddies inspire each other and compel each other to continue charting because they have a shared commitment.

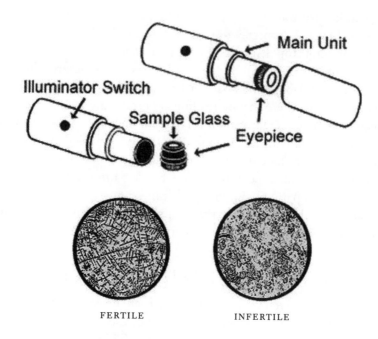

FERTILE   INFERTILE

Why People Don't Chart Enough?

EMOTIONAL AVERSION

It is not uncommon for people to avoid charting enough because they feel an aversion to the entire process of fertility awareness. Keeping track of your fertility signals and documenting them on a chart can evoke many surprising emotions. Therefore, understanding your emotional responses is key to charting well. People who aren't aware of their underlying issues often resent charting and therefore only chart sporadically and ineffectively.

It can be a new and emotionally evocative experience for lesbians and transmen to reconnect to their fertility. At first it can seem quite contrived to have to focus so much attention on the details of your menstrual cycle. Many lesbians have prided themselves on being able to be distanced from fertility, having had no need to focus on pregnancy prevention when having sex. Transmen don't identify with being female and may have even taken hormones to ensure that they don't menstruate each month. For both lesbians and transmen, reconnecting with fertility can evoke uncomfortable memories of body image, sexuality issues, coming out, gender issues and homophobia/transphobia. In the process of reclaiming the option to procreate, it can be beneficial to explore this emotional territory. Some of the common emotional responses to focusing on your fertility cycle include anger, resentment, and self-doubt.

ANGER AND RESENTMENT

One of the initial reactions that most queer women, transmen, and single people of all orientations have to charting is to get angry that straight women (i.e., partnered straight women who don't experience infertility) don't have to go through the ordeal of scrutinizing their bodies in order to conceive. Charting makes us acutely aware that we don't have the heterosexual privilege of sperm being available any time it's needed or desired. This anger can make the process of fertility awareness seem unfair.

Likewise, a lot of resentment can arise about having to focus so intimately on yourself and your body. Some people experience this level of self-observation as demeaning. People don't necessarily like to look at their bodies this closely, since it can make them feel objectified and scrutinized. Likewise, many people feel that by charting they're being judged and rated on a fertility scale.

If you feel angry or resentful about charting, we suggest that you explore your feelings fully and then release them. It's not a life-enhancing stance to feel victimized by your fertility. Take back your power. Fertility awareness is your key to achieving pregnancy. Claim it and chart your fertility signals with pride. This may require an intentional attitude shift, but doing so will be well worth the effort.

It is also common to feel outrage that you were never taught these things about your body by teachers, parents, or doctors. Learning more about your body can evoke feelings of fury and confusion. These feelings are legitimate, feminist, and political, and as a result you may want to educate your friends and families about the wonders of the female body. Likewise, you may find it powerful to commit to raising your daughters (and sons) with all of this information available to them from the start. When used productively and as a motivator, anger will usually quickly transform into excitement and motivation.

SELF-DOUBT

Many lesbians have never felt any need to focus on their ovulation since they ran no risk of getting pregnant. It's common for self-doubt to arise when you're beginning to chart. People are often afraid of discovering that somehow, by not having focused on it, perhaps they don't actually ovulate. Self-doubt can also manifest as fear that you'll discover that you don't actually have the fertility you've taken for granted. This self-doubt can lead numerous people to avoid charting altogether.

SEEMS TOO TECHNICAL

Some people are resistant to charting because they think it's too mechanical. They want getting pregnant to be more of an "in the moment" organic experience, and feel that charting would remove a vital element of spontaneity. This is an important form of thinking to examine, as it often stems from internalized homophobia: having underlying beliefs that the only "natural" way to get pregnant is to have spontaneous sex with a man. Explore if this feels true for you, and don't let it prevent you from conceiving by preventing you from charting.

Charting may also remind you of your relationship to science. If your feelings about science are negative, you might be afraid that you won't be able to chart successfully, since you believe your brain isn't designed to look at yourself this way or you fear you won't be able to read the chart. Charting is actually easy and doesn't require any knowledge of science, but beware of negative internal messages that can undermine your confidence. If you were confused by our descriptions of fertility hormones earlier in this chapter, don't be intimidated. You can chart your fertility whether or not you know the names of these hormones.

When You Find That You Aren't Charting

Remember, many people find charting to be a difficult process. If you find you're not charting more than one or two signs, you've lost your chart for the third time, or you can't remember the last time you wrote on your chart, then it's time to evaluate what's preventing you from charting. *Although charting is optional, it's the single most significant thing you can do to increase your chances of getting pregnant swiftly.*

Timing

Now that you've educated yourself on how much information you have readily available to you about your fertility, it's important to learn how to use the information in your charts. This next section looks at the fertility chart from the view of a person who's on the verge of inseminating. How can you interpret all the data you've gathered? Depending on your method of insemination, the number of times insemination will be attempted, and whether your sperm is frozen or fresh, each chart may need to be interpreted slightly differently.

Most People Inseminate Too Late

Insemination timing is vitally important to achieving pregnancy. Early on in our practice, we'd meet women who'd been inseminating for months or even years without achieving pregnancy. When we examined their charts, we'd often discover they had clearly charted their signs of peak fertility but were inseminating 24 to 48 hours later than we recommend. All too frequently, perceived infertility is nothing more than repeated incorrect timing.

Please remember that if you are going to try to get pregnant from IUI that sperm only lives in the uterus for six to ten hours at most. Conception rates using IUI are highest when performed within six hours on either side of ovulation. Thus, if you are using IUI you must know not only your optimal fertile window, but also you must narrow that down to your ovulation window. For most this requires careful scrutiny.

Remember that when doctors recommend that you (and everyone else they work with) inseminate twenty-four hours and forty-eight hours following a positive predictor kit they also recommend that women over 40 go straight to IVF with donor eggs. You are not generic. You are not infertile just because you are older. Do not abdicate your role in this process; it could be the difference between conception and childfree living.

It's Essential to Inseminate at or Prior to Ovulation

Many conventional understandings about fertility are now outdated. Nonetheless, many fertility specialists still recommend that women inseminate at or after ovulation, despite current research concluding that this is too late. From working with hundreds of lesbian, single, and bisexual women, we've discovered that the peak fertility window is before and up to ovulation. This means you're much, much more likely to conceive if you inseminate prior to or at ovulation than following ovulation. Although it's thought that the egg may remain viable for up to twenty-four hours after ovulation, most studies reveal that this time frame is generally closer to six to ten hours. In fact, miscarriage is more likely if you conceive when the egg is older.

Because fertile mucus plays a key role in not only nourishing but also transporting sperm from the vagina into the uterus, common sense would dictate that you should inseminate when you have abundant fertile mucus. Within hours of ovulation your mucus loses its fertile properties. Thus, if you're inseminating vaginally, the carrier system for the sperm is eliminated and is replaced with a barrier system that's designed to keep sperm out of your cervix and uterus. The body closes up shop. This is a pretty clear message about how the reproductive system is designed. Unless you're using IUI as your means of insemination, your inseminations should always be timed for when you have fertile mucus.

Interpreting Your Fertility Chart

There are four sets of valuable information that your chart can reveal about your fertility cycle:

1. The signs you experience that let you know your fertile window is beginning
2. Your signs of peak fertility
3. Your ovulation symptoms (which will most likely coincide with your signs of peak fertility)
4. The signs that indicate that you've already ovulated

It's important to be able to recognize the onset of your fertile window so that you have ample time to arrange all of the necessary logistics. You might need to forewarn a long-distance donor, give a local donor a first-alert call, order your sperm from the sperm bank, make medical appointments, or keep the anticipated time frame in mind when scheduling your work for the next week.

You'll want to know your signs of peak fertility so that you can inseminate at this time. Peak fertility days are the days immediately preceding ovulation but not after it. Your peak fertility ends with ovulation.

Noting when your body indicates that you actually ovulate is important so that you can time your final insemination. This information can also help confirm your understanding of your peak time in case you don't conceive and want to reevaluate your timing. Signs of ovulation include a rise in your resting temperature and the cessation of strong ovarian awareness and cramping, or the feeling of a localized twinge.

Recognizing the signs that indicate that you've already ovulated also allows you to evaluate your timing and to discontinue inseminating for that cycle. These signs include a basal body temperature that has clearly risen, a cessation of ferning on your lens, a decrease of fertile mucus, a "low" reading on your fertility monitor, and a closed cervix.

Signs of Peak Fertility

Each fertility signal will indicate a peak time of the month, which we've outlined in the previous section. *The goal is to have three signs line up at the same time*. Because your body is different from month to month, it's important to track more than three signs so that you can see which signs indicate optimal fertility for that cycle. You must chart each month that you inseminate, since your fertile window can shift by a few days in either direction. This is a normal and healthy part of the female reproductive cycle. Therefore, do not rely on the day of your cycle on which you inseminated last month to determine the day on which you'll inseminate this month. It may help you to predict the probable week you'll be inseminating, but you can't possibly know the exact day ahead of time. When you're charting sufficient information, you'll more than likely discover what is clearly the best time to inseminate.

Overall Timing Recommendations

For most, the majority of their peak fertility signals occur within twenty-four hours of one another. An ideal picture of a day to inseminate would be when you experience a basal body temperature that hasn't yet risen or is just starting to drop (as long as this is a predictive sign for you); an open cervix; your OPK is just becoming positive or just turned positive, or your fertility monitor has read "high" for a few days or just read "peak"; your sex drive has increased; you're feeling creative; and you haven't yet felt your ovulation sensation.

It's best to time at least one of your inseminations to occur at night so that you can make sure you'll have plenty of rest after your insemination. Studies show that there's also a seasonal influence to the timing of ovulation. In the springtime, 50 percent of all women in the Northern Hemisphere ovulate between midnight and 11 A.M.; in the fall and winter, 90 percent ovulate between 4 and 7 P.M. in their respective time zones. As the seasons change many people notice that their fertile window shifts a little earlier or later in the cycle as well.

Two important points to remember:

1. Inseminate at your signs of peak fertility.
2. Don't delay while holding out for temperature or a positive ovulation predictor kit while the rest of your fertility signals are screaming "peak." This is the worst trap you can fall into.

Always inseminate more than once a month. We feel this increases your chances so significantly that it would be better to skip every other month and inseminate twice in a cycle than to inseminate just once a month. In fact, inseminating three times a month is ideal. However, using frozen sperm can be cost prohibitive, and using fresh sperm is completely dependent on the donor's sperm count. Re-read our creative solution on pages 101–102 for monitoring how frequently your donor/partner can ejaculate.

TIMING RECOMMENDATIONS FOR FROZEN SPERM

It is vitally important to track your signs of peak fertility—not just high fertility—when using frozen sperm. Frozen sperm is only viable for eighteen to twenty-four hours. In addition, each semen sample is purchased in such a small quantity that you'd need to purchase four vials to roughly equal one full ejaculate. Some people choose to inseminate with two vials at a time, thereby increasing the quantity of sperm swimming toward their egg. Because with frozen sperm both the life span is shorter and the quantity is significantly smaller than when using fresh sperm, it's even more essential to chart meticulously so that you can maximize your chances of conceiving. Remember, whenever possible, inseminate when three peak fertility signs line up.

It can sometimes be ineffective to vaginally inseminate with frozen sperm, since if you were to time your inseminations by your increased sex drive or even the peak of your fertile mucus, you may be inseminating too soon. If this is the case for you, and your fertility signals span many days, you may chose to move to IUI, in addition to or instead of vaginal insemination. Lunaception, acupuncture, and affirmations and visualizations are helpful for narrowing your fertility window.

Furthermore, unless extenuating circumstances arise and you feel you may have timed your first insemination early, don't separate your frozen inseminations by more than twenty-four hours—eighteen hours is usually best, in our experience.

TIMING RECOMMENDATIONS FOR FRESH SPERM

Fresh sperm lives in your body and is time released into your uterus for two to three days. Therefore, it's safe to start inseminating with fresh sperm as soon as two of your signs line up. You do, however, want to save your final insemination for as close to ovulation as possible. Most people using a known donor inseminate two to three times a month. But if you're inseminating only once a month, wait until three signs line up or until your intuition strongly guides you. It's a good idea to separate your fresh inseminations by twenty-four hours each time. This is not, however, a hard and fast rule. There's plenty of flexibility when using fresh sperm, so feel free to begin inseminating at your first signs of high fertility. Unless you have confirmed that the sperm count is sustained with frequent ejaculation, we do not recommend morning and evening inseminations over a span of a few days. By the time peak fertility arrives, the sperm count will be next to nothing.

However, with a strong sperm count and a willing donor or partner, some people have success with inseminating every other day from the time they stop bleeding until they get their period again.

Timing for an IUI is much more specific than timing for a vaginal insemination. Because it's believed that sperm deposited directly into the uterus lives for a significantly shorter period than sperm from vaginal inseminations, it's essential to inseminate as close to ovulation as possible. Ideally, you should perform an IUI within eight hours of ovulation. Because this window is so narrow, it's best to have a thorough understanding of your peak fertility signals.

It's our overall recommendation that when using IUI, you also perform one vaginal insemination per cycle. Some people, however, don't wish to do vaginal inseminations. If this is the case for you, don't decide to inseminate just once a cycle. Instead, do two or more IUIs per cycle. One recent study shows that statistically there's only a 7 percent chance of pregnancy when performing one IUI per cycle, whereas there's a 12.7 percent chance of pregnancy with two IUIs. This should be a compelling enough reason to choose two over one. If you do two IUIs, aim for six to eight hours on either side of ovulation.

We know it is absolutely cost prohibitive for most, but when people move to three IUIs a cycle they almost always conceive that cycle. Please realize, however, that this kind of expense from the beginning can actually end up saving you months and months of financial and emotional expense. Some people do this when their donor is at the end of his rope, or when they are contemplating infertility treatments as the next step, or just from the start to save time.

There are some studies that indicate that IUI with fresh sperm has a greater success rate than with frozen sperm. For people with known donors, adding one well timed IUI may significantly increase your chances. However, if your donor has a good sperm count; we usually recommend trying at least a few cycles at home before moving to IUI.

Also, please remember that it is crucial to rest following an IUI. Studies show that it comes close to tripling success rates with IUI.

Working with Your Fertility Specialist

Many times when you look at your fertility from the perspective we offer, you'll discover that your view of your peak fertile days does not coincide with your health practitioner's view of when you should inseminate. Most health-care providers have a generic formula that they recommend to all women in their office such as, "Call me when your ovulation predictor kit turns positive, and we'll inseminate you the next day, or even the day after if it's the weekend or we're too busy." More often than not, this will be too late. Likewise, most practices recommend inseminating just once per cycle. This significantly reduces your chances of conceiving.

If your sense of when to inseminate, based on either our information or your intuition, differs from that of your fertility specialist, you have several options. You could try different approaches for timing on alternate months, instead of trying to reconcile two approaches in the same month. Or you could follow your intuition, if you're able to identify your intuition in the midst of all the recommendations that you're receiving. Some people follow their own timing rather than the advice of their doctors. Ideally, you'll find a practitioner with whom you can work well as a team.

Frequently Asked Questions

I have varying cycle lengths. Can fertility awareness help me?
Absolutely! In fact, when you have irregular cycles, fertility awareness is the best means of knowing when to inseminate. Whether you ovulate on day nine or day twenty-seven, recognizing your fertility signs is all you need to correctly time your inseminations. We have helped dozens of women conceive who had widely variable cycle lengths. These people were commonly told they had PCOS and would not be able to conceive without fertility medicine. We have found that the first thing to determine is whether or not you ovulate each cycle. Most people with a variable cycle length have a variable follicular phase and a consistent luteal phase. This is not the case for everyone. In fact, a number of the clients we have worked with who have consistently elongated cycles go through two full ovulatory cycles before a period. Careful charting, with possible ultrasound confirmation, is often all that it takes to understand what is happening in your body. That understanding is then all that is needed to time inseminations.

However, it is worth mentioning again, that variable cycle length usually indicates hormonal imbalance that would best be addressed. Please read part three on optimizing your fertility.

The medical field offers you the approach of fertility medicine to try to regulate when you ovulate, or to monitor your body through ultrasound to confirm whether and when you ovulate. With irregular cycle lengths you may have to get daily sonograms for weeks to determine this each cycle. This can be practically and financially impossible. If you doubt your signs, you may, however, consider getting ultrasound confirmation of your ovulation when you believe it's approaching.

What do I do when my intuition says I'm fertile but I don't have three match-ing fertility signals?
The Maia approach is to prioritize your internal knowledge. *Your intuition is definitely a primary fertility signal!* If you're using a known donor, it's appro-priate to time at least one insemination as your intuition guides you, regard-less of other corroborating information. Remember that fresh sperm can live in your body for days. On the other hand, if you're using frozen sperm and don't have three matching signs, you may choose simply to note your strong intuition in your chart and examine it at the end of your cycle to see if it indeed was an early fertility signal. Or you may choose to perform one vaginal insemination at this time. We recommend three inseminations for this reason exactly; it gives people the freedom to perform one insemination when the mood strikes them and not to freak out that it may be the wrong time. Three inseminations significantly decrease the stress in the moment. Of course, it does increase financial stress.

What do I do if none of my signs match up?
When you say that none of your signs match up, do you mean they're not all on the same day? Are they clumped together in the same three-to four-day period? When you've tracked your fertility signals for at least three months, you'll have enough information to compare and see if you find observable patterns.

Take the following example: Many people experience an increase in li-bido for a day or two (let's say days 12 and 13) prior to the time that their cervix is the most open and they have the most fertile mucus (night of day 13 and morning of day 14). Their predictor kit might also read positive the next day (day 15) with a slight rise in their temperature, followed by a more significant rise the next day (day 16). This is extremely useful information, as it shows that they probably ovulated somewhere on day 15 or 16, most likely the night of day 15.

Insemination with fresh sperm: One insemination on day 13 when her sex drive increases, and one insemination on day 14 when her cervix and mucus indicate peak fertility, and if she can do three, the final insemination would be as close to the positive OPK as possible.

Insemination with frozen sperm: One insemination when her cervix is the most open, ideally the morning of day 14, and then she could time the second insemination in a number of ways: eighteen hours later or as soon as her OPK reads positive, depending on the other more subtle signs she's tracking.

Insemination with IUI: Time the IUI for as late as possible, ideally after performing a vaginal insemination when her mucus is copious and her cervix is wide open. The IUI could then be performed as late as mid-morning on day fifteen, but no later, since her cervix has passed its most open point, her temperature appears to be increasing already, and her OPK reads positive. If she is planning two IUIs, then the first should be as early as possible on the day the OPK is positive, and the second as late in the day as possible.

If a person truly has no signs of fertility matching up within the same few days, it might be useful to get a hormonal blood panel to rule out any gross imbalances. Likewise, we highly recommend acupuncture and herbs to help fine-tune the fertility cycle. See chapter 12 on fertility inhibitors and enhancers for recommendations.

Please also note that there has been a body of research conducted on women who do shift work and who work at night which indicates reduced fertility. Evidence suggests menstrual irregularities which can directly correlate with fertility. Sleep disturbances can lead to menstrual irregularities which in turn can lead to fertility challenges. If you have noticed changes in your menstrual cycles since working nights or double shifts please consider the potential impact on your fertility.

How do I time inseminations with ultrasounds?

If you are receiving serial ultrasounds from your fertility specialist, we recommend that you incorporate the information gained about the size of your follicles with the information you are already gathering about your body. It is also helpful to know what side you are ovulating on so that you can visualize effectively and roll in the correct direction post insemination. Write down the size of your follicles on your chart so that you can look back retrospectively and learn. Not everyone's follicles rupture at the same size. Also, if you are monitoring your own signs of fertility, it can be helpful in order to effectively guide your doctor for which day(s) you will receive your ultrasound imaging.

We have worked with numerous people who were sent home by their doctors saying they weren't ovulating that month when really they were having a late ovulation. Detecting ovulation with ultrasound seems to be as much art as science. Ultrasonographers can have trouble differentiating the collapse of the dominant follicle after the egg breaks through from the corpus luteum cyst that quickly forms following ovulation. An image of the corpus luteum can be virtually indistinguishable from a ripe follicle. If serial sonograms are taken by the same technician this is less of a concern.

How do I time inseminations with human chorionic gonadotropin shots?

Human chorionic gonadotropin (HCG) is the main pregnancy hormone produced by the embryo. When given mid-cycle by injection, it can stimulate the body to ovulate, just as LH does.

The answer to this question depends on how close to ovulation you were at the time of injection. HCG does not delay ovulation. If your body was already going to ovulate in ten hours, it still will. Perhaps it may even ovulate sooner. All that HCG can do is to set the timing for ovulation to be within forty-eight hours. Each clinic recommends that HCG shots are given at slightly different times. What we have seen, however, is that people conceive most frequently when they inseminate with the peak of their fertile signs and then again eighteen hours following their HCG shot. However, if the peak of their fertility has not arrived but it is eighteen hours following the HCG shot, then we recommend inseminating anyway and following it with a second insemination 12-eighteen hours later.

What aids implantation? I feel like I keep conceiving with no implantation.
This is a broad question. As women age, the zona pellucida becomes harder. This makes it more difficult for the embryo to hatch itself and implant into the uterine wall. Bromelain, an enzyme found in pineapple, may help with implantation, so it is a good idea to eat fresh pineapple (which also has other nutritional benefits). Some research indicates that the consumption of soy around the time of conception might hinder implantation. It is recommended that soy be avoided or reduced for the week around conception. This is potentially related to one of the isoflavones contained by soy, genestein. Some studies indicate that stress can increase the frequency of uterine contractions, making implantation more difficult. The presence of antithyroid antibodies can prevent implantation as well. Essential fatty acid supplementation is thought to create better integrity of the cell membranes—including the egg membrane. If the body is overly acidic, the chances of implantation are reduced as well. Striving to eat a diet that is more alkaline can significantly help if this is the case. It is also thought that a diet too high in protein (more than 120 grams a day) may decrease chances of implantation. There is also a possible connection between low calcium and low vitamin D levels and implantation.

I have a short follicular phase. What should I do?
It is good to have a long enough luteal phase to sustain a thick enough uterine lining, with an endometrial thickness of 9mm. Regular exercise, a healthy diet including essential fatty acids, visualization, lunaception, fertility tea, and vitex seem to make a considerable difference.

I am still nursing. Can I conceive?
With breastfeeding there is a significant increase in prolactin levels. This in turn works to naturally suppress ovulation. However, once menstruation

returns, ovulation usually returns with it. If you are menstruating, or feel like you are ovulating but not yet menstruating, there are ways to naturally regulate your cycle and increase your fertility. At Maia, our favorites are a very nutritious diet, fertility tea, acupuncture, vitex, lots of sex, and lunaception. To date, we have not had to have anyone wean in order to conceive. Upon occasion, if someone wants to conceive before their baby is eighteen months old, we have encouraged night weaning.

I cramp following insemination. Is this normal?
Slight cramping following IUI is normal. Greater than slight cramping will reduce the likelihood of conception. We have worked with women who painfully cramp consistently with IUI. When they move to unwashed sperm and inseminate vaginally, they conceive. If you perform a vaginal insemination remember not to aim directly for the cervix with your syringe. Unfiltered semen moving at high speed directly into your cervix will cause horrendous cramping. This is from the other materials in the semen that are not sperm, such as dud cells and bacteria, entering into your uterus. The sperm is usually separated from the rest of the semen when traveling through the fertile mucus both outside of and within the cervix. Many people end up in the emergency room or go into shock when this happens. It usually passes on its own within a few hours. We hear reports from lesbians and people who have not had sperm in their body for a very long time that following insemination they cramp off and on until they get their period. This is usually more common in the first few cycles and seems to decrease as the body adjusts to the male hormones.

CHAPTER 15

Locations and Methods of Insemination: Choices and Decisions

THIS CHAPTER PROVIDES information on home and clinic settings for insemination, and describes the insemination methods available in each location. It also covers intercourse as a method of conception. Detailed guidance about how to do home vaginal inseminations will help put you at ease if you choose this method. We'll explore ways to make your insemination comfortable and empowering no matter where and how it's done. The goal of this chapter is to assist you in finding your most appropriate combination of locations and methods, taking into consideration your donor choice as well as your legal, emotional, financial, medical, and spiritual concerns. The main body of this chapter is organized into two parts: home inseminations and clinic inseminations. We recommend reading the entire chapter, as you may find it best to use multiple methods and locations within each cycle. Furthermore, if you don't conceive within your first few cycle attempts, you may find yourself changing your plans about donors, your method of insemination, or your location of insemination. However your insemination occurs, our hope is that it is joyful, safe, and comfortable for you.

Deciding Where to Inseminate or Conceive

Sometimes when a person inseminates in an environment that feels wrong or unsafe, they won't conceive. A change in environment may correct this. We've seen this scenario so many times that it's become painful to watch. People who've even gotten to the point of high-tech in vitro fertilization and not conceived have gotten pregnant later through careful tracking and self-inseminating at home. Likewise, people who've spent a year trying to conceive within the comfort of their home often conceive the first insemination they attempt at a clinic. Although there's no wrong or right place to inseminate, home and clinic environments are different from each other in many ways.

Conception isn't inherently a medical experience, nor does it need to be medicalized simply because you don't have easy access to sperm. Because of institutionalized heterosexism, however, queer and single women find themselves grouped in the same category as infertile heterosexual couples. Therefore, assumptions are made that they'll need to conceive with medical help; infertility is assumed simply due to absence of a male sexual partner.

This mind-set is false. All that most women need is access to sperm in order to get pregnant. Of course, that access is often limited and sometimes appears to be restricted to the medical world. Thus, for many reasons women inseminate at a clinic or private doctor's office. This doesn't have to be your only option, though, nor does it necessarily increase your chances of getting pregnant.*You don't inherently have fertility problems because of your sexual orientation or gender identity. Nor do you need someone else to inseminate you just because you're not having intercourse to get pregnant.*

If you seek information from only your ob-gyn or family practitioner, you may be steered in the direction of clinic insemination simply because that's the environment that they're more knowledgeable about or familiar with. If this is the case, you may trust your doctor to decide when and how you should inseminate without even realizing you have additional options. Our goal is to have everyone explore their preferences and options and make decisions about their bodies based on what's right for them. Allow the choices you make to feel life enhancing. If your choices feel depleting or if you feel uncomfortable when you think about your choices, examine why. You may have made the wrong decision or you may need to do more internal work to feel comfortable with your choices.

For example, if you decide it's important for you to inseminate at home in your bed, you may choose to use frozen sperm or have your known donor come to your home despite the possible legal ramifications. But if you hadn't taken the time to explore your feelings about insemination and conception, you might have inseminated in a clinic without thinking twice. Who's to say if it would have affected your chances of getting pregnant one way or the other? It's safe to say, though, that it will affect how you feel about the experience.

Likewise, you may realize that although you'd prefer to inseminate at home, you ultimately will choose to inseminate in a clinic because it affords you the greatest legal security. In this instance it may take you a while to come to terms with this decision, so that you can feel comfortable with your decision, despite making a choice that doesn't feel ideal to you.

So the question is, where do you want to conceive? Where you want to conceive may be a different question than where you'll choose to conceive. We've found that feeling connected to yourself—and your partner if you have one—feeling comfortable in your body, and feeling in alignment with your own spirituality are equally effective in increasing your chances of getting pregnant as making decisions based solely on statistics and your age.

Sexual Expression and Increased Rates of Conception

Many cultures believe that conception is an inherently sexual experience. Although this notion is obviously heterosexually based, science has lent some validity to it. Studies show that if a woman has an orgasm just prior to insemination with male ejaculation, the uterine pull of the orgasm, in tandem with the chemical release of endorphins and other relaxing hormones, actually draws the sperm into the uterus. In fact, studies have shown that a woman's satisfaction during intercourse directly correlates with how many sperm she retains. In this study, half of the women who experienced disappointing sex retained no sperm at all, compared to only one in ten women who enjoyed satisfying sex. Although sexual satisfaction is hard to achieve when being inseminated in a clinic, it may help to be sexually satisfied upon arriving at the clinic. Likewise, it may be helpful to experience sexual satisfaction upon returning home. In this case, avoid penetration.

Arousal has been shown to reduce the acidity in the vagina, making it more hospitable to sperm. The same is true for orgasm. Thus arousal supports conception. Likewise, we have seen time and time again that if we cannot get through someone's cervix in an IUI, if they have an orgasm and then we try again, the cervix is wide open.

Studies also suggest that frequent exposure to pheromones—biochemicals we secrete and react to physically from others—increase fertility and help regulate menstrual cycles. Being sexual with others is a common way to have intimate contact with the pheromones of other people, so the studies examined the effects of sexual activity on fertility. Indeed, they found a correlation. Interestingly, one study determined that lesbians need three times as much regular sex as do heterosexual women to achieve an influence on their conception rates. It is unclear why this is, exactly. Sex with men is defined as intercourse, and lesbian sex is not defined. Anecdotally, a number of single women have reported to us that when they're dating and having regular sex, their cycles are more regular, approaching twenty-eight days in length.

Even though regular sex increases fertility, and sex at the time of insemination can spur physiological and hormonal changes that increase conception rates, not all women want to be sexual at this time. Numerous women don't feel any inclination to have a sexual experience involving sperm.

For others, it's a natural and logical union. It's simply one they may never have considered. In fact, many people fear that sex might interfere with the process. Do what feels right for you, but feel free to be sexual if you want to! Following insemination, however, it's important to refrain from any sexual activities that include vaginal penetration. Anything put into the vagina can disturb the sperm as they swim into the cervix. Pain around or in the uterus can release hormones called prostaglandins, which are unfavorable to conception. When being sexual before or following insemination, don't use lubrication or introduce any foreign substances into your vagina that might have a chemical interaction with the sperm. Also, if you have particularly "explosive" orgasms, the force of your orgasm may expel the sperm from your vagina. If you think this may be the case for you, having an orgasm just prior to insemination might be better than immediately following insemination.

Logistically speaking, sex just before insemination can be a little tricky. If you're using frozen sperm, you might want to start being sexual before you defrost it. But you'll also want to keep an eye on the time to make sure you don't leave the sperm out too long. Be sure to keep the vial on or under one of your bodies so that the temperature can stay constant. If your donor is in your house, you may feel comfortable being sexual while he's in the other room providing a sperm sample for you, or you may feel awkward. If you feel uncomfortable, wait to be sexual until after he's gone.

Some people like to use a vibrator before or after insemination. Others feel the electric currents might interfere with conception. No studies have been done on the effects a vibrator might have on conception. Do what feels right to you.

Be careful—if you're being sexual with a female partner or transman who does not take hormones, make sure she doesn't get pregnant! After handling sperm, wash your hands before becoming sexual with each other. Also, make sure she wears underwear if you're planning to snuggle immediately following insemination.

It's easy to feel pressured to have an orgasm on a time schedule. Also, the excitement and nervousness surrounding insemination can make it hard for you to feel aroused. Therefore, for some people being sexual before or after insemination feels too contrived. For others, however, it's a wonderful way to release the anxiety surrounding insemination and feel connected their body and partner. Remember, do what feels right, what makes you feel good in your body. Laughter releases endorphins into your system as well, so whatever you do, have a good time doing it.

Spirituality and Conception

If conception for you is a spiritual experience, it's important to explore this. What does this mean to you? Will your beliefs influence the location or methods of insemination that you feel most connected with? Will you need to have a certain ritual for the insemination experience? Do you need to feel connected with your egg and the sperm to allow for a more conscious union? Does everything have to "feel right" for it to work? Do you believe that anyone who's with you or touches the sperm will somehow affect the conception and, ultimately, the baby?

We've worked with many people who feel deeply connected with the spirituality of conception. This has meant something different for each person. For some, this spiritual outlook precludes them from wanting to conceive anywhere but at home. It also often precludes a person from wanting to take fertility drugs, which can be perceived as a negative chemical influence in a divine process.

For others, spirituality isn't tied to location or method of conception but rather to a place they enter inside themselves. For these people, insemination is an act of prayer. And still others who feel that conception is a deeply spiritual and personal experience don't feel it's in the least way connected to insemination.

Embodiment and Conception

Something people rarely think about, but which we find to be vitally connected to conception rates, is how a person feels in their body when they're trying to conceive. In our experience wherever you inseminate and whatever method you use, your chances of conceiving are much greater if your body is relaxed, open, and welcomes the experience. If you're uncomfortable or "checked out," your insemination will probably not be enjoyable and will also be less likely to work.

This brings us back to the question of how you make your decisions. If you check in with how your body responds to each of the decisions you make, you'll be less likely to make decisions that ignore the comfort of your body. And you'll be less likely to make decisions based on recommendations from others or what statistics say.

If you find yourself in an environment in which you're scared—be that your home, your donor's home, or a clinic—and you feel strongly that you don't want to switch environments—then it becomes all the more important for you to make peace with your decision. If your decision still doesn't feel right after you do this inner work, you may want to reexamine your choice.

Insemination Choices

The following are brief descriptions of the various insemination methods, followed by an in-depth exploration of the pros, cons, how-tos, and other considerations related to each method (and inherent location) of insemination.

- *Self-Insemination.* Self-insemination, also called vaginal insemination, simply means inserting the sperm into your own body without the assistance of a medical-care provider. The sperm is inserted into the vagina via a syringe without a needle. This method is the most similar to sexual intercourse in terms of the distribution of semen into your vagina. This is the most simple method available. Intracervical insemination (ICI) is the medical term for vaginal insemination (a misnomer as the sperm is not actually put into the cervix, but rather the vagina) although sometimes it involves using a speculum to locate the cervix.
- *Sexual intercourse.* Sex with a man or transwoman for the purposes of conception is less common in some lesbian communities now than it has been historically but is still an option that many consider.
- *Intrauterine insemination (IUI).* Intrauterine insemination places the sperm directly in the uterus through a sterile tube that is passed through the cervix.

Self-Insemination (Home Insemination)

Anyone can self-inseminate; there's nothing to it, as long as you know where your vagina is. And even that is easily taught! The following section explores everything you need to know about at-home self-insemination. At this time, it is in vogue to think that intrauterine insemination is the more effective means of insemination. By no means is this universally supported by evidence. In fact, numerous studies show otherwise. At Maia we see lots of successful self-inseminations at home every year using fresh or frozen sperm for people in all age brackets. Please take the time to examine what is right for you.

Advantages of Self-Insemination

There are many advantages to inseminating at home in a nonmedical environment. One of the primary benefits is that you're the one determining your environment and controlling your experience. You have the freedom to inseminate whenever you want in an unrushed manner, whether it's early morning, late at night, or the middle of the day. You have the freedom to include romance, relaxation, sex, ritual, food, pets, privacy, or friends. You can make it a comfortable, family-centered celebration. At home all emotions are safe; you can giggle, cry, have an orgasm, or even argue. You don't have to worry about being touched by anyone you don't know or trust. At home, you may find it much easier to feel comfortable and safe in your body than you would in an office. For people who have sexual abuse histories this can often make a huge difference in how they feel about the experience. We will discuss this later in the chapter as well.

A main reason people choose to self-inseminate at home is that they wish to receive the benefits of using fresh sperm. For some, these benefits outweigh the potential health or safety risks. In addition, many doctors won't help a woman inseminate with fresh sperm in a clinic unless the sperm comes from her husband, since they don't want to be liable if she contracts a sexually transmitted infection. Finally, people often choose self-insemination at home because it's nearly cost-free. The only cost is your sperm if you're using a sperm bank.

Challenges

There are two fairly significant challenges to inseminating at home. One is severing your donor's paternity rights if you use a known donor who comes to your home. The other is finding a medical doctor—if you choose to do so—come to your home and be present at the insemination. A third challenge, but one that's more easily remedied, is that you need to feel confident that you know how to do the insemination.

Legal security for our families is still new territory, and the precedents are still being established. Each state has different statutes governing insemination and paternity rights. For example, according to the National Center for Lesbian Rights (NCLR), when using a known donor, the safest way to ensure getting sole custody of your children is to inseminate in the presence of a medical doctor. At the time of insemination, if the semen passes through the hands of a doctor before going to the mother-to-be and if a waiver of responsibility is signed, the donor relinquishes any claim to that sperm. To solidify that, however, the sperm donor must sign additional legal papers after the baby is born in order to abdicate any further responsibility for—or claim to—the child.

Prospective parents handle this legal issue in many ways, some within the letter of the law and some possibly on the fringe of it. Many people we work with who use known donors choose to inseminate in a clinic; they say they feel this assures them full custody. Some have a doctor friend come to their house for the insemination or get a monthly signature from a doctor who isn't actually present for the insemination. Other people we work with feel that in order to choose a known donor in the first place, they have to know him well enough to trust him with a signed contract of intent to relinquish paternity. They then inseminate at home without doctor supervision and plan to sign the papers after the baby is born. Some people inseminate at home by default since they want to use a known donor and no clinician will assist them due to the risk of being sued for malpractice. And still others don't even sign contracts with their donors. Of course, it's a very personal decision. Research the current laws in your state and make a legally informed choice about your location of insemination. The NCLR is an excellent resource.

Performing an IUI at Home

We explore intrauterine insemination in depth later in this chapter in our discussion on clinic inseminations. We only mention it here because practitioners will occasionally—but rarely—perform it in your home. If you desire this, it may be worth your while to ask local obstetricians, general practitioners, midwives, and nurse practitioners to see if any of them might be open to the idea. Also, a growing number of people are teaching themselves how to do IUI for their partners. Many people want to do IUI but are unable to find a provider to perform it at home. Thus, they choose to do one IUI per cycle in a clinic setting and one at-home vaginal insemination per cycle to secure the benefits of both.

Making and Setting the Space for Self-Inseminating

Although it's quite easy to perform a self-insemination with fresh or frozen sperm, environmental and logistical elements must be considered and planned in advance.

Insemination is like a prayer. It is praying to get pregnant, to make a baby, to become a parent. When you look at it in this light, it's easy to focus on what kind of mood or environment you might like. Some people set up a beautiful environment in a special place in their home, often the bedroom, that includes flowers, candles, or incense. To them beautifying the space is a way of focusing their intention on conception. Others are less energetically inclined and don't need to tinker with their environment. The possibilities are endless; it's up to you. Here are some practical suggestions:

- Urinate before you begin the insemination so that you can comfortably stay reclined afterward.
- Have plenty of pillows, a blanket, food, and water within reach.
- Disconnect the phone.
- Take care of your pets ahead of time.

Fresh-Sperm Logistics

SPERM-FRIENDLY CONTAINERS

If you're working with a known donor, he needs to ejaculate into a small jar with a lid, if he isn't donating the sperm in your home. The jar doesn't need to be sterile. It just needs to be clean and dry, with no water left inside from washing, since sperm don't thrive when in contact with plain water. Many people give their donor a clean glass artichoke-heart jar. Some use sterile urine specimen cups from a doctor's office, but some prefer not to use plastic. Make sure the receptacle size will work for your donor.

FRESH SPERM, UNKNOWN DONOR

Arrange for your liaison to deliver the sperm to your home. Prearrange a system where they have a special knock and leave it on the doorstep, or arrange a simple hand-off. Since time is so clearly of the essence, it's important not to spend time making niceties. Say all of your thank-yous in advance.

Before you get to this stage, however, if you're going to inseminate in your home, you need to decide where you'd like your donor to ejaculate.

In a separate location? Some women can't imagine a man masturbating in their home. If this isn't a viable option for you, your logistics have to be well thought out. Does your donor live close enough that you, your partner, or friend could pick it up and bring it home? Could he use the nearby home of a friend or neighbor? Is there a local hotel he could use? Would you like him to deliver the sample? Would you prefer to pick it up? Would you like it to be left your doorstep? How inconvenienced is he willing to be?

Same location for ejaculation and insemination. When you and your donor will be in the same location for the ejaculation and insemination, it's helpful to preconsider the dynamics. Although you'll improve this process through trial and error, we've found that discussing some things in advance will make the process smoother. For example, if your donor comes to your home just after work and rush hour, he probably won't want to run to the bathroom and masturbate as soon as he arrives. Do you want to allow for some down time together? Share some food? Talk a bit? It's common to spend fifteen minutes to an hour chatting. If this isn't something you want, however, clarify your expectations in advance.

Show your donor what room you would like him to use and where the sperm container is. Be sure to give him privacy when he enters that room. If possible, try not to be in the next room. The more relaxed and sexually aroused a man is, the higher his volume of ejaculate will be. So if he feels you're hovering by the door, the sample probably won't be as large. One trick in a small apartment is to put on music and involve yourself in something so he won't think you're watching the clock and listening for him. It is usually best, whenever possible, to go out for a walk with a cell phone or to a local café and have him call when he is ready. Let him know that you expect it to take a while, so no worries.

Ahead of time, think about and discuss how you would like the hand-off to be. Some people feel guilty if they don't extend hospitality after the donor ejaculates, yet feel torn since they want to get to the insemination as quickly as possible. Decide if you would like him to knock on the door and leave the container; bring it to you in person, or stay to chat. If he's from out of town and is staying with you, be sure to have discussed these details with him, too. You can avoid awkward situations by being clear and direct ahead of time. Many people we've worked with have felt the most comfortable with a quiet hand-off and the donor immediately going out for a walk or to another part of the residence. They discussed this plan in advance and said their thank-yous and good-byes before the donor went to ejaculate.

Donor masturbation vs. sex with his partner. Sperm volume is often much lower from donors who masturbate than those who are sexual with their partners, so you might agree to invite his partner, if he has one. Some people feel fine about this and like that it's less mechanical and more organic. Others don't want to think about the donor's sex life so intimately. It's up to you. Just remember that the greater his arousal level, the better the sample.

Frozen-Sperm Logistics

Frozen sperm is extremely cold. Use a glove or cover your hand with something when removing the vial from the tank or dry ice. If your sperm comes in a liquid-nitrogen tank, the sperm bank will give you instructions on how to open it easily. The sperm will then need to thaw so that it's at body temperature. After a minute or two it will still be frozen but not too cold to touch. You or your partner should hold the vial of sperm next to your body until it's warm, at which point you should gently turn it and look to see if it's all liquid. Wait until the sperm has completely liquefied before drawing it up into the syringe provided by the sperm bank. Avoid turning the vial upside down as this will disperse the sperm too widely on the sides of the container for optimal collection.

You may be advised to immerse the vial in a bowl of slightly warm water, but it is easier to put the vial under your arm or in your bra and thus bring it to human body temperature than it is to put it in a bowl of water. Placing the vial in water that's too warm can overheat the sperm. The sperm survive the thawing process best if they thaw as quickly as possible. Therefore, don't leave the sperm sitting on the counter to slowly defrost. During the time you warm the sperm, you can be sexual (or not), focus on the baby, get centered, etc. A vial of frozen sperm usually takes eight to fifteen minutes to thaw.

How to Inseminate at Home with Fresh or Frozen Sperm

If you're using frozen sperm, the sperm bank should provide you with a non-latex 1-cc (tuberculin) needle-less syringe. If your sperm is fresh, use a 1-cc, 3-cc, or 5-cc needle-less nonlatex syringe, which you can buy from Maia or get from your health-care provider. A 10-cc syringe is much too big. Use a needle only if the tip of the syringe isn't small enough to draw up the entire sample. Using a 1-cc syringe for fresh-sperm inseminations often requires a few fillings and insertions to use up all of the semen. Before drawing the sperm into the syringe, make sure that the cap is off, that you've expelled any air, and that the needle has been removed.

Prop up your bottom slightly on a pillow so that your hips are tilted up. It doesn't need to be a tall stack of pillows, which might make your back hurt; you just need to be tilted up. Now it's time to insert the syringe. Take a deep breath and exhale slowly and fully. Relax your body and vaginal muscles. Get ready to welcome the sperm and your baby into your body.

Next, guide the syringe into your vagina yourself, or let a friend or your partner slip it in for you. Slide the syringe deeply into the vagina. You don't want to put the syringe directly up to the cervical opening and squirt it force-fully. The sperm needs to find its own way through the cervix; if it doesn't, the fertile mucus inside won't appropriately filter it. If you push the plunger of the syringe in gently, the risk of accidentally doing this is minimal, in fact virtually nonexistent. The more slowly you push the plunger, the less likely it will be that the sperm will run out of your body again. Fertile mucus pools in the back of the vagina and guides the sperm into the cervix, so aiming the syringe is not necessary. If you use a speculum, much of the sperm will get pulled out to the opening of the vagina as the speculum is removed. There-fore, it is not wise to use a speculum. When you're done, remove the syringe slowly from the vagina.

After the sperm has entered your body, relax, breathe, and notice what you feel. Some people can feel the aliveness of the sperm. You should remain lying down for at least twenty minutes; up to a few hours is ideal. After the first fifteen minutes or so, very slowly roll over. Spend five minutes on each side and on your stomach. Then very slowly roll back. In this way, if your cervix happens not to be angled directly into the pool of sperm and mucus, slowly rolling will ensure that it gets coated with sperm regardless of your position. If you know or have a sense of which ovary you're ovulating from, roll to that side first.

Slight cramping after insemination is normal. If you experience severe cramping, which is highly unlikely, contact your health-care provider immediately.

You Don't Need to Rush

Sperm doesn't lose much motility in the first hour after ejaculation. Try not to feel rushed. Sperm thrive in a warm (not hot) temperature and may be somewhat sensitive to light and air. Before insemination, keep the sperm container covered and warm inside your shirt against your body until you're ready to use it. If you're using frozen sperm, thaw it just before you use it, if possible. If you need to wait a little while to inseminate after it has thawed, keep it warm and out of the light, against your body, and inseminate within the hour.

Partner Issues

If you're planning to parent with your partner, please do everything you can so that both of you are present for all inseminations. We've seen relationships damaged when both partners weren't able to be together for inseminations on a regular basis.

We encourage you to make each insemination a beautiful and memorable experience for both of you. Whether or not you get pregnant, each month you inseminate you're solidifying your love for each other and building memories. By claiming these moments as powerfully intimate experiences, you won't let them take over your lives. Instead you'll be left with your love for each other and your desires to expand that love into a bigger family.

To those ends, sharing silence, laughter, massage, and rest in bed are all intimate post-insemination acts. Resist the urge to downplay the meaning of your inseminations. Even if one or both of you have to return to work, take at least a half hour after the insemination to connect with each other. It's worth it!

Self-Insemination for Single Women

There is great beauty and power in being able to say you made a baby all by yourself. It's also a lot of energy to have to hold all by yourself. As mentioned, it's helpful to decide ahead of time whether you'd like a friend to be with you when or right after you inseminate. If not, just make sure you have all of your items of comfort gathered so you won't have to get up after you inseminate.

Many women have shared with us the beauty of the inseminations they've done alone in their homes. The depth of union with yourself and all that comes with can be amazing. More than one woman has described feeling like she was making love with the world. You've chosen to intentionally create new life in your body, so go for it in the ways that are most meaningful for you.

Insemination Tricks and Gadgets

SPERM CUPS

Some women and medical providers use a sperm cup to hold the semen close to the cervix. A sperm cup is like a cervical cap or small diaphragm with a tube that can be attached to the bottom. Once the cup is placed on the cervix, the semen is pushed from a syringe up the tube and into the cup. Then the tubing is removed. The cup remains in place, and you can remove it a few hours after inseminating. Two known brands are the Keeper, and Ensure. Some people use a contraceptive cervical cap or menstrual cup at home to inseminate. It's best not to use ones that are made of latex, since studies show that it is detrimental to sperm.

From the clinical studies and anecdotal information we've examined, we feel comfortable in our conclusion that if you have enough time to rest lying down immediately following insemination, a sperm cup lends no advantage. The vast majority of sperm will travel into the cervix on their own within twenty minutes.

Also, we've worked with many people who've had difficulty using sperm cups as well as cervical devices, including the Keeper and Ensure. In a clinical setting, without a sperm-cup fitting, just a small syringe will be inserted into your vagina. Many women experience emotional and physical discomfort when receiving vaginal and speculum exams, which are necessary when using a sperm cup in a clinical setting; this may predispose them to feeling anxious about the insemination. In addition, many people experience difficulty, pain, and occasionally bleeding when trying to remove the sperm cup. This can traumatize, although only temporarily, your cervix (not to mention your psyche). Likewise a number of people who have used such devices report spillage to be a common problem.

We've found that unless you feel comfortable putting things on and removing them from your cervix, or you absolutely can't lie down for twenty minutes following your insemination, then it's preferable to avoid using a sperm-cup device.

EGG WHITES

Some people we encounter fill a needle-less syringe with egg whites and insert it into their vagina before insemination. Egg whites have a similar consistency to fertile mucus, and some believe they mimic fertile mucus and help guide the sperm into the cervix. Egg whites have a pH of 8.0 which is identical to semen and fertile mucus. We have no data about egg white use, just a few anecdotes. People who use them, however, swear by them. If you decide to do so, bring an egg to room temperature. Draw some egg white up with a needle-less syringe. Insert just enough to lubricate. People report to us that finding the right amount takes some practice. So you may want to experiment at times when you are not inseminating.

ROBITUSSIN COUGH EXPECTORANT

Some people claim that swallowing large doses of Robitussin before insemination helps increase the runniness of fertile mucus. Although we've met people who use this method, we haven't heard that it has helped anyone. If you purchase a cough syrup containing decongestant or an antihistamine, your mucus may actually dry up. We don't encourage the use of cough syrup in this way.

Conception via Intercourse with a Man or Transwoman

Some lesbian, bisexual, and single women and transmen choose to have intercourse to get pregnant. There are numerous advantages and some equally serious potential drawbacks that should be contemplated thoroughly before choosing intercourse as your means of conception.

Advantages

Choosing to have intercourse to get pregnant has some of the same advantages as at-home self-insemination. You're receiving the benefits of fresh sperm, it's a nonmedical experience, and it takes place on your time schedule. You have the freedom to make the experience whatever you want it to be.

People choose this option for a number of reasons. A primary reason is if the person you are having intercourse or making love with is your partner. Others choose this method because it feels more "natural" to or spiritually appropriate to them, or they do not believe sperm is designed to touch air or see light. In addition, intercourse is cost-free. For many, having sexual intercourse is the logical way to get pregnant. This can be an easy decision for many bisexual or single heterosexual women, as their sexual inclinations embrace being sexual with men. Others choose intercourse because they don't want to use a sperm bank or don't have access to or money for a sperm bank. Some people choose this option by having unprotected sex with a man and not informing him of the pregnancy. People who conceive this way often feel this grants them legal safety, as the man won't have to know they conceived. If the man later discovers the woman got pregnant, however, DNA tests can prove paternity and he can then sue for custody.

When choosing this method of conception, it's important to feel connected with your sense of who you are and what feels right. It can be challenging as a lesbian to choose to be sexually intimate with a man in order to get pregnant, and it's often not accepted in most lesbian communities as "appropriate." You might not rationally feel it's right, but intuitively and spiritually you may feel it's best for you. Perhaps you feel that male/female intercourse for conception is human design and anything but intercourse is artificial or unnatural. If you're partnered and feel this way, your partner may have a hard time with this perspective, as she may feel a threat to the intimate connection the two of you share and to the very concept that the two of you are trying to conceive a baby together.

For many it isn't necessarily a sexual or erotic experience they're looking for when choosing intercourse, but simply a means to pregnancy. Others feel the erotic and sexual nature of conception to be intertwined. They feel that a sexual connection with the man who is co-creating the baby-to-be is necessary. This may surprise women who have never had sex with a man or who haven't been attracted to men for a long time. For people who have this conviction, however, all other ways of conceiving seem unnatural.

Challenges of Conception via Intercourse

The desire to have sexual intercourse to get pregnant can be a difficult internal struggle for lesbians. We've seen women use this as a place to get "stuck." They feel that having sex with a man is the "right" way, but they don't want to have sex with a man, or their partner won't hear of it. This enables these women not to move on to a stage in which they are ready to conceive. Some women find that their belief is actually an internalized version of heterosexism or homophobia. They don't feel that making a baby any way but the "right" way counts. Since they think this—but can't fathom having sex with a man—they are left childless. Coming to recognize this as heterosexual enculturation is often the first step in feeling free to think about conception in a way that's unique to you. Some partnered lesbians have sex with a man and let the partnership weather it, while others keep staying stuck. Still other couples who are committed to monogamy can't find a way to get comfortable with one partner having sex outside of the relationship and don't move forward toward pregnancy.

Many lesbian communities embrace a specific "politically correct" method of conception that currently is not intercourse with a man. In fact, many people of all sexual orientations assume that if a woman can have sex with a man, it proves she's truly heterosexual and "going through a phase."

Legal risk. Some women choose to have sex with a friend who will be a known donor or coparent. In these situations most women have prescreened the men for communicable diseases, as they would with any known donor. When you have sex with a man to get pregnant, however, there's no way to formally sever paternity rights until after the baby is born and the donor has gone through a formal court process to relinquish those rights. From a legal standpoint, it's best to at least have signed a contract of mutual consent and intention—a known-donor contract. The fact that you're having intercourse to conceive, however, may negate any legal standing the contract might have. Therefore, the legal risk of using intercourse as your means to conceive is potentially great.

Health risks. If you're having sex with someone you don't know well, or at all, or if you aren't telling him that you're trying to make a baby, there are other challenges that are potentially much more serious, such as health risks. Please consider these carefully, as you're inviting this person's bodily fluids into your body. For more information about this and other potential issues related to anonymous sex, please read chapter 21.

Interpersonal and social issues. When you choose not to tell the man, you face some additional challenges. First of all, will you reveal the man's identity to your family and friends? If so, you run the risk of the information eventually coming back to him, and therefore run the risk of a custody suit. If you don't tell anyone, you'll have to live the rest of your life keeping a secret. Secrets of this magnitude can be hard to keep. If the man was someone you ended up dating for a while or is in your extended social circle, how are you going to make sure he doesn't find out that you're pregnant? This can be a challenge for women in smaller towns. What will you tell your child about his or her conception?

Psychological issues. Some people are nagged by feelings of guilt when they're dishonest. Choosing not to tell the man that you're trying conceive poses an ethical dilemma that each woman must confront. Is it ethical to be pregnant and not inform the biological father?

It's important to note that, just as with known donors with whom you aren't having sex, you may form an emotional bond that may surprise you. In fact, some women have fallen in love with the man they had intercourse with. This can be quite surprising, overwhelming, and complicate matters exponentially. Although these feeling usually pass, they can be quite disturbing at the time.

We had a client who was a lesbian in a longtime monogamous relationship. When we met her she had tried for quite some time to get pregnant in a number of different ways. She had used a sperm bank for more than a year. After that failed, she had been using a known donor's sperm for nearly a year. When that didn't work she decided to try having intercourse with a younger man she knew who had a high sperm count. She felt that something in the physiological process of having intercourse might increase her chances of conception.

When she attempted conception by intercourse her partner felt betrayed. Because the partner trying to conceive framed the act as a sexual experience, the nonbirth mother felt like her partner was "cheating" on her, and she also felt that it destabilized her concept of their sexual orientation. She felt her partner should try fertility drugs instead. The woman trying to get pregnant felt strongly about not taking fertility drugs. This couple eventually broke up because of this—after having tried together for more than two years to get pregnant.

This client continued on as a single woman planning pregnancy while mourning the loss of her relationship with her long-term partner, who didn't understand that she needed a baby more than she needed to be attached to a limited perception of sexual orientation. It was a painful experience for both women.

Because choosing to have sexual intercourse as a means of conception can have many ramifications, be sure to weigh the pros and cons before making this decision, and include your partner, if you have one, in your decision.

Tips for Increasing Your Chances of Conception When Having Intercourse

Some partnered lesbians or transmen choose to involve their partner in the sexual experience of conceiving with a man outside of their relationship. Others aren't out in regard to their sexual orientation or their plan to achieve pregnancy, and therefore they don't involve their partner in the process. Some partners don't wish to be involved.

It is important to note that arousal level and sexual satisfaction have both been proven to increase your chances of conceiving. For an increase in semen volume, the man or transwoman needs to be greatly aroused— ideally at least a half hour of building arousal before ejaculation. As mentioned earlier, studies have shown that for the woman or transman, sexual satisfaction during intercourse is directly related to how many sperm she retains.

Almost all commercial lubricants contain either spermicides or preservatives. They should be avoided when you attempt to conceive. Arousal fluid is the best fluid. After the sperm has entered your body, relax, breathe, and notice what you feel. As we've mentioned, some people can feel the aliveness of the sperm. Try to remain lying down for at least twenty minutes; up to a few hours is best. After the first five to fifteen minutes or so, very slowly roll over. Spend five minutes on each side and your stomach. Then very slowly roll back. When lying on your back with your hips slightly tilted, your cervix will always sit right in the pool of sperm, but if your cervix happens to be angled, rolling will ensure that it gets coated with sperm regardless of your position.

Insemination in a Clinic

Both intracervical (ICI) and intrauterine inseminations (IUI) are performed in an office or clinic. In vitro fertilization (IVF) is also available in infertility clinics.

Advantages

There are many good reasons for choosing to inseminate in a clinic. Some people inseminate in a medical setting because they're using a known donor and feel that, for legal reasons, it's the safest place. Some inseminate in a medical setting because they feel most comfortable there; at home would make them feel too vulnerable or unsafe. Some women live in places where sperm banks will only release sperm to a doctor and the doctor won't allow the women to take it to their homes. Others choose a clinic because they're using fertility medications or receiving medical treatments that are only available in a clinic and they choose to inseminate there as well. People who choose IUI are frequently only able have this procedure performed in a clinic.

Challenges

As we've mentioned, women are often led to believe that because of their age and, unspokenly, because of their sexual orientation, they have fertility problems and must start on a medicalized track. They're often led to believe in no uncertain terms that a medical approach will shorten the time it takes for them to get pregnant. This frequently involves starting with both IUI and fertility medications. Of course this blanket approach to fertility does not apply to all and may not be true for you.

If you choose to inseminate in a clinic because you're scared not to, examine whether fear is the best place from which to make your decisions. If you decide it isn't, take some time to gather more information about your feelings and the procedures offered, and then make your own decisions. Your final decision may be the same, but you'll know you've reached the decision on your own. You'll then be more inclined to remember that the whole process is yours, and you won't be as likely to forget that you continue to have choices every step of the way.

Many people have difficulty feeling fully comfortable in their bodies when inseminating outside of their homes. Some of the most common barriers to feeling comfortable in a clinical setting are those of not feeling you have freedom of sexuality, affection, and expression; feeling the staff is homophobic; reliving past traumas; feeling paralyzed about asking for what you want; and not feeling in control of your conception or health care.

Often some creative work is necessary to reduce or eliminate any of these barriers. We suggest that you start working on any relevant issues as early in the process as possible. Later we'll address some of the most common issues and then discuss what you can do to personalize your experience if you choose to inseminate in a clinical setting. First, however, you'll need to know what an in-clinic insemination looks like. We'll describe both vaginal insemination and intrauterine insemination before moving on to suggestions for increasing your comfort and empowerment.

Logistics of Vaginal Insemination (ICI) in a Clinic

Although there's slight variation from office to office, inseminating in a clinic is a fairly standard procedure. Vaginal insemination is performed as follows: You get up on an exam table, just as you would for a Pap smear. You undress from the waist down. Most likely you are given a paper gown or a paper drape to put over your legs. If a sperm cup is being used, the practitioner will need to fit it manually. This involves finding the correct size cup for your cervix, which can amount to a number of vaginal exams with a little internal movement to get the cup onto and off of your cervix. Then the practitioner may or may not do a speculum exam to see if the sperm cup is placed correctly before he or she performs the insemination. The sperm cup is attached to a tube that comes out of your vagina, to which a sperm-filled syringe will be attached.

Next the sperm is released into your body directly into your vagina via a needle-less syringe or into the tube, if you're using a sperm cup. Review the section on home insemination for a discussion of the pros and cons of using sperm cups. A speculum should not be used during the actual insemination, as the semen can pool in the bills and you'll lose some of the sperm. If it's the protocol of your practitioner to use a speculum, request that he or she not use it. Once the insemination is complete, your practitioner may either ask you to rest for a few minutes or to get dressed right away.

Although many people don't feel it, slight cramping in the uterus is not uncommon after insemination. Whether or not you've experienced cramping in the past during inseminations or during unprotected intercourse with a man, you may experience it now. Breathe into the sensation, relax, open your body up to the sperm, open yourself up to the pregnancy, and allow the sensation to just be there. If it's extreme, however, be sure to alert the medical staff immediately.

Logistics of Intrauterine Insemination (IUI) in a Clinic

Intrauterine insemination occurs as follows: You get up on an exam table, just as you would for a Pap smear, and undress from the waist down. You'll most likely be given a paper gown as well as a paper drape to put over your legs. You'll undergo a speculum exam so that the practitioner can locate your cervix.

Sometimes an instrument called a tenaculum is put on the cervix. This may be used if your cervical opening is difficult to view. A tenaculum has two little clamps that hold the cervix in place. If this instrument is used, you may feel a pinching sensation, which some women experience as painful or uncomfortable. If your practitioner routinely uses a tenaculum with every woman, ask him or her to attempt the IUI without it. The tenaculum is painful and traumatic and causes the release of fertility-reducing prostaglandins.

Once the cervix is in view, some practitioners will wipe it with Betadine—an iodine wash that feels cold and wet and has an astringent-like odor—to clean it. Next, a thin plastic tube called a catheter is put through the cervix and into the uterus. The catheter is connected to a syringe that contains sperm solution. Ideally, your cervix will be quite open, since you'll be inseminating during your window of peak fertility.

Some people don't feel the catheter going through their cervix and into the uterus; others feel pressure or slight discomfort. Still others feel painful cramping. What you feel will depend on the timing of the insemination, the finesse of the practitioner, and the size of the catheter.

After the catheter is inserted into the uterus, sperm is released into the tube and the uterus. Most people cannot feel this directly, though many have a sensation of feeling full. The whole procedure, from the moment the speculum is put into your body until it is released, usually takes between three and fifteen minutes. In some clinics women are offered ibuprofen. Some are given antibiotics, prophylactically, to take after the insemination. You may request not to receive any medication. Once the insemination is complete, the practitioner may ask you to rest for a few minutes or to get dressed right away. All studies conducted on the subject show that remaining lying down for even as little as ten minutes will greatly improve your chances. Given that this is true, if it is not their policy you will want to schedule a longer appointment ahead of time to allow for rest.

Some people feel cramping in their uterus after they inseminate, no matter where they inseminate; others do not. Whether or not you've experienced cramping in the past during unprotected intercourse with a man, you may experience it now. It's a common physical sensation. However, if a person has a reaction to the sperm, the washing solution, or any hormones in the semen that are not thoroughly washed away, she may feel severe cramping following the IUI. If this is the case for you, promptly alert the medical staff.

Advantages of IUI

Physical considerations. Sometimes it may be difficult for sperm to get through your cervical mucus, or the chemistry of your vagina may be not conducive for the sperm. Placing sperm directly into your uterus will improve the chance of conceiving.

Sperm considerations. Some studies indicate that only 5 to 10 percent of sperm make it through the cervix after intercourse; the rest remain in the vagina. Although this is not significant with a normal ejaculate containing millions of sperm, it becomes significant to people working with low-count or low-motility sperm or sperm that experiences agglutination (clumping). Frozen sperm often falls into the "lower sperm count" category, as we've discussed.

Availability of sperm. If only IUI-ready sperm is available, we recommend that you do two IUIs per cycle.

Age. It's commonly recommended that women over 35 use IUI when inseminating with frozen sperm. At Maia we do not make blanket recommendations on the basis of age. However, if you are using frozen sperm and started with vaginal inseminations as your sole method and have not conceived within three months and you are 38 or older, then we do recommend that you try at least one IUI per cycle. If you're younger than 35 and haven't gotten pregnant using frozen sperm within six months with vaginal inseminations, you might consider doing one IUI and one vaginal insemination each month.

For additional information about timing IUIs and the recommended number of IUIs per cycle, see chapter 18.

Challenges with IUI

IUI is an invasive medical procedure, and as such it involves potential risks. The risks, although slight, may include infection and perforation of the uterus. An IUI does not need to hurt. Unfortunately, women often report to us that their in-clinic IUI experiences not only hurt but are often even excruciatingly painful. This does not need to be. If the timing is appropriate and a gentle technique is used during the IUI, there should only be a sensation of slight pressure. Many people feel nothing at all.

There are some good reasons why you should not participate in a painful insemination. When your cervix or uterus is traumatized, prostaglandins are released that cause the uterus to contract in a way that can push sperm out. Thus, a painful insemination may result only in trauma and not pregnancy. Many people, if they can't find a gentle IUI practitioner, feel that a comfortable at-home vaginal insemination is preferable to a painful IUI in a clinic and will more likely result in conception.

Be aware that most clinics don't have weekend hours, so some months you may choose to inseminate at home rather than miss a cycle or inseminate at the wrong time. Likewise, scheduling can prove to be a constant challenge when using IUI. Often the clinic may have restricted hours or be unable to inseminate you at the optimal time. Precision of IUI timing is critical, since sperm only live for approximately eight hours once inside the uterus. Once again, if a clinic setting isn't your first choice, IUI may not be the best method for you.

Finally, IUI can be expensive and most health insurance plans do not cover it.

IUI and Fresh Sperm

IUI does not necessarily increase your chances when you are using fresh sperm. If you have a donor with a good semen analysis, regardless of your age we recommend that you try to self- inseminate for at least a few months before trying IUI. Remember that most straight people try for a year or more before moving to infertility treatments. Because the sperm—whether fresh or frozen—only lives for eight to ten hours in the uterus, if you do add an IUI into the mix be sure to have at least one vaginal insemination as well. The advantage of fresh sperm is the volume and the increased length of survival when inseminated vaginally.

If you are feeling like your fertility is waning, or your lab results indicate reduced fertility, or his semen analysis is poor or borderline, then IUI is certainly the best method of insemination. However, unless you are working with poor sperm quality, continue with a vaginal insemination as well.

Preparation of Sperm for IUI

When a clinic prepares sperm to bypass the cervix and be inserted directly into the uterus, it is washed in order to separate healthy live sperm away from the rest of the semen. Semen contains sugars, salts, antibodies, live and dead sperm, and sometimes bacteria or viruses. It also contains various hormones, including prostaglandins, which can cause the uterus to cramp. The fertile mucus in your cervix is a natural filter that guides healthy sperm through and keeps everything else out. If you bypass the cervix and mucus altogether by doing an intrauterine insemination, the sperm needs to be separated from the rest of the semen. Not washing the sperm can result in severe cramping and allergic reaction.

Please note that rewashing already washed frozen sperm is not necessary and will result in a decreased sample size. It is becoming increasingly more common for fertility clinics to use two vials of IUI-ready sperm to inseminate with. Some clinics will rewash the two together, whereas others slowly fill the uterus to capacity, since they find that for some people 1 cc can go in smoothly and none of the sperm will end up flowing out of the cervix.

Finding the Best Practitioner for You

Unfortunately, in many parts of the country it can be quite difficult to find a physician who is willing to work with lesbians or unmarried women. It's not illegal in any state for a physician to provide you with these services; each physician, however, makes his or her own decision about whether or not to provide those services to you. Many practitioners won't inseminate you if you use a known donor to whom you're not legally married. Likewise, some sperm banks will only release sperm to a physician directly and not to you for home insemination. These physicians may not permit you to take your sperm home with you. Keep in mind that there are sperm banks that will send the sperm directly to your home as long as you have a letter signed by a doctor or midwife, who need not practice or live in your state. If you're having difficulty finding an appropriate practitioner, you may contact the Gay and Lesbian Medical Association at www.glma.org for information or a referral. If you feel that you need IUI, you may have to drive a distance for such services. If you cannot find a local doctor willing to work with you, then you may have to forego the option of IUI all together.

Many health insurance companies are becoming more savvy with their language when defining coverage limits. You may have to be creative in finding loopholes, or you may pay out of pocket if you can't prove you have a male partner who's infertile. The best bet is finding a sympathetic doctor who'll make an ambiguous note in your chart, or have the office staff call your insurance company to clarify that indeed you don't have a partner who has a viable sperm count.

Initial phone screening will save you time and emotional energy. You might want to do interviews over the phone to determine which clinics have worked with queer or single women. If you live in an area where more than one queer-friendly practitioner provides insemination services, take note of how the practitioner and other office staff discuss your sexual orientation, address your partner (if you have one), and address you. If you feel more comfortable working with a woman, seek out a female practitioner.

Perhaps there's only one nearby practitioner or only one covered by your health insurance. If you don't feel comfortable with him or her, you may need to decide what will make you feel the most empowered in the situation. Perhaps you could change insurance plans, travel to a nearby city, or pay out of your own pocket.

Sometimes you may need to continue to work with the provider, letting him or her know your expectations in advance and giving feedback afterward. In some cases, unfortunately, the best you can do is not rock the boat.

Interviewing Practitioners

Even in the Bay Area, where many queer women inseminate in medical settings and many doctors specialize in insemination services, we've heard expressions of dissatisfaction from our clients time and again. Perhaps the doctor is friendly, but the nurses aren't. Or maybe the nurses are friendly, but the doctor isn't. Having a lesbian practitioner doesn't always necessarily carry over to the office staff being sensitive in their care and inclusion of the partner. Finding a supportive, respectful, sensitive care provider can even be a challenge in urban areas, including queer-friendly San Francisco. The key to a good experience is to find a care provider with a warm bedside manner who treats you and your family with respect, maintains eye contact, and does not dismiss your concerns or questions.

We suggest that you have an initial consultation during which you can meet the fertility specialist and discuss your preferences without committing to any services. At this time you can ask to see the exam room so that you'll be able to visualize where the insemination will occur and prepare for it mentally. You can let the practitioner know how you'd like your conception to be and get his or her feedback. Be sure to ask the practitioner what their timing recommendations are. After you hear the response also ask if they recommend this to everyone. (At Maia we have found that not only is each person individual and cannot be generalized but that there are different considerations to keep in mind based on age and fresh or frozen.) It may be worthwhile to ask how they feel about complementary health care as well. If you have a choice of practices and one appreciates the value of acupuncture, you may feel more comfortable there.

At this visit you should ask to meet the other practitioners in the practice, especially if you have a practitioner who might be on call, out of town, or on vacation during your insemination. If you can't arrange to meet the other practitioners, be sure to ask about their experience and comfort level when working with lesbian women. It's quite common for there to be weeks or even months when your practitioner is unavailable, so it's important to feel comfortable with your back-up options.

Along these lines, it's important to inquire about the clinic's hours and what your choices are if you're fertile after hours or on the weekend. Because you can't control which days you're fertile, it's helpful to explore whether there's a clinic in your area that provides weekend inseminations.

At the end of your interview ask that your preferences be noted in your chart so that you can reference them to any other staff members with whom you may be interacting. This is a valuable tool that will help reduce the possibility of stress and miscommunication at the time of insemination. For example, if it's noted in your chart that you and your partner are lesbians, that your partner will be in the room with you at all times, and that you'll be inserting your own speculum, you can avoid challenging conversations by just asking the staff member to look at the agreements that are documented. In the medical world, if a conversation isn't documented, it never happened.

At any point, if you're unhappy with the services provided in your area, consider making a longer drive to have the kind of experience with which you feel comfortable. We live in an urban environment and have clients who drive from towns three or more hours away for our insemination services; some of our clients even fly in from out of state.

Feeling Safe Before Your IUI

One element that affects how we respond to a "medical" or gynecological experience is our life history. Being inseminated in a clinic can sometimes bring up sexual-abuse memories. If you think this may be the case for you, it's best to do some emotional preparation. Perhaps you'd feel safer if you let the practitioner know about your sexual-abuse history in advance. Likewise, bringing a partner or a friend to your inseminations can help keep you rooted in the present. Familiarizing yourself in advance with a speculum may help put you at ease as well. (See pages 245 for step-by-step instructions on using a speculum.) Practicing relaxation exercises can help you feel more comfortable at the time of your insemination. In addition, having a gentle and reassuring talk with yourself prior to arriving at the clinic can help alleviate any anxiety. Likewise, being aware that you may need to take extra time during the insemination simply to process the situation is helpful in planning your schedule.

In-clinic inseminations may also bring up physically or emotionally uncomfortable medical experiences you may have had, particularly in regard to abortions, miscarriage, or pelvic exams. These memories can make you feel out of control. In the past, many people have scrunched their eyes up, gritted their teeth, and held their breath to get through Pap smears or vaginal exams. Many people haven't had Pap smears for years due to past negative experiences or to concern about homophobia or gender concerns.

Although it may not be an altogether pleasing idea, if you address these issues in advance, you may be able to move into a much more comfortable, empowered place, thereby allowing your insemination to be a pleasant experience. This is a novel concept for many. It isn't a bad or shameful thing for a vaginal exam to be comfortable. On the contrary, comfort with our bodies has been taken away; it's time to reclaim it.

Often, connecting with the "baby" and how you'd like to feel when you conceive and bring the baby into your body may provide the incentive for you to do the emotional work necessary for you to become more comfortable with the process. Using a speculum at home can serve as a way of monitoring your fertility, getting comfortable with your body, and demystifying and demedicalizing speculums. It can help increase your awareness of your vagina and cervix. You can do exercises to control your breathing, relax your muscles, and feel more in control. In the clinic you can then insert your own speculum if it feels empowering to do so. Whether or not you insert the speculum, you will be familiar with its movements and more comfortable with the feelings of insertion.

When you bring a health-care provider into your conception process, it may be difficult for you to maintain your decision-making power. Many of our clients share that they never even considered that they had more options than were offered to them. Questioning your care provider or making a decision that doesn't include all the pieces of their plan can often be met with a feeling of disdain from the doctor. This is one of many reasons why it's important to interview practitioners and take note of each practitioner's style and approach. Remember, you can change practitioners at any time.

Feeling Comfortable During the IUI

Some people worry that insemination in a clinic will be physically uncomfortable, rushed, or impersonal. This can be true. There are a number of ways to make yourself feel more comfortable in a clinic. Often none of these possibilities are offered to you—you'll have to request them, which you may find surprisingly difficult at first. It's common for women in a medical setting to feel they're supposed to behave a certain way—to be a "good girl" or a "good patient." Our deference to the authoritative medical system is culturally ingrained, and a self-protective element often leads women not to act in an antagonizing manner toward someone who's going to touch them intimately. Remember that you are hiring your practitioner to help you conceive your baby. You have the right to make it a comfortable and personal experience.

You may receive a disgruntled initial response to requests simply because you are disrupting the normal routine—not because your requests are impossible to fulfill. The medical assistant, nurse, or practitioner may need a moment to compose themselves after your request, so give that person time. Then ask again. Examples of things you may want to request include:

- If you feel uncomfortable or out of control having your feet up in stirrups, you can rest your feet on the edge of the exam table.
- If the room is too cold, you can ask for the temperature to be changed or you can bring a blanket or wear a sweatshirt. You can ask for a blanket if you become cold or nervous while on the exam table.
- You can ask to see your cervix with a mirror. You can ask for your partner to be able to see your cervix as well. Not all offices have hand mirrors, although they should. Bring one from home if you need to.

- You can ask that your partner or a friend be allowed to watch the procedure.
- You can ask for your partner or friend to push the plunger of the syringe in. Remember to go slow.
- You or your partner can insert the speculum and then have the practitioner adjust it.
- You or your partner can insert your sperm cup if either of you feel comfortable doing that and it's something you know how to do.
- You can ask your practitioner to explain exactly what is being done as it's being done, or let you know at the time when something may feel uncomfortable.
- You can keep the top half of your clothes on.
- You don't have to have a drape over your legs if you don't want to. The drape blocks your view of the lower half of your body. There's no reason for the drape other than the idea that it's more comfortable for both the patient and practitioner by supposedly desexualizing the situation.
- Although it's easier to have a speculum inside you if you're not fully sitting up, the exam table doesn't have to be completely flat. It can be raised slightly or you can ask for a pillow so that you'll have a better view of what's happening in your body.
- You can also ask that the practitioner not use a speculum, sperm cup, or a cervical cap if you are receiving an IUI.
- You can request to be alone and do a vaginal insemination on your own.
- If your practitioner is rushed and brusque in his or her speculum- or finger-insertion method, you can ask him or her to stop or go more slowly at any time. If your practitioner isn't receptive, change practitioners. A vaginal or speculum exam need not be painful. We repeat, a vaginal exam need not be painful.
- You can ask to be allowed to rest undisturbed for fifteen to twenty minutes after the insemination.

Intimacy and Personalizing the Space

This is your insemination, the potential beginning of your pregnancy. Claim the experience. Feel free to bring anything that might make you feel more comfortable. Some people like to bring music.

It's valuable to have practiced quick ways of establishing a sense of connection with yourself and your partner if you have one. When practiced, this skill can be called upon. Even in our nonmedical environment, we've found that people often feel vulnerable and even slightly embarrassed at first if they want to have a feeling of sacredness or intimacy during their inseminations. Once they get over their internal self-inhibition, they can be much more affectionate and connected.

Depending on whether the office staff is homophobic, you might not feel comfortable being physically affectionate in any way with your partner. In some cases you might not even be out to your care provider, and your partner might not be present. Or you may be single and closeted and therefore feel you can't be fully present. Although physical intimacy isn't inherently encouraged in clinic settings, there are some ways for you to share an intimate connection with your partner.

If your partner or friend is going to push the plunger, you have a built-in opportunity to look each other in the eyes for a moment and say something personal before releasing the sperm. Likewise, if you're the partner or friend of an inseminating woman and choose not to release the sperm, be sure to make physical contact with her. Hold hands and speak soft words of encouragement to her. Remind her to be open and to welcome the sperm. In your time alone after the procedure, take some time to visualize the conception happening and pregnancy beginning. Make this time special and memorable.

If your ideal conception includes being sexually intimate with yourself or a partner, it's important to come to a peaceful place inside yourself and within your relationship about the fact that you probably won't be able to be sexual at the clinic.

You may choose to be sexual before your appointment so that you enter the space of sexual connection with yourself and your partner (if you have one) ahead of time. This established sense of connection will then have a greater chance of being maintained throughout your insemination. Another way is to maximize your time alone in the room. In most offices you'll probably find yourself waiting, both in a waiting room and in the clinic room. This is the time to initiate contact with yourself or your partner. Most partners become nonsexually intimate at this time, or feel sexual energy without direct physical expression. This can be through holding hands, making eye contact, rubbing each other's back or shoulders, singing silly or meaningful songs, smooching, or doing whatever feels right. Some partners choose to be sexual with each other as soon as they get home.

Clinic Insemination and Partner Issues and Roles

When you're partnered it's important to examine the choices you're making as a team. Established and practiced ways to feel connected become important resources to call upon when you're inseminating—the emphasis being on having established familiar cues. If you choose to inseminate in an environment that isn't your own, you don't have much time in which to create an intimate bond, and established cues will be important.

Working as a team means communicating clearly before, during, and after each insemination. With clear communication you can either consciously resist falling into roles, or consciously embrace a separation of duties, feelings, and roles. In a clinical environment there's an inherent segregation of roles between someone who's conceiving and her partner, simply in terms of who has their clothes off and is up on the exam table and so vulnerable, and who is fully clothed and upright.

With this inherent difference in vulnerability comes a commonly unspoken assumption that the clothed partner is responsible for the physical and emotional well-being and safety of her inseminating partner. Often the person being inseminated doesn't feel comfortable being assertive, expressing when she isn't happy with the interaction, or giving feedback. This role, therefore, gets delegated to the partner.

A person being inseminated may feel very vulnerable—especially when she needs to trust the practitioner with the inside of her body—saying anything that might upset him or her. This may lead to an unspoken expectation that the partner will be the one who expresses anger or frustration about an interaction or who gives feedback. Taking on this role can leave the partner feeling she has to hold all of the negative energy in relation to the clinic staff, and she may not want to shoulder this burden. If the partner is unaware of the expectation, the woman being inseminated can feel let down that her partner doesn't verbalize her feelings for her.

Commonly, the partner who is not inseminating feels ignored or marginalized by the staff. She may also feel blatant or suppressed homophobia from the staff. Often the person being inseminated is so focused on herself in the moment, which is natural, that she doesn't notice this. This is another reason why it's important to communicate with each other before and after each insemination. This way you can decide as a team how the experience felt and what you might like to change next time—if there will be a next time—and how and when you'll address your concerns with the staff.

It's important to discuss in advance any cues you might want to have with each other in the moment. For example, if you're nervous about vaginal exams and it's hard for you to speak up for yourself in those moments, you might have a cue for your partner—such as patting her arm twice—that lets her know you need the practitioner to stop. Having prearranged signals allows you to feel more in control of the experience.

Many couples decide it's unnecessary for both partners to take time off from work, so the one conceiving will go by herself to the appointments. However, we hear time and time again that these same couples don't feel as safe or supported as they would if their partner were there, and so they start to feel resentment and loneliness. The women who inseminate with their partners, however, express feeling safer and more connected to each other and the experience. In chapter 1, we explore how the ongoing process of insemination can undermine self-esteem and relationship intimacy, and why it's vital to be together whenever possible for inseminations.

If there's no possible way you can arrange to be together, we strongly encourage the two of you to establish a special bonding ritual the morning of each insemination. We also suggest that both you and your partner focus on conception during the time of insemination, even if one of you must be at work, and connect by phone just before, during, or after, if you can.

Some people are afraid to go to a clinic with their partner because it would mean acknowledging just how big a step conception is. When a partner can't miss work for financial reasons, there may be an underlying factor of homophobia, both externally feared and internally based. Perhaps she isn't out at work or hasn't told anyone that she and her partner are trying to conceive. It can be difficult to try to reconcile all these areas of our lives. At some point you'll come out, probably, and miss work at the time of the birth, in the first few months thereafter, or if your child is sick. Insemination fits in the same category. This is where partner communication is once again key. If you've established your priorities jointly, while honestly listening to each other, you can decide how to approach these issues. If you don't fully discuss them, you may both be working from inaccurate assumptions. Working together, you can support each other in making decisions that feel right.

The key is to stay honest with yourselves and each other. Allow for your needs and priorities to change and modify as time passes. If you do, you'll be able to feel connected with yourself and each other throughout the process.

Single-Parent Issues and Clinic Inseminations

When you're single it's easy to end up in a clinic for insemination. Many single parents express to us that they don't feel as lonely in a clinic. It can feel like you have someone to share with and talk to. Others don't feel that at all. Instead they report feeling as if the whole world is their partner; they share and ask questions of everyone in their lives. Still other single prospective parents we've met have used a team approach for both insemination and decision making, involving an intimate circle of family or friends for support.

Some people feel empowered by inseminating on their own; it makes them feel more complete. Others feel a loss at such a prospect. If you feel this way, we recommend that you bring a friend or family member with you when you're inseminating in a clinic. Remember that you may also ask a friend to come to your home. Self-insemination is easily done. If you need someone to share with and don't have a friend to talk to, see if a Single Moms by Choice group is in your area, see a therapist, or join a single mothers chat room. Your clinician doesn't have to be your confidante.

Likewise, if you do choose to inseminate in a clinic and go alone, you may feel you have no one with whom to share both the painful and joyful moments. This can bring up the bittersweet nature of single parenting: You get everything for yourself, but you have no one with whom to share it. Have you come out to your practitioner? Or have you chosen to remain closeted? Does your decision affect how you feel in your body during the insemination?

We've spoken with a number of single people who started off inseminating at home but soon switched to inseminating in a clinic so they could decide with someone else what they might do differently. Remember that you can consult with a fertility specialist or give Maia a call, get the information and feedback you need, and still conceive at home if that's what you prefer.

Cervical Awareness and Insemination Effectiveness

Different people have different levels of awareness and sensation in their cervix. Some have sensitive cervices and others don't. Generally, cervical awareness increases insemination effectiveness. When you're at different parts of your cycle, your cervix is either more or less relaxed. Our cervices are emotional. As midwives we see and feel this all the time in birth. We also experience this when we teach women how to do self-exams with a speculum. If you accidentally bonk your cervix with a speculum, it will often retract self-protectively.

You can get fairly deep insights into your emotional state by looking at your cervix regularly and simultaneously noting your emotional state. The cervix is the doorway to the center of woman's capacity to create life. It is a sacred doorway. If you don't feel safe, your cervix may be noticeably tense or closed.

We've noticed this phenomenon distinctly when we perform IUIs. We've seen how much control women have over allowing something to enter their cervix. An apparently closed cervix can open if you relax and focus on deep opening. This not only makes the insemination much more comfortable and quick, but also most likely increases your chances of conception by lessening the hormonal reaction the cervix triggers when it senses pain. Likewise, common sense suggests that an open cervix will more easily allow sperm to swim into it after vaginal insemination. And of course, orgasm can release and open the cervix.

EXERCISE: CERVIX AWARENESS
Each day imagine being open to conception and bringing a baby and sperm into your body. Breathe, visualize, pray. Spend time cultivating this openness. Then imagine you can connect with your cervix. Feel it. Breathe it open. See what message it sends you. It holds our female and sexual histories. Spend time each day checking in with it. It may sound silly or uncomfortable for you at first, but ultimately you'll bring your ability to open your cervix into more conscious control, which will ease not only your insemination, but also labor.

After All the Preparations

First Insemination

A few words of wisdom to share about the first cycle you inseminate: Allow it to be funny—laugh and enjoy yourself. The first month is always comical. You're usually nervous and stressed. If you're at home, your dogs may knock the semen over, you may lock your sperm tank and keys inside your car, you may insert the sperm and watch it come out again. You may have to wait forever for your donor to leave or not have your donor show at all. Also, expect your donor's sperm sample to be meager the first time—he's nervous too. If you're going to a clinic, the first time almost always will be the one when either you or your partner will be stuck at work, the doctor will be busy doing emergency surgery, or the sperm bank will send a vial with a less-than-optimal sperm count. Chalk it all up to gaining experience and laugh at the comedy of it all. Try not to argue, and have compassion for yourself—and your partner and other people involved in the experience—if you end up feeling stressed out.

Partner Tension Cycles

There's often a predictable cycle to the tensions surrounding inseminations. Many couples have either a pre- or post-insemination fight. This seems to be a way of clearing the tension in the air. Crying is also a common component of insemination—especially inseminations performed at home. Maybe it has to do with finding a release that then leaves room for an opening. Perhaps it's about making enough time and space for all of the feelings that come up each time you choose to ask a baby into your body. Intentional ritual might help ease the building tension and expectation. Maybe simply having compassion for yourself and your partner, regardless of what comes up, is all that is needed.

Make It Meaningful!

Insemination can be done at home or in an exam room; with fresh or frozen sperm; by sex, IUI, or self-insemination. Each person makes her own choice, taking into account a variety of factors. Wherever and however your insemination occurs, it should feel meaningful, comfortable, and safe to you—even joyful and celebratory! Insemination doesn't have to look any certain way. It doesn't have to be ritualized or sexualized. It doesn't have to take three hours. Take some time to decide what might make it better for you. It seems that the more time passes without pregnancy, the easier it is to unconsciously prohibit the actual act of insemination from taking up much time or space in your life.

Trying to get pregnant can take over your whole life, making you feel out of control. In some ways the actual insemination is the only part that can be controlled. As a result we've seen people try to take any hope or meaning out of the insemination process itself, relegating it to a task that must be done on a certain day. Resist the temptation to strip your baby's conception of its magic. Claim your conception and make it the internal and external experience you want it to be. Reverse the equation: instead of controlling the insemination as a means of feeling there's something you have a handle on, use that same ability to control it to reaffirm to yourself, and your partner (if you have one), and to the baby why you want to be a parent. Allow each insemination to be a meaningful and memorable experience.

MAIA
Midwifery & Preconception Services
Fertility Chart

Month(s) _____   Year _____   Cycle number _____   Length of cycle _____ (days)   Days of Insemination _____

Day of Cycle	1	2	3	4	5	6	7	8	9	10	11	12	13	14	15	16	17	18	19	20	21	22	23	24	25	26	27	28	29	30	31	32	33	34	35	36	37	38	39	40
Date																																									
Day																																									
Phase of the Moon																																									
Inseminations/Intercourse																																									
Bleeding																																									
Ovulation (pain, pressure, sensation, which side)																																									
Cervical changes (high/low, open/closed, soft/firm, color)																																									
Mucus color & consistency (dry, wet, slippery, fertile, stretchy, sticky, clear, yellow, white)																																									
Lens (ferning)																																									
Ovulation Predictor Kit/ Monitor																																									
Fertility Drugs																																									
Mood changes (anger, contentment, creative, determined, ecstatic, insecure, sensitive, sociable, voluptuous...)																																									
Sexual desire (increase or decrease in libido, masturbation, sex with partner)																																									
Appetite or food cravings																																									
Breast changes (tenderness, swelling)																																									
Cramping																																									
Stress																																									
Sleep changes & dreams																																									

Notes/Comments/Details/Dreams (also see back) _____

2820A Adeline Street, Berkeley CA 94703-2205 • T (510) 869-5141 • F (510) 540-6223

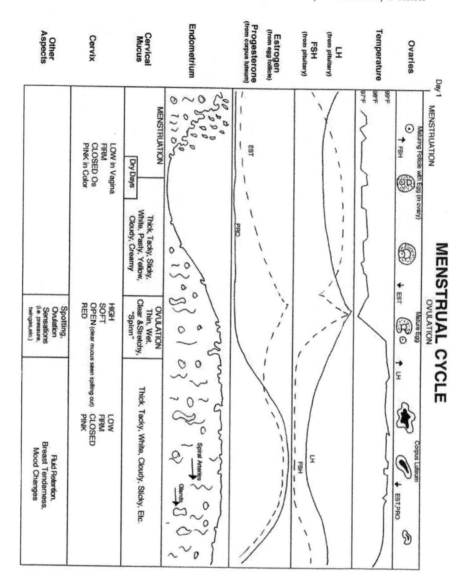

Temp			Day
crampy!	sens.nipples	period cramps	1
crampy!	sens.nipples	period cramps	2
		period	3
		period	4
		period	5
		period	6
		spotting	7
			8
			9
			10
		clumpy	11
insem 1@8pm	ferning	stretchy by 4pm	12
insem 2@8am	ferning	fertile	13
(+1@7pm)		fertile	14
		fertile	15
	horny	yellow	16
	horny	yellow	17
	horny	white	18
			19
crampy	horny		20
crampy	sens.nipples		21
crampy	sens.nipples		22
crampy	sens.nipples	spotting!	23
	sens.nipples		24
crampy	sens.nipples		25
nausea	sens.nipples		26
nausea	sens.nipples	spotting	27
	Im pregnant!	no period	28
		no period	29

THIS WOMAN HAS NEVER BEEN PREGNANT. SHE'S 29 YEARS OLD AND HAS INSEMINATED THREE CYCLES WITH FROZEN SPERM FROM A KNOWN DONOR. THIS IS HER THIRD CYCLE. SHE CHOSE TO USE FOUR VIALS OF SPERM THIS CYCLE. SHE HAD USED LESS DURING THE PREVIOUS TWO CYCLES. SHE CONCEIVED THIS CYCLE.

Fertility Chart

Month(s) MARCH/APRIL   Year 00   Cycle number 12   Length of cycle 22 (days)

Day of Cycle	1	2	3	4	5	6	7	8	9	10	11	12	13	14	15	16	17	18	19	20	21	22	23	24	25	26	27	28	29	30	31	32	33	34
Date	31	1	2	3	4	5	6	7	8	9	10	11	12	13	14	15	16	17	18	19	20	21	23	24	25	26	27	28	29	30	31	32	33	34
Day																																		
Phase of the Moon																																		
Insemination/Intercourse																																		
Bleeding	yes	yes	yes	yes	yes/spot	spot			2½									spot	spot	spot	spot	spot												
Ovulation (pain, pressure, sensation, which side)											1	1								~	~													
Cervical changes (high/low, open/closed, soft/firm, color)						closed	little open	open	less open	high	high + soft	—	closed	closed																				
Mucus color & consistency						slippery	stretch	stretch	slippery	sticky	sticky	—	sticky	—	slippery	little stretchy																		
Lens (ferning)				1	1	1	+	+	+	1	+	1	1	1	+	+	+	+	+	+	+													
Ovulation Predictor Kit/Monitor																																		
Fertility Drugs																																		

THIS WOMAN HAS NEVER BEEN PREGNANT. SHE'S 42, USING FROZEN SPERM, AND HAS INSEMINATED FOR SIX CYCLES BY IUI. HER CHARTS SHOW A NUMBER OF SIGNS OF LOW PROGESTERONE. THE LENS SHOWS FERNING IN THE SECOND HALF OF THE CYCLE; HER TEMPERATURE DOESN'T REMAIN HIGH; AND SHE SPOTS FOR FIVE DAYS BEFORE ACTUAL REGULAR MENSTRUAL BLEEDING STARTS, PRECEDED BY TWO DAYS OF FERTILE-LIKE MUCUS. HER CYCLE LENGTH IS ONLY TWENTY-TWO DAYS, ALTHOUGH THE SECOND HALF (THE LUTEAL PHASE) IS CLOSE TO FOURTEEN DAYS LONG. SHE DID NOT BECOME PREGNANT THIS CYCLE.

Fertility Chart

Month(s) APRIL/MAY Year 00 Cycle number 13 Length of cycle Pregnant! (days)

Day of Cycle	Date	Day	Phase of the Moon	Insemination/Intercourse	Bleeding	Ovulation (pain, pressure, sensation, which side)	Cervical changes (high/low, open/closed, soft/firm, color)	Mucus color & consistency (dry, wet, slippery, fertile, stretchy, sticky, clear, yellow, white)	Ovulation Predictor Kit/Monitor
1	22	S		X	blood				
2	23	S		X	blood				
3	24	M		X X	blood				
4	25	T		X X	blood				
5	26	W		X	spotting				
6	27	T		x	spotting		FIRM		
7	28	F			dry		MEDIUM		
8	29	S			dry		MED.		1
9	30	S			sticky	Full L+R	SOFTER		1
10	1	M			sticky-e.w.	crampy L	SOFT		
11	2	T			egg white	crampy L	SOFT		
12	3	W			sticky-e.w.		SOFT		
13	4	T			sticky		SOFT		
14	5	F			sticky		MED.		
15	6	S			sticky		MED.		
16	7	S			sticky		MED.		
17	8	M			sticky		MED.		
18	9	T			sticky				
19	10	W			dry				
20	11	T			dry		FIRM		
21	12	F			dry				
22	13	S			dry				
23	14	S		x	spotting				
24	15	M			dry				
25	16	T			dry				
26	17	W			dry				
27	18	T		preg test −	sticky		FIRM		
28	19	F		x	spotting		FIRM		
29	20	S		preg test + / x	spotting				
30	21	S			dry				
31	22	M		preg test ++	dry				
32	23	T			dry				
33	24	W			dry				
34	25	T							

THIS SAME WOMAN STARTED USING A SUBLINGUAL PROGESTERONE SUPPLEMENT THIS MONTH FOR THE SECOND HALF OF HER CYCLE. SHE STARTED DRINKING DAILY A FERTILITY TEA MIX AT THE BEGINNING OF THIS CYCLE. SHE CONCEIVED THIS CYCLE. NOTICE THE CHANGES BETWEEN THIS CYCLE AND HER PREVIOUS ONE.

Fertility Chart

Month(s): Nov–Dec Year: 99 Cycle number: 13 Length of cycle: _____ (days) Days of Insemina...

Day of Cycle	1 2 3 4 5 6 7 8 9 10 11 12 13 14 15 16 17 18 19 20 21 22 23 24 25 26 27 28 29 30 31 32 33 34
Date	23 24 25 26 27 28 29 30 1 2 3 4 5 6 7 8 9 10 11 12 13 14 15 16 17
Day	S M T W Th F S S M T W Th F S S M T W Th F S S M T W
Phase of the Moon	● ● ● ● ● ● ● ● (filled circle)
Insemination/Intercourse	
Bleeding	
Ovulation (pain, pressure, sensation, which side)	
Cervical changes (high/low, open/closed, soft/firm, color)	
Mucus color & consistency (dry, wet, slippery, fertile, sticky; clear, yellow, white)	clear / clear / stretchy
Lens (ferning)	⌣ ⌣ / ⌣ ⌣ / → Ø / → + / +
Ovulation Predictor Kit/Monitor	(AM circled); ⊕ test pregnant !!!
Fertility Drugs	
Mood changes	→ happy / → anxious / → grump
Sexual desire	
Appetite or food cravings	→ / → / →
Breast changes (tenderness, swelling)	
Cramping	
Stress	
Sleep changes & dreams	
Notes/Comments/Details/Dreams (also see back)	

THIS WOMAN IS 37 YEARS OLD. SHE CONCEIVED ON HER SEVENTH CYCLE, INSEMINATING VAGINALLY WITH FROZEN SPERM, AND MISCARRIED AT SIX WEEKS. SHE INSEMINATED FOR THREE MORE CYCLES, TWICE EACH CYCLE, WITH FROZEN SPERM. THIS CYCLE SHE INSEMINATED ONCE VAGINALLY WITH FRESH SPERM FROM AN ANONYMOUS DONOR IN AN INFERTILITY CLINIC. ALTHOUGH HER CHART SUGGESTS, BASED ON HER OVULATION PREDICTOR RESULTS ALONE, THAT SHE MAY HAVE INSEMINATED TOO EARLY, SHE CHOSE THIS DAY BECAUSE INTUITIVELY SHE FELT THE MOST FERTILE. SHE HAD THE OPTION TO INSEMINATE THE FOLLOWING DAY AS WELL BUT CHOSE NOT TO, CONFIDENT THAT SHE HAD JUST CONCEIVED.

Part Five
Challenging
Conceptions

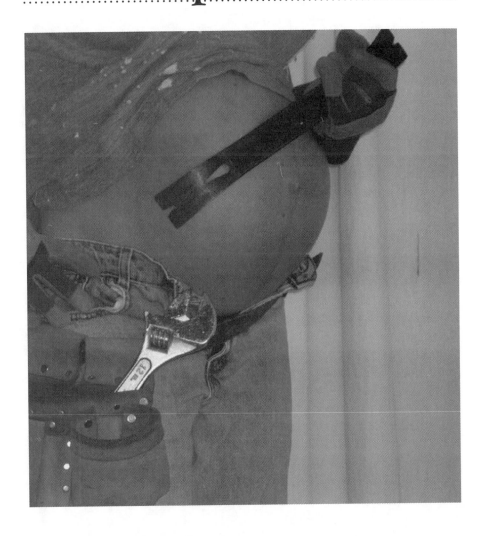

CHAPTER 16

The Emotional
Roller-Coaster Ride

THIS CHAPTER EXPLORES the emotional road map of the insemination period and provides you with tools for making this time of your life
more meaningful and enjoyable. Most people find that the excitement of
creating a baby dominates the first few months of insemination. Each month
that passes without conceiving, however, becomes exponentially harder to
weather. The point at which conception becomes emotionally challenging
is different for each woman and family. Some people don't feel they're in
the advanced stages of insemination until eight months have passed. Others
grow discouraged after one or two cycles. How you react depends greatly on
your temperament and the outlook you have when you begin to inseminate.
Despite the variation in experience, there are some predictable cycles most
people go through each and every month of inseminating.

Most people find the insemination process to be stressful, even to the point
of consuming all aspects of their lives. Insemination directly impacts your
self-esteem, finances, partnership, work life, social life, sex life, your ability
to trust, and possibly your relationship with your family of origin. Thus, if
you experience a lengthy conception period, you may be in a constant state
of chronic stress. Examining the specific stresses involved and identifying
strategies for creative stress management is helpful for many women. If it
feels unnecessary, or even more stressful, to review these stresses, simply skip
ahead in the chapter to the section on tools for weathering stress for helpful
actions you can take during your insemination period.

The Monthly Cycle and Insemination

The menstrual cycle structures the emotional cycle of the months of insemination in a way that is both compelling and universal. This is the template upon
which is superimposed all other aspects of your life for the entire duration of
your insemination period. How you relate to this cycle can change as time
passes, but as long as you're inseminating, you're going through the same basic
cycle as hundreds, probably thousands, of other women do each month.

From the first month of insemination through the last, the menstrual cycle regulates your life. For most people who are inseminating, not a day goes by that they aren't calculating what day they may be ovulating, what days would be best to inseminate, what day they're scheduled to have their period, or which day they could take a pregnancy test. This mental calculating is often stressful simply because of how much time and energy it takes. Let's look at the phases of this monthly cycle.

Phase 1: Fertility Awareness

Each month, from the time you menstruate until the time you inseminate, your emotions build up, much like the lining of your uterus builds to create a potential home for your baby. This first part of the month up until insemination is the fertility-awareness phase. In the first few months of inseminating, the cycle is usually filled with hope and excitement. If you're partnered, this is usually a good part of the month for your relationship.

As you approach mid-cycle you likely become increasingly more consumed with your fertility signals, trying to correctly time your insemination. The planning required to inseminate at the right time takes a tremendous amount of focused attention, and fertility monitoring may make you feel more like a science project than a person. If you don't get pregnant quickly, fertility awareness can move from an amazing learning experience about your body to a confusing jumble of signals whose meaning you doubt. You can begin to feel like your body is failing you, believing that if your fertility signs were adequate you would already be pregnant.

If you're taking fertility medications or receiving other fertility or infertility treatments, this is the time of month spent shuttling yourself from appointment to appointment. As a result, it's common to feel more job stress during the first half of your cycle, as you may be required to miss work multiple times for doctor's appointments.

In general, over time the fertility awareness phase of the month often becomes increasingly difficult. Each month you may find yourself getting cold feet and needing to recommit to having a child. Perhaps you begin to doubt your ability to parent or the wisdom of your choices. It's the time of the month when fears can loom large. These fears and concerns are a natural part of the process—it's common to question what you're doing. But it's also easy for such concerns to play games with your mind. Some people feel that having any concerns about their desire to parent proves that their decision is wrong. Just try to let that go, and if you're partnered, don't allow this to be something you argue about every month. Serious reservations require your attention, but having cold feet is normal.

VISUALIZATIONS FOR BODY AWARENESS

As you start a new cycle be sure to communicate with your body. In affect, tell it how it will be, show it what you would like. This is the power of visualization. You may want to get some photos of what ovulation, conception, and early cell division look like to help you focus your mind.

- *Fertility visualization.* During this time of the cycle your body is preparing for pregnancy. Every day spend some time seeing all of your hormones working together so that all of your fertility signs are heightened and coordinated. Imagine a nice, juicy, welcoming uterine lining beginning to grow. And have your body select an egg that is strong and healthy.
- *Ovulation visualization.* This is the time to visualize a strong ovulation and a healthy conception. Imagine your egg leaving the ovary and the process of the egg and sperm joining together. Imagine a finely coordinated dance that your entire body is participating in.
- *Implantation visualization.* Spend time each day visualizing the tiny embryo being gently swept down your fallopian tube and into the uterus. See it nestling itself into your inviting, rich uterine wall. This is implantation.
- *Conception visualization.* If you are pregnant it is time to congratulate your body on the good work it has done. Keep the visualizing up each day to help support healthy cell division. Sometimes getting a book that has pictures of these early days and weeks can assist.
- *Period visualization.* If you get your period then it is time to release your uterine lining. Allow all feelings to be shed with it. See your menstrual period as a cleanse (which it is) and allow everything that needs to be cleansed to flow freely out of your body. This will help you to prepare for the next cycle.

Phase 2: Insemination

Each month the fertility-awareness phase segues into the insemination phase. How women experience this phase varies greatly, as there are so many insemination methods and approaches to conception. Nonetheless, most people end up feeling some amount of stress from all of the logistics they must juggle. This stress may come from trying to arrange to get your vials of sperm at the right time, trying to arrange for an IUI on the right day, or trying to coordinate everyone's schedules with your body's timing when using a known donor. Despite the stresses leading up to your inseminations, the actual inseminations are, at least initially, usually filled with optimism and hope. For partners, insemination arguments are quite common; they're probably an outlet for the stress of trying to coordinate such an important event.

If you inseminate for a number of months, you may feel increasing tension as you approach the actual time of insemination. Some people feel uptight or desperate. Those feeling uptight may have a difficult time relaxing and being comfortable during the insemination. Those experiencing desperation can find themselves obsessing about coordinating the logistics of the process. For example, they may call their donor six or seven times a day, leaving messages trying to reach him. They may check their saliva with a fertility lens every hour at work, trying to ascertain the exact moment they should inseminate. Although most still feel optimistic and hopeful during this time, many find themselves talking about "next time" moments after they've inseminated. It becomes more and more difficult to remain emotionally open to the possibility of pregnancy and stay in the present.

Phase 3: Waiting

The second half of your cycle is the waiting phase, which is broken into two parts. The first few days are often some of the most exciting days of the cycle. Both in the early months of trying and in the months when you feel your timing is impeccable, these few post-insemination days have a positive, upbeat feeling. The possibility of pregnancy is very real. It's also a crazy-making phase because you'll probably scrutinize yourself constantly for signs that indicate pregnancy. When you focus so much attention on your body, you may discover a plethora of potential pregnancy signs every month—some real and some imagined.

The second half of the waiting period, leading up to your menstrual period (or no period if you're pregnant), is the hardest time for most people. This is when hopes and fears dominate your mental experience. A feeling of depression may set in as many women fear they feel their period coming on or brace themselves for the possibility of seeing blood.

Most veteran inseminators often try hard to ignore this phase of the cycle, hoping to feel less controlled by it. Many people, however, find upon reflecting that it was rare for them to think about possible pregnancy less than fifty times a day. What else in your life do you think about a minimum of fifty times a day? Given the importance that this process has in your life, it may be easier and more meaningful to admit to and honor its significance than to discount it or feel like you're going "crazy."

People in this phase of the month are also often quite superstitious and don't want to do anything that might "shake the pregnancy loose." So, for example, some refrain from having sex, exercising, lifting, eating specific foods, and even having certain thoughts or emotions.

Phase 4: Will I Bleed?

The waiting phase is followed by either the arrival or the absence of the menstrual period. As the conception journeys lengthen, most people feel lower and lower emotionally with each new menstrual period. Some people cry when they see their blood or feel angry or let down by the universe or God. Others don't feel anything and become emotionally numb. It gets more and more difficult to come up, yet again, from this low phase into the hopeful fertility-awareness phase the new month offers. Over time, this aftermath depression may grow longer and stronger. The emotional roller coaster gets crazier as the highs and lows become more extreme.

If you miss your period, or if you get a positive pregnancy test, you're likely to be ecstatic. It's a moment that words cannot capture. If you've miscarried before as part of this roller-coaster ride, then fear may immediately follow this ecstasy.

The insemination cycle is compelling, consuming, and emotionally havoc-wreaking. It's also the monthly pattern of your life until you get pregnant or decide to take a break. Acknowledging this cycle and learning to recognize your emotional responses to each part of the cycle will help you align more easily with the process. Rather than feeling like you're on an out-of-control train, you can become a willing passenger on the ride to parenthood. This acceptance and acknowledgment calms the journey and makes your monthly pattern feel gentler.

Inseminating Affects All Areas of Your Life

We explore here the impact inseminating may have on specific areas of your life, so that you can develop plans for minimizing stress. Likewise, if you've been on this roller coaster for some time, it's helpful to review all of the stresses you're under so that you can appreciate how well you're doing and plan strategies for even better stress reduction. This allows you to anticipate the support you'll need as well as validate the struggles you may be encountering. However, if you need no reminder that inseminating is affecting all areas of your life, you may wish to skip ahead to page 331 for tips on making this time more manageable.

Finances

Conception almost always involves a financial component, and sometimes there is considerable financial strain. In fact, it's not uncommon for us to see women depleting their savings and retirement accounts while trying to get pregnant. It's also not uncommon for us to see less affluent women having to decide between spending money on holiday gifts or on sperm, or having to get an extra roommate or a second job to help finance the project. Unless you get pregnant right away, it will most likely cost a considerable amount for you to get pregnant, whether or not you're buying sperm.

It's difficult to embrace starting your parenthood with depleted financial resources, but that's what many of us face. This stress is unique to our situation. Granted, partnered heterosexual women experiencing infertility have to weather the financial strain of fertility treatments. It still remains true, however, that men make much more money on average than women do. Those of us who don't use known donors have to spend significant amounts of money just to have the opportunity to get pregnant in the first place. Many women feel justified anger at these inequities.

The Impact on Your Worklife

Insemination can directly affect your worklife. The decision to share your plans with your coworkers or boss can be complicated. If you're experiencing an extended conception period, remaining private at work about your conception struggles can feel isolating. Many people are rightly afraid of losing their jobs or suffering in other ways from discrimination, homophobia, or transphobia whereas others simply want to retain their privacy. It can become even more emotionally challenging if you work with pregnant women.

Inseminating can also affect your job if you have to miss work. The stress of trying to coordinate inseminations with your work schedule can be harrying. Business trips, important projects, presentations, and clients' needs aren't always easy to reschedule. People receiving fertility treatments often have an even more difficult schedule, sometimes needing to miss work to attend six or more appointments a month. Not only may your managers disapprove, or your coworkers resent sharing your workload, but also vagueness about why you're leaving may make it even harder to get understanding. Missed work is lost money and a possible threat to your job security. This strain can be significant.

Impact on Your Social Life and Support Circle

At times vital members of your support circle may leave or feel "maxed out." Perhaps you've distanced yourself from some of your friends because it's become more difficult to talk about not getting pregnant than not to talk at all. Sometimes your friends simply cannot relate to the depth of your desire to be a parent. They may judge the choices you make in terms of the time, money, energy, or methods you use to conceive. They may choose to withdraw from you rather than share their feelings, or they may choose to share their feelings and then withdraw their support. Other times your friends may try to be well meaning as they provide you with their interpretations as to why you aren't getting pregnant: You're too uptight, you need to relax, your relationship is no good, you need a partner, you're too old, you just need a vacation. It is a fine balance between being overly interested and providing enough privacy.

Impact on Your Self-Esteem

Unsuccessfully trying to get pregnant eventually affects your self-esteem. Primarily you're faced with the existential question of "Why?" But you can run yourself ragged trying to answer this question. You may become fanatic about your fertility monitoring, exercise, diet, attitude, etc. Becoming rigid and controlling is a common response to feeling out of control. You may no longer participate in any of the activities you once enjoyed, leaving your life as well as your body feeling barren. Until pregnancy is here the underlying question that grows louder and louder is "What is wrong with me?"

Feelings of Shame

If you have trouble conceiving, it's very easy to blame yourself and to feel you're defective in some way. This is the most common emotion that arises during a lengthy conception period. Shame manifests in different ways. Many women say they no longer feel like a woman if they can't conceive. Others regret having had abortions in their younger years and may feel they are now being "punished." A woman may also feel she's letting her partner down if she can't conceive. Shame can also spur feelings of internalized homophobia: "Maybe this isn't meant to be because I'm a dyke."

Although there's much to be gained from self-reflection, there can be a misguided tendency to think that if you haven't gotten pregnant it's because you have a psychological or physical impediment. Although you should strive for mental, physical, emotional, and spiritual health, blaming yourself for not being "perfect" will in no way help you conceive.

Anger

The second most common emotion after shame is anger, which may be very strong. You can feel anger at your body for betraying you, at pregnant women on the street, at heterosexual women for having it so easy, at yourself for waiting so long, at the universe for not supporting your desire, at the potential baby for making it so difficult, and at having to pour so much money and emotional energy down the drain. The inability to get pregnant can feel like cruel and unusual punishment.

It's important to recognize and acknowledge these feelings as they arise. Getting out from underneath the sometimes all-consuming emotional chaos of the insemination period can be quite difficult in and of itself. You may need to go through the motions of doing things that are nurturing for you, so that eventually they will help to alleviate some of your stress. There are quite a few chat rooms on the Internet for lesbian moms in which many mothers-to-be find solace and understanding. Breaking free of the emotional isolation and sharing the struggle with friends and loved ones is worth the effort and perceived risk of doing so.

Stresses with Your Partner

The longer partners are in the preconception phase together, the harder insemination can be on their relationship. This may be especially true if one partner is ambivalent about having children. Because inseminating unsuccessfully month after month can lower self-esteem and increase the likelihood of depression, communication between partners may become more difficult.

In most relationships the partners deal with stress differently. Often one partner wants to talk, share, and process frequently. The other may try to ignore the subject and proceed with life as usual. Some people internalize stress, while others release it inappropriately. Of those that engage with it consciously, some work through it quietly and internally, while others work it through verbally. These are polar-opposite approaches. One partner may be an eternal optimist, seeing all physical symptoms as signs of pregnancy every month. The other may be more pessimistic, convinced that everything about the insemination timing is wrong. Some people don't want to discuss the possibility of pregnancy at all, preferring to wait until the blood does or does not arrive.

Early on it's valuable to discuss with each other your approaches to the insemination process. Some people firmly believe that if you just smile and pretend the stress isn't there, it can't get to you. Some feel that if you "give in" to negative feelings and let the disappointment get to you, you're ruining your chances of getting pregnant. Others believe you need to feel, express, and explore every feeling as it arises. There's no right or wrong approach, but if you can understand each other's natural approaches, you'll have more understanding and compassion for the other's needs.

YOUR SEX LIFE

Your sex life may come to an abrupt standstill during the insemination period. Although some people still have sex during this time, it's often inspired not by sexual desire but by the idea that it might increase the likelihood of conception. If you feel your body is defective, it's hard to imagine anyone else wanting it. Likewise, many people find themselves wary of being sexual during the second half of their cycle out of a fear of disrupting a new pregnancy. Occasionally at Maia we find a couple that's able to maintain a wonderful and active sex life throughout this period, but it doesn't appear to be the norm.

However, bear in mind that regular orgasms increase fertility significantly. So maintaining a sex life—whether partnered or solo—is vital for uterine health and hormonal balance. Likewise, remember that satisfying sexual expression around insemination will greatly increase your chances as well. Find the way back to one another through sex. It is usually the gateway to all of the pent-up emotions. It will be quite healing if you are able to maintain an alive sense of your sexuality during this time.

FEELING IMPOTENT

Many partners of inseminating women feel their self-esteem erode as well. If they're performing the insemination at home, they can feel impotent if they can't get their partner pregnant. Queer conception has many unexpected twists to it, and this is one of them. Feeling impotent in this way can also decrease sexual confidence.

THE ELEPHANT IN THE MIDDLE OF THE ROOM

You'll feel the stresses of the insemination cycle and the desire for a baby are present with you at all times, even when you're not expressing them. This quiet longing, desire, hope, and disappointment is in the air you both share. Many partners try to ignore their sadness or depression and don't realize how stressful this process is for each other and the relationship. The longer it takes you to get pregnant, the harder it is on a relationship. One friend of ours said, "Oh, it's no problem. It's just that we're single-handedly holding up Mount Everest while acting like everything is normal. What a joke!" Most couples say they've never gone through anything more difficult than an extended conception period or infertility.

ROLE SEPARATIONS

Even though you're both going through this process together, a definite separation of roles appears for most couples. An unspoken dynamic that occurs in many relationships allows only the woman trying to get pregnant her vulnerability and emotional expression. Although it's a shared experience, there's a mutual understanding that in some ways it's more the experience of the birth mother.

The nonbirth mom is expected to be strong and supportive. She may feel it's inappropriate for her to share her feelings of disappointment, sadness, and frustration with her partner. Being supportive of her partner can mean not breaking down or expressing her emotional needs. Unfortunately, over time this well-meant behavior can undermine the closeness a couple shares. If only one partner is allowed to feel, two-way emotional communication shuts down. This leaves just one partner discussing practical decisions and plans. It's a brave step to decide to be emotionally vulnerable after keeping to yourself for months, but when you do you'll both be thankful for your regained sense of connection.

WHEN BOTH PARTNERS WANT BABIES

If your partner wants to get pregnant after you do, there's a mutual understanding that the longer you take to get pregnant, the further away her pregnancy will be. Even if she doesn't want to pressure you, she sometimes can't help worrying about it. Sometimes she'll start to share your physical longing for a baby. This particular stress is quite unique to lesbians. It's a sweet possibility to have each of you give birth, but it can also stir up an awkward form of envy and resentment. Keep an eye out for this dynamic.

It may be reassuring to agree upon a date at which point you'll reevaluate your options if you haven't conceived. Still, this agreement alone may not be enough to avoid the serious strain and stress the issue can bring into relationships, especially those in which both people in a partnership have delayed trying to conceive until they are in their late thirties or early forties. If this stress is underlying your actions and stultifying your ability to communicate with each other, you should bring this topic to a couples counselor.

Other Complicated Feelings

Stress from Your Family of Origin

Women commonly experience some stress from their family of origin. Even if you're out to your parents, you may feel the stress of deciding whether to share with them the fact that you're trying to conceive. It's challenging to go through an emotionally draining extended conception period without sharing your news with family members with whom you usually discuss other trying times. On the other hand, if you've told your family that you're trying to make a baby and they aren't supportive, it can be hard on your heart. It can be painful if your family doesn't recognize your partner and therefore your family. Some people are fortunate and have supportive families. As lesbian families become more visible, they'll become more accepted and have the deserved experience of having their parenting choices celebrated by their families. For now, however, remember that you're not alone if you're rejected or misunderstood by your family members.

Shaken Trust

We all start out with hope, faith, and trust that if we really want to get pregnant we will. In fact, most people secretly believe they'll get pregnant the very first time they inseminate. This faith in their bodies and the universe is important to them. But if month after month you go through the cycle of waiting with bated breath only to be disappointed, your trust in life may begin to erode. It's difficult to hold on to hope when you're increasingly afraid that your dream won't come true.

A lengthy insemination period can challenge your spiritual framework. Some people's spiritual beliefs are strengthened through the adversity of a challenging conception. Others feel abandoned by the divine and find little comfort. When you lose trust in all you know to be true, it's hard to find the voice of truth inside yourself that may have helped you to make strong decisions in the past. You may feel like your intuition has failed you. Losing trust in life can happen gradually, but it can also feel like a slippery slope.

Isolation

If you've been inseminating for several months, you may feel like crawling into a private hole until you get pregnant. This desire to isolate yourself can be strong and is also a symptom of depression. It helps to meet with others in the same situation. In large urban areas you might place an ad in your local queer paper to meet with other women trying to get pregnant and form a support group at a local bookstore. If you aren't in an area with many other lesbian or bisexual women, you may want to seek out local infertility support groups. Although you may be the only lesbian(s) in the group and not all of the issues will apply to you, the support and understanding you find may be great.

When you're undergoing fertility struggles it can be difficult feeling so isolated in your experience. Unless you tell people, they can't know the level of stress you're experiencing. Your grief and pain about your infertility become a hidden disability. Although the depth of your anguish is often isolating in and of itself, try to resist the urge to experience this process alone. Withholding your feelings can be tremendously stressful to both yourself and your relationship. You'll find that people can support you even if they can't fully understand the depth of your anguish. Share the burden with at least one friend or a counselor. If you're not reaching out for support, examine your self-isolating tendencies and try to find others you can talk with.

If your partner is the one trying to get pregnant, you're in a category that's even harder to get support for. You're under tremendous strain, yet many people don't even recognize your role. They may consider it your partner's struggle, totally ignoring your experience. Once again, reach out for support in one of the ways we've mentioned.

Racing Against the Clock

When you're getting older or your body is showing signs of waning fertility, you may feel an increased sense of urgency. It feels overwhelming to do battle with the internal and medical messages of infertility. There will be times when you may feel crazy for wanting to try naturally, or wanting to proceed in the way that feels right to you even though your doctor, family, and friends think it is the wrong way. Take the time each morning to just breathe into your fertility. It is your body and your baby. You can do this your way. Sometimes it's helpful not to get any more hormonal tests for a while and trust that you'll get pregnant, if you can, regardless of the numbers attached to your odds.

It can be validating and poignant to realize that stress experts consider the stress of infertility to be equivalent to the stress of having a terminal illness. The uniquely difficult aspect of infertility stems from invisibility and subsequent lack of recognition. If you had cancer, you'd receive much more support from friends, family, and neighbors. The inability to get pregnant is often a hidden and personal burden. The stress of infertility is multiplied when you combine it with possible homophobic reactions from others and the lack of compassion others may have for your partner, if you have one.

Monitor Your Mental Health

People who experience challenging conceptions can often feel a serious strain on their psyches. When you're under this much stress and feel out of control, both old and new responses may arise. You may experience true depression. Please seek professional help and support throughout this journey if you exhibit symptoms of depression. If you have a history of depression, it may be upsetting for you and the people around you to acknowledge seeing some of your old and familiar behaviors.

Likewise, for those who experience anxiety rather than depressive tendencies, infertility and fertility challenges will commonly kick these up in full force. For example, a common fear is that something dreadful will happen if you or your partner doesn't get pregnant. Seek counseling and stress-reduction activities if you recognize your overall state of anxiety increasing.

The advantage of having a history of depression or anxiety is that you've probably learned numerous coping skills. It's important to prioritize these skills and to ask other people in your life to remind you to practice them. Common tools that many women use to help stabilize their mental health include getting regular sleep; eating regularly; exercising and doing yoga; and meditation, visualization, and breathing exercises. If during your preconception period you're showing signs of depression or anxiety for the first time, you may want to join a support group for people experiencing depression or anxiety or enter therapy to help you develop coping skills.

Life Markers

Certain times of the year and important milestones in life may be exceptionally difficult for you. When thinking about getting pregnant you may often create visions of the future. For example, you might imagine that you and your sister will have children who are the same age or that when you graduate from grad school your partner will be pregnant, or when you move to New York for your new job in two years you'll have a one-year-old child. If you're still trying to get pregnant when these events approach, you may feel quite disheartened.

Tools for Weathering Stress

Now that we've outlined how stressful a lengthy conception period can be, it's important to think about what you can put in place to help you to reduce your reactions to stress and to minimize your stress load. Please review chapter 11 For general stress-education tools and techniques that will help you through this time. Here we specifically speak to mental, emotional, and spiritual attitudes and discuss specific things you can do to gain support throughout your journey.

Pregnant Until Proven Otherwise

Our clients have found that one of the most helpful attitudes to adopt is that they're pregnant until proven otherwise. In other words, they honor the entire second half of their cycle as pregnancy whether or not it continues. Although at first this may seem delusional, it can actually be quite validating. In essence it's true that every month you inseminate you could be pregnant, therefore you may choose to act as if you're pregnant during this time. This idea is that a person's mental attitude corresponds with her actions, hopes, and dreams.

This attitude allows each return of menstrual blood to be treated emotionally as a miscarriage, which is often truly what it feels like. This allows more personal room for grief and sadness each cycle, as well as permission to take breaks between cycles when needed. If you don't feel this is a healthy attitude for you to adopt, by all means do only what feels right for you.

Enhance the Overall Quality of Your Life

The preconception period is a protected period of your life that you can use to enhance your health and overall well-being, your relationship to your body, and your partnership. As you spend more time focusing on health enhancement, not only your chances of getting pregnant but also your quality of life improve.

Two of our clients, Sarah and Jamie, expressed to us that although the nine months they spent inseminating were some of the most emotionally trying months they'd ever been through individually and as a couple, they were also their best. The couple started to take nightly walks together, altered their diets to eat home-prepared fresh and healthy foods, practiced yoga in the morning, felt more connected with each other, and felt healthier than they ever had. While Sarah was receiving acupuncture for fertility, she noticed the treatments relieved her chronic headaches and allergies as well. Although pregnancy inspired them to make these changes, they mentioned to us that they were very pleased with their new selves, whether or not they became pregnant!

Prepare for Parenting

Whether you're single, partnered, or preparing to be in a group family, you can use an extended preconception period as a gift of time to more fully prepare for parenting. Take the opportunity to read books on parenting philosophies and to clarify your views on subjects such as discipline, spiritual upbringing, sleeping arrangements, and approaches to health care. If you've always wanted to learn more about a certain element of parenting or have been concerned about a specific phase of parenting, use this time to read about it, talk to other parents, and develop your personal convictions. This will only strengthen your ability to parent when the time arrives.

Keep Living Your Life

Although it's difficult, it's important not to put the rest of your life on hold as you try to make a baby. Resist this temptation. Try to stay engaged with the things that were important to you before you started to inseminate. Continue to make time for the activities and people that feed your soul and let the other things go. This can ease the feeling that your life has stopped until the unknown time when the baby arrives. When you inseminate month after month, you may feel like you're balancing on the edge of a precipice, ready to jump into parenting but never quite getting the chance. This balancing act is truly exhausting. Have compassion for yourself during this time.

Give Yourself Pleasure

Intentionally engage in activities that nurture you and give you pleasure. This may be treating yourself to a massage or taking a hike in the woods. It may be spending the day with friends or going shopping. It may be masturbating. Do whatever gives you joy. There's a tendency for people to avoid pleasure when they're not getting pregnant—which is often a subconscious form of self-punishment. Negative thinking has an addictive quality. Don't foster this addiction; relish the things you enjoy!

Feel the Love You Have

Allow yourself to take regular time to remember why you want to make this baby. Rejoice in the love you already have for this baby. Making a baby is an act of love. Celebrate and grow love in your life. While you're waiting to love this baby in the flesh, allow yourself to feel the love others have for you and the love you have for yourself. Choose to actively love the people who are in your life now; don't reserve all of your love for the baby alone. Many spiritual teachings say love is what brings our babies to us. Include in your daily life a focus on love itself. Living a life that radiates love feeds our souls.

Develop a Spiritual Practice

Making a baby is exciting and amazing. Whenever you feel discouraged, do what you can to keep the energy moving. Make it your goal to expose yourself to new and fresh ideas. Just as you may experience cycles of pessimism, notice the cycles of optimism on your journey. Do what you can to keep an inspirational quality to your quest. Sometimes this means taking an entirely new approach to conception. Try to find books, friends, practitioners, and teachers that inspire you to new ways of thinking. Flowing ideas and flowing energy is renewing. Inspiration—emotional and spiritual—feeds the soul.

Many people we've worked with get trapped in a cycle of negativity during the months in which they're not getting pregnant. They can only talk about or feel the things that are not happening in their lives. It can seem impossible to find a way out of the spiral of negativity. We worked with one couple who had been trying to get pregnant for more than two years. During these years they'd suffered through two miscarriages. They had no hope left, yet they were unwilling to take a break or vacation.

When they came back to see us in four months, they were different people. They still weren't pregnant, but they had discovered a Buddhist meditation practice, which they'd been doing together for three and a half months. They talked about how it had changed their lives and reported having renewed energy. They said they felt much more peaceful and more trusting that the pregnancy would happen when the time was right. The changes were obvious. They talked about how "safe" it had been to be so wrapped up in seeing not getting pregnant as a failure and how threatening it had been to let go of that mental stance. They said they both knew that if something hadn't changed when it did, they wouldn't have survived as a couple. When they realized their relationship existed, and the baby did not, they decided to focus on growing what they'd been neglecting: themselves and their partnership.

Through their meditation practice they experienced a complete shift in attitude. Hope wasn't the only thing that returned, though; they rekindled their sex life, they started socializing again, and they started to have fun again. They, like many women, found that focusing on the positive aspects of their lives was an incredibly helpful act. Living in the moment and appreciating fully the good things in your life will help shift your focus from lack to abundance. This shift is key in maintaining a personal and relationship equilibrium.

Visit Your Fertility Altar

Many people find it helpful to create and maintain a space in their home for their baby. Placing fresh flowers or new items on the baby altar and spending time at the altar is another way to spend time with the baby before he or she arrives. This allows you a physical way to connect with your feelings about the baby.

Take Breaks

Even if you go on vacation during an insemination cycle you'll probably still be affected by the day-to-day awareness of fertility or pregnancy signs. A true break requires taking a month or more off from inseminating. Occasionally taking a month or two off is the healthiest and most supportive thing you can do for yourself (and your partner). It's often difficult to allow yourself to take a break, but you'll find it amazingly renewing. If you're able to, take a vacation during this month, or do whatever your heart desires during this time off. You might make the most of your break by putting your fertility charting aside. Although some things that you may be tempted to do during this month are okay, such as taking a very hot bath or having a glass of wine or cup of coffee, be careful not to reengage with habits you've taken such care to avoid that either undermine fertility on a long-term basis or are ill-advised for pregnancy—such as daily caffeine intake or cigarette smoking. Enjoy the return of sanity and laughter, if you feel these have been lost along the way.

Treat Your Body as You Would Your Baby

Finally, there's nothing better that you can do for yourself throughout this process of preconception and pregnancy than to treat your body as if it were your baby. Nourish and nurture yourself by giving yourself good food, fresh air, and exercise. Take naps, sleep well, play! Have deep understanding and compassion for your feelings. Give yourself lots of hugs and reassurance. You are a sweet, tender, lovable, and needy baby. Giving yourself the love you need will create a profound and healing shift in your self-esteem and prepare you for the tremendous amount of love you'll give your child.

CHAPTER 17

Before Embarking on Fertility Treatments

TODAY'S HEADLINES SHOUT that infertility for both men and women is on the rise in the United States. Current statistics show that one in four women has difficulty conceiving. These statistics include only heterosexual women who have been having unprotected intercourse with men for at least one year and have not achieved pregnancy. We are also bombarded with headlines about decreasing fertility after 35 years of age. We are told to try for a year and yet if we are older to forget trying altogether and go straight to fertility treatments. How can queer and single women relate to this information? We may feel overwhelmed, understanding that we not only share other women's infertility odds but also have additional fertility challenges because of our limited access to sperm. Our chances of conceiving can often seem minimal at best. This is not necessarily true, but it is emphasized so heavily it can feel impossible to avoid internalizing it as true. The fact of the matter is it takes some time for most people to get pregnant. Living in this culture of speed, it is a challenge to be patient. Staying present with the natural process needs to be balanced with the need to enhance fertility both naturally and medically.

As queer and single parents-to-be, if we choose to enter the medical system for help in getting pregnant due to our limited access to sperm, we're automatically labeled as "infertility patients." We're treated as infertility patients whether or not we've ever inseminated and without regard to our true fertility status. Many of us are not "infertile" at all; we simply have to work much harder to get pregnant than partnered straight women who theoretically have unlimited access to fresh sperm.

There is a belief that going directly to fertility treatments or high-tech procedures such as in-vitro fertilization will be the automatic answer. This may be the case for you; it may dramatically increase your chances. However, the stats do not always bear that out. Do your research before making decisions. The number of infertility doctors turning to alternative medicine is on the rise. The mind-body connection is more greatly appreciated than ever before. Many IVF clinics are showing better results with women who receive acupuncture, women who take vitamins, and women who exercise. Clinics are popping up across the country to try to address the more subtle regulation of women's hormones to aid not only with fertility, but also for smoother transitions into motherhood.

This chapter offers a broad range of information for people having difficulty conceiving, for whatever known or unknown reason. We address how veteran inseminators can approach anew the topics of increasing fertility and fertility awareness, and explore the insemination and donor options we've discussed in earlier chapters—capitalizing on the self-knowledge gained so far. We then move on to discuss causes of infertility, available diagnostic tests, and many of the treatment procedures Western medicine offers, including some of the risks and benefits of each. We also answer other questions, such as when to change care providers, and if and when your partner should start to inseminate.

You should review this chapter whenever you haven't gotten pregnant, feel frustrated, and feel ready for a change. It's empowering to remember that there are always new things to try. Sometimes making a subtle shift is all that's necessary to regain your hope and inspiration. Or you may need to reevaluate all of your decisions to date and try a completely new approach.

Although many readers come to this book specifically for the information on infertility, it is very important to read the rest of the book as well, as information given in previous chapters lays the foundation for creating optimal fertility.

We will begin by looking first at how you can refine and improve your efforts to become pregnant, and then we will move on to look at specific health issues that can lead to infertility and what you can do about them.

Examine Your Hesitations About Pregnancy

Many times people are afraid they won't be a good parent or that the responsibility of being a parent is too great. Some are concerned that their own experience growing up has left them without positive role models and that they're doomed to repeat negative behaviors from the past. Others are simply unsure whether they truly want to give up control of their adult lives. And still others are paralyzed by the fear of not having enough time or money to raise a child in the way they see best. Some are greatly intimidated by the prospect of giving birth. And others are conflicted about their choice to be a single parent. Finally, many haven't resolved their internalized homophobia.

Often women are offended if friends suggest they aren't getting pregnant because they harbor hidden ambivalence. We want to look at this head-on, not to "blame the victim" but to acknowledge that many of the people we've worked with who aren't getting pregnant do express to us occasional ambivalence about parenting or pregnancy. This isn't something to be ashamed about, but it is something to recognize and examine. We don't know how the mind-body connection may play into a relationship between ambivalence and infertility, or whether ambivalence simply adds to a person's stress and confusion. In either case, let's discuss what you can do to acknowledge it and resolve it if you notice it's present, before we move on to the topic of infertility. If you didn't feel ambivalent when you started trying to conceive, we're not suggesting that you just weren't aware of it. Unsuccessfully trying to conceive can create looming fears and doubts you may not have had initially. Writing in a journal or talking openly about this issue with friends or your partner can help you gain insight. Ask yourself questions such as: What am I afraid of? What's the nature of my ambivalence? What might enable me to wholeheartedly embrace pregnancy and parenthood? Is there a reason my body may not be open to pregnancy? Coming to terms with these kinds of issues will enhance your confidence in your parenting.

These are complex issues that may require counseling or therapy. However, the people we have worked with who address these issues express greater emotional freedom for having done so. This process has also allowed many people to discern the necessary next step to become parents, whether that's through adoption, in vitro fertilization, or other options.

Measures to Try Without Seeing an Infertility Specialist

We encourage you to reread part 3 of this book for ideas you may not have incorporated into your approach so far. Fertility enhancement is a key component of achieving pregnancy. If you haven't yet incorporated the recommendations in part 3, begin to do so wholeheartedly now. Renew your commitment to enhancing your body's ability to achieve and maintain a healthy pregnancy.

Striving toward greater health not only significantly increases your chances of pregnancy, but also helps you continue to weather the stresses of monthly insemination. The stress of not getting pregnant affects all aspects of health: physical, mental, emotional, and spiritual. The fertility enhancement suggestions help support your body through the specific stresses of the preconception period.

When you've been trying to get pregnant for some time, you may feel tempted to discard all of the fertility-enhancement approaches you've been using because they seem ineffective. Resist this temptation. What you've done so far has helped your body prepare for a healthy pregnancy. It's perfectly appropriate, however, to reevaluate the methods of fertility enhancement you've tried so far. Rotate the methods, incorporating new ideas that you haven't tried and discontinuing methods you've come to resent. This will help you continue to optimize your fertility and health while giving you a fresh outlook.

Track Your Fertility More Carefully

Many people have never charted more than one or two fertility signs during the months in which they've been trying to get pregnant. This is often because the doctors they've been seeing recommend using ovulation predictor kits, ultrasound, and lab work as the only means of fertility monitoring. Many doctors go so far as to claim that to monitor more "subjective" signs such as sex drive or fertile mucus is worthless. Keep in mind, though, that most fertility specialists have learned their trade through working with heterosexual women who have abundant access to fresh sperm. They aren't necessarily specialists in lesbian or single-woman fertility. That's our specialty, and through working with hundreds of clients, we've found that a woman will significantly increase her chances of getting pregnant if she monitors a minimum of three signs, preferably four or more.

TRACKING FERTILITY IS INHERENTLY SUBJECTIVE

It is valuable to remember that in our practice, we consider information gathered from ovulation predictor kits (OPK) and ultrasound readings to be as subjective as any other means of tracking fertility. There isn't a general way of interpreting what a positive OPK reading means; this varies with age and from person to person. Some people have already ovulated at the time of the positive reading, some will in the next few hours, and some will ovulate in thirty-six hours. If you're monitoring your follicle size by ultrasound, it can be difficult to get helpful information without serial scans. In order to determine your particular rate of growth and at what size you ovulate, you must have daily ultrasounds, which is not standard practice. What your follicles look like on any given day, therefore, is also subjective information.

We value tremendously the place these methods have in tracking fertility, but you are unique and must come to learn what each fertility sign indicates for your body. Therefore, the Maia approach is to track more than three indicators of fertility each cycle. Then, when at least three signs line up, you'll have a clear indication of your most fertile window for that month.

Bear in mind that your body changes month to month. It's very rare that a woman is static in the fertility signs she shows each month. Some months you'll have a lot of fertile mucus for four days; some months you'll have fertile mucus for one day. One month you may have peak-fertility signals on day twelve, and the next month on day fifteen. As you become aware of which side you're ovulating on, it's likely that you'll find a more predictable pattern for each side. Keep in mind that your ovulation doesn't necessarily alternate between your left and right ovaries every month. As people age, hormones can fluctuate month to month, causing cycle irregularities. This results in some cycles being stronger than others. These irregularities can usually be smoothed out with the fertility enhancement program offered in part 3.

TRACK MORE SIGNS

The more types of fertility signs you chart, the more accurate your timing will be. If you've been charting fewer than three signs or haven't been getting clear information from your charting so far, try charting more fertility signals. Even if you think you're getting clear information from your methods, it's probably wise to try more, since you haven't yet conceived. Perhaps you're getting clear information that you're interpreting incorrectly, leading you to inseminate a little early or a little late for your optimal fertile window. This becomes obvious when you begin to track additional signals. The more information about your body that you have, the greater your chances of conception.

If you have been resisting looking at your cervix with a speculum, or at your saliva with a lens, you may be ready for that now. Since there are so many fertility monitoring methods, keep adding and rotating methods until you get pregnant. Discontinue charting signs that give you no pattern or valuable information, and add any of the numerous fertility signals you aren't tracking. More than likely, this will add vital information to the patterns you're already tracking. Continue to monitor all of the signs that do show a pattern. The more sources of information you have to work with, the more sophisticated your interpretation will be. You may consider adding ultrasound monitoring or blood work monitoring to your other methods. We will discuss these tools later in the chapter. Maia offers long distance chart analysis for anyone who cannot find a local person to help them review their charting.

Fine-Tune Your Timing

It's best to increase your fertility-tracking methods before you try to fine-tune your insemination timing. This will give you additional information to work with. Even with the most thorough charting, deciding when to inseminate always involves an element of guesswork. For each cycle, it's helpful to write up a short addendum and attach it to your fertility chart, briefly stating why you inseminated when you did. For example: "This month I inseminated twice: once when my cervix was most open, and once when my ovulation predictor kit read positive." This kind of notation is useful to reflect back on when reevaluating your timing if you're not conceiving.

Please, please remember that it's been our experience that people often inseminate too late—in other words, after their fertility peaks. The problem isn't always infertility or the limitations of frozen sperm; you just may be inseminating too late. We cannot emphasize this enough.

Sexual Satisfaction

Studies of heterosexual women show that a women's satisfaction with her sexual experience unconsciously dictates how much sperm she allows into her uterus. Women who were dissatisfied with the sex were discovered to have no sperm inside the uterus. The implications here are many. Please remember that at Maia we see a great increase in conception rates with people who are having at least three orgasms a week. Keep in mind that this is not sex that involves sperm or necessarily penetration. Clinical insemination is inherently nonsexual. For some this may be of incredible significance. Even if you choose the route of medical insemination, it may be worth entertaining the value of self-insemination at home once per month coordinated with some great (solo or partner) sex.

Increase Your Number of Monthly Inseminations

Whether you're using fresh or frozen sperm, you should inseminate twice a month at a minimum. This is especially important if you're using frozen sperm, since it is only viable for eighteen to twenty-four hours. Two vials of frozen sperm do not add up to even one fresh ejaculate in terms of sperm quantity. Ideally you could use three or even four vials of frozen sperm and inseminate two to three times each cycle. We know this can be expensive, but increasing your number of inseminations will increase your chances of conception. Therefore, we recommend using greater quantities of sperm and skipping every other cycle than inseminating just once per cycle. When you step back for a moment it doesn't take much to realize that by increasing the quantity of sperm and spreading out its coverage each month, you're increasing your chances of conceiving. Of course when waning fertility is one of the issues, making a decision like this is compounded by many factors. Each month is valuable and skipping a month may not be in your best interest.

Increasing your number of monthly inseminations is particularly significant if the only insemination you've been doing each month has been an IUI. Some studies show that doing two IUIs per cycle—instead of just one—more than doubles a woman's chances of conceiving. Remember, sperm deposited into your uterus doesn't live as long as sperm placed into your vagina. *Some estimate that IUI sperm only live in the uterus for six to eight hours.* So unless you're within six to eight hours on either side of ovulation, by inseminating just once a month you've lost your chances for the entire month.

Likewise, although fresh sperm lives for forty-eight hours and longer, by increasing your number of inseminations per cycle you'll significantly increase the quantity and the amount of time covered, and therefore increase your chances of getting pregnant.

A number of women have reported to us that increasing their number of inseminations per cycle freed them from the enormous pressure of timing their insemination perfectly, and therefore made the insemination part of each cycle much more enjoyable.

Although it is completely nontraditional, and completely cost prohibitive for most, we have found that for some people who are not conceiving using frozen sperm for IUI that increasing the number of IUIs from two to three was the missing piece. Of course, weighing the cost differential of three IUIs versus one IVF cycle makes the IUIs seem reasonable...

On the other hand, if your donor has an exceptionally low sperm count, or very low motility, you may want to try only one well timed IUI per cycle.

Try One Vaginal Insemination and One IUI Each Month

For people having difficulty conceiving, we recommend they do at least one vaginal insemination and one IUI per cycle. The IUI should be the second insemination, timed as closely to ovulation as possible—ideally within six hours on either side of ovulation. We recommend this in lieu of only doing one or more IUIs per cycle. Even if it's been suggested that due to your age and overall fertility status you should not do a vaginal insemination, we don't agree with this blanket approach.

On the other hand, if your donor has poor-quality sperm, or if the only sperm available to you is IUI-ready, then please only do IUIs each cycle.

There are a number of reasons why adding at least one vaginal insemination to your IUIs will increase your chances of getting pregnant. One key reason is that the life of unwashed sperm is longer than that of washed sperm, so you'll be able to cover a wider window of possible fertility. Likewise, an unwashed sample yields a significantly higher quantity of sperm

BEFORE EMBARKING ON FERTILITY TREATMENTS

than a washed, IUI ready sample. The added time coverage and the additional sperm quantity will greatly increase your chances of getting pregnant. Also, if you're doing your vaginal insemination at home, you may benefit from the dramatic increase of your emotional, physical, and sexual comfort when you're in your own environment. These elements cannot be underestimated in their effect on helping achieve pregnancy.

Conversely, if you have only been doing self-inseminations, it may be of value to add an IUI as well.

Increase the Volume of Sperm in Your IUI

Some clinics across the country are experimenting with using 1 cc of washed semen in their IUIs. For people using frozen sperm this would mean using two vials of IUI-ready samples per IUI. The numbers of conceptions are apparently on the rise. It is unclear whether this is due to the increase of the number of available sperm or to the fact that the uterus cannot always hold such a quantity, so much of the sperm ends up in the cervix where it is then time-released.

Change Your Source of Sperm

If you've been using a known donor and haven't conceived, there are a number of things to consider. If you feel confident about your timing and feel fertile, the problem may very well be your donor's sperm. Has he had a recent semen analysis? Are his sperm count and motility high? Is his morphology good? Is he abstaining from ejaculating for at least seventy-two hours prior to donating sperm? Are you inseminating too frequently and diluting his count at the time you really need it?

How do you know when it's time to change donors? If you've been unsuccessfully trying to get pregnant for six consecutive months, inseminating two or more times each cycle with vaginal inseminations, then it's time for him to get another semen analysis. Remember that there are different gradations of semen analysis. If you've simply had the basic semen analysis up until now, you may want to consider finding a practice that can do a Kruger strict morphology as well as a sperm-penetration assay, which gives more specific information about the sperm's actual functioning by observing how it moves through your fertile mucus. If the tests come back with good results, try six more cycles with one vaginal and one well-timed IUI each cycle. If you haven't gotten pregnant after twelve cycles, it is time to change donors. This, of course, is assuming that you and he have been following our fertility-enhancement program.

If your donor starts off with a low sperm count or low motility, or if the sperm have a high rate of malformation, you need to take a different, more aggressive approach. To begin with, have your donor do all he can to enhance his fertility. (See chapter 9 for suggestions.) Then it's best to begin inseminating with one to two IUIs per month, ideally two if he can produce enough sperm in such a short period of time. With this approach, you are using IUI as a delivery system for closer placement of the available sperm. If morphology is the issue, then the washing process can be tailored to weed out the misshapen sperm from the properly shaped ones.

After three months ask your donor to get another semen analysis to see whether whatever he's been doing has improved his fertility. If there's no improvement in his semen analysis, you need to decide if you'll try a number of cycles more regardless, if you'll use assisted reproductive technology such as in vitro fertilization to overcome his sperm limitations, or if you'll find a new donor. Remember to factor your age into this decision as well. Whenever possible, it is best to not have dual fertility challenges that you are working with.

We know you may be deeply invested in your donor's participation in your family and that you probably don't have donors beating down your door. Nonetheless, to continue with a donor who has a subfertile sperm count means committing to a possibly long, arduous process with significantly decreased chances of achieving pregnancy, or committing to expensive invasive fertility treatments. The choice is up to you.

When You're Using Frozen Sperm

There are a few important points to reiterate when using sperm from a sperm bank. First, if you're using frozen sperm, be sure to rotate which donor you're using every few cycles. Also, be sure to work only with donors whose sperm has resulted in pregnancies before and who have a high sperm count and high motility, and good morphology. Remember, the way to ensure this is to be assertive with your sperm bank. Ask explicitly for the newest samples and those with the highest motility and greatest sperm count. For additional tips about getting the most out of your sperm bank see chapter 9. Make sure that you are only choosing to do IUI with IUI-prepared samples. The only time we suggest ignoring this advice is if you are very fertile or if you do not have access to any other sperm or insemination services. In that case, please use two vials per insemination. In other words, at least four vials per cycle. Do not rewash already washed samples; it greatly reduces the amount of viable sperm.

Whenever possible, increase the number of vials you use each cycle. If you bought six vials of unwashed samples it would still be less than two ejaculates from the average man. Sperm swim in groups; together they propel one another forward. Perhaps there's an ideal number of sperm that swim together, and the arbitrary breaking down of semen into freezable and measurable quantities does not always allow for this. There needs to be enough sperm surrounding an egg to change the biochemical environment so that fertilization can occur. Does the fact that we have seen a number of women get pregnant quickly when they inseminate with two or three vials of frozen sperm at a time bear out the quantity argument? Our statistics are too small to prove this definitively. We know that some studies show that during intercourse only 5 to 10 percent of sperm make it through the cervix into the uterus. Out of the millions, only a few hundred actually swim up the fallopian tube. Because of this, for vaginal inseminations, quantity and quality of sperm are directly related to likelihood of conception.

Even having taken all of these steps, many people just don't get pregnant using frozen sperm. Do other factors exist that can affect a person's ability to get pregnant with frozen sperm? We don't know. Many aspects of the conception process are a mystery, especially for us, because lesbian conception has barely been studied at all.

It's insightful that so many of the people we have seen over the years refer to fresh sperm as "live" sperm—as in, "If only I could find a live source of sperm to use" or "Do you think I should use live sperm?" Frozen sperm isn't dead, but clearly to many women's subconscious minds it is. Many people try unsuccessfully for months or even years with frozen sperm with or without fertility medications and treatments and then inseminate once with fresh sperm and get pregnant. There are conflicting results from studies as to whether or not using frozen sperm decreases a person's chances of conception. Once again, this is due in part to the fact that the fertility studies are primarily of heterosexual women experiencing one form of infertility or another. There are very few fertility studies on fertile people choosing to use either frozen sperm or IUI.

The Fresh-Sperm Advantage

If you've been using frozen sperm with no success, the most effective thing you can do to increase your chances of achieving pregnancy is to find a known donor.

Although we address this earlier in the book, the differences between fresh and frozen sperm are important enough to review again here. Fresh sperm comes in much greater quantities than frozen sperm. Frozen sperm is purchased in quantities ranging from 0.5 to 1 cc, whereas an average fresh sperm ejaculation is 3 to 5 cc. This difference in quantity alone significantly increases your chances of getting pregnant.

Fresh sperm lives at least twice as long as thawed frozen sperm; some sources even say three times as long. This longevity helps buffer possible inaccuracies in the timing of your inseminations. Combine this with the fact that most donors are willing to donate at least two times a cycle and you've increased your chances of conceiving exponentially. Furthermore, aspects of the freezing process, including the addition of glycerol (a buffer), have been shown to decrease sperm's ability to fertilize an egg.

Of course, there are still potential health and legal risks involved in using a known donor, but if you've been using frozen sperm with no success, you may want to seriously reconsider the fresh-sperm option. See chapters 7 and 14 for more information.

Fresh Sperm and IUI

In general we don't recommend using IUI when using a known donor unless you have tried unsuccessfully for at least six months. If one or more of the following applies to you, however, IUI may very well help: (1) You've been using a known donor and doing vaginal inseminations with no success. (2) You're working with a donor with a low sperm count, poor motility, or poor morphology. (3) Your fertility is quickly declining. (4) You're in your late thirties or forties. Although in these circumstances IUI may improve your chances of conception, many queer and single parents-to-be will have a difficult time finding a practitioner to inseminate them with fresh sperm. Of course some people choose to get around this practice by simply saying their donor is their husband. Sometimes the practitioner will be willing if you show that your donor has tested negative for transmittable infections, or if you sign a waiver stating that you won't hold your practitioner accountable if you contract an infection from your donor's sperm.

If you've been using frozen sperm and doing IUIs up until now, there's no need to do IUI when switching to a known donor unless you fall into one or more of the aforementioned categories. In fact, if you've just switched to a known donor with fresh sperm and you're older or your fertility is decreasing, it still may make sense to inseminate two to three cycles vaginally, assuming the challenge has been the sperm and not you, since IUI may even decrease your chances of pregnancy if your timing isn't accurate. Sometimes moving the inseminations into your home makes the necessary difference.

If you have signs of decreased or decreasing fertility and you are using a known donor, you may wish to do one IUI and one or more vaginal insemination per cycle. Adding an IUI is important, since it seems to increase the chances of conception for women with decreased fertility even when the cause is unknown.

Finding a New Known Donor

When your donor's sperm doesn't seem to be working, there may come a time when you decide you need to find a new donor. This can be emotionally difficult for a number of reasons. Perhaps you've been emotionally invested in using this person's sperm. Or perhaps you're afraid you may lose his friendship if you choose to use another person's sperm. Perhaps your donor is also going to be a coparent to your child. Navigating the emotional territory can be challenging, but this isn't a reason to continue with a sperm source that isn't working.

If you'd like to continue a parenting relationship with this person, whether or not you use his sperm, then broach the topic. Once they get over their attachment to biological connection, many men realize the parenting relationship itself is most meaningful to them. Some women, however, feel they need the opportunity to completely reevaluate their options. This would mean ending a parenting commitment with their current donor and prospective coparent in order to be able to foster relationships with others.

Change Your Method of Insemination

If you've been using the same method and location of insemination all along and haven't gotten pregnant, it's time to consider other options. For example, if you've only been inseminating by IUI at a clinic or doctor's office, you might want to try inseminating vaginally in the privacy of your own home. If you've only been inseminating vaginally at home, to no avail, you may want to try IUI. Some people prefer to try having sexual intercourse with a man. Likewise, if you've only been having intercourse, perhaps you need to try a new donor or try inseminating instead.

We've worked with women who had inseminated for more than a year doing only vaginal inseminations, then decided to try IUI, and after one IUI got pregnant. We've also worked with women who began trying to get pregnant in their forties. Aware of their waning fertility, they took fertility drugs and did IUIs from the get-go. Eventually, they ended up in our office looking for a different approach. When we suggested they listen to their bodies, many of them stopped taking fertility drugs and started inseminating vaginally at home. It isn't unusual for these people to get pregnant after one or two cycles. We have worked with numerous women in their forties after unsuccessful IVFs who got pregnant after following our fertility recommendations with one well timed self-insemination and one well-timed IUI per month. Again, review chapter 15 for a through discussion of insemination methods.

Change Care Providers

The fresh energy and perspective of a new care provider may be the missing link you've needed in order to get pregnant. If you have not been able to get pregnant, give serious thought to changing care providers, whether you have a primary-care provider, obstetrician-gynecologist, or reproductive endocrinologist (infertility specialist) if:

- You feel you've surpassed your provider's skill base.
- You feel your provider has lost hope in your ability to conceive.
- Your provider does not respect your choices.
- Your provider is badgering you into trying something you aren't ready for.
- Your provider has only one way of doing things.
- You feel your provider is homophobic.
- Your provider does not have time to answer your questions.
- You are uncomfortable in any way with your provider.

New energy and ideas are always a welcome change when you've been inseminating for what feels like forever. Remember, you don't need to have a reason to change care providers.

Infertility Technology: Considerations

It is important to have a critical thinking framework from which you can read the technical information discussed in this chapter and the next one on fertility treatment options, so we begin with a discussion of how you might approach making decisions about infertility treatments and procedures. We will also discuss the various causes of infertility. This will help you understand the information on diagnostic tests and treatments.

The information we give is complex. You might find it logical or it might be confusing, depending on your background. Don't worry if you don't understand all the details right now. You can ask questions of health care providers and look at other less detailed books and pamphlets explaining infertility. We do suggest reading the whole section through once to get a sense of the field of infertility. If you choose any of these tests or treatments, know that some of the simplest may be completely effective for you in helping you conceive and that you may never need to reread the sections on injectable infertility drugs or in vitro fertilization.

Whom Will You Be Working With

You may be used to seeing a nurse practitioner, midwife, or family practice doctor for regular Pap smears. These health-care providers are perfectly able to provide gynecological care, but they probably don't do much infertility screening or treatment beyond the first set of blood tests. A regular ob-gyn may have a practice that prescribes infertility pills and performs intrauterine inseminations or diagnostic procedures and surgeries such as laparoscopy. Most often, to have a comprehensive infertility screening, receive injectable infertility drugs, or have in vitro fertilization performed, you'll need to see an infertility specialist who is an ob-gyn with a number of years of further specialized training. This specialist is called a reproductive endocrinologist (RE). (An endocrinologist is a specialist in understanding the complexities and workings of hormones.)

Some of any of the above doctors will devise a treatment plan that includes trying low-tech options before moving on to more invasive testing or treatments. Others want to do a very comprehensive workup that includes many of the diagnostic tests we'll describe, before providing any kind of treatment. Others still will have one set way of addressing fertility strictly based on age. You may just see an obstetrician, you may see an RE for a consultation, and then work with your regular obstetrician to complete the steps of the treatment plan you all come up with, or you may see the RE exclusively. It probably depends on which tests or treatments you're doing, your insurance coverage, your preference, and how far you have to drive to see a specialist.

Infertility specialists are listed in your health-care plan, in the Yellow Pages under "Physicians," or through RESOLVE's infertility specialist referral list. Please note that some insurance plans consider infertility a pre-existing condition. Thus if you have used infertility services in the past and want to change insurance plans, you may find that you are ineligible. Check this out before entering into the world of medical treatments for infertility.

Your care provider should:

- Give you full disclosure of the risks, side effects, and actual rates of success of procedures and treatments. Please remember your chances of these procedures working are likely to be much higher than those quoted to you if you do not have fertility problems. They are also likely to be higher if you follow our fertility-enhancement program.
- Be respectful of other healing modalities and practices you feel are useful.
- Encourage you to remain central in the decision-making process.

In addition, if your care provider specializes in infertility, he or she should:

⊚ Have an office staff person help you navigate insurance policies
and payment plans.
⊚ Give referrals to support groups and mental health providers
specializing in infertility issues.

Assisted Reproductive Technology (ART) Is Compelling

ART is on the rise and is very big business. Some of the procedures in wide-spread use have been shown to increase a woman's chances of pregnancy, while others have much more questionable success. A helpful book on the subject is *Beyond Second Opinions: Making Choices About Infertility Treatment,* by Judith Steinberg Turiel. The technological advances of our times have allowed many women to get pregnant who would not have otherwise been able to.

Many women who aren't actually experiencing infertility, however, re-ceive infertility treatment, simply because they're lesbians or single or sim-ply due to their age. Infertility treatment is often presented as if it's a magic pill guaranteeing conception. Lesbian and single women often enter the medical system seeking advice on how to get pregnant. Then, solely because they're using insemination as their means to achieve pregnancy, they're cat-egorized as infertile. Once again, the unexamined heterosexual assumptions of our culture are played out on women's bodies. Because there isn't a sepa-rate fertility field for lesbians and single women, they are instead lumped into a category that may or may not pertain to their actual fertility status.

Because the medical approach is the most widely accepted, many women follow the path their doctor or friends recommend, not stopping to evaluate how they feel about these choices. These same women may end up feeling completely out of touch with their bodies and wondering how this feeling of disconnection could have happened. The most important message we have for you is to stay comfortable with your choices. If you feel you're traveling down a path where you're no longer the driver, step back and reevaluate your decisions.

Deciding Whether Assisted Reproductive Technology Is for You

In lieu of putting yourself on cruise control, take some time to explore whether the medical-technological approach is right for you. There's no universal right or wrong way to conceive, only what's best for you. Some people choose not to enter the realm of technology at all. For some this is an ethical consideration; they feel that if they can't conceive without the help of technology then it's not meant to be. Others feel that it's not "right" to take conception out of the bedroom and medicalize it. For some people this conviction feels like a spiritual belief.

Others are limited by their incomes. Fertility treatments are expensive and aren't usually covered by health insurance. Even without such grand expenses as that of in vitro fertilization, it's not unheard of to spend more than $50,000 trying to conceive. The price of sperm, IUI, ultrasounds, medications, and lab work can add up quickly.

It's perfectly reasonable to set limits for yourself. In fact, it's necessary. Some things may be fine for you, whereas others you will never try. For example, we work with many people who feel fine using fertility medications and getting inseminated in a clinic, but do not resonate with IVF. We have worked with people who are only willing to do IVF with their own egg, since for them an important part of choosing to be pregnant instead of adopting is having a genetic relationship with their baby. Others feel more comfortable using reproductive technology and feel like it increases their options. Some people will choose IVF with donor egg over adoption because they want the experience of being pregnant, giving birth, and breastfeeding. Some people go straight to IVF because their partner has a poor sperm count and they don't want to mess around. Some women start with IVF so that they can conceive a baby using their partner's egg—making the baby "truly" both of theirs.

Self-Reflection

Before you enter the realm of technology, it's helpful to ask yourself some questions. Take the time to write down the responses you have to the following questions. Also, take note of the messages your body communicates to you about each question. If you're partnered, you may both want to do this exercise then get together and discuss what your feelings about technology and this pregnancy are at this point in your process. Answering these questions for yourself can help you to interact with the medical world in a way that is true to your convictions.

- What are my beliefs about conception?
- Are there limits to what I'll do in order to conceive? If so, what are my limits?
- Is there a time limit on how long I am willing to try this for? If so, what is it?
- Are there things I believe are too technical for me?

- How much money am I willing to spend to conceive?
- Do I have a doctor I trust?

If you're partnered:

- Do we have the same feelings and beliefs regarding conception and fertility treatments?
- Are there things we should talk about now to help clarify our beliefs and establish a mutual understanding?
- What will we do if we have differing limits?

Selective Use of Technology

Remember, you're always the one in control of what's done to your body. This is often difficult to keep in mind in the face of the medical establishment. It's even more challenging to assert yourself if you feel your body has failed you. Nonetheless, remember that you have total choice about your body.

Just because there's a standard approach that your doctor takes for dealing with "infertile" women, this does not mean that you have to accept the entire package. It may take considerable effort to assert yourself about what you want. When you do, your doctor should respect your choices. If you feel your practitioner is badgering you, consider changing doctors. Many people find it helpful to bring a friend to act as an advocate. You can discuss your preferences with your friend prior to the visit. This friend can then act with a level head and support you in taking your time to make informed choices that feel right for you.

Technology and Partnership Issues

Some couples reach a relationship impasse when deciding what to do next, after their initial round of insemination attempts have failed. Often the person trying to conceive isn't ready to give up and wants to go one or even many steps further to achieve pregnancy, while her partner isn't willing to go any further. There are a number of reasons for this. The partner of the person trying to conceive often feels more distanced from the process. Perhaps she'd like you to stop trying because she thinks that if you aren't able to get pregnant "naturally," then it's her turn to try to conceive. Or perhaps your partner is unwilling to support your trying other options for ethical or financial reasons. Or maybe she's emotionally exhausted and doesn't share the same emotional stake in biological parenting, leading her to feel ready to adopt rather than to keep pushing to conceive.

Sometimes the couple dynamic is such that it's the partner who isn't conceiving who wants the birth parent-to-be to engage with technology and stop trying so long to conceive "naturally." Philosophical differences in approaches to fertility and conception often become highlighted during extended preconception periods. Perhaps your partner places much more faith in medicine, which drives her to encourage you to receive treatments you don't want or feel ready for. Or she may be growing tired of the level of emotional support required of her each month and is wanting to move the process along. Or perhaps she's eager to get her chance to try and is subconsciously rushing you along in the process.

These kinds of struggles can put a serious strain on a relationship. If you reach such an impasse, it's important that neither of you simply acquiesce to the other. Both of you do need to be on the same page in order to stop or forge ahead. If you can't come to a place of peaceful agreement, enlist an unbiased friend or professional to help the two of you navigate this very emotional territory.

Neither of you wants to look back on this time and the decisions you made with resentment toward the other. Harboring resentment and anger, at either yourself for going along with your partner's choice or at your partner for having all the decision-making power, can ruin a relationship. It's valuable to reevaluate the process by which you make decisions in your relationship and to fine-tune it if necessary. To remind yourself about making decisions see chapter 2.

Causes of Infertility

Infertility problems are fairly evenly divided between male factors, female factors, and the unknown. Sometimes infertility has multiple factors.

Sperm Factors

A man may have been born with a structural or chromosomal abnormality that affects his ejaculation or sperm production. Injury, past disease, current infection, toxic exposure, or nutritional deficiency can also affect sperm production. The sperm can clump up (agglutination) so that they can't swim or they get stuck in the fertile mucus. They may have other problems swimming, be abnormally shaped or low in number, or lack the capacity to do certain biochemical processes that allow them to fertilize the egg. The man may have antibodies against his own sperm that trigger his immune system to destroy his sperm (or the woman may have antibodies against his sperm that lead her immune system to attack them once in her body).

Egg Factors

The other crucial cell involved in conception is the egg. Many infertility challenges are related to ovulation problems. When women run out of healthy eggs that can respond to hormone messages (described in chapter 5), their fertility decreases and eventually they go into menopause. Some women in their twenties and early thirties experience "premature ovarian failure"—meaning they run out of eggs early. This is fortunately not the most common fertility problem. Sometimes the cause is as simple as anemia. Fertility challenges can be related to past sexually transmitted infections. Sometimes there's a problem with the functioning of the pituitary gland, which can affect any of a number of essential ovulation hormones. Other factors affecting these hormones are excess exercise, chronic illness, stress, lack of sleep, nutritional depletion, and weight loss. These factors may affect the delicate balance of hormones in the brain, thus disrupting fertility, without necessarily causing changes in menstrual cycle regularity or length. Sometimes other hormone imbalances hamper fertility, such as those caused by polycystic ovarian syndrome, or those occurring in the thyroid or adrenal glands.

Sperm-Egg Meet-Up Factors

If egg and sperm are both released and functioning well, the next step is for them to meet. Besides the antibodies we mentioned, another potential obstacle is that the woman may not have enough fertile mucus for the sperm to enter the uterus. In addition, both men and women can have blocked tubes. We discuss causes of blocked fallopian tubes in detail later in this chapter. If the egg and sperm meet in the fallopian tube and conception occurs, the tiny developing bundle of cells we call an embryo must travel through the fallopian tube and attach itself to the lining of the uterus and start to grow a placenta. Sometimes implantation is not possible due to the thickness of the zona pellucida. Sometimes structural problems in the uterus prevent the embryo from having a good place to implant. These abnormalities that prevent the lining of the uterus from growing rich and thick and nurturing can include congenital anomalies, fibroids, endometriosis, polyps, or a hormonal problem such as a "luteal phase defect." There are other more rare situations that we don't mention here. Indeed, this may appear to be such an extensive list that it's amazing anyone can conceive. Yet we know many women do, many even unintentionally or despite their best efforts not to. And in fact, many women with infertility challenges do conceive on their own without "high-tech" interventions if they inseminate long enough. The vast majority will achieve pregnancy, with or without fertility treatment, within two years.

Standard Diagnostic Tests and Procedures

The next section describes a number of standard tests for gathering more information about any of the above challenges that maybe apply to you. We then go on to discuss treatment options.

Receiving a diagnosis can feel empowering: finally there is a reason for the challenges that you have been experiencing! After you have received a diagnosis it is important to research as much as you can about the implications it may have for conception, pregnancy, miscarriage, your baby, and breastfeeding. From here you can research medical and alternative approaches to addressing this problem and determine specific ways of boosting your chances of conception. By gaining a comprehensive understanding of the problem, you will be able to become aware of what increases the problem and what can be done to decrease the problem, if anything, Remember that a healthy diet and natural fertility enhancement that focuses on hormonal balance is often all that is needed to remedy many problems.

As mentioned, 40 percent of infertility cannot be explained. So although we outline some of the available diagnostic options, it's quite possible that you may never know why you aren't getting pregnant. This is why we emphasize optimizing your fertility in as many ways as possible. *You do not always need a diagnosis to overcome fertility challenges.*

Blood Tests

If you've been trying to get pregnant for more than six months, and you haven't already had your hormone levels tested, then it's time to do so. This is especially important if you're nearing 40 or have irregular cycles. By irregular cycles we mean cycles that are as short as twenty-four days or longer than thirty-two days, mid-cycle bleeding, very heavy or light periods, or cycle lengths that vary dramatically. If you're in your late thirties or forties, or if you've had questionable levels of any of your hormones in past labs, we recommend that you get your hormones tested two to three times a year.

This information can help you relax if you find you have no significant hormone imbalance or indication of infertility. It can also let you see how rapidly your body is moving toward menopause and help you make decisions that reflect this rate of change. You can use the information to target your fertility therapies as well. Assuming that these tests are all within range then many doctors will move on to the next round of testing. Be sure at this point to have your donor go through an infertility work-up if he has not already. Male tests are much less invasive than female tests and are much less expensive. If he has a borderline semen analysis, be sure that his hormones are tested as well, as hormonal imbalance can affect sperm quality and production.

Some fertility specialists will wait until you demonstrate fertility challenges before offering the following tests, others routinely provide anyone over 35 with these tests regardless of whether they have started to inseminate or not.

Antral Follicle Scans

Sometimes a fertility specialist will recommend visualizing your natural production of follicles each month to make an assessment about ovarian reserve and ovarian function. Although follicle production can certainly vary cycle to cycle, a positive follicle count can certainly be reassuring information. In an unstimulated cycle, the baseline antral follicle count should be between 12 and 30. Under 12 but above 7 may still be possible for conception, especially with stimulation. Fewer than 4 is a greatly reduced chance of conception, even with stimulation. Over 30 follicles may be fine, but may be a sign of either polycystic ovarian syndrome or poor-quality eggs.

The "Clomiphene Challenge"

The clomiphene challenge involves the administration of clomiphene, which stresses the ovaries, and then measuring the hormonal effects of this stress. The challenge consists of drawing FSH and estradiol levels on day 3, taking 100 mg of clomiphene on days 5 to 9 to stimulate the ovaries, and then drawing another FSH on day 10. Ideally at least one ovary should respond by maturing multiple egg follicles. Low FSH and estradiol levels are expected on day 3, and with good ovarian reserve, the FSH will also be low on day 10. An elevated FSH reserve on day 3 and 10, or only on day 10, indicates poor ovarian reserve. An elevated day 10 FSH may indicate that the estradiol was suppressing the FSH on the day 3 reading.

Some physicians feel this is a more accurate test of fertility than simply checking FSH and estradiol levels in the blood during a regular unmedicated (natural) cycle; they feel that poor results on these tests indicate a low chance of pregnancy using one's own eggs. Other physicians don't consider the test particularly insightful.

Hysterosalpingogram (HSG)

An HSG is a medical procedure for checking whether the fallopian tubes are blocked. Three to 6 ml (milliliters) of dye is injected into the uterus and fallopian tubes through the cervix. An X-ray shows whether the dye moves from the uterus into the fallopian tubes and then out the ends. This checks whether the tubes are blocked and properly formed, or whether you may have intrauterine lesions such as polyps, fibroids, an unusually shaped uterus, uterine septum, uterine adhesions, or scar tissue—any of which may impede conception. Scar tissue blocking tubes internally or tangling them externally is usually caused by pelvic infection (often from gonorrhea or chlamydia bacteria), postabortion infection, a ruptured appendix, past tubal pregnancy, or abdominal surgery. Interestingly, almost half of the women whose HSG shows pelvic scar tissue or tubal damage have no medical history of any of these and are suspected of having had chlamydia at some point in the past without displaying any outward symptoms.

Some women choose to get an HSG just to confirm that their tubes are clear. An HSG "washes" out the tubes; thus even for women who have no visible obstructions, it's still possible that undetected minor blockages will be cleared through the procedure. If the tubes are slightly blocked, the increased pressure of the dye can sometimes clear the blockage. As a result, for many women fertility seems to increase during the three months following an HSG.

HSG AND INFECTIONS

It is recommended that a cervical culture for gonorrhea and chlamydia be performed prior to doing an HSG because if there is an infection, the dye being forced into the uterus and fallopian tubes could spread the infection more deeply into the body. The HSG procedure involves a series of X-ray exposures which are directed at your ovaries and uterus.

CONSIDERATIONS CONCERNING X-RAY EXPOSURE

This is a strong reason to carefully consider whether to choose an HSG without apparent cause. Expert texts suggest that three X-ray films (before, during, and after) are sufficient, but many practitioners expose patients to more X-rays to pick up details that are probably insignificant to conception.

HSGS AND ANTIBIOTICS

During the procedure, many practitioners performing HSGs prescribe antibiotics that aren't considered safe for pregnancy. This eliminates the possibility of inseminating during the month of the procedure. If you ask, you may find that these antibiotics are optional. Likewise, although some women feel only slight discomfort, others experience the procedure as extremely painful. If you are allergic to contrast dye or shellfish you should not have this test as the chance of a very severe allergic reaction is high.

Biopsy, Hysteroscopy, or Laparoscopy

If you have pelvic pain, fibroids, endometriosis, or unusual bleeding, sometimes a biopsy, hysteroscopy, or laparoscopy is recommended. These procedures can sample or produce an on-screen image of the endometrial lining and pelvic organs. Hysteroscopy involves looking at the inside of the uterus through a fiber-optic tube inserted through the cervix. Laparoscopy is surgery that shows an on-screen image of the pelvic organs with a fiber-optics tube placed in the abdomen via a small incision. If corrective treatment is needed, instruments can be placed through the incision. Sometimes you can be asymptomatic yet have obstructions in your uterus that prevent you from getting pregnant. During a laparoscopy, endometriosis tissues and fibroids can be removed. Once these are removed, it may be easier to achieve and maintain a pregnancy. The extent to which endometriosis and fibroids affect fertility and the extent to which the benefits of surgery supersede its inherent risks are a matter of much debate. However, presence of fibroids and endometriosis can certainly prevent pregnancy or implantation in many situations. Many factors are at play, including the size and location of the fibroids as well as the location and severity of endometriosis. Not all of these factors may be fully known until the surgery is actually performed.

A regular ultrasound cannot always determine whether fibroids, polyps, ovarian cysts, endometriosis, or other obstructions are present. A sonohysterogram, in which water is injected into the uterus in order to push the walls apart slightly, is a more detailed form of ultrasound that is better at detecting these problems. In fact, a sonohysterogram will often show if the tubes are blocked without subjecting a woman to the X-ray radiation of an HSG. A sonohysterogram is done by transvaginal ultrasound, which involves having the patient lie on the examining table with her feet in stirrups and inserting a transducer, which is about the size of a speculum, into the vagina. Immediately, an image of the pelvic organs will appear on the ultrasound screen. Some women feel vulnerable during the exam and feel discomfort or pain from the internal pressure of the transducer moving around, as well as from the water placed in the uterus.

An endometrial biopsy is the removal of a very small portion of the lining of the uterus through a narrow plastic tube placed through the cervix. A tissue specialist examines it for cancerous cells in order to diagnose the cause of abnormal uterine bleeding. If the biopsy is part of a fertility workup, the tissue specialist will examine the sample for its thickness and progesterone level. Most women find the procedure fairly uncomfortable but very quick. This method of assessing adequate progesterone is considered more accurate than a blood test.

Immunity Tests and Other Infertility Tests

If there are no apparent obstructions in the reproductive organs, and all of the hormonal tests and ultrasounds come back indicating good ovarian reserve, then immunologic tests are often ordered. Some doctors order these tests right from the get-go, others wait until everything else has been ruled out. They are usually quite expensive tests.

ANTISPERM ANTIBODY (ASA)

Antisperm antibodies, possibly present in both men and women, can cause agglutination in sperm. A woman is tested for ASA via a blood test and a sperm donor via a semen sample. Sperm banks screen their donors for ASA. ASA can also attach to the head of the sperm, preventing the sperm from being able to fertilize the egg. If antisperm antibodies are present in a woman—this occurs in 5 percent of the population—then the only treatment is IVF with intacytoplasmic sperm injection (ICSI). This is a procedure where the sperm is injected directly into the egg.

CELIAC DISEASE TESTING

Celiac disease is gluten intolerance. When someone with celiac disease eats gluten, the immune system attacks the villi in the small intestine. The villi are destroyed or damaged, and nutrients from the food are unable to be properly absorbed and reach the bloodstream. Studies indicate that people with undiagnosed celiac have elevated infertility rates, miscarriage rates, and other reproductive problems. Celiac disease is often misdiagnosed as irritable bowel syndrome. Blood tests that can indicate the likelihood of celiac disease are immunoglobulin A (IgA) antigliadin; immunoglobulin (igG) antigladin; and anti-endomysium antibodies. Although there is some debate right now as to whether or not people with gluten intolerance who still eat gluten are truly at an increased risk, we can definitively say that in our practice we have seen it.

25 HYDROXY VITAMIN D

This is a blood test that can most accurately measure the amount of vitamin D reserves in the body. Some fertility specialists measure for vitamin D deficiency because low levels of vitamin D have been associated with PCOS and infertility. There is some indication that suggests that infertility may be explained, in part, by a deficiency in calcium and vitamin D. Ovarian hormones influence calcium, magnesium, and vitamin D metabolism. Studies indicate that people with luteal phase irregularities may have calcium dysregulation as well as vitamin D deficiency. Studies have also established that vitamin D deficiency is widespread in the United States, owing to lack of exposure to sunlight and overuse of sun blockers.

Polycystic Ovarian Syndrome (PCOS)

PCOS is a complex syndrome that results from an imbalance in hormones and is a common cause of fertility problems. There are many lifestyle changes you can make to support the rebalancing of hormones needed to resolve PCOS. This is especially effective early on, but it will also enhance any medical treatment.

Approximately 6 percent of all women of childbearing age suffer from PCOS, but the numbers are much higher for lesbians and transmen. Twenty-four percent of all lesbians and at least 27 percent of pre-hormonal treatment and 70 percent of post-hormonal treatment transmen suffer from PCOS. That is at least one in four. At Maia we have a very high success rate helping people to conceive who have been given a PCOS diagnosis. If you have been given a PSOS diagnosis you may want to follow up with some tests so that you can get a better idea of its possible impact on your fertility.

PCOS can have quite serious implications—an increased risk of infertility; miscarriage; endometrial cancer; breast cancer; type 2 diabetes ovarian cancer; and coronary artery disease.

The groups of symptoms that make up PCOS include male-pattern hair growth (facial hair beyond what is expected in your family), balding, obesity, irregular menstrual cycles, anovulation, infertility, recurrent miscarriage, fluid retention, fatigue, mood swings, and adult acne. Another common symptom is polycystic ovaries, which are ovaries that contain many small cysts from underdeveloped eggs. It is, however, possible to be diagnosed with PCOS without having polycystic ovaries if enough of the other symptoms are present. The National Institutes of Health criteria for diagnosis are:

- Irregular or absent menstruation
- Excess androgens as confirmed by blood analysis
- Lack of diagnosable medical reason for the above two

Medical testing may reveal ovarian cysts, elevated testosterone levels, insulin resistance, type 2 diabetes, elevated LH in connection with a depressed FSH, depressed sex-hormone-binding globulin (SHGB), high cholesterol, and hypertension.

Finally, thyroid levels are often checked to rule out any thyroid dysfunction, since symptoms can look similar.

Researchers have noted that there seems to be a connection between PCOS and high cholesterol. Lowering cholesterol levels to normal range seems to reduce androgen levels.

The Meaning of a PCOS Diagnosis?

PCOS symptoms indicate hormonal imbalance. The two endocrinopathies most associated with PCOS are androgen disorder (excessive testosterone) and insulin resistance. People presenting the symptoms of PCOS are likely to have both of these problems. Hormonal systems are intimately related so that an imbalance in one soon becomes an imbalance in others.

ANDROGEN DISORDER

An androgen disorder is an excess of the "male" sex hormones, including testosterone.

Blood or saliva tests often show an androgen level above the normal range (saliva tests are the preferred method of diagnosis because they show levels of free testosterone, the testosterone that is available to work on body tissues). However, some women and transmen are particularly sensitive to what is considered to be a normal androgen level, meaning that these people will show symptoms of androgen excess with levels that are within the normal range. This is what makes hormonal testing so difficult. The ranges of normal are wide, to encompass human variation, but the amount of hormone needed for optimum functioning in any individual is a narrow window specific to that person's body.

Whether the androgen disorder is caused by excessive androgen production or increased androgen sensitivity, it is responsible for many of the key symptoms of PCOS, including polycystic ovaries, irregular periods, anovulatory cycles, male-pattern hair growth, hair loss, and acne.

Imbalances of LH and FSH, the hormones governing the menstrual cycle, are seen to occur with an androgen disorder. It is unclear exactly how this develops, whether it precedes androgen excess or results from it, because once there is an imbalance in either system, they perpetuate each other.

In a normal cycle, the pituitary sends FSH—follicle- stimulating hormone—to the ovary, which is stimulated to prepare follicles (fluid-filled egg sacs) for ovulation. As the body approaches time for ovulation, the pituitary sends out a surge of LH—luteinizing hormone—to rapidly mature the follicles and trigger ovulation. This high level of LH then encourages production of testosterone by the ovaries.

In women and transmen with excessive androgen, excess testosterone can interfere with normal follicular growth and development. When this happens, no follicle becomes dominant and ovulates. Estrogen continues to be created, and no progesterone is made. The body stays in the follicular, or pre-ovulatory, stage. Instead of releasing the eggs, the follicles become fluid-filled cysts in the ovaries. Polycystic ovaries often have a much harder time converting testosterone to estrogen than healthy ovaries would, and the symptoms of the androgen order are perpetuated.

Eventually, ovulation will occur or menstruation will happen without ovulation and the cycle will begin again.

The risks of an androgen disorder are infertility, due to lack of ovulation; increased miscarriage rates, due to high LH levels; and endometrial cancer, due to excess estrogen production and endometrial proliferation coupled with low progesterone and insufficient shedding of the uterine lining.

INSULIN RESISTANCE

Insulin resistance occurs when the cells of the body stop responding to insulin. This situation is created through chronic high blood sugar levels.

Chronic high blood sugar levels generally lead to obesity, as the insulin works to take the sugar out of the blood and store it in the cells as fat. Eventually, there comes a point when the cells are filled to capacity with fat. At this point, they stop responding to insulin or respond only very weakly. This is insulin resistance. There are high levels of insulin in the blood, but there are also high blood sugar levels.

RELATION OF INSULIN AND TESTOSTERONE

Insulin stimulates androgen production in the ovaries. Insulin also causes the liver to create less of a certain steroid hormone–carrier molecule that binds with testosterone, with the result that more free testosterone is left in the blood to act on body tissues. Obesity also causes less of this carrier molecule to be created in the liver.

This indicates a causal relationship between high insulin levels and elevated androgen levels. Studies show that PCOS sufferers whose insulin levels have been reduced with medicine ovulate more frequently. However, many will show symptoms of androgen disorder before they have achieved insulin resistance. This is because the high levels of blood sugar leading to insulin resistance have necessitated high insulin levels in the body for a long time before insulin resistance is developed.

Causes of the Hormonal Imbalances of PCOS

A combination of factors is at work in those who develop PCOS, including genetics, high stress levels, too much exercise, too little exercise, and poor diet. People whose mothers and sisters have PCOS are more likely to have it themselves. High stress triggers both adrenaline and testosterone to be secreted by the adrenal glands. Overexercise also triggers adrenal-gland production of testosterone. Poor diet—high carbohydrate consumption—is responsible for high insulin levels leading to ovarian output of testosterone.

Medical Treatment for PCOS

The most common treatment is oral contraceptive pills. This regulates bleeding and prevents an excessive buildup of the uterine lining. However, oral contraceptives also further disrupt the balance of female sex hormones, throwing off all hormone symptoms even more.

Treatment of infertility has most commonly been clomid, to induce ovulation. HCG injections are sometimes used for the same reason, though both of these can lead to increased cyst formation in people with PCOS. Current treatment for PCOS infertility is moving away from exclusive use of clomid to a combination of clomid and insulin sensitizers (this tends to be the case if there is a progesterone deficiency in addition to PCOS) or just the use of insulin sensitizers. Insulin sensitizers may be more effective for encouraging ovulation in PCOS patients than fertility drugs—even if blood glucose tests do not indicate insulin resistance. Ovarian surgery is also an option if drug therapy doesn't work. The most common procedure is ovarian drilling. In an outpatient, laparoscopic procedure a laser is used to penetrate the cysts and fluid is drained from the ovary; this eliminates many of the cysts. The amount of androgens is reduced and LH levels decrease. About 80 percent of patients undergoing this procedure will ovulate and about 30 to 40 percent will become pregnant. Patients at or close to ideal body weight tend to have better results than overweight patients. Risks include infection, bleeding, ovarian adhesions and eventual destruction of the ovary, leading to ovarian failure.

IVF is another option that is pursued in the medical model for those with PCOS and fertility problems. However, because people with PCOS tend to produce many small follicles, there is an added risk of ovarian hyperstimulation with IVF medications.

There is little chance of success in rebalancing the inherent imbalances of PCOS with medical approaches unless necessary lifestyle changes are undertaken.

Alternative Treatments for PCOS

Despite some genetic implications in PCOS, the condition is very much a lifestyle-based endocrine disorder. Thus, PCOS sufferers have great opportunities for healing themselves. The primary way of doing this is nourishing the endocrine system. Hormones are made from proteins, cholesterol, and fats. The body needs sufficient fats and proteins to function properly. Many people inadvertently damage their bodies and throw off hormonal balance by following a low-fat diet.

Alternatively, some people take in plenty of fat in the form of trans-fats or rancid oils. These damaged fats create problems for the body and are not able to be used in the production of hormones and other biochemicals.

The body *needs* fat and cholesterol from the food it takes in. If the body is not getting enough cholesterol, it will manufacture its own from sugar. This cholesterol is different from the kind gleaned from butter or eggs in that it is much more easily oxidized. Oxidizing cholesterol, fat, and body tissue is the foundation of many health problems.

A diet that nourishes the endocrine system is a balanced diet. A diet rich in healthy fats (this includes saturated fats such as butter, eggs, meat, coconut), protein, carbohydrates from whole grains (as opposed to sugar or overly processed white-flour products), and vegetables. Ideally, every meal should have something from each of these four groups. If that is not possible, try to blunt blood-sugar spikes by consuming carbohydrates together with a fat and protein. There is a great deal of fear about getting fat by eating fat, but it is primarily excess sugar that the body stores as fat. Further, excess carbohydrate consumption throws off the metabolism and gives rise to weight gain. Throwing carbohydrates out is not the answer. The key is to be balanced. Complex carbohydrates are essential for healthy function, just like fats, proteins, and vegetables.

REDUCING STRESS TO BALANCE HORMONES

Emotional, physical, or psychological stresses all trigger the same hormone response in the body. The adrenal glands release a combination of stress hormones—adrenaline and cortisol—and testosterone. Adrenaline is a short-acting hormone to deal with immediately stressful situations. Cortisol is designed to deal with more long-term stresses. Elevated cortisol levels over long periods of time can cause all kinds of problems for the body—diminished immune function, depleted neurotransmitters (negatively affecting mood), and decreased fertility. Cortisol stimulates the production of prolactin; this hormone stimulates breast milk production and curbs fertility.

Stress has become a kind of buzzword that is heard so often that it becomes easy to dismiss. Managing stress, whether it arises from physical illness or injury, environmental conditions, or emotional turmoil, plays a primary role of the endocrine system. Maintaining balance is what the hormone interactions are all geared for. When the demand for maintaining balance becomes too great, the endocrine system shuts down nonessential functions in the body (such as reproduction). The wisdom of this response is in attempting to prevent women from the demands of pregnancy during a time of famine or war. However, this hormone response becomes undesirable when everyday stress, even the very stress of trying to become pregnant, can become a part of the infertility problem.

Since chronic stress has detrimental health effects far beyond the realm of fertility, this can be a useful time to strengthen stress-reduction skills that will be health-promoting for a lifetime.

FERTILITY CHARTING

Just focusing awareness on the body processes and signals can be enough to boost fertility. Many people with PCOS diagnoses are able to achieve pregnancy easily with some lifestyle changes and careful charting. Coming to understand when in the extended cycle you may ovulate and what those signs are is vital to being able to conceive with PCOS.

Also, elevated LH can make ovulation-predictor kits an inaccurate means of tracking ovulation. Some people can register a surge throughout their whole cycle. Fertility monitors may be a better option as they calibrate to your LH and Estradiol.

Temperature charting can be helpful in determining if you are ovulating, within the context of erratic menstrual cycles or if you are anovulatory. Lunaception is particularly helpful for people with PCOS.

EXERCISE

A regular exercise program is great for stress reduction, blood sugar stabilization, and for endocrine and overall health. Body fat actually works as an endocrine gland—it stores hormones and it converts hormones. A certain amount of body fat is necessary for proper endocrine function. However, too much body fat can be detrimental, it can also be the result of an endocrine system that is out of whack. Eating well and following an exercise program are the best ways to achieve a optimum body composition and hormone health.

SUPPLEMENTATION AND HERBS

Chromium picolinate. Take 200 mg daily to help create greater insulin sensitivity. Also in prunes, mushrooms, liver, beets, whole wheat, and bee pollen.

Vitex. This wonderful herb is a tonic for the pituitary. Some people recommend against its use in PCOS because one of its effects is to increase LH, which is already elevated in a person with PCOS. However, as a tonic it promotes balance. This balance takes time to manifest. It is common for the first cycle of vitex to result in more irregularity. The first sign of positive results may take up to three months to show up. In addition to increasing LH, vitex increases progesterone, which is lacking in women and transmen who are anovulatory or having very long cycles. Vitex also decreases prolactin, which is a result of chronic stress and a big part of fertility problems. Vitex can be taken in tincture form. It can be taken daily for several years with no adverse reactions. However, since it decreases prolactin, it is best to stop taking it in the last months of pregnancy so as not to interfere with milk production.

Maia fertility blend of red clover, nettles, oatstraw, and red raspberry leaf. These herbs are all great nourishing tonics for fertility and pregnancy. They provide many minerals, stabilize blood sugar, and regulate the endocrine system with many hormone precursors. The best way to take these herbs is in an infusion. Infusions can be made with single herbs in rotation or with all four combined.

Cinnamon. One half teaspoon with each meal may help with insulin and blood sugar levels. A USDA study indicated that it appeared to increase glucose metabolism about twenty-fold.

B-complex vitamins. These help with the insulin-glucose balance.

OTHER HEALING MODALITIES

Acupuncture provides an entirely different understanding of the symptoms of PCOS. Treatments are geared around unblocking energy flow and nourishing different body energy systems.

Chi-nei tsang is Chinese organ massage. It focuses on moving energy through the organs and regulating function.

Essential oils can be rubbed into your belly daily. A good combination for PCOS is the following formula (combine drops with the oil):

⊙ Clary sage — 10 drops
⊙ Fennel — 10 drops
⊙ Geranium — 10 drops
⊙ Rose — 3 drops
⊙ 2 tablespoons of carrier oil (olive oil, almond oil, etc.)

PCOS FACTS

PCOS and miscarriage. People with PCOS have an increased risk of miscarriage. Estimates range from percentages of 30 to 65 percent increased risk. Two theories are suggested for why this is: One, high levels of LH may be responsible; two, elevated insulin levels may impede implantation. Some doctors are suggesting using insulin sensitizers during pregnancy until fetal cardiac activity is confirmed via ultrasound.

PCOS and pregnancy. There are some significant pregnancy risks associated with PCOS. Due to insulin resistance, there is some speculation that PCOS patients may be at a higher risk for developing gestational diabetes. Also, because both elevated cholesterol and clinical obesity is common in people with PCOS there is speculation that there is also a greater risk for pre-eclampsia. The good news is that for some people with PCOS pregnancy seems to normalize the hormone levels and PCOS symptoms never return.

PCOS and birth. People with PCOS are more likely to give birth to "small for gestational age" babies; the rate is 12.8 percent in PCOS sufferers and 2.8 percent in non-PCOS sufferers.

Breastfeeding. The hormonal imbalance that characterizes PCOS may reduce the ability to exclusively breastfeed. In fact, this is a common occurrence. Milk production can be enhanced with metformin and a good regimen of herbal support. If you have PCOS it would be good to ask your doctor about metformin and contact the local La Leche League or a lactation consultant prior to birth. However, many with PCOS have no trouble breastfeeding and for some people with PCOS, breastfeeding may in fact improve glucose tolerance and insulin resistance.

Endometriosis

Endometriosis, found in 15 percent of women in the United States, occurs when normal endometrial tissue—the mucous lining of the uterus—grows in places outside of the inner lining of the uterus. Most commonly, tissue is found in uterine tubes, the abdomen, and ovaries. However, it has also been found in as far away as the nose and lungs.

Endometrial tissue is what is shed during menstruation. With endometriosis, the displaced tissue is still responsive to hormonal fluctuations and breaks down and bleeds each cycle. Unlike the blood that comes out of the uterus and exits via the vagina, this blood has no place to go. Inflammation, pain, and occasional formations of cysts or scar tissue can result from this stagnant blood.

Diagnosing Endometriosis

Endometriosis is diagnosed by looking at symptoms and contributing factors and ruling out other possible causes. The only way to definitively diagnose it is to do a laparoscopy (small abdominal incision into which a camera is inserted) or laparotomy (larger abdominal incision) to examine the endometrial tissue outside of the uterus.

Ultrasound is used by some practitioners to diagnose endometriosis, but other practitioners discount a diagnosis made in this way. Ultrasound can reveal inner deposits of endometrial tissue that are not able to be seen even in surgical procedures. Ultrasound can be done trans-abdominally or with a vaginal or rectal probe. Ultrasound can also miss endometriosis that is outside of the uterus, but interfering with fertility.

Sometimes a HSG will indicate signs of endometriosis, but these same signs could also be seen as a result of pelvic inflammatory disease or nonspecific adhesions.

The symptoms of endometriosis include the following:

- Pain before and during periods, sometimes from ovulation through menstruation
- Pain during and after vaginal penetration
- Infertility
- Fatigue
- Painful urination during periods
- Other GI problems (diarrhea, constipation, nausea)
- Chronic pelvic pain

Causes of Endometriosis

The cause of endometriosis is unknown, but there are numerous different theories. On theory focuses on retrograde flow, where the menstrual flow is forced backward out of the uterus and back up the tubes, carrying endometrial tissue which implants and grows, and another focuses on decreased immune function. Endometriosis is strongly affected by hormones, especially estrogen. Maya massage and chi-nei tsang practitioners feel that incorrect placement of the uterus causes retrograde flow.

Its Affect on Fertility

Endometrial migration to the ovaries causes blood-filled cysts that can impair egg development, ovulation, and luteal production of progesterone. Endometrial tissue deposits in the uterine tubes cause scarring that can obstruct the path, preventing the egg and sperm from meeting. Misplaced tissue also produces prostaglandins, which cause spasms of the tubes. In this case, even if an egg is fertilized, it may be rushed through the tube too quickly and will not be ready to implant when it reaches the uterus. There are also problems with increased prostaglandins causing uterine contractions and increased miscarriage rates. Finally, endometrial implants within the muscle of the uterus can cause problems for implantation of the embryo.

Treatment of Endometriosis

In severe cases, surgery to remove the endometrial tissue can double pregnancy rates. With mild endometriosis, the risks of surgery may counter the benefits.

Outside the medical model, there are many ways to strengthen the body to deal with the multidimensional causes of endometriosis. A basic program would involve the following:

NUTRITION

Follow our recommended fertility diet. Focus especially on the following:

WHAT TO INCREASE
- Vegetables of all colors.
- Protein-rich foods.
- Essential fatty acids in flax and fish are of prime importance in reducing inflammation

- Evening primrose oil, black currant oil, or borage oil. These oils contain gamma linolic acid, which is key in the production and regulation of prostaglandins. These chemicals play a major role in the cramping and pain associated with endometriosis, but also with infertility.
- Intake of fiber.
- Intake of filtered water.

DECREASE
- All nonorganic animal fats—meat and dairy.
- All foods containing sugar, caffeine, chocolate, or alcohol.
- Avoid pesticides and heating food in plastic containers.

DAILY SUPPLEMENTS
- Vitamin C: 1 to 2 g
- Vitamin E: 400 to 800 IU
- Flaxseed oil, borage oil, evening primrose oil: 300 mg each
- Beta carotene: 50,000 to 150,000 IU
- Selenium: 200 to 400 mg
- Fish oil: three 1,200 mg gel capsules per day

HERBS
- Vitex tonic
- Dandelion tonic

AROMATHERAPY

Aromatherapy can be a very self-nurturing way of promoting health as it can be added to relaxing baths or self, partner, or professional massage.

ACUPUNCTURE

Acupuncture works off an entirely different understanding of the symptoms of endometriosis. Treatments are geared around unblocking energy flow and nourishing different body energy systems.

HEALING MASSAGE

Chi-nei tsang or Maya abdominal massage can be especially helpful with endometriosis. It focuses on breaking up scar tissue and adhesions in the abdominal and pelvic areas and restoring health to the organs there.

Dealing with Endometriosis Emotionally

Endometriosis is often seen in women whose emotional needs are in conflict with what the world is demanding of them. Endometriosis may be the body's message that it needs self-nurturance.

Many women with endometriosis have developed antibodies against their own tissues. Auto-immune diseases are not well understood in Western medical models, but the basic message that the body has turned against itself is significant. These kinds of illnesses are much more common in women in our society, who are being taught in many ways to hate and deny themselves. It makes sense that lesbians and transmen would be at even greater risk for these conditions having to deal not only with messages of misogyny but also homophobia and transphobia.

You now have the framework to understand whether infertility treatments are right for you. In the next chapter, we explore your options thoroughly.

CHAPTER 18

Infertility Treatment Options

WHETHER YOU HAVE a diagnosis for why you are not conceiving or maintaining a pregnancy or if you are experiencing unexplained infertility or repeated miscarriages, the Maia approach to increasing fertility will complement the following treatment options. In this chapter, we cover not only fertility medications and in vitro fertilization but also the intricacies of using your partner's egg or her getting pregnant.

Orally Administered Fertility Medications

The use of fertility medications has become so widespread for women who use insemination to achieve pregnancy that it's almost scary. Fertility medications have serious potential side effects that often aren't discussed with the people who will be taking them. Often women are automatically prescribed clomiphene (Clomid, Serophene) or one of the injectable gonadotropins (Follistim, Gonal-F, Bravelle, Repronex, and Menopur) before they begin to inseminate, simply because they're over 35 years old. If a woman of any age hasn't achieved pregnancy in a few months, all too frequently the blanket recommendation from fertility specialists is to take fertility drugs. This is often recommended instead of suggesting that a woman inseminate more frequently in a cycle or change her insemination timing. These options are rarely, if ever, mentioned, which just goes to show that the field of infertility is heterosexually biased. Fertility specialists often don't take into consideration our special circumstances, such as the decreased quantities of sperm we are often using, and the fact that working with frozen sperm and working with fresh sperm require two entirely different fertility plans and approaches.

We have found that some people do not respond favorably to fertility medications while others seem to respond quite favorably. For those who are more sensitive to them, the entire menstrual cycle may be thrown into mayhem. Some people find that they are unable to menstruate on their own following even one cycle of fertility medications. The cycle of medicines then just increases as she is put on hormones to trigger menstruation. We have found that about one in four women tend to react strongly to these medications in a negative way. If you are someone whose menstrual cycle gets disturbed from flying, if you are very sensitive to other medications, and if you tend to bring stress into your body you may be more likely to have a negative response to these medications. You may want to consider other options. If you do have a negative reaction, acupuncture seems to be the most effective means of rebalancing the body quickly and effectively.

Clomiphene

Clomiphene, known by the brand names Clomid and Serophene, is a drug that's usually taken from day 5 to day 9 of the cycle to promote ovulation. Some medical consumer advocates feel clomiphene is over prescribed and that women are under informed about its potential risks versus benefits.

HOW CLOMIPHENE WORKS

Clomiphene is a chemical that blocks cells from recognizing estrogen. The pituitary gland in the brain produces follicle stimulating hormone (FSH) to stimulate the ovarian follicles to mature eggs. The follicles in the ovary, in response to FSH, produce estrogen when stimulated. One of the jobs estrogen has is to let the brain know the FSH message was received. When the brain gets the estrogen signal, it knows it's producing enough FSH to prepare the eggs in the ovary for ovulation. If a woman takes clomiphene, the cells in her pituitary gland can't receive the estrogen message since the drug is connected to the receptor sites (where the estrogen message is received) on the cells instead. Thus, the brain continues to produce higher and higher levels of FSH, "thinking" that the ovaries aren't responding. The effects of clomiphene last longer than the five days during which it is taken, since it stays bound to brain cells for weeks.

If a woman isn't ovulating but has eggs and the ability to make FSH, clomiphene can help stimulate ovulation. There's some thought that clomiphene can also help women who are almost ovulating or whose eggs aren't maturing quite enough before ovulation. This can be a cause of "luteal phase defect" or low progesterone during the second half of the cycle. Clomiphene is routinely prescribed for this.

In addition to the aforementioned specific purposes for which clomiphene was designed, the drug is often prescribed to any woman who's having trouble conceiving. Studies haven't shown, however, that clomiphene increases the chances of pregnancy in women who are already ovulating. Clomiphene should be started at a low dose, which can be increased if ovulation or conception does not occur.

Checking FSH and estradiol levels and getting ultrasound just prior to ovulation to check on follicular response are useful in monitoring whether clomiphene is actually helping ovulation occur. Many experts, however, consider it adequate proof if a woman's basal body temperature charting shows a clear temperature rise in a way that indicates ovulation. Keep in mind that clomiphene is much less successful in increasing conception rates for women over 35. Nearly all pregnancies for women over 35 who are taking clomiphene and using IUI occur in the first four months of use.

SIDE EFFECTS OF CLOMIPHENE

Although it's called "cheap, safe, and effective" in fertility textbooks, clomiphene has some significant side effects. Five percent of women taking it experience abdominal pain, 1.5 percent experience vision changes from decreased blood flow to the eyes, and many women experience mood changes. Each woman responds differently to the drug. Although some women don't experience mood shifts when taking clomiphene, many experience depression, uncontrollable rage, paranoia, and hysterical crying. These common side effects are usually downplayed, if mentioned at all, when clomiphene is prescribed. If you experience these emotional reactions to taking clomiphene or any fertility medication, we suggest you mobilize a support network. If you're seeing a therapist or psychiatrist, notify him or her about your medication. It's essential to be cautious about making significant life decisions, such as quitting your job—or murdering your partner!—during these cycles.

Clomiphene can cause ovarian cysts, which usually, but not always, recede after stopping use of the drug. In addition, 5 percent of women taking clomiphene experience significant ovarian enlargement, since their ovaries are so stimulated. This is called ovarian hyperstimulation syndrome (OHSS). Hyperstimulation greatly enlarges the ovaries with fluid, which can leak into the abdominal cavity and cause serious side effects, including shock, respiratory distress, kidney problems, and even death. Symptoms may include severe pain in the pelvis, abdomen, and chest; nausea; vomiting; bloating; weight gain; and difficulty breathing. Call your doctor or go to the nearest emergency room immediately if you experience any of these symptoms while taking clomiphene.

Ovarian hyperstimulation can take seven to twenty days to fully resolve. Women diagnosed with it are usually advised to avoid penetrative intercourse, gynecological exams, and exercise until the ovaries return to normal.

Although clomiphene stimulates ovulation, conception rates with clomiphene are surprisingly low. Clomiphene can limit the ability of the cervix and uterus to respond to estrogen just as it does with the brain, which can lead to a decrease in fertile mucus and changes in the endometrium.

Some studies have shown an increased risk of certain kinds of ovarian cancer in women who take clomiphene or other fertility drugs. These results are up for debate, but current protocol is not to prescribe ovulation-stimulating drugs for more than six months total. If women take clomiphene for three to four months and then take injectable fertility drugs for a number of cycles, their total number of months of exposure can easily exceed six months.

The only studies on the potential fetal effects of clomiphene have been analyzed with data from observable defects in newborns at the time of birth. There are few if any longer-term studies. It's also important to note that up to 10 percent of women conceiving with clomiphene have twins.

CLOMIPHENE AND INSEMINATION TIMING

Usually when a woman takes clomiphene, her ovulation changes from its normal day to anywhere from day 14 to day 21 of her cycle, usually occurring on day 16 or 17. We've seen some women ovulate sooner rather than later, usually around day 10. It can be difficult to predict ovulation and to time insemination when using clomiphene, since a woman's ovulation date will probably occur later than usual, her fertile mucus will be decreased, and the drug may affect the results of her ovulation predictor kit.

Femara

Femara is also known as Letrozole. Femara works similarly to clomiphene. The company that makes Femara sent out a warning letter in January 2006. There were reports of birth defects as a result of this medication. Should a doctor prescribe this to you, please be aware of the risks. Many reproductive endocrinologists no longer prescribe this drug.

Injectable Fertility Drugs

Injectable gonadotropins (fertility drugs) are useful for women who aren't ovulating because of insufficient hormones, or for women whose eggs need extremely high levels of hormones to respond. Fertility medications are either synthetic or distilled from menopausal women's urine. These medications push your body to mature multiple eggs each cycle.

Fertility drugs can cause discomfort at the injection site. Like clomiphene, they can also cause hormonal mood swings. Some people find that they are not safe to drive or operate any form of machinery on these medications.

When taking injectables, it's also common to experience extreme physical tension, and many people on these drugs suffer from very sensitive breasts. In addition, mild to severe ovarian hyperstimulation syndrome (OHSS), which is discussed in more detail in the previous section, is a possible side effect. OHSS is more common with gonadotropins than when using clomiphene.

It's common to ovulate significantly earlier or later when using fertility medications than during nonmedicated cycles. Fertility medications are very expensive, as are the monitoring tools needed for each medicated cycle. So before you decide to use medications, make sure it's the best choice for you. Some people choose to alternate between a medicated cycle and a regular cycle to give their body and psyche a break.

Insemination Timing and Injectables

It is crucial to use your body awareness even when you are using injectable fertility medications. A number of our clients have been told that they were not ovulating with the injectables they took that cycle. This was determined by ultrasound monitoring. However, they called us a few days later with extreme sensations of ovulation. (Many people feel ovulation very strongly when their bodies are stimulated with fertility medications.) We recommend that they inseminate—and nine months later they are holding their beautiful baby in their arms. Do not abdicate your central role in this process!

HCG Injections

Although HCG is a hormone produced during pregnancy, it happens to also function to signal the body to ovulate, like LH. Because HCG is easier to concentrate than LH, it's sold by prescription pharmaceutically to be given by injection to trigger ovulation when a person on ovulation-stimulating fertility drugs has fully mature egg follicles. Some clinics routinely administer HCG shots to help with the timing of insemination; others do not use this technology.

Some people choose to get an HCG shot when they're monitoring their cycles by ultrasound, even if they aren't using fertility drugs. The rationale is that they can tell by ultrasound when the eggs are in the optimum state to be ovulated and trigger ovulation with the HCG shot. Although this isn't our general recommendation, it is a way of inducing ovulation, and your inseminations can be scheduled, to some extent, based on when you receive the shot (see below).

On the other hand, people occasionally choose to decline the HCG shot. Some people feel there isn't enough conclusive evidence that it will help them conceive. Others feel that the fertility medications they're taking interfere enough with the natural process and that their body will ovulate when it's ready.

It's important to realize that since HCG is the pregnancy hormone that urine pregnancy tests monitor, if you perform a pregnancy test too close to the time of your HCG injection you may receive a false-positive result. Likewise, symptoms of pregnancy may appear as HCG runs through your bloodstream, although you may not necessarily have conceived.

Ultrasounds for Fertility Monitoring

Some people monitor a cycle with ultrasound but decline fertility medication. By following a cycle with ultrasound, ovulation can be confirmed. With this information you can time your inseminations effectively by correlating the ultrasound information with the signs you've been monitoring to see if your timing has been correct.

Others decline the ultrasounds early in the month and only use ultrasound closer to ovulation to reduce the amount of time spent in the doctor's office and to reduce their exposure to ultrasound.

Often ultrasounds are ordered for people using fertility medications, not necessarily to time ovulation but to see if the drug is working in the desired way. One scientific article suggests that a woman using clomiphene to ovulate or to overcome a short luteal phase doesn't need an ultrasound to find out if the drug is working if she charts her basal body temperature. If her BBT remains high for at least eleven days after ovulation, this is considered adequate information to determine that the drug is working. If her BBT is questionable, her progesterone level can be checked in the second half of the cycle to see if it's high enough. However, most fertility practices prefer to visualize the ovaries in order to see how many follicles are developing and the monitor their size. It is through this form of monitoring that they decide when to administer an HCG injection.

Blood Work for Fertility Monitoring

In some fertility practices it's routine to have your blood drawn every other day in the follicular phase of your cycle. This blood is analyzed for information that is used to monitor your hormonal shifts throughout the month and help determine the timing of the HCG shot. This can be quite helpful as you can gain much information about your body and hormone levels. Some people, however, decline these monthly rounds of labs. Many of these women believe they aren't necessary or are too time-intensive, or they're afraid of having blood drawn. Some people choose to monitor a cycle this way once or twice a year; others monitor their cycle this way whenever they're using fertility medication. And still others decline the medications but feel that the hormone-level information, in tandem with the ultrasound information, is invaluable in helping them diagnose subtle imbalances and more effectively time their inseminations. Pick and choose what feels appropriate to you. It will most likely be presented to you as a package, but you can decline whatever does not feel right for you.

MAIA RECOMMENDATIONS ON FERTILITY MEDICATIONS AND MONITORING

If you choose to take fertility drugs, it's important to maximize your chances of conception, since each cycle you spend on the drugs carries increased health risks. Thus, if you're on the fertility-treatment track, be sure to inseminate *at least* two times each cycle. Consider doing the first of these at home vaginally to increase your time coverage and follow it with one or even two well-timed IUIs.

If you plan to take clomiphene, do so for only three to six cycles at the most. Do everything you can during those cycles to optimize your chances of conception: inseminate more frequently, stay lying down for a longer period of time afterward, and definitely don't compromise on your timing.

Do not take fertility medications without monitoring your cycle by ultrasound or hormone labs. Monitoring your cycles by ultrasound can help you to recognize ovarian hyperstimulation early on and can confirm that the medications are indeed working at the dosage being given. Many doctors prescribe clomiphene to any woman who's not getting pregnant, without informing her of the health risks or offering fertility monitoring. We strongly suggest that you request or do some type of monitoring if you choose to take any fertility medications.

After receiving an HCG shot, it's important to adequately time your inseminations. All too many fertility clinics recommend a woman inseminate just once, 36 hours after an HCG injection. At Maia, we feel this is too late for some women. If you're relying entirely on the fertility monitoring of the ultrasound and blood draws as your signs of fertility rather than on your own signs, then the ideal approach would be to inseminate three times: once when you receive your shot, once eighteen hours later, and once between twenty-four and thirty-six hours after your injection. Or you can inseminate two times, once at eighteen hours post-injection and once at twenty-four to thirty-six hours post-injection. *Remember, the HCG ensures that you will ovu-*

late within a set time period, however, if you were already going to ovulate earlier, you still will. It does not delay ovulation.

Many people who are monitoring their own fertility experience a discrepancy between when their body starts to exhibit signs of peak fertility (fertile mucus, open cervix, high sex drive) and when they're told to give themselves their shot. The body usually indicates high fertility earlier than the time recommended for the injection and subsequent insemination. Thus, we recommend that you do an at-home vaginal insemination when your body indicates that it's the best time—especially if you are using a known donor. Don't fret if this is sooner than your doctor recommends and sooner than the injection is scheduled; this insemination will release viable sperm for the next eighteen to seventy-two hours. The IUIs can then be timed according to the shot.

We've worked with many people who finally got pregnant when they incorporated an at-home vaginal insemination at the time they felt the most fertile or an at-home insemination eighteen hours post-injection. This insemination is in addition to the IUI.

In Vitro Fertilization (IVF)

In vitro fertilization occurs when conception takes place outside of the body. It's a treatment for a variety of infertility problems, both male and female. Depending on your age and fertility status, either your eggs or a donor's eggs are "retrieved" and then the donor sperm is mixed with the available eggs. The remaining eggs, as well as the extra embryos, are then frozen and saved. Some people adopt other women's embryos and have these embryos implanted into their uterus instead of using their own eggs or a donor's eggs and a donor's sperm.

When it's time for insertion into your body, multiple embryos are placed into your uterus—usually two to four. After implantation occurs, a sonogram will be used to determine how many embryos have implanted. Then, if more than two embryos have implanted, you may choose to have a procedure called selective reduction performed. This is the procedure by which certain embryos are vacuumed out of your uterus so that you are not carrying too many embryos at once.

Women under the age of 35 have a success rate, on average, of at least 30 percent for each cycle. Women 39 or older, when using their own eggs, have at least a 10-percent pregnancy rate per cycle. The rate of multiples (mostly twins and triplets) is often around 35 percent, depending on how many embryos are transferred. Chances are higher yet for older women, if donor eggs are used. All these statistics are approximate, since they are influenced by each clinic's protocol and each person's body. And if you follow the Maia approach to fertility, your chances will be much higher. We always recommend two IVF cycles if you choose IVF. If you're seriously considering IVF, there's a wealth of information available on the subject.

Advantages of IVF

Some people feel it's absolutely necessary for them to carry a baby and to give birth. It is a biological drive that feels like destiny. For these women, IVF provides an opportunity to do so when nothing else has worked. If they can afford it, some women choosing IVF prefer to use donor eggs and get pregnant rather than adopt or live without children. These women believe strongly that the bonding with a baby that you gestate, birth, and nurse is radically different than the bonding possible through adoption. This incredible procedure affords them the opportunity to bond with their infant right from the start. Sometimes a lesbian choosing IVF is able to use her partner's eggs. This is a remarkable benefit of infertility—perhaps the only benefit— as it is biologically a way of making a baby together. You grow, birth, and nurse the baby that carries your partner's genes.

Disadvantages of IVF

In vitro can cost $8,000 to $25,000 per cycle and even more if you're using an egg donor. Some people actually find that it's less expensive to travel outside the United States to receive IVF. And, unfortunately, despite all the time, energy, and money you may invest, there's no guarantee that IVF will work for you.

Another significant consideration when using IVF is that the process of selective reduction is emotionally excruciating. The women we have worked with who had multiple pregnancies have all reported back to us that they wished they had been counseled more thoroughly about how grueling this decision-making process would be. Some women have reported that they would not have chosen IVF had they known it would be so emotionally wrenching.

Using Your Partner's Eggs or Using Donor Eggs

In lesbian families we have a unique option available to us—we can gestate a baby that is formed from the genetic material of our partner. This is the closest that science has come to affording us an option to create babies together. Because of the remarkable nature of this option, some couples begin their conception journey with IVF. Others end up here after unsuccessful tries to conceive and yet a burning desire to grow, birth, and nurse a child. This is common when the partner whose eggs will be used is younger than the partner who is unable to conceive.

Although this looks quite romantic at the start, we have found that the complexities of this dynamic are consistently much more than anyone imagined they were going to be. Pregnancy seems to be the same as any other IVF pregnancy. However, it is postpartum when the challenges arise. Some birth moms feel a sense of despair or disconnection with their baby—fearing that the baby is not really theirs—but someone else's. They may feel that despite the fact that they birthed the child, that the child is actually adopted. Or that the baby will prefer its genetic mom to them. They can feel out of place in the family picture. Ironically, they have a similar experience to many nonbirth moms, coupled with the complexity of having birthed the child. This can lead to identity crisis and a slow bond with the baby and even to postpartum depression or partial rejection of the baby.

Postpartum is always a very intense time as it is full of hormones and major life transitions. This is especially true if you are an older parent who has had an established adult life for decades that is now being completely overhauled by a new baby. It is often a time of identity crisis and overwhelming to begin with. But it seems, from experience, that when families add the element of using their partner's eggs it can be quite heightened. We have seen a similar presentation for any woman using donor eggs, but in that case the fear is not of the baby bonding more with your partner. Rather it is a generalized sense of disconnection.

The irony, of course, is that you really wanted to use your partner's eggs, and you really want the baby and her to be deeply bonded. That is not actually the problem. What is the problem are the feelings of displacement and the questions of personal validity.

If this happens in your family, please seek counseling and postpartum support. It seems to be a time-limited situation when handled head-on. Most families feel that it has resolved by the time the baby is a few months old.

USING A PARTNER'S EGG: A DIALOGUE

LINDA: We had a hard time deciding who would give birth first. I'm older, I was forty at the time, but we were concerned that if I "went first" then by the time we were ready for a second child Randine might not be fertile. We considered what aspect of having a baby was most important to each of us. It meant a lot to Randine to have a genetic child and to me being pregnant and giving birth was most compelling.

IVF was the way we could start our family and both feel a bodily connection to the child we were creating.

Having a part of Randine growing inside of me was really an incredible experience and it's an ongoing thrill to see so much of Randine in our son.

RANDINE: I was the "egg donor" and Linda grew the baby inside her and delivered him to the world. For me it's been a wonderful way to become a family. Although my partner is the one he has the strongest bond to, through gestation, nursing, and she is the primary caregiver, I feel very secure that I'm just as much his parent. I love seeing myself and my family carried on in our baby's features. I imagine it's a lot like being a "dad." He's my son, and I'm totally in awe of my sweetie for producing him.

All that said, the actual process of IVF was hard, and we won't do it again. We both had to do hormone therapy to synchronize our cycles and get our bodies ready. It was like extreme PMS/menopause for both of us. We cried a lot—I've never been so overwrought in my life. Once Linda was pregnant she had to continue taking hormones and getting daily injections throughout the first trimester. Also the whole process was very medical—there was not much room for intimacy in the conception, and there was tremendous stress about how many fertilized eggs to transfer, because we really wanted to get pregnant, and we only wanted one baby.

She got pregnant with multiples that were reduced down to one. That was the most awful experience of both of our lives.

||||||||||||||||||||||||||||||||||||||||||||||||||||||||||||||||||||||||||||||||||||||

I love my son, but I'm sure I would love him just as much if we weren't genetically related. That bumper sticker "Love Makes a Family" has it right. Next time we may adopt. —LINDA, 43, AND RANDINE, 45, EL CERRITO, CALIFORNIA

||||||||||||||||||||||||||||||||||||||||||||||||||||||||||||||||||||||||||||||||||||||

Changing Which Partner Becomes Pregnant

When pregnancy cannot be achieved by one woman in a couple, some lesbian couples have the opportunity to have their partner try to get pregnant. Not all women, however, are able to get pregnant, and not all women want to get pregnant. It's very common to have a female couple in which one woman has always wanted to get pregnant and the other is thrilled to have her partner get pregnant but would never consider bearing a child herself. There's a cultural belief that anyone with female anatomy automatically wants to get pregnant. This is far from true. Some families find themselves at this crossroads when the other option is IVF.

We strongly encourage you to take the time necessary to make the best decision for your family. Some women will never feel complete if they do not know that they tried everything possible to get pregnant. If they do not do IVF they will always have that longing feeling of "what if?" It is a hard life to live with regrets.

The option of having your partner try is uniquely lesbian. It is complex and confusing. Navigate this territory carefully, and seek the help of a counselor if it is getting too difficult to sort out on your own.

Claudia and Kenya

For many years, Claudia and Kenya both wanted to be parents. Claudia wanted to experience pregnancy, while Kenya did not. After inseminating for five months, Claudia conceived. They were delighted to be pregnant. Claudia and Kenya went to their genetic counseling appointment to discuss testing for chromosomal anomalies of the baby, because Claudia was almost 39. They chose to have an amniocentesis. The results came back showing that the baby had Down syndrome. They decided to terminate the pregnancy, and Claudia had an abortion at nineteen weeks. They started attending a support group to work through their grief.

After six months, they felt ready to try again. Claudia inseminated for six more cycles without conceiving. They were feeling pulled apart by the stress of insemination and some unresolved grief about their first pregnancy. They chose to not move into more medical realms of infertility technology, but to take a few months together to focus on their relationship. They both felt reconnected at the end of this time after having done some counseling work. Having moved through those issues, they felt ready to explore adoption, both feeling relieved to share more equally in the process, and both ready to move toward bringing a baby into their lives in a more definitive timeline. They applied to adopt internationally, and within nine months went to Vietnam to bring home their daughter.

Having Your Partner Try: A Mixed Blessing

Deciding to stop trying to conceive and have your partner try instead is a difficult transition for most couples. The dynamic is slightly different if your partner has wanted to get pregnant anyway but you were planning to have the first baby than if your partner is willing to give it a try even though she's never felt the biological drive, need, or desire to get pregnant. If your partner has always wanted to get pregnant, an underlying sense of competition may permeate your choices. Perhaps you wouldn't choose to stop trying at this point if you were the only one who could or wanted to get pregnant. Likewise, if your partner has never really considered getting pregnant but is willing to offer her body up to the cause, you may feel anger or resentment at her lack of appreciation for the amazing opportunity she's being given.

Either way, when your partner starts to inseminate you're relinquishing the possibility of getting pregnant yourself, at least for now. Letting go in this way can be painful. You may feel tremendous loss as you let go of a dream you may have had your entire life. It's vital to honor these feelings and not sweep them under the rug. This may be a good time to enter therapy or search out other forms of support. Although you'll still be parenting, you won't be pregnant or give birth, and this realization can trigger extreme feelings of loss. If this is the case for you, please read the section in chapter 15 on loss and coming to terms with what your body is never going to do.

Take Time Off Before She Tries

When you come to this decision as a couple, it may be in your best interest to take some time off from inseminating before your partner begins to try. You may hear "internal voices" telling you not to skip a month, since you'll be another month further from having a baby. But it's unnecessarily emotionally straining to have your partner get pregnant before you've taken the time to process your own feelings.

Take at least one cycle off, and take a vacation together, if you can. Allow time for the two of you to reconnect. Spend time sharing with her how you feel about letting go and the depth of your loss. In addition, take the time to reflect together on the months that you've spent inseminating so far. Are there fond memories you'll both be taking away from this time? Are there things you may like to do differently in the future? And most important, are you sure you're ready to let go? If you're not truly ready, it's essential that you discuss this.

The transition from one partner trying to conceive to the next can be wrought with emotions. Take the time now to do your personal and joint emotional work so that you can move freely into the present and the future. You'll be grateful you did.

Your Partner's Choices

When it's your partner's turn, you have the opportunity to reevaluate together the choices you've made to date. For example, do you want to use the same source of sperm? You may find that your partner is inclined to make different choices than you did. This may be due to differences in nature and attitude toward conception. It may also be influenced by the experience you both have already been through. If her choices bring up negative feelings for you, it's best to get this out into the open.

When Your Partner Gets Pregnant

When your partner gets pregnant it may be hard for you to fully embrace the pregnancy with excitement. If she gets pregnant right away, you may feel angry at how easy it was for her to do so. Although surprising, it's perfectly normal to feel resentment and jealousy. In fact, these emotions are often overwhelming. But you can reduce them if you spend time together sharing your feelings prior to insemination. Some women, however, find it difficult to fully recognize or process their own grief until their partner actually finds that she is pregnant.

Once again, resist the urge to sweep your feelings under the rug. They'll explode when you least expect it, or they'll interfere with the intimacy you're able to have with your partner during pregnancy. Use your feelings as a catalyst for self-exploration. Have the motivation to be able to bond deeply with the baby.

Challenges in Your Partner's Conception

Another rocky situation to navigate is when your partner experiences conception challenges or miscarriage. If you felt anger or resentment toward your partner when she became pregnant, you may feel guilty if she then miscarries. The miscarriage isn't your fault, of course, but it's easy to feel like you both will always remember the pregnancy as one you weren't ready for.

If she has inseminated unsuccessfully for just as many cycles as you did, you may feel that it's your turn to try again. But just as it may have been difficult for you to stop trying when she started to inseminate, it may also be difficult for her to relinquish now that she is so personally invested.

This can feel like a weird power struggle. You're both supposed to be on the same team trying to work together to make your baby, yet it can feel like a competition over who will actually get to do it. Remember, adoption is always an option. Also remember that you're in an adult relationship, so if the process doesn't feel consensual or fair, stop and reevaluate.

We can't stress enough how valuable personal and joint therapy can be for you at a time like this. Don't let the stress of an extended conception, combined with the stress of being unable to get pregnant yourself, break up your relationship. Seek support. Remember that you're probably just regaining trust in your own body for not having allowed you to get pregnant. If now your partner has lost trust in her own body, it can feel like the two of you are lost at sea.

Some couples decide to alternate who is trying each month, some set an arbitrary amount of months each partner is allotted to try for, and some base it on who has better health insurance to cover fertility problems. Some talk until one of them is ready to actually let go and let the other forge ahead. Some decide to adopt.

Stay Connected to Your Body

If you have been unable to conceive so far, and if you were to throw all of the "shoulds" to the wind, how would you try to get pregnant right now? It's important to ask yourself this periodically. Take the time to really listen to your answers. Then give serious consideration to what your heart says. This may include trying fertility medication when you had previously thought you never would. This can include giving yourself permission to take a break.

People come to us to help them find a more "natural" approach to conception. Often all we do is help them listen to their bodies. This can include stepping off the compelling wheel of technology and returning to the privacy of their own homes, with their own emotions and biorhythms initiating a new sense of self-discovery.

For these people, whether they ultimately end up conceiving or not, a healing has taken place so that they feel once again that their body is their friend. Your body is all that will stay with you for this life, and you must befriend it to have a happy life. This isn't always easy when you're experiencing conception struggles. Nonetheless, do all you can to strengthen your connection to your body and to increase your awareness of your body. Your body isn't separate from who you are and how you feel. We are our bodies. We must trust our body wisdom. When you listen to yourself, you'll know when it's time to try something new, when it's time to move on, and when it's time to let go.

Part Six:
Pregnancy,
Birth,
and Beyond

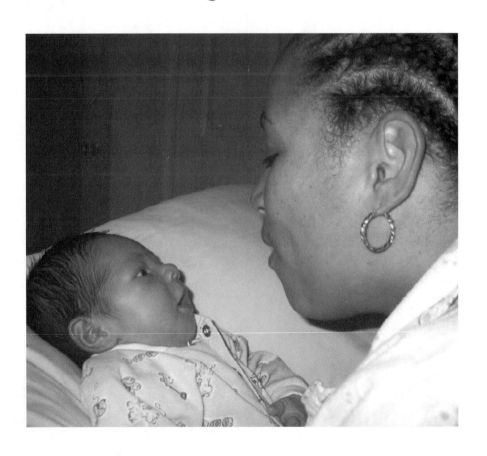

CHAPTER 19

Adoption and Child-Free Living

DECIDING TO STOP inseminating and move into the next phase of your life is probably the most difficult decision you'll ever make. It can be very scary to choose to stop inseminating. What if pregnancy is just a month away and you stop now? It's a deep challenge to let go of this hope. For many women their entire sense of self is inextricably linked with being a biological mother. Letting go of this possibility can feel like letting go of an essential piece of yourself. It's common to feel afraid that if you stop inseminating, you'll cease to exist. Despite the agony of relinquishing your dream of pregnancy, it's important to recognize when it's just not happening for you.

Acknowledging that it's time to make a change and move on can be a gradual realization or a sudden understanding. In any event, when you're unable to conceive or sustain a pregnancy, the time eventually arises when you must recognize this. It takes courage and strength to leave the possibility of pregnancy behind. But moving forward, whether toward adoption or toward child-free living, is a powerful step.

When you're single you may delay the inevitable because of the fear that it will mean continuing to live alone, when you were so desperately ready to share your love with another human being. Single women can fear that adoption will not be feasible due to legal or financial constraints, so continuing to inseminate often seems like the only possible route to parenthood.

If you're partnered, it can also be difficult to imagine moving on. After many months or years, the process of the insemination cycle may feel like it is the basis for all aspects of your relationship. For couples who have devoted years of their lives to trying to get pregnant, there's a fear that stopping inseminating may reveal that there's no longer any spark or connection remaining in the relationship. Thus, the thought of moving on can be filled with the fear of this loss. Not only do you face losing your dream of being pregnant and giving birth to your child, and perhaps your dream of having children at all, but also you face the fear of losing your primary relationship. The fear of losing your partner is often sublimated and can unknowingly cause you to continue inseminating for longer than might otherwise feel right for you.

How to Tell When It's Time to Move On

Deciding when the time is right for you to move on to the next part of your life is deeply personal. Some women inseminate for three cycles and then choose to adopt or live without children. Others devote years of their lives to inseminating. Their journeys may have included multiple surgeries, multiple miscarriages, and multiple IVFs. Some women will have depleted their entire life savings and become emotionally deadened before effectively being forced to give up. In other words, some women move on as part of a prearranged timeline, some move on because the roller coaster of insemination is too emotionally devastating, and some move on only when they've depleted all their available resources. For most women, however, deciding to move on comes from a place that feels much more vague and is a combination of the above scenarios.

Regularly checking in with yourself is important, since there are no established, universal indications to tell you when the right time is for you to stop. When you're losing hope and perspective and feel you can't take any more emotionally, it's important to step back and reevaluate. This is best done by taking a break from inseminating. During a break you'll find a more accurate reflection of how much more time, energy, and money you're willing to give this dream. In addition to losing hope, there are other signs that indicate that the time may be close for you to stop inseminating. Take note if you're experiencing any of the following:

- You check in with your body, and it no longer feels fertile to you.
- You find the idea of pregnancy has lost its appeal and that you would actually be relieved to move on with your life.
- You're realizing that a child-free life sounds appealing.
- You hardly remember what life was like prior to inseminating.
- You're so depressed that you're having difficulty functioning in daily life.
- Your fertility signs and tests have shown that your body isn't fertile, and you've tried unsuccessfully for more than eight cycles.
- Your partner is threatening to leave if you don't stop inseminating.
- Adoption sounds more appealing than inseminating.
- You have depleted all financial resources and are getting deeply in debt.

Deciding to Move On Is Not a Failure

Although it's often heartbreaking, deciding to stop can feel empowering. You're never obligated to try for longer than what feels right to you. Likewise, you don't need to stop just because everyone in your life tells you you're crazy for continuing. You must be ready and willing to take the step yourself. If you make the decision to stop trying to get pregnant due to external pressure, you may feel resentful and may be unable to reach resolution with this part of your life. When you decide the time is right to move on, you've completed this phase of your life and it's easier to reach a place of peace.

Pursuing Adoption While Inseminating

Some women have known from the start that if they're unable to conceive they'll become a parent through adoption. If this is the case for you, it's important to inform yourself of potential age and financial restraints so that you won't unknowingly exclude yourself from the option of adoption. Numerous adoption agencies don't allow women to adopt if they're over 40. Common age limits for international adoption are 43 to 45 years old. Private adoptions often end up costing $20,000 to $50,000.

Some women choose to pursue adoption at the same time they're inseminating. Although this is a lot to think about all at once, adoption can be a lengthy process, and sometimes a parallel path feels best. Many women pursue a joint path for a while, while they research what kind of adoption interests them and begin to fill out the paperwork. This way they allow the possibility of conception to occur right until the last minute.

This decision can be stressful, however, because you run the risk of achieving pregnancy just as your adoption is finalizing and thus run the risk of bringing two new children into your life simultaneously or losing a hefty deposit for your adoption. Likewise, it can be expensive to pursue fertility treatments and adoption concurrently.

Many couples find that pursuing adoption and conception simultaneously can help jump-start their relationship, since they once again feel hopeful about building a family. Many adoption agencies provide classes that can help you feel like parents already. The excitement and inspiration of these classes are contagious qualities.

Other women feel strongly that starting the adoption process would dilute their intention to conceive. They prefer to dedicate all of their focus and intention on conceiving. Such women don't allow themselves to even begin exploring adoption until they've chosen to stop trying to conceive.

Often it's a good sign to yourself that you may be nearing the end of inseminating when you begin to look into adoption.

Loss and Letting Go

As we've said, deciding to stop inseminating takes courage and strength. We wholeheartedly validate and celebrate your courage to do so. When you make the decision to stop inseminating you'll find that you're not the same person as when you began. Grief, pain, longing, hope, and disappointment have transformed you permanently. You are a survivor. You've been on a journey that only others who have experienced infertility can truly understand.

At first the pain and grief are devastating, but over time you regain a positive outlook on life and begin anew. Some women have been through the stages of grief and loss while inseminating; they're able to start life fresh the moment they decide to stop. The length of your grieving process is unique to you, but allow yourself a full year to reemerge from your cocoon after you stop inseminating. If it takes less time, celebrate. If it takes longer, seek the support you need.

Many women describe experiencing infertility as feeling like a part of their heart has been shaved off, while a callus has grown over the rest of it. Women sometimes describe feeling defective, dry, barren, or not being a "true woman."

In a partnership, the feeling of being barren isn't restricted to the woman trying to conceive. Both of you have been yearning for so long that you both share the feeling of being let down by the universe. For both individuals and couples, a feeling of flatness can consume your entire existence.

The grieving process of infertility is akin to the grieving process surrounding the loss of a child. Just because you haven't conceived or held a pregnancy to term doesn't mean you're not a grieving parent. When you allow yourself to feel the depth of your loss and make room for the grief as you'd expect of any parent who has lost a child, eventually you'll more fully be able to move on. Although extreme feelings are to be expected with such letting go, please monitor your mental and emotional state of being. Seek help at any time, but especially if you're unable to function or feel things are getting worse.

EXAMPLE: KELLY AND JOSETTE

Kelly and Josette had been talking about having children off and on throughout the 10 years of their relationship. When Josette turned 36, they decided to begin inseminating.

Josette had a history of endometriosis, for which she had been taking birth control pills. She'd had surgery for it when she was 27, which had given her relief for a few years. Her period, when she wasn't taking the pill, was very irregular. She tried to conceive for two years, with much medical intervention but no success. After a lot of discussion they decided that Kelly would try to conceive, and she became pregnant the first cycle. Kelly spotted throughout the first trimester and miscarried at twelve weeks.

Josette felt a lot of guilt about the miscarriage, because she had been feeling ambivalent about the pregnancy. She had expected to be done with her feelings of loss about her own experience inseminating and be thrilled that they'd have a baby with the help of Kelly's body. Instead she felt resentment, estrangement, and more sadness. They sorted out each of their own experiences and felt ready to try again.

Kelly conceived fairly quickly three more times, each time miscarrying between eight and fifteen weeks of pregnancy. Each time she miscarried, the fetal tissue showed a different kind of chromosomal abnormality. A perinatal specialist advised Kelly that as she was 42 years old, her eggs were "just too old," and she should look at doing in vitro fertilization with donor eggs from someone younger. Josette was not a suitable egg donor because she was also considered too old.

Kelly and Josette had relatives who were willing to donate eggs, but they didn't know if they were willing to go through more of this. When they took a vacation together, they remembered all the fun they used to have together, before they had devoted the last four years to trying to conceive. They remembered all the reasons they each had been ambivalent about having children earlier in their relationship. They thought of all the extended family and friends whose children they were close to, and how they could love these children in a way that left them free to do lots of grown-up playing. They decided to live without children and invested the very last of their "baby funds" into backpacking equipment.

Although their friends and family had to go through their own grief process, by the time Kelly and Josette decided not to have children, they felt amazingly relieved and ready to move on.

Regaining Trust

After you stop inseminating, it's natural to feel that your body has failed you. If you feel betrayed, whether by your body, medicine, or even God, the journey back to trust may be long. This is important to recognize. When you acknowledge your loss of trust, you're able to have more self-compassion. It's especially important to be aware of your loss of trust if you're quickly moving toward adoption, as it may directly influence your parenting. Don't allow your heart to close down to love, as painful as it may be to stay emotionally open and vulnerable. Love will heal your pain. Closing down will only push the pain further inside.

Whether you decide to adopt or to live without children, dedicate some of your newly available time to rebuilding inspiration and confidence in your life. Start up a new hobby or activity. Perhaps it will be physical activity such as rock climbing or mountain biking. Maybe you'll learn to design furniture, remodel your bathroom, or take a dance class. Give yourself the gift of learning something new. If you're partnered, this may be a wonderful opportunity to take up a new interest together as well as individually. Finding something new to bond over can shift your dominant shared experience away from trying to conceive to a completely new and refreshing focus.

Relief

When you decide to stop pursuing pregnancy, it's also perfectly normal to feel as if a huge burden has been lifted. Many women are surprised by this relief and respond by feeling guilty, because they think it means they must not have really wanted to be pregnant. This is far from true. Relief is a good sign that you're letting go; relief indicates that you're beginning to acknowledge just how intense a project you've been undertaking. Remember, infertility is commonly considered to be as big a stress as terminal illness. Of course, then, you'll naturally feel some relief when you choose to move on with your life.

Allowing Yourself to Feel Happy Again

It can take active effort and intention to permit yourself to feel happy again. Most women who have experienced infertility have become so accustomed to sadness and disappointment, and to monitoring their hope so that they won't feel so devastated month after month, that they don't remember what happiness feels like. This often results in an instinctual response of fear when happiness does come their way. Happiness can be so unfamiliar that they instinctively guard themselves against it. Keep an eye on this tendency. Feeling good and enjoying life does not discount your grief. You're allowed to feel both! Still, you may need some help with this. Being spontaneous in your joy may make you afraid that your sadness will be unleashed. Let go of this control over emotional expression. Practice laughing and smiling. Watch funny movies, do silly things. Through ever-increasing bursts of happiness, joy will return to your life. Happiness doesn't need to be rationed—give in to it whenever you can!

Rebuilding Your Relationship

The journey to and through infertility can seriously impact a relationship. Strengthening and rebuilding your relationship can take time and concerted energy. Some partners have had the foresight to enter therapy together before this point and have worked hard to maintain their intimacy throughout the insemination and infertility journey. Others have not. Regardless as to where you are at this point, it takes dedication to nurture your partnership after having undergone such emotional turmoil together.

Emotional Intimacy

Infertility often causes people to shut down emotionally as a way of handling overwhelmingly difficult feelings. Although this intentional or subconscious tactic can provide a sense of self-protection, it also means separating yourself from having any positive feelings. You become emotionally numb. A side effect of this coping mechanism is becoming distanced from your partner. If this has happened to you, you must slowly find your way back to each other, which can be frightening. Having a satisfying relationship, however, requires emotional availability. If emotional disconnection has been your means to self-protection, it's a good idea to seek support from outside sources as you come back to yourself, since you may find many feelings flooding forth in the beginning. Women find counseling, support groups, and online support groups to be helpful ways of sharing the intensity of their feelings.

Recognizing Limiting Roles

Many couples fall into roles during the preconception process that can become deeply ingrained over time. Often the person who is to become the birth parent, in her role, needs to be sheltered and taken care of. She is the one whose emotions have been given top priority. Likewise, the nonbirth parent-to-be has usually taken to processing her emotions outside of the relationship in order to allow more space for her partner's feelings. She has often been acting as the "knight in shining armor," taking on a protector role. After a number of months she often stops sharing her feelings both about the conception process and about the rest of her life.

Although these roles seem to serve women through the preconception process, they don't necessarily nurture the relationship in the long run. When you stop pursuing pregnancy, your roles may often be very unbalanced and no longer appropriate. It's important to recognize if the two of you have slipped into any such roles so that you can change your interpersonal dynamic to one that more appropriately reflects your current situation. It takes effort to come together as equals again, and it can take time to relearn how to share emotional and daily issues that don't pertain to pregnancy and fertility.

Sexual Intimacy

Many women stop having sex in the very early days of inseminating. In fact, for lesbians this seems to be the norm. If you've been inseminating for more than six months, the odds are probably low that you're maintaining an active sex life. Regaining a sexual connection can deepen intimacy, togetherness, and even emotional healing. Regaining sexual intimacy can also be one of the hardest things for couples to do.

Sex is emotional. Making love can release such strong emotions that we can automatically shut down sexual response when we shut down emotional response. It makes sense that by limiting the vulnerability you're willing to experience, you're able to feel safer and more in control of your world. Ironically, by shutting down this venue of connection you're also shutting out a rich source of comfort, pleasure, and release.

Many couples find that after a lapse in sexual activity it helps to discuss the awkwardness and shyness they each feel. Often the sexual intimacy in relationships disappears for reasons that are complicated and full of history. Although you may feel shame and guilt that you're struggling with this issue, it's very common. Honor that your subconscious intention is to protect yourself, and seek ways that are gentle and safe to explore returning to your sexuality. Dedication and love, including self-love primarily, are the key ingredients to regaining sexual intimacy. Therapy, either alone or as a couple, will probably be very helpful. Self-exploration is key.

It can take time to learn to trust yourself, your body, your partner, and life enough to let go fully. Don't judge yourself for this. A simple first step is to make regular dates with your partner. In the beginning these dates may just be time set aside specifically to touch in a way that feels comfortable, perhaps snuggling and massaging each other or relearning how to open up and share. Often these regular dates, coupled with finding safe ways to communicate honestly, go a long way toward regaining an active sex life. With these steps, you'll be able to regain this wonderful part of lesbian love.

New Beginnings

When you've decided to stop pursuing pregnancy, life opens up with new possibilities. What do you want to do with your life? Although many women know they want to adopt, others aren't as sure about what they want to do. It isn't always easy to decide between adoption and living without children. Child-free living may mean choosing to live without parenting and without children having primary roles in your life. For other women child-free living means finding other ways in which a child or children can have a significant place in their life.

Whether or not you're clear about what your next step will be, now is a good time to take a break for a few months or take a vacation. Find a way to honor the long journey you've been on and lay it to rest. You're beginning a new chapter in your life. Immediately, or over time, you'll probably be struck by the profound freedom you have to choose what to do with the rest of your life. So much potential feels amazing!

Once you've taken some time away from pursuing pregnancy, you'll usually find that you already know whether you would like to adopt. Allow your heart to show you what you would truly like to do. It's perfectly fine to adopt; it's perfectly fine to live without children. It's your decision—there's no "right" or "wrong" way to live your life. Choosing to live without children does not invalidate your long-standing desire to parent.

Once you've decided which path you're going to take, you reach the often overwhelming task of telling all the people who knew you were trying to get pregnant. Many women find that aside from their closest friends, it's easiest to tell people all at once. Some women send a letter or email to any relevant people. Some use this time as an opportunity to acknowledge the distance friends and family may have felt during the latter part of the pre-conception period by explaining how consuming the process has been. This kind of letter is a broad way of both opening up to support and reducing the number of times you bring up the subject of infertility.

Adoption

There are a few issues that are important to consider when you decide to pursue adoption after having experienced infertility as a lesbian, bisexual, or single woman or transman.

If you choose to adopt, you must be completely clear that you want to adopt and that you're ready to become a full parent in this way. When adoption is your second choice after pregnancy, you may feel that your adopted child is a substitute or second-rate in comparison to a biological child. If you have these feelings, we urge you to seek counseling prior to adopting and throughout the first year after adoption. It's very important that you bond fully with your child and that your child isn't led to feel that she or he is second-rate. Feelings such as these can obviously interfere with your ability to bond with your child. These feelings usually are actually perceptions of self-inadequacy that are projected onto your child and need to be addressed so that you can have the necessary self-esteem and confidence to parent to your highest potential.

Adoption Considerations for Lesbians

In all states in this country it's legal to adopt as a single mother, although Florida bars adoption even by single lesbians and gay men. In some states, two partnered women can jointly adopt a child at the same time. In others states two partnered women must choose one to be the legal adoptive parent, and then complete a second-parent adoption, if available, for the other parent. In all international adoptions at this point, one woman adopts the baby as a "single" parent. In addition, some countries are now barring adoption by lesbians and gay men, even as single parents. Once the child is in the United States, you can pursue a second-parent adoption for the other parent, if this option is available. Women choosing to adopt privately must decide whether or not they'll be closeted to the caseworker and the birth parents. Whether or not both women will legally be allowed to be named on the finalized adoption papers, they may choose to be out as a couple to prospective birth parents and adoption agency workers. This lessens their chances of being selected but allows them to be honest about their family structure.

When partnered lesbians pursue adoption there are a number of factors to consider. One of the benefits of choosing to start the adoption process is that the partner who wasn't trying to get pregnant can take the lead for a while and start researching options and making appointments. This can be a huge relief, since the bureaucratic elements of pursuing adoption can be quite time- consuming and women who have been inseminating for a long time often aren't ready to undertake such efforts right away. They may be thrilled, however, to have their partner do this work. The woman who wasn't trying to get pregnant can finally feel like she's able to do something practical that will further the process instead of just having a supporting role.

Another benefit to adoption is that you can be more flexible about how you divide parenting responsibilities, as neither of you will automatically breast-feed. Even if you choose to nurse through a supplemental nursing system, you could both choose to nurse your baby if you wanted.

This new flexibility can become complicated if the partner who was try-ing to get pregnant was planning on being the stay-at-home parent, or pri-mary caretaker, and she doesn't want to relinquish the role, although the other partner wants to renegotiate how they share the parenting duties.

Another potential site of renegotiation is who will be legally recognized as the parent. In all but a limited number of counties across the United States, only one of you starts off initially with this status. This is due to the fact that same-sex marriage isn't legally available at this time. If you wish to share legal parenting rights, you'll need to go through second-parent adoption to secure equal parenting status under the law, if it's available in your state.

This may be tricky emotional territory for both of you if one assumes she'll be the legal parent because she would have been previously, or if she newly understands the feeling of legal insecurity that her partner was preparing to face if pregnancy occurred. Walk softly together through the experience of living in a homophobic society. It hurts and it's scary, yet this is something you—and all other partnered same-sex couples—are in together.

Child-Free Living

Some women want to pursue adoption; others don't have or desire the op-tion. Living child-free after wanting to be pregnant and having chosen to parent is a very painful process. Over time you come to find new focus and direction, but initially your whole life can feel like a void. Some women choose to bring children into their lives in other ways so that they can have the spark and joy that children embody around them. Women do this in different ways. They may become a "super-aunt" to a child of one of their friends or relatives; most parents welcome all the support and help they can get. It's possible to create a situation where you and a child dear to your heart spend one afternoon a week together, have a sleep-over, or take a vaca-tion together. In this way you become involved in this child's life. Many par-ents would love to have a special aunt like you, and any child would love it! Other women choose to bring children into their lives in a less committed way: they may volunteer as Big Sisters, tutor children at the library, or teach art classes to kids in their home. There are many ways to bring children into your life. Focus on what kind of a relationship you would like to foster and make it happen.

Choosing to live without children is a powerful choice. As life moves on you'll continually find new pursuits and things to explore that you wouldn't have the time for if you were parenting full-time. Enjoy your child-free life. Over time you may even find that you feel lucky!

CHAPTER 20

Early Pregnancy and Miscarriage

WHETHER YOU'VE BEEN trying to conceive for two years or two months, the moment you realize or confirm that you're pregnant is a wonderful, exciting, and possibly scary time that you'll never forget. Nothing can describe the overwhelming flood of emotions you experience when you realize you're going to have a baby.

This chapter covers early pregnancy, miscarriage, and how to find a care provider. Because on average every one in four pregnancies results in miscarriage, we feel it's important to include this subject in the initial discussion of pregnancy.

Signs of Pregnancy

Some people realize they're pregnant at the moment of conception and actually describe feeling sensations of conception. If you're one of these people and doubt what you feel, remember how long you've focused so intently on your body sensations, and remember that women feel many other similarly subtle events such as ovulation. You may not feel conception itself on a conscious level, either physically or energetically, but within twenty-four to forty-eight hours following insemination you may start to experience symptoms of pregnancy. *Most* people do not experience pregnancy symptoms this early but do feel some new sensations by the last few days preceding their expected period. Sometimes, however, after paying such close attention to your body for many months, you may no longer feel confident in interpreting what you feel anymore and will be taken by surprise the day your pregnancy test reads positive.

Am I Crazy or Am I Pregnant?

Sometimes initial symptoms of pregnancy—such as breast enlargement or tenderness and mood changes—are confusing because they're also signs of PMS. It can be difficult to believe that your symptoms indicate pregnancy, or to receive validation from others around you, until you've missed your period and gotten a positive pregnancy test. People are often reticent to believe that it is possible to experience such a strong response to early pregnancy, so they try to persuade you that you're physically manifesting wishful thinking. Unfortunately, you may find it easy to doubt your unique body experience because our culture commonly resists acknowledging intuition. Furthermore, because fully half of conceptions don't progress past the first seven to ten days, and thus don't ever produce a positive pregnancy test result, you may feel pregnancy symptoms but then receive a negative pregnancy test and experience a seemingly normal period. For this very brief but consuming experience of early pregnancy you may find virtually no external validation of pregnancy. But many people do experience it and can describe in detail the difference between a month with conception and a month without.

Pregnancy Symptoms

Hormonal changes during early pregnancy cause breast tenderness and enlargement, nipple sensitivity, and mood changes. Some women and transmen get weepy or angry in completely uncharacteristic ways long before their period is due. Others can't even lie on their stomachs or be hugged, due to the sensitivity of their breasts. Many can't specify how they feel different, exactly; they simply don't feel like themselves—they feel pregnant. These same hormonal changes, incidentally, also cause the basal body temperature to remain elevated.

The next set of noticeable pregnancy symptoms includes appetite changes and fatigue as well as sensitive smell reactions, sleep irregularities, sex-drive changes, indigestion, constipation, and even an awareness of the cell division and initial formation of the embryo. Remember, some people experience all of these symptoms prior to missing a period, whereas others exhibit no signs of early pregnancy other than not starting their period.

Pregnancy and Menstrual Periods

Some women and transmen continue to have menstrual-like bleeding, even though they're pregnant. This is most common during the first month of pregnancy. Usually, this bleeding is lighter and shorter than a normal period. If you're having pregnancy symptoms, or your period is uncharacteristically light, you'll want to take a pregnancy test to make sure you're not already pregnant before inseminating again, or before discontinuing progesterone supplementation.

Pregnancy Tests

Home Pregnancy Tests

Most home pregnancy tests are quite sensitive and can usually detect a pregnancy anywhere from ten to fourteen days following insemination. These tests monitor the level of the hormone human chorionic gonadotropin (HCG) in the urine. HCG is produced in large amounts within a few weeks of early pregnancy; however, the test needs to detect a certain amount of HCG to read positive. For some pregnancies, this HCG level takes some time to show up in the urine: therefore, on rare occasions a positive reading may not come until a few weeks after missing your period. It is therefore possible to get a false negative on a home pregnancy test. Most people receive a positive reading before they even miss their menstrual period, or within a few days thereafter.

You may choose to wait until you've already missed your period before taking a pregnancy test, since the absence of blood is one of the best signs not only that you're pregnant, but also that the embryo has successfully implanted into your uterine lining.

Although a pregnancy test may give false negatives if you test too early, it's quite rare to have a false-positive result. Thus, even if you are almost certainly pregnant, positive home test results are usually confirmed with a test from your health-care provider.

Blood Tests

Blood tests are more sensitive than home tests. They can be used to confirm pregnancies if your home test reads negative even though you've missed your period and feel like you're pregnant. A blood test, however, will only read positive a few days earlier than a urine test will and most clinics will not test for pregnancy until you have missed your period or until you have a positive home pregnancy test.

Reactions to Pregnancy

Of course, many people react to pregnancy in ways they've expected; they feel glee, elation, and ecstatic joy. Others, however, are then shocked to discover that after only a few moments they move into numbness, fear, panic, disbelief, and uncertainty. This is normal. It's also normal to feel "crazy" about wanting to get pregnant in the first place, even if it has taken you an exceedingly long time to get pregnant. Pregnancy is a big deal. Don't judge these unexpected feelings: they're a natural part of the adjustment period.

If it's taken you a long time to get pregnant, you may only allow yourself a few minutes of joy before you find yourself bracing for the possible disappointment of miscarriage. When your trust in your body has been deeply shaken, it can be difficult to allow yourself to trust that it will be able to sustain a pregnancy. Try to have compassion for yourself. Let your joy and fear coexist.

Early-Pregnancy Management by Fertility Specialists

A number of issues are specific to people who have been having difficulty conceiving or maintaining a pregnancy. We cover a few of the initial considerations in the following section. Even if you haven't had a challenging conception but have accessed sperm or insemination services through an infertility clinic, you should also read the following section. Regardless of why you contacted the clinic, you may have been treated as if you have been infertile.

People who have sought infertility treatments to assist them in getting pregnant are at an interesting crossroads in early pregnancy. Just because conception was difficult does not mean that their pregnancy is necessarily "high risk." Likewise, just because a person is older does not mean the pregnancy is "high risk". An increasing number of fertility patients, however, continue to see their fertility specialists after conception until their pregnancy has been fully established. The care given during these early days and weeks is dramatically different than the routine care provided by obstetricians and midwives in early pregnancy. Fertility specialists often recommend numerous sonograms and blood tests in the earliest days of pregnancy. Although a limited number of people find these procedures helpful, most find them traumatic. We will explore the advantages and drawbacks to these increasingly common procedures, typical responses to these procedures, and some personal exploration questions to help you decide in advance whether these procedures are for you.

Routine Procedures

As soon as pregnancy is confirmed, fertility specialists often recommend undergoing repeat vaginal ultrasounds as well as repeat blood tests that check HCG, estrogen, and progesterone levels every few days. Some of these tests may even begin prior to missing your first period. Some people receive serial ultrasounds until a heartbeat is detected, usually around four weeks after conception. Others receive them throughout the first twelve weeks of pregnancy to confirm normal growth patterns.

ADVANTAGES

The advantage to these repeated tests is confirmation that the pregnancy is progressing adequately. Likewise, tests can confirm that you're producing enough progesterone to sustain an early pregnancy. If your progesterone numbers are too low, supplementation can be started or increased. Sometimes adjustment of progesterone doses, even at the last minute, can prevent a miscarriage those who have unusually low progesterone levels. For people with a history of miscarriage, if the current pregnancy also miscarries, these types of procedures may be able to suggest if this miscarriage resulted from unusual cell division or insufficient hormone levels.

DRAWBACKS

When you've just discovered that you're pregnant, it may be quite disorienting to have to go to the doctor's office every forty-eight hours. The initial days of pregnancy are some of the most rapid days of cell division for the entire pregnancy, and ultrasounds may have potential effects on cell division. Ultrasounds may demonstrate that miscarriage is likely due to improper development of the fetus. Ultrasounds can't prevent miscarriage, however, because there's no treatment for an irregularly growing embryo—which is the most common cause of miscarriage. Thus, the value of such ultrasounds is questionable because of the invasiveness of vaginal probe, the potential risk to the growing baby, and the inability of the ultrasound to prevent miscarriages.

HCG levels that aren't increasing as much as expected can indicate a pending miscarriage, because it can signify that the embryo isn't developing well. Once again, however, having this information cannot prevent a miscarriage from occurring.

It is expected that HCG levels with double every forty-eight hours in early pregnancy. It is a sign of a healthy pregnancy when the HCG increases at a rapid rate. However, this is an average rate of expected growth. It is not uncommon for a doctor to recommend a surgical termination of such pregnancies. It is very important to note that some healthy pregnancies that carry to term were pregnancies where the woman refused to get the recommended surgical miscarriage and decided to wait and see what happened on its own.

Common Responses to These Procedures

Because these procedures are routine for people who consult fertility specialists, most pregnant people don't question their value until they've been done. Numerous people have called us in total panic because their joy of pregnancy has been replaced with the fear that something may be wrong. They report phone calls from nurses insisting that they return the next day to have more lab work done, because their results are unclear, but they aren't offered a specific explanation until they see the doctor in person.

After receiving questionable results, people feel like they're in limbo for days while waiting for the next sets of test results to indicate whether their HCG levels have reached the expected levels for this early stage of pregnancy or have remained low enough to confirm miscarriage.

For people who ultimately miscarry, all who have reported to us expressed firmly that this approach of repeated tests and ultrasounds afforded them no peace, no time to *enjoy* being pregnant, no time to realize that their body finally conceived. Instead, there was only a moment to experience being pregnant before the pregnancy became a relationship to tests and to numbers. They say this approach removed any sense of celebration of finally being pregnant and replaced it with more guilt that their body didn't work right. Most people with whom we've spoken who did miscarry say this approach was a complete nightmare that they would never choose to repeat.

On the other hand, for those who have had multiple miscarriages in the past, having confirmation that this pregnancy isn't going according to plan allows them to have a "surgical miscarriage," rather than wait for an inevitable natural miscarriage. Likewise, if this pregnancy is growing in a healthy way initially, it provides reassurance that perhaps it will work this time.

Those who get positive results from the beginning have reported mixed reactions to us. Some feel that the procedures carried unnecessary risks and that they would not have chosen these procedures had they known of these risks, whereas others feel that the positive information they gained about the pregnancy right from the start gave them courage to believe that their body does work and will be able to sustain a pregnancy. They say these tests gave them significant emotional relief.

Questioning These Procedures

Before you actually get pregnant, it's valuable to ask your care provider about his or her approach to early pregnancy. Knowing this, you can decide which routine procedures you'd like to receive. Spend some time envisioning how you'd like your initial days of pregnancy to be. Are you the kind of person who'd be reassured by visiting a doctor's office every other day and waiting for test results, or would this medicalized approach drive you crazy?

Do you have enough information about the effect of ultrasound on newly developing fetuses to make an informed decision about whether to undergo repeat vaginal-probe ultrasounds? How would these procedures serve you and your pregnancy? What might be the drawbacks of these procedures to you and your pregnancy? If you're partnered, be sure to discuss these issues and concerns ahead of time. Choosing to inform yourself about routine medical procedures in order to decide whether they're right for you is part of being a responsible parent. Declining to receive certain treatments is not a betrayal of your baby. You should never feel guilty for asserting your opinions and choosing the form of care you wish to receive. This is both your right and your responsibility as a parent.

From a Highly Managed Conception to a Low-Risk Pregnancy

It's hard to believe that having difficulty conceiving doesn't inherently mean that you'll have difficulty during pregnancy and birth, but it's true. Regaining faith in your body and trust in life itself isn't always easy. Nonetheless, it's important work to be done. Some people who see fertility specialists for conception are immediately transferred to "high-risk" obstetricians for prenatal care. Often, though, those who've been seeing a regular obstetrician gynecologist for fertility care plan to continue seeing the same ob-gyn for prenatal and birth care.

We encourage you to see a practitioner, whether it's a midwife or obstetrician, who can separate the circumstances of your conception from your pregnancy. Sometimes that means changing doctors during your pregnancy when you come to realize that you're having a healthy "low-risk" pregnancy but are being treated as "high-risk."

People who have had fertility challenges find it extremely beneficial to see a therapist, with a partner or alone, throughout their pregnancy to help them manage their fears and move to a place of trust with their bodies again prior to birth.

Choosing a Care Provider and Where to Give Birth

Self-care during pregnancy is the most vital part of prenatal care, whether you've just inseminated and are in the window of possible pregnancy, or you know for certain that you're pregnant. Eat healthy, nutritious foods and pay special attention to your vegetable intake. This is a good time to review chapter 12, on nutrition. Take a good prenatal vitamin. Get plenty of sleep and exercise. Feel free to be sexual if it feels desirable.

Take the time you need to find the right care provider. There's no reason for you to rush this process. If you want genetic screening and you have not yet found the right care provider, get the tests and continue searching.

To find the right care provider for your pregnancy and birth, you must first decide where you'd like to give birth. Many people end up choosing a hospital by default because they know nothing of the other options, and everyone they know has given birth in the hospital.

There are actually three options available in most areas of the United States: in a hospital, at home, or at a birth center. As midwives, we feel it's important for every pregnant woman and her partner to explore each of these options before deciding where to give birth. Only through such an approach can you be fully informed in your choice of setting and care provider. It's our goal to have each person give birth in the setting that makes him or her feel most comfortable, with a midwife or doctor well suited to their needs.

For lesbian and bisexual women and transmen this is especially important, since we have unique considerations as a result of our "alternative" family structures. Each option affords different levels of built-in comfort and support for our families. People reading and researching the subject prior to pregnancy are surprised to learn that home birth is statistically safer than routine hospital birth for low-risk pregnancies. Likewise, in many Western nations—and around the world—people receive care from a midwife unless their pregnancies are considered high-risk enough to warrant consultation with a doctor.

Once you've informed yourself about the available options, do some preliminary imagining about your comfort level in each specific setting. The following self-exploration exercise will help you learn your body responses to each setting. We recommend reading *Immaculate Deception*, by Suzanne Arms, before you try the following exercise, especially as representations of birth in mainstream media are often quite unrealistic.

EXERCISE: CLARIFYING YOUR BIRTH VISION

The goal of this exercise is to help you clarify your ideal birth vision. Having a vision can help you move toward manifesting the key elements of your vision. Allow your mind to imagine freely. Resist the urge to step in and correct your vision; just let it flow. Imagine yourself in labor. Conjure up your greatest feelings of safety and love. Who is with you? What's the quality of your connection with that person, those people? What are you doing that helps you feel safe and helps you work with the strong sensations and pain you experience? What are you wearing? What are you doing? Where are you? Is anyone touching you? Is anyone comforting you?

How do you see the arrival of your baby? What's important to you? What qualities of contact with your close friends and family are important to you? How about immediately following the birth? What do you see happening? Be specific about the feelings you're having when you envision your first few moments with your new baby. Write down the images and qualities that are clearest to you.

Now that you have a strong sense of your ideal birth, try placing the important qualities of the experience into each setting: home, hospital, and birth center. What do you feel, on a body level, as the advantages and drawbacks of each setting? Are you able to maintain the same quality of connection with your partner or close friend(s) in each setting? Take note of what you feel you might sacrifice by giving birth in each location.

Once you've completed this exercise, write down what you've learned about your vision and how it aligns with your available options. Many people prioritize intimacy with their partner. They want the physical and emotional comfort of home but can't imagine giving birth there because they're afraid to do so. In this instance there are a few options: One couple might choose a birth center. Another might explore what they could do as a team to ensure that the most important qualities of connection can be maintained in a hospital setting. They might work with a hospital-based midwife or hire a labor assistant to help them maintain the emotional and spiritual qualities that are of primary concern. A third couple might educate themselves further about the actual risks and benefits of both home birth and hospital birth, then choose to birth at home with a midwife.

Keeping your emotional priorities in mind, you can begin your search for a care provider who not only shares your philosophy of birth, but also is sensitive to a pregnant lesbian's specific needs.

As a lesbian, bisexual, or single pregnant woman you deserve to have health care that is suited to your specific needs. You have the right to have your family structure acknowledged without judgment. This must remain in the forefront of your mind as you begin looking for care providers in your area.

Networking to Find a Care Provider

If you know any lesbian parents who live in your area, the best place to start is to ask who their doctor or midwife was and what their experience was like. The Gay and Lesbian Medical Association in San Francisco has nationwide referrals as well. Their contact information is listed in the "Resources" section. Many people choose to find a pregnancy-care provider before they're pregnant, expecting that it might be a challenge to find a lesbian- and trans-sensitive provider in their area. Also, when you're not pregnant you might feel less vulnerable expressing your needs and desires.

Why Seek Prenatal Care Early?

Because the overwhelming majority of our pregnancies are planned, we know we are pregnant from very, very early on. Making it through early pregnancy isn't always emotionally easy. As pregnant queer and single women and trans-men we have many unique issues that extend greatly beyond the universal elements of the first trimester, such as choosing your place of birth and a care provider. Establishing care early can help to address some of these needs and concerns and to begin the process of feeling safe with a care provider. It is common for prenatal care to start at the end of the first trimester. However, if you are interested in early genetic screening or testing options you will want to make an appointment as early as the sixth or seventh week of pregnancy. If selective termination is a consideration for you, please research the newer options of nuchal fold translucency screening (done at eleven to fourteen weeks of pregnancy) and chorionic villi sampling (done between ten to twelve weeks of pregnancy). These are not always offered in every location but may be of interest to you and worth the drive to receive such options.

Be Honest About Your Needs

You may be the first lesbian family in your town, or at least the first out family, or you may be the first transmen to become pregnant in your area. If so, you'll be the one doing the original research. We recommend a proactive approach: come out from the start. This is especially vital if you're partnered so that your partner will feel able to participate as a parent and not be regarded as just a friend. If you're out, at the time of birth you can celebrate the birth of your child together. If you're closeted, only one of you will get the recognition of motherhood, and each of you will be relegated to having her own private entry into motherhood rather than a shared experience.

Screening Care Providers

You may never have had to come out in a medical environment before. Even if you're uncomfortable with the actual thought of coming out, it's best to do so at the initial interview visit. When you come out to a care provider—or to anyone, for that matter—it's helpful to remember that your comfort in discussing your family structure will directly influence their comfort in discussing it with you. When you explain the nature of your family it's helpful to follow with questions such as the following:

- Are you comfortable working with our family?
- If not, can you refer us to anyone in the area who may be comfortable working with us?
- Have you worked with lesbian clients? If so, do you have any past lesbian clients we could speak with?
- Have you worked with transgendered clients before? If so, someone in our situation?
- Have you worked with single mothers before?
- If this is a group practice, can you speak for the comfort level of each doctor or midwife?
- Is it best that we interview each of the different members?
- If one of you is uncomfortable with my family, how can we assure that this person won't be the one providing us care or be at the birth of our child?

Just because someone says they're comfortable working with you, you shouldn't immediately breathe a huge sigh of relief and look no further. On the contrary, you've passed the first hurdle and are now moving into the more subtle arenas. In fact, we recommend that you interview at least three practitioners so that you can compare their nonverbal and verbal comfort levels. Do they say the word "lesbian" or do they skirt around it? If you're partnered, can they look both of you in the eye? How do they refer to the nonpregnant partner? Do they ask you questions to clarify your family structure? Do you like and feel comfortable with them? Do their philosophies and practices align with your own?

These are all good starting places for screening a care provider. Unfortunately, most care providers aren't as queer-sensitive as we would like. This by no means always stems from homophobia or transphobia; it usually comes from ignorance or lack of culturally specific education. Once you've chosen a care provider, you can then decide how much education you're willing to provide the clinic's staff. If you're partnered, after each visit it's a good idea for both of you to talk about your respective comfort levels and whether you should be more or less proactive about your needs.

WHAT IS GOOD PRENATAL CARE?

Good prenatal care…:

⊚ recognizes that the pregnant client is the central decision maker, not the health-care provider.

⊚ involves and acknowledges the importance of the pregnant client's partner, other children, extended family, and community to the pregnancy and birth process.

⊚ educates and supports a pregnant client so she can choose and maintain healthy lifestyle habits.

⊚ focuses on monitoring for potential illnesses and complications so that they can be diagnosed and treated, while understanding that for most, pregnancy is a healthy life process, not a disease state.

Midwife or Obstetrician?

In general, midwives spend considerably more time with you during each visit than physicians. Most midwives spend anywhere from fifteen minutes to an hour with each patient. Midwives, although not specifically trained in understanding gay culture, are trained in psychosocial issues and do tend to ask personal questions. The combination of their training and the time they spend with you allows you greater opportunity to educate your midwife about your family structure and to address your unique issues of pregnancy and general concerns and questions.

On average, doctors spend five minutes with each patient. Most midwives are women, whereas obstetricians are either men or women. Many women, especially lesbians, prefer to work exclusively with female practitioners. In some clinics a nurse practitioner provides all of the prenatal care, and a doctor, whom you may never have met, attends the birth. This is especially common in urban areas. Although this affords you continuity with the nurse practitioner during pregnancy—which is wonderful—it leaves you with a stranger at the time of birth. If you have a choice, we don't recommend this model of care, because it includes too many unknown and unscreened people at the time of birth. However, even in practices or settings—such as Kaiser—where this is the only available option presented to you, there are possibilities. Due to the unique needs of your family—as a pregnant transman or the first lesbian in a very homophobic town—you can usually arrange to have continuity of care. It just may take some effort on your part to help them to value your need and find a way to work their system to accommodate your family.

Remember, this is your pregnancy and birth experience. You don't need to acquiesce when finding a care provider. If you can't find a suitable care provider in your area, search outlying areas. If you find a more sensitive provider, it will always be worth the drive. If you discover that your care provider isn't working out, change providers. You're a consumer purchasing a very expensive product: good care. You have a right to quality and comfort. This is the birth of your child; don't compromise!

Choosing a Midwife

The midwifery model of care embraces the components of good prenatal care listed in the box on page 311. On average, in the United States, midwives spend a total of fifty to sixty hours with a client from pregnancy through postpartum, compared to the average four to five hours spent by physicians. In the five nations with the lowest perinatal mortality rate, more than 70 percent of pregnant women are attended by midwives. The World Health Organization has called on the United States to shift its approach to pregnancy and birth care to a midwife-centered model, incorporating obstetricians only in their rightful role as high-risk providers. The reasoning is that the midwifery model of care is more comprehensive and less expensive, and less often subjects mothers and their babies to unnecessary medical interventions.

Is Home Birth Safe?

For low-risk pregnant clients—who are the vast majority of pregnant clients—birth at home with a midwife is as safe as if not safer than giving birth in the hospital. Midwives do not view age alone as making someone high-risk. Numerous studies have shown that those giving birth at home have better birth outcomes than those who give birth in hospitals. They experience fewer severe vaginal tears, cesarean sections (and therefore fewer surgery complications), postpartum hemorrhages, and birth injuries to babies.

The medicalizing of birth in the United States has not been a story based on best practice and has been strongly influenced by lobbyists, economics, power struggles, sexism, and media campaigns. Many people don't have access to accurate information about home birth, nor is home birth accurately portrayed in the media. Home birth, however, offers safety as well as familiarity, comfort, privacy, and family focus.

Miscarriage

On average, every one in four pregnancies results in miscarriage. With age this proportion grows higher, reaching as high as one out of two pregnancies by age 40. Thus no discussion of early pregnancy is complete without covering the topic of miscarriage. Miscarriage is an occurrence in the lives of most women, yet it still seems to be a taboo subject. In fact, it isn't until you experience a miscarriage that you discover how many women you know have also miscarried. Although finding this out may offer you support, the knowledge often comes to you after the fact. Therefore, when faced with it is common to feel like you're the only ones who have ever been through such a trauma, which can seem isolating. Because of the lack of openness surrounding its normalcy, miscarriage has become unnecessarily medicalized.

Signs of Impending Miscarriage

Although some people are warned of an impending miscarriage through HCG lab work or a sonogram, most first become concerned that they may be about to miscarry when they see blood. There are a number of reasons for bleeding in the first trimester, many of which are normal and resolve on their own. Therefore, when you first see blood on your toilet paper or underwear, it doesn't necessarily mean you're miscarrying. Brown spotting, or pink spotting with clear mucus is much more likely to resolve than seeing red blood. Sometimes you may bleed or spot for a couple of days or even weeks and maintain your pregnancy. In fact, 50 percent of women who bleed during early pregnancy continue to grow a healthy baby. If cramping begins, however, it is more likely that you are beginning to miscarry.

Preventative Measures

Unfortunately, there are few preventative measures for miscarriage once you are pregnant. Most miscarriages are caused by improper cell division, which makes the pregnancy no longer viable. But living a fertile lifestyle may help prevent miscarriage to a certain degree. Hormonal imbalance is a cause of up to 15 percent of all miscarriages. We thoroughly discuss diet, lifestyle, and herbal ways of maintaining hormonal balance. Experts find that women who exercise have a 40 percent lower chance of miscarrying than those who don't, most likely because of the increased health of the body overall. See part three of this book for ideas. If you're bleeding or spotting, immediately lie down and relax. If anything can prevent a pending miscarriage, it is relaxation and visualization—imagine your uterus relaxing, and completely relax your body and mind. Take the Bach Flower remedy "Rescue Remedy"—available at all health food stores—every few minutes to a few hours, as it has a calming affect on the uterus.

Although bed rest may not ultimately prevent your miscarriage, it will allow you time to feel your feelings and pay attention to your experience. Above all, it's vital to remain connected to yourself during trying times.

If you have been pregnant for less than ten weeks and begin to spot, taking a progesterone supplement can be of great assistance in preventing a miscarriage. If you're not already taking oral progesterone or progesterone suppositories, a topical progesterone enhancer cream (which you apply on any soft, fatty spot on the body, such as inner thigh, tummy, or inner arm) can be purchased at your local health food store and used until you can secure a stronger form. This supplementing will only help if the bleeding is related to a progesterone deficiency.

Treatment Options for Miscarriage

Most people don't have a midwife or a doctor at the time they miscarry. As a result they feel like there's no one to call to ask what to do. Even if you do have a midwife or a doctor and you call their office, you'll likely reach their answering service or a receptionist who will be unable to give you the information you're looking for. Therefore, unfortunately, most people end up in the emergency room.

MEDICALIZED MISCARRIAGE

If you see a doctor when you're miscarrying or think you're miscarrying—whether in the emergency room or in a private office—they'll perform an ultrasound to check whether the baby has a heartbeat. If there's a heartbeat, they'll send you home and tell you to come back if you start to bleed heavily or your cramping becomes severe. If there's no heartbeat, they'll most likely perform a surgical procedure to remove the contents of your uterus. This is an option you may choose or you may decide to return home and miscarry in a nonmedical manner.

Miscarrying in the emergency room can be traumatic. In the overwhelming majority of cases, miscarriage isn't an emergency; thus, you may wait for hours to be seen. Being in the hospital when you're losing your pregnancy can be emotionally painful: an extremely traumatic—yet normal, private, and healthy—experience is taking place in your body, yet you're in public and don't know exactly what is going on. You're going through a huge internal crisis and navigating the medical world at the same time. Unfortunately, in the hospital there's rarely any acknowledgment of the intensity of your grief about losing your pregnancy.

While in this crisis, you may also need to decide how to represent your family structure, and you may have to filter through possible homophobia or judgments about single mothers, which, more than likely, will only add to your stress.

NONMEDICAL MISCARRIAGE

If you choose to miscarry at home, you may appreciate the emotional safety and privacy that isn't afforded in the hospital. At the same time, some people don't feel completely safe being unattended, due to the blood loss of miscarriage. Miscarriage is very much like the pain of a mini-labor with the bleeding of a heavy period. The pain of a miscarriage is intensified by grief and fear.

Most women don't know what a miscarriage feels like—what amount of pain and bleeding is normal. If they did, more would choose to miscarry at home. Many home-birth midwives provide the valuable service of assisting people, both in person and over the phone, to safely miscarry at home.

A miscarriage is the body's way of emptying the uterus of a nonviable pregnancy and is a very normal physical process: a combination of cramping and bleeding. Cramps—the sensation of the uterus rhythmically contracting—have a wavelike sensation, may be quite strong, and may last a number of hours. Many people find themselves rocking on the toilet for a few hours and then feel much better. Some people cramp for up to twelve hours. Again, for most women, the bleeding is like that of a heavy period, with a couple hours of concentrated cramping, bleeding, and pain.

Not all miscarriages are safely conducted at home; thus, if you completely soak more than one maxipad per hour for more than two hours, it's best to contact a medical professional immediately. Likewise, because blood loss is involved, we don't recommend that you miscarry without a partner or friend in the house.

What Did I Do Wrong?

After a miscarriage, it's common for guilt and self-blame to arise. People often wonder what they did wrong. If they're partnered, they may feel their partner will blame them for not being able to maintain the pregnancy. The need to point to something that caused the miscarriage can feel more settling than living with the fact that it was unpreventable.

Some people go to all lengths to blame themselves or their partner for the loss of the pregnancy. "It was that fight we had." "It was the spicy food we ate the other night." "It was the sex." "It's confirmation that I don't work right." "It's because I'm too old." "It's because I'm gay." Miscarriages happen.

This desire to place blame comes from feeling out of control and is a signal you can use to recognize that you may have underlying feelings that need to be addressed.

Grieving

Grieving is a deeply personal process and varies in duration for each person. It isn't something that can be rushed. Usually, the longer the duration of pregnancy before the loss, the longer the grieving period. It's important, especially if you're partnered, to recognize that everyone grieves differently. Having compassion for each other's style and timeline for grieving will help deepen your relationship and compassion for each other. Trying to hasten a grieving period can breed resentment.

If you're partnered, it's best not to try to get pregnant again after a miscarriage until you're both ready. After a miscarriage, you may not want to try again, since the process may be too grueling. Some people follow miscarriage with adoption, knowing they couldn't withstand more loss. Others don't feel emotionally prepared for many months to resume striving for pregnancy. In fact, it's common to want to wait until after the estimated due date of the pregnancy you lost.

Grieving takes on an additional dimension when you realize you're basically starting all over when you inseminate again. You begin at the first cycle, knowing that once more it may take up to a year (or longer) for you to get pregnant. This can feel overwhelming.

Others aren't as consumed by the grieving process and are ready to begin inseminating again as soon as possible.

When to Start Inseminating Again

The answer varies. If you were only a few weeks pregnant and miscarried at home, it's probably sufficient to skip a full menstrual cycle and then resume inseminating. If your period is abnormally light or heavy, it's best to wait until your cycle is normalized. If you had a medical miscarriage, it's best to wait at least two full menstrual cycles to allow your uterine lining to build up again. If at that time your cycle is still not regular, wait until it is. If you do not wait until your body has had time to recover, you run an increased risk of a second miscarriage.

Because of the hormonal changes during early pregnancy, a frustrating side effect of miscarriage for many women is that their cycles change. Your body may not menstruate for two to eight weeks after you miscarry. After any pregnancy, no matter how brief, your cycle can change dramatically in length and nature. It is common to go from a thirty-two-day cycle to a twenty-eight-day cycle, or from having no fertile mucus to having a lot of fertile mucus, seemingly overnight. This can be disconcerting. You may feel like you've just gotten the hang of reading your body and now it's totally different.

At Maia, we strongly recommend that everyone who has experienced a pregnancy loss, no matter how early on, receive treatments for hormonal balancing. We think that acupuncture is incredibly effective at this time. If there were no complications with the miscarriage, often three or four treatments is sufficient. If you dealt with extended blood loss or repeated medical procedures then a longer course of care is going to be more effective. In addition, it is valuable to continue drinking your fertility tea and to focus on renourishing your body. Pregnancy loss can be experienced as a depletion and create hormonal chaos. It is always best to head this off at the pass if you are planning to start trying again as soon as possible.

Serial Miscarriages

The vast majority of women who miscarry twice in a row don't miscarry a third time. If a woman miscarries three times, many tests can be done to try to determine the cause(s). This area of obstetrics care is new but quickly growing. Many theories are controversial, and treatments go in and out of vogue rapidly. If a woman chooses to see a high-risk specialist, we encourage her to take a team approach in which she also sees a practitioner who can evaluate her diet and overall health, as well as a therapist or other emotional support provider.

Celebrate the Fact That You Were Pregnant

One thing we like to celebrate with women, although it can be very difficult to do, is that they did get pregnant. This is really, truly wonderful and may get lost amidst the grief. Each woman relates to her pregnancy and miscarriage differently. Women may refer to "my first baby" or "my first pregnancy" or "my twelve-week pregnancy," or may base everything in relation to the pregnancy—"after my miscarriage" or "before my miscarriage." Pregnancy loss is a big marker in women's lives.

One of the support groups we led decided to adopt the idea that pregnancy, no matter how long, is an accomplishment worth honoring and celebrating. They discussed trying to hold the attitude of self-support when facing pregnancy loss: "Good job, body! Way to go! The baby wasn't developing right, and you knew just what to do."

CHAPTER 21

Pregnant Life

PREGNANCY IS A joyous and phenomenal time of creation. The idea that you can actually create another human being is a miraculous concept! Layered within this joy, however, are innumerable physical discomforts and hormonally induced emotional fluctuations that are an inherent to pregnancy. Add to this blend the issues specific to being a lesbian or transman and the ways we must navigate the mainstream, and you have a very consuming and complex phenomenon. Welcome to pregnancy!

This chapter explores issues that may arise for pregnant lesbians, transmen, bisexual women, and single women of any orientation. Some issues are just added twists to the universal themes of pregnancy, while others are unique to a lesbian pregnancy.

Sharing the News of Your Pregnancy

Telling people the exciting news of your pregnancy can fill you with many conflicting emotions. You may be concerned about what exactly you'll tell people. You may be afraid of receiving a negative response to your wonderful news. Of course, you'll want the people in your life to be as excited as you are about the news. Living in a straight world, however, has probably taught you to proceed with caution when discussing lesbian issues or publicly displaying your love. This is a challenging dichotomy. It's helpful to explore in advance the emotional and practical elements of telling others that you're having a baby so that you can, as much as possible, prepare for this sometimes awkward phase of pregnancy.

||||||||||||||||||||||||||||||||||||||||||||||||||||||||||||||||||||||||||||||||||||

"We have found ourselves having tension around who we are telling and what we are telling them. Mikki told her mom I'm finally pregnant. That was fine, but she also shared with her the complete donor profile of our sperm donor. I feel like the profile is private and at the very least we need to discuss who, if anyone, we would consider sharing these intimate details with. I felt betrayed when she shared them with her mom without even telling me first. We're working it out, but we approach this subject really differently. She's outgoing and forthcoming; I am shy and private." —MIKKI, 33, AND GERALDINE, 41, HONOLULU, HAWAII, SIX AND A HALF WEEKS PREGNANT

||||||||||||||||||||||||||||||||||||||||||||||||||||||||||||||||||||||||||||||||||||||||||

Telling Immediate Family Members

No matter how you choose to tell your family, it's normal to feel nervous about sharing the information. Often at least one person won't receive the news wholeheartedly or with the enthusiasm you'd like. On the flip side, we've found that most lesbians have at least one supportive family member who has been following the progress of their family-making and eagerly awaits the pregnancy.

WHEN THEY KNOW OF YOUR DESIRE TO PARENT

Many queer women have shared with close family members their desire to parent from the beginning of their process. These people are blessed with open and progressive families who acknowledge and support their relationships and choices to raise children. For these families, the news of the pregnancy is welcomed with glee. As a result, these people usually tell their families as soon as they find out they're pregnant. An embracing family provides these women the wonderful and much deserved experience of having their loved ones react to a planned pregnancy with excitement.

Unfortunately, not every lesbian or bisexual woman, by any means, can rely on receiving a positive response from their entire family. Many people have mentioned to their family, prior to pregnancy, that they plan to raise children, but have chosen to keep private the intimate details of their conception period. If this is the case for you, the news of your pregnancy may come as a surprise to family members who didn't really understand that you were serious about becoming a mother.

We've worked with many people who have guided their parents and other family members through the "appropriate" response to the news. For example, Marina and Jennifer told Jennifer's mother over the phone in this way:

Hi, Mom! Marina and I have some really exciting news to share with you. We wanted you to be the first to know because we know you'll be as excited as we are. I'm pregnant! We're thrilled! We thought you might want to tell Dad yourself, but what do you think is best?

In trying to elicit the desired response, some women choose to tell their parents and other pertinent family members first by letter or e-mail. Although this may feel too formal or distanced for some, others feel it allows their family members to have their individual responses alone and to adjust to the news before responding. Women who choose this tactic often expect less-than-thrilled responses and feel the situation will be mitigated best by allowing family members the time and space to react before responding.

WHEN THEY DON'T KNOW OF YOUR DESIRE TO PARENT

Many lesbian and bisexual women choose not to inform their family members that they're trying to get pregnant or even that they're hoping to parent. Some delay telling family members until after the window for miscarriage has passed or until genetic tests have confirmed that the pregnancy is one they wish to continue.

Letting family members know at this point in the process has distinct advantages and disadvantages. Your news will be the first they've heard of your desire to parent.

We've found that people choose to keep their family out of the loop during their preconception period primarily because they feel the news will be met with a negative response and they want to delay that response for as long as possible. These women hope that when their pregnancy is clearly established, their family members may feel less comfortable voicing negative opinions, since the decision has already been made and it would be rude to do so. Thus, by not disclosing their intention to parent until pregnancy, they are able to protect themselves emotionally during the sensitive periods of conception and early pregnancy.

Unfortunately, waiting to tell family members until the pregnancy is under way often backfires. Often close family members are hurt when they discover they haven't been included in such important elements of their daughter or sister's life. Even if they're also homophobic, they may feel hurt by being left out. Likewise, some people have such an enormous amount of processing to do about the concept of a lesbian pregnancy that finding out about the pregnancy may end up delaying the overwhelming reaction and only serve to concentrate it during pregnancy. Family members with a lot of processing to do may be unable to appropriately contain their reactions and fears from the pregnant woman or her partner. This can lead to a highly stressful pregnancy.

With time, most family members will come around to accepting that you're a parent. Nonetheless, there are the few who may excommunicate you for your decision. Some families will never acknowledge that you're a parent if you aren't the one giving birth. Biology means everything to them. And there are some families who will accept you as a single parent but refuse to acknowledge your partner as a parent. In some families this process takes years or even an ultimatum that they'll lose their relationship with you and their grandchild if they don't acknowledge your entire family. It has been our experience, however, that most families will come around in time.

If you choose to delay letting your family members know of your intentions to have children until you're pregnant, you're also delaying the time it takes them to integrate and process this information. When you do tell them, you may want to provide them with books and resources on the subject so that they can process this information on their own and not feel the need to do so with you exclusively.

WHEN ONE SIDE OF THE FAMILY IS WELCOMING AND THE OTHER ISN'T

When you're partnered it's particularly hurtful if only one partner's family accepts the child. It's especially difficult if the nonbirth mother isn't acknowledged as a parent, because she is less likely to be recognized as a parent by society at large, whereas the birth mother is always seen as a mother. Each lesbian family deals with this issue in their own way, but it's often difficult to live in a culture that doesn't recognize our family structures as valid and to live with that same homophobia in our immediate families.

WHEN THE NONBIRTH MOM ISN'T RECOGNIZED

We recommend being direct in your communications with your immediate and extended-family members, clarifying the significance of each of your roles and setting out parameters for how you'd like each parent to be treated and named. If your family still insists on not recognizing that both of you are equal parents to your growing child, you have some tough decisions to make. Many families choose to discontinue contact with these family members until they're willing to recognize their family as valid. Others encourage their families to accept their family before making such a big decision, knowing that growth sometimes requires time.

It's particularly painful if your own parents reject the notion that you're a parent. We've met more than one nonbirth mom whose family completely ignored the fact that she was a parent until the formal second-parent adoption went through. After she had completed the adoption, the family recognized her parental status because the state recognized it. Having your parents reject your parenthood is one of the deepest wounds you can receive. If this is the case for you, don't hesitate to seek counseling to help you through this time.

WHEN THE PREGNANT MOM ISN'T ACCEPTED BY HER FAMILY

When you're pregnant you'll more than likely feel a universal sense of connectedness with all women who have been pregnant before, especially your own mother. If your mother rejects you now or rejected you when you first came out and hasn't reentered your life, this pain can be overwhelming. This hurt may be intensified or restimulated by your own transitioning into motherhood, and these wounds can be very difficult to heal. Even if you were rejected fifteen years ago, these wounds may reopen during pregnancy.

Telling Extended Family and Friends

It may also be a challenge to figure out how to tell extended family and friends. Many people in our lives appear to accept us and our sexual orientation, but for some heterosexuals, the idea of lesbians raising children nudges our "lifestyles" into the unacceptable. Pregnant lesbians seem to push more "primal buttons" than nonpregnant lesbians. To avoid having to witness any anticipated or unexpected negative responses from the people in our lives, it's becoming more and more popular for lesbians to announce their pregnancies via postcard or email. Akin to a birth announcement, some families send out a "We're having a baby" card. This form of mass announcement allows you to do the majority of your "coming out" about the pregnancy in one fell swoop, but not face to face.

UNEXPECTED RESPONSES

Some women experience the seemingly positive, although disconcerting, response of suddenly being brought back into the fold of their family or having an instant circle of friends as soon as they share the news about the pregnancy. It's as if some invisible barrier has been broken down when lesbians do something that heterosexual people can relate to.

Women share with us the mixed feelings that arise when their mother or sister suddenly communicates with them on a daily basis and sends them letters and baby clothes, whereas prior to pregnancy they only communicated on birthdays and holidays. Or how strange it is to instantaneously be invited to many more social gatherings than they were before because their straight friends feel they can now share with them in ways they could not before. It's also quite common to become the "lesbian poster-child family" for your friends or neighborhood, with everyone wanting to show off their lesbian friends who are having a baby so they can prove how liberal they are, even if their motivation is subconscious.

Although these responses may be touching, they can also feel infuriating. These responses can be especially poignant if your partner isn't included in the lavished attention, or if the past homophobia of these same people isn't even mentioned because you've now become "acceptable."

HOW TO HANDLE HOMOPHOBIC REACTIONS

At some point in time most lesbians encounter a directly homophobic response to the news that they're pregnant. It can be startling to excitedly share your news and have people not know what to say. It's confounding to realize that these people to whom you've been out for so long have been judging you the whole time. Their response may be silence or a simple "Oh" followed by a change of subject. Or it may come as a homophobic diatribe blasted at you. All of these responses are difficult to deal with. When someone reacts negatively to the news of your growing family, it's hard to imagine what continued place they'll hold in your life. Their response puts them into an entirely new category. Thus, you feel not only the pain of their response, but also the pain of losing these people as trusted members of your life.

It may be necessary to give these friends or relatives the ultimatum that if they can't leave their criticisms out of their interactions with you, you'll discontinue the relationship. As painful as leaving a meaningful relationship is, continuing to expose yourself—and eventually your children—to homophobia on a regular basis is not only painful but also self-hating and disempowering for your kids. Although most relatives and friends can agree to disagree and not discuss it, there's no denying the altered place they now hold in your life. Sometimes it becomes easier just to let that person out of your life than to have to pretend their judgment and rejection aren't really there simply because you've agreed not to discuss it.

Homophobic responses usually feel like they come out of the blue, and you're rarely prepared for them. If you're in public and someone you don't know discredits your life—as may well happen at least once during your pregnancy, and certainly during your parenthood—you have two choices: directly call them on their homophobia or swiftly leave the scene. If the negative response comes from someone you know, it's important to be brave enough to cut them off and not let them continue. This can be done with statements such as the following, which you can practice ahead of time:

- ⊙ "I hear you have a strong opinion on the subject of lesbians having children. However, we are very excited about our family and are not asking for your opinion."
- ⊙ "Please don't criticize my life. I have made my choices from love. If you can't accept this, I'd prefer that you keep your feelings to yourself."

These statements will stop most people in their tracks and help them realize the inappropriateness of their reaction. Some, however, will continue on. If they must, and you've been direct, then to maintain your integrity you must leave the conversation by walking away or hanging up the phone. It takes courage to confront someone's homophobia midstream, but the only way we will make this a safer world for ourselves and our children is to do just that.

There may be times when you feel comfortable and confident discussing someone's concerns about your family. This is always your choice. You can choose with whom you have such conversations, and you get to decide when enough is enough. Having someone respectfully discuss their questions is a completely different scenario than having someone attack your family. Nonetheless, it's important to remember that you're not obligated to educate anyone about the validity of your family; you can say this to them and remind them that you don't ask them to justify their choices to you. Likewise, there's the option of saying you don't want to address their concerns but are willing to give them a referral, such as to Parents, Families, and Friends of Lesbians and Gays (PFLAG), where their concerns can more appropriately be addressed.

Telling the World That Your Partner Is Pregnant

Your pregnant partner has the luxury of deciding how much to reveal to any person at any given time when she tells them she's pregnant. As a female nonbirth parent, when you tell the world you're becoming a parent you inherently come out each time. If you haven't directly discussed your homelife and sexual orientation with everyone in your life, the announcement of the pregnancy will often be an official coming out as well.

Each nonbirth mother chooses to navigate this issue differently. We encourage you to resist the urge to keep silent out of fear or discomfort. In choosing to become a parent, you've chosen to take on society's homophobia and claim your right to parenthood. Pregnancy allows you the opportunity to become confident in your coming-out process, so that by the time your child is born you will be better equipped to be a lesbian or queer family.

Telling the people you work with is important, even though many non-birth moms think that not discussing the pregnancy at work is also an appropriate decision. We disagree. How will you advocate for yourself to get parental leave when your baby is born if management doesn't know your partner is pregnant? How will you investigate whether the baby can join your insurance plan if your employer doesn't know you're having a baby? How will you take time off when your child is sick if they don't know you're a parent?

Granted, perhaps you have good reason to believe that if you came out you would lose your job or suffer irreparably. If this is the case, you may want to investigate how important it is to you to continue working at that job. Could you get a job where you could be an out parent? These are personal decisions, yet ones that should not be overlooked.

As a nonbirth mother, you may feel negated if your partner chooses not to disclose that she is partnered and parenting with you, her loving partner. How do you think she (and your child) would feel if you didn't acknowledge them in your worlds?

Whereas "passing" may have worked for you in the past as the safest way of avoiding awkward moments, it may now serve to undermine your family unit. Give this thought and attention. We must do everything we can to strengthen our personal relationships so that they make it through the challenges of early parenting. Taking pride in your family is one of the strongest steps you can take to do just that.

Still, it isn't always easy or comfortable to constantly be asked, "What do you mean you're having a baby? You're not pregnant! Are you adopting?" Having to always explain that your partner is pregnant can feel like a lot of work when all you're trying to do is share your joy about the pregnancy.

If coming out in this way makes you uncomfortable, consider practicing what you're going to say. Likewise, try coming out about the pregnancy to people you encounter but don't know in everyday life. For example, when you're buying ice cream try mentioning to another customer that your partner is pregnant and try to strike up a casual conversation about it. Does he or she have kids? Did anyone he or she knows have the same ice-cream craving during pregnancy that your partner has? Situations like these are perhaps safer settings where you can attempt to become more comfortable and familiar discussing your family.

Telling People That Your Partner Is Pregnant When You Were Unable to Conceive

If you haven't been able to conceive or maintain a pregnancy yourself, it can be emotionally agonizing to tell others that your partner is pregnant. Telling people can often be followed by holding back (or breaking into) tears about how you yourself couldn't get pregnant. You may have not kept everyone up-to-date on the progress of your own fertility struggles, so when they hear that your partner is pregnant they may be confused and ask what happened. Thus, sharing the news of the pregnancy may also mean sharing the news that you were unable to conceive or hold a pregnancy yourself. In many instances this means unexpectedly being more emotionally vulnerable than you had wished with any particular person. This can make telling people very poignant and sometimes heart-wrenching.

If you're having a hard time telling people — or even entertaining the idea of telling people — of the pregnancy and your partner is ready and eager to let everyone know, this can put a strain on your relationship. She is undoubtedly less conflicted about the pregnancy and being public about the news. Although she'll most likely understand your feelings and be supportive, she may also want you to let go of your feelings and fully share in the newness of this pregnancy. Talk about and share your feelings compassionately and respectfully. Clear the air as soon as possible so that resentment and anger don't color your experience of pregnancy. If necessary, seek joint or individual counseling to resolve this issue.

How to Handle the Barrage of Personal Questions

As a pregnant lesbian or single parent, you will more than likely face numerous personal — and sometimes inappropriate — questions when you share your news with others. It's helpful to prepare yourself so that you won't feel so taken aback when they arise. Sometimes you may feel the subject is none of their business. Remember, you're under no obligation to answer personal questions. To maintain your integrity it's important to answer only the questions that feel appropriate and to have pre-established responses to questions that are hostile or invasive. Commonly posed questions include:

- "How is it possible for you to be pregnant?"
- "Did you mean to get pregnant?"

- ◎ "What does your partner think about this?" (implying that you were having an affair with a man and accidentally got pregnant)
- ◎ "Did you use a sperm bank?"
- ◎ "Don't you know that sperm banks are dangerous and only down-and-out men looking for fast money go there?"
- ◎ "What if you have a boy? How are you going to raise a son?"
- ◎ "Tell me all about your donor."
- ◎ "Did you have sex or use a turkey baster?"
- ◎ "How could you choose to raise a child with only one parent?"
- ◎ "How can you live with the guilt of inviting such discrimination into your child's life?"
- ◎ "Don't you think it's unfair to have a child when you know that lesbian relationships don't survive and that your child will live in a broken home?"

Knowing that personal questions will come your way allows you to explore for yourself and with any relevant family members how you'd like to respond. For example, many families don't want to give out any information about their donors. They feel that doing so misdirects the focus from a female-parent family to a traditional heterosexual model. When you're asked questions about the donor, a pat reply such as "We're keeping that information to ourselves" or "The identity of the donor isn't what is important to us about our child" will often stop further questioning.

Deciding for yourself how much is appropriate to share is a personal choice. Once again, it will probably be most helpful to check in with your body's response when you're answering questions. Notice when you feel tight, defensive, or nervous. This may indicate that you're sharing more than what's comfortable for you. For more suggestions for how to handle these and other public experience read *The Queer Parents' Primer*, by Stephanie Brill.

Coming Out as a Single Mother

Single lesbian mothers are caught in a very interesting place. Many women have chosen single motherhood because they haven't found a suitable partner and their biological clock is ticking. Others want to be parents and have no intention of partnering. Still others had relationships that dissolved during their pregnancy. The majority of single lesbian mothers we've worked with fit into the first category.

Even today, single motherhood carries a cultural stigma. Although in the U.S. women aren't officially allowed to marry other women, partnered parents are often held in greater regard than single ones. Although there are millions of single mothers of all sexual orientations in our country, rampant stereotypes surround them. The prejudice and discrimination faced by single mothers of any sexual orientation is often just as great as or sometimes greater than the discrimination faced by partnered lesbians. Many people are willing to accept that a couple, of any gender, is more equipped to raise a child than a single woman is.

Single mothers by choice are often given a hard time initially by friends and family who can't understand why anyone would want to parent on their own. When you tell people you're pregnant and that you'll be a single mother, you'll face a variety of responses, from outrage to pity. It's common to have to repeatedly assert that you're a single mother by choice—if you are—and that you're sharing positive, joyous news.

If you're a single lesbian, the additional overlay of homophobia colors the responses of others. It's your choice whether to disclose your sexual orientation in any given situation. If you're not out—and plan to stay closeted—you may answer these personal questions more evasively than if you're out or planning to come out. Numerous single mothers-to-be have expressed that the greater issue is that they're single rather than that they're lesbian or bisexual.

Lesbians with Surprise Pregnancies

A number of lesbians every year get pregnant unintentionally. These conceptions predominantly occur when lesbian-identified women have sex with men. A surprise pregnancy for a lesbian usually comes as a complete shock. Because it's so completely unexpected, it can feel overwhelming. Apart from the shock, there's also the recovery from denial. When you aren't planning to get pregnant and if you barely realize it's a possibility, it's easy to deny the symptoms of pregnancy until you're quite far along. If this is the case for you, it may not be an option for you to terminate the pregnancy, even if you would have chosen to do so. Therefore, a small but significant number of lesbians each year find themselves not only with surprise but also with unwanted pregnancies.

When you have a surprise pregnancy that you intend to continue, everything in your life turns around. This includes trying to elicit support from friends and family members. The stress of discovering that you're suddenly going to be a parent is compounded if you aren't out or if your circle of friends is judgmental of lesbians who have sex with men. Nonetheless, finding support is crucial. Resist the urge to keep the pregnancy a secret until you've sorted everything out. It may take the entire pregnancy to feel you have a grip on your life changes. If you find that your identity, circle of friends, and body are all changing too rapidly for you to keep up, be sure to seek counseling.

Most lesbians take years preparing to be a parent. When you're suddenly dropped into it, you may feel paralyzed by the enormity of the endeavor. It helps to know that you're not alone. We see a number of lesbian-identified women each year who unintentionally get pregnant and choose to continue the pregnancy. There are many of you out there.

||||||||||||||||||||||||||||||||||||||||||||||||||||||||||||||||||||||||||||||||||||

"I work construction. I've always been one of the guys. Most of the guys I work with don't even know I'm a woman. I like it that way. Well, one day after a few too many beers after work I ended up having sex with my best friend on the job. It was a mess, he was married, and I am a dyke. We vowed to forget it and not to tell anyone. Anyway, I ended up pregnant. I was stunned. I didn't want to admit it could possibly be true. I surprised myself and everyone I know by deciding to have the baby. True to our promise, Bob and I never discussed it again. I assume he knows he's the father but we don't go there." —JAMIE, 32, TEXAS

||||||||||||||||||||||||||||||||||||||||||||||||||||||||||||||||||||||||||||||||||||

Pregnancy as a Time of Physical and Emotional Transformation

Pregnancy is an amazing opportunity for personal growth. It has been said that the "inner work" possible during pregnancy is equivalent to three years of therapy. As the body undergoes a radical metamorphosis, so do you on your journey to becoming a parent. The physical and hormonal changes of pregnancy provide a natural time to deepen and explore all of your relationships. Commonly explored relationships include those with your partner, your body, and your mother. These relationships are explored by all pregnant women, and are thus universal themes of pregnancy. For lesbian and bisexual women, however, there are usually specific twists to these themes. In the following sections, we'll discuss common physical and emotional changes that arise during pregnancy as well as issues that are specific to lesbian couples.

Life as a Pregnant Dyke

It isn't always easy to maintain a sense of queer visibility as a pregnant mother. In fact, your pregnancy can easily consume your queer visibility and identity. Because you've joined the club of pregnant women, you may often be assumed to be straight. If you are femme you are often assumed to be straight. If you ordinarily pass as a man nothing changes until the end or until you turn around. As the nonpregnant mom, you maintain your queer visibility but are invisible in terms of the pregnancy. If you're bisexual and partnered with a man, you're perceived as straight. And if you're a single pregnant woman of any sexual orientation, you're usually assumed to be straight. These assumptions often come equally from within the queer community and from outside it.

These same transformations and questioning of your queer identity may happen inside yourself because you no longer have the same identity markers to depend upon. Our identities change as we become parents, and there may be an awkward period while you try on a variety of self-projections until you find a balance between your parenthood and lesbian or queer identity. Internally it's not so much a question of what your sexual orientation is, but rather how you continue to express your queer identity while pregnant.

For example, many women we meet during preconception have a specific image of what a mom looks like, and it's usually quite different from their "hip dyke" self-perception. Women often face some outward overhauls as they try to reconcile these two images. Many women strive for "mommy hair" or a more feminine style of dress in order to feel they're ready to be a mother. Usually, over time each woman finds her own comfortable style, but there are often some comical interpretations along the way.

Life as a Pregnant Butch, Gender-Queer Person, or Male-Identified Woman

Many of the issues of gender, and sexual orientation are highlighted if you're butch. This is true when not pregnant, but add pregnancy into the mix and the complexity of your existence deepens. If you've always felt most comfortable expressing yourself with masculine traits and appearances, blending an incredibly female body experience and feminine cultural experience with your butch identity can be a challenge. If you're mistaken for a man when you're not pregnant, it may feel very surreal to still be mistaken for a man now that you are or feel so obviously pregnant. Likewise, if you often pass as a man to the general public and enjoy it, you may be discouraged if you no longer pass anymore. Maintaining a butch persona throughout pregnancy inherently questions the outside world's stereotypes, and possibly your own, of what it means to be a pregnant woman. In fact, the experience of pregnancy can lead some formerly butch-identified women to realize that they actually feel more comfortable identifying as a man. Thus the transgender identity solidifies itself through the pregnancy experience.

If you identify with a more fluid gender concept and perhaps don't add any pronouns to your self-concept you can feel internally pressured to identify in a fixed fashion during the pregnancy and breastfeeding time period. We would like to suggest that this is not necessary. Your gender-fluid or queer-gender existence remains the same. You will not damage the baby by being yourself (this seems to be the primary concern we hear voiced). The binary of gender is culturally imposed and not based on anything real. Please entertain the idea that rather than confusing or damaging your child, you will be doing him or her a great service by reducing the amount of buy-in they have to make to the gender construct. There is such power in being yourself.

||||||||||||||||||||||||||||||||||||||||||||||||||||||||||||||||||||||||||||||||||||||

"I found that I loved being pregnant! It was great!
The hard thing was that for the first time, really, I didn't feel safe. I remember one rainy night I was using a pay phone at a gas station. Some guys were hanging around drinking, no big deal. At one point they asked me a question. When I turned around to answer them my trench coat blew open revealing my very pregnant belly. They took it in immediately. I went from being a man to being a freak. They started approaching me with that look in their eyes and uttering verbal abuse. I panicked and virtually fled to my car with my heart pounding. As I drove away I had so many feelings all at the same time. I felt exposed, vulnerable, and afraid for the baby, angry, weak, and scared. My gender expression had always been mine up to that point. That experience made me feel like public property."—DYAN, 38, SAN FRANCISCO

||||||||||||||||||||||||||||||||||||||||||||||||||||||||||||||||||||||||||||||||||||||

Body Changes and Their Accompanying Emotions

Breast Growth

For some, the rapid rate of breast growth during pregnancy feels overwhelming and alienating. If you've always prided yourself on not needing to wear a bra, suddenly having large breasts can make you feel like you're living in someone else's body. You may feel overly feminine or overly sexualized simply by having larger breasts. This early physical transformation is true preparation for the tremendous changes your body will undergo throughout the pregnancy and birth experience. Staying connected to your body and trying to embrace these changes will ultimately make pregnancy, birth, and nursing much more pleasurable experiences for you.

I Have to Wear What?!

It can be equally challenging for a pregnant dyke to find appropriate clothes. Maternity clothes are usually very feminine. If you're accustomed to wearing more butch or "masculine" attire, it can feel awkward to have to purchase feminine clothes that don't reflect your self-perception. Likewise, continuing to dress in the same fashion as prior to pregnancy means wearing oversize clothes that fit your growing belly, which can make you feel dumpy instead of pregnant. Suspenders and low cut pants are often a good option in lieu of maternity pants.

The unexpected flip side to the challenging issue of butch pregnancy clothing is that the impact of being pregnant, whether hormonal or cultural, may cause you to gravitate toward clothes more feminine than you ever would have considered wearing while not pregnant. To start sporting dresses and leggings may throw your identity for a loop if these are radically different from your nonpregnant attire. Occasionally, however, you may not even notice the stylistic differences that are so obviously apparent, sometimes disconcerting, and definitely surprising to your partner and friends.

If you typically dress as a femme, maternity clothing styles have broadened sufficiently in the last few years that you probably won't have a huge problem finding clothes that suit you during pregnancy if you have a sufficient budget. Many of us find maternity clothing costs untenable, especially since we don't wear them that long. Thus, we borrow clothes from relatives and friends. The older styles in general were often very desexualized and little-girl-like. No matter how you usually dress, invest the time, money, and creativity necessary to obtain one basic outfit that fits you well and doesn't drive you crazy stylistically—it's important to your self-esteem and body image. By the end of pregnancy most people are down to wearing the same one, two, or possible three outfits every week.

Maternity clothes, in all sizes and styles, can now be found at many online retailers.

Adapting to Physical Limitations

As for most pregnant women, there will probably come a time when you're no longer able to do the activities you've always been able to do, whether it's opening a jar, lifting a heavy object, balancing yourself on a ladder, or having sex in a certain position. With these limitations your identity may be thrown for a loop. Many women deeply enjoy their ability to lead active and athletic lives. Many feel that their competency and strength have marked their lesbianism and have helped them create an identity that feels empowered and comfortable. Having to work with the concept of physical limitations may often be confused with being "weak."

The crisis part of this shift seems to lift when you're able to recognize that you're not weak, but rather you're pregnant. Your identity as strong and capable in a physical sense is superseded for a brief interlude by the strength and capacity to grow and nurture a baby. Ultimately, you'll gain a broader respect for yourself and your body by acknowledging the qualities needed to grow a baby—but perhaps not without a few stumbling blocks along the way.

The physical changes during pregnancy are tremendous, and they are the most apparent transformations that accompany pregnancy. Adjusting to your body changing shape every day for month after month, however, isn't always easy to do. We've discussed the inevitable breast changes, clothing challenges, and physical limitations that are a large part of the adjustment of being pregnant. But your inner relationship to a radically different body shape is also a major part of pregnancy.

Many people think they're going to love the physical changes of pregnancy. In actuality, they usually experience a mixed bag of emotional responses to these changes. No longer knowing your body and its limitations can feel disturbing on a core level. One mom recently expressed to us her utter panic when she realized she could not even walk down the block without getting winded. She was previously accustomed to riding her bike fifty miles at a time and then going dancing that same night. The complete reversal of what she could depend on from her body shook her deeply.

If you have traditionally been the one in your couple who has been the caretaker and the emotional rock it can be quite disconcerting to feel the need and desire to be taken care of. This can also create stress in the relationship as the role reversal can create some bumps in the road as each of you learns a new facet of giving and receiving. People are often vaguely aware that they'll grow emotionally and spiritually during pregnancy, but rarely are they aware what this growth may demand of them.

Food, Food, Food

During pregnancy and postpartum, food is love. A pregnant mother feeds the baby directly from the food that she eats, as does a nursing mother. Feeding yourself so much quality food is a full-time job. It can be difficult to maintain this level of food preparation and intake all on your own, and the effort is magnified if you're experiencing morning sickness. However, eating nutritiously and regularly is the number one thing you can do to ensure not only the health of your baby but also your own emotional and mental stability. It is quite common to feel like an emotional wreck or to feel like you are losing your ability to hold your life together when you are pregnant. Please, please take to heart that this is a side effect of not eating enough food frequently enough. Your sense of self will increase dramatically if you increase the quality, quantity, and frequency of your eating. Please take the time to reread chapter 10.

If you're single and don't have roommates, you'll need to figure out how to feed yourself when you're too hungry or sick or tired to cook. This is where friends can pitch in easily. They can drop off prepared food. If you approach your friends and family directly about how supportive it would be if they could help you with food, you can then create a schedule that you can rely on. There is comfort in knowing that Joe picks up take-out and comes over to eat with me every other Tuesday. My sister drops by a meal on the doorstep on the way to her shift at the hospital on Thursdays. Have Tupperware on hand to freeze meals and just leave one or two fresh portions out to eat. Most people when they are pregnant won't eat the same thing three times in a row, so making a big pot of stew that will last you the next four days will no longer be the most successful way to cook for yourself. If you need to forgo spending money on fancy baby items to make way for expensive, healthy, prepared food, do it. Your baby is made from what you eat, and you'll feel loved and nourished if you feed yourself well.

If you're partnered, a large part of your partner's responsibility and joint commitment to the pregnancy is to help feed you. This isn't an easy job, since pregnant women are especially choosy about what and when they want to eat.

If the nonpregnant partner fails to do her part in keeping her partner well fed, the pregnant mom is likely to feel unloved. In fact, low blood sugar may spur many of the fights you may have during pregnancy. Thus, if your pregnant partner is being unreasonable but persistent, feed her before she blows her top. Often her desperation stems from nutritional depletion, and things won't look so bad on a full stomach.

It isn't easy to realize that so much depends on your ability to feed your partner. This is especially so if she's the one who has usually prepared household meals. But just as she has the baby in her body and is lending her life energy constantly to growing the baby, whether or not she's in the mood to do so right then, you need to try your best to keep her well fed—whether or not you're in the mood to do so. And remember, this is the primary way that you can participate in the pregnancy.

Sexual Abuse, Eating Disorders, and Body Issues

Even if you think that your eating disorders or your abuse histories are well processed parts of your past, please, please know that they may nevertheless arise during pregnancy. Hormones, rapid weight gain, morning sickness, and body changes often trigger past eating disorders and sexual-abuse traumas as well as overall negative self-esteem body-image issues. Our culture seems to hold less respect for pregnant women's privacy than other people's. While pregnant, you'll probably hear many comments from strangers, family, and friends about your size and weight gain. You'll receive not only unsolicited advice and unsolicited disclosures of others' experiences, but also direct judgment and criticism. It's common to be told in the same day that you're both too big and too small, regardless of how average your weight gain and growth may be. In fact, we've never worked with any client who was able to completely avoid a barrage of feedback from random people about her size. In this way society's true obsession with size becomes fully apparent. Thus, it's no surprise that old weight and size issues may reappear for you, even if you've done a lot of work to resolve them. In fact, some pregnant women with strong anti-fatphobia attitudes are surprised to recognize their own issues about weight and size and body image that they may never have felt.

There is an insidious side to eating disorders, as any of you who have experienced them well know. Please be on the vigilant lookout for your typical signs that your eating issues are manifesting and but pay special attention to the tendency toward limiting your food intake, controlling eating behaviors, and overexercising as well. People who have significant eating disorder histories know that while in the throws of it the compulsions are quite compelling and thus you are highly unlikely to reach out for help. The best way to handle a eating disorder and pregnancy is to have planned for it ahead of time and put prevention measures in place. Please see chapter 10, on food, for specific ideas.

The reemergence of issues of sexual assault and abuse may come as more of a surprise, especially if you thought you had safely put these issues away. Still, the hormones of pregnancy, coupled with common underlying pregnancy feelings of being out of control, bring these issues to the surface for some women. Because these are past issues, it may take some time for you to recognize the emotional impact they may have on your pregnancy. It's helpful to be on the lookout if you think these issues could come up again for you and to seek counseling if necessary. Your sexual abuse or assault history may show up in the form of memories, which is easy to identify. However, during pregnancy some warning signs that your history may be negatively impacting your pregnancy also include feeling like you are not alone in your body, perceiving the baby as a foreign invader, generalized fears—especially of going to sleep—and feeling disconnected from the pregnancy.

Often being aware of, naming, or expressing these feelings to someone is all that's needed to keep these issues at bay. Some people, however, feel as if they're being flooded with past traumatic memories or unable to maintain their healthy eating habits. If this is the case for you, remember to have compassion for yourself and to seek necessary support and counseling. If these issues arise, we've found that it's best to assume that they'll remain an active presence throughout nursing as well.

Emotional Changes

Increased Emotional Instability: Feeling Crazy

Exhaustion, discomfort, and nausea are the physical underpinnings of the cacophony of hormones and emotions that mark the first trimester of pregnancy. Many pregnant people express feeling scared and overwhelmed by the sheer intensity of all their feelings. Although some people are more sensitive to these hormones, and some are more prone to emotional expression from the start, every pregnancy brings elevated emotions. The altered mental and emotional state brought on by pregnancy hormones is almost impossible to describe to a nonpregnant person. Commonly the pregnant woman finds it difficult to recognize how "abnormal" she is feeling and acting. This level of emotional instability can make you and everyone around you feel like you're on an emotional roller-coaster every day.

Usually, you and your loved ones grow more adjusted to the whole experience as you move into the second trimester, and your hormones will ease up a bit. Nonetheless, a fair amount of emotional volatility continues throughout the entire pregnancy. If having such strong emotions sweep over you triggers panic, anxiety, depression, or past trauma, you may consider seeking therapy. Sometimes this emotional instability can prove too much for a relationship or work environment, so without hesitation seek support if you need it.

Although the stereotype of the crazy pregnant woman is just that—a stereotype—the emotional swings during pregnancy can be wild and unsettling. If you know you tend to have significant mood swings when you're not pregnant, you may want to plan ahead for the kinds of support you and your partner may need during this time.

||||||||||||||||||||||||||||||||||||||||||||||||||||||||||||||||||||||||||||||||||||

"I honestly didn't recognize her anymore. I kept wondering where my girlfriend had gone and who this crazy person was in her body. I found myself bracing every time I came home from work. I just could never know when she was going to fly off the handle. Finally our midwife sat us down and said some of this was to be expected (and I would have to live with it). However, some of it seemed to be related to hormonal and emotional extremes. We came up with a much better system for Carla to get decent food every few hours. That meant I would wake up early to pack her a huge—and I mean huge—lunch to take to work each day. Our midwife recommended weekly acupuncture. That was so amazing, she would get so relaxed and gentle afterwards. She was instructed to drink her pregnancy tea every day for hormonal regulation. And I started to give her nightly ten-minute massages. That was my favorite part, as it often became a doorway for making love. These things made a night and day difference. I now tell everyone I know—have your wife do these things right from the start." —HELEN, 44, LOS ANGELES

||||||||||||||||||||||||||||||||||||||||||||||||||||||||||||||||||||||||||||||||||||

Control

If you've always prided yourself on your emotional stability, or if you've been the rock in your relationship while your partner has been more emotional, you may be in for quite a surprise. Being at the mercy of your emotions can make you feel out of control. When you find yourself crying over dog food commercials or because you wanted lasagna and not a casserole for dinner, you may no longer recognize yourself.

Feeling weepy and easily overwhelmed, as well as more physically limited than usual, can make you feel like a "helpless female." This usually feels quite scary for a person who's always considered herself in control. Pregnancy helps you recognize how much being in control is an illusion. Maintaining control is crucial to many person's sense of safety; it is usually a coping skill learned much earlier in life when "out of control" times were perhaps truly dangerous. Being pushed by your pregnancy to accept new truths about yourself and the interdependency you share with others can feel overwhelmingly unfamiliar. The gift of this lesson is that parenting involves intimate daily interaction with another being, and therefore can't and shouldn't be solely in our control. Any new awareness, acceptance, and accommodation to feeling out of control will ease your transition to parenthood.

Self-Centeredness

Pregnancy, although in many ways readily visible, is for the most part a very internal process that requires considerable personal reflection. You may feel like you're never alone in your own body and thus start to develop a full relationship with the one inside you. You have an evolved instinct to put the needs and presence of your baby first, and your body has an evolved capacity to make you feel its pregnancy needs are undeniable. The combination of the two can make you appear self-centered to the rest of the world, and this isn't actually unhealthy.

Many nonpregnant partners, however, feel tried by how everything revolves around the pregnant partner: where she wants to go, what she does or doesn't want to eat, what she does or doesn't want to do. Many nonpregnant partners also feel like they've lost their partner. The pregnant partner may appear to be interested in nothing other than herself and her growing body and baby. When this happens, the nonpregnant partner may feel unappreciated and invisible. Add this invisibility to her inevitable societal invisibility, and it's easy for her to doubt what her role in this whole process is.

These feelings of having lost one's partner are certainly heightened in lesbian relationships where the partners have a strong level of "merge." To have one's role in the relationship replaced by the baby can leave the non-birth mom-to-be feeling left out in the cold. What's hard to accept is that the pregnant partner usually doesn't even realize just how self-centered she is during pregnancy, or how this level of self-centeredness can transform into the same level of nurturing capacity to the baby. In fact, the pregnant partner can feel unsupported and unrecognized for all of the work she's doing, wanting the nonpregnant partner to put out more emotionally, regardless of whether she's capable of reciprocating.

This dynamic takes a lot of integrity to navigate as both of you are becoming parents and have strong needs from each other. If you're the nonbirth partner, you may feel this whole situation is more than you bargained for. You may feel exhausted, unappreciated, clung-to, bossed around, or ignored. Furthermore, your best friend and lover, to whom you'd normally turn for support, is the cause of the trouble. Get some support just for you. There are beautiful, incredible experiences to be had while sharing a pregnancy, and acknowledging the challenges in no way denigrates the miraculous aspects, so don't feel guilty expressing your feelings about the difficulties that may arise. It just may be best to go outside of the relationship to do so.

This is the emotional reality of the first trimester and usually at least part of the second trimester. Some couples get a reprieve during the second trimester when they feel like they can reconnect again. Other couples, however, don't feel they reconnect until the baby is a few months old.

MAIA TIP ON RELATIONSHIPS DURING PREGNANCY
At Maia we provide relationship pregnancy counseling for queer families. One of the best techniques that we offer is to suggest that at all times you are mindful of turning towards your partner. In any given situation you have the opportunity to turn away or to turn towards another. We recommend the meditation of always turning towards your partner. This requires letting go of the need to be right and the need to further an argument just to get your point across. It requires love to be your guiding force.

Mother Issues

Many queer people are alienated from their mothers simply because of their sexual orientation. This alienation may be a reaction to the pregnancy or may be a reality you've lived with throughout adulthood. Regardless, every pregnant woman seems to have a primal need for her mother. This need and longing seem equally strong whether your mother is dead or if she's your daily confidante. If you're adopted, you may find yourself revisiting your desire to know more about your birth mother. There just seems to be something about becoming a mother that triggers a woman's need for her own mother.

The pain of not being able to make the kind of emotional contact with your mother that you long for can be indescribable. It tends to cut to the quick of all of the abandonment issues each of us carries within. This unexpected need for a mother's love can often cause women to reach out to their estranged mothers at this time. Although some are well received when they choose to do this, many are painfully rejected again. In truth, it appears that what we are often longing for is the universal mother, the mother we wish we had, not our own actual mothers.

If you're partnered and one of you has an involved mother, she can act as a surrogate mother to the other. However, if she refuses, or even fails to recognize your partner as part of the family, the pain will only be magnified. She may be willing to step into this role for you if you take the initiative to directly invite her to do so and tell her exactly what you appreciate about what she does or can do that would feel motherly.

Some people find that it's most helpful to spend time in quiet introspection exploring what qualities they're looking for from their mother. Once they've come up with these qualities—be they unconditional love or a warm, understanding embrace—it's easier to work to fill the need. It can be helpful to ask for those behaviors or qualities from a partner or friend.

For example: Joanne finally got pregnant. She and her partner Deborah had been trying for more than two years to conceive. Deborah was in contact with her family on a regular basis, but they lived across the country. Joanne hadn't seen her own mother in fifteen years. During pregnancy Joanne felt an almost desperate need to contact her mother. But she knew that to do so would be self-defeating. One day she and Deborah sat down and made a list of all of the things Joanne felt she was missing by not having a mother. Deborah encouraged Joanne to be as specific as possible. Her list—after a good cry—looked like this:

⊙ Delicious, warm brownies made from scratch
⊙ Nighttime back rubs as I fall asleep
⊙ Hugs that let me know everything will be OK
⊙ Someone to cook for me without me feeling I have to reciprocate
⊙ Approval and unending excitement that we're having a baby

When Joanne had completed the list, she and Deborah looked at it together. Joanne felt much better being able to name what was missing for her. Just making the list had been painful yet cathartic. Deborah realized that although she would never be Joanne's mother—nor did she want to be—there were things she could do to help Joanne fill certain emotional gaps. Deborah got the recipe for the special brownies from Joanne's sister and baked them on a regular basis. She also gave Joanne nightly back rubs. As often as possible she swept Joanne into her arms and said reassuring things.

And she took over more of the meal preparation. Joanne and Deborah asked Deborah's mother to help with the cooking when she flew out after the baby's birth and to express a great amount of approval and excitement to Joanne specifically on the phone whenever she called.

These things, of course, weren't a replacement for Joanne's mother, but they did allow Joanne to feel unconditionally loved and to further heal the pain of losing her mother. Deborah and Joanne found that an active approach to healing Joanne's emotional wounds was best. It brought them together even more closely as a couple and invited Deborah's mom more fully into the grandmother role, which she herself found reassuring.

Donor, Sperm, and Coparent Issues

At some point in the second or third trimester, people usually revisit their donor or coparent choices. If you used a known donor's sperm or plan on coparenting, you may find yourself revisiting whatever choices or options you had for legal protection of your parenting autonomy. You may be surprised by feeling threatened, in a way you hadn't previously, by the idea of having any contact with the sperm donor or coparent. Don't worry, this feeling is perfectly normal. First, you may be developing your protective mothering instincts. Second, if you're the one who's pregnant, you're probably beginning to realize that your twenty-four-hour-a-day physical relationship with your baby is going to change at the birth. Most people face this prospect with a great deal of relief, but also with a fear of not being able to protect the baby adequately on the outside, and loss of the constant intimacy now shared with the baby. The possibility of the baby's new relationships with others that begin to develop at the moment of birth can get mixed up with your impending feelings of loss, and therefore feel threatening. It's helpful to reread any journal writing you've done or any part of a contract you wrote with your coparent(s) that reminds you of the reasons you chose to create life in the way you did.

Another common response, if you're planning to coparent with others, is to feel as if the coparents aren't helping out during pregnancy and to resent the idea that they'll show up at the day of birth to start partaking in all the fun. They may not realize which kinds of help would benefit you now during pregnancy. They may not have yet realized that paying for a house cleaner for you or shopping for you or paying for prenatal massage is in fact caring for the baby. It seems a hard leap for people to make, especially those who haven't been around many babies or pregnant women. Remind your coparents of any agreement you made along these lines or spell it out for them very specifically now. It is common to harbor some resentment along the lines of "They think they just get to show up at the birth after they said they were too busy to attend the childbirth-preparation class and too busy to help feed me." Make sure to start the parenting relationship off well by being extra clear in your communication. Often we think we're being heard more clearly than we truly are, so express yourself whenever you need to and be specific when asking for help or support.

If you've chosen to use sperm from an unknown donor, a number of issues may arise now that the baby seems more "real": What will she or he look like? Did we choose the right donor? Are we sure we made the best choices about the ethnicity of the donor? Talk out the issues once again as they arise, even if you spent a great deal of preconception time deciding carefully. You probably had very good reasons for making your decisions, but fears don't disappear by being ignored. Voice them and rediscover your trust.

Emotional Themes of Single Motherhood

The beginning of pregnancy can often be challenging for single women, as it is a time requiring great support when neither the support team nor the "asking for help" skills have yet been refined. It may help to know that for most women the first trimester of pregnancy is the absolute hardest, with great improvement often arriving around ten to fourteen weeks after conception. In the interim, contact every person who has ever offered to help and solicit them to pitch in, even if you're not sure what they could do for you. They might be more clearheaded than you and come up with lovely offers. Often the hormone changes at first carry feelings of aloneness, isolation, and abandonment. You may feel these more acutely if you live alone. Or you may feel secure because you've developed many skills and resources for both enjoying alone time and creating connections when you need to. Good for you if you have. If you haven't, here are some aspects of pregnancy that seem particularly difficult and are just the places to ask for help.

You'll probably want one or a few special people with whom you can regularly share all the subtle details of your exciting great time of change. Consider choosing one or two of them and asking if they'd be your companions in the adventure—they might be who you call at 7 A.M. when you first feel the baby kick, or who you call at 11 P.M. when you can't sleep because of heartburn. Some single parents-to-be have a developed strong network or friends—almost a tribe for themselves. These are usually very social people who prefer to do things within community. For these parents the challenge is usually about getting specific about asking for the kind of help you need. However the more solitary single parents-to-be have a greater challenge of breaking out of solo tendencies in an attempt to widen the circle of support.

Nighttime

Nighttime can feel particularly lonely for many pregnant women. You may be up in the middle of the night with insomnia, nausea, or heartburn. Hormones exacerbate fears and worries, and these can loom in the dark of night when you feel it's too late to call anyone for support. If you experience this, be gentle with yourself. Have a warm bathrobe by your bed and a space heater if you need to feel cozy when it's cold. Be willing to get out of bed, make yourself some food and a warm drink, read a bit of a comforting book, or even take a warm bath instead of lying in bed feeling miserable. Prepare anything you may need for this special 3 A.M. time and place it within reach. It's a magical time to experience that most of us in regular life don't have the opportunity to be conscious for. Sleepless nights can be a beautiful time to journal. We encourage all pregnant people to keep a journal. Pregnancy is a time of amazing intuition; later you'll want to be able to recall the insights you had. You need a variety of ways in your life to express and receive acknowledgment of the beautiful work you're doing growing your baby.

Avoiding Isolation

If you become too tired to do anything but work and sleep, let your friends know that you would like them to make an extra effort to maintain their friendships with you and to help you not fall into the self-defeating cycle of isolation: "I haven't seen my friend because life has been consuming. I can't call her now just to ask for help." Let your friends know you really want and need to spend time with them and explain that the time you spend probably needs to be a bit different than usual. They could show up after work with a meal to share with you, and then tuck you into bed by eight. They could socialize with you at the Laundromat, or in your kitchen as they help you prepare food on the weekend to freeze for weekday dinners. You may need to do your socializing in these ways so that you can get things done, connect with people, and still get as much sleep as you need (which is as much as possible).

In general, you'll find that your focus will be quite introspective: you'll probably want less and less to be in big loud groups. You'll probably be content to spend many minutes watching birds feed outside, letting your mind wander. This is the beautiful inward journey of pregnancy. It's essential to leave spaces of unstructured time in your life that permit this to happen.

Work During Pregnancy

You may feel under particular pressure not to call in sick to work when you'll be the sole financial provider for your baby. The time to think about budget and financial considerations is when you've just eaten and slept well the night before, not when you're throwing up at 6 A.M. Most people find working while pregnant is sometimes fine, sometimes fulfilling, and sometimes utterly exhausting. If you absolutely must work full-time, you'll find ways to organize the other parts of your life to let that happen. Getting a lot of sleep on the weekends and going to bed early during the week will be crucial. You'll probably do less socializing, and your house may not be as clean as you'd like. You may not get every closet on your list organized before the baby comes, and that's okay.

Asking for Help

During your insemination process, you may have already done the hard work of learning to ask for help. If you haven't, now is your chance. Sometime—and probably a number of times—in your child's first few years, you'll have to ask for help, whether it's carrying the stroller off the bus or tending to your child's needs when you have the flu. Does it seem impossible to ask friends for these levels of support? In reality, you're probably more hesitant to ask than they are to accommodate. You may have friends who feel that if you couldn't do it all on your own, you shouldn't have chosen to become a parent. These people will probably not remain your friends for long, and although it will be a sad loss, the loss is truly theirs. You'll find that you have other friends who are thrilled by your pregnancy. Whether they know very much or very little about children, they'll tell you they're excited to welcome your new child into the world. These people would love to help you, if you specifically tell them what you need.

As soon as you're pregnant and parenting, you may feel that the help you need is obvious and if anyone wanted to do it they would. This is simply not true. People who aren't parents often have no clue about parenting. They just need to be told. Because of this, some of your best help will probably come from other parents, especially single parents, who have the most to juggle yet know the most about how to support you. Get involved in a support group for pregnant and new moms, join Single Moms by Choice. People in these groups are your best source of after-hours support, because they're used to being woken up in the middle of the night. You may be surprised, but people often feel blessed by the opportunity to help, as long as they have some idea of what you need.

Queer Community vs. Community of Parents

Pregnancy may bring a loss of friends in your LGBT community. Many feel their queer community gets replaced by a community of other parents. In most areas of the country, lesbian parents are still few and far between. This is certainly not the case in most metropolitan areas or certain other smaller communities. But, at least for now, it remains true for most of the country. When you become a parent your priorities change, how you spend your time changes, and what you have the time and energy to do changes. As a result, you'll probably seek support and friendship from parents with children the same age as your own.

When you become pregnant these shifts begin to take place. As your need for rest increases and your desire to focus on "all things baby" increases, many of your nonparent friends may drift away. Although this is a natural process, it's still painful. Likewise, you can feel arbitrarily thrust into a community of heterosexual parents, unsure whether either of you want each other. It takes time to develop new friendships. Although in her book *Lesbian Mothers* Ellen Lewin documents that the priority for lesbian parents often shifts from having lesbian friendships to parent friendships, most lesbians would never consider straight parents to be a replacement for their queer friends. These are not interchangeable communities. Both serve specific needs.

If you find yourself outgrowing your queer community or if your queer community isn't child-friendly and thus has left you, try to make contact with other LGBT families in your area. For some this is easier than others. Actively making contacts during pregnancy, when you have more time than you would with a new baby, is a fruitful project to undertake.

Connecting with other queer families can be accomplished by placing an ad in a local newspaper or putting up a notice on a billboard at a bookstore or community center, or online. Be persistent in your search. It can seem as if there are no other lesbian parents in your area, but more than likely there are. Even in our haven of queer parents in the San Francisco Bay Area, we've encountered many women in our groups who didn't know a single lesbian parent before coming into the group. Many lesbians we meet don't even know other lesbians. *This isolation needs to be broken.* Meeting other gay and lesbian parents is a good way to start to get more comfortable in coming out. The more people you ask, the greater the chances you have of finding LGBT parents. Finding and connecting with other queer parents is essential not only to your own comfort and well-being, but also for the comfort and well-being of your children.

Partner Issues

If you're partnered, your transformations during pregnancy will undoubtedly include your relationship with your partner. Change isn't always easy. In fact, more often than not it's downright stressful. If you are a same-sex couple planning to have children together, it's important to look at the big picture. You'll need to make the health of your relationship a priority, as the universal stresses of pregnancy and the first year of life with a baby are tremendous. Add to that the pressure of internal and external homophobia, and you'll see that you're going to need to actively affirm your love for each other regularly in order to strengthen your relationship. There's a tendency for couples to give in to the stress of this time and break up because of it. *Get support if you're nearing the point of breakup. If you felt your relationship was strong enough to sustain having children, then it probably is.* We don't advocate staying together at all costs—being true to yourselves is the most important thing you can model for your children. Nonetheless, couples who make it through the baby's first year often regain what was fulfilling about the love relationship. By then life will usually have settled into a familiar pattern, and you'll be thinking about your next child instead of breaking up.

Some couples find that the growth changes during pregnancy help strengthen their relationship. They say they have never felt closer, that their love seems to blossom exponentially. Their sex life is great. Their physical intimacy is deeper than ever. These couples only have the physical aches and pains of pregnancy to deal with. These are the lucky couples.

Most couples—of all sexual orientations—have much more on their plates than just pure pregnancy bliss. Although they may be thrilled to be pregnant, the intensity of change goes hand-in-hand with their excitement.

When One Partner Is Ambivalent About the Pregnancy

It's difficult to weather the emotional and practical demands of pregnancy when you're in a relationship in which only one of you is excited about becoming a parent This can be grounds for much resentment if this has not been planned for ahead of time. Both of you need to provide room for the ambivalent partner to grow into parenthood. Pregnancy often becomes more exciting as it becomes more noticeable, which can lead to a deepening interest in the entire process for both partners. We strongly encourage couples and individual counseling for couples in this situation. It is best to gain clarity about how to support one another early on and what realistic expectations are right from the start. This provides the pregnant partner the opportunity to devise another plan for support if needed.

Many pregnant women, however, realize the ambivalence of their partner isn't working for them as they'd hoped it would. Perhaps they assumed that once pregnant, their partners would come around, but they haven't yet. Or perhaps they realize that for them it's too painful to deal with a lack of commitment to the most consuming thing they've ever done and what will soon be the most important aspect of their life. In these situations, unfortunately, breakups are common.

Where Did the Romance and Physical Intimacy Go?

Many people experience intense morning sickness and other discomforts during pregnancy. The loving, active, nurturing partner can suddenly be replaced with a napping, snappy, uncomfortable, vomiting partner who goes to bed each night at seven. This is all a normal part of pregnancy, yet it doesn't often gel with the romantic notions of creating a baby together.

Some couples are able to maintain an intimate physical closeness throughout pregnancy. They mutually enjoy the body changes of the pregnant mom-to-be and love to snuggle and hug and are constantly physically close. Other women feel like being touched during pregnancy is the last thing on earth that they want. They need to sleep with a variety of pillows in order to feel comfortable, and they're alternately hot or physically uncomfortable, so although they might want physical intimacy, their personal comfort precludes their desire or ability to be physically close. This can be emotionally difficult for the nonpregnant partner who wants to maintain the physical closeness but feels rejected in her attempts to do so.

Sex, Sex, Sex

FIRST TRIMESTER

Most pregnant women don't want to have sex during the first trimester. They may be concerned about triggering a miscarriage or simply feel too sick and tired to have sex. Sex is perfectly safe during the first trimester as long as you are not spotting or showing other signs of pending miscarriage. However, we recommend that sex be more gentle in nature during the first trimester. Clitoral stimulation is always fine. It's important to be gentle with the cervix during pregnancy, especially during the first trimester. If you feel your penetrative vaginal or anal sex is gentle and doesn't roughly bump the cervix, then it's safe for you.

THE REST OF PREGNANCY

Many pregnant people do have a strong sex drive during the second trimester of pregnancy, especially as increased blood flow increases vaginal and breast sensitivity. Some people don't want to have partner sex during pregnancy, as it triggers too many emotions for them. Sometimes people are too physically uncomfortable to want to have partner sex and are not with their partners during the few hours of the day when they feel good. In addition, some nonpregnant partners are turned off by their pregnant partner's new body or don't think it's "right" to have sex when pregnant or with a pregnant woman.

Many pregnant people lead an active sex life with themselves through masturbation. This can be disconcerting if you are accustomed to and want partner sex and your pregnant partner is content with solo sex.

At the end of pregnancy, when the baby's head is low in the mother's pelvis, penetrative sex needs to be gentle, especially with dildos. Myths about avoiding oral sex during pregnancy are unfounded; what should be avoided is blowing air forcefully into the vagina. Unless hemorrhoids interfere, anal sex is also fine during pregnancy. In fact, in later pregnancy many people find anal sex more pleasurable than in the past due to the hormonal relaxation present throughout the body. Another point of sexual interest is that breast milk may drip from the nipples when a pregnant woman is aroused. This is no reason for concern. It's an amazing thing!

Remember that the sexual spectrum is broad. What you desire sexually may change from month to month. You may feel awkward about not being able to physically get comfortable in your familiar positions if you're used to always being a top or a bottom. You'll need to get creative with your ever-growing pregnant belly and ever-changing hormones!

ORGASMS

It's common for the pregnant woman not to be able to achieve orgasm. She may experience much sexual pleasure but physiologically be unable to achieve climax. Likewise, some people find that their breasts and clitoris are so sensitive that they can become overstimulated quite quickly. And some have painful—though not dangerous—contractions when they orgasm, thus abruptly concluding the rendezvous. The painful, crampy feeling that occurs in the uterus when pregnant women experience an orgasm is a type of contraction. The uterus has many kinds of contractions that serve different purposes. The contraction felt during orgasm, although uncomfortable, is nothing to worry about and usually lasts a few minutes before relaxing.

For all of you folks who enjoy fisting, we are oh so sorry to let you know that it may not be safe for pregnancy. We know that many of you enjoy fisting as a regular part of your sexuality. We also know that plenty of people fist throughout pregnancy with no negative side effects. However, our recommendation regarding fisting stems from the fact that every case of late miscarriage we have seen (past fourteen weeks) and many of the preterm labor situations we have worked with in our communities, have been following a night of great sex that involved fisting, which has stimulated uterine contractions. Thus, we must caution you against the practice during pregnancy. Perhaps very gentle fisting with no power attached to it and little if any cervical contact would be okay. It is hard to know if it is the force, the filling of the vagina so fully, or the increased surface area of what can come in contact with the cervix, or something else entirely that causes the uterus to start contracting following fisting.

BONDAGE, S&M, AND PREGNANCY

Little research appears to have been done on BDSM and pregnancy. Are you surprised? This subject is a very interesting one, as there are the physical safety issues to consider, the hormonal issues to consider, and the potential emotional impact on the baby to consider. Let's start with safety. There are some general safety issues to keep in mind. First, no bondage or restraints that cut off blood circulation. No activity that decrease oxygen to the pregnant player. No impact to the torso, especially avoiding the stomach area. As for spanking or other high impact on the body, it is best to only make contact that will not reverberate into the pelvis and to the baby. Intense nipple play later in pregnancy can spur preterm labor. It is important to note that overexertion in pregnancy can also spur preterm labor.

We recommend that heavy players get into other forms of play during pregnancy such as role playing, light to medium sensory play, and easily removable bondage. If you restrict who you play with in pregnancy to people you love and trust, then you have the greatest chances of being fully present—thus deepening your opportunity to listen to your body. As with all sexual and nonsexual activity during pregnancy, it is essential to be open to changes in your preferences and comfort levels.

As for hormones, please note that both adrenaline and endorphins cross the placenta and enter the bloodstream of the baby. It has been documented that elevated levels of adrenaline decrease blood supply and oxygen to the baby. Endorphins generally create a greater sense of well-being. So it is important to examine the forms of play you prefer. There are definite concerns surrounding repeated elevated levels of adrenaline during pregnancy. Thus, it goes without saying that it will be best to play in the realms of endorphins. However, the release of adrenaline and endorphins often go hand in hand with kinky activities. Babies born from chronically stressed mothers have been documented to have adrenal stress at birth. Some studies have also shown that if a pregnant mother is experiencing adrenal stress she may actually pull hormones from the unborn's adrenals. So be careful and consider the effect of your sexual choices on the fetus.

It is believed by many that even during fetal life an infant starts to experience, becomes a participant in, and shares some aspects of the mother's emotional states, owing in part to the crossing of the placenta of emotional hormones such as adrenaline and endorphins. Likewise it is established that babies in utero can hear. Their response to music and voices and the ability to recognize different languages has been well documented. Likewise, there is an ever-growing understanding in the birth and psychology professions that babies have the capacity to experience pain—both emotional and physical—in the womb. And, perhaps most important, it is becoming more accepted that babies remember their prenatal life and key events during pregnancy. This is perhaps the most provocative piece of the BDSM conversation because it calls into question the issue of consent on the infant's part to your activities.

SEXUAL AROUSAL AND THREATENED PRETERM LABOR

If a person shows signs of preterm labor or is at high risk for preterm labor due to factors in her medical history, she'll be made aware of this by her health-care provider and be educated about the signs of preterm labor. People who are at risk should refrain from sexual activity. If the care provider is uncomfortable discussing lesbian and queer sexuality, he or she may not mention this. The activities to avoid if the pregnant woman is at increased risk for preterm labor are penetrative vaginal or anal sex that stimulates the cervix directly (the wall between the vagina and rectum is thin); nipple stimulation that causes the release of uterine-contracting hormones; semen getting on the cervix, since it contains cervix-softening prostaglandins; and any kind of clitoral stimulation, including vibrator use. Some people think that stimulating their nonpregnant sexual partner but not being touched themselves is safe behavior if they are at risk for preterm labor. Although this may be true for you, and you will have to monitor if it increases your contractions to know, for most ANY sexual activity is too much. This includes sexual thoughts and reading or viewing porn. For those without specific preterm labor risks, none of these sexual activities will put you at risk for premature labor.

Vaginal Infections and Discomforts

Some people get yeast infections more easily during pregnancy. If this is the case for you, be careful to avoid using lubricant with glycerin, which may encourage yeast growth. Many people have extra vaginal secretions when they're pregnant and don't need as much lube. These clear white secretions are normal and aren't a sign of infection as long as they're not itchy, bubbly, foul- smelling, yellowish green, or brownish. After giving birth, hormone changes related to breastfeeding will often cause a natural decrease in spontaneous lubrication. If this happens, keep lubricant handy, depending on the sexual activities you enjoy.

Some pregnant women get herpes outbreaks more frequently than they did before pregnancy. If you fall into this category, try to notice if there's any correlation between friction or irritation of the skin and your outbreaks. In addition, people sometimes get purple swollen varicose veins in their labia and vagina during pregnancy. These should be treated gently with minimal touch or friction. Since pregnancy increases the chance of bladder infection, it's a good habit to urinate after sex so that you'll wash any bacteria out of the urethra that may have found their way up. Natural remedies and prevention tips for yeast, herpes, vaginal varicosities, and bladder infections can all be found in natural pregnancy books.

Nonmonogamy and Dating During Pregnancy

If you're single and dating, or partnered and nonmonogamous, there are some things to consider during pregnancy. First, it's crucial to remember that practicing safer sex is important before, during, and after pregnancy. This is especially true during pregnancy, as any infection that you contract can have an impact on your pregnancy as well as the birth and potential health of your baby. Second, whereas you may have been comfortable with casual sex before, many people discover that during pregnancy they're no longer able to have sex without forming a strong emotional bond with their sex partner. Third, many pregnant people in nonmonogamous relationships become very insecure and want their partners to at least temporarily be monogamous during pregnancy. Likewise, many nonpregnant partners don't want their pregnant lover being sexual with others while she's carrying their baby. Be sure to check in with each other's feelings about nonmonogamy during this time so that you'll both be as sexually respectful and responsible as possible. Take the time to project into the future, recognizing that the first six months postpartum are likely to feel even more vulnerable than pregnancy. Many couples declare the first six months to a year after the baby has been born as sexually exclusive time—even if you are not sexual with each other much during that time—to safeguard the primacy of the couple's relationship.

Affairs

Just as with heterosexual couples, numerous women who are monogamously partnered with women become aware that their partner is having sex with someone else at the end of the pregnancy. Sometimes nonpregnant partners stray out of fear of the huge commitment and intimacy before them, and sometimes they do it out of a need to receive attention instead of give it, and sometimes they are looking for a way out of the relationship altogether. This is a painful time for all concerned if it disrupts the trust in the relationship just before birth of the baby—which is a heightened time of emotional need for the pregnant woman. It also raises concerns about risks of sexually transmitted infections if communication and honesty aren't practiced. Get some counseling if any of the above issues seems more than you can deal with by yourselves.

Pregnancy as Preparation for Birth

Pregnancy provides you with a daily opportunity to prepare for birth and parenting. As you learn to surrender to your body, you prepare to give birth. As you learn to ask for help from friends or a partner, you prepare to give birth and to parent. As you work with the numerous discomforts of pregnancy, you prepare for birth. As you come to love the growing baby, you prepare for birth and parenting. As you adapt to the constant presence of the baby in your life, you prepare for birth and parenting. Birth is the crowning experience of pregnancy, yet it's only the beginning of the journey you've been wanting for so long. In the following chapter we explore specific lesbian issues pertaining to birth and new motherhood.

CHAPTER 22

Preparing for Birth

BIRTH IS AMAZINGLY universal, regardless of sexual orientation or gender identity. Preparing for birth as a lesbian, bisexual, or single woman or transman of any sexual orientation is similar, although not identical, to preparing for birth as a partnered heterosexual. This chapter pays specific attention to the unique aspects of the experience for queer families within the context of the deep transformations that lie ahead.

The end of pregnancy is a complex time. Most pregnant people are physically uncomfortable, with numerous aches and pains throughout the day and night. Although some people still enjoy being pregnant at the end of pregnancy, many are ready to no longer have to navigate carefully with their ever-growing body. The discomforts of the end of pregnancy allow women to look forward to the next phase of the process: giving birth.

Most pregnant women become very introverted during the final months of pregnancy, not realizing how consumed they are with their bodies and their growing baby. This preoccupation often leads to a desire for quiet introspection. When time permits, a pregnant woman may realize she's spent the past two hours staring off into space. On the outside, nonpregnant partners experience this phase of pregnancy as a departure from the external world and thus a departure from any meaningful interactions that don't revolve around the baby.

Unfortunately, most pregnant people don't have the option to stop working as early as they'd like. Most pregnant people would be thrilled to stop working around the sixth month of pregnancy. In fact, many report feeling uninterested in their job from the early months of pregnancy. Due to financial realities, however, people don't usually stop working until two weeks before their due date, and many work right up until the time they go into labor. At Maia, we suggest that you look into your state disability benefits as you may be able to get paid leave from as early as four weeks before your due date. We recommend that every pregnant person take at least the last three weeks off, if at all possible. It will greatly ease your transition into parenthood and actually decrease your chances for experiencing postpartum depression.

Working during the last month of pregnancy doesn't always allow sufficient time to emotionally prepare for birth. And if a pregnant woman is partnered, work schedules don't often provide built-in time to prepare together for the big event. In this chapter we cover ways in which you and your partner can prepare for birth together and as individuals in spite of leading busy lives.

Ways to Prepare for Childbirth

Childbirth Education Classes

We recommend that everyone giving birth for the first time take a formal childbirth education class. These classes provide a wonderful opportunity to educate yourself about the labor and birth process. The first step for a childbirth education class is to find one suited to your needs.

At Maia we teach childbirth education classes specifically for queer families. Just to be able to bask in the glow of a room full of pregnant queer folk and same-sex couples is an amazing experience for all who attend. We know that in most areas you may not even get to meet another pregnant lesbian. If you live in a town or city with a significant lesbian population, consider placing an ad asking other pregnant lesbians if they'd like to form a class with you. It's not difficult to find a childbirth educator who's willing to teach a group of people who have already gathered together.

When looking for a class, there are a number of things to keep in mind. In general, we recommend looking for private classes taught by childbirth educators rather than classes at hospitals. A private instructor will usually have a more holistic, integrated approach to birth that includes a greater emphasis on teaching you pain-management techniques and ways to avoid unnecessary medical technology. If you have difficulty locating such a teacher or class, contact local midwives for suggestions and referrals.

When you've found out about available classes, it really pays to do some screening on the phone. Come out about your family structure in your conversation and ask the teacher whether she has any experience working with families like yours. Likewise, whether you're partnered or not, ask whether she regularly has single women in her classes. You may also want to ask about the ethnic diversity of her classes. Pay attention and take notes on how she responds to these questions. Her comfort level will have everything to do with your comfort level in the class. Keep calling instructors until you've reached one who has at least an open respect for all family structures.

If you're having trouble locating such an instructor, or the idea of being the only single mother, lesbian mother or couple, or pregnant transman in the class is intimidating, or you don't feel comfortable coming out in this kind of group environment, we encourage you to find an instructor who's willing to provide private classes just for you. Most childbirth educators offer private classes upon request. A good childbirth education class should help you feel much more educated and prepared for your birth. These classes are often emotionally provocative and can help you determine your hopes and dreams for the birth experience. The best book we have found on this subject is *Birthing from Within*, by Pam English. Besides attending a comprehensive childbirth education class when preparing for birth, it's helpful to explore the following issues.

Processing the Conception

When preparing to give birth, spend some time reflecting on the conception of your baby. How do you feel about the entire conception process? For people who became pregnant quickly and easily, there might not be much to reflect upon except gratefulness. If your conception journey was long and arduous many painful feelings may still be lingering. In fact, even though your pregnancy is almost over, you may still be traumatized from the conception process. Trauma doesn't disappear overnight. Depending on the particulars, this trauma can last for years. The intersection of feelings about conception or previous pregnancy loss and feelings about your current pregnancy can be multifaceted and interconnected. Fears, self-doubt, and feelings of inadequacy left over from an extended conception period can undermine your trust in your body. This impacts how you feel about your ability to birth your baby. Likewise, if one partner in a couple was unable to conceive or hold a pregnancy and now the second partner is ready to give birth, this can retrigger the nonpregnant partner's feelings of inadequacy, resentment, or envy that she isn't the one who's about to have the baby.

This is a fruitful time to explore individually and as a team what impact the conception process or previous pregnancies still have on you and in what ways it might influence how you feel about giving birth. Some people have residual fears about using an unknown donor. When they are subconsciously wondering if they make appropriate decisions it can also affect their ability to feel confident around the decisions they make for birth. So it is worth re-examining your feelings. By exploring these feelings you may be able to release some of their unconscious hold on you.

Empowered Birth

Giving birth is truly amazing. It's miraculous that live human beings, nurtured from our blood, come forth from our bodies. Our culture, however, doesn't always revere women's innate power to create and bring forth life. If it did, society probably wouldn't be so misogynist or antichild. Unfortunately, modern-day birth practices, which have developed within the context of our culture's view of women, often leave women feeling disconnected from their bodies and traumatized by the entire experience.

When we educate ourselves and take birth back into the hands, bodies, and hearts of women, where it belongs, birth takes on an entirely new meaning. (It is from here that our culture will one day embrace the concept of the pregnant man.) It's a life transition, an initiation on all levels. We are trained to believe that birth will be too painful to withstand and are encouraged to consider pain relief through drugs. As midwives, we've seen hundreds of women amaze themselves as they discover that, with support and knowledgeable assistance, they can give birth without the help of drugs or machines. When they discover they can do this, they feel they've been given the gift of themselves. Their self-respect soars, and they begin parenting on sure footing.

Nonpregnant partners helping and witnessing their pregnant partners consciously giving birth have a greater respect for life, their own role in the family, and the power of their partner. This shared experience also strengthens familial bonds.

Our goal for you is to experience the power of birth and for the birth of your baby to be one of the greatest events of your life. Your birth may take place in your home, a local birth center, or a hospital. You may use no medications to help with the pain; you may use many. You may give birth vaginally; you may have a cesarean section. Regardless as to what the outside appearances of your birth may be, we want you to firmly realize that you're the one who brings forth life.

Claiming your right to bring forth life onto the planet, rather than have your baby "delivered," is much more than just semantics. It takes education and trust. Claiming this power is definitely a lesbian and feminist thing to do, but often it seems harder for lesbians to claim than for heterosexual women. Perhaps this can be traced back to the conception and preconception periods in which lesbians and single women are routinely seen in the infertility clinics simply due to their lack of access to sperm. This pathologizing of our bodies right from the start can subtly or blatantly undermine our trust in our bodies. Making our conceptions medical events rather than intimate life experiences lays the groundwork for a medicalized birth.

This way of thinking about our own bodies is often carried over to the birth process, where we can naturally assume that we are "high risk" as a result of having gone through a medicalized conception. As midwives, we've heard numerous people explain that they would strive for a natural birth or choose to give birth at home but that this pregnancy was so hard to achieve that they can't risk anything during the birth of their child. This fear-based attitude is erroneous and keeps people from educating themselves about the actual facts and statistics. It provides them with the false sense of security that somehow abdicating responsibility for their birth experience makes it inherently safer. These fears may stem from the belief that since their intuition and opinions seemed to have had no positive affect on their ability to conceive, their intuition and opinions have no purpose in helping them secure a positive birth experience.

Empowered birth cannot happen if you fully abdicate your role in the process. By necessity, empowered birth is about the inner responsibility each of us has for educating ourselves about the pros and cons of routine procedures and for forming preferences about how we would like our birth to proceed, barring complications. This is empowered birth, and you have the power to actualize it.

Clarifying Your Birth Vision

Although birth doesn't always look or feel the way you hope or expect, it's valuable to spend time clarifying your vision for the birth of your child. You may want to review your answers to the birth vision exercise in chapter 20. Or you may wish to do the exercise again now from a new perspective closer to giving birth, before reading what you wrote in early pregnancy. In any event, creating a current birth vision is important.

If you're partnered, this exercise is best done individually and then as a team. Creating a concrete vision with as many details as possible is one way of claiming your power. This doesn't mean your birth will turn out exactly according to your vision. It does mean, however, that you've devoted the time and energy to examine what your heart's desire is in regard to the birth of your baby. It's highly valuable for all pregnant women to engage in this exercise prior to giving birth. It's especially valuable if you're partnered so that as a team you can visualize what's important to you in bringing your new baby into your family and the world.

EXERCISE: BIRTH VISION

Take some time in quiet introspection or meditation, focusing on the perfect birth of your baby. Allow yourself to fully experience whatever feelings or images arise. It doesn't matter what you see or feel or how that pertains to the choices or outside world; simply allow this vision to be just that—a vision. Notice how you feel during the labor. What helps you feel more comfortable? Where are you? What time of day is it? Who's with you? Are there smells or sounds that you're enjoying, that help you to relax? If you're partnered, where is she? Do you feel connected and close? Is this feeling important to you? If you're single, be sure to notice who's with you. Do you feel supported and safe? When you've spent the time to fully allow yourself to experience these feelings, write them down on paper.

If you're the partner of the birthing woman, do this same exercise, focusing on the labor and birth from your position. What does your partner's ideal labor and birth look and feel like to you? Ask yourself the same questions the birthing mom asks herself.

When you've completed this exercise, share your vision with your partner and your birth team. Which of these elements do you imagine will be easy to create? Which will be harder but worth striving for, and which will have to remain in the realm of your vision or be symbolically represented in other ways?

The Last Months of Pregnancy: Common Partner Issues

The discomforts, work schedules, and hormonal upheavals during the last months of pregnancy can create rifts between partners at a time when they'd like to feel closest. Though this is a common dynamic, it's often quite painful to feel emotionally distanced during such an important time of your life. Part of the rift comes from the distinct separation of roles.

Clash of Roles for Pregnant and Nonpregnant Moms

At the end of pregnancy, the nonpregnant partner often confronts the "provider" issues that fathers-to-be usually face. It can be stressful for the nonpregnant mom to embrace the traditional expectations of the father to provide financially for the family. Although this may not be the expectation within your own family, the nonpregnant partner will undoubtedly embrace this expectation to some extent as a way of providing additional security to the birthing mother. Because on average a woman's earning capacity is still much less than a man's, this stress can be great.

Nonpregnant partners may also feel an overwhelming compulsion to complete projects before the birth of their child. They're just fulfilling their own need to nest and provide for their pregnant partners a safe place to have a baby. To the pregnant mom, who often just wants time and attention with her partner, these projects may seem irrelevant. Each partner has different needs to fulfill to prepare for the baby's arrival. These needs, however, are often conflicting because the pregnant mom is more inwardly focused and the nonpregnant mom is often concerned with the practical "outer" elements of life. An understanding of the separation of duties at this time can help ease frustrations or fears that the nonbirth mom doesn't want to be involved.

Feeling Left Out

The end of pregnancy is often emotionally challenging for the nonpregnant parent, due to so much focus being placed on the pregnant mom. Feeling left out of the attention lathered on pregnant women can spur feelings of disconnection and isolation. Many nonpregnant partners wonder what their role will be in their baby's life. Will the baby love them? Will they share the connection that biological mother has? Will they always feel like the third wheel? Will they love their baby as much as if they had given birth? When their role is overlooked by strangers—and family and friends—their fears of exclusion may become heightened.

These feelings may be conscious or subconscious. Often the nonbirth mother-to-be finds ways to confirm her unimportance in the family by excluding herself; she may make herself very busy or start arguments with her partner. It's important in a lesbian partnership to discuss the nonbirth mom's feelings and to do everything possible to encourage her to feel and be included. The slights of well-meaning people can seem subtle to the unobservant eye; when the slights are daily, however, they add up and may cause a great deal of resentment and pain.

Approaching parenting inclusion as a team is the only way to combat societal neglect of the nonpregnant mom. For example, although baby showers are often traditionally given only for the biological mom, in two-parent lesbian families there are two moms. In three-parent lesbian families there are three moms. In gay male families there are two dads. Make sure the shower reflects and celebrates your family

The language you use to discuss the baby, pregnancy, and birth set the tone for others. For example, if you're in public together and someone asks when your baby is due, you might say, "Carrie and I are ready for this baby anytime now" (while touching Carrie). This includes a partner more than just saying, "My due date is next week!"

As the pregnant mom, you can easily get so consumed with the baby and your pregnancy that your partner can feel like she's not a part of the experience. Take the time to explore her feelings and to encourage the team aspect of the pregnancy and reaffirm your desire to have children with her.

Do what you can to help your partner feel more secure about her role and importance to you. You both will feel closer if you take the time to imagine what it's like to be in the other person's shoes and care for each other from that place of love.

Encourage Intimacy

Despite the various obstacles, encouraging intimacy throughout pregnancy is crucial to maintaining a healthy relationship with your partner. Therefore, it's important to do small things to help the two of you feel connected. For example, a nightly back or foot rub exchange is a nice connecting activity. Many couples claim they're too busy for such things; however, it's essential to find at least ten minutes a day to connect as partners. If you can't find the time and make it a priority to spend a few minutes together now, before the birth of your child, how will you find time for each other after the baby arrives?

During the massage exchange the two of you can share your thoughts and feelings about the pregnancy, upcoming birth, or parenthood. Try to center your conversation on something "baby focused." Making each other a priority will help you ease into the birth experience together in the spirit of intimacy. In addition, make it a point to ask each other for what you need and what feels good, what could feel better, and what kind of touch doesn't work for you. These tactile and verbal communication skills are helpful tools for achieving intimacy and connection during labor. Remember, birth is potentially a time of great intimacy between a pregnant woman and her partner. If you enter the birth feeling alienated from each other, it's more difficult to achieve this intimacy during labor. Conscious preparation is usually necessary for most couples.

||||||||||||||||||||||||||||||||||||||||||||||||||||||||||||||||||||||||||||||||||||||||||||

Maia Relationship Tip: The essence of our relationships is love, and yet we can forget to tend to and nourish that essence. When time gets short for connecting—the end of pregnancy and life with a new baby—it is vital that you still be able to actively feel loved by your partner. The love hasn't changed but the available time there is to express it is often greatly reduced. Without knowing it, we often express love to our partners in the ways we'd like to receive love ourselves. At these times we can really benefit from a love map of our partner. At Maia we recommend the following exercise to all couples.

EXERCISE: LOVE MAP

Individually make a list of all the things that make you feel loved. This list may include things as varied as: when you make me tea, when you call to tell me you love me, when you touch me, when you clean my car, when you buy me presents, when you initiate lovemaking, when you leave me love notes, when you hold me, when you do house projects with me, when you cook dinner on my night to cook, when you tell me I'm hot.

From this list, prioritize and mark the top three ways of being loved that you absolutely must have or you start feeling insecure. Share these lists with one another and talk about them. Make an internal commitment to show love to your partner in one of those ways every day. Keep these lists handy in the days and months to come. Feel free to adjust and edit as it becomes clearer to you what makes you feel loved.

||||||||||||||||||||||||||||||||||||||||||||||||||||||||||||||||||||||||||||||||||||

The Last Months of Pregnancy: Single Moms

When entering the last months of pregnancy as a single mom-to-be, many women are faced with the enormity of their decision to birth and parent on their own, which can make them feel isolated. Although feeling alone is generally not the governing theme for pregnancy up to this point, as your body gets bigger and it's harder to do things for yourself, it's easy to become jealous and resentful of partnered pregnant women. This is often highlighted when taking a childbirth education class, as the classes are usually full of couples.

Thus, preparing for birth and making it through the end of pregnancy are often one and the same. You'll need to enlist the help and support of people who love and care about you. You'll need to think about which of your friends or family members you'd like to be with you while you give birth. This same person or people should be willing to attend your childbirth education classes with you.

A single mom we worked with recently enlisted her friends to come over at the end of her pregnancy to help her clean her apartment. It was getting to be too big of a job for her to do on her own, yet she was having strong nesting urges for an immaculate environment. Likewise, in addition to forming her birth team, she had her church community and friends create a postpartum support plan for her. This plan included a list of people who took turns bringing food to her every day for the first week and then every second or third day for the next three weeks. Each person who brought food would stay for thirty minutes to help around the apartment doing small chores, washing clothes, or taking care of the baby while she showered. She had people lined up to spend the night at her apartment every night for the first week if she wanted it. This plan was completed in the beginning of her ninth month so that she could relax and get ready to give birth without worrying about how she would manage postpartum.

The Last Months of Pregnancy: For Coparents

Sometimes women choose to invite their male coparent(s) to the birth. If this is your wish, share your vision with each person who will be attending the birth so that everyone can be aligned with the spirit of your vision. We've found that it's essential to discuss, in advance, your birth philosophy with your coparents. Likewise, it's important to spell out how decisions will be made during the birth: whether you'd like their participation or whether their role will be that of observing, non-decision-making participants. Without this discussion, unnecessarily tense moments may arise during the birth.

For example, say you come to a point where you're ready for an epidural and have requested one, but your coparents feel drugs are harmful to the baby. If you haven't specified that you're making these decisions and that their role is to support you through the process no matter what, they may feel it's appropriate to inundate you with their opinion that you're doing damage to the baby. This can lead to open hostility at a time when harmony and unity are of utmost importance for all involved—especially the baby.

If you anticipate your birth philosophies to be radically different from those of your coparent(s), you may consider not asking them to the birth but rather inviting them to see the baby soon after the birth. You're not obligated to invite your coparent(s) to the birth. In fact, in our experience as midwives, if a birthing mother isn't entirely comfortable with her choice of birth attendants, no matter who they are within the family, labors that are longer, harder, and more complicated may result.

One lesbian family we know whose donor is an active coparent explained to him that they weren't inviting him to the birth, just as he had not invited them to his ejaculation. When put in such graphic terms, the donor immediately understood why they didn't want him present.

The Last Months of Pregnancy: Preparing for Birth Legally

How to protect your family legally is a dynamic topic as changes in legislation and court precedents occurring frequently. It's also a topic that varies significantly from state to state. We refer you to the National Center for Lesbian Rights (see the "Resources" section) for the most recent information. Here we give a brief overview of preparations to consider.

Durable Power of Attorney

Everyone should have a durable power of attorney, a document that empowers another person to make legally binding decisions for you *in case you should be incapacitated and unable to make such decisions.* The document should include information on your preferences concerning life-extending measures and organ donation, and, most important, who will make decisions about your medical care if you're incapacitated. This is especially crucial for gay and lesbian couples, who aren't recognized as spouses or partners in almost every state, and therefore don't have visitation or decision-making rights guaranteed without this document. Though it's highly unlikely that giving birth will incapacitate you, we recommend that you fill out this simple document for peace of mind and bring a copy with you to the hospital if that's where you're giving birth. You don't necessarily need to see a lawyer for this; sample documents can be found online. Regardless of your planned place of birth, have these documents drawn up and notarized early in the pregnancy.

Birth Certificates

If you're married in Massachusetts, or in a civil union in Connecticut or Vermont, or in a registered domestic partnership in California, your partner's name will be placed on the birth certificate, and your partner automatically will be considered your child's second legal parent. Despite this automatic protection, however, attorneys who specialize in this area strongly recommend that you and your partner also obtain a second-parent adoption to ensure that your partner's legal status will be respected in other states. See the next section for information on how to do this. In other states, the non-biological mother's name will be added after a second-parent adoption is completed, if you have this option available and choose it. Currently, there are only two blanks for the names of parents on a birth certificate. Some women see if they can get their name put in the "father" box, but this doesn't enhance their legal parental recognition in any way. In fact, if you decide to complete the second-parent adoption process, your lawyer will probably ask you to refrain from doing this until the process is complete. Each state sets its own policy for what can be entered in the "father" box. Some of the options in your state may be: unknown, withheld, D.I. (for "donor insemination"), A.I. (for alternative or artificial insemination), or the father's name.

Second-Parent Adoption

Although logically this process of securing legal recognition for a nonbirth parent should be similar to stepparent adoption, which is fairly straightforward, it's instead awkwardly modeled on traditional adoptions. Therefore, it usually requires home visits from the state social worker, counseling for all parties, a lawyer, a court visit, and numerous fees (which may be a few thousand dollars). Depending on your area, these may all be a friendly formality or they may be quite nerve-wracking. If the donor is known, he must sever his paternal rights and responsibilities as part of this process. The final legal statement entitles the nonbirth parent to the same full and equal legal recognition as the birth parent. Many partnered women choose to go through this process to obtain legal parental rights for the nonbirth mom. This is especially important for her when dealing with schools, medical providers, homophobic grandparents, or airlines, in terms of having decision-making authority. It also protects her claim to custody in case of a breakup. This process cannot be completed before the child is born and can take up to nine months to complete. Second-parent adoptions are available in about twenty-five states. As domestic-partnership and civil-union laws change in each state, the process may soon become much simpler in some states. In California, for example, same-sex couples who are registered domestic partners can now use the same adoption procedure used by stepparents.

Uniform Parentage Act

This is a recent legal precedent in California and in some counties in a few other states. It's a simple court order that acknowledges both the biological mom and nonbirth mom as legal parents based on their decision to have and raise a child or children together. To determine whether this option is available where you live and whether it makes sense for your, you will need to consult a lawyer.

The Big Event: Preparing for Labor

Labor and birth are tremendous, life-changing experiences. After giving birth, many women express that they've never done anything more powerful in their lives. Many nonbirthing parents express awe when they recall the birth of their children, saying that it was one of the most amazing events of their lives. In the following section we cover some of the issues that are specific to lesbian and single women giving birth.

From the hormonal research being conducted on the differences between lesbians and heterosexual women and birth, it seems that lesbians (and we would say single women as well), especially older lesbians, have prolonged pregnancies and labors. Our midwifery experience concurs with this research, while denoting a difference between women who are more practiced at letting go and those who maintain a high level of control in other aspects of their lives as well as their labors. The two factors that seem to reduce the tendency for these longer labors are: taking herbs prenatally to help the uterus be ready and preparing emotionally well in advance for letting go. There are many ways to herbally prepare for labor. If this is of interest to you, you may wish to read Susun S. Weed's *Wise Woman's Herbal for the Childbearing Year*. The herbal tea we recommend you take preconceptionally should be taken every day during your pregnancy as wonderful preparation for labor. See chapter 12 for the recipe.

Labor and birth involve a tremendous amount of letting go. Giving in to the sensations of labor and letting the contractions move through your body without fear or resistance are key to experiencing a straightforward labor and birth. It has been our repeated experience that many independent, autonomous women have a difficult time surrendering their control to the process of labor. This emotional theme of needing to be in control seems common for our communities. Perhaps this is largely due to the fact that in order to be a lesbian parent, trans-parent, or a single parent by choice, you must be inwardly strong and feel ready to confront the judgments of the outside world. People of such strength have often cultivated this strength in the face of great opposition. Experiencing birth, where strength is equated with total surrender into the unknown, often runs counter to the survival skills that have guided many women up until this point.

Thus, one of the best forms of preparation for labor is to practice letting go, surrendering, and asking for help. On a daily basis during pregnancy it's vital to cultivate these skills. You can do this through the simple act of finding an inner sanctuary of quiet, calm, safety. You can do this by asking a friend for a back rub or by taking a nap at work. In any event, it's important to practice the skills of letting go, surrendering, and asking for help.

Studies of the brain and neural pathways suggest that humans automatically respond to any given situation in the ways that are most familiar and most frequently used. Thus, unless you cultivate new responses to pain, fear, and the unknown, you'll slip into your trained responses. If you regularly practice creating new responses, you'll be more able to access these responses during labor. This is just like exercising a muscle: if your muscles aren't in shape, your stronger muscles must compensate for the weaker muscles. So, your best preparation for birth is to strengthen your muscles of surrender.

Emotional preparation also involves coming fully to terms with your decision to parent. Keeping the baby inside your body helps delay the inevitable: that you're going to be a parent. If you're still holding on to strong levels of internal homophobia or concerns about your donor choice, or worries about being a single parent, it's worth your time to process, process, process. This will not only help you become more comfortable with your choices, but also will likely help you shorten your labor time and not go too far past your due date.

||||||||||||||||||||||||||||||||||||||||||||||||||||||||||||||||||||||||||||||||||||

Maia Meditation Tip: At Maia we recommend that every pregnant person meditate for at least five minutes every day as preparation for birth. This can take place in bed, in the shower, sitting comfortably. The purpose of the meditation is to intentionally cultivate a new response to stress and pain: peace. Close your eyes and take a few relaxing breaths. Let your exhale be longer than you inhale. (This relaxes the diaphragm and resets the parasympathetic nervous system.) As your breath deepens begin to imagine your place of peace. For some this may be the feeling after an orgasm, for others it may be sitting by a stream in the woods, to others it may be listening to beautiful music. Find you place of peace and go there in your mind. Experience it. Enjoy it. As your mind wanders bring it back. Continue to enjoy your peace for as long as you can. In the beginning two minutes may seem agonizingly long, as you have to train your mind to stay focused. Over time, with daily practice, five minutes will bring you a profound sense of inner calm. Once cultivated you will be able to go there when you are in line at the store, while you are on hold on the phone, when you stub your toe, when you start feeling anxious, when you are in labor. Your place of peace is your serenity. It will become readily available; it only takes practice.

||||||||||||||||||||||||||||||||||||||||||||||||||||||||||||||||||||||||||||||||||||

Preparation for a Home Birth

If you're planning a home birth, you've most likely chosen a midwife who's familiar with and supportive of your family structure. If you're partnered, your midwife has undoubtedly encouraged the two of you to freely express yourselves as intimately as you wish. If you're single, she's probably helped you devise a postpartum support plan and encouraged you to invite a friend or family member to be your birth partner.

Because people often choose home birth for the comfort factor and have found midwives with whom they're comfortable, there's usually no context for homophobia to arise. It's important, however, to explore these issues, since there's always the possibility that you'll have to be transported to a hospital. So be sure to read the following section and discuss the pertinent points with your midwife.

Preparation for a Birth Center Birth

Birth centers are usually small operations with a few midwives and several doctors. So once again, although there isn't the same assurance that the staff is totally familiar and comfortable with your family situation, it's quite likely that every staff member has been briefed on your situation and is prepared to have you in the center. As a result, it's unlikely that you'll encounter any virulently homophobic or transphobic staff members. Some uneducated employees, however, may unknowingly offend you. Read the following section on hospital birth for suggestions to prepare yourself to respond to any such situations.

Preparation for a Hospital Birth

A hospital is by far the most common and complex birth environment for our families. In a hospital setting our families have to navigate many unique issues. This is primarily because there are so many people involved whom you've never met. You can prepare for some things in advance, but most must be dealt with in the moment.

As a part of your prenatal care, cover with your practitioner in detail who's in your family, what each person's role will be in the birth, and what their titles are. Once you feel comfortable with your doctor or midwife's understanding of your family, find a way for the other practitioners in the medical group to also share an understanding of your family situation. This can be done by scheduling prenatal appointments with the other practitioners and by typing up a "cheat sheet" that spells everything out for your provider to include in your chart. This enables whoever works with you, if they look at your chart, to have a basic understanding of and be able to use the appropriate language for your family.

SAMPLE CHEAT SHEET FOR HOSPITAL BIRTH
⊙ We are a lesbian family
⊙ Margo—birth mom
⊙ Joanne—other mom
⊙ Danny—Dad
⊙ Jeffrey—Dad

Margo and Joanne are partners. They inseminated to get pregnant. Although they used Danny's sperm to get pregnant they do not consider him more of a dad than Jeffrey. Margo and Joanne are the primary parents. They are partners. The focus of the staff's attention should be on Margo and Joanne as the parents. Staff members should treat Danny and Jeffrey as auxiliary family or friends are treated. Joanne and Margo are both going to be called Mom.

THE BENEFITS OF HAVING A LABOR COACH

We highly recommend that anyone planning a hospital birth use a professional labor coach, also called a doula. A labor coach is a professional birth attendant, a person you hire to stay with you throughout your labor and birth. She has many functions, one of which is being your personal advocate in the hospital. Studies have shown that having a skilled birth attendant at your birth will reduce the time you are in labor and reduce the likelihood of unnecessary interventions.

Having a trained professional who loves birth allows you and your partner or birth team to focus on the birth, knowing that your advocate will be working on your behalf to help you have the birth of your choice. A labor coach usually meets with you at least once prior to the birth to review her skills and your birth vision. Then during labor she'll either meet you at your home or the hospital and remain with you the entire time. It's emotionally satisfying to have a labor coach at the birth for numerous reasons. She'll advocate for your wishes medically, support partners and friends emotionally, and offer nonmedical suggestions to reduce pain and increase effective contractions. Nurses and hospital staff are often helpful, but they aren't with you throughout the process; usually, they just drop in on you from time to time.

Another benefit to having a labor coach is that she can act as your filter. She can ensure that hospital staff members have familiarized themselves with your family structure. She can ask for a new nurse if you have a nurse with whom you feel uncomfortable. She can come out for you to new staff during a shift change. She can be your buffer. If you want her to have this role, however, you must specify this ahead of time in detail and ask whether she is comfortable and able to do so. It is, of course, most helpful, but not necessary, if she has worked with other families like yours in the past.

LABOR ITSELF

Be sure to bring a few copies of your family cheat sheet to the hospital at the time of birth. One of these can be attached to the outside of your door, another to your labor chart. These will be visual cues for the staff to familiarize themselves with your family prior to coming in contact with you. You'll also want to bring copies for the pediatric department and the postpartum ward.

It goes without saying, yet it bears repeating—homophobia is their problem; there is nothing wrong with you. It can be hard not to internalize nasty looks, avoided eye contact, tense body language, and so forth... This is not something that you need to put up with.

Remember, you're a consumer who is hiring the hospital and staff to provide a service for you. Therefore, you're the one with the power. It's important to remember this, because if at any point you feel or experience homophobia or transphobia from any member of the hospital staff, you can ask for a replacement. Usually, in these situations both you and the person in question will feel relieved

We've heard of women who gave birth at a hospital where they hadn't met the doctor ahead of time claim that lesbianism was their religion and that they must only work with a female doctor. Although this doesn't guarantee a lesbian-friendly doctor, it does eliminate the possibility of having a male doctor, if that prospect is uncomfortable for you.

COMING OUT

If you're the partner of someone in labor, it's important for both of you to come out to each relevant person who enters your hospital room. When you're looking forward to the baby's birth, this can seem like overkill, but in the moment you'll understand the importance. If a nurse, anesthesiologist, or doctor is going to be providing you with care, they should understand who is a part of your family. Otherwise they'll only direct the conversation to the laboring mom and assume that you are her sister, friend, etc. If there is a man in the room, the staff will assume he is the father unless otherwise stated. If you don't come out, they'll ask you to leave whenever they perform routine procedures. You'll be excluding your partnership from the experience. If you take the initiative and introduce yourself and your partner to each person who enters the room, there will be little room for confusion. Having everyone understand the nature of your relationship opens up the freedom for intimate expression. Although you can certainly be physically and emotionally intimate without explanation, we often feel more uncomfortable and inhibited if we don't come out.

PHYSICAL INTIMACY

Holding and being held, giving back rubs, looking deeply into someone's eyes while breathing through more difficult contractions, and other kinds of physical intimacy are all meaningful parts of labor—as are terms of endearment, loving hugs, and hand holding in the silence between contractions. If you're not out or feel uncomfortable with public gestures of affection, you and your partner may withhold such intimate expression—but to do so only hurts you both. To hold back out of fear of others' judgments is both understandable and sad. Remember, this is the birth of your baby. This is your mutual entrance into motherhood. This is your experience.

If you anticipate that expressing physical intimacy in the hospital may be hard for you, you may want to spend time before the birth practicing being more intimate in public. Use this time as preparation. If you usually don't hold hands or hug in public, push yourselves to try to do so in places that feel safe. Labor support involves a lot of touch and kind, loving words. You'll both feel much closer if you're able to share this form of intimacy during the birth of your baby. A labor coach can help provide a buffer of sorts allowing you to achieve greater physical intimacy. She can also help you to work on this if she knows it may be hard for you.

Partner Issues: Dealing with Your Partner's Pain

Your partner giving birth is a tremendous event to witness and share. It is not, however, always easy to see your partner in so much pain. In fact, many nonpregnant moms-to-be find that they wish that their laboring partners would take pain medication just to give them a break! It's important to discuss in advance your philosophies surrounding pain medication and other important topics so that you're able to work as a team. If you, the nonpregnant partner, are "pro pain relief" and she wants a "natural" birth, you must find a way to respect her desires and support her through the contractions. The same holds true if she's "pro–pain relief" and you're invested in a "natural" birth. The person in labor should make the ultimate decision about what level of pain she's willing to endure. If you do have a philosophical difference here, you may need to do some concerted personal growth work surrounding letting go and allowing the pregnant mom her birth experience. This can be especially difficult if you plan to give birth in the future or if you had hoped to give birth but were unable to conceive or sustain a pregnancy.

Nonbirth Mother's Personal Issues

Sometimes seeing your partner in so much pain, or seeing how out of control she feels, or seeing various tubes and monitors attached to her body, can trigger personal sexual-abuse issues. Although this can be surprising, it's actually a common experience. If you recognize this may become an issue for you, it's best to take a proactive approach. First, seriously consider hiring a labor coach and informing her of your abuse background. Second, enlist the support of a friend whom you can call or ask to be at the birth—if only in the waiting room—so that you'll have someone to talk to if you need to work through your feelings during the birth. If you assume you'll just stuff your feelings down and tough it out, you won't be fully present for your baby or your partner.

Birth can be painful to witness as it becomes more and more medicalized. Some birthing women or partners of birthing women see many of the procedures as dehumanizing and even humiliating. Some birthing women and some partners find that the birth of their child resembled more of a rape than a joyful experience. If this is the case for you, you may need to do some fast growth work during the labor and immediately postpartum. If you're the nonbirthing partner, these feelings are usually best kept from your laboring partner. As hard as it may be to not share with her, at this time and during the vulnerable postpartum period, it isn't appropriate for her to have to take care of your feelings around the birth.

When the Baby Is Actually Being Born

When it's time for the baby to be born, everyone in the room is usually very excited. Make sure you have a spot where you feel included in the experience—whether that means holding your partner up as she pushes, holding one of her legs and being able to both look into her eyes and watch the baby emerge, or helping to catch the baby. Many hospital staff may enter the birth room at the last minute; don't let this overwhelm you to the point where you feel excluded. Assert yourself into your desired position so that you feel you are an integral part of the birth.

We've noticed that some couples plan that the nonbirth mom will be the first to hold the baby when it is born. This is a special touch they feel will increase their bonding. However, the majority of birthing women instinctively need to hold the baby right away. Then, when they're ready to let go, they hand the baby into the arms of the other mother. You may want to discuss these options together ahead of time.

If your baby needs to go to the nursery or the pediatric station in the room, it's best if the nonbirth parent accompanies the baby through all times of separation from the birth mother. If you're the nonbirth parent, you'll provide a reassuring presence and voice that your baby will recognize. Spend this time talking out loud or singing to your child. Your partner will manage without you. Although it may be hard to separate from your partner at this time, this will be a very significant bonding time with your baby, and your voice will guide the baby through all of these new experiences.

To prepare in advance to accompany the baby to the nursery, make sure you have drawn up your legal papers beforehand and have brought them to the hospital with copies, and that you've received the appropriate identification bracelets that allow you to enter the nursery as a parent.

Coparents and Known Donors

If you choose to invite your coparents or known donor to the birth, discuss openly and honestly what you'd like their roles to be and how you'd like them to identify themselves to the staff. Just as it's important to discuss this with your care providers, it's even more important to discuss this with the coparents themselves. Often women, especially partnered lesbians, don't want the donor or male coparents to receive the primary attention from the hospital staff. Because our culture is heterosexually biased, it feels natural for people to refer to a baby in relation to its biological parents. Thus, everyone must be reminded to focus on your true family model in order for something other than the standard "mother and father" assumptions to arise.

Be specific about how you'd like your coparents to interact with others at this time of joy and vulnerability. The nonbirth mom can feel especially vulnerable now, so it's vital to support her role as primary parent. Discussing possible scenarios in advance as a team will help prevent any misunderstandings later on.

Single Mothers

As mentioned, it's best if a single mother has at least one close friend or family member who's committed to being her birth partner. When setting up such a commitment, it's essential to clarify that this person will be available regardless of time of day or day of week. If she does have time restraints, you'll need to arrange for a backup person. Make sure your support person understands that you'll probably also want them to stay for the first few hours after the baby is born. In fact, whether you give birth at home or in a birth center or a hospital, it's best to have friends lined up who are willing to stay overnight with you the first week.

Although no one ever wants to have a cesarean section, it's always a possibility and therefore should be planned for ahead of time. If you do end up requiring a C-section, you may need around-the-clock support for the first week or even two weeks after the birth. This may include the time when you're in the hospital as well. In order to keep the baby with you twenty-four hours a day rather than have him or her put in the nursery after a cesarean birth, you'll absolutely need companionship because you'll need help lifting your baby to your breast.

It can be emotionally agonizing to think of asking for that much support as a single mom. It's much easier, however, to plan for these events in advance rather than to scramble for the support you need when you're most vulnerable. Contingency plans are essential. In the event of a difficult birth or a cesarean, many people have a backup plan for a long-distance friend or relative to be on standby to fly in and stay for a week and help out during this time of need. It's by no means admitting failure if you need to ask for help. It's best to plan ahead so that you're already prepared. A good way to do this is at your baby shower or to have an on-line schedule that people can use to sign up for shifts.

In Conclusion

The experience of childbirth can encompass every physical sensation and emotion that humans are capable of feeling. It can be incredibly challenging and incredibly triumphant at the same time. If you're partnered, explore all the ways you can do the beautiful work of staying connected as lovers and as a family during the birth. Whether or not you're partnered, organize adequate support for yourself and anyone else in your family so that you can focus on being fully present for the amazing power of this experience.

CHAPTER 23

Welcome to Parenthood!

CAN YOU BELIEVE IT? You're finally a parent! After all your dreams, plans, and attempts to get pregnant, after the long pregnancy and the labor and birth, your much-loved baby is here. Congratulations! Most people spend their pregnancies thinking of birth as a culmination rather than a beginning. With such a focus on getting pregnant, being pregnant, and giving birth, many new parents aren't prepared for the reality of being a parent. Postpartum — loosely, the first three months of your baby's life — is challenging for all new parents. For queer parents it can be a particularly stressful time, especially for nonbirth mothers. The personal challenges of postpartum are unique to each family, influenced by family structure, amount and quality of community support, financial stresses, challenges of the birth experience, and the difficulty of learning breastfeeding, to name just a few. Despite the wide variation of personal factors, many common issues arise during this time.

The postpartum period is amazingly rich: full of new love, new identities, little sleep, and more hormonal changes than you may have expected. Little is written, taught, or acknowledged about this special time. In this chapter we describe some of the issues that arise for most women, as well as experiences specific queer families. Each family will find creative solutions and support for their particular challenges beyond what we have the space to suggest here. Often, however, just reading a description of something similar to your own experience can help you feel less isolated and reassure you that no matter how difficult your challenge, you need not feel any shame or embarrassment or failure in asking for help.

When Can We Get Back to Normal?

You may only have a few other women's stories against which to measure your own experiences, since modern medicine doesn't recognize or educate about the complexity of the postpartum experience, nor do most pregnancy books. In fact, Western culture is unique in not embracing the first forty or so postpartum days as a sacred period in which mothers require special help, nurturance, and support. The dominant myth that women in agrarian cultures give birth in the fields and go right back to hoeing is based in part on observations by U.S. soldiers of women during war, and European observations of women whose traditional practices had been destroyed by colonialism or slavery.

In reality, although women remain active through pregnancy and early labor in most cultures, the birth itself and the postpartum period are respected as an extraordinary time of family life. In most cultures, families are protective of the mother-child unit, not requiring regular daily tasks and activities from the mother until about six weeks postpartum. Within that six weeks, mothers are traditionally massaged, fed special diets, allowed to rest, kept warm, and exempted from cooking and cleaning. Babies are held and massaged, and both mother and child are kept inside and away from drafts and strangers (and foreign germs).

The modern-day "superwoman" image many women aspire to involves greeting multiple visitors, keeping house, and losing weight, all while getting to know the baby, learning to nurse, adjusting to being a new mother, and healing from birth. Often, this also involves returning to work full-time outside the home within weeks of birth, leaving the baby in the care of nonfamily members. Many aspects of this "superwoman" role deny the birth mother's physical and emotional needs as well as the needs of the baby, the other parent, and siblings.

Moving through the physical and emotional transformations of birth requires and deserves patience, care, and attention. It doesn't make sense to try to return immediately to business as usual, because bringing a new person into the family isn't an everyday experience. Becoming a parent isn't an everyday occurrence in your household either, whether or not you gave birth. New rhythms, routines, and communications need to evolve, and the way to discover and integrate the ones that best suit your particular family is to give yourselves space to explore, experiment, feel, and heal. You'll find a new sense of "normal" over time, step by step. Some steps take a few weeks; some take a number of months.

The First Couple of Weeks

The first days may seem an endless blur, because day and night don't feel much different to the baby—and therefore to you. This time period is magical, yet challenging. You'll do almost nothing else than eat, sleep, nurse, and take care of your baby's needs. In the midst of these wonderful tasks you'll encounter a wide range of emotions, which are heightened by hormones and lack of sleep.

In addition, your body's physical changes during the postpartum period may surprise you. Healing from birth takes time and gentle nurturing. Although birth is not an illness, it's a huge transformation involving an amazing amount of physical exertion and occasional medical intervention. Each person heals differently, at a different pace. Each family gels differently, at a different pace. Patience and trust are much needed throughout the postpartum period.

The Importance of Bed Rest

We strongly recommend spending the first week to ten days almost entirely in bed. This advice takes many families by surprise because of the dominant culture's lack of respect for the postpartum period. In our practice, we've seen that women who spend the first week resting adequately and focusing without distraction on themselves, each other if they're partnered, and their babies have fewer breastfeeding problems, a lower risk of postpartum infection, and significantly less postpartum depression. People who do not rest initially run on adrenaline; when they have overwhelmed their adrenals a few weeks later they plummet into depression. For a healthy start to parenting it is best to rest and nurture yourself.

Eliminate any need to leave the house the first week. The goals of this precious time in your life as a family are to rest, bond with the baby, and learn to breastfeed. By spending this time in bed you will get to know your baby in a very deep way. You will gain the confidence of parenting by taking uninterrupted time to recognize your child's signals for hunger, discomfort, and pleasure. You will allow your bodies and spirits to heal from the birth. And you will ensure a more graceful entry into parenthood. Take this time to sleep whenever the baby sleeps. Rest is vital to mental and emotional health. You will be amazed how much there is to do, even when you are spending all of your time in bed! You have to nurse, gaze at the baby, change the baby, gaze at the baby, sleep, gaze at the baby, eat, gaze at the baby, nurse, gaze at the baby, change the baby, gaze at the baby, eat, gaze at the baby, sleep. It doesn't sound like much until you are there. Once you are there you'll see how all of your time is taken up in this cycle.

Make this time happen for yourselves. Ignore the comments made by other generations and do it for yourself, for your couple, for the baby. To do so takes planning ahead; at your baby shower get your friends to sign up for shifts on the meal brigade. Arrange for meals to be dropped off every day for the first two weeks after the baby is born. If you have older children you will also need a schedule for people who will come and take care of them or take them on an outing or to the park.

This rest period is especially important for queer families, as it lets the family relationships solidify within the home before you all move out into the world together. These relationships are so new and emotional at first that they need special nurturing; they won't get this nurturing if everyone is distracted and exhausted. The nonbirth mom especially needs a lot of time and recognition within the family unit and the partnership to ease any fears and insecurities she may have about her role.

If you're partnered, both of you may find it difficult to just be with each other and the baby and feel all the feelings of new parenthood. A common response at first is to feel as though you might go stir-crazy or need to run away. Using activities to escape feeling emotions usually doesn't resolve anything; it just sets you up for postpartum depression.

You're in the liminal newness of parenthood, and it feels unstable emotionally, hormonally, and perhaps physically. Be gentle and patient with yourself. Over time you'll get to know your new self with the same deep familiarity you may have been used to previously. Instead of engaging in your previous activities right now, just sit with your feelings, write in a journal, or do some artwork that allows your feelings to arise.

Postpartum and Breastfeeding

During the immediate postpartum period, you need to eat as well and as much as during pregnancy in order to establish a good milk supply and heal torn tissue. Extra iron intake is also important if heavy bleeding occurred during the birth of the baby. Drinking extra water helps avoid constipation and keeps the urine diluted, both of which are important for comfort if a birth tear or episiotomy is healing. New parents should drink a large glass of water every time they nurse as well as with each meal, to ensure that they're well hydrated.

Nursing parents need to be fed during their first few weeks postpartum in order to feel loved and nurtured. Making breast milk and nursing a newborn are acts of incredible giving. Nursing parents will feel emotionally and physically replenished if friends and family nourish them with food and drink. Low blood sugar along with sleep deprivation and hormone changes can make the early days of parenthood feel overwhelming. During postpartum, nursing parents need to have food and drink by their bedside throughout the day and night. The emotional vulnerability of early postpartum can often be alleviated by providing a nursing parent with nourishing food on a regular basis.

Arranging to drop off cooked meals during the first two weeks after birth is the most essential support friends and family can provide a new family. Even if a partner can be home from work to cook, she herself has just become a new mother and should focus her attention on bonding with the baby, getting enough sleep, and helping the biological mother with tasks such as bathing the baby and changing diapers.

A Nursing Diet

Some infants are sensitive to certain foods that are absorbed into breast milk in the first five to ten weeks postpartum. These may include spicy foods; cruciferous vegetables such as broccoli, cauliflower, and cabbage; beans, garlic, or onions; caffeine; and chocolate. These foods often upset the newly developed digestive system. Less often, a baby may be sensitive to wheat or dairy products during the entire breastfeeding period. These reactions fall more into the category of food allergies. This will be apparent if the baby continues to show signs of discomfort past the first few weeks and seems frustrated or cranky while nursing as well. These babies are often called "colicky," when more frequently than not they're suffering from an allergy to dairy, wheat, or caffeine. Sensitive babies often react with gas pains within an hour or two of nursing. Passing this information on to whoever is organizing the food brigade will help avoid unnecessarily challenging evenings with a cranky, crying baby.

Visitors and Support

If you've asked others to help out once you give birth, now is the time to get that help. They can be bringing food or helping to do a load of laundry or dishes if they have twenty minutes. If you are single, they might hold the baby while you take a shower. They might stay with you for a couple of hours so your partner or you can catch up on sleep. If your guests aren't actively helping out, they should probably limit their visits, if at all, to ten minutes. More than ten minutes is actually physically and emotionally draining for the birth mom, leaving you weepy and frazzled after the guests leave. It may be helpful to note that your cervix stays open for ten days after birth. Make sure that any and all visitors you invite over are ones that you want to take that deeply into your psychic space. Unfortunately, a classic dynamic we see all too often is that a guest comes to socialize and hold the baby, and focuses all their attention on the baby and the birth mom, while the nonbirth mom ends up feeling like a hostess or servant. Remember, if you're partnered, you both are new parents, and your guests should reflect that by providing support to you as a family.

Without adequate help and adequate acknowledgment of her primary parenting role, it's easy for the nonbirth mom to feel that all she does is cook, clean, run errands, and help out, but not truly parent. The nonbirth mom may resent her partner for treating her like the helper and herself like the "real" mom, or may feel resentful of others who see her in this way. If she's doing all of this in addition to working full-time, she may experience her own unique form of exhaustion that compounds all of her emotions. Whether or not the birth mom graciously thanks her, she should know that she's doing an essential part of parenting with all her logistical support as well as the direct love and caring she gives the baby. This extreme division of labor usually changes over time.

If you're the nonbirth mom, when your friends and family stop by, ask them to go ahead and heat up the food they've brought and feed it to both of you. Let them know that, like the birth mom, you're in bed or on the sofa because you're also doing the night shifts. Ask good friends to do any out-of-the-house family errands that would otherwise take you away from home at first, even if these errands are not birth- or baby-specific. In these ways, you can also receive support during this great time of love and transition.

Support for Single Moms

If you're single, remember the great postpartum support plan of action you created and be sure to activate it. If you haven't organized help, delegate this task to a good friend who likes to organize. All you need to do is give a list of names and phone numbers to her or him, and don't be shy. Your friend will ask others to organize meals, help with housekeeping and shopping, and help you and the baby heal and nurse.

It is especially nice to spend some of this time with other single moms by choice who have been through this before. This time is mixed with overwhelming excitement, awe, joy, and terror. The twenty-four-hour a day reality of parenting can seem quite daunting in the early days of recovery and hormonal fluctuation. It takes a while for new parents to get their sea legs. Don't panic. All you need is time to heal and adjust to your new life. If your friends and family do not come through for you, please hire a postpartum doula. You must be supported and cared for during this time. The love and nurturance you take in—whether from people you know or from people you hire—will help you refill your own internal stocks.

Body Changes

Tremendous physical changes take place in the postpartum period. Your pregnancy hormones will drop rather suddenly after birth, producing a variety of symptoms. These usually occur in the first two to five days, sometimes lasting through day 7. The most notable two symptoms are that your breast milk will fully come in—which may be uncomfortable and make breast-feeding temporarily difficult—and you may feel especially weepy and overwhelmed. Back to our mantra about limiting visitors during this tumultuous period: spend time alone with your partner or a good friend and the baby, resting and eating good food until the milk comes in all the way.

Many women don't recognize their vulvas after they give birth, and can become quite upset the first time they look with a mirror or touch themselves. Their partners may have the same response. Don't fear! The swelling will recede, skin tags from hemorrhoids or stitches will shrink, and normal muscle tone will return. At that point you will have newfound respect for your body. One client we had looked at us after giving birth and said, "Quick, grab a camera and take a picture of my wonder pussy." Celebrate your wonder pussy!

Breastfeeding Challenges

Breastfeeding can almost always be successful if you have adequate support. If you have a difficult time, call other moms who have nursed, your local chapter of La Leche League, or a lactation consultant. Call sooner rather than later. Some nipple pain is normal, but intense and frequent pain means you need some help. Trouble getting the baby to latch on, or concerns about not producing enough breast milk, can be alleviated with some experienced advice and enough support. Support for breastfeeding means being encouraged with confidence and patience on the part of others around you. It means that others bring you food and drink so that you have all the calories you need and are well hydrated. There's much more to say about the physical and emotional pleasures and challenges of nursing than we have room for here.

Dealing with Upsetting Aspects of the Birth

Birth can sometimes leave a person feeling raw and traumatized. Many women have to open their hearts and souls to give birth, confronting some of their biggest physical challenges in life and the accompanying emotional changes. In the midst of this they may be touched disrespectfully or invasively by care providers they have or have not met previously. Sometimes the birth goes in directions a woman would have rather avoided. Sometimes the "hugeness" of birth can feel shocking, no matter the details. Birth can stir up old memories of times that felt painful, out of control, shameful, vulnerable, adrenaline-filled, or frightening. And sometimes during birth we learn things about ourselves that are poignant.

If you're the partner of someone who gave birth, you may also have these responses. You may have doubts about the adequacy of the support you provided. You may feel great pain or disempowerment about not being able to fix or rescue your partner from the challenging aspects of the experience. It's crucial that you too get to acknowledge all of your feelings so that they don't create a rift between you and your partner. Your partner is healing from giving birth and processing her own journey and is therefore probably not the best person with whom to do all of your emotional work. However, both of you taking responsibility for working through your own birth feelings, and sharing with each other where appropriate, will bring you together as a couple even more deeply.

Whether you're the birth parent or the nonbirth parent, find the safe places and people in your life with whom you can do this emotional work. Not all friends will be open, supportive listeners. Find those who are and take the time you need to tell and retell your story. You may find it helpful to write in your journal or to process your birth with a local midwife. Ignoring the trauma of birth is hard on our self-esteem. As queer parents in particular, we need to start out our parenting with high self-esteem to weather the inevitable stresses that arise.

To approach this healing, be gentle with yourself about your birth experience. Let yourself feel any and all the emotions you need to. You may feel angry or sad about the smallest details as well as the largest. Give yourself permission to feel it all, but find compassion for yourself when you might instead reach for shame or self-blame. You may need to make peace with decisions you made that in retrospect don't seem ideal. Welcome to parenthood! Claim all the powerfulness and good work you did in labor as well as the hard parts, so that you don't tell your story to yourself wholly as a victim. Feel as much love for yourself as you do for your baby. You're as perfect as the child you made! You have all the time in the world to slowly unravel this birth story and all it has to teach you. Don't rush through it!

Sibling Bonding

If you already have children, it's important to focus on the process of sibling bonding. In queer families, our children may or may not be biologically related. You may be acquainting a much older child from a previous heterosexual marriage with your new baby or you may be introducing siblings with different birth mothers or even more part-time siblings who live primarily with other parents. In any event, it's important to foster their bonds and connections with each other. This is usually quite easy and natural to do.

It's important to make sure, if the first child or children were not birthed by this newest baby's birth mother, that they don't feel as though they become stepchildren to her now. In other words, the mother who just gave birth needs to be aware of including her existing children in her bond with the new baby. The biological connection between the current birth mom and the new baby can seem consuming and alienating to the other children and cause them to question their own relationship with this mom. This is a subtle but incredibly essential piece to keep an eye on for family harmony. The focus on biology from the outside world can sometimes underscore the feelings the older children may be having. For example, if visitors are constantly exclaiming about how now that she's a mother she understands this or that, the older kids can wonder why they did not make her a mother previously. Be aware that all siblings are sensitive to being displaced, and this added dynamic makes it extra necessary to provide constant reassurance of the invaluable role of each member of the family.

Fear of Intimacy

You may have never loved anyone as much as you love your baby. How wonderful and special to have your heart feel so full and open—and how terrifying! If you realize that this much love could be lost should anything happen to your child, you'll probably feel some panic. You may imagine this in the form of sickness, injury, or the death of your baby, or as the loss of your baby if you don't have guaranteed legal parenting rights. You may even feel trapped, realizing it's too late to stop loving this deeply; you developed this deep love in pregnancy or the first time you held the baby and couldn't deny it if you tried. In this situation most women find some resolution by looking deeply into any spiritual beliefs they have that allow them a sense of trust or faith in something larger or higher than themselves.

This process is important to recognize in a couple situation because either parent can experience it, and the response can often include pulling back emotionally from the partner. This pulling away can simply be a response to a fear of deep intimacy or it can come from the unfamiliarity of feeling so close to more than one person. When you recognize this, talk and share so that neither of you takes the other's reaction personally, but can instead support the other to remain embodied and closely connected.

Postpartum for the Nonbirth Mom

Vulnerability

It's important to understand that the emotional backdrop for new parenthood for all involved is vulnerability. In fact, looking back, most parents realize that they've never in their lives felt more vulnerable. Although in heterosexual families a man certainly experiences monumental emotional changes as he becomes a father, his role is clearly culturally established, and there's built-in recognition from peers about what it's like to have a wife postpartum and to live with a new baby.

For lesbian two-parent families, the birth mom and baby are just as vulnerable as those in heterosexual families, but in addition, the nonbirth mom is equally vulnerable. Because she has no legal or culturally recognized role, she can feel completely and utterly vulnerable in all ways. Thus, there's no one person in the family holding a clear sense of self, and therefore emotional stability, to ground the family as a whole.

Another easily overlooked component of added vulnerability is hormonal resonance. Your partner who gave birth is excreting a cacophony of hormones. For most nonbirth partners their own hormones get wacky in response. Birth moms, however, have the added benefit of prolactin when they nurse that calms them and fills them with a feeling of peace. To ease the hormonal vulnerability it is quite beneficial for the nonbirth partner to get acupuncture regularly postpartum.

If you're the nonbirth mom, you may feel quite vulnerable from the lack of public recognition of your parenting role. Others may ignore your role and your feelings, especially during the initial postpartum period. Innocuous questions such as "How was the birth?" or "How are you feeling?"—if only posed to the birth mother—can certainly leave you feeling excluded. When your emotions are so tender and new, especially from lack of sleep, the most well-meaning people relegating you to the invisible can feel heartbreaking. This is only compounded if your legal parenting status is unclear or unrecognized. Discuss your feelings and your experiences with your partner. Despite her best intentions, she too may exclude you in ways she doesn't recognize, which only heightens your feelings. With good communication she can be your most ardent supporter.

Out in public after your first few weeks at home, nonbirth moms are often assumed to be the child's grandmother, even when this is an inappropriate guess based on your age. It speaks to the extreme lack of openness straight culture has to perceiving family outside of rigid norms. Being mistaken in your role with the child may continue for some time, especially if you don't share the your child's last name. As your child grows older, he or she and you together will find ways of identifying or introducing yourselves that feel true and clear about your vital mother role, leaving less room for guesswork on others' parts.

Your partner who just gave birth may be feeling a newfound connection with the other women in her life, both family and friends, who have shared the experience of birth. This divide may be especially painful to you if you tried unsuccessfully to get pregnant before she did. Seek help from someone other than her on this one. Honor your experiences as different but equal. She has had a unique physical experience that she needs the opportunity to hold and reflect on.

If every postpartum woman, whether birth mom or not, could hold the awareness and compassion for the extreme vulnerability of each other in the postpartum period, weathering this time would be a lot easier.

Work

It is common for nonbirth moms to experience postpartum depression. In fact, in our families, if the birth mom is able to rest in bed for the first few weeks, it is more common for the nonbirth mom to experience depression than for her partner! This is due in part to the emotional sensitivity and the hormonal matching of the nonbirth mom. For the fortunate families where the nonbirth parent is able to take a few months off from work after the baby is born, this is not so common. But in more typical families where the partner must go back to work after one to two weeks it is typical.

The best course of action is to see if there is any way of extending your leave from work. However, for many families that is not an option. If this is the case for you remember that self-care is essential during this tender time of life. Remember to eat regularly. You may need to let your partner know that you are an emotional wreck and need a break from some of the nighttime parenting until you are more able to manage work outside of the home and sleeplessness. Take time each day for a quick walk and some centered deep breathing. Straddling the luminal world of new baby and the busy world of work can be a great challenge. Honor yourself and take good care.

Feelings About Breastfeeding

Nonbirth mothers may feel many mixed emotions about your partner's breastfeeding. You may feel jealous that the baby is so intimately connected to a part of your lover's body that she had previously shared only with you. This is normal. If many visitors and family want to hold the baby at first, their time with the baby comes out of the time you spend with your baby, because the baby's nursing time isn't negotiable. Therefore, it's reasonable for you to be protective with your time holding the baby. Understand that initially while your baby is awake it will probably almost exclusively be breastfeeding. And although at first the baby will be spending many more hours asleep than awake, a number of those hours will probably be spent sleeping on your partner's breast. In time the baby will space out its nursings and be awake for longer stretches. Meanwhile, the first eight weeks or so can easily seem like an eternity of waiting to have more contact with the baby, especially if you imagined that as soon as the baby was born you'd be able to begin a fifty-fifty relationship. The fifty-fifty concept is a setup for frustration for two reasons. The first is that in reality the parenting effort both of you will put out is about two hundred–two hundred! Second, each of your 200 percent will look different from the others because of the biology of breastfeeding. This does change over time, even though you may not be able to see that far ahead with confidence.

Feelings of Exclusion or Losing One's Partner

Many nonbirth moms feel that the birth mom has gained someone to love in the form of the baby, while the nonbirth mom has lost the love of someone, namely her partner. The birth mom and baby may appear an inseparable and whole dyad, complete unto themselves. Fathers feel this way as well, but they at least have their own socially accepted and unique title and role.

Nursing a baby, especially at first, can so saturate a birth mother's need for human touch that it may replace all the adult opportunities for physical intimacy and snuggling. Try to recognize this and don't internalize it as rejection. If you feel threatened, it's much better to acknowledge these feelings by discussing them rather than building up resentment that shows itself in other less healthy ways.

This is an important time for you both to stay connected to the idea that you made the baby together out of love and that you love each other through the baby—and also adult to adult. You may only have thirty seconds here or there to express your love for each other, but try to do it every day, whether by saying "I love you" or by acknowledging each other in other special ways. Give each other a lot of positive feedback and appreciation, whether it's about each other as mothers, lovers, or just as wonderful people.

Bonding with the Baby

The nonbreastfeeding mom may have many concerns about her own bonding with the baby at first in the absence of the breastfeeding connection and within the time limits that breastfeeding imposes. She may have strong fears that the baby won't need or recognize her. This may be compounded by the birth mom's attitude toward sharing the baby. Many people don't realize that mothering instincts, driven most likely by hormones, compel many women to keep their newborns within hearing and seeing range. Indeed, feeling that the baby is too far away or gone for too long is very excruciating. If your partner just gave birth and is feeling this short psychic umbilical cord, she may seem to be acting irrationally by not allowing you to take the baby outside or even into the front room of the house. This attitude has little to do with her trust for you and more to do with her inexplicable emotional needs.

These deep intuitive parenting senses may seem exaggerated and un-necessary now, but women who can stay open to them will be developing a most useful parenting tool. You all may have to laugh at the ridiculous aspects while still trying to honor these instincts because you don't want to close off or distance yourselves from the place they originate. The non-birth mom will develop her own maternal intuition in time as well. The birth mom would do well to try to communicate exactly how she feels to her partner whenever possible. Be very conscious about allowing the non-birth mom to develop her own style of parenting and providing space for her to figure out how to parent the baby on her own. You may be tempted to interpret the baby's cries or quick to correct her, but try to resist impulses such as these so that she can develop her own parenting style and problem-solving intuition.

One aspect of parenting that is often particularly challenging is comforting a crying baby. Regardless of the reason the baby started to cry, a nursing mom can often comfort the baby at the breast, while a non-nursing mom or coparent will have other ways to comfort the baby. The non-nursing mom may feel she is inadequate because the baby is so easily comforted at the breast. Babies are directly and passionately expressive of their feelings. Try to relax your shoulders, take three or four deep breaths, and while you physically hold the baby, energetically hold some safe space around it as well. That way, your child can feel whatever he or she needs to feel without being "fixed" or silenced. If your baby is crying for reasons other than hunger, everyone needs to be patient and supportive of the non-nursing mom's ability (and that of coparents as well) to develop her own connection with the baby, including a variety of ways to be with the baby when he or she is crying.

In general, each parent will need her own time and style of bonding with the baby. Sometimes because of living arrangements or the number of parents, each may feel he or she isn't getting fair share. It's helpful to remind everyone before the birth that the baby will primarily be with the nursing mom at first. Each parent is essential for the other roles she provides, even if they don't all involve one-on-one time with the baby. Nonetheless, there's plenty to do with the baby while the breastfeeding mom rests, including diapering, bathing, massaging, and holding it so the nursing mom or one of the other parents can nap. Over time, bonds will form organically. Each parent will have his or her own unique way of understanding the child and responding; the baby will recognize each parent's voice and style of touch. This may be hard to remember and trust in the beginning, but be patient and you'll be rewarded with beautiful parent-infant relationships.

If you're the birth mom in a family situation involving multiple parents, you may have agreed to a fairly specific structure of sharing in the care of the new baby before you became pregnant. Now that you're in the reality of new motherhood, this structure may be perfect or may feel wildly inappropriate. Renegotiate, if you need to, in light of this new awareness. Parenting arrangements need to be dynamic, changing to accommodate new needs and awareness as they arise. To discuss new or different plans than you had previously doesn't mean you negotiated in bad faith; it means you now have a much more realistic view of your unique new parenting reality and can more accurately represent both your own needs and what you perceive your baby's needs to be.

Second-Parent Nursing

If you intend to share breastfeeding with the birth mom, you'll probably find that the only information available is for adoptive moms. This isn't entirely relevant to you, because you won't be the only one breastfeeding. Nonetheless, read through any available adoptive nursing information and integrate it with the information we provide here.

Many women want to share in the breastfeeding experience for the unique bond it can create with the baby or for the physical experience of nursing. Some women have heard that enough nipple stimulation can cause their bodies to produce breast milk, even if they haven't recently given birth. This can occur, although in most cases women nursing in this way won't produce enough milk to be the sole nutritive provider for the baby. Nursing, however, doesn't have to meet all of a baby's caloric needs to be fulfilling. Nursing also provides comfort and connection, even if you don't produce breast milk. Babies have an intrinsic need to suck that is often greater than their need for milk. In other words, they love to suck, even if they're not hungry. They won't only suck on a pacifier or a pinky finger in these situations; they often will latch on to and nurse at a nonlactating person's breast, even if it's differently shaped or sized than their birth mom's breast. With this in mind, read on and then think carefully about what your particular interest in nursing entails so that you can decide as a family how to approach breastfeeding. Don't be surprised if the mom who gave birth has different questions and concerns. You should both learn as much as possible to start the conversation.

The birth mom needs to establish a good milk supply and breastfeeding technique with the baby, since the nutritive value of her milk will be primary for the baby. We recommend that she nurse exclusively "on demand" for the first four weeks of the baby's life. After this, a mother can begin to share feedings. Keep in mind that for some nonbirth mothers, the experience of nursing a baby they did not birth stimulates a heightened sexual response and it is not possible to nurse the baby. This is a form of direct sexual stimulation, which is quite different than its function as a backdrop of sexuality that is present with all lactating moms.

‖‖‖

I was very excited when I discovered the concept of second-parent nursing, though my partner was initially hesitant. After further discussion and research, and reassurance from our doctor that this would be safe for us to try, she decided it was a good idea, and was willing to try allowing me to share nursing.

Early on, I decided not to attempt to lactate on my own, due to the fact that I had already had my own health issues with hormones and was taking medication at that time that was contraindicated with nursing. So, my first challenge was to find the right equipment for nursing.

I'm kind of embarrassed to admit it, I was concerned that I had inverted nipples, though I discovered many women do, and so in preparation for nursing, I started to wear nipple shields in order to prepare my breasts for nursing. After some additional research, I finally settled on the Lact-Aid nursing device, and ordered one in anticipation of our daughter's birth.

My partner and I attended a lesbian and bisexual birthing class, and shared with our instructor our intention to co-nurse. She actually cautioned us to be aware of what kind of feelings this might bring up for my partner as the birth mom. She suggested that I be open to not co-nursing if my partner felt, once the baby was born, that she was unwilling to share nursing. Though I couldn't entirely understand this at the time, now that I'm nursing my own birth-child, I can see where some moms might have mixed feelings about someone else, even a partner, nursing "their" baby. Fortunately for us, my partner was comfortable with our co-nursing choice, and we had no problems in this area.

I so distinctly remember the first time our daughter latched on to my breast-I was sitting on the couch holding her not long after she was born, and we were both undressed, having skin-to- skin time, when all of a sudden, "pop" and she was comfort-nursing on my breast. I was startled, but it didn't seem to faze her one bit.

I found that our daughter was primarily open to nursing with me when my partner wasn't home. One of the most important lessons I learned through our process was to be sure I was prepared, because trying to check to make sure the milk was fresh, filling the milk container, taping the tubes to my nipples, all took valuable time when I had a screaming hungry baby on my hands. I was also surprised at how long it took to nurse-I found it hard to sit still long enough sometimes.

My partner had to go back to work when our daughter was three months old, and soon after, our nursing ended (though my partner went on nursing our daughter for two and a half years). I was really sad when she no longer wanted to nurse with me, but then, and now, I'm so very grateful for having had the experience.

Our daughter is four and a half now, and I gave birth to our son seven months ago. I'm the only one nursing this time around-and again, I'm feeling grateful that I had the experience that I did with nursing before, as some of the fear and concerns some first-time birth moms have with nursing just weren't there for me—so, with my increased confidence (and a former nursing mom to offer me advice) I look forward to a continued successful nursing relationship with our son." — DOREEN, 36, MODESTO, CALIFORNIA

|||||||||||||||||||||||||||||||||||||||||||||||||||||||||||||||||||||||||||||||||||||||||||||||||||||

WHAT TYPE OF NURSING WILL YOU DO?

It is best to prepare your breasts for breastfeeding at least one month before the baby comes. In order to determine what methods of preparation will be best for you, it is best to start by deciding whether you plan to nurse for nutritive purposed or simply for comfort. If you would like to be able to feed the baby you then need to decide whether to attempt to lactate/relactate or to just use pumped milk (or formula).

PREPARING YOUR BREASTS

If you plan to simply provide comfort-nursing or to use supplemental nursing devices, you may not need to do much nipple preparation ahead of time, unless you have very sensitive nipples. If you nipples are sensitive, try going without a bra whenever you can to get them used to friction. Touch them and stimulate them throughout the day.

SUPPLEMENTAL NURSING DEVICES

The supplemental device is a small container filled with breast milk or formula with attached tubes that are taped to the mother's breast. The milk flows down the tubes from the container, which is hung around the mom's neck, and into the baby's mouth as it sucks on the nipple. You can fill the device with breast milk expressed from the lactating mother, or formula if needed. This allows for nutritive nursing without the need to stimulate lactation.

LACTATING AND RELACTATING

If you plan to try to lactate, then it is vital to stimulate the breasts. A study of 240 adoptive mothers showed that women who used no breast pumping at all did as well in terms of milk supply as the women who faithfully pumped. In fact, studies of prolactin secretion (the hormone needed for milk production), infant suckling, self-stimulation of the breasts, partner suckling, and breast pumping all showed that nursing a baby of course scored the highest; next was massage and self-stimulation. Breast pumps scored the lowest.

If you have nursed before but are not pregnant this time, it is probably going to be relatively easy to relactate through nursing the baby alone. Although at first the baby will be dry sucking, with stimulation relactation will occur.

Take the time a few times a day to manipulate your nipples and massage your breasts. Do so in a relaxed manner while changing your clothes, bathing, while in bed. This will also help to emotionally prepare you for the intimacy of nursing.

BREAST PUMPS

There's some controversy about using the breast pump to stimulate milk production. Some feel it's unwise to prepare with a pump because it will distract you from the experience at hand and because the slight amount of milk produced, if any, can discourage you easily and lead you to give up. If you choose to pump anyway, start pumping a few weeks before latching the baby on. Moisten your nipples and start slowly pumping with a breast pump. This will help increase the elasticity of the nipples and areola and get you used to the feeling of nursing. Electric pumps such as the Medela Lactina work best because you can double-pump (pump on both breasts simultaneously) which will increase the levels of prolactin in your body. Pump three times per twenty-four-hour period, gradually increasing to eight times per twenty-four hours. Pump three minutes on each side, gradually increasing to six minutes per side.

HORMONES

Some doctors prescribe hormones to stimulate breast-milk production. These hormones, however, haven't undergone much clinical testing, and there are a number of drawbacks to using them. For starters, they're expensive and not always effective, and they may cause undesired side effects. In addition, the use of these hormones requires physician supervision and is not advisable for women with low blood pressure or depression. As an alternative, many nonbirth mothers take safe and gentle herbs to boost their breast-milk production.

Herbal extracts and tinctures can be used in combination with regular breast stimulation to encourage milk production in nonpregnant women. Goat's rue increases mammary tissue, increasing the ability to produce milk. Fenugreek seed, blessed thistle, nettle leaf, and fennel seed can be used to increase milk production and flow from already developed mammary tissue, but should not be taken while pregnant. Raspberry leaf and alfalfa leaf are gentler herbs that can be used in pregnancy to encourage milk production after birth. MotherLove sells a variety of breastfeeding support products, including More Milk Special Blend, which contains five herbs especially for women who have limited or no milk production.

The Next Weeks and Months
Returning to Work

This topic warrants thorough discussion, since work arrangements may greatly influence the structure and quality of family life. Sexism and the inherent lack of respect for children in our culture unnecessarily limit our options. Usually, state disability will reimburse the birth mom a portion of her regular salary from up to four weeks before the due date to six weeks after the baby's birth (eight if birthed by cesarean). The Family and Medical Leave Act allows a parent up to twelve weeks of unpaid leave to care for her child. Some workplaces offer a longer paid maternity leave than six weeks. Others offer the option of taking more time off unpaid. Still others expect you back at work six weeks postpartum. If you're partnered, your partner should inquire about her company's maternity and paternity leaves to see which she may qualify for or prefer to use—believe it or not! Many progressive companies are recognizing new mothers who haven't given birth, through awareness of domestic partner families and families formed through adoption. Don't let your own homophobia prevent you from exploring and obtaining the most leave time you can both for emotional security and depth of bonding.

You may choose to go back to work when your leave runs out, or sooner. You may choose to stop working entirely for six months, one year, or longer. You might try to job-share, reducing your hours to part-time and asking your workplace to hire someone for the other hours. Perhaps you can work from home or telecommute part-time. Some workplaces are amenable to your having the baby there at least part-time until he or she starts to crawl, although you should realize that you'll work more slowly and less efficiently this way. Perhaps you and your partner or coparents can arrange your schedules so that you don't have to hire a child-care provider. Once the birth mom's milk supply is well-established—at six to eight weeks after birth—she may choose to return to work and express milk so that the nonbirth mom can stay home with the baby. Or perhaps you're single and must work full-time relatively soon after you give birth in order to keep your job security or pay the bills.

Explore as many creative child-care and work options as possible, daring to ask your boss for arrangements they may not usually offer, just to have the options that best suit your family. Good child care is difficult to find and isn't subsidized, so we often have to settle for something less than ideal. Nonetheless, listen to your heart. If your situation doesn't feel right, go back to the drawing board. Ask other parents about local resources or arrangements they may have discovered.

Gender-Queer Parenting

More and more families have at least one parent who does not identify within the established gender binary. Some people are aware of their own gender twists but some are not. In either case, these new parents may have assumed that they would feel more "motherly" once the baby was born. As someone in a female body, it is common to assume that you will feel like your child's mother. When the baby arrives, however, it becomes clear to many people that the term "mother" is not something or someone they resonate with. In fact, they can feel alienated by the very association. For some, this association is subconscious and they fear they may be resisting parenting or rejecting the baby. It may take a while to realize the reason you don't feel like your child's mother is because you don't feel like their mother, *not* that you don't feel like their parent. Gender-identity issues are complex and confusing, especially if you have not directly confronted this within yourself before.

Take the time to really explore what you are feeling. Many, many of the parents we work with feel great relief just in knowing they are not alone with this feeling. Over time you may come to feel more comfortable with "mother" terminology, but you may not. You may choose a more typical masculine connotation for parent or you may come up with your own gender-neutral name for yourself. We have met Babas, Dadas, Papis, Momos, Papamamas—the list goes on.

Of course, as you gain clarity you must share that clarity with your friends and family so that they don't continue to refer to you as Mommy if it makes you cringe!

Postpartum Depression

Many different theories look to specific hormonal, physiological, or emotional causes of postpartum depression. The unique combination of all the above is, of course, relevant to each woman suffering this hardship. The brain biochemistry of some women is deeply affected and perhaps unbalanced once the surging hormones of birth drop off suddenly and are replaced by breastfeeding hormones. Lack of sleep and frequent low blood sugar can feel destabilizing mentally and lead to feeling blue or overwhelmed. Always germane are the psychosocial issues we've described that come to bear during the postpartum period: old memories of trauma or abuse, past birth issues, how you were or were not loved as an infant, and isolation or lack of support through a very challenging time of transition involving your most core identity. Many women feel periods of blueness, sadness, or even surges of grief, anger, or fear in the postpartum period.

This form of depression is often greatly relieved by increased rest, increased nutritive intake (you need even more calories now than when you were pregnant), acupuncture, drinking your tea every day, and gentle herbs such as motherwort. Postpartum care providers are able to provide assistance to your family even months after the birth if you just need someone to nurture you.

Clinical depression, however, is usually more constant and can move from "low" feelings to general apathy, sleep disturbance, lack of caring for or about the baby or yourself, loss of appetite, and a downward spiral of isolation. Please reach out for help if you have these signs and they're not disappearing. Please seek assistance if you're the partner or friend of someone with these symptoms. Call a local counseling hotline, ask your midwife or obstetrician for a referral, or even ask for a referral from your local hospital's labor and delivery unit.

The nonbirth mom isn't immune to depression herself. She faces similar new parenting stresses and lack of sleep, as well as often having to return to work before she's ready. She has many roles to balance—with very few roles models—as she her way through issues that both mothers and fathers experience culturally. She too may need support and counseling.

Postpartum Sex

When your body may be ready to have sex often has little bearing on when you're emotionally ready to have sex. It's safe to resume vaginal penetration and oral sex as soon as the birth mom's postpartum bleeding has completely stopped. When bleeding stops, the uterus has closed and healed and is no longer at risk for infection by germs that may enter the vagina. This can happen anywhere from two to six weeks after giving birth. Before the bleeding has stopped, women can get in a well-cleaned bathtub with plain water or water and specific herbs that speed up the healing process (called sitz herbs), but should avoid putting anything in the vagina, including fingers, swimming-pool water, vibrators, and tampons. Clean vibrators or clean fingers can be used for external clitoral stimulation if it feels comfortable.

After a woman gives birth vaginally, the inside of her vulva is different than it was before. All of the folds inside the vagina were stretched to capacity and then reshaped themselves once the baby was born. Nerves that received pressure may take up to six months to regrow, and after they do, many women experience new and different areas of vaginal sensation. Newly healed tissue is very sensitive. Initially, it may feel too sensitive for any stimulation, but eventually it may feel pleasantly extrasensitive. Each time we give birth vaginally, our vaginas change significantly, and we get to explore them anew when we are ready. If you had a cesarean birth, you may also feel changes in your vagina if you labored to the extent that the baby's head came low into your pelvis.

As a result of these changes, our internal markers of pleasure often have changed, leading to our feeling new and vulnerable about sex. Don't count on liking or desiring the same kind of touch or sexual stimulation as you did prior to pregnancy and birth. Sometimes it's frightening or upsetting that nothing feels familiar. Instead, try to think of sex as a new opportunity for exploration and variation of pleasure. Postpartum sex is about rediscovery. Therefore, you'll need to be extra sure to communicate verbally what feels good and what doesn't. If you're breastfeeding, the new hormones will suppress some of your estrogen production. This means you may not self-lubricate as much when you're sexually aroused as you did previously. If your partner counts on your vaginal wetness as a sign of your pleasure, she may be confused, and so may you. This may no longer be a reliable marker of sexual arousal. So use extra lubricant if you need it and communicate to your partner that you're turned on!

Some women like to have a lot more vaginal penetration after they've given birth because it's more comfortable than it was previously or their vaginas are more sensitive now. Other women feel exactly the opposite. Still others may enjoy penetration but need it to be much slower or gentler. Breastfeeding moms and nonbirth moms alike often feel as if the birth mom's breasts are no longer a sexual object: they've become functional and sacred for the sole use of the baby. Although this is true for many women, others experience newfound sexual sensitivity in their breasts and enjoy nipple or breast contact tremendously. Most women will leak milk, especially early on, when sexually aroused. Check out how sexual breast contact feels for you before deciding to avoid it all together.

Not only the physical aspect of sex after childbirth is difficult for many women—the emotional side is often just as challenging. Just because a woman has healed physically doesn't mean she has emotionally. If the birth involved trauma or vaginal tearing, or postpartum or breastfeeding challenges, it may take quite some time before the birthing woman is ready to have anyone—including herself—touch her vulva. This reconnection to the body and emotions may take many months to complete. In fact, the desire to resume sexual contact often does not occur before deep emotions about the birth begin to be resolved. These feelings may take up to a year to surface.

Likewise, the nonbirth mom can also have issues that arose during the birth that make it difficult to resume being sexual again. Sometimes just watching your partner go through so much pain is hard to let go of. Any intimate contact can bring you to that memory, possibly bringing up sadness, anger, helplessness, or even guilt. Having witnessed vaginal trauma such as tearing, episiotomy, or suturing can be enough to quell the libido for some time. Sometimes having watched your partner's vulva stretch so widely and have a baby emerge from what used to be her "honey pot" may put you in too much awe to touch it. If during labor you watched many people touch her vagina—especially if they did so roughly or nonconsensually—either you or she may feel as if it's not hers anymore for herself or for you. You may have just as much healing to do as she has, and the things you find difficult may be entirely different from her experience. Talk about this, if not with your partner then with others, including your midwife or a counselor if you need to.

Many women feel uncomfortable with their bigger bodies after they give birth, which affects their ability to perceive themselves as sexually desirable or their desire to be naked. Body image, self-esteem, and libido go hand in hand for many women. Being able to talk about this openly with your sexual partner can help to relieve any shame or negative feelings.

Some mothers are unable to let go in a sexual fashion after giving birth. The vigilance of new motherhood has grabbed them in a deep way. In this case it is important to go slowly and relearn the way to sexual surrender. It is okay to be a mom and have sex; it is not being a neglectful parent to let your guard down. Turn the baby monitor up and go into another room if you are unable to get in the mood with the baby asleep in the same room with you.

Some nonbirth moms find that after childbirth they're no longer sexually attracted to their partner since they see her as a mother instead of a lover. Sometimes birth moms feel the same way. They're too exhausted and consumed with breastfeeding to even think about sex. Prolactin, the nursing hormone, can really dampen sex drive, although sex drive usually resumes for all involved at some point during the first year after childbirth. Often for the birth mom it coincides with either her nursing hormones dropping as the baby eats more solid food or experiencing lifestyle changes that allow her to spend more time alone replenishing her reserves, so that she feels more capacity to share her body not only with the baby but also with her partner. Although partnered lesbians may spend some time with their sexual desires out of sync with each other, they'll eventually match up. However, finding time and energy logistically as well as emotionally to make love while parenting is a whole new ball game. Take it when and where you can, and in the interim remember that there are many nonsexual ways to express physical intimacy and nurturing with each other. If, however, either mom is delaying any sexual expression more than ten months postpartum it may be a good time to seek therapy to help resolve the underlying issues.

Sex and Single Moms

Most single moms are content with solo sex for a long while after giving birth. The length of time that this feels complete varies widely from woman to woman. Many single women don't have the time or energy to date at all in the first year postpartum and feel just fine about that. Some don't want to have sex with anyone until they've met someone who could potentially be a long-term partner, whereas other single moms are much more interested in casual sex, since they're not presently able to even think about putting energy into a potentially long-term relationship. Dating nonparents usually involves a lot of explaining and educating before you can both share similar expectations of the type and schedule of time you'll have together. Dating other parents can be logistically challenging, although potentially more emotionally supportive. Don't worry—you will have sex again. Many, many people find moms sexy.

CHAPTER 24

Parting Words . . .

AMIDST ALL THE awkward changes, diapers, and sleepless nights, you'll find moments stretching into hours of pure ecstatic love. You'll hold your baby while she or he sleeps, watching your child inhale and exhale, and your heart will feel full of compassionate love. You might catch the way your baby's breath quickens at the sound of your voice when you enter the room or how your baby's eyes stare into yours when you bring your face near, and you realize at that moment your child loves you just as fully as you love him or her. If you're partnered, you might see the tenderness with which your partner holds the baby, and you'll feel the adoring love you have for her well up in your heart, realizing you've embarked upon a miraculous journey together. You might find yourself in a moment feeling fully present and competent as you care for your child or reflecting on the pride you have at growing and birthing your baby, and you'll realize you have a newfound deep unconditional love for yourself.

This deep sense of love and joy can be found many times a day in parenting. It's from this place that you'll renew your monumental parenting patience when it runs low. Sometimes we do a funny process of limiting how much happiness or joy we feel, whether we're afraid to lose that joy because we don't trust that it's sustainable or because we don't feel we deserve that much joy and love. Joy and love are our birthrights. They're the deep rewards of parenting. Soak them up.

AS MIDWIVES WHO have helped thousands queer and straight people create family, we feel it's safe to say that the people who spend the most time prior to parenting clarifying their intentions, goals, and expectations from each family member are the families who start parenting on the strongest footing. They are also the families who have the greatest chances of staying together through the daily challenges of parenting. Conception, pregnancy, and birth are truly just the beginning steps of the lifelong journey of parenting. It is hard to imagine that birth is just the beginning when you have come so far to get to the point of giving birth! Clarity in this part of the journey, however, carries over to deeper confidence and clarity in the second half of your life: actual day-to-day parenting.

We hope that this book has allowed you to feel that the path to pregnancy, birth, and parenthood is a little clearer, easier, and more accessible. We also hope it has guided you through the many decisions you as a lesbian, bisexual, trans-person, or single woman of any orientation, have to make in order to become parents—thereby helping you identify your own unique path to parenthood. And most of all, we hope that this book has allowed you to recognize, value, and celebrate the love that you have to share with a baby. Keep growing that love from the inside out—this is your greatest gift to your children.

Although there are many struggles we each face when we choose to parent in a predominantly heterosexual culture, once we become parents we realize that those struggles—when addressed consciously and with compassion—just help to lay a solid foundation for our family. Remember to take the time to congratulate yourself for being one of the pioneers of intentional parenting outside of traditional heterosexual relationships or marriage. When times are rough, slow down and appreciate the internal and external struggles you face and applaud your bravery to become a parent in the midst of these challenges. When you're feeling alone, keep in mind that there are millions of us already out there parenting our children with pride and love, and millions of people just like you, on the verge of becoming parents. You are not alone.

So wherever you are in the process, check in with yourself to make sure that you're coming from a place of love and confidence as you create the foundation for your parenthood. Nourish yourself and your relationships as you nourish your body—the future home for your baby—and as you nourish your baby-to-be. Take the time you need to firmly feel that the decisions you're making are the right ones for you.

As you read these last words, some of you will be awaiting the imminent birth of your baby, and some of you will have read this book cover to cover before even beginning to inseminate. Regardless of where you are in the process at this moment, we hope that all of the information we have shared with you has been both informative and inspirational. Take what you have learned and share it with others.

The experience and wisdom you gain from your path to pregnancy will start you off way ahead of the game. The challenges of parenting still await you, but you are well prepared. Honor how far you have come and take a deep breath...the joy you have so dearly been wanting is awaiting you.

So we send you off on your adventure with well wishes. Whether you're at month 10 or year 10 of your journey at the time of reading this, just pondering parenting or due in two weeks, we hope you find your joy and love at each step of this daunting and rewarding experience. The intention of the book has been to provide as much information as possible about the wide diversity of experiences and choices queer families have available to them and to take this information and make their own true and unique best decisions. Our goal in presenting the topics holistically is to encourage everyone to value the connections between their emotional, physical, and spiritual selves throughout conception, pregnancy, and birth, and to find ways to feel comfortable and safe in their bodies. We wish you great happiness amidst all the challenges queer parenting (in fact any parenting) includes, and we know you'll raise your children with great love and pride. Good luck!

Appendix:
Queer-Family Resources

Organizations and Programs

Gay and Lesbian Medical
    Association
459 Fulton St., suite 107
San Francisco, CA 94102
415-255-4547
www.glma.org

ACLU Lesbian and Gay Rights
    Project
125 Broad St., 18th Floor
New York, NY 10004
(212) 549-2627
www.aclu.org/lgbt/index.html

Center Kids: The Family Program
    of the Lesbian and Gay
    Community Center
208 W. 13th St.
New York, NY 10011
(212) 620-7310
www.gaycenter.org

Lesbian, Gay, Bisexual, and
    Transgender Family and
    Parenting Services
Fenway Community Health Center
7 Haviland St.
Boston, MA 02115
(617) 267-0900
www.fenwayhealth.org

COLAGE (Children of Lesbians
    and Gays Everywhere)
3543 18th St., #1
San Francisco, CA 94110
(415) 861-5437
www.colage.org

Family Pride Coalition
P.O. Box 65327
Washington, D.C. 20035-5327
(202) 331-5015
www.familypride.org

Lambda Legal Defense and
    Education Fund
120 Wall St., Suite 1500
New York, NY 10005-3904
(212) 809-8585
www.lambdalegal.org
*Offers many free documents and
    publications on their website.*

Men's Resource Center for Change
236 North Pleasant St.
Amherst, MA 01002
(413) 253-9887
www.mensresourcecenter.org
*They have a great book for potential
    known donors to read.*

National Center for Lesbian Rights
870 Market St., suite 370
San Francisco, CA 94102
(415) 392-6257
www.nclrights.org

Human Rights Campaign
1640 Rhode Island Ave., NW
Washington, D.C. 20036-3278
www.hrc.org/familynet

Gay and Lesbian Advocates and
  Defenders
30 Winter St., Suite 800
Boston, MA 02018
(617) 426-1350
www.glad.org

Alternative Families Project
442 Warren Wright Road
Belchertown, MA 01007

Fresh Semen by Mail

OverNite Male™ Program
University of Illinois at Chicago
  Andrology Laboratory
Call the andrology coordinator at
  (312) 996-7713
www.uic.edu/com/mcsr/androlab/
  overnite.htm
*They send fresh semen donations via
  Federal Express.*

Rainbow Flag Health Services
(510) 521-SPERM
www.gayspermbank.com
*Donor identity released when baby is
  three months old.
Has openly gay and bisexual donors.*

Lesbian-Friendly Sperm Banks

The Sperm Bank of California
2115 Milvia St., 2nd floor
Berkeley, CA 94704
(510) 841-1858
www.thespermbankofca.org
*Will work with gay-directed donors.
They have an open-identity donor
  program.*

Austin TX Branch Laboratory
4201 Marathon Blvd., suite 303A
Austin, TX 78756
(512) 206-0408
www.fairfaxcryobank.com

New England Cryogenic Center
209 Harvard St., 2nd floor
Brookline, MA 02446
(800) 991- 4999
www.necryogenic.com
Has an open-identity donor program.

California Cryobank
11915 La Grange Ave.
Los Angeles, CA 90025
(800) 231- 3373
www.cryobank.com
*Has a partial open-identity donor
  program.*

Cryogenic Laboratories, Inc.
1944 Lexington Ave. North
Roseville, MN 55113
www.cryolab.com
(800) 466-2796

Pacific Reproductive Services,
San Francisco office
444 De Haro St., suite 222
San Francisco, CA 94107
(415) 487- 2288
www.hellobaby.com

Pacific Reproductive Services,
    Pasadena office
65 North Madison St., suite 610
Pasadena, CA 91101
(626) 432-1681
Has open-identity donor program.

Xytex Corporation
www.xytex.com
Has open-identity donors.

Midwest Cryobank
4333 Main St.
Downers Grove, IL 60515
(630) 810-1201
www.midwestcryobank.com
They have no open-identity program.

Fairfax Cryobank
3015 Williams Dr., suite 110
Fairfax, VA 22031
(800) 338-8407

CryoGam Colorado
2216 Hoffman Dr., unit B
Loveland, CO 80538
(800) 473-9601
www.cryogam.com
*Does not have an open-donor
    program; will work with gay-
    directed donors.*

Fertility Enhancement Resources

Chi-Nei Tsang Institute
www.chineitsang.com

Maya Massage
www.ofspirit.com

Safer Sex and Sex Toys

Safersex.org
www.Safersex.org
Good Vibrations
(800) 829-8423 (customer service)
(800) BUY-VIBE (mail order)
www.goodvibes.com

Babeland
707 E Pike St.
Seattle, WA 98122
(800) 658-9119
www.babeland.com

Sexuality.org
www.Sexuality.org

Alternative Menstrual Products

Glad Rags Cotton Menstrual Pads
P.O. Box 12648
Portland, OR 97212
(800) 799-4523
www.gladrags.com

Green Marketplace
800-439-5506
www.greenmarketplace.com
*Sells nontoxic tampons and
menstrual pads made by Seventh
Generation and offers other
nontoxic household and body-
care items.*

Ovulation-Predictor Kits (OPKs)

Cue Ovulation Monitors
(800) FOR-CUES
www.zetek.net

Clearblue Easy Fertility Monitors
(800) 321-EASY (3279)
www.clearplan.com/fertilitymonitor
ovulationpage.cfm

Speculum and Fertility Lens

Maia Midwifery and Preconception Services
23 Altarinda Road, Suite 215
Orinda, CA 94563
(925) 253-0685
www.maiamidwifery.com

Glossary

FOR MORE DETAILED information on specific terms and concepts (some of which may not be listed here), consult the index.

ASSISTED REPRODUCTIVE TECHNOLOGY (ART) Usually refers to the process of in vitro fertilization, although it also refers to placing an egg and sperm surgically together in the uterus or fallopian tube.

BASAL BODY TEMPERATURE (BBT) The lowest temperature of the body on a particular day, usually early in the morning immediately upon awakening. Women monitor their BBT as a method of tracking fertility and predicting their day of ovulation.

BIOLOGICAL FATHER A man whose sperm was involved in a child's conception. Does not necessarily imply parental involvement.

CHEM PANEL A blood chemistry test that assesses someone's overall health. Most laboratories print out a range of normal values next to the test results so it's fairly easy to see when a result is abnormal.

CHLAMYDIA A bacteria that can infect the reproductive tract, urethra, lungs, and eyes. It is most often sexually transmitted. It can create scar tissue, causing infertility, and often does not produce any symptoms. It can also be transmitted from mother to infant during birth.

CLOMID The brand name of clomiphene, a drug taken in pill form at the beginning of the cycle to stimulate ovulation.

COPARENT A term with many definitions. Usually refers to an adult who shares parenting responsibilities but isn't romantically involved with the birth mother, or to an adult who shares parenting responsibilities but isn't the primary parent. The verb coparent means to parent together.

CORPUS LUTEUM The gland formed by the ruptured follicle following ovulation.

CYTOMEGALOVIRUS (CMV) A virus to which many of us have been exposed at some point in our lives. It usually will only make you sick if your immune system isn't working well. Getting an active CMV infection while pregnant can cause birth defects such as central nervous system damage, brain damage, and hearing loss.

DOUBLE OVULATION When ovulation occurs more than once a cycle, often seven to ten days apart.

DOULA Another name for a labor coach or postpartum care provider, a professional nonmedical birth and postpartum attendant who helps the entire family practically and emotionally.

EGG DONOR A woman who takes fertility drugs to mature a large number of eggs, which are retrieved with a minor surgical procedure and combined with sperm during in vitro fertilization. The embryo is then placed in the uterus of another woman who wishes to parent. Usually, women who are older and have few healthy eggs left are encouraged to consider using a donor's eggs if they have fertility challenges.

EGG HEALTH Refers to whether or not the egg is able to respond to the hormone message from the brain that tells it to mature and ovulate.

ESTRADIOL One form of estrogen, produced by the ovaries that can reveal information about a woman's level of fertility.

ESTROGEN A hormone that stimulates the development of female secondary-sex characteristics.

FERTILE MUCUS A substance produced by the cervix, that serves as a natural filtration system and allows healthy, well-formed sperm into the cervix.

FERTILITY DRUGS Medications that induce the ovaries to produce many eggs. Except for clomiphene, all are administered by injection.

FOLIC ACID (FOLATE) One of the B vitamins. Key in the formation of the baby's neural tube, which becomes the spine. Women are encouraged to take a folic acid supplement during preconception, as the neural tube forms in very early pregnancy.

FOLLICLE-STIMULATING HORMONE (FSH) Hormone produced in the pituitary gland in the brain that triggers the follicles in the ovary to mature eggs so they can be ovulated.

FOLLICULAR PHASE The first half or so of the menstrual cycle, from the first day of the menstrual period to the point of ovulation.

FRESH SPERM Sperm that has just recently been ejaculated and will be used for insemination immediately without freezing.

FROZEN SPERM Sperm that has been cryogenically frozen at a sperm bank or fertility clinic and is thawed before insemination.

GENETIC TESTING May refer to blood tests that check for genetically inherited diseases in a man or a woman, such as cystic fibrosis, Tay-Sachs disease, or sickle-cell anemia. May also refer to various tests such as amniocentesis done during pregnancy to diagnose chromosomal abnormalities of the fetus, such as Down's syndrome or any of the aforementioned diseases.

GO-BETWEEN Someone who works with a woman to screen a sperm donor to some extent and maintains the confidentiality of both parties by picking up and dropping off the donated semen.

GONORRHEA A contagious inflammation of the genital mucous membrane caused by sexually transmittable bacteria. It can be transmitted from mother to infant during birth.

HUMAN CHORIONIC GONADOTROPIN (HCG) The main pregnancy hormone produced by the embryo. This is the hormone that pregnancy tests check for. When given mid-cycle by injection, it can stimulate the body to ovulate, just as LH does.

HYSTEROSALPINGOGRAM (HSG) A series of X-rays taken after opaque dye has been placed in the uterus through a tube in the cervix in order to diagnose a number of irregularities, particularly tubal blockage.

IDENTITY-RELEASE DONOR A sperm donor from a sperm bank who has authorized the bank to release his identifying information to the child upon his or her request as an adult.

IN VITRO FERTILIZATION (IVF) Conception that occurs in a laboratory with an egg retrieved surgically from the uterus.

INITIAL HORMONE TESTS Tests a woman may undergo before inseminating to check if her hormone levels are optimal for conception.

INTERNALIZED HOMOPHOBIA Shame, self-doubt, guilt, or not feeling deserving of first-class treatment because of a lesbian, gay, or bisexual orientation.

INTRACERVICAL INSEMINATION (ICI) Often a fancy word for vaginal insemination, although sometimes it refers to finding the cervix by using a speculum and then depositing the semen right at the opening of the cervix, instead of injecting in the back of the vagina without the use of a speculum.

INTRAUTERINE INSEMINATION (IUI) A method of insemination that involves washing the sperm to separate it from the semen, then placing it directly into the uterus with a sterile plastic tube that is passed through the cervix.

KNOWN DONOR A sperm donor whose identity is known, or a sperm donor obtained through a sperm bank whose identity will be released to the child upon his or her request as an adult.

LUTEAL PHASE The second half or so of the menstrual cycle, from the point of ovulation to the day before the next menstrual period.

LUTEINIZING HORMONE (LH) Hormone produced in the pituitary gland in the brain that triggers ovulation. Ovulation predictor kits test for LH surges.

MENOPAUSE A physiological state women go through as their ovaries run out of eggs and their hormones change in response. Women may menstruate regularly for a number of years with very decreased fertility due to having few eggs left before the onset of menopause.

MIDWIFE A traditional birth attendant. Almost always a woman, she may practice at home or in the hospital and be trained holistically or medically from a variety of educational models; she may also be a nurse. A midwife provides complete prenatal and postpartum care, and offers education and support to the entire family. Most women in the world, historically and currently, give birth with a midwife in attendance, not a physician. World Health Organization statistics show that on average the best birth outcomes occur at home with a midwife in attendance. Statistics in the United States reflect this as well.

MYCOPLASMA, UREAPLASMA Bacteria that can be found in the reproductive tracts of women and occasionally men. They do not cause any symptoms but are suspected of increasing a woman's risk of miscarriage. They both can be transmitted sexually but are easily treated with oral antibiotics.

NONBIOLOGICAL MOTHER A woman who is not biologically related to her child. Usually used to identify the partner of the birth mother. This term is not preferred by most women, who usually just call themselves "mother" or use a more positive term that does not identify them solely by what they are not.

OVULATION The release of the mature egg from the ovary.

PITUITARY GLAND Gland located in the brain. This is the site of production of many reproductive hormones including FSH and LH.

PRECONCEPTION COUNSELING Education and support on any of a variety of topics, including fertility awareness, nutritional needs, pre-pregnancy, avoidance of birth-defect-causing substances are common topics. Lesbian and bisexual women often also receive information on sperm donors, legal issues, insemination methods, and many other issues specific to them.

PREMATURE OVARIAN FAILURE When a woman runs out of eggs to ovulate and experiences menopause at a relatively very early age.

PROGESTERONE A hormone that is produced in either the ovary or the placenta. It has many roles, one of which is to "tell" the uterus to maintain its fertile lining in the second half of the cycle in case an embryo is on its way to implant in it.

PROLACTIN A hormone made in the pituitary gland that is best known for its role in stimulating breast milk. High levels of prolactin can inhibit ovulation.

PROSTAGLANDINS Natural chemicals essential to the working of the muscle in the ovary to release the egg.

QUARANTINE Sperm banks often hold a donor's sperm for six months, after which they repeat his tests for sexually transmitted infections. If the tests are negative at that time, the sperm is released from quarantine. This process increases the accuracy of the testing; as some infections take weeks to months after exposure to show up on a test yet are transmittable immediately.

REPRODUCTIVE ENDOCRINOLOGIST Professional term for an infertility specialist, an obstetrician gynecologist who has specialized training in causes of infertility, reproductive hormones, and infertility treatment technologies.

RUGAE The folds of the vaginal walls.

SECOND-PARENT ADOPTION A legal process available in some states that gives full parenting rights to a nonbiological mother in a lesbian partnership.

SEMEN ANALYSIS A test, known by many people as a sperm count that examines many other components of semen than just the number of sperm.

THYROID Large endocrine gland located at the base of the neck that produces the hormones thyroxine and triiodothyronine.

UNKNOWN DONOR A sperm donor who will always remain anonymous.

VAGINAL INSEMINATION Method of insemination in which the semen is deposited via a small syringe into the back of the vagina so it can swim into the uterus. Sometimes the syringe is held in place by a cup placed over the cervix.

YES DONOR See IDENTITY-RELEASE DONOR.

Index

as preparation for birth, 452
preparing body for, 47–48, 222
in queer community vs. community of parents,
445
sexual abuse memories and, 435–436
sharing news of, 418–419
single motherhood, 427–428, 442–444
surprise, 428–429
telling extended family and friends, 422–424
telling immediate family members, 419–422
telling the world about your partner's,
424–426
tests, 402
as time of physical and emotional
transformation, 429–431
vaginal infections and discomforts, 451
pregnancy, early, 400–417
choosing care provider, 406–412
confusion around symptoms of, 400–401
from high-risk conception to low-risk
pregnancy, 406
management by fertility specialists, 403–406
menstrual periods and, 401
miscarriage, 412–417
pregnancy tests, 402
reactions to, 402–403
signs of, 400
symptoms, 401
premature ovarian failure, 354, 504
prenatal care. see also pregnancy, early
good, 411
preparing for hospital birth, 467–468
seeking early, 409
prescription drugs
antidepressants and anti-anxiety, 184
coping skills and, 185–186
fertility drugs and psychotropic drugs, 187
fertility inhibitors, 137
safety of, 185
support for getting off, 186–187
preterm labor risks, and sex, 449–450
probiotics, 210–211
progesterone
defined, 504
hormone tests, 60–61
identifying imbalance with BBT charts,
234–235
preventing miscarriage, 414
supplementation for, 234–235
programs, queer-family resources, 506–507
prolactin, 496, 505
prolactin luteinizing hormone (PLH), 61–62
prostaglandins, 298, 505
protein, 163–164
psychological issues
around lengthy insemination period, 331
feeling safe before your IUI, 302–303
with known donors, 293

when couples cannot conceive, 385–386
psychotropic drugs, 187
pycnogenal, 141
pyridoxine (B-6), 165

quality of sperm, from sperm banks, 130
quarantine, 505
The Queer Parents' Primer, 22

race, and donor choice, 124–125
Rainbow Flag Health Services, 87, 122, 139–140
Rapid HIV tests, 115
RE (reproductive endocrinologist), 349, 505
red clover tea, 208
red raspberry leaf tea, 208
relatives
coparents managing relationships with, 24
as known donors, 90–91
telling about your pregnancy, 419–426
relaxation, 413–414
relief, after infertility, 394
reproductive endocrinologist (RE), 349, 505
Rescue Remedy, 413–414
resentment, charting, 265
RESOLVE, 349
resources, 506–509
alternative menstrual products, 509
best practitioner for insemination, 300
fertility enhancement, 508
fresh semen by mail, 507
lesbian-friendly sperm banks, 507–508
organizations and programs, 506–507
ovulation predictor kits (OPK), 509
safer sex and sex toys, 508
speculum and fertility lens, 509
riboflavin (B2), 165
Robitussin cough syrup, and insemination, 290
roles
coparents/known donor at birth, 472
nonbirth mother being mistaken for
grandmother, 483
pregnant/nonpregnant moms, 458–459
rebuilding relationship after infertility,
395–396
romance/romantic relationships
coparenting and, 16
donor coparents and, 77
known donors and, 96–97
parenting and, 5–6
room, setting up baby's, 215
RPR tests, 53, 116
Rubella, 53
rugae, 505
Rule of Three, 228

S&M, during pregnancy, 449–450
safety
embodied decisions and, 39

About the Photographers

CATHY CADE Personal Histories & Photography
I help people tell their stories. 407 Orange St. #101 Oakland, Ca 94610
http://www.CathyCade.com 510-251-2774

JENNIFER LOOMIS is an award-winning and internationally recognized photojournalist and fine-art photographer known for her groundbreaking work with the pregnant nude. Jennifer got her start photographing pregnant women after a referral from Annie Liebovitz's studio—where Demi Moore was photographed pregnant for *Vanity Fair*. Since she began working 14 years ago, Jennifer has photographed more than 900 mothers, including the wife of pro-golfer Rich Beem among other celebrities.

Identified in 2003 as one of the emerging photographers of the northwest, Jennifer uses her training as a fine art photographer and her expertise as a documentary photojournalist to tell the story of each woman.

"More than a portrait, I want to photograph a feeling that captures and celebrates each individual woman's beauty of motherhood," she said in an interview with *Sunset Magazine*. Her business motto "Feel Beautiful" came about because many women said they felt beautiful during and after photo shoots. This saying is important to Jennifer because she is passionate about changing the way pregnant women see their bodies as well as the way society sees pregnant women. Contact Jennifer Loomis at www.jenniferloomis.com.

JILL SHENKER is a photographer and community organizer living in the Bay Area. She learned the art of photography through her father and stepfather, and blames her artistic bent on her mother. It has been her honor to photograph important life passages in her friends and families lives, including weddings, commitment ceremonies, political actions, and the births shown in this book.

She has facilitated youth arts activism projects through the Gay-Straight Alliance Network (www.gsanetwork.org) and COLAGE (Children of Lesbians and Gays Everywhere www.colage.org.

Contact her at jill.shenker@stanfordalumni.org for inquiries to show/ publish or take photos.

About the Author

STEPHANIE BRILL is director and cofounder of Maia Midwifery and Preconception Services (23 Altarinda Road, Suite 215, Orinda, CA 94563; (925) 253-0685; www.maiamidwifery.com).

Maia has achieved national recognition by helping thousands of lesbian, gay, bisexual, and transgendered individuals with every aspect of creating family, pregnancy, and parenthood. Maia has also helped hundreds of single and coupled heterosexual women to conceive and is renowned for helping older women to conceive using their own eggs.

As a leading Bay Area midwife, Stephanie has helped more than five hundred babies to be born at home. Stephanie presents regularly at state and national midwifery conferences. She regularly contributes to *Midwifery Today*, and international professional magazine for midwives.

Stephanie is also the author of *The Queer Parents' Primer: A Lesbian and Gay Families' Guide to Navigating the Straight World.*

Stephanie also provides comprehensive training and consultation for health professionals on the subjects of fertility and lesbian reproductive health care. She presents at PFLAG meetings, queer health forums, mental health organizations, and medical schools, and provides in-services for schools on issues of queer parenting and gender identity in young children.

She has four amazing children and a fantastic partner. They live in Orinda, California.